ALSO BY ROBERT M. CRUNDEN

The Mind and Art of Albert Jay Nock (1964)

ℂ A Hero In Spite of Himself

❩ A Hero In Spite of Himself:

BRAND WHITLOCK

IN ART, POLITICS, & WAR

❩ ROBERT M. CRUNDEN

ALFRED · A · KNOPF / 1969

NEW YORK

FRONTISPIECE

Brand Whitlock in 1900
from the Toledo Public Library

THIS IS A BORZOI BOOK
PUBLISHED BY ALFRED A. KNOPF, INC.

First Edition
Copyright © 1969 by Robert Crunden

Library of Congress Catalog Card Number: 73-79316

Manufactured in the United States of America

For the Memory of

Allan B. Crunden, Sr.

[CONTENTS]

BOOK ONE

"The Father of All"

AMERICA, 1869 - 1913

ℭ CHAPTER 1

A Boy and His
Grandfather (1869-1890)

THE SMALL BOY SENSED ADVENTURE. The day was
hot even for an Ohio August, but his grandfather, having
finished his nap, said that the boy could accompany him uptown.
The prospect was especially welcome because Grandmother always
drew down the heavy green shades while Grandfather slept, and
the house rested in the somnolent silence of a small town. Besides,
trips with Grandfather were welcome not only to escape boredom
but also to get the present Grandfather always gave him afterward.
Grandfather combed his thick, white hair and then promptly
ran his fingers through it to make himself look a little savage. The
pair then set out. He wore broad, low, polished shoes with buckles
and was entirely in black except for an immaculate, starched white
waistcoat. The lowest of the pearl buttons was fastened, and from
one of the upper buttonholes hung a long gold watch chain from a
large gold hook. With his white beard and large panama hat
weathered by much summer use, the old gentleman made a companion any boy could be proud of.
The boy held Grandfather's hand firmly, especially when they
passed through the Swedenborgian churchyard, because a ghost
dwelt there which he had once seen clearly. Grandfather was a

3

brave man, however, and the precaution was unnecessary. As a former soldier, he was still called "Major," even though everyone knew he was now mayor; his trips uptown were to town hall. The main street stretched ahead in hot and interminable white dust. A bronze cavalryman marked the square to the north. The fairgrounds were off in the far distance to the south. Grandfather wiped his perspiring face several times with a large silk handkerchief.

Town hall was in Market Square; it was a low, brick building containing most of the local institutions, including an auditorium, city council rooms, jail, and fire department. In back were shady eaves where the firemen, city marshal, and occasional visitors spent their time playing checkers. Across Market Square was a line of brick buildings, in a state of quiet decay, slowly turning a faint pink in their old age. In front of a line of saloons were several carts, driven by Irishmen from Lighttown, and drays, driven by Negroes from Guinea or Gooseville. But on that day no one was in sight; no one was playing checkers or laughing or walking. The heat had driven away everyone.

Everyone, that is, but a dusty, drab figure with an old felt hat and a mass of rags for clothes, his trousers tied to him by irons and a ball and chain. He made aimless little gestures with a broom at the dust surrounding him. The little boy knew that the man was a prisoner and that therefore he was Bad, and had been "made so by Rum." He knew also that the man lived in the calaboose, which was somewhere in town hall because anyone who looked hard could see the faces that sometimes pressed against the bars.

From the shade of the broad eaves, Grandfather motioned to the prisoner. The man showed sudden energy, dropped his broom, picked up his ball, and came so close that the boy could see the sweat that drenched his forehead, matted his arms, and stained his shirt. He dropped the ball, took off what was left of his hat, and looked at Grandfather.

"How many days did I give you?" asked Grandfather.

"Fifteen, your honor."

"How long have you been in?"

"Three days, your honor."

"Are you the only one in there?"

"Yes, your honor."

Grandfather paused and looked at him. "Pretty hot out there, isn't it?"

"Yes, your honor."

Grandfather looked around and saw no one else. "Well, come on into the office."

They went in. Grandfather went to a drawer, fumbled for the key, stooped and unlocked the chains, but did not remove the irons. Then he sat down and leaned back in a squeaking, cane chair.

"Now, you go out there in the Square—be careful not to knock the leg irons off you as you go—and you sweep around for a little while, and when the coast is clear you kick them off and light out."

The man looked back dumbly, opened his lips, closed them, swallowed.

"You'd better hurry, I don't know what minute the marshal . . ."

The man quickly picked up his ball and held it with great tenderness and care as he shuffled out. He stood for an instant framed in the glittering sunlight by the door, looked back, and then disappeared. Grandfather put on his glasses and turned to his work. The minutes ticked by in the still, hot room. Then Uncle John Brand, Grandfather's brother, a large man almost the same age but with a longer beard, appeared in the doorway and announced breathlessly:

"Joe, he has escaped!"

Ignored, he cried again: "Joe, he's gone, I tell you; he's getting away!"

Grandfather looked up calmly. "John, you'd better come in out of that heat and sit down. You're excited."

"But he's getting away, I tell you! Don't you understand?"

"Who is getting away?"

"Why, that prisoner."

"What prisoner?"

"The prisoner out there in the Square. He has escaped! He's gone!"

"But how do you know?"

"I just saw him running down Main Street like a streak of lightning."

Grandfather wiped his face with his silk handerchief and said: "To think of anyone running on a day like this!"

Uncle John stood and gazed at his brother in despair. "Can't you understand," he said intensely, "can't you understand that the prisoner out there in the Square has broken away, has escaped, and at this minute is running down Main Street, and that he's getting farther and farther away with each moment that you sit there?"

The boy was helpless. He knew that Uncle John was right but he liked his Grandfather better.

"But how could he get away?" Grandfather asked. "He was in irons."

"He got the irons off somehow," said an exasperated Uncle John. "I don't know how. He didn't stop to explain!" He found some relief in this sarcasm and then asked: "Aren't you going to do anything?"

"Well," said Grandfather with rare irresolution, "I suppose I really ought to do something. But I don't know just what to do." He sat up and looked around carefully. "You don't see the marshal, do you?" John displayed great disgust. "Just look outside there, will you John, and see if you can find him? If you do, send him in, and I'll speak to him and have him go after the prisoner."

Uncle John Brand could find no appropriate words, and left. After he was gone Grandfather leaned back in his chair and started to laugh, and he laughed until his ruddy face became much redder even than the day's heat had made it.[1]

LITTLE JOSEPH BRAND WHITLOCK received many things from his grandfather Joseph Carter Brand, but this incident was his favorite. The event made such an impression on him that he made it the opening scene of his autobiography. During his lifetime, Brand Whitlock always saw in his unconventional but merciful grandfather and in his conventional and moralistic uncle symbols of two kinds of men; while his mind often acknowledged the truth in the position of his uncle, his heart always sided with the mercy and tolerance of his grandfather. The adult Whitlock often found himself in conflict with the established order, and, try as he would, he always sympathized with the underdog, whatever his crimes. Yet as he did so, Whitlock was always torn between a head that found for him reasonable theories for life and a heart that was entirely romantic, that knew little but human sympathy. The odds always favored the prisoner whenever Whitlock was judge, but he always felt a bit guilty afterward.

The event described above also gives us a picture of Whitlock himself. The imaginative boy always needed a hero to lean on whenever he found himself in a scary graveyard and, so, found himself repeatedly worshipping a figure more magnetic and assertive than himself. Throughout his life, a life in many respects one of the most exciting that a member of his generation could have led, he was most often detached, an onlooker, even when most obviously involved in the fray. He was there, and he did his best, but he was forever the artist absorbing material for art and not an adventurer sampling life for its own sake. Some of his critics would call him ineffectual and helpless. Really he was only a sensitive artist who seemed to be doomed, like some innocent orphan, to wander in the gloomy world of misery, guilt, and war.

Finally, both he and his grandfather were men of pity. "I am sure that no one was ever long with Joseph Carter Brand, or came to know him well, without learning that rarest and most beautiful of all the graces or of all the virtues—pity." Pity, or empathy, or whatever it is called, "it was that divine quality in man which enables him to imagine the sorrows of others, to understand what they feel, to suffer with them." Whitlock the novelist, as well as Whitlock the social reformer, had to be able to put himself in the other man's place—to be, in short, a small boy who was himself a hot, sweaty, miserable offender of the petty codes of society, who had to run for his life before the town marshals of the world could arrive.[2]

WITH THE EXCEPTION of "the bit of Scottish blood inherited by an ancestor who foolishly went out in the '45," the Whitlocks were all English.[3] Brand Whitlock's own favorite ancestor was Bulstrode Whitelocke, "who was no mean politician since he succeeded in keeping office under Charles, under Cromwell and under the Restoration," a feat which took on added luster to a diplomat appointed by Woodrow Wilson and quietly dropped by his Republican successors. The extra *e* in the name had no apparent justification, for Bulstrode's father, a judge of the King's Bench, and most of his descendants did not retain it. Old Bulstrode was also something of a diplomat, if that is the word for it: After he achieved an appointment to a mission to Sweden, it was said that "he taught the ladies the art of kissing." Before and after his Scandinavian forays, Bulstrode and his relatives came from Wiltshire, and from there Whitlock's original American ancestor emigrated eight generations before Brand to the wilds of New Jersey.[4]

Grandfather Elias Whitlock, as his grandson later recalled, was "a large, gaunt, silent man, who spoke little, and then mostly in a sardonic humor." In normal pioneer fashion, he had spent his life clearing his own farm in Montgomery County, Ohio, and then retired to Piqua, not far from where his grandson grew up in Urbana. Whitlock later suspected that his grandfather's taciturnity was due to a distaste for political discussion which doomed him to silence in the partisan atmosphere of post-Civil War Ohio. Once a devoted Democrat, Elias Whitlock had campaigned for Buchanan with such great enthusiasm in 1856 that "he had kept his horses' tails and manes braided for a month that they might roll forth in noble curls when they were loosened" in order to celebrate the election of his hero with the proper flourishes. Buchanan's subsequent performance so disillusioned his Piqua supporter that he "renounced forever his interest in political affairs, and, like Henry I., never smiled again."[5]

Grim pioneers were often prosperous and religious, and Elias Whitlock was both. He was the acknowledged township leader, and the first Methodist services in the area took place in his house. He and his wife, Mary Johnson Whitlock, reared four future clergymen. One, William Francis, whom his nephew Brand later remembered—because of a portrait in the school chapel—for his "great smoothly shaven face" with a "smile of quizzical humor," became president of Wesleyan University in Delaware, Ohio. A regular visitor, Uncle William would come to his brother's fireplace, warm his hands, and produce a book for old Elias to read. He was fond of carrying papers in his high hat and seemed to carry an endless succession of eyeglasses, which he forgot regularly on some table or another and promptly replaced from his waistcoat pocket. After his death he became a symbolic puritan forebear, for to young Brand Whitlock—the "Joseph" was soon forgotten—all his forebears were big puritans, over six feet tall, "strong and rugged men, inflexible, obdurate, much enduring, stern pioneers whose like is known no more."[6]

Elias D. Whitlock was William's dutiful and self-sacrificing brother and the father of Brand. Born on a farm sixteen miles west of Dayton, Ohio, on November 12, 1843, he was the youngest of seven children. He attended Ohio Wesleyan as did most of the family but interrupted his education for Civil War service in the 145th Ohio and did not graduate until 1866. He did a little teaching, and a little law. He was a high school principal in several Ohio towns and finally entered the Methodist ministry in 1874, five years after Brand was born. While principal of the Urbana high school, he met the daughter of the town mayor and married her. Mallie Lavinia Brand Whitlock then accompanied her husband on the dreary round of constant movement from hamlet to town to hamlet, while he was first a principal and then a circuit rider for the Methodist Church. In time, he was often presiding elder of his district, a continually influential delegate to the General Ohio Conference, and sometimes delegate to the national General Conference.

In each town Elias D. Whitlock gained a reputation as a stern and able minister with a good heart, and as such a man he earned and received the devotion of his son. He was moody but sympathetic, his son remembered, "one who knew the value of silence in a noisy and jabbering world," a man with humor enough to be "the life of any party." Always careful about his appearance, he made "a noble and handsome presence, a presence that fairly radiated cleanness and wholesomeness." He was deeply emotional, but as a good Anglo-Saxon he hid his emotions and kept them under control. A loyal family man, he managed to be strong and rugged as well as gentle and affectionate, with the circuit rider's particular fondness for a spirited horse. He had a firm grounding in the classics and grew more liberal and not less so as he grew older. Both unworldly and independent, he was utterly devoid of self-seeking. His other most prominent trait, one that was appealing to his son, "was a devastating and withering scorn of any kind of pretentiousness, social, intellectual or moral. I have never known a man who had greater natural simplicity; there was not the least shade of affectation about him."[7]

Whitlock rarely wrote about his mother, but fortunately she has left several letters that paint a better portrait of the woman than pages of description might have. Mrs. Whitlock was a woman of good education, unlike most of the women in her husband's parishes, and her letters are full of good humor, pointed and accurate description, and a zest that seems quite unlikely in the wife of a Methodist circuit rider. She was capable of joking about sermons—not a common practice in rural Ohio—and about her son Will, Brand's brother, who grew up to be distinctly unsuccessful in his career, a socialist in politics, and a freethinker in religion. Her best joke was the anecdote she tells on herself in a letter to Mrs. Brand Whitlock written in 1910. She and another woman decided to visit the former's birthplace, and while there they went over to the church graveyard: ". . . to do which we had to climb two barbed wire fences—the gate was tied and barred for it had not been used for years . . ." There, while reading the inscriptions, they found one that read: "Mary C. Morrison . . . I have gone home, let me alone!" Mrs. Whitlock "roared with laughter, hollow as it sounded in that ghoulish place."[8] A remarkable woman indeed, to climb barbed-wire fences when she was well past sixty and write well of her laughter.

Mallie Brand was fortunate far above most Ohio girls, for her father, Grandfather Brand to young Whitlock, was a highly cultured man who made sure that his family had a thorough grounding in the humanities when they were young. The house was always full of the love of books and music, and everyone was encouraged to use the available resources. Presumably, his mother and her influence led Brand Whitlock, in his later fiction, to cast the mothers of his boys as the mediating, sympathetic influence which helps the poor children to enjoy life even as the stern father tries to prevent all pleasure, as being sinful. Mrs. Whitlock produced four children, three boys and a girl. Of this group, brothers Will and Francis both had occasional contact with Brand in later life. Sister Mary died when she was only twelve.[9] Unfortunately, not even culture could supply the one thing that both Whitlocks and Brands lacked for a full life—money—and the families were pinched for funds. Brand's decision to work rather than attend college may well have had a financial basis.[10]

Of all Brand Whitlock's relatives, however, Grandfather Brand was the most important. The descendant of Scottish immigrants, who grew up to be mayor, freer of prisoners, and man of pity, had renounced his Kentucky patrimony of slaves and come north, leaving Bourbon County where his branch of Brands had settled after their Jacobite exile from Forfarshire, Scotland, and a long stay in Virginia. He first came to Ohio briefly, returned to Virginia to marry Lavinia Talbott, and then returned to the farm he called "Pretty Prairie." A personal friend of Henry Clay, he was soon deep in Whig politics and served in both houses of the Ohio legislature. He knew and admired Governor Salmon P. Chase, and was deep in the abolitionist movement and in open defiance of the Fugitive Slave Law. He was good enough with a rifle to snuff out candles with it, and when a runaway Negro named Ad White found himself under fire from a group of United States marshals from Cincinnati, Brand and his friend Ichabod Corwin went and drove off the marshals. The Negro escaped, but the marshals returned to capture his two defenders. They barely managed to escape severe legal retribution, while Ad White settled down near Urbana to become a living legend from the exciting past. Joseph Brand meanwhile joined the Republican Party and attended the Pittsburgh convention in 1856, his roommate at the convention being his friend Cassius M. Clay of Kentucky. Four years later he was an enthusiastic supporter of Lincoln and, when the war broke out, joined the 66th Ohio Volunteer Infantry to back his vote. He later turned down command of his unit because he felt he knew too little. All his sons saw some service; one was a captain in the 66th. The family itself was split, however, for the Brands still in Virginia were unblushing rebels. After some service he was transferred to the Commissary Department in Washington, where he knew Lincoln at least fleetingly. At Appomattox he was the first man to give food to the surrendering Confederates, and he did it proudly, for he still regarded them as his own kin. His respite was brief, however, for Chase soon requested him to become President Grant's consul in Nuremburg; in 1870 he set out for Germany with wife and daughters. Upon his return he began the acquaintance with his grandson, a friendship "which lasted until his death, and was marred by no misunderstanding, except, perhaps, as to the number of hours his saddlehorse should be ridden on the gallop, and the German he wished me to read to him out of the little black-bound volumes of Schiller and Goethe, which for years were his companions."

Joseph Brand conducted his large family in a grand and patriarchal manner, and they gathered often around the piano—bought in Berlin—for evenings of music. But what interested the mayor more than anything he had discovered in Europe was politics, and, even if one of the great advantages of his office was the free time it left him to read German poets, he was still fascinated by his profession. Like everyone else in the world, or so his grandson assumed, he was a Republican. In those days, in that place, "it was natural to be a Republican; it was more than that, it was inevitable that one should be a Republican; it was not a matter of intellectual choice, it was a process of biological selection." The party was not a faction or group but an institution, "a fundamental and self-evident thing, like life, liberty, and the pursuit of happiness, or like the flag, or the federal judiciary." The name was "merely a synonym for patriotism, another name for the nation," and in Urbana, one became "a Republican just as the Eskimo dons fur clothes." Democrats lived in Lighttown or in Alabama, but they were never your friends.[11]

Just how Republican his state was, and how tied was this Republicanism to religion, the letters of Brand Whitlock's brother Francis indicate. Unlike Brand, Francis went to Ohio Wesleyan University where Uncle Will was a professor, and he painted an unforgettable picture of the place for his brother. It was, he wrote a "*dear old Republican* institution." "Say, it is something awful here. The feeling of Republicanism, I mean. Really, they think a Democrat will go to hell sure! (Excuse me, but that is just what they think)." He overheard several of the faculty, including Uncle Will, talking politics, and they all agreed that the Lord would not let Bryan be elected: "Think of people who are supposed to have a little mind anyways thinking that the Lord has anything to do with politics." Theodore Roosevelt had recently visited and spoken and tried to overpower everyone who was not a Republican, with the obvious approval of the school. Then, when two Bryanites came, they were given a greeting scarcely civil. "I suppose that the next branch they add to this school will be a school of Republicanism."¹² As Elias D. Whitlock wrote his son Brand the same year: "There are a great many preachers as well as laymen who are Republicans first and Christians second. It is a sad but true observation."¹³

But the Republican Party had once been a party of real social change, and Ohio had been a center of reform from the days when Grandfather Brand knew Governor Salmon P. Chase. Only the corruption of the Grant era enabled the Democrats to make some headway in spite of everything the Republicans could say. The issues were often revivals of the crusades of the days before the war, issues that often dominated the Whitlock house and gave Brand some of his best material for fiction on the period. The Hayes administration had suffered from labor unrest and strikes, and in 1878 a party was formed in Toledo to fight for inflation. Some local governments were notoriously under boss rule, like Cincinnati under George B. Cox, Cleveland under Mark Hanna, and Fostoria under Charles Foster. But the real battle that occupied rural Ohio and America when the urge to reform was strong was that against alcohol, and the fight was particularly appealing to women. Drink came to stand for the sins of the times, whether rising atheism, corruption, depression, or sons that could not be disciplined and left for the city. It was

> Pimple-maker, visage-bloater,
>   Health-corrupter, idler's mate,
> Mischief-maker, vice-promoter,
>   Credit-spoiler, devil's bait.

Prohibition became the new abolitionism and ran particularly strong in devout Methodist homes like the one kept by Elias D. Whitlock.¹⁴

Brand Whitlock moved with his father throughout this Ohio, to posts in Delaware, Findlay, Kenton, Defiance, and other small towns, and larger places like Bellefontaine and Toledo. But when he thought of home he meant Urbana, and when he came to write of small-town Ohio he pictured Urbana and called it Macochee. Urbana itself felt self-sufficient, "and it cared so little for change that" by 1912 it had "scarcely changed at all, save as one misses the faces and the forms one used to see there in other days." The

town did achieve some fame, however, for it could boast of its
university, a Swedenborgian college that was probably more of an
academy. There, in the flourishing days before and just after the
Civil War, it achieved enough of a name to attract the young tutor
who lived there briefly and later signed his novels and essays—
works much appreciated by Brand Whitlock—with the name
Hjalmar Hjorth Boyesen. A Norwegian immigrant, Boyesen came
to America a few months before Whitlock was born (1869) and
settled in Urbana because of the relatively large number of Sweden-
borgians there. By September 1870, he was a tutor in the university and was full of dislike for the town and its people, mud, and
drabness. He recalled its inhabitants as "mostly small, harsh,
cramped village souls, made up of petty pretensions, appetites and
vanities," with only a few exceptions. "Men and women were
rigidly circumscribed in their ideals and sympathies, and exhibited
toward an alien nothing but thorny prejudice or offensive though
well-intentioned condescension. To talk with them was like con-
versing with a stone wall."[15] Another citizen, somewhat older,
became better known and in later life stayed as far from the town
as he could. Until Whitlock, sculptor John Quincy Adams Ward
was the most famous man of this unsympathetic town. As a boy
Ward had done much modeling at a clay bank near the Urbana
sawmill, and the village potter had noticed him and let him work
in his shop. In classic, small-town fashion, his family had disapproved such useless time wasting, and the neighbors remembered
him only as queer. Like many other young artists in small towns
all over America, intellectual Urbana boys had to go to the city to
escape their background and achieve fame.[16]

Peculiar incidents remained in Whitlock's mind for years after
he left Urbana. He had a particular fondness for the "little bob-
tailed street cars that went teetering and tinkling, at intervals of
half an hour, out a long street that ran within a block of my
home." The street cars came to mean much to him, for he could
see in their evolution one example of the course of history,
"affording a means by which to measure that progress in material
efficiency which is so often mistaken for progress in speculative
thought." The little car would proceed, leisurely and deliberately,
often waiting a few minutes for a hurrying, puffing woman to
catch up with it. With her safely aboard, the driver would slowly

unwind the brake, "cluck to his horse, the rope traces would strain and the car would bowl along." In winter the car was the coldest place in the city, particularly when it passed near the icy wind coming off the lake. The floor was padded with straw to keep feet warm, but it never did. Up front the driver stood, "slowly rocking from one foot to the other, bundled up in old overcoats, with his cap pulled down and his throat and chin muffled in a repulsive woolen scarf, hoary with the frost of his breath, and nothing of him visible except the shining red point of his frosted nose." Whitlock had read once of a driver in Indianapolis who had come into the yard "at the end of his run, never moved, but kept right on standing there, and when the barn-boss swore at him, it was found that he was dead, frozen at his post." He was sure that at some time he too would see his driver frozen, "but nothing exciting ever happened on that journey."

Different men then owned each of the two car lines, and Whitlock heard a man say once that each new family that moved onto a line meant $73 a year to its owner. Slowly the families moved in, and men made their fortunes or went bankrupt. One by one, the pioneer owners sold out to one man or a small group, and eventually these groups in all the Urbanas in the country each incorporated themselves and "thus could jointly rejoice in all the individual rights and privileges of a person, without any of his embarrassing moral duties and responsibilities." No one heard of individual owners any more, the horses gave way to mules, and the mules to cable cars and elevated railways and the hideous disfigurement of electric-power lines and trolleys. Conductors no longer waited for puffing housekeepers, and people, Whitlock felt, "grew dimly conscious that somewhere in the whole complicated transaction an injustice lurked." After years of frustration, "this hidden injustice became the chief public concern of the people of the town, and an issue in local politics for more than a decade." The battle against street-car monopolies became one of the chief interests of the progressive period, and Brand Whitlock led and partly won it in Toledo.[17]

To discover what rural Ohio meant to Whitlock requires a trip to Macochee, his fictional Urbana. It was "a typical Mid-Western community," and in its conduct "a provincial strictness prevailed, and the standard of morals, though perhaps not always achieved, was that of the primitive Methodists." To the average member of this average town, "all pleasure was sinful; it was wrong to dance, to play cards, to attend the theatre, to go to race-meetings." The "sins of others" provided "the most interesting subject of conversation" and "privacy of course was resented."[18] As the son of the Methodist preacher, Whitlock saw the community at its strictest, and his story of "The Preacher's Son," about a boy whose father would not let him go to the circus for moral reasons, has an autobiographical overtone that is inescapable. All the places of joy proved to be places of immorality, and many of Whitlock's ideas were obviously formed in opposition to the values of the somewhat inhibited Methodist parsonage of Macochee.[19]

Even more of the short stories deal with the Civil War and its aftermath than with the moral prohibitions of his family. The town had been well represented in the war, and Whitlock's family presumably had more than its share of stories to tell. For example: Colonel Wade Clayton is in love with beautiful Laura Sheldon, but she deserts him for another man who dies a coward; the Colonel shows his true devotion by making the man who displaced him a hero so that his Laura would have to bear no shock and could cherish her memories. Or: A young boy, drafted to lead the Yankees through unknown country, manages to put them off onto the wrong road because so many of them are asleep as they ride. Whitlock often has an undertone of romance in his stories, Civil War or otherwise, and Macochee is full of young lovers who are happy and old lovers who have a fleeting sense of the joy they might have shared. Sometimes the issue of whether or not to leave the small town appears too, as in "The Question," where two men who courted the same girl take different paths. One settles down and marries her, the other remains a bachelor, goes off, and becomes well known. Nothing of great significance ever really happens, as people who live in small towns always complain in Whitlock's short stories. Life in Macochee is not all unhappy, however, and at times Whitlock would remember it with longing; but he never went back for very long, and most of the time felt little nostalgia for it.[20]

The stories are at best a fragmentary means of recapturing Macochee, but the novel *J. Hardin & Son* is not. J. Hardin is a devout Methodist harness maker, devoted to both a business and a system of morals which are doomed to extinction by the twentieth century. His son Paul rebels, sometimes with success and sometimes not, against this system, yet stays with the town and does not leave. Paul acts in ways that suggest that Whitlock is toying with the idea of what might have happened to him had he stayed. The parallel in character is not close, but the parallel in conditions is. J. Hardin and those like him "had the bucolic conviction that early rising was, perhaps, next to total abstinence, the highest of moral virtues," and made a point of abiding by sun time, "God's time," rather than by Daylight Saving Time. In the midst of local mores, "Paul felt himself as one abandoned, like the last forgotten man left in the world after the day of judgment. . . . He was kept by prohibitions." Soon, the Reverend Mr. Sparrow conducts a revival, and Mr. Popple, with his putrescent breath, makes a special effort to convert Paul. Paul finds that he has "to wrestle with one of the problems of that existence which to the sensitive and imaginative is always in some sort a tragedy." Seeing her son miserable and unconverted at the revival, Mrs. Hardin demonstrates qualities which probably indicate some of Whitlock's feelings toward his own mother. "Logic, of course, irritated her, as it does most women, and most persons who have intuitions so much deeper and wiser than mere logic can ever be." Paul pretends to conversion, and thus "saved his face, if not his soul," but he would never feel comfortable in his family, "where expression was so constantly repressed."[21]

The town tries to suppress expression, but it never quite succeeds. The book opens with the death of an actress bearing an illegitimate child and Paul's shock at the town's attitude of disapproval of sin rather than sympathy for suffering. The real sign of immorality is not sex, however, but the saloon and its frequenters like Malcolm Dyer and Wade Powell. There Paul finds a life different from that in his home, and in the "fine, free world" of the saloon takes his first tobacco and liquor. When the bastard girl of the dead actress grows up, the town children make a sport of chasing her, and Malcolm Dyer—not a Methodist!—is once her rescuer. When Paul, who watches this rescue, comments that "they are depraved," Dyer replies: "They are worse than that, my boy, they are moral." A chill he catches while rescuing the girl develops into pneumonia, and Dyer dies. J. Hardin finds Paul in the saloon and exiles him to a friend's farm.[22] Soon Paul returns to his father and joins the family harness business. Freed from some of his business cares, J. Hardin dilutes his fierce Republicanism with prohibition, and in company with a ministerial failure, the Reverend Mr. Theodore Wilde Brackner, begins organizing "dry" campaigns. Paul escapes his father's preoccupations by courting Winona Dyer, daughter of the man who died saving the actress's daughter. Soon, Whitlock talks of the "desolate farmhouses wherein the dumb, obdurate tragedies of remote and monotonous lives dragged themselves out in rural isolation" and of the feminine heart, which possesses "a force, more powerful than conscience, which even the Protestant spirit has never mastered." The same division that the little boy noticed in himself when his grandfather freed the prisoner has reappeared: Whitlock's warm and irrational heart is always opposing harsh fact. He knows too that the division is not a simple one between male and female or classic and romantic, for he finds even in John Wesley—whose religion he detested—"the great truth" that "there is a need in man which reason and logic cannot supply . . ."[23]

The rest of the story is less relevant here, as Paul prospers financially and declines morally, always in opposition to local mores, yet never strong enough to assert himself against them in any satisfying way. His father's campaign against drink gets progressively more repulsive, and public opinion soon becomes the real villain of the book. Despite his yearning, Paul is victim of it, and one can sense in him some of the feelings of isolation which any imaginative boy must have suffered in such an environment: "How dreadfully alone in life was every human being; they had to go through it in the dark, and go through death in the dark. There was nothing more terrifying than the awful isolation of every human soul . . ."[24]

Life was grim in retrospect, perhaps, but Whitlock could always remember moments of excitement. He had a "noble friend" in Gus Wright, an old sailor invested with great glamour who had hunted whales in the South Pacific and sailed the Seven Seas. More important, he made the hero-worshiping little boy two miniature vessels, "one a full rigged ship, the other a bark."[25] As a boy he also loved the writings of Mark Twain about the Mississippi and the romantic melodramas of Bartley Campbell, especially *The White Slave*. Whitlock never forgot how he sat enraptured "in the mystery and romance of life on the Mississippi" with its accompanying steamboats, plantation hands, singing darkies, moonlight and the jasmine flower; the handsome and cruel master, in fierce moustache, slouch hat, and top boots, was always taking a beautiful octoroon to unnameable destinations, the girl "so lily white and fragile that it should have been patent to all, save perhaps an immoral slave-holder, from the very first scene, that she had no drop of negro blood!"[26]

Of all his youthful excitements he remembered Buffalo Bill the best. Already acquainted from reading nickel libraries about the hero, he could scarcely believe the man really existed when he headed down to the hotel where Buffalo Bill was to stay and found him there "with his enormous cream-colored sombrero and long hair, smoking a cigar and reading a newspaper." Whitlock gazed enraptured, and then came the inevitable disillusionment: "For there in the crown of the cream-colored sombrero, was a large dark grease spot!" During his stay, the hero later redeemed himself in a western melodrama in which a man, trapped by "a gang of desperadoes with the most villainous countenances," was rescued by a bearded man who arrived, defied the captors just as they were hanging the man, whipped off his beard, and, as Buffalo Bill, made a significant rescue—"Oh, but it was magnificent and thrilling!"[27]

But life in Urbana was often dull and boring despite these occasional interludes, and Whitlock was glad when the family moved to Toledo, where he could attend a good high school. Like most towns west of Philadelphia, Toledo was still young and a little raw in the period after the Civil War. Lucas County had been established only in 1835 and by the next year still had fewer than one hundred inhabitants. Cholera plagues in 1852 and 1854 and the panic of 1857 slowed down growth, yet by 1860 the county had 13,000 people. Toledo was incorporated in 1837 as its county seat and early developed a busy industrial life, with bankers, brickmakers, sawmillers, grain millers and car makers all prominent. By the Civil War the area also had foundries, tobacco works, and a gaslight and coke company. Later, when Whitlock's family settled there, Toledo also had the reputation of being politically unorthodox, and it regularly violated the precepts of political-party loyalty. In the 1870's, it even elected a Greenback mayor and city council—which seemed quite radical to more conservative observers.[28]

Whitlock attended high school in Toledo but preferred to enter the field of journalism rather than go on to Ohio Wesleyan. He worked for several Toledo papers and finally landed a relatively permanent spot as a roving commentator for the Toledo *Blade* with the flattering right to sign many of his contributions. Like most schoolboys with more brains and talent than training, he was addicted to parody, puns, and shallow witticisms of the clever country-boy variety. His regular column he called "The Blade's Spectator," but he also contributed short fillers called "Sharpened Blades" and, irregularly, longer works. Once, he parodied Longfellow in commenting on some news from Africa:

> Near the silver Lake Nyanza
> In the country of Uganda,
> Uganda, ruled by King Mewanga,
> (Ruled by him, how e'er no longa,)
> In the late month of Octoba,
> When the moon was in fourth quarta,
> Did the guards of King Mewanga,
> Rise and swipe his throne from unda
> Him, and give it to his brotha
> etc.

More often he was just wordy, banal, and affected, as when he wrote about Washington, on April 30, 1889: "In allowing my thoughts to amble back through the corridors of time, to the occasion which was of so great moment to the incipient Republic, I can but marvel at the unqualifiedness of the man whose inauguration we are commemorating today," etc. Or: "Young Mr. Count R. Jumper, whom everyone probably knows as a prominent society man of the Third ward, went gaily forth the other evening, humming a jocund lay, to see Miss Angy Collingwood, to whom, as is also well known, he is affianced." Add to these satires on local events a series of weather reports put into light verse, and Whitlock's career as a writer might have seemed doomed at the start. Fortunately, as soon as he came of age he went to Chicago to toughen.[29]

All was not satire, however, even in Toledo, for at this time

Whitlock found his second hero—after Grandfather Brand. Out of the "Black Swamp" area of Ohio "had risen a young, fiery, and romantic figure who ignored the past and flung himself with fierce ardor into a new campaign for liberty." Frank Hunt Hurd irritated the contented Republicans of his state, who knew that liberty had been won in 1865 and were convinced that free trade was the sign of Southern sympathy, treason, and the devil. A Democrat, he served several nonconsecutive terms as Toledo's representative in Washington, and Whitlock ranked his speech on free trade in the House, February 18, 1881, as "the classic on that subject, ranking with Henry Clay's speech on 'The American System.'" Whitlock could not praise Hurd too highly, and in his speech on Hurd he sounded like a politician himself. When normal adjectives ran out, he said, and "the American passion for picturesque alliterative nomenclature must needs at last be indulged, there was but one name to call him, and he became the Demosthenes of Democracy."

Whitlock first saw Hurd when David H. Locke, better known as Petroleum V. Nasby, introduced him during a patriotic orgy on July 4. He delivered his oration, and "anyone who ever heard Frank Hurd deliver an oration never forgot it afterward." Whitlock could never remember what Hurd said—a typical outcome of many political and patriotic speeches, no matter how inspired—"but his black hair, his handsome face, his beautiful voice, and the majestic music of his rolling phrases were wholly and completely charming." Everyone told the teenager that "Frank Hurd was wrong, if he was not, indeed, wicked, and the subject possessed a kind of fascination for me." More and more perplexed, the boy finally reached the momentous decision to take his perplexities to the man himself and ask him. One summer, when Hurd had just returned from Washington, Whitlock, then eighteen, worked up his courage, found his man, and asked to be instructed about free trade. They sat together in the big leather chairs in the lobby of the old Boody House, met again and again, and "it was not long until I was able, with a solemn pride, to announce at home that I was a Free-Trader and a Democrat."

The Hurd that Whitlock recalled was "a modest, almost a timid man." He told Whitlock repeatedly that even after his many years of public speaking he could never face an audience without discovering himself shaking from fear and finding at the end that he had forgotten what he most wanted to say. Whitlock himself later suffered even more terribly in Toledo and remembered Hurd all the more sympathetically because of it. A true gentleman, Hurd was a close friend of the devoutly Republican Locke, and although the men had hardly an opinion in common they both enjoyed talking endlessly about their terrible differences at the old Draconian Club. Finally defeated in politics for the last time, Hurd retired to his legal practice, "where his love for truth, and liberty, and justice, and his great sympathy with the unfortunate prevented his attaining the riches that were continually held out to him by the corporate interests he found it against his principles to serve." An example, in short, that would solace Whitlock during his long, lean career as lawyer and mayor.

After his conversion to the Democrats and free trade, Whitlock went to Urbana to visit his favorite grandfather. The house was cool, even in the summer, and he prolonged the preliminaries as long as he could. He went through rooms and out into the garden. He visited the stable and the horses, but the time had to come. At last the two sat in the living room, in the cool half-light of the late summer afternoon, on the Nuremberg furniture. Grandfather Brand sat and looked at him, stretching forth his hand in the gesture he made when, during their Socratic conversations, he came to the inevitable sign of ignorance in his grandson and said, "Let me instruct you." This time, after they talked idly for a while, he sat and looked at Whitlock and asked: "Do you understand this tariff question?"

The proper and expected reply was "No, sir," and Grandfather had already stretched forth his hand for the inevitable "Let me instruct you." Teenagers are always uncooperative. "Yes, sir," Whitlock said.

Grandfather drew in his hand, touched the end of his large nose with his long fingers. "I am in favor of Free Trade, sir," said his grandson.

Joseph Carter Brand did not extend his hand. He stared a moment and then said: "You are quite right; we must support Mr. Cleveland in the coming contest."

If Grandfather Brand and Frank Hurd were in agreement, Whitlock's conversion to free trade could never be reversed. For old Mr. Brand few such opportunities to express his political views remained. Soon after, he was kicked by one of his horses and was an invalid until he died. Since he could no longer participate in politics he read about it, and more and more he took to reading poetry, even replacing grace at the table with a stanza or two. In 1896, when he supported William Jennings Bryan, his devout Republican neighbors said: "Poor old Major Brand! His mind must be affected!" They had no such excuse for his errant grandson, but by then he had gone away. After high school and the *Blade*, Whitlock had had enough of Toledo, and in 1891 he left for Chicago. Through Frank Hurd's influence, he had a job as a reporter on the Chicago *Herald*, the principal Democratic newspaper.[30]

《CHAPTER 2

The Education of a
Whitechapel Wit
(1890-1896)

FRANK ALGERNON COWPERWOOD, Theodore Drei-
ser's best-known hero, left his native Philadelphia in disgrace.
All the logic of geography and opportunity led him to Chicago, "a
seething city in the making," where there "was something dynamic
in the very air which appealed to his fancy." In one passage of
Dreiser's somewhat overwrought rhetoric, Cowperwood sees parallels there to Athens, Rome, and Babylon, and even to Troy and
Nineveh. The actual vision more resembled Sodom and Gomorrah;
Chicago was "a city packed to the doors with all the riffraff of a
thousand towns. Flaring were the lights of the bagnio; tinkling of
the banjos, zithers, mandolins of the so-called gin-mill; all the
dreams and the brutality of the day seemed gathered to rejoice
(and rejoice they did) in this new-found wonder of a metropolitan
life in the West." Cowperwood found an ugly world full of dirty
politics, epic forces, widespread corruption, and sexual irregularities. He met it unafraid and fully initiated. Brand Whitlock met it
as a young, sensitive, highly impressionable man just passed twenty-
one. He found it his college.[1]

College, however, has never been quite as it appears from the
outside. From the point of view of the student, Whitlock had

ample resources. His chief "teacher," continuing the work of Frank Hunt Hurd and Joseph Carter Brand, was his newspaper boss, Horatio W. Seymour. The "administration," admirable in both intentions and grandeur, was that of the imperturbable Carter Henry Harrison. Best of all, the "fraternity," refuge from the philistinism of the world, was the legendary Whitechapel Club, a source of countless anecdotes, shenanigans, and lifetime friends.

Horatio Seymour, editor of the Chicago *Herald*, was the elder brother of one of Whitlock's closest friends and himself carried on an irregular correspondence with Whitlock for many years afterward. Born in New York, brought up in Racine, Wisconsin, he rose quickly on the staff of the Milwaukee *Daily News* and achieved enough of a reputation to receive an invitation from Wilbur Storey to join the Chicago *Times*, then a radical Democratic paper. After four years as telegraph editor and four more as night editor, he quit to join the *Herald* in 1883, and was editor or managing editor until 1895. He wrote most of the articles which gave the paper its reputation and political coloring and was the chief creator, as Whitlock put it, of "a newspaper famed for the taste and even beauty of its typographical appearance." No paper, he thought, had so much influence in helping the Democrats to their 1890 landslide victory, and no single set of articles was so important as the one which Seymour wrote on the tariff. It was, Whitlock notes significantly, "one of the delights of Frank Hurd."[2] Whitlock was continuing his education in liberal theory.

Every writer has his favorite words, and Horatio Seymour's were *moral, principle,* and *privilege.* He viewed the world in moral terms and measured all ideas against moral principles. Privilege was always the enemy, a perpetual bête noire that haunted his editorials. In general terms he compared Privilege to the Slave Power, and he showed how one aspect or another of each power hurt the laborer, the farmer, or the businessman. The words helped mold his view of present circumstances. The America he saw was dominated by greed, "a spirit of gain so eager and reckless that, even in its effects upon men as individuals, it long ago excited the condemnation of the world" and made the era one "that will be forever memorable for the remorseless aggrandizement of wealth." Greed created Privilege, for Privilege was the institutionalization of greed. Tariffs, in whatever form of subsidy, tax, monopoly, or grant, "are the basis of Privilege as it exists in America today."

Tariffs were the real villains. "Privilege's first sweeping triumph in America was the passage of the protective tariff bill of 1862." While men were fighting for union and liberty, a selfish few were preparing to feast at the public trough. The next bill, that of 1864, "embodied every selfish device that the human mind could suggest. It was the most stupendous measure of taxation ever known on this planet." The people were not consulted, and only sneaky special interests knew enough to ask for what they wanted. "No avarice was too great to meet instant endorsement; whatever tax this man or that man had the hardihood to demand, that tax was laid by a body that was quick to do the bidding of Privilege."[3]

Seymour based his objections on a firm faith in moral laws, Christian principles, and faith in the goodness and ability of the middle-class Democratic American. He had praise for the golden rule, equality and brotherhood, and stressed the moral fiber of the individual man. "Privilege is morally wrong," and "the security of free government demands its utter and immediate extirpation." Privilege, represented by the tariff, "the practice of taxing one man for the benefit of another man is wrong—wrong in morals, wrong in politics, wrong in business, wrong in government." Yet Seymour was no radical and did not even approach socialism. For all his anger, his ideal was pure American bourgeois. People had to reform themselves first, for "people who cannot or will not reform themselves will not undertake to reform their government." No one should look to Washington for help, and those who did were as guilty as the monopolists. To ask for government aid was to fall into "the error so industriously propagated, that it is the duty of government to provide work and wages for all." Privilege was evil also for the other usual middle-class reasons. "It teaches labor of the most degraded type to look for its reward to legislation rather than to industry and frugality," and thus leads to sloth and waste. It "is destroying the self-reliance of the American people as surely as it is corrupting our youth, exasperating our labor, and polluting our politics." Finally, it took men from fruitful labor and caused "too many people in the United States" to seek to "live by their wits; too many people in the United States with a capital of a few thousand dollars, or with no capital at all, are attempting to live without work."[4]

Such views had obvious parallels with the Forgotten Man ideas of William Graham Sumner and formed the backbone for popular support of much later progressive social reform. Nothing was less radical. As in earlier days the middle class led the way and prevented class warfare, for it was "as profoundly interested in the abolition of Privilege as, in the days of slavery, the middle class of that period was interested in the abolition of that institution." What people had to do was force the Democratic Party to live up to its duty as the opponent of Privilege and "return to first principles, and with uncompromising firmness cut away every new growth that does not harmonize with their everlasting truths."[5] How much of all this Whitlock believed, how much he took for granted, and how much he rejected out of hand no one can say definitely; but he was certainly prepared by Grandfather Brand and Frank Hurd for such doctrines, and the close relations between Hurd, Whitlock, and Seymour seem to indicate that the men agreed at least in their devotion to the Democratic Party, free trade, and a mild, civil-service variety of reform. Certainly Whitlock's autobiography indicated that he took Seymour's ideas, if not Seymour's expression of them, for granted. Surely Seymour's unbendingly moral tone repelled Whitlock, as such arrogance of expression later did in the mouths of Whitlock's opponents in Toledo. Yet despite this probable aversion, Whitlock frankly acknowledged his debt to Seymour's ideas in letters to Seymour long afterward.

Seymour was not the only influence on young Whitlock. During much of the time he was in Chicago, the city's mayor was Carter Henry Harrison. The parallels between the Harrison administration in Chicago and the later Whitlock administration in Toledo are too many and too close for mere coincidence. Seymour talked about morality and principles, but the more congenial practices of Carter Harrison had a more lasting effect. Chicago was a raw city, with all the moral inhibitions of a Frank Cowperwood, but the varieties and the spirit of reform were many. Reform mayors repeatedly tried to close down the drinking places, but most of the people would not stand for it, and genial judges paid by gamblers more than once arrested the puritanical raiders and freed the so-called criminals. Carter Harrison, being neither fool nor puritan, was no reformer.[6]

Born in 1825 in a log cabin near Lexington, Harrison came from the most beautiful part of Kentucky. His father died early: his mother raised him, sent him to Yale, and watched him try and then abandon law, travel to Europe, resume law practice, marry, abandon law again, and go into real estate. He was, as a rule, a Henry Clay Whig with no violent political convictions and ran during his life as a nonpartisan, a Liberal Republican, and a Democrat. He held minor local office and twice was a Representative in Washington. In the spring of 1879 he became mayor as a Democrat, the first of five terms. He quickly began setting precedents for the future mayor of Toledo. Finding the city insolvent, he began an austerity regime and found himself in the first of many battles against franchise-grabbing railroads. By so doing, he won upper-class support for his thrifty administration. A true libertarian, he was soon under attack by some of the "better elements" of the town—the middle class—for his frankly liberal, laissez-faire attitude toward vice and crime. This attitude in turn won him lower-class and foreign voters. The press and professional reformers generally shouted against him, to the point where he made his third campaign on the single plank of "personal liberty." Naturally, this offended the middle class. He was a moderate on free trade and a deep believer in the educability of the mass of the people. They almost always repaid his confidence by re-election, just as they would later repay Samuel M. Jones and Brand Whitlock.

Chicago during his administration was full of anarchist and socialist propaganda, and the good people frequently fretted loudly about it. A supremely tolerant man, Harrison refused to interfere with anyone's civil liberties and even appointed some socialists to high posts in his regime. Despite his tolerance, graft did not run riot; if anything, it remained static or declined. With fewer laws to enforce, fewer policemen found the opportunity to request bribes. "You can't legislate morality," he said. "So leave it alone. Those who think that the morals of a great crowded city can be made pure by law are as much dreamers as the mad anarchists who imagine that crime can be destroyed by killing law."

Worn down by sickness and death in his family—he buried two wives and six infant children during his life—and by the constant attacks upon him by newspapers and clergy, Carter Harrison retired after four terms to make a trip around the world and get back his health. Chicago was in his blood, though, and so was a sense of grandeur. Along with James Scott and others, he helped to bring the World's Fair to his beloved city. "Chicago is my bride! I love it as a young man loves his chosen one!" he once declared in a speech, and he meant it. A dashing man, he yearned to represent the city as its symbol during the World's Fair years, so he ran again in 1891, only to lose. He promptly bought the Chicago *Times* and began campaigning for the next election. He won, the Fair arrived, and he gloried in it. Then, an energetic sixty-eight and engaged to be married for the third time, he discovered an unexpected reward for public service. After an active Saturday at the Fair, he returned home, answered the doorbell, and was shot three times by an insane office seeker. Neither Chicago nor Brand Whitlock ever forgot him.[7]

The contest for the allegiance of Brand Whitlock between the moral, earnest, and humorless democracy of Horatio Seymour and the easygoing libertarian democracy of Carter Harrison might well have been close, but the Whitechapel Club tipped the scales firmly toward tolerance. Whitlock was admittedly naïve and uninitiated when he arrived in Chicago, and Whitechapel introduced him to a new world. "They were boys in spirit, though in the knowledge of this world they were as aged men, some of whom had seen so much of life that they were able to dwell with it only by refusing any longer to accept it seriously." The nucleus of the group was the newspaper clique, with numerous artists, musicians, physicians, and lawyers in vocal minority. None of them "were in any sense reformers, or actuated by the smug and forbidding spirit which too often inspires that species." They were often radical, Rabelaisian, and even grotesque in their sense of humor, and lived the Bohemian life with a flair that was rarely matched even in the later heyday of New York's Greenwich Village.[8]

The list of men who belonged, as members, hangers-on, or honorary members, is impressive even today, when the lesser-known figures have disappeared into the unread pages of their friends' autobiographies. For Whitlock, one of the chief attractions was Horatio Seymour's younger brother, Charles, "the center of the coterie, a young man with such a *flair* for what was news, with such an instinct for word values, such real ability as a writer, and such a quaint and original strain of humor as to make him the peer of any, a young man who would have gone far and high could he have lived." Smiling under his red hair, with his "comedian's droll face," he would recount the many adventures in his life, "whether on one of his many journeys as a war correspondent to the region of the Dakotas when his friends among the Ogallalla and the Brûlé Sioux were on the warpath again," or in some local tragedy with glamour, such as a murder in South Clark Street. The club had its headquarters in the rear of Henry Koster's saloon in Calhoun Place, more commonly known as "Newspaper Alley," near the *News* and *Herald* buildings. It was nameless for a while, but one afternoon as several of the group were sitting in the rooms, a newsboy passed through the alley and cried: "All about the latest Whitechapel murder!" Seymour, sitting with Frederick Upham "Grizzly" Adams, raised his stein of beer halfway to his lips, paused, and said: "We'll call the new club the 'Whitechapel Club.' " The name stuck. The connotations of the name presumably led to the practice of collecting relics from events that the men reported. After he had returned from a trip to the Dakotas, where he had covered the Sioux War, Seymour donated a number of Indian skulls and blankets drenched in blood, which the members hung on the walls. As soon as they heard of the practice, sheriffs and newspaper men everywhere began to send anything they had of that kind to the Whitechapel Club. The place was soon full of ropes used in hangings and photographs of the execution of Chinese pirates. Within a few years it had a large collection of the skulls of criminals, and some of the learned medical members whiled away the time deciding on the differences between the skulls of men who were caught and those of men who were not.[9]

Another Whitechapel devotee with much in common with Whitlock was George Ade. Born in Indiana of parents even more fundamentalist than the Whitlocks, Ade too became an infrequent churchgoer, and, in the classic manner of the young artist, caused his parents great concern by his perpetual dreaminess. He soon teamed with John Tinny McCutcheon, and his new friend persuaded him to move to Chicago, where Charles H. Dennis hired him on the *Morning News* less than a year before Whitlock arrived. Ade too joined the Whitechapel Club, which he later termed "a little group of thirsty intellectuals who were opposed to everything." He soon became friends with Whitlock, finding him tall, quiet, and good-looking, with "a searching eye and a whimsical smile," who deserved admiration for his "bantering, fantastic, mock-serious, spoofing stuff," and he predicted a good career for the boy as a humorist. If Whitlock's editor wanted to poke fun at some ceremony or some celebrity, Ade wrote, he gave the assignment to Whitlock, and some of his reports became classics. Whitlock's reputation in Chicago was that of a "witty commentator," although at the Club he "was one of the sedate and temperate members who sat back and enjoyed the ribald talk, but did not have much to say."[10]

Ade and Whitlock often worked together, and they kept in touch sporadically after they separated. Ade recalled in 1911 that he and Whitlock covered the 1892 Minneapolis conventions together. Both were members of the Sigma Chi fraternity, and they found this allegiance of great value when trying to interview the reclusive Matt Quay. After the two men had been refused an interview, they spotted a fraternity key on Quay's secretary and declared that it would be most unfraternal to prevent loyal brothers from doing their jobs. They got their interview. Ade's memory indicates that the prose Whitlock wrote for the Toledo and Chicago papers masked a witty and thoroughly enjoyable young man. In those days, Ade recalled, Whitlock "was a brilliant fellow. But there was never anything about him that suggested the seriousness that later developed in his work. He was always kidding everything."[11]

Of all the Whitechapelers, only Finley Peter Dunne became a long-time friend. Two years older than Whitlock, Dunne grew up in a middle-class, Irish Catholic neighborhood in Chicago. His parents were as devout as the Whitlocks, and Dunne was as tolerant and skeptical about religion as his friend. He was not quite seventeen when he went to work for the *Telegram* as an office boy, but his knowledge of the Chicago tenderloin areas, and police routine in general, soon enabled him to be the "police" man for the paper. One of his stories caught the eye of the managing editor of the *News*, Henry Ten Eyck White, and Dunne shifted papers and got a raise for his trouble. Dunne was something of a congenital sloth and routine bored him, but he soon won approval for his offbeat feature articles and even some short editorials—anything, in fact, that was not routine. Charles Seymour was then already suffering from the tuberculosis that killed him, but he and Dunne soon became close and shared an unconventional Bohemian life. Together the two men gained fame early as they traveled with local baseball teams and revolutionized the art of sports reporting.

Baseball soon bored Dunne too. A good offer from Wilbur F. Storey brought him to the *Times* to switch to political reporting. When he became better known through his Mr. Dooley columns, Dunne did a piece on his former paper. Storey, he wrote, "knowed what th' people wanted. They wanted crime, an' he give it to thim. If they wasn't a hangin' on th' front page some little lad iv a rayporther'd lose his job. They was murther an' arson till ye cudden't rest . . ." Storey lost his mind, and James J. West reorganized the paper, soon gaining the dislike of other publishers by his nasty remarks about them. Dunne's work was so good that West made him city editor when Dunne was just twenty-one, but West's enemies were soon after him and when he had to leave the paper Dunne was forced to leave with him. The *Tribune* quickly hired Dunne as a reporter, and by 1890 he had risen to editor of the Sunday edition. Finally, the next year, James Scott brought him back into the Democratic fold to do political articles for the *Herald*. There, besides Whitlock and Seymour, the group included cartoonists Charles Lederer, Thomas E. Powers, and Horace Taylor, inventor "Griz" Adams, and poet-critic Wallace Rice.

Dunne's chief contribution to the Club, aside from his personality, was his mercilessly critical tongue, a tongue that would lash millionaire, businessman, politician, or one of his best friends whenever the occasion seemed to warrant it. He set the tone for the Club's habit of dissecting the great reputations of the day, and Whitlock in all probability learned his skepticism at the side of this most skeptical of all American humorists. The great interest of many of the members was in writing, and their guides were Robert Louis Stevenson and Rudyard Kipling. Dunne and the others could be murderous on prose that fell too far short of the mark set by the masters. Constantly they pounded at a sentimental view of life, bad prose, and sloppy observation. George Ade was once so offended by Dunne's tongue that he shunned his company for some time, until he realized the basic kindness of the man and the honesty of his views. Poor, huge, kindly Opie Read never did realize it. When one of his trivial novels went under the knife, he walked out and never came back. "When the heavy firing began across the table," John Prindiville recalled later, "it was time for the man of weak broadsides to climb a tree. No one had an opportunity to take out his knitting when framing a reply. And the retort always had to be proof against a comeback. Those Whitechapel sharpshooters were the most expert in the business anywhere."[12] Obviously they missed hitting at least one man's mixed metaphors.

The club soon grew in popularity and leased a small building up Calhoun Place with a great oak door trimmed in wrought iron. In the main room of the first floor was a huge table, built in the shape of a coffin lid and studded with big brass nails. Upstairs was the symposium room, with a big table shaped like a mule shoe. "Griz" Adams was the respected mayor of Whitechapel, elected on the platform: "No gas, no water, and no police."

Macabre immortality was only a matter of time, for when the members overdid it, they overdid it in a way to make any college fraternity green—and not only with envy. The victim was Maurice Allen Collins, a disappointed agitator who had fallen in with Honoré J. Jaxon, then a minor politician and sidewalk contractor. Jaxon, a half-breed Indian who had been secretary of state in the Louis Riel uprising in Canada, was not a member, and he asked permission to show his friend Collins the famous Chicago club. Once admitted, Collins got the idea that he was in a radical organization devoted to death—not an unreasonable assumption, considering the skulls and coffin lids around. At the time, Collins had been talking about suicide; as the result of a severe railroad accident he was a chronic invalid, and his money had been stolen by a corrupt lawyer. His visit to the club decided him. He went home and wrote a letter willing his body to the club for dissection or cremation and put a bullet through his head. The resulting events indicate, better than any others, the environment that took Whitlock out of his Methodist home and gave him the reputation as a humorist and witty commentator that Ade had remembered.

The club decided to cremate Collins. One member, demonstrating his wide reading, remembered that the poet Shelley had been cremated on the shore of the Mediterranean at about that time of year. Someone looked up the exact day, and it was convenient. A committee found a suitably wild spot on the shore of Lake Michigan, not far from Miller's Station, Indiana, just beyond the state line. Someone looked up a discussion of how the Greeks made funeral pyres, and they all constructed one accordingly: eight feet long, four feet high, and four feet wide, with timbers pointed inward so that in the collapse all the ashes would fall inward. They soaked the structure in oil and wine, and swathed Collins' body in a Greek robe with the right arm arched over and resting on his chest. The Whitechapelers then stood around and listened to impassioned speeches from those members who were so inclined, under lights supplied by blazing pine knots.

Jaxon then lit the pyre; as the heat grew intense, the rigidity of the body relaxed and the bent arm rose and waved goodbye to the assembled club members. Several Scandinavian fishermen, who had seen or heard what was going on, prayed hysterically on their knees in their fear at the event. A rival local newspaper man, who had somehow heard of the ceremony, was tied to a tree with telephone wire so that the scoop could appear first in the *Herald*. The club, whether from adverse publicity, too many members, or the transfer of several of the wittier men, soon broke up, its immortality assured.[13]

His years in Chicago thus taught Whitlock much. With a background in Civil War Republicanism and narrow Methodism, he had broken away to Grover Cleveland and free trade, under the eyes of Grandfather Brand and Frank Hurd. In Chicago, Horatio Seymour reminded him of this democratic heritage and gave it vocal if sometimes extreme expression. Increasingly, this heritage found its counterbalance in the tolerant, laissez-faire amusement of Carter Harrison with his confidence that no one should legislate morals or endanger civil liberties out of fear or prejudice. Finally, the Whitechapelers introduced Whitlock to the world, the underside of a crude and corrupt city. They would tolerate everything but sham, sentimentality, and poor writing and taught the plain style, conciseness, cynicism, and skepticism which a basically romantic and impressionable artist needed to balance his natural tendencies. Certainly, his later success as a public figure, both as mayor and diplomat, owed something to his training as humorist and raconteur for this last most demanding of audiences.

As an education, moreover, life on the *Herald* did more than introduce its employees to the slums and clubs of the city. It also sent its more capable reporters traveling with famous men of the region and sometimes made them its representatives in Springfield or some other area of interest to local readers. During the fall of 1890, on a snowy morning shortly before the election, Whitlock went into Indiana to accompany James G. Blaine, President Harrison's secretary of state and one of the acknowledged leaders of the Republican Party, on a campaign trip. Blaine was a tired, sad man, his face, hair, and beard all of a gray pallor, and already he was gloomily predicting the defeat which the Republicans soon suffered in the 1890 Democratic sweep. Despite his total opposition to Blaine's high-tariff views, Whitlock had a certain admiration for the old man and sympathized with him during his dreary trip through the farm country. In the hope of winning the admiration of Pete Dunne and Charlie Seymour, he wrote a report lovingly detailing some of Blaine's more rhetorical extravagances. Blaine, fearing that he had indeed said too much, requested the privilege of editing the story, and Whitlock felt just a little ashamed of himself for the piece. Despite his opinions, he had come to like the man. He refused the request, but felt badly about it.[14]

Ultimately more important was Whitlock's assignment two years later, during the 1892 legislative sessions, to the post of Springfield political correspondent for the *Herald*. The most obvious result of his years in Springfield was his use of the town and its legislature as the raw material for two of his novels and several short stories. *The Thirteenth District* and *Her Infinite Variety* were both concerned with Illinois politics, the first with the moral problems of political life and the second with politics merely as background for a light satire on woman suffrage. The ever-present theme of politics in Whitlock's stories almost always had the smell of decay and corruption about it, and many stories were specifically about that smell in Springfield. "That Has-Been" was about an old man and his memories of dirty politics in the legislature and the effect the environment had on a nice young man. "The

Vindication of Henderson of Greene" was about lawyer-lobbyist
George R. Baldwin, the corrupter in more than one of Whitlock's
short stories, and his attempts at bribery. "Senate Bill 578" was
about stalwart Bronson Meredith of Chicago, who defeated a foul
plot to ram through a corrupt franchise plan during a rump session of the legislature; a devout and admiring young page ran to
tell him of the plot and saved the day. None of these stories was a
bit more distinguished than the synopses indicate, but they did
show the almost visceral dislike which Whitlock was acquiring for
politics and politicians.[15]

Also in Springfield, he carried on a lightning romance with
young Susan Brainerd. He met and married her so swiftly that
they had no time to be long separate and to write letters that
would help future biographers determine what she was like. Anyone who has read many of Whitlock's earlier, lesser-known works,
knows of his intensely romantic frame of mind and its preoccupation with young people deeply in love. It comes as no shock to
discover that he himself lived as impetuously as some of his characters. His stories rarely end with tragedy, however, as his marriage did. For four months later, Susan Brainerd died.[16] Perhaps
she died of consumption, the nineteenth-century name for what is
now usually tuberculosis; one report has her dying of convulsive
vomiting of early pregnancy. But whatever the cause of death,
Whitlock never forgot Susan, and decades later her birthday
would bring forth in his journal a sad and agonized exclamation,
though nothing more. He was young and resilient, and he recovered and remained on good terms with Susan's family. Beyond
that, nothing is known.

Springfield also contributed to Whitlock's political education.
As a Chicago man Whitlock had already been discovering how
cities often found themselves shortchanged by rural domination
of the state legislature, so deep was the belligerent rural hatred of
the corrupt, foreign, dirty, and generally undesirable people that everyone knew lived in cities. When a rural clique in the Springfield
legislature attempted to cut off funds for helping Chicago with the
World's Fair, Whitlock was instrumental in getting *Herald* publisher James Scott to send down a lobbyist capable of talking rural
language. Down came the man, Colonel James A. McKenzie, a
small-time Kentucky politician whom Whitlock met in connection

with work on the fair, and who had more inflated rhetoric and
sheer political charm than most legislators could handle. The
Colonel arrived, "and after he had associated with the members a
day or so, and they had seen him draw Kentucky 'twist' from the
deep pocket of the long tails of his coat, and on one or two
occasions had watched him gently pinch into a julep the tender
sprigs of mint the spring had brought to Springfield, the appropria-
tion for some reason was made."[17] The wheels of the Republic
apparently ran on soft soap, and this lesson was not lost on the
cynical yet idealistic young member of the Whitechapel Club.

Politics may have been messy, but newspaper work seemed, to
Whitlock, little better. The modern metropolitan newspaper,
Whitlock soon wrote, needed more energy than intellect or talent
from its employees. When the young used up their supply of
energy, they soon got shoved aside for new and more industrious
arrivals. Their pay was poor, and no future advancement made up
for early privations. Soon the work lost its fascinations and became
mere drudgery, and the young man became tired unless he could
find connections which enabled him to use his newspaper work as
a stepping stone. Anyone who really had journalistic ambitions,
Whitlock commented sarcastically, indirectly explaining his resignation from the *Herald*, ought to "accumulate a fortune in the
packing of pork or the manufacture of neats-foot oil from the
carcasses of diseased animals . . ."; then, "with social position
assured," he could later "buy the souls of other men in the market
places, casting upon them the burden, and reserving for himself
the seat at the banquet board . . ."; there he "may pose to his vain
heart's content," and appear "as the true exponent of a profession
which he is not qualified to follow, of which he knows nothing,
and to which he was only admitted by his ability to hire."[18] A
stronger indictment of Chicago's editors and their belligerent conservatism, lack of culture, and unconcern for the welfare of their
employees would be hard to find, yet Whitlock himself was not
mistreated, he did not dislike his own relatively liberal paper, and
he did enjoy many friendships. More likely, he was beginning to
feel the first rumblings of a frustration that almost enervated him
during the next decade: What would he ever make of himself?
What was he most fitted to do? How could he do it? Never capable of making quick decisions in anything but love, and yearning

to be left alone to write and dream, he was in 1894 older than
many settled professional men. With a new marriage and possibly
a family on his mind, he felt boxed in. He even turned against
Chicago and soon spoke of "the horror of living in the place
again." Yet he always retained a feeling of attraction to the city,
"with all its hopelessness and horror," and yearned for it at times
when he was subconsciously sure he could not go there.[19]

He had to make one last unconscious gesture toward what he
had learned from Horatio Seymour and Frank Hurd. Although he
later recalled that the 1894 campaign was "fun," he did not
exactly agree at the time. He went on the stump for the Democrats, on "soft autumn evenings, over the soft roads," roads that
became especially soft in the rain, campaigning for free trade, "at
the top of one's voice, in remote country schoolhouses of the
backwoods," in an attempt to "inject tariff doctrine into the slug-
gish intellect of the benighted farmer along the Sangamon . . ."
Worse than all this, he was hard put to explain why the Democratic minority in the Senate had just betrayed the principle which
he was expounding, and he suffered more than a little heckling;
sometimes the heckling took the form of a removal of all the nuts
from the axles of his carriage wheels and sometimes mere verbal
combat.[20] Why, in this campaign, did a young man who hated
much of politics, who knew of this betrayal of principle, and who
knew from his friends that all this oratory was sheerest wind
nevertheless go out and stump?

Grandfather Brand, Frank Hurd, and Horatio Seymour were
at the root of the matter with their teachings on free trade, but the
question, Why was free trade so important to Whitlock?, remains
puzzling. The answer lay less in the subject itself than in what it
symbolized to the many reformers who campaigned for it. Just as
Andrew Jackson had campaigned against the United States Bank
because it was a thing of evil, a symbol of the wealth and aristocracy that opposed his ambitions and his idea of democracy, the
tariff reformers campaigned against a symbol of all that was corrupt in the Gilded Age. Even as late as 1913 Whitlock could look
at the action of those Senate Democrats in 1894, as when they
campaigned for free trade, then voted against it, and say that "no
greater moral wrong was ever committed in America." The betrayal was so evil because it meant endorsing a system of favorit-

ism for the industries which had lied to labor, driven women into the mills, and fed children "to the Moloch of the machines . . ." Laborers had finally learned that the insolent hypocrisy of the capitalists meant that labor received no protection, and the laborers had turned to the Democratic Party for relief. Once elected, the Democrats betrayed them "with the brutal cynicism such a cause as theirs demands," and the deed was "little short of dastardly."

The tariff seemed so important in 1894 because its attackers saw it as the one fundamental question. Because of the tariff, big businesses had only to join together to fix prices, inflate stock, and bilk the public. They could do this because the tariff made it impossible for foreign goods to compete with them. Thus the way to prevent huge monopolies—and all the graft, corruption, and unlovely greed that came with them—was to enact free trade and allow foreign goods to keep American companies honest. Then, with the enactment of civil service reform, all politics would become once again pure, as it supposedly had been in the days of Jefferson—the man most free-trade Democrats admired more than any other.[21] To be sure, the picture seems simple in the twentieth century; it seemed a little naïve even to Whitlock only a decade or two later. But at the time it seemed all-important. All Whitlock's future intellectual development tended to add to his tariff views, not to replace them, with some results that would not be visible until the New Deal. Meanwhile, 1894 marked the last time any reformer could intelligently concentrate solely on tariffs. Labor problems soon replaced them.

THIS NEW IMPORTANCE of labor, both as a social fact and as an element in Whitlock's mental development, marked his transition from Chicago newspaper work to Springfield political work. The prominence of the labor problems, in fact, made any great concern over the tariff faintly ridiculous. The importance of these problems and the men he met in confronting them are of incalculable importance in tracing Whitlock's intellectual growth. The first inkling he remembered having of these problems came to him from but two words spoken by a newspaper crony: "Oh, nothing." That was all, "the exact words, just those two, and yet a negative so simple contained within itself such an affirmation of an awful truth," that Whitlock was never able to forget them.

He and a companion, some time in 1891, had gone to a little Chicago restaurant late in the night, and in idle gossip one of the reporters asked where Whitlock had been at the time of the Haymarket affair.

"In Toledo," he answered.

"What did people think of it there?"

"Of the hanging?"

"Yes."

Whitlock looked at him in astonishment. What could have been sillier? "Could any question have been more stupid, more banal? What did any people, anywhere, think of it? What was customary, what was proper and appropriate and indispensable under such circumstances?" He was at a loss for words. Everyone knew how much the evil anarchists deserved their fate.

"Why, they thought it was right, of course," Whitlock answered promptly.

The man lit a cigarette, and the yellow flame lit a dark face with a closely trimmed and pointed beard. About his puckered lips played a faint, illusive little smile, quite disconcerting to a country boy new to the city.

"Why?" Whitlock asked, now ill at ease.

"Oh, nothing," he said.

The boy from a respectable, Republican, Methodist family suddenly had discovered that there were two opinions on a subject he had never heard debated. In the presence of the man, Whitlock felt "as though there were secrets from which one had been excluded, as though there were somewhere in this universe a stupendous joke" which he alone "lacked the wit to see. It gave one a disturbed, uneasy sensation, a *mauvaise honte.*"

The man offered little in the way of help. All he would say further was, "ask some of the boys." With the sense that his closed and certain world was changing irrevocably, Whitlock was shocked, "shaken for days." He wandered out into the cold Chicago midnight ready to learn new ideas, of which he had never even dreamt in Urbana.[22]

He was ripe, that is, for a new hero to replace Grandfather Brand and Frank Hurd and their outmoded emphasis on tariffs.

All through his life, Whitlock's intense desire to have a man somewhere that he could admire, often in the most romantic and passionate way, cropped up, now in the form of these men and later
in Golden Rule Jones, Tolstoy, Woodrow Wilson, and King Albert of Belgium. He seemed to have an uncontrollable need to find
someone whom he could endow with all the ideal qualities he
admired and thus reassure himself that a life in conformity to his
ideals was possible and that perhaps he could lead such a life if
these other, obviously greater men could do so. That he thus saw
qualities in men which escaped less enraptured observers was undeniable. Certainly, in John Peter Altgeld he found a man almost
equal to his exacting standards.

One cold, raw morning in Springfield he met Democratic State
Senator Joseph P. Mahoney, who said to him, in a phrase which is
still cliché, "Come with me and I'll introduce you to the next
governor of Illinois." For once he was right.

Whitlock went with him into a narrow little building on
Adams Street, where, upstairs, "in a very much crowded, a very
much littered and a rather dingy little private room, at an odd
little walnut desk, sat John P. Altgeld." The man was not impressive, with his matted hair and trimmed beard and the least hint of
a sinister quality which cartoonists would soon use to scare their
readers. "It is one of the countless ironies of life that a face, sad
with all the utter woe of humanity, should have become for a
season, and in some minds remained forever, the type and symbol
of all that is most abhorrent." The face, full of suffering and
despair, was saved only by the obvious intelligence in the eyes.
Rarely did it express joy or humor.

The Chicago *Herald* and its bourbon-Democrat owner John R.
Walsh opposed Altgeld, and ultimately Walsh helped to defeat
Altgeld politically and to ruin him financially. The paper was
devotedly Democratic on the issues of free trade and general reform, however, and so after Altgeld's nomination for governor it
gave him the lip-service support expected as the minimum for a
party organ. The summer of the campaign showed that Altgeld
was slowly gaining strength, and Whitlock's persistent attempts
gained him permission to write an article on Altgeld in which he
tried "to describe his personality and to give some impression of
the able campaign he was making." Horace Taylor illustrated it,

and Altgeld enjoyed it so much that he sent for its author and asked for the pictures. Then he hesitated for a moment, as if from fear of showing weakness, and told Whitlock that he intended to have the article republished in a newspaper in Mansfield, Ohio, his home town, where he had taught school and met his wife. The two men talked for a while that afternoon and soon cemented a warm friendship.

After Altgeld's victory, Whitlock declined an offer to become his secretary, fearing, or so he says, that he would get a reputation not as Brand Whitlock but as Governor Altgeld's secretary; and his devotion was not so great as to desire that. Whatever rationalizations he made for himself, however, this refusal is intriguing psychologically, for Whitlock's devotion to Altgeld was unquestionable. Perhaps Whitlock's decision indicated that he needed a certain distance between himself and his ideal; that his devotion was more to the ideal than the embodiment and that he did not wish to confuse the two. He did accept an offer of a job in Secretary of State William H. "Buck" Hinrichsen's office, which he hoped would give him a chance of completing legal studies and also give him time to write—two ambitions which a demanding newspaper chief or a demanding governor would not allow time for.

He liked Springfield, particularly in the spring, "and it was a relief to escape the horrid atmosphere of a great brutal city which as a reporter it had been my fate to behold for the most part at night." The quiet town, with its green avenues, had a sense of spaciousness as well as a pleasant society, which included the Brainerd family, and two impressive libraries—a vital consideration to a very poor and aspiring young law student. Governor Altgeld also brought a touch of culture into the philistine wilderness of a state capital, and with him Whitlock could discuss his new literary enthusiasms: George Meredith, Thomas Hardy, and William Dean Howells.[23] But to understand the effect which Springfield eventually had on Whitlock, knowledge of three aspects of life in the 1890's is vital: What was the attitude of the men in power, whose words shaped the thought and reactions of lesser men? What were the local conditions which produced the Haymarket, Lemont, and Pullman strikes? Finally, just what was going on in that sympathetic, intelligent, and stubborn mind that occupied the governor's chair?

Oddly enough, for an era so notoriously and profitably devoted to the loving pursuit of money and success, the key word in the business mind during the 1880's and 1890's was *fear*. The reasons are not hard to find, and are inevitably tied to the economy and the social changes of the period. Two of the most severe depressions of the nineteenth century struck in 1873 and 1893, and another one only slightly less severe came in the mid-eighties. One student has surveyed the years in terms of contemporary reaction to the events and concluded that fourteen of the twenty-five years between 1873 and 1897 should rate as either "recession" or "depression" years. Most histories have emphasized the working man's suffering during these years, but few have discussed the effect of these troubles on employers. With the exception of the few prosperous years, firms failed at the rate of about 100 per year for every 10,000 firms, and contemporary commentators estimated that 95 per cent of all capitalists failed at one time or another. The extraordinarily successful men had most of the acumen and money; they have received most of the academy's attention. The larger majority of more vulnerable entrepreneurs, remarked E. L. Godkin, were in just as "precarious a position as other classes in the community." Mrs. John D. Rockefeller recalled the period as the "days of worry," and her husband recalled the time in words that would be poignant if uttered by a lesser man: "You know how often I had not an unbroken night's sleep, worrying about how it was all coming out. All the fortune I have made has not served to compensate for the anxiety of that period."[24]

This fear made it imperative for men to hold firm to whatever intellectual or psychological security they could find, and one result was an almost belligerent emphasis on "eternal" principles. Americans created for themselves a rough version of natural law, fashioned in part from their religious past, to gain the sense of stability they needed. To endorse their predilections some men still called on God directly, but most acted as though they were now in a deistic, mechanistic world governed by inflexible laws. The social Darwinism preached by Herbert Spencer and his American popularizers had little direct effect on any businessman, with an occasional exception like Andrew Carnegie. The true prophets were the English laissez-faire economists, especially Adam Smith, David Ricardo, and Thomas Malthus, and many American businessmen specifically mentioned Smith when they wished to prove a point. The liberal thought of these men easily joined with the Enlightenment heritage of an orderly, mechanical world which God had begun and for which He had endowed man with reason enough to manage while He merely watched. Thus one Henry Wood, a businessman with no academic training, could publish *Natural Law in the Business World* in 1887 and feel assured that the men of capital would understand him easily. This is the world of allied business, politics, and religion that Francis Whitlock so mocked and that Brand Whitlock had to fight so bitterly as mayor of Toledo.

Within this system, the law of trade was an expression of natural law, and the chief commandment was: Do not interfere with it. Men spoke of these laws as "business principles," but they were, in fact, "the laws of human nature"—"human nature as it is, and not as it ought to be, or as we would like to see it," as Godkin remarked. The chief law, which men referred to in all contexts and with a sublime disregard for relevancy, was that of supply and demand, and it somehow seemed to explain labor unrest, overproduction, slums, and everything else. The laws were immutable; human nature was immutable. Thus, the best of men could only sit back and watch, for God knew best and no one should tamper with His handiwork. When Henry Demarest Lloyd made his famous attack on the Standard Oil Company, Charles Elliott Perkins, president of the Chicago, Burlington and Quincy Railroad, wrote to his friend Edward Atkinson in irritation at "the donkeys who can't see the operation of natural laws in fixing rates of transportation . . ." He hoped that someone who could write would answer Lloyd and his deluded readers to "show what I suppose to be the fact, that the Standard Oil Company is simply a product of natural laws and laws which it is not safe to touch." He had, he emphasized truthfully in closing, "*no* knowledge touching the Standard Oil Co. more than what I read in the newspapers."[25] Facts, in short, did not bother him. Only the theory was important.

Tied with the theory was a myth. Benjamin Franklin was its chief prophet, although scholars often trace its origins to the protestant ethic of puritans like John Cotton and Cotton Mather. By the time of the Civil War, Franklin's *Autobiography* had reached a phenomenal audience, and those who missed it could hear watered-down versions on every side. The myth of the self-made man meant that the average American believed that his country offered each man an opportunity to succeed in the glorious struggle that was life under capitalism. Poverty was an advantage that taught the young aspirant certain indispensable virtues. As the myth developed, the young man was born in a rural area with an angelic mother who gave him the moral training necessary for life; after rudimentary instruction, the young man left for the world, usually a city full of opportunity and corruption, where, due to his rural virtues and his mother's training, he would succeed because he had Character.

Everyone knew the qualities of Character as well as the undeniable fact that they were not inherited, or dependent on immutable gifts like intelligence, but were rather always attainable by an act of will. Character meant that a person was self-reliant, industrious, and persevering, eager to help his employer at any time, and alert for chances to strike out on his own. A man with Character knew that idleness was shameful, that frugality was a virtue, and that smoking and drinking and trivial amusements led to a richly deserved poverty. He knew that he must be punctual, dependable, obedient, and meticulous, and that he then could achieve—never inherit—a heavenly home in the best district in town for his devoted, beautiful, and exceedingly proper wife. Salvation, in short, had become economic. The employer was God, and the employee could choose to be saved or damned. Altgeld, and later Mayor Whitlock, never heard the end of the attacks made on them for ignoring this myth.

The ties of business and religion were never closer. Clergy of most protestant faiths were among the success ethic's most constant and repetitive boosters. Let Baptist Russell H. Conwell stand for all the men and values Whitlock came to detest. In no sense a bloated capitalist, Conwell was loved by many and admired and followed by more. He had but one sermon for his fans; in fact, he repeated "Acres of Diamonds" over 5,000 times in his lifetime, making the two-hour speech a likely candidate for the longest cliché in history. He came, he told his audience, "to tell you what in God's sight I believe to be the truth," in the hope that his common sense might be theirs, for "never in the history of the world did a poor man without capital have such an opportunity to get rich quickly and honestly as he has now in our city." The city might change—in the printed speech it is Philadelphia—but the message never did. "I say that you ought to get rich, and it is your duty to get rich," and all who complain about Christian ministers saying such a thing should know that "to make money honestly is to preach the gospel." The rich man is on the whole honest and trustworthy and deserves his money, and all should imitate him. "I say, then, you ought to have money. If you can honestly attain unto riches in Philadelphia, it is your Christian and godly duty to do so." Poverty was an irrelevant issue, and sympathy for the poor almost sacrilegious. "To sympathize with a man whom God has punished for his sins, thus to help him when God would still continue a just punishment, is to do wrong, no doubt about it, and we do that more than we help those who are deserving." Everyone should remember that "there is not a poor person in the United States who has not been made poor by his own shortcomings, or by the shortcomings of some one else." Russell Conwell started from scratch, made his fortune, built the Baptist Temple in Philadelphia, and founded Temple University. Go, and do thou likewise.[26]

Russell Conwell seemed scarcely aware of it, but America had changed from the days of his youth, and these changes form the second element of the America that Whitlock saw in the 1890's. The era after the Civil War saw one of the greatest industrial expansions in history. Between 1867 and 1893 the country acquired 150,000 miles of railroad track alone, and railroads were only the most conspicuous of its industries. A given year, say, 1871, might see over $100,000,000 worth of American securities marketed in London alone, and by 1893 the country owed more than $3,000,000,000 abroad. In any period of such great change, waste and inefficiency were perhaps inevitable, but in America they passed description. The endless competition, with its accompanying cycle of high prosperity and low depression, meant a chronic imbalance between production and consumption and led to the fear which characterized the businessman's mind of the period fully as much as it did the laborer's. The result was that the more skillful businessmen destroyed each other or formed pools, combinations, and trusts to lessen the terror inherent in free competition.[27]

The growth of industry meant the growth of the laboring

force, and factory workers in anonymous working clothes replaced the artisan who knew the boss by his first name. The distance between employer and employee became as great as the distance between progress and poverty, and for related reasons. Workers were no longer men, with families and problems, but were cogs, parts of a greater whole. Samuel Gompers claimed one manufacturer had told him: "I regard my employees as I do a machine, to be used to my advantage, and when they are old and of no further use I cast them in the street." A New England wool manufacturer showed more by his tone than any amount of statistics could hope to show: When workers "get starved down to it, then they will go to work at just what you can afford to pay." The division between master and man even kept intelligent contact to a minimum, and many of the rich honestly had no conception of what had happened; "I defy any man to show that there is pauperism" in the United States, Andrew Carnegie remarked in 1887, at the time of some of the most severe suffering Americans ever experienced. In 1883-4, the Citizens' Association of Chicago investigated the tenement areas of the city, and demonstrated how little Carnegie knew of life outside his steel plants. Its report spoke of "the wretched conditions of the tenements into which thousands of workingmen are huddled, the wholesale violation of all rules for drainage, plumbing, light, ventilation and safety in case of fire or accident," and decried "the neglect of all laws of health, the horrible condition of sewers and outhouses, the filthy dingy rooms into which they are crowded, the unwholesome character of their food, and the equally filthy nature of the neighboring streets, alleys and back lots filled with decaying matter and stagnant pools."[28] This was the life of Chicago that Brand Whitlock found so moving and so depressing on his newspaper rounds and that made his retrospective comments so acidulous and so despairing.

These conditions, combined with the severe depression of 1882-6 and the religiously intolerant economic notions of some employers, meant that an explosion could come at any time. Union agitation for an eight-hour day conflicted with management determination to destroy the union. On the sidelines, anarchist groups talked in flaming rhetoric that either amused or terrified the average man, depending on the current state of labor relations. On Wednesday, May 5, 1886, in a time of strikes, lockouts, and clashes with police, the spark finally lit at Haymarket Square. During a peaceful meeting of labor supporters, a group of police led by a notorious labor-baiter tried to break up the meeting. An unknown person threw a bomb that killed and wounded numerous policemen. The next day all public opinion condemned the anarchists, assumed their guilt, and condoned the purge that quickly began.[29]

The story of the orgy of righteousness in which the police and most of the people indulged themselves in the months after the bomb exploded has been exhaustively and accurately told and need not be repeated in a life of Brand Whitlock. The outline of events is clear. After a roundup of everyone known to have any possible connection with anarchism, eight men were finally tried and convicted of conspiracy to commit murder. In a trial full of irregularities, with a blatantly prejudiced judge and equally prejudiced jury, the men never had a chance. August Spies, George Engel, Adolph Fischer, Louis Lingg, and Albert Parsons were sentenced to death, Michael Schwab and Samuel Fielden were sentenced to death and then pardoned to a sentence of life in prison, and Oscar Neebe received fifteen years. The trial remained the most famous miscarriage of justice until the Sacco-Vanzetti case of the 1920's.[30]

One of the more heroic aspects of the whole nasty business was the act of William Dean Howells, then well known and socially respected as a writer and editor, and in real danger if certain important people should decide that he was too radical. In a public letter to the New York *Tribune* he denounced the act of the courts in convicting the men and in upholding the conviction. He pleaded in vain for clemency, and one of his few readers was young Brand Whitlock, who found his statement in the archives of the State House during the Altgeld administration. Howells's public plea was brave and intelligent as it stood, but he toned it down in an effort to win public support for the men. He almost printed another letter, however, that indicated his *real* views; it has only recently been printed. This second letter retains value today not only for what it shows of Howells's character and why Whitlock later loved him, but for the insight it displays into the events. The document contained brilliantly scathing descriptions, unfortunately all too accurate, of the prosecutor, the judge, and the evidence, and demonstrated how the logic of the court, applied to the abolitionists, would have resulted in the hanging of Emerson, Thoreau, Garrison, and others for the act of John Brown.

But the key insight of the letter was the analysis of why the men died, for it was more than halfway to the truth. *"They died, in the prime of the first Republic the world has ever known, for their opinions' sake,"* he wrote. "It is useless to deny this truth, to cover it up, to turn your backs upon it, to frown it down, or sneer it down. We have committed an atrocious and irreparable wrong. We have been undergoing one of those spasms of paroxysmal righteousness to which our Anglo-Saxon race is peculiarly subject . . ."[31] The opinion was brave and correct as far as it went, but Howells did not have quite the insight necessary to explain it all. For the terror of American reaction to anarchism was hard to explain racially, despite the nativist tirades of the *Tribune* and other papers. What had happened was in fact a crisis in religion and morals and not a matter of fear for property or of superpatriotism. The fear which had become endemic in the business mind in the years after the Civil War was caused partly by economic insecurity but also by the slow collapse of real religious faith. Unable to believe in the God of their grandparents, Americans had made him a businessman and accustomed themselves to regarding economic laws as only a modern form of the eternal moral laws. God and gold became hopelessly intertwined; ministers like Russell Conwell made the confusion official. When faced by foreign anarchism, American reaction was not only an economic, patriotic, or racial fear, but also one that was essentially religious; that is why the reaction was one of such total horror. Chicago, after all, was a large, corrupt city, well used to violent death and ruthless business practices. The murder of a policeman or two was scarcely a two-day sensation under normal circumstances. But the anarchists had committed a greater crime, and thus the legal maneuvers were peculiarly irrelevant. Many people admitted that the men were innocent as charged, but demanded the hanging anyway. They did this quite consciously out of no fear for their property or for their lives, although some may have said so. They did it because of the opinions which Howells pointed out. Thus, to the public the anarchists did indeed deserve death, for their crime was not murder or conspiracy, but blasphemy. Their denial of the

American dream of possible riches for the poor man, their insistence on the poverty of the workingman's life, was a threat to the whole moral order of American life. The Haymarket affair was the first American Inquisition since the Salem witch trials.

The third important component of Whitlock's world, John Peter Altgeld and his mind, faced the legacy of hate from the Haymarket affair. Altgeld was born in a peasant family in tiny Nieder Selters in southern Germany and came to America when he was three months old, in the spring of 1849. The family settled in the Mansfield, Ohio, farm country, and Altgeld grew up there in a poor family. His father was strict, even abusive, and intensely opposed to education for his son. But Altgeld displayed a stubbornness that was always with him, and obtained an education mainly through tenacity and the surreptitious aid of his mother. He was not scholastically outstanding, nor was he physically attractive. He had a slight harelip, which sometimes impeded his speech, and his hair was so matted that reporter Nellie Bly later remarked she had seen hair like it only on "boys who had gone swimming and had no comb when they came back." Altgeld was only half joking when he once remarked: "Hell, if I had to depend on my looks I'd have been hung long ago!"[32]

After several *Wanderjahre* and a hitch in the Union Army during the Civil War memorable chiefly for the disease he caught and could never quite cure, he taught school and acquired legal training, more by sheer industry than anything else. He settled for a while in Missouri and dabbled in politics with success as a bourbon Democrat with at least a sympathy for populism. No one could become rich and famous in a small Missouri town, however, and Altgeld was as ambitious as any of the heroes of the trash fiction of his day. In 1875 he went to Chicago and promptly rented offices in the Reaper Block, one of the most prestigious buildings in the city. He was soon a moderate success as a lawyer, a complete success as a husband, and a millionaire as a real-estate investor. He joined several of the local clubs, became socially prominent, and seemed a perfect example of the men Henry George would make famous as those whose progress meant poverty for the masses.[33]

He was soon bored with business, so he re-entered politics. He campaigned for the Democratic nomination for Congress from the heavily Republican Fourth District, was nominated and spoke often as a Cleveland Democrat, and lost by 3,000 votes in the Republican sweep of the state that overwhelmed both Cleveland and the gubernatorial candidate, Carter Harrison. During the next years, the years of the McCormick and Haymarket incidents, he remained quiet, made no reputation as a labor or socialist candidate, and did nothing which could be interpreted as radical. He appeared to be a rising young conservative lawyer with ample private means. He did nothing during the Haymarket trial and did not even sign the appeals for clemency which 60,000 Chicago citizens, including many eminent local lawyers, presented to the governor. His motives for this silence were unknown, but were perhaps evident in a remark he made to an ardent defender of the anarchists. "You know," he said, "I have some of the same ideas that you have. But if I talked now as radical as I feel, I could not be where I am. I want to do something, not just make a speech. . . . I want power, to get hold of the handle that controls things. When I do, I will give it a twist!" Meanwhile, he won election to the bench of the Superior Court of Cook County, with labor support. One of his colleagues was Judge Gary, who a month before had sentenced the anarchists.[34]

For all his outward success, Altgeld, like Whitlock, was always a lonesome man, an outsider. Whitlock was an outsider in the sense that he was always the somewhat timid little boy, looking on while others acted, then going to his room and writing about it. Altgeld was an outsider as a foreigner is an outsider, because he came from afar off, talked in a peculiar manner, and had queer ideas. He also had an acute sense of mission, and his isolation increased rather than decreased the tenacity of the views he held. "Self-denial and self-control are essential to achievement," and "great endurance is impossible where there is great indulgence," he once wrote, in his little book on oratory, in words that sound pilfered from a timely success tract. But then he continued: *"Isolation is the price of greatness, and the stars are all the friends an orator needs."* With this sense of loneliness he combined a feeling for the underdog that was almost messianic: "All the great speeches ever delivered were protests against injustice and appeals for the public welfare. Generally they were on the losing side. Defeat is often the baptism of immortality . . ."[35]

But to be stubborn, righteous, and alone was a dangerous combination for a man hoping for material success, a combination likely to combine disaster with its immortality.

Altgeld was quiet in the 1880's; he was thinking and writing, and his ideas reached men like Brand Whitlock, Clarence Darrow, and George Schilling, all of whom would have a role in the Altgeld administration. Altgeld was concerned, for instance, with the lack of justice he saw in the local judicial procedure, and his example proved important to Whitlock and his own later reforms in Toledo. Altgeld objected to the common practice of reversing and delaying decisions not on the merits of the case but on procedural technicalities. He objected to the long delays common in lawsuits, which enabled the guilty to elude payment and punished the wronged by preventing them from collecting damages. He objected to laws which impeded the instruction of the jury by the judge. He wanted faster, less expensive procedures, majority rather than unanimous jury decisions, an attorney-fee assessment against the loser in a lawsuit, and a change in the custom of overruling decisions for any reasons other than a miscarriage of justice.[36]

He was even more concerned with the common conceptions of criminality. He attacked the basis of the current system, which he said was based not on any idea of rehabilitation but "on the idea of expiation," that is, "paying for having violated the law . . ." The true function of justice required an examination of the history, environment, and character of the offender, which should result in making the person a decent citizen again. Instead of this humane procedure, "we treat those who are not vicious, but have been unfortunate, and have been guilty of some slight offense, in almost the same manner that we treat the vicious who have been guilty of graver offenses; and we put both in a condition in which it is next to impossible for either to make an honest living when they have been once imprisoned."[37] Such ideas bore less fruit in Altgeld's Illinois than they did in the Toledo of Brand Whitlock and Sam Jones, the Cleveland of Tom Johnson, and the nation in the many trials of Clarence Darrow.

The great majority of offenders in Chicago (for 1882 all but 190 out of 7,566), were in jail for nonpayment of fines, not for any serious offense, and thus were in jail solely because they were poor. Of these, the great majority were under thirty and came

from homes with one or both parents missing; the inevitable conclusion was that bad home influences and poor education were the
chief causes of crime. Inevitable, perhaps, but in total opposition
to everything which American tradition taught about individual
responsibility and the poverty that comes from sin. An outsider,
Altgeld did not care. "The truth is, that the great multitudes an-
nually arrested for the first time are of the poor, the unfortunate,
the young and neglected; of those that are weak and, to a great
extent, are the victims of unfavorable environments." In other
words: *"Our penal machinery seems to recruit its victims from
among those that are fighting an unequal fight in the struggle for
existence."*

Once the first offender was in jail, he seemed lost, for the
number of repeaters was far too large. Is there not, he asked,
something wrong with a system that makes matters worse rather
than better, a system which, "instead of being reformatory and
preventative," is really "debasing and productive?" Against unnecessary arrests and the badgering of unconvicted men he protested in a way that would receive a graphic fictional representation in Whitlock's novel, *The Turn of the Balance*, as well as in
his own career. "Remember, *brutal treatment brutalizes* and thus
prepares for crime." The important thing is to save "the weak and
neglected from becoming criminals," and the only way to do this
was "to develop and to build up their self-respect—their manhood
and womanhood." Without this respect, they can only sink. "In
the entire history of the human race there is not a single instance
in which cruelty effected a genuine reformation. It can crush, but
it cannot improve."[38]

Altgeld began sending up trial balloons for the Democratic
nomination for governor as much as a year before the 1892 elections. The Republican Governor "Private Joe" Fifer was a colorless nonentity, and the unpopularity of the Harrison regime in
Washington augured well for Democratic chances. Altgeld, as a
wealthy man with some solid labor support, was also attractive to
certain intellectuals because of his ideas on prison and legal reform. His real attraction was somewhat less grand, however; he
had just finished erecting the well-known Unity Building in Chicago, and politicians looked on him not as a social reformer but as
a sugar daddy who could hand out financial sweets during a cam-

paign. He received the nomination along with the expected denun-
ciations from Republican sheets like the *Tribune* and the bourbon-
Democratic sheets like Whitlock's *Herald*. Despite this opposition,
Altgeld won the support of the ward bosses and the reformers, he
ran in a Democratic year, and he spent an estimated $100,000 of
his own money in an indefatigable campaign. Not the least of the
ironies of Altgeld's career was the enormous amount of money he
had to earn and spend to get himself in a position to be denounced
as a viper, and anarchist, and a demagogue.[39]

Winning, Altgeld celebrated quite unspectacularly in a round
of social affairs and then went to bed with a severe illness. He was
so sick that many thought he would never live to be anything more
than governor-elect, and he barely managed to take his inaugural
oath without fainting. Even after his recovery he was no radical.
His first message was cautious, and only those hunting carefully
for possibly radical statements could make much of any concern
for labor in it. Conservative elements saw nothing to alarm them,
and radical elements became restless in anticipation of what they
hoped their leader would do. Trouble, however, was soon at
hand.[40]

WITH ALTGELD ELECTED, Whitlock settled quickly into
his job as secretary to Secretary of State Hinrichsen. The work, car-
ing for state archives and answering mail in connection with them,
was not difficult, and he found time to study law and enjoy the
company of women. He began writing for national magazines and
received his first rejection slips. In 1894 he was admitted to the
Illinois bar. His heart, however, never left the home of Mr. and
Mrs. Gideon R. Brainerd, and he was the best of friends with
Susan's sister Ella and her good friend Octavia Roberts. Ella—or
Nell, as everyone called her—soon replaced her dead sister in his
affections. In 1895 Elias D. Whitlock officiated at the marriage of
his son and Nell Brainerd in the home of the bride's mother in
Lincoln, Illinois. June 8 was a sunny day, perfect for a wedding,
and the local paper termed it "one of the prettiest which has
occurred in Central Illinois for a long time." The couple left
promptly for Springfield, "where a cosy little home had been previously prepared for them on South Second, between Allen and

Scarrett Streets." The marriage proved close and happy, and they were rarely apart from each other until the day Whitlock died.[41]

Despite his lack of interest in the law, Whitlock pursued his studies doggedly. He took some time out to write trivial letters to inquirers about state coats of arms, seals of state, and other interests of the "Chief of the Index Department," as he signed his letters. He had decided on the law for a career, however, and spent most of his free time obtaining enough training to pass the bar exams.[42] The chief document that gives an idea of what he was like at this time, though, is not a state letter or a clipping about his legal career, but, predictably enough, an unpublished story about a sensitive young lawyer and his involvement in politics.

"Davis McGowan, Attorney at Law" is the story of a young courtroom lawyer who is very weary and discouraged about the possibilities of rising to the top. He is a weak, vacillating character of the type later made famous by James Thurber in his story about Walter Mitty. McGowan is a dreamer, and he enacts his dreams before a mirror in his room, clinching arguments with devastating aplomb, winning the hearts of beautiful women, and attaining the pinnacle of political influence in the sanctuary of his hotel room. Like his creator, he is constantly involved in politics, forever distracted by dreams of women when he should be studying, and deeply moved by a sensually stimulating church service. He attempts to break into Republican politics and is hired, as a matter of course, by the traction company to do lackey work for them which, he is assured, will in no way conflict with his political ambitions.

The few obvious changes from real life only seem to confirm the autobiographical nature of the story. McGowan has few literary ambitions, but they would only have complicated the story unnecessarily just as they complicated Whitlock's life. McGowan joins the Republican Party, but does so only to provide a way for Whitlock to attack it as being most in league with the traction companies. McGowan breaks away from a strictly Methodist upbringing to enter society, much the way Whitlock entered the world of the Brainerds. He learns the art of social dancing. He enters politics, but balks at the bribery of voters and finds himself ostracized. Finally, the traction company has a mission for him that is not strictly proper on the surface and looks increasingly like corruption the more McGowan looks at it. He balks, and thus he dooms both his political and his legal ambitions. His dreams exploded, he gives up his ambition to succeed in the city and returns to a small-town practice in little Circleville. Whitlock returned regularly to all these themes in his early work and quite obviously was himself concerned with political morality, as well as with the chances of a young and dreamy lawyer for success. He was ambitious, but not absolutely devoted to his career; his own character was in fact only half formed, and he seemed to realize it. The misery and indecision that plagued him through the 1890's are all apparent and explicable to one who reads this early story. As literature, it was not much better nor much worse than most of his works, but it had one severe fault that always plagued him as much as his indecision: He seemed incapable of writing a short story. "Davis McGowan" ran on to seventy-three typed pages, far too long for any magazine of the period yet far too short for separate or serial publication. Whitlock simply could not confine himself to twenty or thirty pages of material with any success, and not until magazines agreed to print his work in two or three installments did much of it get published. Even then he received many rejection slips, and a good deal of anguish. The pattern repeated itself in all parts of his life: He had to do things in his own way—in art, ideas, or politics—and no one seemed interested; he could conform only with great reluctance and was always breaking away. Like Davis McGowan, he was doomed to more disappointment than a sensitive man should have to bear. The world never quite fitted the man.[43]

Whitlock quickly got far deeper into politics in his real life than McGowan ever did, as he and Altgeld soon tasted the blood of the labor problems created by the 1893 depression. The first outburst came from Lemont, where eight years earlier troops called out by Governor Oglesby killed two men in putting down a strike of quarry workers. On June 9 trouble came again, as armed scabs killed two strikers and wounded many others. Whether the trouble came from the strikers or from *agents provocateurs* of the employers, no one knew, but the public immediately cried for intervention. Altgeld believed in the traditional Democratic doctrine of local rule, and he refused to send in troops unless local authorities telegraphed their assertion that they were unable to handle the situation. Late that night a telegram arrived, signed by three county sheriffs. Altgeld immediately asked how many deputies had been sworn in and whether or not anyone other than a striker was injured. Only one sheriff answered, and on receipt of his claim to have 120 deputies under service, Altgeld sent in 550 militia. He then left the capital for Lemont, taking Whitlock and Lieutenant Jewett Baker with him.

Altgeld's great fear was that the troops would only make matters worse. What he discovered was a patent abdication of responsibility on the part of local authority. He found that when the trouble occurred, only eight deputies had accompanied the three sheriffs, and that the sheriff who had telegraphed so desperately for help had only twenty-two deputies on duty. The day was cheerless, and the crowds were sullen in the presence of the militia. Everyone remembered 1885. The soldiers were all dressed in blue, and Whitlock and Baker stared at them in fascination until they noticed a crowd of people around the body of one of the men who had been shot. He was a foreigner, and his wife was on her knees beside him, incapable of speech in any language. She rocked back and forth in dumb grief. Among the people there were several Chicago reporters, including old Whitechapeler Eddie Bernard, who told Whitlock that the man had reached Lemont only days before and had been happy that he had found a job so soon in the land of promise and freedom. Bernard looked at the man and his wife and captured the situation in a Whitechapel sentence Whitlock could never forget: "The land of the free and the home of the brave!"[44] Labor problems expressed in statistics held no meaning for an artist, but one dead immigrant and his wife were unforgettable. In his imaginative life, his only *real* life, Whitlock was already unalterably committed to progressivism.

Altgeld soon calmed the workers, and he demonstrated his obvious sympathy and intention of keeping the militia strictly impartial. No other governor had dared to walk among the workmen and ask them about their problems. He walked everywhere, including railway embankments and quarry pits, and even traveled awhile on a train crew's handcar, legs dangling with no concern for dignity, while workers cheered. Despite the pompous nonsense of the *Tribune*, which placed all blame on the strikers, Altgeld pointed frankly at the employers who had armed the scabs as the ones really guilty. He did not neglect the other villains either: The local authorities shared at least as much blame as the employers, and their neglect of duty was inexcusable. Had they acted in any sensible manner, all the violence could have been prevented and the state need never have sent in troops at all. Even the *Tribune* agreed with him in that.[45]

Lemont was not the only thing on Altgeld's mind. Ten days after he took office, while still sick, he asked for the files on the Haymarket anarchist case and a complete transcript of the court records. As the months passed and he did nothing, friends visited him to encourage whatever action he might take. He told them to wait. He insisted on making a thorough sudy of the matter himself and would not make a snap decision. Likewise, he ignored, or prevented the delivery of, petitions of clemency. He made only sporadic attempts to get the public support of famous men, although he could have done so. With the moral fervor of a puritan preparing to receive grace, he ignored all intermediaries and palliatives and insisted that the matter concerned him alone. If the cause proved just, he would so decide and make no attempt to sway the public opinion. If the cause proved not, he would do nothing. His course was courageous, but without tact or diplomacy. A man can ignore the people when facing God, but to ignore them while in their service is suicidal, no matter how morally just the cause.[46]

Meanwhile, Whitlock was working away in the musty archives. Many of the state documents were rotting, and he was in charge of sorting them before moving them to a new, insect-proof vault. The job was monumentally uninteresting until the file for the anarchist case turned up. It held all the petitions for mercy and demands for execution, and it revived memories of the wild hysteria that had shaken the state at the time. Many prominent names appeared on the documents, "but there was no appeal stronger, and no protest braver, than that in the letter which Mr. Howells had written to a New York newspaper analyzing the case and showing the amazing injustice of the whole proceeding." The job introduced him to Howells, whom he grew to love. It also involved him in the Haymarket pardons.

One morning in June, he got a call from the governor's office.

When he arrived, Altgeld's secretary told him to make out the pardons for Fielden, Neebe, and Schwab. Altgeld had finally made his decision. "And do it yourself," the secretary added, "and don't say anything about it to anybody." Dumfounded and full of hazy emotions, Whitlock went and got the proper papers, and before the executive clerk, whose work it properly was, had arrived, he made out the three pardons "in the largest, roundest hand I could command, impressed them with the Great Seal of State, had the secretary of state sign them, and took them over to the governor's office." He went into Altgeld's private room and found there also a Chicago banker, E. S. Dreyer, who had been unwearying in his petitions for the anarchists. He had also been, unknown to Whitlock, foreman of the grand jury that voted the murder indictments against the anarchists. Dreyer was standing, and very nervous. The moment meant much to him. Altgeld looked over the papers, signed his name to each, and handed them to Dreyer. The man tried to thank him but was too choked with emotion to get out a sentence. Altgeld made an impatient gesture and looked out the window in silence. He took out his watch and told Dreyer he would miss his train. Dreyer nervously rolled up the pardons, picked up a small valise, shook hands, and headed for Joliet to deliver the pardons to the men in person.

On Governor Altgeld's desk was a high pile of proofs that George Schilling and others had gathered for him. Whitlock admired the pardon message, but Altgeld was unemotional. Whitlock records nothing further for that day, but the next day he met Altgeld riding. The governor smiled "that faint, wan smile of his," and came over to the curb.

"Well, the storm will break now," Whitlock said.

"Oh, yes," he replied, with a not wholly convincing air of throwing off a care. "I was prepared for that. It was merely doing right."

Whitlock wanted to say more and could not, and he always regretted his inability to do something to make Altgeld's burden easier. The governor rode away, still with his wan, persistent smile, into the hurricane that was waiting for him, "but I never again heard him mention the anarchist case."[47]

The pardon document was fair, just, long, and wholly undiplomatic. Altgeld emphasized that the jury was packed for the sole purpose of achieving a conviction; that the jurors were not legally competent, and that therefore the trial was illegal; that the defendants were not proven guilty of the crime charged to them; that the conviction of Neebe, in particular, was obviously unjust even to the state's attorney, and he should never have been indicted; and that the judge was so prejudiced, or so subservient to those who were prejudiced, that he did not conduct a fair trial. Altgeld was asking for martyrdom, and he got it.[48]

The pardons were a complete surprise to the country, for no one had broken secrecy. One reaction, written in Schwab's hand, came to the governor a week later. "Your excellency have given us back wife and children home and liberty," he wrote. "You did this after having carefully considered the facts which could be known. Having weighed evidence against evidence you pursued the course dictated by your conscience, regardless of the torrent of abuse which you knew would be the consequence of your courage. This was the deed of a brave heart, and it will live as such in history." Schwab was right, about weighing evidence, about conscience, and about abuse. Not a great many Chicagoans loved Altgeld for it. Edward Osgood Brown did, and so did Clarence Darrow, although Darrow agreed with Jane Addams that the attack on Judge Gary was unfortunate.

The Chicago *Tribune* did not. Altgeld was of course an alien, without "a drop of true American blood in his veins. He does not reason like an American, does not feel like one, and consequently does not behave like one." Medill always had a talent for irrelevant belligerence, but he soon outdid himself. Altgeld, the millionaire businessman, was now an anarchist himself, with un-American feelings that finally broke out "in this hysterical denunciation of American principles, law, judges, executive and judicial officers and of people who deliberately and conscientiously approved of them." Altgeld was also "Demagogue!" and "Socialist!", "Apologist for Murder!" and "Fomenter of Lawlessness!", "A Viper," and "A slimy Demagogue." the vast majority of the nation's newspapers agreed. By basing his pardons not on mercy but on the faults of law, Altgeld had questioned whatever was left of American religion. He had endorsed the men who would destroy that which God had ordained in His natural law, His Constitution, and His Courts. The Reverend Mr. H. A. Delano of the

First Baptist Church of Evanston used his pulpit to discuss "The Shame of our Governor." "A Nero in Rome, a Paul of Russia, a Napoleon in France showed more care for the people than has this man by this deed," he said. "Thank God, ours is the very form of government which makes possible a change!"

In the face of this nonsense, one turns almost with a sigh of relief to the editorial which Carter Harrison wrote personally for his newspaper. Once again mayor of the city he called his "bride," Harrison had been at Haymarket the night of the riot, had followed the trial, and most of all understood both human nature and the role of law. He applauded the pardons and quite justly criticized the language in which they were phrased. Governor Altgeld, declared the *Times*, "has done no more than right in giving them freedom for the rest of their days."[49]

At least nobody died from the Haymarket pardons. They did in the next crisis, which newspapers named the Debs rebellion and history remembers as the Pullman Strike. Pullman was the town that George Pullman erected to be a monument to himself, his company, and his thoughtfulness. On a deserted region of the prairie south of Chicago he set up a model town for his workers that was soon world famous as an experiment in planned living. In a time in which living conditions were usually disgusting for the majority of workers, Pullman erected decent homes in a city with parks, a church, a library and compulsory decency. The houses were furnished with gas, water, and good sewerage facilities and were designed for fresh air and exposure to sunlight. They were usually clean, five-room structures with sink, toilet, water tap, and plenty of closet space. The town cost about $8,000,000 and was judged the most perfect in the world by the presumably unbiased jury of the International Hygienic and Pharmaceutical Exposition of 1896 held in Prague, Bohemia. George Pullman was proud enough of this achievement; he was just as proud of the fact that the town was not a charitable organization and that he expected as his just reward a return of 6 per cent on his investment. Altgeld was bothered by the legal as well as the moral aspect of the town, and he had assigned Whitlock the job of looking up and analyzing the legal basis for the town even before the trouble broke out. Unfortunately, Whitlock's report has not survived. Later, when the crisis came, Altgeld appointed him "an

aide-de-camp, general staff, with rank of colonel, the appointment
to date from June 26, 1894." In this capacity Whitlock soon
visited all the Pullman troop areas and saw the Debs rebellion
from a good vantage point.[50]

Unfortunately, as Whitlock discovered, the place was not quite
a utopia. Pullman refused to permit labor unions. He allowed no
liquor stores or bars to operate. He exercised an almost absolute
veto over every aspect of community life, and as the owner of all
the homes his workers rented he could command more authority
than many European dictators. Company spotters apparently
checked up regularly to watch for subversive activities, and an
encyclopedic lease forbade more activities than the average British
preparatory school. Tenants had to enter and leave their homes
quietly, were forbidden to enter with muddy feet, to hammer,
pound, or split wood indoors, or to use musical instruments after
bedtime. They must not indulge in boisterous behavior or loiter in
stairways; they could not smoke in cellars or forget to care for
their stoves. A lovely place the town was, clean and pure enough
to drive a decent working man mad and far from the rude democracy that the average American was used to before his arrival. As
one man put it: "We are born in a Pullman home, fed from the
Pullman shop, taught in the Pullman school, catechized in the
Pullman church, and when we die we shall be buried in the Pullman cemetery and go to the Pullman hell." During the depression
of 1893, more than one man had a good idea of the location of
that hell.[51]

In the midst of all this began one of the biggest labor wars in
the country's history. Debs led his men in a strike that was for the
most part as orderly as a weak union with good intentions could
make it. The violence and damage that did occur was apparently
the result at least as much of industry provocation and sabotage,
in an effort to make the unions look bad, as it was of the actions
of Debs or his men. Nevertheless, most of the publicity was violently anti-union, a good deal of damage was visible, and most
Americans were dismayed and even terrified by what they thought
was happening. The court involved was distinctly unfriendly to the
strikers; the attorney general of the United States, Richard Olney,
plainly loathed them, and the cooperation of the court and of the
federal government brought national troops in to stop the strike.

Grover Cleveland simply stood by, either misinformed or unwilling to intervene except to endorse Olney's policies. The strike, and the subsequent judicial farce that sent Debs to jail, made a deep impression on Whitlock. He had spent the summer in the midst of the trouble and long remembered "the long lines of idle freight cars, charred by incendiary flames," and "the little groups of men standing about wearing the white ribbons of the strike sympathizers . . ." One morning, in the office of the mayor of Chicago, he saw Eugene Debs, "tall, lithe, nervous, leader of the strikers, his hair, what there was of it, sandy, but his head mostly bald, his eyes flashing, his mouth ready to smile, soon to go to Woodstock jail . . ."[52] How like Whitlock it was, to remember the little details of the scene, with the chief impression that of character! Whatever his duties, he could not resist looking on life as raw material for literature, finding heroes as he went.

C h i c a g o a n d S p r i n g f i e l d had given him quite an education. He learned first that free trade was no longer the most important of issues and that, at least for the moment, the labor problem was. The two issues were related, but the change of emphasis was important, for it was the first significant break in the process that led from the reform of the Cleveland Democrats to the progressivism of the new generation. Whitlock was one of the earliest to realize the change, along with Altgeld and the young Robert La Follette. He learned, too, to distrust appearances, for his Whitechapel skepticism deepened when he noted the nationwide misunderstanding of the acts in which he and Governor Altgeld participated. The good people were *so often* wrong, and the dirty anarchists *were* on the side of justice. Appearances then led him to reconsider the value of the law and to question its abuse by the large corporations and their robed stooges, who would give out injunctions against—and jail sentences to—men who wished only to have enough to eat. Altgeld had taught him also of the need for pity and understanding in handling poverty and the law and shown him how often the environment had more to do with imprisonment than depravity. An artist had to be able to put himself in the place of his characters, and Whitlock was exposed while in his early twenties to the poor, the miserable, and the persecuted, as well as to the man who championed them. He learned of the need for reliable local responsibility and how outside intervention was often only an aggravation and a goad to the people concerned. Had local officials acted intelligently, Altgeld need never have intervened at Lemont; had the local authorities acted responsibly, Richard Olney and Grover Cleveland would not have dared to send in the troops that only made matters worse. Whitlock learned, too, to detest newspapers for their willful perversions of the truth. His own paper, the Chicago *Herald*, was not the least offender, despite its reform record, and when its detestation of Altgeld found support in the *Tribune* and other papers around the country, who that loved Altgeld could love the newspapers too?

But Whitlock's chief impression was that politics was filthy—a lesson that has been learned by many novelists. Politics was "mean, and while I do not intend to say that this meanness bowed me with despair, it did fill me with disgust, and made the whole business utterly distasteful." Politics was personal, and its moral atmosphere "was foul and heavy with the feculence of all the debauchery that is inseparable from privilege." Its people were low and philistine and bovinely stupid, and they positively scorned virtues. Lobbyists and lawyers were allied with the great corporations and the political leaders, and the worst feature was that "no one seemed to care, or if a few did care, they did not know what to do about it." Whitlock saw state politics at its least lovely, at a time when corruption was the style, not the exception. He grew so familiar with these battles that he wrote stories based on the events of those days, quite apart from the lessons he gained and later used in Toledo. His most vivid memory of these years was of corruption and of Altgeld as the hero fighting it. Altgeld deserved the admiration despite his faults, and his record and ideas served the young secretary well when his time came for exercising authority, fighting corporate and governmental corruption, and protecting the poor from justice.[53]

ℂCHAPTER 3

Life with the Iron

Madonna (1897-1900)

T HE YEARS WITH ALTGELD were full of events of national importance, but while they quite naturally made up a
large part of Whitlock's memoirs, they scarcely occupied all his
time. Furthermore, the Haymarket pardons, the Lemont and Pullman strikes, and the meetings with famous men took only a few
weeks altogether, and Whitlock was in Springfield for three years.
Much of his time he spent with the Brainerd girls and Octavia
Roberts, getting his first introductions into the social life of the
middle-class capital, and enjoying and suffering the years of his
marriage, widowerhood, and remarriage. His chief function, aside
from sorting papers in the archives, was answering mail—usually
the inane variety from old women of both sexes who wanted to
know about obscure points of genealogy, local history, and anti-
quarian trivia. The letters deserved at best a barely civil reply from
a servant paid by the state and sometimes did not even get that.
The tongue that was trained in Toledo *Blade* sarcasm and toughened in the Whitechapel Club was not the most subtle of instruments, and the few letters that survive indicate that Whitlock was
often sarcastic and never servile in the performance of his duties.
His sole literary achievement of the period was an article, "The

65

Great Seal of Illinois," which appeared in two installments in the Chicago *Times-Herald* for Sundays, April 12 and 19, 1896.

Politically, he was just important enough to be pestered by the first of what proved to be a long series of applications for political office. Altgeld's notoriety reminded Toledo of its old reporter, and his old friends made him a member of the Toledo Press Club, apparently with no effort or even interest on his part. He demonstrated a pardonable vanity by ordering from the M. C. Lilley Company of Columbus "one pair of fine gilt U.S. Army regulation shoulder straps for Colonel and A.D.C. on the general staff," for use in his role as roving colonel for Altgeld during the Debs Rebellion. In fact, he was merely a political lackey, given unpleasant jobs. Chief among these was the chairmanship of the Finance Committee of the Democratic County Central Committee for the 1894 elections. He managed to collect all of $133 by early August.[1]

Politics unfortunately seemed to hold no more permanent attraction as a career than had newspaper work. Even in his twenties Whitlock started talking about giving up politics, and he apparently meant it. No one expected Altgeld to win re-election, and the new Republican secretary of state would want his own secretary. Whitlock told everyone that he was preparing for a career in law and devoted at least as much time to it as his unfortunate Davis McGowan—probably a good deal more. He was never too enthusiastic about the law as a career, but he could see no future for himself now in either politics or newspapers—though he often dreamed of renewing both careers—and could see no other alternative. He was no scholar and without a college education could scarcely follow Uncle Will into teaching. He was thoroughly disenchanted with Methodism, and thus had no desire to follow his father into the ministry. His brothers mailed him letters telling of their hatred for their poverty and blue-collar jobs, and Whitlock had not the build nor the temperament, and certainly not the desire, for a life of manual labor. He wanted to write and knew that it would not keep him or a wife alive. Where else could he go but the law?

The study of law meant that he needed a teacher, in those days before law students needed either a college degree or a law school. Whitlock started with the uncle of his wives: big, burly, grandfatherly Senator John M. Palmer, one of the most influential and respected men in the state, and not unknown nationally. Palmer was an ideal teacher for the man educated under Grandfather Brand, Frank Hurd, and Horatio Seymour. Born in Kentucky, in an antislavery family of Jacksonian Democrats, he and his family moved to Illinois in 1831 to free land. He soon learned the law, joined the bar, and fathered ten children. As an early opponent of Illinois Democratic Senator Stephen A. Douglas's Kansas-Nebraska Bill, he was elected to the state senate as an Anti-Nebraska Democrat and played a leading role in the formation of the Republican Party in Illinois. He served the North in the Civil War and achieved the rank of major general. Returning to law in Springfield, he was elected governor of Illinois as a Republican in 1868, only to find himself snowed under a pile of corrupt, special-interest legislation passed by a subservient legislature only too typical of the Gilded Age.

He talked continually of his states' rights beliefs, fought valiantly against corruption, and ultimately was so disgusted by his own party that he bolted to support Horace Greeley and the Liberal Republicans in the 1872 revolt against Grantism. Then, in the prompt collapse of that party, he became a Democrat and retired for a few years from public life. He ran and lost in 1888 as the Democratic candidate for governor, but, three years later, in one of the most grueling elections in state history, he became senator after a bitter fight. Always a man of rigid principle and integrity, he was a leading possibility for the Democratic nomination that went to Cleveland, and he supported Cleveland loyally even when it meant political suicide. In 1896, in the face of a state then far more radical than he, Palmer supported and then led the Illinois Gold Democrats in the revolt against Bryan. He was the Gold Democrat candidate for President in 1896, getting only 130,000 votes—including one from his devoted law student—and was not the least disturbed by his defeat. Like Cleveland, he stuck to his principles regardless of party. Whitlock never forgot this independence, and his distaste for partisanship is traceable at least in part to his studies with Palmer.[2]

He was, Whitlock remembered later, "a simple man with simple tastes, and his very simplicity was an element of that dignity which seemed to belong to other times than ours." He was a familiar and popular figure in the streets of Springfield as he went along in his great broad hat, "a striking figure with his plentiful white hair, his closely trimmed chin whiskers, the broad, smoothly shaven upper lip distinguishing a countenance that was of a type associated with the earlier ideals of the republic . . ." At home, where Whitlock often met him, he had a viol and would play if there were not too many people around, mostly old songs that he had learned as a boy in Kentucky. He liked poetry that was not too modern and introspective and was one of those legendary, heroic figures who actually did read all of Scott's novels through every year.[3]

Palmer taught Whitlock enough law to get by, and Whitlock formed a practice in Springfield with former Illinois representative William J. Butler as a partner. The practice did not flourish, quite possibly because Whitlock had little interest in it. Judging from the surviving evidence, he spent most of his time collecting bad debts and trying to get damages for a client who had been sold a defective horse. Whitlock wanted to write novels and have the law support him; the law refused to support him without a certain minimum effort, even in a small town. The predictable result was that Whitlock's career caused him even more depression, and his was a mind that depressed easily. He flirted, and continued to flirt for several years, with the idea of going to Chicago and a possible partnership with Judge David J. Barker and his son John, or some other acquaintance from political life. He fully intended to go to Chicago, but his prospects there did not work out as he had planned and he was afraid to go without a firm partnership because he thought the temptation of returning to his newspaper career might be too great. Horatio Seymour assured him that he could always have his old job back, and that was precisely what Whitlock feared. Habit, if nothing else, drew him back to Toledo, and by the end of 1896 he was sending out letters to several established men there inquiring about his chances. He also requested information about the difficulty of passing the Ohio bar exams. Obviously, bad debts and decayed horseflesh could not keep a man in Springfield when his job ran out, as it did in January 1897.[4]

Finally, the approach of the Republicans forced him to make up his mind, and one dour morning in January he and Nell waved goodbye to Octavia and the Brainerds and went off to Ohio. For the next three weeks, he luxuriated in the inertia forced on him by an attack of the grippe, "coddled myself with the blues, deep down in huge chairs, with books, and took wildly to cigarettes"— a habit his mother-in-law had discouraged in Springfield. He went to Bellefontaine to stay with his parents while he prepared for the bar exams. Most of the time, at least if his letters to Octavia are at all accurate, he spent reading the current fiction of the day, most notably Harold Frederic's *The Damnation of Theron Ware*, a devastating portrait of Methodist life that made Whitlock jealous of its skill, critical of its being "not as distinctly elevating in tone as I like a book to be," and a little shocked that Frederic had managed to write so well about an environment that Whitlock hoped to explore himself. As he remarked, with considerable insight, "I begin to despair of myself—I procrastinate so—I am distinctly in the future imperfect tense."[5]

Meanwhile, he was upset about where he would practice law when he settled down. Full of uncertainty and indecision, as he usually was over any problem more serious than reading a book, he found himself in "a state of nervous prostration—almost dementia." He loved Springfield, but he could find no opening there. He felt drawn to Chicago, but a visit reopened all the wounds from his newspaper days. His character "so contemptibly vacillating," he decided on Toledo, visited there, and promptly decided that Chicago was attractive again. Nell disapproved, and his father grunted in contempt; his mother was pained and surprised. As usual, he became something of a walking bruise, as the indecision lingered on. "Women smile and girls snigger as I pass. The public treats me with badinage. Children revile me in the streets as a man without a purpose and a hope. The finger of scorn is aimed at me. I slink along in shadows." If nothing else, he had the artist's power of self-dramatization.

Finally, the force of circumstances took the job of deciding his fate. He had to wait until June, at least, in Bellefontaine, because the Supreme Court did not sit until then and he could not join the bar any earlier. On the assumption that he would pass, he and Nell would then go to Toledo, and if the town seemed hospitable they would remain—otherwise, back to Chicago. Presumably the bother of moving twice in a brief period made the eventual decision for him, and Toledo gained a mayor and world figure in large part because he did not have the energy or ambition to leave town. Meanwhile, Nell proved to be the least neurotic and most helpful of wives and quite enjoyed her visit to her in-laws. She helped her husband, he wrote, putting him through paces of the law "with a quiz book like a drill-sergeant." She read George Eliot. He apparently read Goldsmith; at least, he compared his life at Bellefontaine with the monotonous round of the Vicar of Wakefield, finding both lives equally dull.[6]

In early June, almost a nervous wreck, he went off to Columbus to take his exams. He then returned, exhausted by the heat and his own unstable constitution, to Bellefontaine and the comfort of a gift of Browning's poetry which Octavia had sent along to solace her friend during his ordeal. He promptly and gratefully lost himself and his troubles in the reading of that poet, with whom Whitlock shared a curious combination of psychological realism and romantic idealism. Yet even without Browning, Whitlock survived —he soon discovered that he was one of the thirty-eight out of ninety applicants who passed. Even that pleasure palled quickly, though, for Whitlock really wanted to write, and each success in law only took him farther from his books. At least at first, neither career paid him enough to live comfortably, so his activities were doubly unrewarding, since not even the legal services he did for money gave him any. His father had none to spare, and Whitlock was both very poor and very much on his own. As he wrote of his only real consolation, inscribed wryly in his Christmas gift to Nell that year,

> And in this year, dear wife, what cheer?
> Have we in purse some poorer grown?
> Well—times are at hand—but never fear
> We're rich in head and heart, my Own.[7]

Nine of his old Toledo newspaper friends fêted him on his return, but even that did not make him entirely at home in the city where he had lived through most of his teens. By March 1898, he was again seriously considering a move to Chicago and thought he had a definite opening. He and Nell went there, but again became discouraged by the prospects, and returned. Whitlock then took immediately to bed with a nervous dyspepsia and went back to Bellefontaine and the security of his parents. By August, he was writing of his dislike for Toledo and his fear that somehow he would rot there. Yet, despite his stomach and his most unmilitary physique, he seemed quite eager to enter the army to fight in the Spanish-American War. He wrote to John M. Palmer, who promised to write to President McKinley and try to get Whitlock into a volunteer spot with troops at the front. Whitlock also offered his services to the governor of Illinois and received nothing more than a polite acknowledgment. Finally, in June, the U.S. government refused; no vacancies were available.[8]

Certainly the law proved less than scintillating. Slowly, he left fledgling status and gained acceptance both as a lawyer and as a possible candidate for social standing. Each time he beat a lawyer in a small case he earned just a little more respect and he and Nell were invited to one more tedious dinner in a prominent Toledo home. Silly society women were bad enough, but men who could talk about nothing but shop turned his stomach even more sour than usual. A local club asked him to join, "which I did not do because I am too poor"; certain Democrats wanted him to run in the primaries, but he refused because "I am sick of politics"; and a church asked him to join, "which I did not do because the members were too effusive and unduly apprehensive concerning the destiny of my miserable soul." His practice was picayune by any standard; his law register indicates that he had few cases and received only $5 for the great majority of them. Rarely did he ever get as much as $25, and even these petty cases were scattered over many months. Except for the fall of 1898, which was moderately busy, he had far too much time to think for his peace of mind. Nell, as usual, kept him going with love, encouragement, and most of the family backbone.[9]

Whitlock worked from a lonely little office in what Toledo called a skyscraper. The walls held pictures of Howells and Tolstoy and other writers, rather than those august Founding Fathers or dead judges who depressed clients in most offices. He had a few books and a small digest of the law of evidence, which the Ohio courts had evolved. Chiefly, he worked on his fiction, staring occasionally out of his window at the cheerless walls of the brick buildings across the way, one of which reminded him of the world outside with its sign: MONEY TO LOAN AT 6 PER CENT. The chief case he remembered from the first few years came to him as the attorney for the local humane society, a charitable position usually foisted on young lawyers with more sympathy and time than resistance. A young German immigrant, Maria Rusch, came to him to complain that her husband Reinhold was neglecting her and the three children and drinking too much besides. Full of righteous indignation, the young attorney promptly had Reinhold arrested and brought to trial. On the evidence of Maria and a tall young German shoemaker, Reinhold, quite unable to speak English and probably much confused about the whole affair anyway, went to the workhouse for his antisocial behavior. Whitlock, as the indignant young protector of women and children, had a good press. A local paper wrote: "After Brand Whitlock, appearing for the prosecution, had drawn a heart-rending picture of the pitiable condition in the Rusch homestead, all the jurymen save Charlie Stevens were in tears."[10]

Whitlock felt bad about the whole affair afterward. It all seemed so pointless, putting a man in jail for neglecting a family and thus forcing him to neglect it more. Finally, Whitlock went and had Reinhold paroled, and he disappeared into the West. Meanwhile, Maria lived on, helped by grants from the Humane Society, clothes made for the baby by Nell, and free visits from a friendly doctor. Next spring, when Reinhold's neglect was patently permanent, Maria applied for a divorce and obtained one from an old bachelor judge who thought all people should be single for their own good. Whitlock was her lawyer. It all looked lovely until the next day, when Maria and her shoemaker—the one who had testified against poor, drinking Reinhold—promptly got married. The affair, Whitlock learned, had been at the root of those inarticulate cries which Reinhold had made in court the previous fall. Why should he not neglect a woman who was carrying on with the shoemaker, and why should he not drown his sorrows and ignore her requests for his check? Whitlock never heard from Reinhold again but he owed him a debt, for the young lawyer "discovered that whatever other men might do, I could never again prosecute anyone for anything; and I never did." He kept his vow and lost, in addition, most of whatever faith he had kept in the law. Forever after, he was on the side of the so-called criminal, devoted to explanations that stressed the relativism of right and wrong and environmental determinism. Maria and her shoemaker, quite oblivious, were happy and prosperous together and quite devoted to each other.[11]

Whitlock's handling of the Rusch case, his immediate reaction of sympathy, his willingness to take quick action, and his ultimate discovery of his deception all indicate that as a lawyer he was an extremely imaginative artist. The man who had seen in Eugene Debs not a hero of the working classes but a character in a novel of real life was obviously uncomfortable as a lawyer, and he certainly knew it. Whitlock soon discovered that his creative and reform impulses were so intertwined that he himself could not tell them apart. He knew that his life was often legal and sometimes political and that his basic ambitions were all literary; aside from that, he could not really verbalize his predicament. The key to an understanding of his life and his art in these years lies in his inability to divide his life and his art: His art thus included the actual events that happened to him, while his life soon attained an artistic significance as part of a mission of reform. Eventually he came to believe that his real job was to combine the two: He was to use his sensibility to make the life of his city into a work of art in itself. All its people would thus be able to lead lives as beautiful as the world permitted, and in this sense *all* would be artists. It proved to be a compelling vision, but Whitlock's first steps toward it were shaky and uncertain, and nowhere were they as uncertain as in his fiction.

EVEN AS A MINOR FIGURE in the Altgeld administration, Whitlock was already writing his first stories. Using his own experiences in the law and in politics, he wrote his story about Davis McGowan. With Altgeld all but in the next room, he wrote about the governor of a state and the pardons he had to consider in "The Pardon of Thomas Whalen." Looking back on his life in rural Ohio, he wrote in "Blue Jacket" of the rivalry of a young teacher and a student for the love of a beautiful girl student. Using the careers of three of his inseparable cronies in Springfield—the brother of his then-prospective Chicago law partner John Baker; a lieutenant in the army; and Octavia's cousin, Lieutenant Roberts, who had attended West Point— he wrote "A Daughter of the Dunkards," a study of the love which a Catholic West Pointer has for an illiterate but lovely Dunkard girl. Unfortunately, for some time the only reader he had was the faithful Octavia, who cherished ambitions of her own. The two young people wrote frequent letters of encouragement to each other, and Whitlock particularly doted on the solace which even one sympathetic person can give to a self-conscious and sensitive and quite unsuccessful artist.[12]

While still in Springfield, Whitlock finally made a contact. A Whitechapel crony, Arthur Henry, knowing his ambitions, told John S. Phillips, editor of *McClure's*, about Whitlock. Just before Altgeld's defeat, Phillips wrote Whitlock and asked for stories— having to apologize immediately because *McClure's* had received an unsolicited Whitlock story the previous spring and had lost it while moving into new offices. Phillips suggested that Whitlock write ". . . a series of short stories that would deal with the incidents and characters of political life, from the ward caucuses and ward managers up to the chairmen of important political committees and men elected to important offices." He was, he added, dissatisfied with many of the more established writers and was looking for new blood. Whitlock answered that he had long been considering such a series and that "The Pardon of Thomas Whalen" was the first of the set. A month later, Phillips returned the story. It was "very promising" but too long for *McClure's*.[13]

Length was certainly a problem, for Whitlock wrote novelettes rather than stories; most of these early works run on to an unpublishable 20,000 words—and except for the ones he cut, most of them never did get published. Unfortunately, he soon discovered another problem that was harder for him to solve. Just after his earliest correspondence with Phillips, Whitlock submitted "The House Across the Street" to Robert Underwood Johnson at *The Century*. Johnson sent it back, for it was "not quite enough of a *story* to meet our present wants, and at the same time has the disadvantage of being on a very sad theme, which is also an objection at a time when we are trying to make the magazine gay and cheerful." Whitlock changed the envelopes and mailed the story off to Phillips as "a character study on the realistic side." Then he faced the dismal prospect of moving from Springfield and preparing for the Ohio exams. Taking a respite from writing, he read voraciously, in Oliver Wendell Holmes and George Eliot, and in James M. Barrie, Gilbert Parker, and S. R. Crockett—demonstrating the lack of selectivity he was prone to, if nothing else—and even some in Dickens, whom he generally disliked.[14]

He also revived his interest in Kipling and promptly found himself defending that hero of the Whitechapel Club to the disapproving Octavia. "Kipling is a realistic poet," he emphasized. To him, he was "the Poet of Manhood," and he had that in his work which "appeals most strongly to me, to my manhood, to my sense of honor, to my innate love of adventure, and as his poetry thunders and sweeps along, like a rush of cavalry, I go down before it." This was the mood, presumably, in which he offered his services as an officer in the Spanish-American War. He doted also on Browning, apparently more as a breviary of comfort than as a poet. He found much to admire in Robert Louis Stevenson, and a few things he did *not* like in a man he admired more: "If Mr. Howells has a fault—and it pains me to accuse him of one," he wrote Octavia, "it is that he makes, at times, his art his all, he is coldly classical, he seems to be showing one how perfectly, how calmly, how composedly, he can set life before you, but it is apt to be after all icy and cold." Real life, as Whitlock knew it, was full of warmth and excitement, and he could not find in Howells "the blood and fret, the noise and vehemence of life" that he had experienced. Only Browning and certain French and Russian realists, particularly Tolstoy, met with his complete approval.[15]

In July 1898 he read a collection of essays, *Literary and Social Silhouettes*, by the young immigrant who had been unhappy working in Urbana when Whitlock was a baby. Hjalmar Hjorth Boyesen had remained in America and made a successful career as a professor and novelist, and Whitlock could find in Boyesen's book certain reasons for the continued rejection of his manuscripts. Certainly his friendship with Phillips did not result in any stories immediately finding their way into *McClure's*, or anywhere else. In the fall, William George Jordan returned a story with the usual solace that did not console. "The Old House Across the Street" was "the best piece of realistic work which I have read for a long time," but it was not suitable for the *Saturday Evening Post* because of the "popular audience such as the *Post* has to cater to . . ." In October, the *Atlantic Monthly* turned down a story. Whitlock then sent off "Davis McGowan, Attorney at Law" to the Herbert S. Stone Company and "The Pardon of Thomas Whalen" to the *Post*. Jordan returned it because it was too long, but said that he liked it and would be glad to see more. He then offered the sort of advice that spoiled Whitlock's digestion. Forty-five hundred words was his "best length," he said. But then he continued: "I like to avoid the morbid, the sordid, and the erotic, so far as possible, and of course for a popular audience clear and satisfactory endings are best." As the new year began, the Stone people made it unanimous by turning down poor Mr. McGowan as being only one third of a novel—which it was—and suggesting that Whitlock finish it. At the time Whitlock did not even have legal clients to help him fill the day. No wonder he needed Octavia.[16]

Whitlock's second literary opportunity was to come about also as a result of his being in Springfield. The man who had so stupidly murdered Chicago mayor Carter Harrison during the 1893 World's Fair had been swiftly tried and condemned to death. Several days before the day of execution, Pete Dunne and some of the other Chicago newspapermen telegraphed Whitlock, as a man close to Governor Altgeld, to ask him to use his influence to get the sentence commuted to a life term. Everyone agreed that the boy was insane and that his case had been bungled by his attorney. At the time, Altgeld was out of the state, and the acting governor was Joseph B. Gill, a loyal Democrat who was especially popular with newspapermen. Whitlock loathed capital punishment and Gill was the soul of kindness, so the case did not seem hopeless. The next morning Whitlock went over to find Gill and told his secretary what he wanted. When he stated his errand, a man in the same room jumped up and asked Whitlock why he was interested in the case. Whitlock replied that he had no interest, he just did not want the boy hanged. "On the man's face, tired, with the expression of world-weariness life gives to the countenance behind which there has been too much serious contemplation of life," a face "prematurely wrinkled, there suddenly appeared a smile as winning as a woman's, and he said in a voice that had the timbre of human sympathy and the humor of a peculiar drawl":

"Well, you're all right then." The secretary then introduced Whitlock to Clarence Darrow.

D A R R O W   A T   T H E   T I M E was neglecting his own legal career to come and plead with his friend Altgeld for clemency for the Harrison assassin. He and Whitlock promptly went into another room and discussed the case. Despite their pleas, however, Joe Gill refused to relent, and the execution went forward. Darrow, there for the day, spent the rest of his time with his new friend, and they talked books until midnight. When he boarded the train Darrow had "The Pardon of Thomas Whalen" under his arm. The two men became lifelong friends, and out of their friendship came an introduction for Whitlock to Howells and a meeting with Mark Twain.[17]

Darrow and Whitlock indeed had much in common. Both shared years of experience in Chicago, a sympathetic knowledge of the ideas of Henry George, and an adulation of John Peter Altgeld. Darrow's affection for Altgeld was indeed unbounded, particularly for his treatment of criminals not as a social type but as normal human beings who were the victims of economic circumstances. But strangely enough, literary similarities more than political ones seem to have been strongest in drawing Whitlock and Darrow together. Darrow's later reputation as a criminal lawyer and small-town agnostic has overshadowed the more literary part of his career, and few remember him as a critic. Yet at the time he met Whitlock he was lecturing at the Chicago Single Tax Club on the novels of Tolstoy, for whom he had much sympathy and deep intellectual agreement. Whitlock nowhere states when he first discovered the doctrines of Tolstoy, but it seems probable that Darrow first introduced the greatest living novelist to him.[18]

In his lectures, Darrow spoke of *Anna Karenina* and *Resurrection* in particular, but he always emphasized the moral message rather than the aesthetics of the books. Tolstoy, he said, "will live in history for his philosophy of life. Brilliant though his novels be, these are but the gold and tinsel which flutter at the theatre to beguile the crowd." Tolstoy's real greatness came only after the age of fifty, when his conscience made his aristocratic life unbearable for him and he became the conscience of the world. He became a type of Christ: Only rarely do such men come, and when they do "they have been crucified in one age, to be resurrected and glorified in the years to come." Darrow's discussion was frankly religious in its import, and Tolstoy's philosophy was a secular form of religion. This philosophy permeated the writer's greatest art and made it great, for, wrote Darrow, "no true art exists that does not have as its fundamental purpose the desire to better and serve mankind." Like Whitlock, Darrow too had his vision of the better world, a vision like the good and beautiful life and nothing at all like what one might expect from the caustic Darrow of the McNamara and Scopes trials. The tone was worthy of Tolstoy himself: "In that day no man will compel the service of his fellow man, but each will gladly labor for the whole, moved by the righteous power of Love . . ." Then "art will become a part of daily life and daily life a part of art. To make one pair of shoes for weary feet will be as worthy in the sight of man as to write an epic poem or compose a deathless song," Darrow wrote; "to thatch one roof, as great as to paint the brightest hues that the sunset ever wrought; and to cool one parched tongue or hold out one hand to guide your fellow mortal through the dark, more than all the sermons ever preached by man."[19]

Darrow's views on Tolstoy are of more than passing interest, for both an understanding of Whitlock and of much of progressivism. Historians have tried to explain the movement in terms of class conflict, status resentment, a deep commitment to conservatism, and other notions that seem to miss the point. Each explanation has just enough truth to be superficially convincing, at least in the particular case at hand. But with Whitlock, Jones, Darrow, Altgeld, and many of Whitlock's later friends, an explanation of the movement—one that would seem most convincing to them, as well as to the modern student—is in their religious vision of the world. When these men used words like *love* and *harmony* and *fundamental democracy* and *the free city*, they were simply labeling parts of the vision which they all had of the Kingdom of God on earth—to use a phrase reintroduced by Tolstoy. For most of them, the source of this vision began in their youth with Lincoln and some variety of abolitionism, developed into the free-trade Jeffersonianism preached by Frank Hurd and John Palmer, and moved into modern times with the concern for labor problems under Altgeld. By the time Whitlock became mayor of Toledo, all of these men had read and absorbed Tolstoy, as well as the occasional American book—like Altgeld's *Our Penal Machinery and Its Victims*—which seemed to fit in with Tolstoy's vision. They were utopians moved by religious fervor, and they conducted not political campaigns but crusades, gave sermons instead of speeches. They developed a new ethic of primitive Christianity adapted to modern urban-industrial life to oppose to the tired, acquisitive virtues of Russell Conwell and Andrew Carnegie. Their battle was less for legislation than for the minds of men, since the burden of their argument was religion and religion needed conviction and conversion before it could do anything else. Toledo's future mayor and Whitlock's future mentor, "Golden Rule" Jones, seems an incredible figure to succeeding generations, but he knew what he was about, and that was the saving of souls. When even the most notorious agnostic of the time, Clarence Darrow, was talking about Christianity and using language appropriate for a revival, the influence of Darrow's ideas on the young Whitlock takes on even greater importance.

Darrow spoke for most progressives, as his choice of Tolstoy books showed, for if progressives could agree on a single book that they loved, it was *Resurrection*; when the time came for Whitlock's best progressive statement, *The Turn of the Balance*, correspondents from all over the country—including many he never met—instinctively used *Resurrection* as their yardstick for his achievement.[20] *Resurrection* was, first, a great tract, made art by the genius of one of the world's greatest novelists in his later days when he gave up the writing of novels and turned to the giving of sermons. He wrote it, in fact, chiefly to make enough money to help the persecuted Dukhobors leave Russia. In it Tolstoy voiced sentiments that most American progressives could agree with. He attacked all institutionalizations of society—government, army, prisons, and the church all came under sharp attack and helped make the book the best seller of all Tolstoy's books in English-speaking lands up to that time. Tolstoy had a greater influence in England, and particularly in America, than he did in any other country including Russia, and the pilgrimage to Yasnaya Polyana became the progressive American equivalent of the trip to Mecca: It was the "sacred dream" of Henry George to get there, although he never succeeded, and his son could make the trip only after George's death; Ernest Crosby, a close friend of Golden Rule Jones, came, and Jones himself corresponded with Tolstoy; William Jennings Bryan came; and Jane Addams found the influence of Tolstoy and her trip there worthy of an entire chapter in her autobiography. Fortunately, the more prickly side and the more than colorful past of the holy man were heavily masked by distance and devotion, and the anarchistic Christianity of the man could shine all the more inspiringly for the lack of solid biographical information.[21]

Oddly enough, American thinkers influenced *Resurrection* at least as much as it in turn influenced them. Thoreau received a brief mention therein, and the British-born but American-appreciated Herbert Spencer received several. The real inspiration for the book, however, and the man whose ideas formed the intellectual superstructure of the plot, was Henry George. George's influence in the book was so pervasive that *Resurrection* may well have played a material role in the spread of George's ideas in America and helped sanctify the economic theories that many Ohio reformers already knew something about. The theme of the book was the moral self-reform, or resurrection, of Nekhludov for his single act of immorality—thus appealing to the predilection of the progressives for moral interpretations of the world and to their intense individualism. Nekhludov came to believe what Whitlock himself would put into more abstract terms in his later works: "Now he saw quite clearly that the only sure means of salvation from the terrible wrong which man has to endure is for every man to acknowledge himself a sinner before God and therefore unfitted to punish or reform other men." Or, as Nekhludov put it somewhat earlier, about Maslova: "She is not the one I want to reform. It is myself."[22]

Given this individualistic moralism, the rest of George's theory followed. When Nekhludov first saw Maslova, he was a third-year student writing his thesis on land tenure. The early, radical ideas of the *Social Statics* of Herbert Spencer deeply impressed him. The arguments were "lucid and unanswerable," and they were later "brilliantly confirmed by Henry George . . ." He found himself making vows about what he would do with his estates, now that he saw the injustice of aristocrats living off unearned increment. He came to believe that the people's misery "arose from the fact that they do not own the land which would support them, this land being in the hands of men who take advantage of their ownership to live by the work of the people." Or, as Nekhludov "vividly recalled the fundamental principles of Henry George and his own former enthusiasm for them": "Land ought not to be subject to private ownership any more than water, sun or air. Every man has a right to land and to all the benefit that can be derived from it." A small vignette perhaps tied together all the religious, economic, and social issues. Nekhludov began to explain Henry George's single-tax theory to some common people: "The land belongs to God," he began. . . .[23] One scarcely had to go on, although Nekhludov did for another page.

WITH THEIR COMMON INTERESTS in Tolstoy and re- form, Darrow and Whitlock remained close and visited and corresponded regularly. Whitlock thought enough of Darrow's critical acumen to write that he "should have devoted himself to literature," and in practice entrusted many early manuscripts to Darrow's critical eye. In January 1898, Whitlock called on him in Chicago and gladly complied with Darrow's request that he leave stories that he might find worthy of recommending to his friend Howells. "Davis McGowan" and "Thomas Whalen" still remain- ing, Darrow took them, along with "The Lynching of Lincoln Brooks," a story of love and mob justice, and "The Old House Across the Street," about a funeral. Like most of Whitlock's shorter works, these were not impressive, and Darrow wanted numerous changes made before showing them to Howells. As Octavia had made similar comments and Whitlock was as uncer- tain as ever about his work, he took the judgment in good stride.[24]

At the same time, Arthur Henry was again helping. He ap- parently knew most of the magazine world, and he succeeded in interesting *Ainslee's*, as well as *McClure's*, in Whitlock. Richard Duffy, an *Ainslee's* editor, soon became a one-man cheering section for Whitlock's work, tirelessly encouraging, compli- menting, and consoling a man who needed all the attention he could get. "The Pardon of Thomas Whalen," after its reading by Darrow, was again turned down, this time by *Munsey's*, on

January 25, 1899, so Whitlock promptly popped it into yet another envelope and sent it to Duffy. There, after much pruning, it achieved print, the first success of Whitlock's career. Once the story was safely published, its proud author could admit to some doubts about his good fortune: "*Ainslee's* is undeniably a cheap magazine in many respects, and yet it is young and growing, with plenty of capital behind it, and I believe it has a future," he wrote to Octavia. "I prefer *McClure's* to any of the cheaper magazines, and yet Mr. Duffy has been so kind to me that I must do all in my power to repay him." In other words, he can have everything I write if he wants it, and what a relief finally to have something to be proud of! Together, Whitlock and Duffy decided that a series of political short stories might have a market, and Whitlock agreed to write them.[25]

Meanwhile he was reading again, sharpening his taste on Howells and Henry James and Cervantes, and comforting himself with Browning. He deeply admired Clarence Darrow's essay on realism, where Darrow demonstrated that realism and liberty grew together and were dependent on each other. Whitlock toyed with the idea of writing a political novel, based on the career of Senator, railroad builder, and one-time Democratic national chairman, Calvin S. Brice, but he looked on the prospect of a sustained work "with much diffidence and dread." He greatly admired Frank Norris, especially the Norris of *McTeague* and *The Octopus*, while having certain serious reservations about the vulgarity and coarseness of parts of the latter. Finally, he "resumed the study" of French "with a most charming little Frenchman, M. Philippe A. Roi, after having been away from French books, of which I never knew much anyway, for four or five years." He could read it readily and was indulging in the novels of François Coppée and short stories of Guy de Maupassant. The latter, he wrote, "has taught me a great deal about the art of writing short stories, for he is without doubt the greatest of all miniaturists." Whitlock had at least one admirer for his own work besides Octavia. Pete Dunne analyzed his old friend's letters and wrote: ". . . you are rapidly becoming the Samuel Johnson of Toledo. I think your epistolary style is improving every year and I strongly advise a collection of letters to friends. I am sure they would be widely read in Sangamon County, Illinois."[26]

As Dunne wrote, Whitlock was enjoying some success in places more populated than Sangamon County. Although George H. Perry of *Everybody's* turned down "The Old House Across the Street" because of "its somewhat lugubrious undertone, which I do not think consistent with the policy of a magazine which avowedly confines itself to light matter for quick and pleasant reading," as the new year arrived Whitlock received a few letters actually requesting stories. Both Duffy and the Appleton Company suggested that he get started on a novel, and in July the *Saturday Evening Post* bought "Jamie The Page Boy" for $75. Early in 1900 he actually did begin work on a story that he thought might grow into a short novel. The story concerned a politician, and the morality of politics, society, and sex. Whitlock was, however, afraid of certain unstated inhibitions of the American publishing establishment, which he was afraid would not dare to publish such a story: "Oh! the irksomeness of having to write cheerfully and innocuously for the pretty little American school-girl!" Even if it were published, Whitlock feared that its theme would cause him to get "misunderstanding, criticism and abuse," and he was never quite strong enough to take these without pain. Even his beloved Howells demonstrated this American prudery. Darrow finally sent him a Whitlock story, and Howells replied directly to Whitlock in a letter that sounded hopeful but hardly enthused. In that peculiar prudery that was part of Howells's own eccentric realism, he cautioned Whitlock against the use of sexual themes in his stories. Howells frankly did not want what he called French Realism, and he told Whitlock: "I believe there is a lot of *clean* truth in life."[27]

W HEN EVEN THE DEAN of the realists began to caution young writers about their emphasis on sex, it was time to ask what had happened to American fiction. Why did magazine editors turn down Whitlock stories because of their lugubrious undertones, unhappy endings, and lack of moral uplift? What brought on Whitlock's despair at having to please the pretty young American girl? Why, in fact, did realism seem so important to men who wrote at the turn of the century?

The chief literary obstacle to realistic success was what all critics recognized as the female audience for American fiction.[28]

The American public, as Boyesen noted sadly, was the female half of it when it came to literature. "The readers of novels are chiefly young girls, and a popular novel is a novel which pleases them . . ." The author knew what the ladies like and so had to write to please them, or he made no money and ran the risk of seeing his works go completely unpublished. He therefore had to refrain "from discussing what, according to the boarding school standard, is unsafe or improper." Novelists had to ignore most social problems, for they displeased; their social conscience was inhibited— or their purse suffered. Whitlock encountered just this sort of opposition to his chosen themes, and his disgust at the pretty young American girl was quite well founded. This young American girl, Boyesen concluded, "is the Iron Madonna who strangles in her fond embrace the American novelists; the Moloch upon whose altar he sacrifices, willingly or unwillingly, his chances of greatness."[29]

Whitlock and his fellow realists were half convinced, by the time of Howells's *Criticism and Fiction* in 1891, that the war against sentimental idealism was over and won. With Howells pointing an approving finger at every writer who made even a slight effort at the realistic method and exercising a benevolent autocracy concerning which European books were worth the time of Americans, the battle all but died out—until almost the exact time when Whitlock started writing fiction. Then, about 1894, the fashion changed, and instead of epics of the kitchen Americans had epics of the weird and far away. Earlier writers like Charles Reade, Augusta Jane Evans, and Elizabeth Stuart Phelps had required that their readers suspend disbelief to fathom everything from religious truth to elegant Bohemianism to murder and baby farming. Now nothing exotic escaped, and the realists found themselves outnumbered by writers who wrote such escapist trivia as: *Trilby, Ben-Hur, Quo Vadis?, Little Lord Fauntleroy, King Solomon's Mines, When Knighthood Was in Flower,* and *Alice of Old Vincennes.* In the time of religious and social crises that the realists wished to discuss, these books gave sensation-hungry readers an uncomplicated escape into the world of foreign aristocracies, where rich American girls often married; into an endless series of pocket principalities along the Danube, full of feudal trappings, moats, and masked balls; and into the world of beautiful women, melodrama, and a good dungeon for spice at midnight.[30] Realists were forever spoofing the genre, whether in its earliest form, as with Huck Finn finding a wrecked boat called the *Sir Walter Scott* and the pictures of Gothic sentimentality painted by Emmeline Grangerford; or in its later phases, as in the whole apparatus of *A Connecticut Yankee in King Arthur's Court*; or in the domestic phase, as in the many disparaging anti-escapist remarks made by Howells's characters, most noticeably in *The Rise of Silas Lapham*. Even in some of Whitlock's early fiction, the almost visceral distaste for the stuff reappears at times. Whitlock's and others' spoofing often concealed pain, however, and indicated the presence of a real dislike for men who would distract people from the needs of a democratic, urban society that needed all the reform it could get.

In such an atmosphere, Whitlock's work was depressing and unpopular. Who wanted to read of lynchings, funerals, the pardons of criminals, or the struggles of daydreaming young lawyers when a whole medieval panorama was waiting in another magazine?— apparently only Howells, an occasional young editor like Richard Duffy, and devoted friends like Octavia. Fortunately for Whitlock, Howells was one of the most important critics in the country, and with his public and private encouragement Whitlock managed to find success of a sort. Late in 1900 Howells wrote Darrow to ask if "that Toledo friend of yours" had "a novel of actual American life in MS" that he would like Howells to consider for publication by *Harper's Monthly Magazine*. When Whitlock saw the letter, he experienced a "flush of joy" and promptly sent it off to Octavia. Unfortunately, he had no finished novel at hand and was only part way through what he intended to be a short novel about a congressional campaign, "more realistic than anything I've done." Nevertheless, such attention after so long a series of disappointments made all the difference to him. He wrote Darrow: "For years and years, as you are aware, Mr. Howells has been my literary divinity. I have followed him timorously from afar, I have shivered in the realization that much of my stuff has been a weak imitation of his work, and I have despaired of ever doing anything original." He then concluded: "And now I catch my breath to think that I am actually near to attracting his attention, and am fearful that I fail to reward his generous interest by proving worthy."[31]

Whitlock's literary misery at being a realist in an age of romantic fluff had its "real life" parallel in his legal career. The fact that the Maria Rusch case had been one of the most memorable cases of his early career perhaps gives some indication of how scintillating his other cases were. Yet neither Whitlock's own literary tastes nor his legal problems are entirely comprehensible without a certain amount of background in what was happening in America as a whole at the end of the century. Whitlock was reasonably cultured and widely read, but even he was only half aware of the important changes taking place that soon began him on the career that made him famous both as writer and as reformer. In all probability he did not even expect that he would have an important role in these changes. To understand Whitlock's emergence in the first decade of the twentieth century, one must be aware of three related developments, two of them national and one of them state.

AT THE NATIONAL LEVEL, the most obvious changes were economic and social. For two decades after the Civil War, America remained largely a rural country, conservative in its politics. In the 1880's, however, the first of a new group of immigrants began arriving who played a crucial role in the development of the West: In the 1880's alone more than 400,000 Germans arrived, settling predominantly in Illinois and Ohio and surrounding states. In that decade, their arrival plus the forces of industrialization changed America from a country with only one person in five a city dweller in 1880 to one person in three in 1890. Not all the new urban dwellers were Germans or even, subsequently, Eastern European. The tedium and labor of rural life soon had little attraction for the brighter sons of the farmers, and the city became a mythic destination to which one escaped when work or parental domination became too onerous. Still, as one of the chief historians of the period has pointed out, by 1890 about 20 per cent of the inhabitants of the United States were of alien birth, and a great many more were the sons and grandsons of earlier immigrants. In that America, "urbanization for the first time became a controlling factor in national life," and the city became "the supreme achievement of the new industrialism."[32]

Unfortunately, the rise of the city was not a thing of beauty.

Since the Civil War slum conditions, disease, and the lack of sanitation, food, and clothing in the city had haunted those who were aware of them. Some public health efforts produced improved sewerage facilities, public vaccinations, and efforts at halting female and child labor. The poor, the insane, the criminal, and the animal all had champions, and reformers who cared more for abstractions than people could exhaust themselves in the agitation for woman suffrage and prohibition.[33] In subsequent years, success occasionally followed concern. In New York, in particular, the Reverend Mr. Charles H. Parkhurst made some progress in reforming the city, while upstate at Elmira, in an experiment that won the approval of John P. Altgeld, Z. R. Brockway was initiating the first of modern American prison reforms. Yet, viewed as a whole, the record was so uninspiring that such occasional exceptions seem only a mockery. Both indirect evidence and occasional court testimony indicate that nearly every city hall was hiding the peculations of its inhabitants and that much of this corruption originated through outwardly respectable businessmen. The result was generally the worst city government that America had ever known.[34]

From all sides, contemporary writers agreed. James Bryce gave a much-quoted indictment in his widely read study of America. Andrew White wrote that, with no exaggeration, "the city governments of the United States are the worst in Christendom—the most expensive, the most inefficient, and the most corrupt." Everyone agreed that cities were ugly, dirty, congested, corrupt, and diseased. What then could be done? Not—as might seem obvious to people living decades later—take a study, appropriate money, and go after the poor for their own good and the good of society. The approved path was that of moral principle and the method that of education. White, Godkin, and most other commentators were at least subconsciously the heirs to the mental processes of Russell Conwell and the champions of wealth, incapable of looking at anything except in terms of good men and bad men, rich men and poor men. Godkin wrote that ". . . the work of municipal reform is really a work of education. No change in the machinery of government would do us any good without a radical change in the way of looking at municipal administration on the part of the more intelligent class of voters." White preferred business methods to good men in office: "My fundamental contention is that a city is a corporation; that as a city it has nothing whatever to do with general political interests; that party political names and duties are utterly out of place there."[35] Both men, of course, were partially right, and Whitlock could agree with at least some of what they said, especially the part about nonpartisanship at the local level. But what about the poor? Somehow, they seemed to be less people than irritating statistics; at their most human, they were little more than a bad smell and a court record. White and Godkin, in short, were reformers, not progressives, tinkering with the old system and not trying to find a new one and thus much prone to thinking in abstractions. Whitlock would meet men similar in their thinking habits in Toledo, and the confrontation would make him miserable.

Equally important for the course of Toledo reform was the rise of social Christianity, both in America and the world. Before the Civil War, the churches had been deeply involved in reform movements of every conceivable variety. Then the war itself soaked up all the religious energies of the people. But in the years after Grant, religion again became a great force for reforms of many kinds. Indeed, until World War I religion was the greatest single force supporting the principal humanitarian and reform movements. The Unitarians had long been producing critics of American society, but now some of the force for change had evangelical roots. The New Haven theology, rooted though it was in Jonathan Edwards and Timothy Dwight, produced Nathaniel Taylor and eventually Horace Bushnell as it slowly lessened its emphasis on sudden-conversion experience and life as a preparation for another world and began to concentrate on living life in the present world. Soon, a growing and vocal group of clergymen was questioning unrestricted competition and laissez-faire economics, doubting that labor was as wholly depraved and malicious as it appeared in the speeches of the apologists for wealth, saying frankly that business ethics often left something to be desired, emphasizing that the relations of labor and capital were perhaps more important than the morals of the poor, and discovering that urban problems were the task of their generation.[36]

The first leader of the Social Gospel, as this movement was called in America, was Washington Gladden. A man of deep and sincere piety ever since his youth, Gladden had grown up in the ferment of abolitionism and prohibitionism. All around him was a Calvinistic, individualistic, otherwordly, hellfire religion, but he felt little drawn to it. He preferred "a religion that laid hold upon life with both hands, and proposed, first and foremost, to realize the Kingdom of God in this world." Educated at Williams College, he entered the Congregational ministry and promptly demonstrated his independence by taking an unorthodox, secessionist Methodist church in Brooklyn. An early enthusiasm for Lincoln reinforced his social conscience, and the reading of Horace Bushnell and Frederick W. Robertson influenced him still further. Bushnell even gave the ordination sermon when Gladden moved to North Adams, Massachusetts. From there, Gladden moved to New York and a brief stay as religious editor of the New York *Independent,* where he took a vocal role in the anti-Tweed campaign. Then he went back to Massachusetts to preach the importance of labor and the applicability of Christianity to social conduct. Often he found himself a target of heresy hunters, even for his enlightened views on harmless amusements. Finally, in a move crucial for Toledo reform, he moved to Columbus, Ohio, in 1882, bringing his message to the Middle West. There his work attracted the attention of the man who became Golden Rule Jones, and the two men kept up a regular correspondence throughout the years that Jones was mayor of Toledo.[37]

Jones particularly approved of Gladden's emphasis on living a life of service to others and not wasting it in selfishness. Gladden himself applied his views to Columbus city government, just as Jones and Whitlock did in Toledo, and campaigned for a city government led by an elected mayor with full responsibility, just as Jones did. He even served for two years as a councilman from the seventh ward (1900-2) and shared his experience with Mayor Jones. He helped get a street-railway fare of seven tickets for 25¢ with a sliding scale for balancing fares and profits, just as Whitlock did years later. He was instrumental in getting what Jones and Whitlock always wanted, a municipal electric plant, for he was sure as he could be "of anything that the municipal ownership and control of public service industries is the right policy,—the only policy under which there is any hope of preventing corruption and oppression." He also had a strongly ethical stance with which to attack the homilies of Russell Conwell, even as his resembled theirs in moral rigidity: "We shall get it hammered into our heads one of these days that this is a moral universe; not that it is going to be, by and by, but that it is moral now, moral all through, in tissue and fibre, in gristle and bone, in muscle and brain, in sensation and thought; and that no injustice fails to get its due recompense, now and here." Finally, Gladden even emphasized what became the Jones trademark. He had, he wrote, the conviction "that the Golden Rule is, after all, the only workable rule of life. . . ."[38]

George Davis Herron, the other important Social Gospeler of this period, was a considerably more flamboyant figure. He first attracted national attention in 1891 after a speech on "The Message of Jesus to Men of Wealth," an earnest appeal for the application to business of Christian ethics, in total opposition to Conwell's "Acres of Diamonds." Later, he became even more controversial for his highly unconventional sexual activities and his work in World War I and the subsequent peace. Those, however, were in the future. For Jones, who read his books, particularly *The New Redemption* time after time with great admiration, Herron preached a God who was at work in this world producing the Kingdom of God. He was a man highly sensitive to social wrong who preached the stewardship of man for his fellow man through social sacrifice. He was a man who attacked capitalism fiercely, called competition selfish and anarchical and thought it in direct conflict with Christian teaching. Always, he campaigned for a church committtted to social justice and emphasized the compatibility of true Christianity with certain of the tenets of socialism. Eventually, Jones and Herron became friends, and Herron's picture hung in Jones's office when he became mayor. As Jones's biographer has written: "Most of Jones's ideas may be traced directly to Herron."[39]

IMMIGRATION AND URBANIZATION and the social gospel, then, were the chief *national* factors influencing Toledo reform. The chief *state* influence was unglamorous, negative, and inevitable: the political background. Ohio, the maker of Presidents, was always in some kind of political ferment, and had been since before the Civil War. When Jones and Whitlock began their careers in Toledo, Ohio Democrats were in their usual ineffectual disarray, an impotent minority that only occasionally could produce a Frank Hunt Hurd to challenge the dominant Republicans. The majority party, in its turn, was split, often with great bitterness, between factions supporting Mark Hanna and his chief rival, Joseph Benson Foraker. Foraker, otherwise known as "Fire Alarm Joe" and "Boomtara" for his bloody-shirt oratory, first found himself the leader of a Republican faction in 1887, when despite his announced support of John Sherman for the Presidency some people suspected Foraker of having designs on the vice-presidential nomination: One position made the other untenable. (The Constitution forbids, in effect, a President and Vice-President from the same state.) Mark Hanna, as a chief of the Sherman faction, first opposed Foraker in that year and, in his subsequent support of William McKinley, continued to oppose Foraker with some bitterness. The two groups divided state politics between them, as Foraker and his friend Asa Bushnell were both governors whereas Hanna was a senator and McKinley a representative and President. Foraker and his lieutenants were particularly strong in Toledo, and in 1896, with Asa Bushnell just nominated for governor, Foraker was at the height of his power.[40]

In Toledo the leader of the Foraker men was Mayor Guy G. Major, a linseed-oil businessman who also had the support of the anti-Catholic American Protective Association, which had one of its strongest chapters in Toledo. But, when the time came for the 1897 nominations for mayor, he was unable to keep the Foraker forces from splitting severely; after a lengthy fight, Samuel Milton Jones, a genuine dark horse, won the nomination. Jones was, as one observer wrote, a "sterling business man, the friend of labor, the friend of the poor, and a self-made honest man—the noblest work of God." Obviously, he was straight out of "Acres of Diamonds," businessmen would take heart, and the Republicans would stay in power for a few more years.[41]

❰❰CHAPTER 4

Golden Rule Jones and the

"Great Suspender"

(1900-1905)

IMPROBABLY ENOUGH, this unknown businessman in a
very short time became the greatest single influence on the life
of Brand Whitlock. He was one of seven children of a Welsh slate
quarrier who had emigrated to America when Jones was still an
infant. He had scarcely thirty months of schooling, and an intense,
orthodox-religious upbringing which he promptly renounced. Extremely poor at the start of his career, he never forgot the raw life
he had encountered in the oil-boom towns where he began work
and from which he rose to wealth.

In 1891 Jones took out a patent on his invention of an all-metal
sucker rod, intended to replace the old hickory devices then used
in oil fields to connect the pumping mechanism at the bottom of a
well to the engine on the surface. No one was interested in producing his device, so he set up shop himself at 600 Segur Avenue,
Toledo, in an abandoned factory. A year later, in 1895, he incorporated the Acme Sucker Rod Company. Toledo was then still
deep in the 1893 depression, and Jones was shaken by the misery,
poverty, and servility among the men who tried to get work in his
plant. They appeared soon after Jones, as a fifty-year-old businessman, began his reading of reform literature, and they received the

benefit of his discovery of Morris, Ruskin, Mazzini, and, most of all, Tolstoy and Herron. Armed, if not bruised, by his reading of these men, Jones accepted the doctrines of Christian love applied to the modern world, the ugliness of competitive society, the joys of equality and cooperation, and the nonexistence of any class war. In practice he paid his men more than his competitors did; he tried to help men he could not hire; he eliminated work bosses and time clocks and ran his factory on the honor system to promote equality; he experimented with fringe benefits, such as company picnics, to boost morale and self-respect; he instituted a bonus system which he called profit sharing; finally, in the act which gave him his name, he grew exasperated with the tedious prohibitionism of most factories, tacked up the Golden Rule and said he had no others. Herron had written: "He who builds a mercantile establishment upon the basis of the Golden Rule is a greater and wiser philanthropist than he who founds hospitals for the poor out of the gains of selfishness," and Jones believed in this as literally as he believed most statements he loved. He became an extremely soft touch for beggars, often hiring the worst of the derelicts because, he said, no one else would. Fortunately for his wife and children, his factory produced equipment protected by monopoly patent and made money almost against the will of its owner. Naturally, the men he helped soon remembered their benefactor at the polls, as well as in their prayers.[1] One of his strongest supporters was soon Brand Whitlock, the young lawyer with nothing to do; elements of Jones's thought soon permeated the mind of the younger man and permanently stamped his outlook.

After his election as mayor in 1897, Jones built a Golden Rule Park and Playground out of his personal fortune and regularly invited liberal speakers from all around the country to speak there Sundays. He established an eight-hour day, forty-eight-hour week at his factory, late in 1899. He visited Jane Addams at Hull House and imitated her work by setting up Golden Rule House across the street from the factory and park, with his sister Ellen in charge, in 1898. He tested plans for a cooperative dining hall, a cooperative insurance plan, and a week's vacation with pay, in days when such proposals were not even thought worth ridiculing by many of his competitors. In 1901 he even began a Golden Rule Band, for he found in music a principle of harmony symbolic of his vision of the cooperative life. Throughout all his attempts, he tried to give men a chance at the beautiful life and shrugged off all the complaints that people made about the men he picked up off the streets. He preferred saving souls to making money. He received both laughter and votes in return for practicing the business and politics of his vision.

Unfortunately, Jones had several character traits that made many of his ideas impotent when the time came for actual legislation and that left a tradition which hampered Whitlock when he became mayor. Rather than fight for jobs or a bill that he and his supporters wanted, for example, Jones would orate for it, disdaining any back-stairs conniving. Such an Olympian attitude made for much purity and no progress and caused some of Jones's supporters to declare, probably unjustly, that all Jones cared about was the publicity. What he and Whitlock really cared about was the Kingdom of God, and, with their great faith in the capacities of the people for self-government and self-improvement, they devoutly believed that Jones's function was less to do certain things than to preach. When Whitlock attained power in his own right, he managed to shed much of Jones's tendency to say rather than to do, but not all. Certainly the political speeches of both men were really homilies, sermons and not pleas for votes. To them, politics and religion were one and their attitudes in these areas emphasize one of the most important aspects of Toledo politics, for, viewed from Toledo, the progressive era is but the political phase of the social gospel.

One of the reasons Jones seemed ineffectual to Toledo was his lack of faith in social reforms of a certain type. The Major regime had openly tolerated many violations of the state blue laws, and in the German sections of the town especially, Sunday drinkers, gamblers, and the inhabitants of the "wine rooms" (a euphemism for houses of prostitution) had little to fear from city police. Goaded by many of his Republican supporters, Jones made rather ineffectual attempts to talk the proprietors of these places out of wrongdoing, getting many pledges and no noticeable compliance. Jones soon decided that most of the things people wanted were not all that wicked, and although he never drank himself he was soon tolerating most of the liquor-law violations and not worrying much about other infractions. Whitlock heartily agreed, and continued the policy when he became mayor. Jones was certainly not helped, however, by the need to go to court to defend his police chief, accused of drunkenness and profanity while on duty. The case had its bright side, however: When Chief Raitz was acquitted, Jones had a lifelong friend who incidentally controlled a large portion of the saloon vote and was a powerful voice in ward politics; the mayor never had to worry too much about re-election thereafter.

Despite his tendency to talk rather than act, Jones did achieve some reforms. He took the clubs away from the police and gave them sticks instead, leaving it to Mayor Whitlock to take the sticks away a few years later. With the help of the Toledo newspapers, he educated the people about the blue laws, showing that such laws were undemocratic, enacted not by the city people but by rural farmers in the state legislature who did not have to live with them. He made city treatment of tramps more humane. Chiefly, however, he talked about love, Christ, and the glories of municipal ownership of public monopolies. He talked in Golden Rule Park and Golden Rule Hall and around the country at places where his friends were, like Hull House in Chicago. Soon, he attracted national attention.[2]

When the time came for Jones's renomination in 1899, he found himself repudiated by Walter F. Brown, leading Republican boss in Toledo, and by the Hanna wing of the party. Jones promptly walked out, taking the tenderloin and Foraker vote with him. The result was a kind of high comedy. The Methodists then brought in evangelist Samuel Porter Jones to hold a revival in the midst of the campaign and thus underline and expose all the horrible vice that was rotting the city under Mayor Jones. The vice issue, now attached to Jones for good, remained to haunt Mayor Whitlock throughout all his campaigns. Jones, however, set Whitlock a good example by ignoring all the attacks on town morals and insisting that the real issues were public education about the values of love and cooperation, made specific in municipally owned public utilities. Soon, organized labor and Negro groups swung behind him, deserting their traditional Republican allegiance; then came the Germans and other ethnic groups. Chief Raitz worked so hard for Jones that he came under attack for making the police a Jones machine, which it soon was.

All the newspapers opposed Jones, but he managed to carry every ward in the city and every precinct but one. He received 69 per cent of the vote. Unfortunately, he disliked politics so much that he refused to have any running mates, so the Republicans held their usual majority of lesser offices.[3]

Whitlock wrote later that he and Jones were drawn together by their "interest in the disowned, the outcast, the poor, and the criminal," as well as by common intellectual and emotional commitments to the writings of Tolstoy, Emerson, Whitman, and others. The struggling young lawyer knew of his mayor at first only as he was painted by the institutional voices of Toledo; and by 1900 the press, the pulpit, and the businessmen were all united on the mental inadequacies of their mayor. No one since Altgeld had been such a terrible man. One day, as Whitlock was writing fiction in his empty law office, in stepped Jones himself and, with his startling, abrupt manner, took a chair and sat down. Once Jones had taken off his hat for a charwoman and been laughed at for it, so now he took off his hat for no one. There the big Welshman sat, with his huge, workingman's hands still cracked from his days of poverty, his large, cream-colored slouch hat, and his flowing cravat. He was planning a program for Golden Rule Park and wanted Whitlock to speak.

"On what subject?" he asked.

"There's only one subject," Jones said with his radiant smile, "—life."

Whitlock said something about preparation.

"Prepare!" he exclaimed. "Why prepare? Just speak what's in your heart."

What could you do with a man like that? Whitlock went, for he was a sucker for any appeal to his emotional sympathies, and kept coming back to speak for years. His public career had begun.[4]

The two men quickly became close. Together they toured the city workhouses and prisons, talking to the inmates and trying to find out how to free them. The two men made a small agreement that if Jones would pay incidental fees, like stenographic costs, Whitlock would represent the people in court. Hard and time-consuming work—and Whitlock's law partners were forever grumbling—but he loved it. The results were quickly apparent. No longer were the police quite so quick to run people in on suspicion, when they knew that they would perhaps be made to look silly by a probing defense counsel in court. They also soon stopped the habit of holding people for no reason and for no specific charge. And that was not all. Toledo law said that, in the absence of the police judge, the mayor or a man appointed by him might sit in his place and dispose of the cases. That is where the publicity started.[5]

Beginning as early as January 1900, and regularly by the summer of 1901, Whitlock sat as police-court judge when Lyman Wachenheimer, the elected judge, was on vacation or sick. Jones had made a policy of letting just about every criminal go, and Whitlock scarcely needed conversion. The great majority of culprits were simply poor people who had bad records as tramps, gamblers, drunks, prostitutes, and petty thieves. Jail and fines quite obviously did no good at all, for, whatever the sentence, the people were always back the next week. Punishment seemed pointless, especially when men who regularly milked public monopolies and watered stock enjoyed the respect of the community even as they helped create the conditions that made the poverty, and thus the crime, unavoidable. Altgeld had taught Whitlock enough about crime to dispose of the moralistic ethic of Russell Conwell; Jones now gave him a new ethic to practice. Soon the local papers were running articles, complaining about the "sarcasm" of the new substitute judge when he talked about the rights of railroads and corporations: The pillars of society would crumble because of the sportin' women and loiterers he was loosing on the streets; why, he even let some little Polish boys go, when they were brought in for stealing 60 cents' worth of coal from the poor, vulnerable railroad! As the Toledo *Times* wrote, in the first of a long series of unfriendly notices, "Whitlock is called the 'great suspender' because of his unequalled record while presiding on the police court bench in the absence of Judge Wachenheimer, when it is said he suspended sentence on almost every culprit, exhibiting decided socialistic inclinations."[6]

His friendship with Jones immediately awakened the politicians, eager to capitalize on a winner. In March 1900 he was nominated for police commissioner "as a young Democrat of the old school" but lost to local saloonkeeper William E. Enteman. As the *Blade* remarked, he was "too much of a 'kid glove' for the unwashed." During the next months the local press mentioned him persistently as a possible candidate for some office or other. On May 6, he took the job as attorney for the Humane Society that led to the Maria Rusch case. Late in the summer he was a prosecutor (before he knew the full story of Reinhold and Maria) against William Taylor, accused of unlawfully docking a horse's tail. Increasingly, people wanted him to speak on public issues, and he campaigned vigorously against McKinley, imperialism, and militarism in the 1900 elections. He handled several cases of personal injury, winning $7,500 and $3,500 from the railroads for two of his clients. With fellow attorney J. W. R. Cooper, he helped defend Jacob Blase on a charge of attempted murder; he was also counsel for Tony Preve, suspected of a particularly juicy axe murder.[7]

In private life he was miserable. He took some solace in the summer of 1901 when Nell became pregnant, but aside from the joy of expectant fatherhood his spirit was not up to the misery inherent in the job that Jones had given him. The little boy, who in his imagination was the miserable convict that Grandfather Brand had freed, now found himself the friend of a poor delinquent boy, a deserted wife, or an injured workman. Had not Nell been around to look after him, he would probably have taken to bed with one nervous disease or another—often he did, anyway. He was thin, ascetic, and highly strung, quite unlike the burly, healthy vegetarian and cultist of physical fitness in the mayor's office. As he wrote Octavia after a day in police court, his heart was "lacerated and torn by squalid stories of vice and poverty told over and over again," his soul "torn by the tears of mothers over wayward boys," and he was "very weary." Soon, he was more than weary. Late in January, 1902, tragedy struck him again; the child was born dead.[8]

Despite his personal tragedy Whitlock kept working, for he and Jones were involved in a case of great importance for all Ohio cities. The Ohio legislature had a long tradition of making laws applicable to only one specific Ohio city, in express violation of the state constitution. By framing laws for, say, all cities with a population of not less than 42,000 people, or more than 44,000 people, they circumvented the constitution and made law for the one city that had, of course coincidentally, 43,000 people. The fight against this practice was a fight for home rule, mayoral autonomy, and in the long run for the "city beautiful." The first round of the fight began when a few citizens of Toledo, fuming at the habit of Jones and Whitlock of releasing arrested men, persuaded Toledo representative Harold W. Fraser to introduce a bill at Columbus depriving the mayor of his right to sit on the police bench or to appoint anyone to sit there for him. Instead, only the clerk of the police court could fulfill the function Jones had exercised. The bill was a blatant piece of special legislation, and everyone knew it. It passed after some fierce opposition from Jones, Whitlock, and others on April 19, 1902. Another bill, to deprive Chief Benjamin Raitz of power, was engineered into law by Walter Brown. It passed April 17, 1902.[9]

Acting accordingly, Governor Nash appointed a perfectly respectable police board. Jones and Raitz fought strongly to retain their powers and refused to hand over anything to the new appointees. Joined by lawyer Clarence Brown, Whitlock and Jones decided to take the problem to the state Supreme Court on the grounds of unconstitutionality. Whitlock was highly pessimistic over their chances, knowing as he did how close the Ohio judiciary was to corporate and Republican interests, but he had an unknown friend who helped him out. Mark Hanna was then in the midst of his battles against Tom Johnson in Cleveland and desperately wished to remove the legal foundation that gave Johnson some of his powers. The Jones-Whitlock campaign, if successful, would eliminate the legislation that set up the charters for all Ohio cities (all were equally special in their legislative creation). With both Hanna and Jones in agreement the case was simply and easily won, and Toledo was free of the laws it disliked.[10]

That fall, the legislature re-established the legal basis for Ohio urban governments, incidentally incorporating some reforms Jones and Whitlock had long desired. On October 22, 1902, the state passed a new municipal code, which required Toledo to replace its old cumbersone councils and committees and boards of this and that with a more simplified, controllable arrangement. Toledo acquired thirteen wards, each of which elected a delegate, plus three delegates at large elected by all the wards, making a single council of sixteen, plus a president at large who would be acting mayor when needed. Three boards replaced the earlier fourteen, and the mayor now had the power to appoint, and thus assume responsibility for, these boards of health, public safety, and public service.

Only one provision caused some alarm. The governor, in frank circumvention of home rule, could appoint public officials if the mayor's appointments were not confirmed by council. Jones and Whitlock began anew the fight for home rule, for they knew that Jones, facing a Republican council, would soon face trouble. Besides, the issue had become by now a part of their vision and could not be dropped. As a whole, though, the bill was at least a step toward home rule.[11]

Meanwhile, Whitlock's private career developed. He early formed a partnership with L. C. Cole of Bowling Green and then with J. R. W. Cooper, who worked with Whitlock in arguing several of his more important criminal cases. Cooper soon dropped out, and Charles M. Milroy took his place in January 1903. In May 1905 the final change in the partnership established the firm as it lasted until Whitlock's departure for Belgium, when Lewis E. Mallow replaced Cole. Also during this period Whitlock received the Democratic nomination for state senator in the 1901 elections and lost, as expected, in a Republican district. His old friend Clarence Darrow wrote to ask him to join his Chicago law firm, replacing John P. Altgeld. Whitlock could not accept. Not only did the law depress him, but he wanted far more to write fiction. He was also involved in some important criminal cases which he did not feel he could drop. Besides, Chicago depressed him even more than Toledo did; and Jones needed him.[12]

His law practice was improving, and these new cases helped further his career, gained him a citywide reputation, and provided material for his novels. His first entrance into banner headlines came when Mrs. Dora Lightner, a tiny woman of only twenty-five, but looking much older in her pictures and weighing between eighty and ninety-nine pounds (depending on your newspaper), took a shoe knife to Miss Lucy Wheeler, a rather ugly, husky creature, somewhat younger. Each woman, the papers said, had made unkind remarks about the chastity of the other, and the result was a wonderful newspaper bonanza: "Ghastly indeed was the sight witnessed by a News reporter as he gazed on the dead body of the unfortunate young girl," reported the *Daily News*. ". . . horrible is no name for the gruesome sight. The face of the victim was stained a crimson hue. The couch on which she lay was a mass of clotted blood," etc. The *Bee* headlined succinctly: BLOOD-

THIRSTY TIGRESS. Whitlock soon discovered that the dead girl had also been physically threatening the married woman, had indeed been tormenting her out of a sheer malicious vindictiveness, and that the murder came only when the girl had been physically attacking the smaller woman. By December the *Bee* was writing that Whitlock "made one of the best arguments that has ever been heard in Toledo. It was characterized by clear, incisive English, careful and logical arrangement of facts, penetrating analysis and keen sarcasm." Apparently Whitlock dwelt primarily on the poverty of Mrs. Lightner and the misery of her life. When he got her acquitted, on December 11, 1902, the *Blade* wrote: "Mr. Whitlock's argument was a masterly effort. Keen shafts of sarcasm, a pathetic character sketch of the life of Mrs. Lightner, from the cradle to the present time, a scathing arraignment of some of the witnesses for the state, an attack upon the police court and a dispassionate, logical analysis of the testimony, characterized Mr. Whitlock's speech." He had moved the jury to tears. He was a public figure.[13]

Next, in February 1903, Whitlock represented chicken thief Al Wade, accused of killing Kate Sullivan in a particularly revolting murder. The crime, in a deserted farm area where Kate lived with her sister, was supposedly for money that Wade thought she had hidden. Wade pleaded that his brother and another man had done the actual killing and that he had only watched. Whitlock, in a characteristic maneuver that he probably took from reading Tolstoy and talking to Golden Rule Jones, argued not that Wade was innocent but that the death penalty was evil, and he used not legal precedent but the Sermon on the Mount for his evidence. Despite his plea, which the *Bee* called in a headline ONE OF THE MOST BRILLIANT IN COURT ANNALS, Whitlock lost, and Wade was convicted of murder in the first degree. Then, in his cell, Wade promptly converted to Christianity, and, amid wide publicity, the fight for his life began. Despite all Whitlock's efforts, however, this attempt failed, and Wade was executed on July 13, 1903, after many delays. Wade gained an uncertain immortality, however, for Whitlock later used his case for a major episode in *The Turn of the Balance*. In a subsequent case, the murder of bartender William Marshall by Walter Crosby, Whitlock did succeed in getting only a life sentence for his client.[14]

Meanwhile, Whitlock was also involved in somewhat less glamorous but less bruising activity. He campaigned with some success for prison libraries, to help the convicted men educate themselves into becoming again the plain people he was convinced they were. Long before he began his correspondence with Denver judge Ben Lindsey, Whitlock was instrumental in getting Toledo a juvenile court, and he worked hard to get truant homes opened to keep children guilty of petty crimes out of the jails, which only contaminated them with hardened criminals. Regularly, the local press mentioned him in the filler columns of political news, as a possible candidate, usually on the Democratic ticket. He lectured often in Golden Rule Hall, most successfully on one widely reported occasion when he spoke on lynching, and he campaigned for Jones whenever he could. He also helped the many small boys and erring girls whose parents came running to him, usually without money. Money, in fact, was a constant source of worry. The state gave him one of his highest fees, all of $200, for his months of work for Al Wade.[15]

Meanwhile, the Independent movement was in trouble. In 1902, Jones was seriously ill with inflammation of the bowels, pleurisy, and bronchitis. Jones's sickness meant that the movement was sick, for no elected officials would carry on his work. He was a strong man, however, hardened by years of physical work in the oil fields, and he did not kill easily. Certainly his spirit was willing. He took up a regimen of cold baths and exercise as soon as he was well enough and then went to a retreat in rural Michigan to recover. He grew, if possible, even more eccentric and became addicted to standing on his head, often in his office, occasionally in the public parks, and on one memorable occasion on the busiest street corner in Toledo. To the dismay of the inmates, he imposed his diet on the city jail, allowing them only two meals a day, one of them a dry cereal called U-Need-Me and another called U-Ought-To-Eat-It, with corn syrup poured on. He began opposing compulsory vaccination for smallpox, despite a local epidemic. Regardless of everything he did to himself, he recuperated, ran for re-election, and succeeded, although his margin of victory was not as spectacular as in earlier years. Throughout the bitterly cold spring campaign, Whitlock was always by his side, as they drove from one meeting to another in a little buggy drawn by an old white mare named Molly. Despite his throat, Jones campaigned eagerly. He would blanket Molly and then rush into the hall, say, in the Polish section of town where he was especially popular. The men would jump up with a shout when he entered, for they unblushingly loved him, and with total scorn for conventions, introductions, and other trivia he would lean over the front of the platform and say:

"What is the Polish word for liberty?"

The Poles, huddling around the stove in the middle of the hall, with strange clothes and puffing pipes, would shout together: "Wolność!"

Jones would pause, listen, and cock his head again. "What was that? Say it again!" Again they would shout it. "Say it again—once more!" And again it would come. "Well," he would say, "I can't pronounce it, but it sounds good, and that is what we are after in this campaign." Corn grows in all languages, but it grows fastest when its planter has absolute faith in his work. Jones was wholly serious, and he never played down to his audience.[16]

Freedom, to Jones in this campaign, meant an end to the traction company and the start of municipal ownership. The company had offered six trips for 25¢ and universal transfers. The Toledo Chamber of Commerce wanted the five-cent tickets to be available at a discount price of eight for 25¢ and universal transfers, the alternative being profit sharing with the city. Jones and Whitlock held out for three-cent fares, with no need to buy twenty-five cents worth at one time. The *News-Bee* and its editor Negley Cochran kept up a steady drumbeat, for the traction company was disliked by many in the city, and the fight against it sold newspapers. The council passed a franchise bill calling for a twenty-five-year lease and eight trips for a quarter. Jones vetoed it, saying it was morally wrong to give away city property, especially for so long, and that he frankly hoped that soon a two-cent fare would be possible; and that, when the current franchises expired, they would revert to the city and make municipal ownership possible. The public disliked the traction company so much that it apparently did not much care how hard Jones squeezed it, and so they followed him. No one could know that rising wage scales would soon make the council wage rates look highly desirable.

On September 21 the council met to consider the veto. Egged

on by Cochran and Johnson Thurston, a crowd of Jones supporters staged what progressive mythology was later fond of calling "a
petition in boots," simply a group of citizens exercising instant
democracy by attending meetings en masse to make clear their
displeasure over an expected council action. The bill, which the
company had never wanted anyway, did not pass. As will be clear
later, Whitlock's autobiographical description of this whole campaign was more art than fact. Certainly the petition provided little
political assistance. Despite the Jones victory, the Republicans
swept the state, Myron Herrick became governor, and Mark
Hanna easily won re-election to the Senate. Then, it suddenly
seemed as though the world tired of its current leaders and demanded new ones, at least in Ohio. On January 15, Asa Bushnell
died of a stroke. Exactly a month later, Mark Hanna died of
typhoid fever. Jones and Whitlock, never stopping, campaigned to
outlaw capital punishment, in the form of a bill introduced by
Toledo representative John C. Jones; this attempt also failed. Then
in late June, Golden Rule Jones contracted pleuropneumonia.
Brand Whitlock and his friends were constant visitors. A local
brokerage house advised its customers to buy traction-company
stock. Finally, Jones died, Wednesday, July 12, 1904.[17]

Two days later much of Toledo and many friends from the
whole country attended the funeral. Newton Baker was there, and
Tom Johnson, as if to underline the unity of Ohio reform forces.
Thousands of people packed the Jones lawn and the street, lining
the whole way to the cemetery. Whitlock and Baker both agree
that all classes were apparent among the mourners, "judges, and
women of prominence and women he alone would have included
in humanity, there were thieves and prize-fighters—and they all
stood there with tears streaming down their faces." Jones had been
mayor, friend, and father to the city. Whitlock pointed out two of
the crowd to Baker: "They all loved him. That woman represents
the best we have in Toledo of culture and refinement. The giant
near her is a saloonkeeper who closed his saloon at midnight and
never allowed a man in it to drink more than seemed good for him,
because Sam asked him not to, and in his way, he, too, was trying
to follow the 'golden rule.' " Whitlock himself gave the eulogy of
the man to whom "religion, politics, business and life were one, he
could not separate them nor distinguish them." The hulking sa-

loonkeeper stood motionless, "his face tense with grief," and "stared straight ahead of him, unconscious of the crowd and manifestly with no thought but a sense of woe at his personal bereavement."[18]

Everyone spoke of Whitlock as Jones's logical successor. He even took Jones's place on the board of the Samuel Milton Jones Company and was appointed guardian of Paul Jones, one of the mayor's children. Immediately, he began speaking more often, first in Golden Rule Hall on Tolstoy and later on a whole range of subjects. He made a withering speech on the tenderloin district, emphasizing that the good people lived in their lovely houses because the prostitutes and saloonkeepers paid them rent. He campaigned for the perpetuation of the Independent movement, for the equality of the sexes and woman suffrage, for equitable and fair treatment of the indigent, and for more humane treatment of the merely poor. He took a leading role in the off-year elections, helping men he thought loyal to "fundamental democracy." Unfortunately, Jones and the Independents were the same thing, and no real organizations survived. Elisha B. Southard began a revival by calling several meetings, and along with Whitlock, Johnson Thurston, and others loyal to Jones began a new Independent movement. As Thurston wrote many years later: "The Independent Movement was organized by four or five non-politicians with purely altruistic purposes." Several petitions in boots as well as a veto of a franchise bill by Acting Mayor Robert H. Finch, gave added publicity and support in these early stages.[19]

The new group managed to field a full slate for the fall campaign, offering Whitlock the nomination for councilman at large. He declined. The Republicans won most of the state and nine city offices to three for the Independents and none for the Democrats. All the Independents could win were two ward council seats and one at-large seat. Clearly, they had to find a good man for mayor or go under, and just as clearly Whitlock was the only man that all Independents—and Democrats—could agree on. Whitlock was uninterested in the job and he said so. As the election campaign approached, the Democrats became desperate. Always a minority, they had been all but wiped out by Jones and could hold on only through state patronage, which was sparse indeed under Republican governor Herrick. Furthermore, they needed the approval of state boss Tom Johnson, who was close to Jones and Whitlock.

Within the Toledo Democrats, the Independent problem split the party. The Bolan-O'Dwyer faction were party loyalists and would hear of no alliance with the Independents. The Manton-Seney faction, on the other hand, favored fusion and survival. Some Independents on their own began promoting Acting Mayor Finch as a reward for his veto of the traction-company franchise, hopeful that a man rumored to be at odds with Walter Brown might be a good bet; Whitlock remained the choice of most Independents and Democrats despite all the maneuvering. Several appeals to his duty and his conscience won him over. He easily won the nomination, and announced that the chief issue was the people vs. the bosses. Even though the Democrats decided to nominate a ticket, Democratic leader John Pattison cabled Whitlock his congratulations, upsetting the local faithful but underlining for those who needed it Whitlock's political origins and the source of much of his support. The struggling young lawyer had at last achieved a career in the world outside his art. The days of waiting in his office were over.[20]

But the end of his waiting for cases in the office also meant the end of his free time for the writing of fiction, and that was a more serious problem. His major difficulty as a young man in Springfield had been that, aside from lack of sureness about the writer's craft, he had not lived enough to have sufficient material for the stories he wished to write. The realist had to write about what he knew, and, while Whitlock knew in a journalistic sense a good deal about Midwestern puritanism and political chicanery, he had not yet digested the experiences, or really experienced enough, to create artistically with this material. In the years of his work with Jones, however, Whitlock apparently did reach the point where he knew enough to write properly. The chief irony of the situation, of course, was that a writer could write about events in his own life only after they had happened, and in Whitlock's life this ability to look back began only shortly before his duties as Jones's successor began using up his writing time. He thus found himself in the position of being able to write creatively only when he had no time to write; his social conscience thus worked to destroy his art, and it is scarcely any surprise that the resulting dilemmas made his temper short and his health precarious.

His short stories had attracted the attention of several magazine publishers before the turn of the century, but only when his hero of long standing, William Dean Howells, began to show interest and to offer encouragement did his career really begin. The first fruit of this attention was the long story that grew into his first novel. Whitlock completed the manuscript entitled *For Congress, Jerome B. Garwood* on June 11, 1901, after a month of extensive cutting—and promptly mailed it to Howells. Howells read it and replied quickly that he could not assure its publication, but that he was sure that Whitlock had "written a great, honest, powerful story" which he read "with intense interest. It is easily the best political story I know." He also offered his help in finding another publisher should Harper turn it down. Whitlock promptly sent them the book and the predictable happened. J. H. Sears of the editorial staff wrote with tentative approval, but he found the novel depressing and thought some of the problems not adequately solved. He finally requested that, along with other revisions, Whitlock should add a chapter of love interest to make the novel salable to young girls; on the stipulation that the chapter would not compromise the realistic principles of Mr. Howells, Whitlock agreed. All through the summer he worked on that chapter and the further revisions, and when he finally sent it to Harper they declined it, ignoring all the promises Sears had made to publish it with the revisions. The exhausted author became quite ill, and for two months he was all but unable to function. For a while he got precious little encouragement. In May, Howells wrote a note offering his moral support, and in July the Bowen-Merrill company expressed interest in the novel, but that was all until October. Then, the Harper refusal at hand, Whitlock sent the manuscript to Bowen-Merrill, one of the most successful publishers of the new romances in the country—"the most 'hustleful' publishers in the country," Whitlock wrote. Howells thought he would be lucky if they took the book; he was. Late in November, "the bluest day I ever knew, up to a certain hour in the afternoon, my nerves, every one, were vibrating like tuning forks, and I thought I was going to die," but they telegraphed that they would take the book. He was too ill to go to see them, so editor Hewitt Hanson Howland came to Toledo with a contract and, thus, began a long career as Whitlock's unofficial editorial adviser.[21]

Howland liked the book, but was frank to criticize parts of it.

He thought the title dull and suggested the one finally agreed on: *The Thirteenth District.* During January and February, 1902, he and Whitlock exchanged numerous letters about galley proofs and about Howland's dislike for some of Whitlock's dialect—dislike that a reading of the book proves quite well founded. Such minor problems either solved or ignored, the first copies of the book were ready by the end of March, and the eager publishers were after Whitlock to get Howells to give them "an epigrammatic, short sentence that we can have every body in the country learn by heart." Whitlock cringed from such a request, finally made it anyway, and was turned down politely by Howells. The publishers dug up a Howells quote from one of Whitlock's older letters to them and used it without permission from either one of them. Whitlock was mortified and made an abject apology to Howells, but the older man appeared unconcerned. He invited Whitlock to see him either in New York or at his summer place in Maine. The publishers meanwhile added to their reputation by sending out hundreds of complimentary copies, including one to each member of the House of Representatives; they were trying everything but tact to sell the book, and after the first gaffe Whitlock had little to complain about there.[22]

The Thirteenth District WAS A NOVEL Howells could read with pleasure, for it used the same techniques that realists had been developing for thirty years. It was most obviously a novel with an autobiographical basis, about Whitlock's career and the men and problems he knew at first hand. Realists had long sought to portray actual life so that when readers knew enough, they could work to improve that life; and in delineating Jerry Garwood's moral dilemmas, and the qualities a man needed to survive in American politics, Whitlock had added to the sum of knowledge. Furthermore, the reform impulse was tempered by a love for America; and Whitlock's concern for the facts, the sounds, and impressions of average, commonplace life, were in the realistic tradition. Romantic and idealistic impulses did not dominate the story, and when they were present they often received satirical rather than serious treatment. The Howells method, which worked so well in *The Rise of Silas Lapham* and *A Modern Instance,* of portraying change in moral character through an infinity of small detail and unobtrusive action, Whitlock successfully realized in his tracing of Garwood's decline from man into political derelict. Whitlock had no romantic uplift and little to cheer up the readers, as the Harper people had complained, so the reading of the book was more experience than catharsis, a presenter of knowledge rather than a builder of sentiment. It was also, finally, part of the realistic parallel to pragmatism, with moral absolutes disappearing and truth taking its definition from relations of sensed objects and not abstract ideals. There was no overt moralizing—forbidden by Turgenev and Howells and the rest—and yet the moral position of the author toward his characters was as clear as Tolstoy's usually was.[23]

Yet, as Howells must have realized, the novel also added new territory to the domain of realism. Howells's notion of the normal, commonplace experience of Americans, formed as it was in rural Ohio and Brahmin Boston, was not modified as greatly in his later work as some critics might have readers believe. Howells became concerned with problems of labor and capital, but the more concerned he became the more poorly he wrote: His experience was totally middle class or even upper class, and he knew nothing firsthand of the life of the industrial poor, the grinding pain and boredom of rural farm life, or the whole underworld of professional immorality. Yet to many people these worlds were commonplace, the normal life of the author's own experience, and each writer Howells encouraged added new territory. Stephen Crane wrote of the life of a common soldier and prostitute, Harold Frederic of the power of sex and the decline of Methodism, and Frank Norris of the animal nature of man and the strangling of western wheat farming by the railroads. Whitlock here wrote of politics, and he wrote of it in a way no one else ever had. In *The Thirteenth District* all the petty details of backroom maneuvering made it extremely difficult for the best man to win. Newspapers sold their support for favors. A candidate (at least in the original draft) used a man's past sexual irregularities to betray his best friend and join his avowed enemy. He needed to live in a way that almost broke up his home as well as his moral character. Never had politics been so believably dirty or lawmakers more like the poorer half of democracy. Whitlock's highly disillusioned years in Springfield and Toledo were showing clearly.

He wrote *The Thirteenth District* in a way that had become habit from his short stories. A story, written in pencil at about one hundred words to a page, grew into a huge and unwieldy novel. Then someone, probably Nell or a secretary from his law firm, typed over this heap on long sheets of paper, triple-spaced, and the corrections began. Whitlock was a tireless reviser, and almost always wrote far more than he could use, consciously planning on wholesale excisions—even though it always hurt him to make them. Two characteristic qualities of his revisions were, first, the movement of whole sections of narrative from one part of the book to another, leaving a second draft that resembled a tattered patchwork, and, second, his attack on his own persistent tendency to overwrite pages of natural description—the parade of scenic interludes, with their "spangling skies" and "autumn's crispness," and so on, usually ended in the discard.

Next, he began work on the effusive use of awkward phrases that gave his earlier drafts of *The Thirteenth District* a sound bordering perilously on that of a sentimentalized political novel like Paul Leicester Ford's *The Honorable Peter Stirling*. Ford was popular and his prose showed it. He would not have seen anything wrong with Whitlock phrases like "the laugh had a little tinge of the bitterness Rankin had carelessly dashed into his cup when it was sweetest" or "Anna [Anna later becoming Emily] was listening with flagging attention caused by her effort to penetrate the mysteries of balloting and delegations." Nor would he have recognized the inherent melodrama in "Garwood's heart seemed to turn white within him in fright, and turning, he crushed Anna in his arms" or, further on in, "He held her more closely still, fearing to let her go. Should he tell her now, and have it done with? She was lying so still so peaceful upon his heart. Could he bear to break her joy?" Whitlock quite obviously had a romantic temperament, even without the stimulus of an environment that applauded *When Knighthood Was in Flower*. In the 1890's, no one could avoid knowing about the trash everyone was reading, and Whitlock's early drafts showed he was no exception; fortunately, he crossed out all of the passages quoted above.[24]

Whitlock also had trouble keeping himself separate from his hero. Henry James had all but eliminated personal reference from his novels, and Whitlock as a constant reader of James may have obtained the lesson firsthand. Thus, he eliminated impersonal asides like ". . . as it is apt to do with all of us . . ." as irrelevant intrusions by the author. But he had a more persistent trouble with Garwood. In the early versions Garwood was always coming out with pure Whitlock, reminiscent of the *Blade's* remarks about his sarcasm. He quoted the Bible or the classics and used a kind of pompous phrasing that seemed intentionally ironical—yet which came from a petty politician who had no real sense of humor, few brains, and no classical education. Thus, Garwood says to his wife: "No—he's an orator, one of the old kind, who talk with fine, rolling tones—orotund I believe the elocutionists call it—just two hours of magnificent platitudes and glittering generalities, 'He seized with a politician's voracity on the conventional phrases of his kind' . . ."—just exactly what the final Garwood would not do. Often, too, Whitlock's own autobiography, which as a good realist he felt justified in using extensively, made his novel poorly proportioned. Politicians and their petty round of official functions took more place than they should in a study of character, and newspapermen played a far greater role than they had any right to, always offering the sort of homely analysis that smelled of the cracker barrel and the decaying skulls of Whitechapel.

Whitlock also had trouble of a more serious nature when he touched on personal relations, particularly of those people who knew each other well. Women had a tendency to get together in domestic coziness and talk for chapters, in ways that illustrated nothing in the novel and nothing very important about Whitlock's own past life. Entire chapters of such matters were deleted, or drastically cut or rearranged. The core of Whitlock's problem was the corruption which a decadent romanticism had caused in the way people described emotions; the teary scenes between mother and daughter—and daughter and almost everyone else in a best seller like *The Wide, Wide World*, to take one of the more notorious examples—were the "slop, silly slop" of Howells's mockery in *The Rise of Silas Lapham*, but ridicule had not stopped the crying even by 1900. Whitlock's prose became awkward and involved in moments when lovers talked or close friends confided, and he veered suddenly toward an absolute profundity that resembled platitude. Thus, Emily and Dade and their feelings for each other:

Had this restoration been possible, it would not have been necessary of course, for such a declaration of intention, and their fitful intercourse had been rather a tribute to their old interest in each other, than a witness to its present existence. But Dade, with her ever active interest in life, itself, had none of that difficulty in giving her demeanor towards Emily that semblance of reality that we usually feign in our hypocrisy [sic] towards the friends of a bygone day and stage of development; who distress us by the duty we seem to owe them when in their presence, but who are ineffective, and unprofitable, save as measuring rods to tell us how we ourselves have grown. If, unhappily, the growth has been theirs, we call them affected, so it amounts to the same thing in the end. It is probable that if the dead could return, we could find it impossible to adjust them to our altered circumstances, and vote them bores.

No doubt he knew what he meant when he started the passage, but such sentences defy analysis, and Whitlock's own taste apparently agreed.

The Thirteenth District, despite all these corrections, remains seriously flawed. Many of the sentences are still awkwardly phrased, too long, too bumpy, and too full of ideas. Trying to write about Emily's cultural alienation from her early boyfriends, Whitlock has:

Failing in literature, a few of the more determined of these youths essayed music, but when she played for them Chopin's nocturnes and asked if they liked Brahms, whose name they could never learn to pronounce, they gave her up, and fled with relief to the banjo, the mandolin, and the coon songs that echoed not inharmoniously on summer nights along the borders of Silver Lake, as they called the muddy pond where the aquatic needs of Grand Prairie society are appeased.

Whitlock obviously has too many memories for him to get them all into one sentence, and he makes matters worse by using language that is too affected either for the intelligent Emily or the boorish auditors. A Grand Prairie swain would never "essay" anything, and the thought of playing "not inharmoniously" on the banjo would never occur; the social status of the lake is quite irrelevant to Emily's own social status; and "aquatic needs" is a term more appropriate for a struggle over water pollution than for swimming and boating—or would be, if anyone in Grand Prairie would ever have used the term. The ironies are forced and carry little conviction. Too many passages are equally bad.

Even more unfortunate is the character of Dade Emerson, apparently the result of Whitlock's conference with Harper editor Sears. Dade speaks a deplorable dialect, too excruciating to be entirely fictitious, and wanders through the book meeting Emily or Garwood as she passes through town with her hypochondriac mother. She performs her sole useful function when she is Emily's bridesmaid, and does nothing more. Her love affair with Baron Wolf von Waldenburg, in Europe, and her extended engagement to Lieutenant Beck play no part in the central moral issues that are the proper concern of the book. She is a concession to the pretty American girl, and Whitlock should never have consented to develop her. He was too sick, when Harper declined the book, to delete the offensive material, and simply mailed the manuscript off to Bowen-Merrill without correction. As publishers of many of the best-selling romances of the day, they were hardly likely to object to such fluff. Dade's dialect, like Rankin's, is not always consistent and may have been dragged in in imitation of Mark Twain or the local-color story writers whom Whitlock had read. Many realists tried dialect, often to the regret of modern readers, and, with the rare exception of *Huckleberry Finn* and perhaps a few other books, most of the works would be better off without it.

A third difficulty is more central. Jerome Garwood despite all the corrections remains a rather unappetizing prairie politician half the time and Brand Whitlock in disguise the other half. In early life he does some social work and has liberal ideas, just like Whitlock. Late in life, in a moment of despair, he quotes poetry and finds solace in Epictetus, like Whitlock. The rest of the time he has no culture at all, and the plot requires that he be a morally obtuse man who slowly deteriorates in politics. With the irrelevant sensibilities deleted for the moment, Garwood is a believable portrait of the decent midwestern boy with a little ambition and luck, sentimental enough to cry when he is cheered, but who has not enough stamina to retain his character under pressure. He is the first case in Whitlock's fiction of the man whose character develops not

through any inner structure but from exposure to outside influences: to Rankin, to Emily, to Pusey, and to Washington. This
theme will be of great importance in *The Turn of the Balance* and
is only suggested here, but it is a subtle point, well made; it is a
pity that it should be marred by a confusion in the mind of the
author about who his character really is.

The book, however, is far from all bad, and parts of it are
good. Many of the minor characters are drawn quite as realistically
and perceptively as those of George Eliot, who probably gave
Whitlock the inspiration for them. Rankin, the cynically realistic
politician with the heart of gold, should be a type, but he is not; he
becomes the moral center of the book, and readers can tell quickly
to what stage of decay Garwood has arrived by discovering what
his relation to Rankin is. The old banker father of Emily Harkness
is not the nasty, whining miser of much fiction but a person who
lives with these qualities and yet is quite believable. Like Garwood's fundamentalist mother, he has problems and emotions that
give him all the reality, and about as much attractiveness, as the
inheritance-obsessed women in *The Mill on the Floss;* they are
understandable but hard to like, and the ability to create such
characters is an achievement of much difficulty.

Another minor character who is successful is Zeph Bailey, and
his presence points to another good part of the book. Whitlock's
political scenes pleased Howells and many reviewers for their realism, and they are still real. Bailey, the shambling man who helps
nominate, and then later defeat, Garwood, quite dominates the
convention, and with his unimpressive physique, extensive knowledge of the rules of order, and manner of speaking that is idiosyncratic without being boring, he is the political creation of a man
who knew both his politicians and his people and knew which
qualities to combine to create men who were private as well as
public figures. In the build-up of considerable detail about the
minute facts of the political process, Bailey stands for the best in
the book. He is both a type and a man, and rather enjoys being
both, much the way other public figures probably look at themselves. No American had ever looked at state and local politics
with such success before, and Whitlock was right to be proud of
his achievement.

The remainder of the book is of interest chiefly for historical footnotes. The sex escapade which Pusey blackmailed Garwood with in the manuscript became merely a case of boodling, presumably in deference to Howells's qualms about "French Realism." Emily Harkness, who is even more like Whitlock than her husband, makes the typical realist stab at the sentimentalists in preferring Browning and Realism to "the most widely advertised novels of the swashbuckler school" (p.30), and she will subsequently prove her devotion to Howells by sticking to her husband and by accepting a suitably depressing ending and not forcing a tragic, sentimentally satisfying one. In Freeman Pusey, the most stereotyped of all the characters, Whitlock pictured the realist's idea of the newspaperman; not since Tolstoy had realists had a kind word for newsmen, and Howells went out of his way to make them unappetizing. Pusey is fully as disgusting as any of his predecessors. Finally, in a technique that Howells must have recognized, Garwood's moral decay quickly finds expression in his physical appearance, and like Bartley Hubbard he eats and drinks to show his lack of moral fiber. Realists had to see things physically to make themselves believe them, and the bulging stomach and flushed cheek show where Garwood is headed.

One leaves the book with two moral lessons and a good deal of insight into Whitlock's later political views. The first lesson is that politics is a public career which forces men to give up their private principles if they wish to win. Rankin, Emily, and Garwood himself all discover this at one time or another, and Whitlock obviously agrees. Politics is dirty not because of the boodling, the deliberate lies, and the barroom deals—although they all contribute—but because of what it does to a man's moral character. Rankin remains true to his concepts of morality, and loses his post office; Garwood swims with the tide, and loses his character even as he wins public office; in the end he loses that, too. The second lesson is that of the nature of politics itself. Nowhere are any real issues discussed, any real problems brought out as issues. Politics becomes purely personal, and men vote because of a tradition of partisanship, the promise of a favor, or a small donation. Economics and prejudice control the voters, and nowhere do the issues that meant so much to Whitlock have any place. From this picture, Whitlock and other progressives took the immediate lesson that education and a change of heart were more important than anything else for them to work for. In the twenties and thirties, many of them would lose faith in basic democracy completely and oppose political actions demanded for economic reasons by masses of people. Even here, in its earliest of phases, progressivism had a distinctly conservative tinge to it, muted in tone as that may have been.[25]

AS A FIRST NOVEL, the book was a respectable achievement, and despite its faults it is still read for its insights into the social and literary history of the period. Of perhaps more importance to its author at the time, it opened the doors of the mighty. Grover Cleveland wrote Whitlock to thank him for a copy, and assured him that he had read the book with "keenest interest and pleasure. I am especially struck by the thorough and accurate familiarity of the writer with some of the incidents that often accompany the particular phase of politics of which he writes." The best news came from Howells. Early in August, 1902, Whitlock and Nell went to Kittery Point, Maine, for a visit with the master. Whitlock was often more effusive than he needed to be in his letters, but for once his description is probably not exaggerated, at least as it sums up his own attitude toward Howells. "Now I have reached the heights; I have drunk tea with him, I have dined with him, he has shown us the dear old town of Portsmouth, and for hours I have sat with him and heard the principles I loved so long, and have tried, in my poor way, to stand for, stated by the lips of the master." He met all the members of the Howells family who were not sick and got to know Howells himself quite well for the few days of the visit. Six months afterward, he was still happy about the long walks and long talks he had with his hero. The young writer who had had so many stories turned down suddenly felt like a success. He had found the literary counterpart of his political heroes like Altgeld and Jones, and he was happy. "That such a friendship should have come to me seems almost unimaginable, when I stop to reflect on it."[26]

Thanks also to Howells, Whitlock received a letter of introduction to Mark Twain; one Saturday he went up to Sewall's Bridge and for an hour sat on the porch of Twain's summer house drinking tea and smoking cigars. Twain, ready to receive anyone sent by his long-time friend Howells, regaled the visitors with story after story while his daughter Jean poured the tea. Whitlock long remembered this most famous of all realists, as he sat there in his blue coat and white trousers, his beautiful plume of white hair, heavy eyebrows, and twinkling eyes. Twain later wrote a brief note to Howells stating that he had enjoyed himself with the Whitlocks, so the visit appears to have been a success on both sides. Whitlock, characteristically, was quite dazzled.[27]

On the same trip Whitlock cemented a friendship with a family friend, John D. Barry, in Boston. Barry, then a *Collier's* drama critic and free-lance writer, took the Whitlocks around town and one memorable day to Concord, where Miss Emerson "wildly said she could 'make no exceptions' when we tried to visit her house." After this minor defeat, the three of them went all over Hawthorne's house and then visited the place where the Alcotts once lived. The visit with Barry was all too short—only a week—and for Whitlock the time was dear, for he knew few people he could talk politics and art to with any success, and Toledo was all but barren of intellectual companionship for him. Several months later Barry visited them in Toledo for three weeks, and they all corresponded regularly; but that was not enough. By the end of 1902, Whitlock was talking about moving to New York so that he could find some sort of stimulating company. It was only talk, of course, but he was discontented despite his success, and the taste of Howells and Twain and Barry only made more plain to him the provinciality of northwestern Ohio.[28]

Meanwhile, Whitlock went immediately to work on two more novels and several short stories. The first novel was one of those manuscripts of uncertain length that he seemed unable to stop writing. *Her Infinite Variety* was the only one of them ever published in anything like its original form. The book was more skillful and much less important than *The Thirteenth District*. The characters are sketched with economy, and the stereotypical women are perfect for the intended satire on women as lobbyists for and against woman suffrage. The suffragette is feminine, attractive, and lucid; her opponents are stern and full-busted, monumentally stuffy. The antihero, Morley Vernon, is a Davis McGowan (and Whitlock) slightly grown up into an Illinois state senator. He is boyish, dreamy, enthusiastic, and terribly susceptible to women.

He is at first enthusiastic for the bill, under the influence of the lady who supports it. Then, when his fiancée and several Chicago matrons descend to oppose it, he manages to miss the important vote; he then becomes reconciled to his fiancée. The style is crisp, and some of the social confrontations between the ladies and the rougher politicians well done. Perhaps because he tried to propound no deep truths, Whitlock avoided the awkwardness of some passages of his first book, and in that sense *Her Infinite Variety* is an advance. But it added nothing to literature, and did little for Whitlock but win him publicity and money. Howells wrote "to tell you how extremely well done, I think it, how restrainedly, guardedly, admirably. Without committing yourself for a moment, you have conveyed the impossibility, the valuelessness, from every high point, of the lives, and have put us in possession of a true picture of American public and private life." Howells, perhaps too generous to his new protégé, nevertheless had grounds for pleasure, for Whitlock was doing for Illinois politics what Howells had done years before in his lesser-known comedies, such as *April Hopes* and *The Coast of Bohemia*. The valueless lives were those of the useless society folk that dominate the novel, but their lack of social utility is not really the point or subject matter of the novel. Howells was reading too much of what he knew of Whitlock's politics into his art.[29]

The prestige of Howells and the Harper name encouraged Whitlock to keep trying to get Harper to publish his books, but the best he could do was get Harper's to accept some of his short stories. Yet he tried, with a persistence amounting to masochism. The revisions of *The Thirteenth District* wasted a summer's work and put him into bed for two months. Despite that experience, he sent *Her Infinite Variety* to them. It came back promptly. So promptly that Whitlock must have suspected something. Some nitwit in the mailing room, or else an inexperienced editor, had sent it back with no one having read it and possibly without even unwrapping it. Sears, when he found out about it, apologized, but by that time Bobbs-Merrill had the book, and they finally published it. With *The Happy Average*, Whitlock's third book, the comedy continued, and despite explicit praise for Whitlock's work, Sears found it not worthy of the Harper imprint. Off it went to Bobbs-Merrill, who apparently had hustle but no prestige. Harper never did publish a Whitlock book, despite the long correspondence of its editors with Whitlock.[30]

The Happy Average has yet another version of Davis McGowan in Glenn Marley, an impressionable young lawyer and journalist who falls in love at first sight with the daughter of a local judge. Like his predecessors, Marley is not Whitlock; he is rather a part of Whitlock that is made to stand for a whole person. What he lacks are the qualities which later made Whitlock an important man in history—his intellect, his acute social conscience, his ability to succeed almost despite himself, and his talent for making life into art. Marley has Whitlock's secondary qualities, and those not intensely. He, too, is the alienated son of an itinerant Methodist minister, bothered by his lack of a career, attracted toward yet awkward with women, boyishly appealing to mothers, sincere and well meaning, tempted and yet repelled by the prospect of making a career in Chicago. In this book, readers can discover the atmosphere, if not a precisely accurate record of the years Whitlock spent as a boy and young man in Urbana and Springfield. His mother and father are kind yet distant, not much understanding their son yet not too severe with him. He suddenly falls in love with a girl more knowledgeable and socially established than himself, and she returns his feeling. The Judge is not sympathetic, for he sees no prospects for the boy, and he is more than half right, and the boy knows it. Marley studies with and befriends Wade Powell, a lawyer who both drinks and scoffs at certain church doctrines; he thus arouses fear in people that he may fall into bad hands. All the elements that Whitlock probably knew, either at first hand or by imaginative projection from the conditions of his own life, are there, and the atmosphere is genuinely autobiographical.

Historically the book was the second reversion to an old style of realism, that in which Howells had concerned himself with the smiling aspects of common American life and in which the portrayal of normality was the ideal of achievement for a writer. Social issues intrude only from a distance, indirectly, and have little bearing on the plot. Macochee in its sleepy way is normal America, and its greatest problems are whether or not to marry and how to find a job. The everyday round of life includes swimming parties, boating, an awkward interview with a possible father-in-law, and tears at the inability of generations to communicate with each other. It ends with a happy marriage that is not too sentimentalized. Of the later Howells, it most resembles *Indian Summer* and *The Kentons*, which in their turn recalled the days when *Their Wedding Journey* and *A Chance Acquaintance* first set forth realistic ideas in fiction. Nothing much happens, and nothing is supposed to happen. Whitlock once referred to it as "simple, and I think, sane, and as uneventful as the most exacting realist could wish it." Howells was naturally pleased. "I have never read a sweeter or truer book than *The Happy Average*. . . . The perfectly unaffected simplicity of the style, the plain, good outlook, the absolute fidelity of the fiction to the facts, are quite beyond praise. Every character in it, and every situation, are felt with entire accuracy . . ."[31]

Howells was right. The book was good realism, but it was nothing more. Consequently, few people have even heard of it today. A book that adds nothing to the scope of the novel and has no shock value whatever is rarely remembered, and Whitlock's book is no more deserving than thousands of competent professional performances. Biographically, its importance is in the adjective: Whitlock was with this book a "professional," in that he had produced a novel written not because he had any great message, or whim, but because he wanted to write and did so. The result was well written, with none of the faults of style or characterization of *The Thirteenth District*. The problems perhaps solve themselves too patly, and too much may be narrated indirectly through letters, but the work leaves the total impression that its author knew what he was doing and did it. He had proved himself. He was now ready to write a novel worth remembering, and promptly set out to do so.

ℂ CHAPTER 5

The Life of Art (I):

Sin (1905-1907)

I N THIS NEW NOVEL, written chiefly during his first campaign for mayor in 1905, Whitlock could feel more and more
secure. He had had the encouragement of an artist like Howells, as
well as that of a public figure like Grover Cleveland. His ambitions
were literary and not political, and he knew he was suited to the
life of a writer. He made the outline of the new novel on a large
scale, using his recent experiences to make into art his own developing political and social views. But the talented artist with deep
social commitments always faces an agonizing problem: If he believes in his ideas, why does he not go out and work to see them
fulfilled? Why does he sit in his room all day, "doing nothing," or
nothing but writing? The problem becomes almost unbearable when
the novel becomes itself a part of a campaign, a work of propaganda
as well as a work of art. The new novel that Whitlock was now
working on in effect became two achievements: a widely read and
vigorously denounced novel, and a political career that attempted
to put the novel's ideas into effect even as it was being written. The
conflict between making life into art and making art into life all but
drove Whitlock to distraction for the next eight years, and he
never did manage to separate his two functions properly.

Even though he preferred art to life, conditions in Toledo soon demanded his total commitment. He was the obvious heir to Golden Rule Jones, and even his enemies knew it. "Well, Walter Brown is with us, too," wrote his new friend and regular correspondent Lincoln Steffens. "All his talk with me bore upon that one point. He said things to me, which he evidently intended me to carry to you, and they all were meant to keep you from running. He dreads your candidacy and that is about all he does fear. Whence I conclude: That you could be elected; you are the one real menace to the plans of the machine; and,—therefore,—you are in duty bound to consider seriously and not too selfishly the idea Brown dreads." Whitlock needed the encouragement as well as the call to duty, for he knew he was a novelist and not a politician. The overwhelming preference shown by the Independents for him was decisive; Steffens's assessment of the Toledo political scene, accurate. The campaign, like the various alliances that nominated candidates, was determined to a large degree by the past. The Republicans harped persistently on the questions of gambling and vice, and Whitlock and the Independents just as persistently refused to talk about vice and instead spoke only of boss rule and fundamental democracy. From afar, Steffens loudly supported Whitlock in nationally published articles and public letters and received prominent newspaper play locally for his views. Meanwhile, at least one obvious proof existed of *Blade* charges of uncontrolled vice: all the newspapers, and apparently large numbers of voters, cared more about the gambling odds on the outcome of the election than about issues. The very papers that decried Whitlock's subservience to the vice rings were overwhelmed with speculation and odds statements.[1]

To the tunes trumpeted by the Pulaski Polish Band, two thousand Independents held their final meeting on November 3; five hundred people were turned away. There, "professional men, laborers, clerks, railroaders, stenographers, dockhands, women, colored men, clergymen, office holders"—representatives of all Toledo groups—demonstrated the classlessness of the Independent appeal. Governor Joseph Folk of Missouri sent his best wishes, and Whitlock announced as he always did, election after election, that "the issue in this campaign is as great as has ever been before the people. It is the issue of the man against the machine." 1905 proved to be a progressive year. Bossism, even in Boss Cox's Cincinnati, went down to defeat; in Toledo, as 92 per cent of those registered voted, Whitlock carried every ward but the twelfth and the thirteenth, achieving a five-thousand-vote plurality and nation-wide publicity. Only Lyman Wachenheimer, the Independent candidate for prosecuting attorney and usually the greatest vote getter, did slightly better than Whitlock. The great and the poor from all over the country wired their congratulations, including convicts #36325 and #35620, Joseph Dwyer and Walter Crosby, from the Ohio State Penitentiary in Columbus. T. E. Powers, echoing the persiflage of the Whitechapel days that he and Whitlock shared, telegraphed: "Water Commissioner for me police for Dunne Adams Street Commissioner I CONGRATULATE YOU."[2]

Whitlock then suffered the immediate inundation that engulfs most public officials upon their emergence from obscurity. He was asked to speak at countless luncheons, meetings, and clubs, and accepted several of these, including ones for the Peoples Forum of Toledo's Negroes, who strongly supported him, a group of Jews celebrating the two hundred and fiftieth anniversary of the settlement of Jews in America, and the Toledo newsboys. The newsboys, led by Whitlock's friend John Gunckel, all but mobbed him in their enthusiasm, and when Whitlock finally reached home his "right hand was literally black from the pawing of their grimy little hands—they all, five hundred of them, insisted on shaking hands." Candidates for jobs poured in, and aspiring female writers requested that the handsome young mayor read and comment on their productions. Whitlock, for his part, worked at a novel about his recent legal experiences and regarded most of the new intrusions as irritations that signified not a new importance, but the old annoyance of not having enough privacy in which to write. Furthermore, his whole notion of democracy did not permit him to draw the line between his public and his private lives, so he was doomed to suffer because his conscience would not let him hide from the people. To him, as to Tolstoy and Sam Jones, "even if I am in politics, I am still in art—and . . . they may indeed very much mean one and the same thing—and mean religion, too." Clearly, Toledo could expect more of its peculiar brand of the politics of vision.[3]

Whatever Whitlock might have preferred, politics soon de-

manded most of his time. He was appointed to a ceremonial post
for the inauguration of Democratic Governor-Elect Pattison, underlining for those who were unfamiliar with Toledo and Whitlock
just how independent the Independent movement was, at least at
the top. Whitlock in fact was only repaying Pattison for a congratulatory telegram received during the campaign that outraged
local Democrats and certainly did not hurt Whitlock. Also on the
state level, and considerably more important, Whitlock joined
three other mayors or mayors-elect in calling for a meeting to plan
a campaign for home rule. Joining with Tom Johnson of Cleveland, E. J. Dempsey of Cincinnati, and D. C. Badger of Columbus,
Whitlock signed the invitation for the December 4 meeting in
Cleveland. This gathering soon became known as the Association
of Mayors of Ohio Municipalities, and Whitlock was quickly
named to the committee to gather information for the revision of
the Ohio Municipal Code. Whitlock and Dempsey both spoke
while Johnson presided. The group had at least the tacit approval
of Governor-Elect Pattison, but the time was not yet ripe for reform. Pattison was mortally ill, and anti-reform Republicans organized the state House of Representatives. Nevertheless, the meeting
brought like-minded men together, gave them publicity for home
rule, and marked the second stage of the battle to free the cities—
after the victory in *Knisely vs. Jones* in 1902. Steffens attended,
giving the meeting national publicity. Upon his return to Toledo,
Whitlock publicly stated his goal: "We are going to make more
great big cities, with better feelings, more brotherliness and greater
kindness among the people who inhabit them. This will come, not
so much through the amendments to laws—I don't imagine that
people want more radical laws—but through a mild form of home
rule, to which we are growing, that will give the cities opportunities
to express themselves and to develop the individual."[4]

Locally, the new mayor took hold quickly. As soon as he was
inaugurated, the Rail-Light Company announced the abolition of
free passes for city officials, almost at the minute that Whitlock
was announcing that he would not accept them. He forbade boxing
within city limits and refused an offer of free telephone service for
his office. He gave orders that all saloons should close at midnight,
but refused to say anything at all about Sundays. The issue, he
said, was trivial, for "it is of much more import that thousands of

wretched children are sucking at withered breasts in this country than whether a man takes a drink at midnight or at 1 o'clock A.M." He also took steps to close the "wine rooms," openly prostitutional as they were, by proposing a law that would forbid the serving of liquor to women in closed rooms. He went after violators of the smoke ordinance who were fouling Toledo air, and turned down requests that he shut the theatres. Persistently, he refused to talk at all about vice and the pressures on him to do something about it. Aside from not wanting to be bothered, he wished to give his opponents none of his own words with which to attack him. He succeeded, and maintained his silence throughout his terms as mayor, infuriating the righteous. About all they ever made him say was the sentence: "Just so long as the Toledo saloons keep within the bounds of prudence they will be permitted to open on Sunday." He was simply continuing a Jones policy of giving the people what they so plainly wanted and ignoring the outcries of rural legislators, professional agitators, and the claque surrounding certain protestant clergymen. The issues and alliances of the Jones years clearly had not gone away.[5]

Whitlock also continued the Jones policy of not giving in at all to any of the requests of the traction company, on the grounds that such grants violated the rights of the people and encouraged special privilege. Thus, on January 29, 1906, he vetoed "An Ordinance granting to the Toledo Railway and Terminal Company, its successors and assigns, the right to construct, operate and maintain a railroad track in and along a portion of George street in said city" because it granted the right in perpetuity, and this seemed to Whitlock entirely unwarranted. Likewise, he vetoed a dock-extension bill on February 23, firmly establishing himself as an independent in action as well as label. More to his interest, he also joined the Board of County Visitors for two years. This post enabled him to go, without compensation, to all Lucas County charitable and correctional institutions supported by public funds and then to recommend needed changes. Through it all, he worked at his new novel; he also managed to spend part of each day at his law office.[6]

The city that Whitlock found himself governing was the fastest-growing city in Ohio, full of all the problems created by the urbanization of America and the new immigration. It was a coarse, industrial city full of transients and businesses, with a tough lake-port area and large numbers of poor workers. The tenderloin area, around lower Summit, St. Clair, Superior, and Lafayette streets, did a roaring business. Its most notorious spots included Dixon's Inn, or "Fort Dixon," nos. 44-8 St. Clair, and "Wildcat Run," in the old State Street district. Many of the places were popular with underworld characters. There were bordellos, around six hundred saloons, faro banks, crap joints, policy shops, and pool rooms—more than enough to keep certain respectable people exercised for months.[7] The city was also full of immigrants and the first native-generation offspring of earlier immigrants. According to the 1900 census, the total city population was 131,822, of which 78,083 had foreign parentage and only 53,739 had native parentage. Of these, 102,350 were people native to the city; yet, even among these natives, almost exactly half had parents who were not American citizens. There were also about 1,700 colored, i.e., Indian or Asian or undetermined, and about the same number of Negroes. Most of the immigrants and their children quickly became citizens, or were born citizens, for in 1900 Toledo had only 1,145 aliens.

An analysis of the adult males of voting age shows what certain of the electoral issues would be, even without the reading of a single newspaper. Of the 38,257 male citizens of voting age, only 14,489 were of native parentage, while 23,768 were of foreign parentage. In other words, no one could be elected in a citywide election without substantial support from foreign-born or first-generation Americans, and anyone offending these groups, as Guy G. Major did with his A.P.A. associations, was courting defeat. Of these foreign immigrant groups, the Germans easily predominated, with 11,376 males over twenty-one; of the rest, 3,484 were Irish, 1,965 were Polish, and 1,812 were English in their ancestry. The German and Polish figures were slightly deceptive, because of a large number of German Poles: In the city as a whole, 12,373 people had actually been born in Germany, almost 4,000 in German Poland, and just over 600 in other Polish areas. Thus, discounting the dozens of other countries that were represented in the city, down to the Wales of Golden Rule Jones, the two chief groups of foreign-language voters were Germans and Poles, and no one could hope to run the city for long without their support. When fractional parentage is taken into account, the figures become even more lopsided: In the entire city 62,653 had at least one foreign parent, and of this group 30,653 had at least one German parent.

These people often had their own churches, their own saloons, and their own social groups. They also had their own politics, and tended to vote in blocks. The Germans were the controlling factor, and as they were largely liberal in sympathies and Republican in pattern of *national* voting, they could easily swing to the Democrats or Independents, should the Republicans appear to turn against their interests. As it turned out, Toledo voters were historically unpredictable, and the city had had a long history of splinter groups, independents, greenbackers and other populist groups, to which voters turned when the dominant Republicans seemed about to begin one of their periodic spasms of puritanism or bigotry. German pressure apparently had thrown the Republican convention to Jones, known as a foreign-born man of liberal sympathies, and kept out Major and his chosen successors. When Walter Brown and his henchmen managed to deny Jones renomination by one vote two years later, the Germans were instrumental in giving Jones his landslide independent victory. This Jones heritage gave Whitlock the core of his support. The Germans and Poles were not about to close their saloons and sedately observe a Methodist Sunday when they had the power and a sympathetic mayor. The more the clergy fumed, the fewer were their voting supporters, and so a shrill note of desperation resounded during each election. Whitlock really did not have to answer the pleas of the pure; he had the votes. He also took care to distribute campaign literature in German and Polish and to continue Jones traditions such as making Polish workers shout their own word for *freedom*.[8]

The most important single issue of Whitlock's terms was the status of the traction-company franchise, another legacy from the Jones years. From 1888 to 1900, Toledo converted from a chaotic transit system, with many companies and horse-drawn cars, to a single Toledo Traction Company, using electricity. The necessary electric-generating plants were in turn also consolidated into a central plant owned by the Toledo Consolidated Electric Company. Albion E. Lang was president of both companies. The traction company needed franchises for the use of the city streets, and the issuance of these franchises gave the City Council the power to demand certain concessions on fares, location of lines, track gauges, taxes, and payments of profits to be shared with the city. Public and private interests were thus open to constant friction and pressure. Many people criticized the company for inconveniences and high fares, while the company replied stressing the cost of new installations brought on by technological improvements. Both sides were right, for the services cost much to install and yet were often inadequate, expensive, and inconvenient. The company had to make a profit, and the people resented its monopoly. The resulting friction divided the city for years, was the cause of regular caustic newspaper editorials, and proved to be the greatest problem for the Whitlock administration.

Most lines had been built too fast, too expensively, and too far out from the city, and the fight to consolidate them into a profitable monopoly reminded Toledo of its past troubles with the Rockefeller monopolies and local natural-gas industries. Soon the persisting pattern of the campaign had established itself. Jones and the *News-Bee* (or its predecessors, the *News* and the *Bee*), attacked the company as an inexcusable monopoly, demanded a three-cent fare with universal transfers, and frankly proposed municipal ownership. The company and president Lang, aided by the *Blade*, replied promptly that talk of municipal ownership was radical nonsense and that only a five-cent fare could reimburse the company properly for all its expenses. Jones and Whitlock campaigned for municipal ownership every two years, the Democrats and their leader Negley Cochran's *News-Bee* came out for regulation, and the Republicans remained discreetly silent. The result was a stalemate that lasted until the franchises began to run out, as early as 1900. Jones fought a few battles against the company, chiefly through his sermons, and lost. The great majority of franchises did not run out until the years of Whitlock's third and fourth terms, but fear that they would not be renewed kept the company and its bondholders pleading for franchise extension so that loans could be negotiated. Whitlock played for time; he was politically secure, and the company was financially shaky. He wanted the city to own the whole industry, and its imminent financial failure did not disturb him for a minute.[9]

The great majority of Toledo residents apparently accepted the perennial charges of the *News-Bee* that the company stock was heavily watered and believed that allowing new franchises at the five-cent fare was quite unwarranted. The prevention of the franchise extension was the purpose of the famous petition in boots (see p. 104) and became a standard feature of Toledo politics; it was largely nonpartisan. The parties were often inert, and an Independent movement seemed the only way to keep the traction company from gouging the people. Jones himself thought he needed no machine, and thus his work was doomed to be merely educational and had little bearing on actual law. His chief supporters, men like Elisha B. Southard, William J. McCullagh, Frank Greer, Oren Dunham, A. E. Overmyer, and Johnson Thurston feared that Jones's death would rob the people of their veto power, so they quickly organized a ticket for the coming elections. There were more petitions in boots, and no candidate who frankly avowed support for the company was elected in the 1904 off-year elections. The next year, with Whitlock at the head of the ticket, the Independents elected eight councilmen and all the rest of the city administration except auditor, one state senator, two state representatives, county treasurer, prosecuting attorney, and infirmary director. Thus, Whitlock had eleven of eighteen councilmen supporting him. The pressure of his success on the Republicans was so great that they promptly began talking of formerly ridiculous measures such as direct primaries and even began mentioning, on occasion, previously forbidden topics like watered stock. They were led by the inevitable Walter Brown, state committeeman from Toledo, G. P. Waldorf, collector of internal revenue, Sam Cohn, chairman of the Republican city committee and superintendent of the Free Employment Bureau, Frank L. Baird, oil inspector, and Charles H. Nauts, city clerk.[10]

By 1907, all the gas interests had also merged, and on June 25 the Rail-Light stockholders approved a merger that made a mammoth gas-light-railway monopoly. During the fall election, the Independents campaigned against this ready-made issue, while the Republicans followed their usual policy of talking heatedly about the awful vice that was corrupting the city. Whitlock won, the council was firmly Independent, the bonds of the company dropped almost 10 per cent, and the stock fell from 19⅜ to 9 by the end of the year. Clearly a battle was coming, and the alliances formed in this fight often spilled over into related issues.[11]

Meanwhile, Whitlock faced his first city crisis, made a complete success of it, and earned the votes of most Toledo workers whether they spoke English or not. In the years of Whitlock's youth, Toledo was under consideration as a possible automotive center, and the Albert A. Pope family of Hartford, Connecticut, established a huge plant on Central Avenue to make bicycles, then steam cars, and then gas cars. The Pope-Toledo was a luxury gasoline-model car, made in Toledo, that sold in the $2,800–$11,000 range. The factory employed between twelve hundred and fifteen hundred men, and during the early years of the century working conditions were so amicable that the factory was often advertised as a means of attracting other industry to peaceful Toledo. Appearances deceived; the International Union of Machinists, A.F.L. was making inroads, and the National Association of Manufacturers countered by sending J. W. King to Toledo to organize employers into resisting unionization. To help the employers, anti-union local citizens formed Citizens' Alliances to bring in strikebreakers and resist boycotts. William Boettker stated group policy: "When a man joins a union, he sacrifices his country, his home, his family." Allied with these groups was the National Metal Trades Association, just organized locally expressly to fight the demands for a closed shop. With good reason these groups feared that Whitlock would not give them the sort of protection they received in other towns, and they announced publicly that they would use strikebreakers, the blacklist, and the injunction to fight the unions.

Late in August, about 250 members of Local 105 walked out, or only about one fifth of the labor force then employed. The immediate cause was the dismissal of two union men, one a foreman with ten years' seniority. Harry Leymann, assistant manager of the plant, announced: "We discharged the man because he was taking our time to talk union among the other men and departments." Most observers agreed that the issue was unionization and not wages and hours. The strikers began around-the-clock picketing, and the company imported strikebreakers and tried to keep going. All the workers, new or old, who remained at work were held within the plant and not allowed to leave. Strikebreakers had to sign an ironclad contract agreeing not to quit for two months and pledge all their personal possessions as collateral for money advanced for transportation to Toledo, until they should pay it back from salary deductions. Despite the new men, the strike slowly wore down the company, and it had difficulty filling orders. Strikers discovered a labor spy in their midst but showed remarkable forbearance by turning him over unharmed to the police. Guards attacked picketers for trespassing, and they in turn intimidated and sometimes beat strikebreakers. Yet even when a Pope guard fractured a striker's skull, there was no serious retaliation and the guard also was turned over to the police unharmed. The strike was rather tame, and the peacefulness of the strikers in the affair was matched by the Pope general manager, who publicly deplored the conduct of the man who harmed the striker.

By October, the company was suffering enough to go to court to seek an injunction to bar the union men from picketing and keeping strikebreakers from getting to work. Judge Taylor of the United States Circuit Court ruled first that no union member could be individually held responsible for any damages, and second that picketing was legal when peaceful. Law had come a long way since the Debs Rebellion: Judge Taylor denied the motion for a sweeping injunction, but issued instead a temporary order forbidding six of the 276 men named in the injunction "to use force or intimidate legitimate workers." Three of these men were later cited for contempt when they beat and injured a Pope employee. Whitlock, meanwhile, was subjected to periodic visits by capitalists, who demanded that he provide police protection to the strikebreakers. He replied that strikebreaking was not the business of the city government, that he represented all the people and not just the rich, and that he would attempt to keep law and order but would not protect a nonunion shop. His temper did not improve when he received pathetic requests from strikebreakers left destitute and without work when the company was through with them. He and his secretary, Bernard Dailey, each made the men small personal loans, but could do little more.[12]

Whitlock made repeated offers to mediate, but the company ignored him. Several newspapers suggested that the employers disliked Whitlock as mayor and were prolonging the strike to make him look bad. By February 1907, the pressure of a new car season brought a brief peace, but then the strike broke out anew. This time it was more serious, as about one thousand men, or 90 per cent of the work force, went out, including both strikebreakers and nonunion men who sympathized with the persecuted union men. Whitlock again intervened and worked with his industrialist friend, Marshall Sheppey, of Berdan and Company, and Frank Mulholland, attorney for the union, to reach a settlement. By March 10 the strike was over, Whitlock received praise for his actions in all the papers, and the men returned to work. The agreement did not provide a closed shop, but it did reinstate all fired men, forbade discussion of union matters during work hours, provided for no interference with properly conducted union activity and for no discrimination against union men—it thus managed a good compromise giving neither side what it really wanted. What it did do was establish the right of labor to organize in Toledo, a right which few would have conceded a year earlier. Unfortunately, it also weakened an already unhealthy company past mortality; Pope-Toledo sold out to Willys interests in 1909, and the national company was liquidated in 1913. What fewer people perhaps realized, the strike also gave Whitlock a permanent place in the affections of workingmen. Toledo's mayor, unlike so many others, had not used the police against the unions, had not contrived an anti-union settlement, and had listened to union grievances as though the men who made them were human beings. With the support of the News-Bee, the Germans, and the Poles, he scarcely needed a machine after the unions joined him, thus continuing their allegiance to Jones. As Jas. W. Kline, president of the International Brotherhood of Blacksmiths and Helpers wrote him immediately after the strike settlement: "The part that you played in this case is one that will elevate you in the minds of the wage earners of Toledo, as well as those all over the country . . ."[13]

During the long months of the strike, Whitlock also dealt with other real problems and some manufactured criticism. When he spoke in favor of the abolition of capital punishment, the Blade reprimanded him sharply for coddling criminals and pointed out that as he was speaking criminals were committing burglary in Toledo. Whitlock also continued the work begun as a lawyer as he tried to improve prisons, establish prison farms, soften the treatment of children who were city wards, and speed other reforms originated by Altgeld, Jones, or Tom Johnson and his men in Cleveland. He received less criticism for his other activities, such as organizing aid for the help of San Francisco earthquake victims, promoting a successful campaign for a safe and sane Fourth of July, taking action against bad beef when Upton Sinclair's *The Jungle* pointed out just how bad some meat could be, and hearing complaints of police graft. Of these activities, only the latter received much publicity and caused controversy, but the charges slowly died when several of the officers were tried and acquitted. None of these issues, in fact, proved to be more than a three-day wonder in the newspapers. Even the traction company did not cause more than a sporadic uproar. But sin did.[14]

Sin seemed to fascinate the protestant clergy and the *Blade.* They could not speak too much about it, for they knew how rotten the town was with it, how immersed in it were all the children, and how many the fallen women who practiced it. The infuriating thing was that most voters seemed to approve of the evil—to positively enjoy it—but of course they were foreigners and workers and thus without the American morals of decent folk. Jones had been nominated and elected first with the help of these outraged citizens, for he was a known teetotaler, a churchman of unsullied reputation, and a self-made businessman. Obviously he would rout the devils from their dens and make the tenderloin safe for those who merely owned the buildings to walk by at night. Jones, however, demonstrated a monumental lack of zeal in imposing his own moral habits on others and saw no reason why a law enacted in Columbus by farmers distrustful of the city should have any effect on good Germans who liked their Continental Sunday, complete with beer. Whitlock, educated in the libertarian doctrines of Grandfather Brand and Frank Hurd and matured in the Chicago of Carter Harrison, felt no more desire to support the prejudices of Toledo's middle class in 1907 than he did when that same class condemned the anarchists and the man who pardoned them. He maintained silence; they fumed.

By late March, 1906, the anguished cries were written down, when the law and order committee of the Toledo Church Federation presented its petition to the mayor: "The undersigned, residents of the city of Toledo, O., respectfully and most earnestly pray that you will exercise the functions of your office in the enforcement of the Sunday laws of the state of Ohio, which today are being ignored in our city to the extent that the security of the best interests of our homes are being endangered. We pledge you our heartiest support and co-operation in any effort you may make in this direction." They were particularly concerned by the Sunday theatres, baseball, and alcohol. Whitlock replied: "I have nothing to say." The German Central Bund promptly set about getting a rival petition to encourage the mayor to leave the town open. The next week, the Reverend Mr. Cyrus Townshend Brady was calling for Whitlock's impeachment if he refused to enforce the laws. On April 4, a meeting of the reformers became so full of irritation, that presiding officer Solon T. Klotz had to say, "I believe that we should hold a few minutes of prayer to calm some of these excited souls . . ."[15]

Whitlock meanwhile acted as he saw fit. In April new local "wine room" laws became effective, as he wished, and he enforced them in his quiet and effective way—not by police raids and mass arrests, in the manner of sentimental romance and the dreams of Mr. Brady, but simply by placing, daily, a large, uniformed policeman at the door of each place, armed with a pencil and paper and nothing else. He took the names of every person entering and leaving, for whatever purpose. Nothing was ever done with the names, because nothing was needed; the knowledge that they might have a place in local history so discouraged the clientele that they ceased coming, and the offending places either obeyed the law—thus removing the policeman—or closed. Despite these undramatic gestures Whitlock received no approval from the clergy, and their criticism persisted, Sunday after Sunday. By January 1907, the campaign revived to the extent that the *Times* could headline TO CALL MEETING FOR A WAR ON SIN and write about the efforts of Dr. George R. Wallace of the First Congregational Church and Dr. E. B. Allen, pastor of the Washington Street Congregational. Mayor Whitlock refused comment. As if for comic relief, news soon reached Toledo that a man impersonating this mayor who would not put vice dens out of business was drinking heavily in Texas and indulging in some light swindling on the side.[16]

By June the clergy were at it again, as Dr. C. T. Robinson of the East Side Presbyterian Church accused Whitlock of being soft on criminals, gamblers, drinkers, and so on, and said that he demonstrated no respect for the law. When queried about these charges, Whitlock answered, "I have heard none of Dr. Robertson's [sic] sermons and have read no reports of them," and that was all. The next month, with perhaps more than a purely disinterested zeal, the police arrested the supposedly respectable citizen Mr. Edward V. E. Rausch and accused him of owning a whorehouse and of knowing about it. Instead of arresting the ladies in question, the police called them as witnesses for the prosecution. Police chief Perry Knapp was too intimate a member of the Jones-Whitlock organization, and the trial too close to earlier suggestions of the two mayors, for there to have been no connivance between the police and the mayor's office. The *Press*, at any rate, predicted some fireworks, "as it is known that a number of the houses in the downtown district, which are rented to these women, are owned by some of the most prominent and the wealthiest citizens of Toledo." That, of course, was the whole point, but it was perhaps lost on the clergy. By election time, the *Citizen* took over from the *Blade* as the paper most exercised about local whores. CITY'S MORALS ARE FRIGHTFUL, they headlined. They asked Whitlock if he would make a statement on law enforcement. "No, I will not." Would he close "wine rooms" and gambling houses? "I will make no statement at this time." Cyrus Townshend Brady erupted promptly, and one paper headlined his remarks: THE CITY REEKS WITH SHAME. Throughout the campaign the *Blade* ran cartoons of saloon windows full of Whitlock posters, with captions such as: "Where Whitlock is popular." They were right, for Whitlock was easily re-elected; the *Blade* informed its readers of what had really happened: "Mr. Whitlock ran ahead of his colleagues on his ticket because he had the endorsement and support of the Brewery Merger and all its immoral tributaries. This gave him the vote of the saloonkeepers and their following, of the wine room proprietors, of the gamblers and of the policy kings." In the fall of 1907, Toldeo was clearly a corrupt city with a popular mayor.[17]

Under all this goading Whitlock finally decided to make his reply. Orally he would still say nothing, but his written answer became one of the most intelligent polemics written by a progressive and received nationwide circulation and publicity. Vice, he wrote in "On the Enforcement of Law in Cities," a pamphlet he published and distributed himself, is a problem that will be solved

only by removing its causes: those forces which deny the good life
to everyone. Badness arises largely out of conditions for which the
individual is not responsible, goodness appears in those who have
opportunities to be good, and "it is our duty to see to it that all
men have this chance and this incentive multiplied more and
more." The responsibility for widening the chances for being good
rests on everyone and not just on the wrongdoer. Quite aside from
sin itself, Whitlock also insisted that the issue about vice arose
chiefly because some people wished to distract attention from the
depredations of privilege. This last charge has some truth in it, but
obscures the basic truth that lay behind the whole squabble:
Whitlock and Jones, both in their relations to the traction company and to the vice issue, represented an ethical view that opposed the ethical view of much of Toledo respectability. Those
who held to the old view regarded vice as something to be made
illegal and private enterprise as the economic aspect of religion.
The mayor's supporters were working toward a new ethic. Charges
of ministerial implication with traction interests were thus gra-
tuitous and unenlightening. Whitlock was of course sincere in his
charges, for both the clergy and the traction industry opposed
him bitterly and often used the same language and the same
newspapers in their attacks.

The key distinction Whitlock made in his pamphlet was that
between the *malum in se*, or act that almost everyone agrees is
wrong, and the *malum prohibitum*, or act which is not wrong in
itself but is merely illegal. Most everyone agreed (in time of
peace) that murder or robbery was wrong. But perfectly decent,
respectable people did not agree on issues like baseball or the
theatre on Sunday, drinking beer at times deemed immoral by non-
beer drinkers, or even working on the Sabbath. Laws against these
latter were enforceable only with far more violence, misery, and
confusion than the offense warranted. The result of all the agitation for the enforcement of these laws bred, in the intelligent man,
a hatred of reform and a feeling that the men so concerned with
the activities of others were more worried about their precious
laws than about the people the laws should be made for. The
whole issue left the mayor cold. "Somehow, the sins of others, the
mistakes and the failures of others, cannot excite in me that moral
indignation which exists in the breasts of some, nor can it in me be

artificially provided by an affectation of that impersonal precision, which as it is supposed, should replace in an official all human feeling." Golden Rule Jones had said that a law was what the people would back, and Whitlock agreed. The people, in their faith, were the ultimate repository of the virtue of which true law was made. To some of the more prominent progressives this faith in the people meant little more than a faith in the initiative, the referendum, and the recall. To Whitlock it meant that society had its own laws, and that the discovery of them was the business of its elected officials—this was Altgeld and *The Cost of Something for Nothing* brought up to date. According to Mayor Whitlock: "Just as there are in nature certain eternal and immutable laws, governing in the field of physics and biology, so there are laws which govern in the field of sociology." Man could at best still only approximate them, but this approximation was the proper function of the lawmaking power. When large numbers of people violated a public ordinance with no pang of conscience whatever, they merely trespassed a statute; they did not break a law. The statute should approximate the law; no one should try to force the people to resemble the statute. Laws were made for men, not men for laws.

In making statutes and moral laws into the same thing, the legislator had to appraise the intimate relations between so-called vice and environment. The problem of prostitution would not be solved "by pretending an outraged morality, nor by hounding the prostitute," but by starting at an examination of it as "merely one of the many evils of industrial slavery and legal privilege." The poverty of the girls and the income that their activity gave to the rich men who owned the houses were far more important than the mere repression of the more open aspects of the profession. Or, consider the liquor issue. A farmer, working outdoors all week, did not mind a quiet Sunday in his living room, and his religion encouraged this indoor lassitude. But the laboring man came from a different environment, often a different country; he had different customs, languages, and religions. Upon reflection, his activity on Sunday was as explicable and as moral as the farmer's; it was merely different. "Again, when we reflect upon the intensity of the modern struggle for existence, the rigorous demands made upon the vital forces of men in the economic conflict, the long hours of toil in close and often ill-ventilated shops, stores and factories, the nervous strain, the risk and danger in operating machines, it will be seen that some relaxation is necessary, and this fact, more than any other, explains the search for amusement, the theatre, the ball game and all that. These things become a necessity under the economic conditions of today." The saloon, in its turn, "is the only public place where many men may meet freely as equals and enjoy each other's society," and its presence "is found to be due to the necessity for stimulation decreed by the same insatiable machine, which, by exhausting men's bodies in the mad greed for profits, drives them to stimulants in an impulsive effort to restore their wasted forces and exhausted bodies." In other words, men were not born immoral, predestined to become drunkards or criminals by their inheritance; nor did they choose their fate out of perversity or love of evil; they were labeled evil because the force of circumstances and environment affected them as normal people in such a way that evil became unavoidable. In short, in direct opposition to Russell Conwell and most Americans, Whitlock declared that the environment largely determined the individual. In the course of intellectual history this theory was a distinct advance; that it proved less than adequate as an explanation of human behavior in later years should not obscure the fact that it was an important contribution that had to be tried before more sophisticated ideas could evolve. Whitlock, Darrow, Jane Addams, Ben Lindsey, and a host of others worked on roughly similar ideas at about the same time and shared these ideas both privately and in works like the pamphlet "On the Enforcement of Law in Cities." Few had to face Whitlock's task of putting the ideas into public practice. His success, both in running a decent city and in enunciating the reasons for his actions, was all the more remarkable when one considered that the whole subject made him often physically sick, frayed his nerves severely, and kept him from the only thing he really wanted to do: write novels.[18]

The article gave Whitlock more publicity than most of his novels; and this was publicity from public and political figures, not from literary critics. Requests piled in for copies of the pamphlet, and it was as widely reviewed in national newspapers as most books. The ministers said they would answer it and apparently spent weeks in trying to do so, but gave up, and the issue died down slightly. Whitlock's reputation as a progressive thinker as well as a novelist was secure. In Baltimore, H. L. Mencken gave his unmistakable imprimatur. The pamphlet, he wrote, "is one of the sanest, bravest, most truthful discussions of a public problem ever published in America. Mayor Whitlock is a thoughtful and an honest man, and in addition he knows how to write. Compare his intelligent, straightforward exposition and argument to the puerile, ungrammatical balderdash of our own elected Solomons. Discover for yourself that a man may hold high public office in a republic, and yet not be a tedious, booming ignoramus."[19]

VICE AND THE TRACTION COMPANY thus provided the main issues of Whitlock's first years as mayor, but he also took a great deal of punishment for another, more predictable issue: He was a dreamy literary man who did nothing but write and play golf, neglecting his duties. This charge had a great deal of truth in it, although Whitlock and his supporters hotly denied it. Whitlock disliked public office and often said so with unpolitical frankness. He was finishing the first draft of his major novel about crime and the law when first elected and spent the early months of his first year in office revising it. He did not, however, begin another novel, although he wanted to; and his mayoral responsibilities did take much of his time. Whitlock also loved golfing, and he enjoyed the game so much and so often that the *Blade* replaced its critical barroom scenes of Whitlock posters with long series of pictures of a dreamy, sophomoric mayor, smoking absentmindedly on the golf course, ignoring ugly but pressing issues like sin. The criticism became common enough for the *News-Bee* to send a reporter to the mayor's office to write about just what the mayor did do with his time.

Whitlock proved to be busy indeed, and the resulting article painted both a typical portrait of him and a landscape of his political machine. His first caller was an old man whose son, forty-five years old, was in the workhouse for drunkenness. The old man was a rheumatic cripple, and the boy was the sole support of the family. The mayor explained that he had no power to pardon or parole, but the man was convinced that he could do anything, and remained unpersuaded. The next visitor was a young man fresh from the penitentiary, who wished to go straight and hoped the mayor could get him a good job. Whitlock made several telephone calls and secured a place for him. Later, it developed that the work was too heavy for a person weakened by a term in prison; the mayor promised to try for something lighter, and the boy went away, leaving the mayor with a fear that a tired, sick, and discouraged man with a record and no job might not resist temptation.

The next visitors included: a young workman who had lost his job and had come to the mayor to get train fare to Chicago—no one else could help him; a woman, well-dressed, who wanted to sell some tickets for a series of concerts; and an old lady, feeble and infirm, who had had her horse and wagon stolen. The last lived seven miles out in the country, and she was convinced the thieves came from Toledo; the mayor should either recover them or get her new ones. As these people talked the phone rang persistently, and everyone had to speak to the mayor personally. One woman said that her neighbor's back yard had fallen into such bad condition that it was a health menace; she wanted the Board of Health to take up the matter, but was very anxious that her neighbor should not know who complained. A man wanted the mayor to do something at once about Clark Browning's bulldog. An old woman, behind with her room rent, wanted the mayor to pay it; her son was in prison, and she had been turned out of her house and had had her property seized.

As the phone kept ringing, in came reporters from the three evening papers to ask about whether a fireworks show would be permitted in the city. Two school teachers wanted the mayor to use his influence to have Mr. Carnegie give some money to the old mother of a school teacher who lost her life trying to save two friends from drowning. A delegation arrived to discuss compelling interurban cars to stop at every intersection, but they soon went into conference with the city solicitor. Isaac Kander came in with a Russian immigrant whose wife had been detained in Philadelphia by the immigration authorities; the mayor immediately sent over a man to the Probate Court to see about the man's naturalization papers and the obtaining of affidavits; meanwhile, Whitlock wired Philadelphia himself. He was scarcely off the phone when the harbor master came in to say that if the harbor hearing was set as dated it would be impossible to put the question properly before the government. The mayor struggled for some time with the phone and managed to get Colonel Townshend to postpone the meeting. An old man, meanwhile, forced his way in, asked for money to pay his rent, and was asked politely to wait a few minutes.

Public officials added to the confusion. Franklin Macomber of the Board of Public Safety was in to talk about some matters of importance in the fire and police departments. The chief of police wanted some advice on a few matters, and got it. The superintendent of Forest Cemetery had a few small problems, and he and the mayor conferred. Then the people flocked in again. A pedlar wished to complain about a license, but his English failed him and no one precisely knew what he did want. A woman on the east side wanted the mayor to keep her son out of the saloons; he recalled the chief of police and discussed the problem. Two young men came in to complain that a local store had promised them jobs if they paid for suits; they never got the jobs. Two visitors from somewhere who knew of the mayor's books came in for a chat about literature, the East, and the weather. Another man came in to complain that the Independents talked wrong in Walbridge Park and wanted the mayor to make them talk different. The old man who was waiting then became impatient and said he wanted the money for his rent now; he was asked to tell the landlord to come to the mayor's office.

Meanwhile, the mayor was unable to open any of the heap of mail on his desk, and he began to worry about the message he had to deliver to council and had not yet started. He had no chance. The fire department wanted to know where the men were whom the mayor appointed to vacancies; they had not reported, and after Whitlock checked, he found that one was out of town and the other somehow missing. Two policemen came in, sent by the chief to be disciplined. A boy came in to sell two tickets to a raffle for a blind man. The mayor bought them without a murmur, although he already had five of the same raffle tickets. Two more women came in to sell tickets to still another raffle, then left angrily because the mayor only took two. Still another woman arrived with tickets, and Whitlock again took two. She then started to work on Secretary Dailey, who declined to purchase on the grounds that he had already done so; she was sorry she had demeaned herself by addressing him and left wishing women could vote.

Then an attorney came in to urge that the mayor sign an ordinance passed by the council which conferred certain sidetrack rights; they went over the legislation and blueprints carefully. Finally, at five o'clock, he rested while a sergeant brought in the day's newspapers, then saw how he had been "roasted." His digestion then suffered still further as he found he must skip dinner to deliver an address of welcome on behalf of the city shortly after six and then go quickly to the other side of town to talk once more. He reached home at eleven, too tired to eat. At one, his phone woke him up. A man said that there were two horses in the barn next to him and that he was certain they had not been fed since morning; he wanted to know what he should do about it. The mayor suggested that he feed them himself and rang off with dispatch. The golfing and smoking littérateur had finally retired for the day.[20]

Whitlock's day showed quite precisely where his electoral support came from. The most obvious source was in his own open door. He was always there when the people needed him, and he was willing to put himself out to help alleviate the special personal problems of each Toledo citizen. He plainly cared, and he treated them as people who were fully as worthy as the town aristocracy but who were just bogged down for the moment by circumstances. He frankly believed in their worth, he cared about their sorrows, and his personal involvement did more than any campaign issue to win him votes. Soon, in fact, he was regarded as a friend on first-name basis with most of the city. Women, particularly those from immigrant homes, learned quickly that he would listen to them and fix whatever was wrong. They imposed on him easily; he in turn often became so involved with his petitioners that he was emotionally exhausted even before the regular demands of his office made him physically exhausted. To all of troubled Toledo, he was, in the words of the wife of a convict petitioning for her husband's release, "the father of all." This utter confidence appeared in numerous ways, some comic, some pathetic, and all evidence of why "respectable" Toledo was helpless against him. Thus, when fourteen foreign-born residents were getting their final citizenship papers one Saturday morning before Judge Brough,

chief naturalization examiner Merton A. Sturges of Detroit asked:
"What is the chief officer of Toledo called?"

"Whitlock," they all answered. No one said mayor.

One enthusiastic Hungarian then went on to say that he was
sure that Whitlock was also the name of the chief officer of the
United States and the chief officer of Ohio.[21]

After he had been in office a few years, everyone knew him
and his plump wife, who somehow managed never to leave him
for more than an hour or two. They lived in a simple two-story
cottage, behind a lawn edged with plants, at 629 Winthrop Avenue, in contrast to the luxurious mansions that often housed his
mayoral opponents. Everyone in town felt perfectly free to call
him Brand, and his campaigns eventually became mutual admiration meetings between the people and their friend downtown.
When he rose to speak, often in a big tent—an idea borrowed
from Tom Johnson's Cleveland campaigns—some workingman in
the audience called out: "Put on your hat, Brand. Don't speak
with your hat off. You'll catch cold." After this had happened a
number of times "Put on your hat, Brand" became a standard
campaign joke. His health usually was precarious, and his illnesses
quickly became the concern of the town. Nell managed to take
care of the trivia that took up much time in his private life, and
she was particularly solicitous about his stomach, which was
known citywide for its unreliability. Often the mayor could digest
only crackers and water instead of a meal, and he found great
difficulty eating at all before a speech. In January 1911 he even
had a bout of appendicitis, with daily newspaper reports in some
detail about his every moment under the knife and during con-
valescence.[22]

He was, in short, the sympathetic uncle of his town, and three
anecdotes show why he never had a moment's respite for his
writing and never needed to fear about his re-election. His funeral
oration for Golden Rule Jones had been so moving that a few
days later an elderly lady, poorly dressed, came into his law office.
Her son, a workingman of twenty, had just died. She wanted
Whitlock to make the funeral address.

"Why, I couldn't do that," he said gently. "I didn't know your
son; I wouldn't know what to say."

The poor woman took out her pocketbook. "I'm not asking it

for nothing, Mr. Whitlock," she said, hesitatingly, while tears rolled down her face; "I'm able to pay; but I want the best for my Johnny."

He refused the money, of course, but he could not refuse the poor woman, and forever after he was the only acceptable speaker for countless funerals. Toledo was probably the only city in the world where the mayor was expected to give funeral orations as a regular function of his office.

Then there was the time when a young man and woman appeared at the Whitlock home bearing an infant in arms. Whitlock had already married more people than any of the local clergy, and young people, particularly immigrants and their children, came to him often in preference to a clergyman. It was Sunday morning, and Nell answered the door. After several rather halting exchanges, due to the barely sufficient English of the visitors, she suddenly realized what they wanted. She assumed a resolutely cheerful expression and went upstairs to where "the father of all" was toying with a razor. He had callers, she said. When he came downstairs, the young couple greeted him with smiles.

"We come for you to baptize our baby," said they, beaming happily. The mayor was startled.

"Why my good people," he exclaimed. "I can't baptize that baby. I'm not a clergyman."

The young couple were highly disconcerted at the astonishment in his voice. They feared they had said something to offend the mayor. Their smiles faded.

"You marries people—and buries them—we thought you could baptize our baby," faltered the man.

The mayor explained the difference.

The girl began to cry. "He iss our first baby," she said; "we wass so poor before he came. My man had lost his job. We had no fire, no bread one day. Then you got him a job, and we had comfort for the baby; we wanted you to baptize him—and name him Brand."

The mayor could not baptize, but all over Toledo by the end of his term in office were babies named Brand Whitlock and girls named Ella.

Finally, there was the campaign story that bore fruit. In his attempt to get his Tolstoian message across to the voters, Whitlock was fond of using an anecdote. The story was that one morning a tramp called at a clergyman's door, asking for food. The man gave him two slices of bread and asked, "Can you pray?" "No," was the answer, "I don't know any prayer." "Will you pray with me?" asked the minister. "Certainly," said the tramp. The man led his visitor through the Lord's Prayer. At the conclusion the tramp said, "When you say 'Our Father,' do you mean your father and mine too?" "Yes," said the preacher. "Well," answered the tramp, "don't you think it's pretty mean to give your brother a cold handout when he comes around to breakfast?"

One morning the Whitlocks were eating a late breakfast, but before it was ready two men called. They were obviously unemployed, but apparently not yet tramps. They had not come to beg and so had knocked at the front door, wishing to see the mayor about getting a job. They were ushered into the dining room, set up for brunch.

Mrs. Whitlock was fully as tactful as her husband. "We're very late with our breakfast this morning," she said to them; "I expect you've been to breakfast already." Both said they had, and both were plainly famished. She went upstairs to where Whitlock was dressing.

"Two of your brothers are downstairs," she said; "the table is all ready there, and I know they haven't been to breakfast. They've undoubtedly heard you tell that 'brother' story a dozen times. What are you going to do—send them to eat in the kitchen, or have them sit down with us?"

"Why, ask them to sit down with us, of course."

The two men, properly urged, enjoyed griddle cakes, sausage, and coffee. With their fiction respected, they felt free to take just a bite to be sociable. At the end, one of them, an old man with his pride quite melted, looked up: "That's the first mouthful I've had since yesterday morning," he said.[23]

Given such a place in the affections of his people, Whitlock was in an ideal position to preach to them of his new ethical formulations. Jones had given them a living example of a life not led along the lines of "Acres of Diamonds," and Whitlock slowly developed that life into a common-sense philosophy that he hoped would replace the "Diamonds" ethic. In these early years, he concentrated on four themes—capital punishment, prison conditions, nonpartisanship, and the success ethic—that prepared the way for the ultimate formulation of his philosophy in the vision of the free city, during his second two terms.

Capital punishment concerned him first. Shortly after his inauguration he went to Columbus to lobby for a bill outlawing it. He came very near to success as the bill passed the Senate, but it was later buried in the House and subsequently defeated when it was put on the ballot for statewide voting. Unfortunately, Whitlock was too emotionally involved in the issue to give a very logical statement of his reasons for his bill: He hated state murder not from logic but from his intense feelings and involvement with the executed. Some of these executed men had been his clients and, after a fashion, his friends, and he was wounded himself every time they were imprisoned and died a little whenever one of them died. In print, he founded his distaste on natural law. The physical and moral worlds were one, and the laws governing them should not be abused by men. "There is a principle that has its origin in the bosom of God, where the great mystery of life resides, which declares that it is wrong to kill: it is a principle inherent in the very nature of things, a principle that is attuned with the harmony of the universe, and this principle is boundless, infinite in its operation." He took a great deal of space quoting men who agreed with him and examining and dismissing somewhat cavalierly arguments that did not. Implied was the psychological idea that he thought was behind much human activity: He was afraid that certain people, watching the state kill, might themselves commit murder out of imitation. Man was not strong, but weak, and the victim of circumstances: Do not tempt him. The important thing was always mental attitude: "The spirit that was in the murderer's heart is the same spirit that is in society that kills the murderer, and no good can ever come from a spirit that is but an accumulation of hatred and revenge, and so long as that spirit is kept alive in the world, just so long will there be killing in the world." Captial punishment, in short, set a bad example.[24]

He next turned to criminology. Jones had stopped much of the brutality of police treatment of arrested men; he had taken away their clubs and given them canes, reprimanded them severely for arresting men and women merely on suspicion, and made every effort to make more humane the life in prisons. In Cleveland, Tom

Johnson and Harris R. Cooley continued the Jones (and Altgeld) policies by viewing offenders as the creatures of unfortunate circumstances, as people to be helped more than to be punished. They granted pardons and paroles freely to men imprisoned for nonpayment of fines, and Johnson, like Jones, often paid the fines himself out of his own fortune. Drunks were walked home and not arrested. A farm colony cared for many who were simply old, sick, or delinquent in a minor way and tried to rehabilitate offenders away from debilitating prisons. In this context, Whitlock contributed most to the movement for prison reform by portraying prison conditions dramatically, in *The Turn of the Balance,* but he also wrote and spoke publicly on the subject. He stressed the close connection of poverty and crime, as well as the historic inability of punishment to stop crime. The average man, he said, thought that the criminal class was somehow set apart by its innate depravity and was not like other classes, and that the way to keep it from sinning was to punish, threaten, or abuse its members to frighten them from their chosen professions. Nonsense. The criminal class was simply a group term for men who had been caught, and "there are no people who are wholly one thing or the other." Some men did wrong often, all men did wrong occasionally, and many did not feel that they had done wrong even though society may say they had. The so-called hardened criminal "has many kindly, generous, even noble impulses, but perhaps has had little chance of developing them, or little incentive to do so." At any rate, the wealthy businessmen who corrupted legislatures and owned brothels should not be the ones to cast stones.

Professional criminals became that way because society would not let them do otherwise. A man got into trouble for trivial reasons and went to jail, often because he could not pay a trifling fine. When freed, no one would befriend or hire him, for he was an ex-convict and a proven criminal. If he wanted to eat, he must return to crime; there he gained social rewards from associating with fellow criminals, the only people who accepted him as a person. "This is the only semblance of a criminal class; society makes it, and perpetuates it, and then hates and complains of its own work." Jail hardened but did not deter. Men saw thieving guards, corrupt judges, bribed policemen, and protected political grafters and were subjected to the water cure and solitary confinement for crimes they knew were less important. Besides, when a convict was free, society had not forgiven him; he was often arrested on suspicion and told to leave town. If he obtained a job someone soon informed his employer, and he was fired. In an argument that drew as much from Altgeld, Darrow, and Howells as from Johnson and Jones, Whitlock wrote that society had better not concern itself too much with punishment, for no man was good enough or wise enough to judge another. "Only Omniscience can plumb those mysterious and awful depths. Man's attempts to do so are profanations. All that society has a right to do is protect itself by restraining those of proved dangerous tendencies; it has no right to hurt them while doing so; and its duty is to do all it can to help the erring, wandering souls back into the right path."[25]

Whitlock next turned to a Toledo specialty: independent political action. Jones had been denied Republican renomination for his second campaign, and he was convinced by this defeat—and by his following victory at the polls—that partisanship was both pernicious and unnecessary. The whole subject became inextricably entwined with his faith in the people, in their ability to judge when properly educated, and in the wickedness of the forces that preyed on them through the regular parties. In practice, Jones had received most of the Democratic vote and a large dissident Republican vote, but his refusal to build an organization had led to the regular defeat of his plans in council and to his poor showing when he ran for governor. Whitlock knew far more than Jones about politics and machines; unlike Jones, he cared as much for the actual legislation as for the proper moral tone and, as he was chosen by an independent organization, he could scarcely disavow the principle behind all organizations. In the state, Tom Johnson was boss of the Democrats and Whitlock was his close friend and collaborator, so nonpartisanship during the Whitlock years meant an informal group of citizens and jobholders in Toledo and a *de facto* allegiance to acceptable Democratic candidates in state and nation.

The intellectual basis for nonpartisanship was frankly Jeffersonian—if a man could go to heaven only with a party, he should not try to go there at all. Individual integrity was far more important than party regularity or success at the polls, and men who belonged to parties "are not free; they are owned. And unless the men in it are free, a country cannot be free. And when men cease to be free, democracy fails, and an oligarchy is established. This is what has happened in our cities; thus have they become the shame of democracy." Partisanship and party regularity could lead only to boss rule, for the man who controlled the nomination then controlled the city, and the individual was helpless. The material costs of a Tweed or a Cox were great enough, but "the spiritual cost has been immeasurably greater, and, of course, of immeasurably greater importance. For the most valuable capital, the chief asset, of a city is the character of its citizens." Individual integrity, furthermore, was one with the same moral laws that determined his stand on other matters, such as criminology and capital punishment. The worst effect of boss rule was "the withering of character, the wasting of strength, the disintegration of personality, which is the punishment that inevitably, inexorably and remorselessly follows the violation of law that is real Law—not the printed statute, which is oftentimes something very different from Law, but the law of the moral world, which no legislature can enact or need repeal, which requires no executive to enforce it." The chief of these laws was "that of spiritual cause and effect, according to which evil can produce only evil, and hate more hate, so that all the bitterness and malignity and intolerance of partisan conflict can never bring forth any good thing in men or in their government. Instead of all this strife and hatred, there must be brotherhood and love; instead of this disunion, there must be union and solidarity. Then good will come."[26] Yet, for all this, the conclusion was all but inescapable that Whitlock's own personal following, and not his dogma, made these views as popular in Toledo during his terms as they were. Had he espoused other reasonable ideas, with all probability they too would have proved acceptable, if only he had spoken for them. Despite all the rancor of the *Blade* and the *Citizen* about city morals, Toledo politics in practice had more to do with the love of one man than anything else. When people name their children after a man, they will often vote for him no matter what he says, and in this way nonpartisanship became a Toledo ideal in which many people believed. For, when Whitlock left, his ideas apparently left with him, people returned to the old parties, and few seemed aware of the ideas they had voted for in an earlier election.

His final ethical statement of these early years was his most obvious blast at the ethics of "Acres of Diamonds." Tom Johnson's once vast wealth had been shrinking visibly under the strain of his Cleveland campaigns, and people were freely predicting that the millionaire mayor might well end his days impoverished. The Cleveland *Press* asked for Whitlock's comments on these rumors, and his reply shows just how far he was from the beliefs that many Ohio citizens still held. Privilege, he wrote, "demands that its servitors give that best which potentially was in them," like "self-respect, manhood, all the nobler things of the soul, all that gives charm and beauty and real meaning to life"—a sense of humor, sympathy, understanding, and love. The man who pursued wealth by allying himself with the interests gave up "the power of spiritual appreciation," and found himself with no ability to recognize the beautiful. "He who lacks that is an unburied corpse, walking the earth in his own shroud, the ghastly victim of a tragedy he himself has written and staged and managed, and now forever must enact." Johnson's wealth was thus never of the financial variety, although he had plenty of that. It was a spiritual wealth, obtained by a man who gave his life and money for the serving of others.

The real issue was thus not Johnson's money but the American ethic of success. "We have made a god of money, worshipped it as a fetich, measured what we call 'success' by it, and counted men great chiefly in proportion to their ability to grab and gobble." Anyone who could take the most from the people has been held up to small boys as an example for them. Thus the whole question of Johnson's wealth presupposed the importance of a fraud. "Why, it is an ideal no better than a flock of magpies or a herd of swine could evolve. Our mad, profit-seeking, anarchic system presents, as its fruit and flower, men merely rich, with acquisitiveness abnormally developed, having a genius for organization, no doubt, but devoted to selfish ends." With such an ideal, a people must give up its democratic faith, for its "inevitable end is plutocracy, with its shams, and vulgarities, and ignorances, and brutalities."[27]

Whitlock's first term as mayor thus helped him formulate his new ideas before a local, and sometimes a national, forum, and gave him his first real opportunity to put those ideas into practice.

In his early skirmishing with the traction company, his energetic defense of the right of the people to enjoy the decent pleasures of life without the legal interference of a bigoted fundamentalism, his personal care of the needy people of Toledo, and his written articles, he gave notice that the gospel of wealth was a faith unfit for decent men even in an industrialized country. The making of money was no replacement for the making of men, and in these early years, as in his later years, the development of the spiritual qualities of individual men was Whitlock's first goal. Too many Toledoans were too poor and needed food and money too much to concentrate on less vital qualities of life; for them Whitlock had to get jobs, money to pay the rent, and even an occasional baptism. His goal was not material, however, despite the material nature of these preliminary tasks. Jones had cared most for parks and music and good fellowship, and Whitlock's discipline was implementing his vision with more realism and acumen than Jones himself ever displayed. He was, in fact, trying to produce a kind of Kingdom of God on earth, and it is only appropriate that his office, occupied by the mayor who was "the father of all," had lettered in gold at its entrance the words of the author of *Resurrection:* "Men think there are circumstances when we may deal with human beings without love, and there are no such circumstances. One may deal with things without love. We may cut down trees, make bricks, hammer iron without love. But you cannot deal with man without it."[28]

ℂ CHAPTER 6

The Art of Life:
The Underworld

(1 9 0 5 ' 1 9 1 3)

WITH THE END of his first years in office, Whitlock had begun the arduous process of turning his artistic vision into reality. Despite the complaints of the religious middle class, he had achieved a certain success, and both he and Toledo knew it. If Whitlock tried to make his mayoralty into a work of art, he also tried to make his art into an accurate distillation of the life he was leading. The result was at times deeply confusing, and deeply moving, but it was always an important insight into his character and the character of the progressive mind. The key to this confusion of life and art lay in a myth that was slowly developing around the independent movement, a myth that helped the movement at each election. At the heart of the myth was Jones, the sort of man who could not be forgotten; one of his acts was its central feature.

The bare facts concern a proposed bill regulating the town street cars several years before Jones died. The issues were the price of tickets and the length of the franchise that the city would offer the company. The final bill, as the City Council considered it, was a compromise measure that satisfied no one and so was probably fair. But Jones regarded the measure as a conspiracy against

the people's rights; the company and its representative, Barton
Smith, also found it unacceptable, for the fares were too low. The
bill was thus doomed, since neither side thought it acceptable. But
then, the great event happened. A group of citizens led by Jones
came to the council room en masse to lodge a citizens' protest
against the measure. This petition in boots more or less prevented
any council action, and Jones and his men were convinced that
they had won a great victory for direct democracy. Others, including Negley Cochran, the antitraction, proreform editor of the *Bee*,
thought the whole affair smacked of mob rule. No one seemed to
realize that the bill in question would not have passed in any case,
and that, far from plotting to seize a franchise through the bill, the
traction company opposed its passage.

The event would have been but a minor and forgotten footnote
to the history of Toledo reform, except for one thing: The reformers were sure of their great victory, and they never stopped talking
about it. The result was the legend of the petition in boots, which
reappeared again and again, in each election, as the living example
of the evil practices of the traction company and the virtues of the
people and their direct democracy. Soon after the event, Whitlock
wrote a brief article on the affair for *World's Work*. Analysis of
this story gives a remarkable insight into the psychological machinery of Toledo reformers and helps to explain how Whitlock's
mind worked, as well as what was wrong with the fiction he wrote
at the time. The key section of his description runs:

> Toledo's battle with her street-car company is but a repetition
> of all municipal battles. Here were the big corporation, with its
> mysterious agencies, a political machine, a suspected council, a
> citizenship trembling, uncertain and afraid—and Golden Rule
> Jones. Last summer, when the traction company had its council pass
> an ordinance, renewing its franchises, Jones promptly vetoed the
> ordinance. Then the council, guarded by husky conductors and
> motormen, the doors barred against the public, prepared to pass the
> ordinance over the mayor's veto. The citizens stormed the doors,
> thrust back the traction company's employees, and burst into the
> suffocating council-chamber, with Jones at their head.
>
> "I suppose, Mr. Jones," sneered the attorney for the traction
> company, in one of the lulls of the human storm, "that this is the

kind of government we should have under the Golden Rule."
"No," replied Jones, on the instant, "this is the kind of govern-
ment we have under the Rule of Gold."
The council did not pass the ordinance over the mayor's veto.[1]

Anyone who remembered Whitlock's story of the small boy
watching his grandfather free a criminal would find himself on
familiar ground here. On the one side, Respectability and Justice,
working in a suffocating room, guarded by hoodlums, hiding from
view; on the other, the slightly disreputable but virtuous Man of
the People, leading his men in defense of real justice, not justice as
Respectability would have it. Whitlock's adjectives imply a powerful council and a cowed people, when actually the people were
obviously greater in number and power; the adjectives imply that
a plot had been hatched, and that the company was seizing what
did not belong to it, when in fact it was in the process of defeating
the bill in question. Even the repartee is nicely prejudiced, not
only giving Jones the last word, but giving the people a pat slogan
with which to fight: the Golden Rule vs. the Rule of Gold. Indeed,
the only real deviation from the episode of Grandfather Brand,
mutatis mutandis, is that Whitlock's loyalties are no longer divided. Although his head had supported his legalistic uncle before,
now both his head and his heart supported Jones. He had committed himself to the Independent side, and this commitment guided
his actions throughout his term as mayor; it provided him with a
great deal of righteous energy, but it prevented him from seeing
Toledo as it really was; ultimately, it led him to all but destroy the
traction company, before he reached a saving compromise. Like
most legends, this one inspired, but it also blinded. In retrospect,
the importance of this vignette is less its truth or falsity than the
insight it gives into Whitlock's mind.

This process of dramatization, of translating fact into art almost without thinking, shapes all of Whitlock's writings in this
period and much of his correspondence with close friends. To
Octavia Roberts, he is always effusive, far too effusive for modern
tastes, too full of emotion, frustration, nerves, and disappointment. Had he actually lived in such a romantic confusion of inten-
sities, he would never have survived his first term. Perhaps he read
too much Carlyle—both he and Nell had read the complete let-

ters—but whatever the reason, this realist in fiction saw himself in
a romantic setting, beset by powers and influences that attacked
him. The romantic tone was not confined to his letters on literary
subjects to Octavia; it was just as prevalent in the more political
correspondence with Lincoln Steffens. Steffens replaced Darrow as
Whitlock's friendly mentor and proved more faithful than Darrow
in answering letters and visiting regularly. To him Whitlock
poured out his heart about Toledo politics, prisons, vice crusaders,
and his novels, and from him he received in return an assurance
that the world would notice him, and that an intelligent member of
the world thought he was worth bothering about. Steffens, always
traveling, brought news of reforms in other cities, relayed personal
messages from one reformer to another, and was a one-man cheering squad for the isolated men who were trying to improve American cities.

Steffens fed Whitlock's need for praise and encouragement
with a master hand and had a positive genius for drawing Whitlock out on his favorite subjects. Consequently, Whitlock's early
letters were about his reading and his illnesses. He loved *De Pro-
fundis* and Conrad and was always feeling nervous and unable to
function properly. He struck the typical romantic pose of a man of
feeling oppressed by the cares of the world: "I'm getting better,
but I need a rest; too much work and worry this winter—too
much concentration, and involution, and introspection, and all
that kind of thing." Translated into his public life, this attitude
found conditions in Toledo and Ohio intolerable and subsequently
gave rise to a peculiar conflict in Whitlock's mind. In several
places he mentioned the evils of Coxism and the need to educate
the people and reform city politics; yet in the same letters he will
remark that, when all is said, you cannot tell anyone anything that
they do not already know. This attitude, if taken seriously, leads
to inertia. As a result, Whitlock was easily discouraged by politics,
and was forever finding relief in talking about his writing. Politics
was "too often unwholesome" and only delayed "my book, and
you don't know how wholly my ambition is literature!" When in
1905 he made his abortive campaign for the gubernatorial nomination eventually won by Pattison, he summed up a feeling which
persisted throughout his political career: "I came out of it all
feeling that among politicians I am considered a very good litté-

rateur, and among littérateurs a very good politician." As self-analysis, that is a remarkably perceptive statement.[2]

By the 1905 campaign, Whitlock's effusions were noticeably on the pattern of the conflict between the heroic people and dastardly privilege. His romantic vision even painted a perfectly decent, if uninspiring, man like Robert Finch, the acting mayor of Toledo, as a tool of the enemy. Finch showed good qualities, Whitlock wrote, but he did not come out against the machine; he was not a big enough man to do it. Reduced to its basic presuppositions, Whitlock's argument about Finch becomes: Step one— if a man is honest and does not agree with you, he is a fool ("A man of uncouth presence and gesture, no education, but honest enough if he gets started right and wise enough to have a stenographer who can correct his grammatical blunders. When he was a foreman over at the American Bridge Company he was known among the men as 'the Bull-Head.'"); step two—(as a fool) he is weak and easily used ("The plaudits of the press and the people because of his attitude on the franchise made him tremendously conceited. The night before the Republican convention, having his eye of course on the Independent nomination, a platform was prepared for him by friends which declared for municipal ownership of the lighting plant, no extension of street railroad franchises and the abolition of machine rule in politics . . ."); step three— this was all an obvious plot, for a man who is not with us is against us, even when seeming to agree with us (". . . Finch said to the machine bosses that unless they adopted this platform he would not accept the nomination. This being made public of course he appeared instantly in the role of a great hero, throwing as it were his ball of pitch into the jaws of the dragon."). But the poor man was foiled, "for our dragon is a sophisticated, modern dragon, and swallowed the platform and Finch with it. The convention was in the hands of the machine absolutely. They nominated Finch, they adopted his platform and then nominated for the rest of the ticket machine men." For Whitlock, the hero's duty was then clear: "I then told the Independents, those who came to see me, what I had not told them before that I would take their nomination, and they gave it to me unanimously." The people tends to become a singular force when it supports the right side, for when properly educated the people act as one. That Finch had carried out Jones's policy and done quite creditably as mayor was only misleading. The real issue for Whitlock was not how Finch acted, but what he thought—in short, had he experienced his "religious" conversion? Whitlock's religious background betrays itself in a habit of thought which persisted even after he had rejected religious dogma. If Finch were not "converted" to the principles Whitlock believed in, all his good works could not redeem him in Whitlock's eyes. Therefore, these principles became the chief issue of the campaign. "I am trying to force to the front the issue of representative government," he said, despite the many people, particularly businessmen, who thought Finch should be reelected on his record. "That is, they're thinking of good government and not of representative government and I am trying in all my speeches to make them see the distinction."³ One can see how a poor businessman, wanting only a city government that did its job and left him alone, would need a good many speeches before being convinced of this vital distinction. Whitlock thought his election vindicated his principles and his belief in the people. In fact he proved only that they loved him as the successor to Jones, another man who would be their friend in city hall. Finch they knew little about, and he was admittedly not persuasive.

Once in the 1905 campaign, Whitlock half suspected what was going on in his own mind: "By Jove, what a political novel I could write now! Realism, and romance—good reality, stirring romance —all in one, for what swashbuckler ever fought a battle so hard as these, and with such weapons!" Heroes tend to win in romances, and Whitlock swept to victory. Steffens, in return, did his required part admirably, by showing Whitlock the cosmic role which he was performing: ". . . we, the American people, carried ourselves at last, and the beginning has been made toward the restoration of representative democracy in all the land. No victory of them all is more significant than yours in Toledo . . . You are the most advanced leader in American politics today." The next week, he indicated, in passing, the other dimension of the issue: "I have found another Christian in politics. He is Mark Fagan, the mayor of Jersey City."⁴

If his correspondence with Steffens gave Whitlock the opportunity for dramatizing events in Toledo, his correspondence with prisoners gave him more than enough material to write about, even aside from his political activity. Whitlock was a good friend of several men in prison; to many of them he was their only friend outside their immediate families. His well-publicized ideas about prison reform and capital punishment were widely known in prisons, and men he had never met, often in out-of-state jails, wrote asking for his help, his references, or his aid in assisting a wife left in the outside world without money. He could never refuse them, and the result was a lengthy, time-consuming correspondence with the men themselves, their wardens, their families, and their possible employers. Sometimes he even implored the governor of the state to help as well. If this continuing association with the underworld regularly disturbed him, it also contributed immeasurably to his understanding of human psychology and his transformation of that psychology into art. In his writings about criminals Whitlock was the true realist writing from autobiographical experience. Despite the charges leveled at him for exaggeration, he made a regular policy of toning down the drama he adapted from life to make it less extreme and more convincing.

Whitlock's early correspondents included: Samuel Jackson, who seems to have been the first; Hugh Campbell, who is the subject of one of the few published letters (p. 47) available of this large collection; and Walter Crosby, his old client from a Toledo murder trial of 1904, convicted of second-degree murder and sentenced to a life term. Crosby, quite aside from his having been a Whitlock client, has an added importance for Whitlock's biography: He was the man whose letters gave Whitlock the documentary proof he needed to write about the tortures used in Ohio prisons. In one letter in particular, Crosby wrote extensively about wrist-hanging, common penalties, prison food, medical practices, and all the petty details of prison life that made *The Turn of the Balance* such a bitterly attacked book. Crosby certainly had brains and a gift for dramatic and vivid description, and his letters supplied realistic material for the prison troubles of the book's chief criminal, Archie Koerner. They also specifically vouched for the existence and use of the water cure, which many wardens indignantly denied when the book came out.[5]

Nothing, however, quite illustrated Whitlock's fascination with the underworld as did his friendship for William H. Wheeler, alias Curly Williams, alias Frank Pollard. Curly was a Canadian from the Toronto area, who had had careers in both the British and American armies before joining the underworld. By the time Whitlock knew him in Toledo, he seemed more like a rogue escaped from the England of Fielding or Smollett. Whitlock had defended him on a murder charge, and Curly was understandably grateful for his acquittal. Whitlock liked him immediately, simply as a person, and soon had several of his respectable correspondents fascinated by the continuing serial. Curly would wander into the mayor's office for a chat, often for hours, describing his exploits and narrating future plans, and then go off, no one knew where, for months. Then he would return and repeat the process. On one occasion, he came in with a box of cigars for the mayor:

"I was throwing off some bolts of silk from a freight car, and seeing the cigars I thought I'd take a few boxes for my friends."

The mayor replied, resignedly: "You and I must understand each other; I like you but I don't like your business."

Curly helped Whitlock learn underworld argot and taught him that criminals were also people with a moral code that in its crazy way made some sense. Whitlock was delighted, not disapproving, when he wrote in his new-found slang: "I thought I would fly you a kite to give you the sad news that our friend Curly was bagged by an elbow last Saturday for heisting tags on a John O'Brien down at Port Clinton, a little town down in the jungle. He was put in the boob, and the beak here had a rap against him for suspicion . . ." Whitlock was always worrying about Curly, and felt he should be shocked at what he did. In a way he was, but Curly did not help his ethical absolutes by agreeing with him that he was indeed in a bad way. Whitlock lay awake nights trying to understand his friend, with no success. As a character in Whitlock's *The Turn of the Balance* and "The Fall Guy," Curly seemed overdrawn to the critics, too romantic to be believed. But Whitlock felt he was only doing justice to this extraordinary personality. "If he had lived in the seventeenth century, he would have been a great hero and today would be figuring in romantic novels that were among the six best sellers instead of drawing down condemnation upon the head of a humble realist." Believable or not, he kept turning up, destroying the last vestiges of faith Whitlock might have had in the current platitudes about congenital criminality and moral debasement. The following incident is typical of the occa-

sional encounters that kept Whitlock from accepting easy definitions of right and wrong and applying his own cherished principles
too rigidly.

"Curly Williams was in yesterday after a long absence. He was
accompanied by two dogs, not his own, and was much touched by
the fact that they loved him if nobody else did." He was looking
for his mother with "tears in his eyes." He was $700 in debt, "and
says that he has to go out and steal this money to pay his creditors, and after that he does not care what becomes of him. Isn't
that a confusion of good and bad for you?"

As Curly was about to leave, Whitlock said to him, "Curly,
you are a good fellow, and there's only one thing the matter with
you."

"What is that?"

"You are a damn fool."

"I know it," he said, and he pulled his hat down over his eyes,
called his two dogs, and went out. Now he would not see him any
more for months.[6]

Here, then, are the basic ingredients for Whitlock's fiction
after he returned to Toledo: a sense of the dramatic, a clearly
defined moral viewpoint, a hero, a knowledge of the underworld
and an evaluation of it as at least as good, on its own terms, as the
world of crooked politicians and corrupted businessmen. To the
average American, Whitlock's comparison of the underworld with
the political and business worlds seemed lopsided, overdrawn,
melodramatic. Whitlock, however, believed his works were realistic, grounded on common, everyday experience. His stories were
taken from his own life, which simply happened to include such
people as Curly, crooked politicians, and greedy businessmen. As
they stand, *The Turn of the Balance* and his autobiography, *Forty
Years of It*, are both based on life and both transformed into art,
in about equal measure; a comparison of the two works says much
about the use the realist made of his own autobiographical data
and just as much about the way his own romantic tendencies
transmuted those facts.

Whitlock began work on *The Turn of the Balance* shortly after
completing *The Happy Average* late in 1903, about eighteen
months before his first campaign for mayor. The idea had been

growing in his mind for some time, generated by his legal experience with personal-injury and murder cases—cases which form
the background of the story. His contact with public and private
charity and his hatred of the depersonalization he saw in them
also played leading roles. The writing of the book proved to be a
long ordeal, taking several years from conception to publication
and 200,000 words to complete. He finished the first draft in the
last days of 1905, just before his inauguration, and spent much of
his first year in office laboriously deleting more than a quarter of
his manuscript. The first-draft chapters totaled perhaps 250,000
words—almost as many as *Anna Karenina.* The final draft was
closer to the length of *Resurrection.* He finished his revisions
sometime around June 1906, completely exhausted.[7]

He had set out to write a book to demonstrate that "the spirit
of our whole system of dealing with crime and criminals is funda-
mentally wrong because it is founded in hatred and fear," and that
"it is impossible to create any kind of system or formula from
which personality can be excluded, that is, that the court is just
what the judge happens to be, etc. . . ." Unfortunately this intention did not produce an appropriate title instantly, and he spent
days conferring with William C. Bobbs and Octavia Roberts about
the possibilities of *The Balance, The First Stone, The Strength of
Sin, The Letter of the Law, The Ends of Justice, Judge Not,* and
Blind Justice, among others. He was satisfied with none of these,
but liked *The Balance* best, taking it from Robert Burns:

> Then at the balance let's be mute,
> We never can adjust it;
> What's done we partly may compute,
> But know not what's resisted.

Bobbs thought the title had too much commercial overtone, while
Whitlock stood on it because he thought its reference was clear
enough. They compromised on *The Turn of the Balance,* a title
first suggested by Bobbs. The Bobbs-Merrill readers were split
violently on the merits of the book, about half disapproving of it
thoroughly and even some of the favorable ones finding it somewhat one-sided and occasionally redundant. Whitlock reread the
book in an attempt to meet some of the more reasonable criticism,

but his creative impulse was spent and he could do no more. The book finally appeared in March 1907, toward the end of his first term as mayor.[8]

THE WRITING OF THE BOOK gave Whitlock enormous trouble. He was still haunted by the bad habits he had contracted unconsciously from the sentimental idealists and the more extreme romantics. He was all but unable to control his urge to write at great length about visual phenomena—*snow* particularly set the ink flowing too freely. Occasionally he also slipped into pathetic fallacies, and even in the completed book the snow seems to imitate the mood and the characters' emotions a good deal too closely for true realism. He was still wordy and given to the same awkward circumlocutions that plagued him in *The Thirteenth District*. More than ever, his first drafts and later corrections indicate that he wrote as a romantic and then revised and criticized as a realist. For example, he was inordinately fond of the romantic habit of abrupt transitions, making violent emotions and actions come and go with all the unreality of the action in Schiller's *Die Räuber*. On one first-draft page he had to delete a "suddenly," a "starting up," a "hastily" and an "instantly." His corrections always bring back most of the common sense of reality: "As she spoke, she seemed, in the glance that she gave her husband, to fear her position before the whole company, and she appeared to be shrinking into her black gown" became "As she spoke, she glanced at her husband, and seemed to shrink in her black gown." Or, upon the news that Archie was in jail: "To Gusta the news was a blow that stunned her. She felt in the great love she had always had for Archie, an instant desire to go to him, but when she mentioned this, her father turned on her so fiercely and berated her so soundly that she did not dare mention it again" became "But Gusta, in the great love she had for Archie, felt an instant desire to go to him, but when she mentioned this, her father turned on her so fiercely that she did not dare mention it again." Often, the corrections lessen the air of gothic gloom that the plot encouraged but realist principles discouraged: "For Gusta it was so still, so quiet there, so commonplace; her mother sitting there quietly, the two women looking on. The great tragedy seemingly remote and unreal, not present or visible, and yet hovering over them, dark and oppressive, like some mystic fate that hung unseen above them." Perhaps this is only the influence of Thomas Hardy, whose work Whitlock loved, but it sounds suspiciously like Anne Radcliffe. The realist in Whitlock then made it much quieter and more effective: "It grew still, quiet, commonplace. Gusta bustled about, her mother sitting there quietly." The facts, stated economically, allow the reader to supply the proper mood of horror; the prose just narrates these facts and does not become overwrought.

Whitlock was also hampered by his habit of seeing metaphors in everything and then harming his style by trying to wedge in all the suggested emotions he himself experienced from a simple scene. Marriott, Whitlock's alter ego in the story, is thinking about Elizabeth's brother Dick, a deadbeat:

> He shrank from preaching; he could take no priggish or saintly attitude; he had too much self-consciousness, too much imagination for that; and he flung away his cigarette as if it to him symbolized the problem, and he sighed when he thought that Ward, after all, would have to make his way alone and fight his own battles, that the soul could emerge into real life only through the pangs that accompany all birth and often present a crisis which that life cannot survive; like some chicken struggling in pitiable agony to free itself from the shell it has blindly and instinctively pipped and as often failing as succeeding; the whimsical uncertainty of the process that might have been governed by some bungling fate. . . .

. . . and so on for five more lines of unhelpful analysis. The trouble with all this is first, that it is autobiographical and the author has not thought out his own emotions to such a degree that he can write about them clearly. He knows what he feels, though what he feels is not yet a thought but an emotion extremely difficult to convey. The emotion affects him as an impression, in the figure of the chicken, but until the impression becomes an idea that he can verbalize clearly it remains only an extended series of half-crystallized feelings that are connected only by the semicolons Whitlock tended to overuse whenever he found himself in a tough spot. Yet this tendency to think in metaphors rather than ideas is only part of Whitlock's problem in making his frequent revisions.

Another part is his difficulty in objectifying his own personal emotions in order to attribute them in clear form to Marriott. Often, too, the metaphors and similes are strained and self-conscious, as though he felt he had to think in them even when it was not natural: "He felt a spiritual relief from thus pricking his wound like that sense of physical relief that comes from probing an aching tooth"; or, "These noises seemed to excite the inmates, and the discords resembled that which occurs when a menagerie is being differently disposed . . ."[9]

Aside from his personal difficulties as an artist, Whitlock shared a perennial problem of the realists. If one is to write about material reality—building a mass of descriptive detail about the commonplace—one runs the risk of building great houses without any people in them, to take a criticism from Virginia Woolf's article on Arnold Bennett. The physical, material surrounding—the atmosphere—is there, but the people are seen from the outside only, while their thoughts and feelings and agonies are present only as they are reflected on faces or in gestures. Whitlock had great difficulty in describing what was going on in someone's mind, and finally crossed out most of the interior monologue he wrote for his characters. Marriott of course does much of this, but Elizabeth provides particular difficulties for she is an upper-middle-class girl who realizes at least some of the inadequacies that are obvious to Marriott, and she is torn between her environment and background and her perceptions. Her confusions and indecisions often become the reader's, rather than a part of the story. The opposite side of the problem is the realist's tendency to dwell too long on the obvious physical details: Whitlock was abnormally conscious of clothes and frequently indulged in long digressions on the appearance of a criminal or a girl or the inside of a jail.

Autobiography also intruded where it did not belong, in the plot and description, just as it had in *The Thirteenth District*. The legal scenes that remain are but part of the many originally in the text, both about police and legal niceties and courtroom procedure. Whitlock's dislikes were at first far more obvious: The jury was far stupider, and the police, especially Kouka, far more brutal, in the first drafts. Thus, the turnkey, "with an air that showed his contempt for the constitutional provision that gives an accused man the right to see counsel . . ."—an obvious example of author prejudice and quite uncalled for—is deleted. And then, there is the bright young Whitechapel wit popping up: "Four miles from the city, where the high white pike that leads westward across the low mud road that leads nowhere is the Lulu Corners, a name bestowed on the crossroads by some trivial and feeble intelligence long ago . . ." This becomes to the mature realist: "Four miles from town, where a white pike crosses a low mud road, is Lulu Corners. There is little at this crossroads to inspire a name less frivolous . . ." The remaining autobiographical deletions have value chiefly for Whitlock's biography and would be useful if the evidence they contain were not available elsewhere: Marriott's misery at the pain and poverty and injustice he sees, his depressions, his indecisions, his disgust at anything institutionalized or otherwise depersonalized, all reflect the feelings of the author.

One final criticism which many readers raised about the book remains relevant and needs explaining. The great realists, despite their admitted prejudices, created a world balanced in its proportions of good people and bad people, rich people and poor people, happy people and sad people. Tolstoy detested the lives led by Vronsky and Anna, yet he portrayed those lives at great and convincing length and simply balanced them against the lives of Levin and Kitty, who had much in common with Tolstoy and his wife, Sonya Bers. Tolstoy approved of Levin but did not unbalance his book by concentrating on him unduly. George Eliot did the same with Rosamond Vincy in *Middlemarch*, balancing her against Dorothea Brooke Casaubon; even her minor characters are relatively well balanced, giving a picture of a world of mixed good and evil that is thoroughly believable. Likewise, each character is mixed: a Fred Vincy engaging but weak, or an Ernest Casaubon somewhat musty and boring—but hardly an ogre—and comprehensible on his own terms. In *The Turn of the Balance* Whitlock at first attempted to follow this pattern; he tried heroically, in fact, and that was why his manuscript was so long. In Marriott he created his alter ego, the sensitive young lawyer trying to help the poor and suffering when they suffered; opposite him, Eades, the prosecutor, not a bad man really, but too willing to institutionalize himself and actively stifle any twinges of real personal involvement with a poor man. Elizabeth, the woman both Marriott and Eades court, is the well-to-do young girl who is bothered by poverty and tries to do what is right; opposite her, her wastrel brother, drinking and whoring his way through the book, breaking his father's heart. The wealthy Ward family, presented in detail, was to balance the Koerner family with its tragedies of poverty, sin, and accident. The result might seem somewhat contrived, thus anatomized, but it was in many ways convincing and a notable achievement by most standards. But Whitlock feared greatly that, as his book grew, its salability and even publishability decreased, and so he cut. But he did not cut evenly, realistically. He cut out the scenes he really did not care about, and as he cared so much more for Archie and Gusta and the Koerner family in general than he did for the Wards, who were rich enough to take care of themselves, and Eades, who was a prosecutor and thus unworthy of sympathy, they soon all but disappeared, while the Koerners usurped the space. The result, while realistic in the sense of being true and autobiographical, was false in that it was not complete. The book became one-sided, with the evil portrayed in far greater detail than the good. The criminals seem far less wicked than the police, and the defendants less guilty than the lawyers, jury, and judge. It was not life seen steadily and seen whole, but the underworld seen in passion and excused with spirit. The result makes for exciting reading, but the excitement comes as much from the melodrama as from the characters and narrative. In short, the book is effective because it resembles romance at least as much as it resembles realism. Not for nothing were some readers reminded of Dickens and Charles Reade, even though neither writer had an honored place in Whitlock's library. To many progressives the book was realistic, but that view said more about their own bias than about the book itself.[10]

The result of all this suffering and revising was a book that seems in retrospect one of the better novels produced by American progressivism. It is one of those books that triumphs over its own admitted flaws because of the convincing and intense vision that drives it and the effectiveness of its narrative. Even as a tract, it was not without literary merit. Consider, for a moment, the opening scene in the snowstorm, the same snow that caused much of the overwriting in the earliest drafts. It is in print an unpretentious and effective device for delineating the views that the novel will encompass in its development, and it provides brief and effective introductions to the chief characters and their social environment. Elizabeth Ward is radiant, enjoying its glory; the rich townspeople are out in their sleighs, admiring each other; broker Stephen Ward finds it refreshing; the women at his party find it romantic, but their businessmen companions can think only of the interruptions to business; Marriott, who is Whitlock in disguise, finds in it the subject for an epic. The rich at play take such things as the weather as conversation pieces. Then suddenly the pretty maid, Gusta Koerner, screams, and with her scream the world of poverty appears briefly, disconcerting Mrs. Ward, who finds such interruptions intolerable. To the poor the cold is bitter, and in the snow Papa Koerner has fallen into a railroad frog and had his foot mutilated by a train. Gusta, on her return, finds the poor struggling with frozen pumps, unshoveled paths, and frozen wood; they face a bleak day indoors huddling by the only source of warmth, the kitchen stove. Otherwise, the saloons alone provide protection against the cold.

This opening is superb realism, done with economy and attention to small detail in the physical world. The meaning is plain in the narration, without sermonizing by the author. Slowly the view shifts, and the world seen whole becomes the world seen from the underworld, the world of the rejected and the criminal. The Ward family takes on less importance, the Koerners more. The world view becomes the Koerners': the law is full of delays, and a man like Reinhold—a good worker and a good man—cannot get payment from the plainly negligent railroad. The law is unjust, for it hounds Archie when he is innocent and tortures him when he is in prison, even as the guards graft off the prisoners. The law is cruel and unfeeling, imprisoning the totally guiltless like Gusta on a charge of mere suspicion. Above all, the law is frustratingly impersonal, and Marriott realizes many times that it seems made not for people at all but for something called justice, which seems to have no connection with people. Business is equally malign. Its leaders are disposing of stolen property, turning in small embezzlers while operating on the grand scale in the next room. It is a world much like the underworld, and one of the more effective passages Whitlock creates is the discussion of the status rituals and the nepotistic network that keeps order in the underworld much as similar tribal customs do in the business world. Finally, the rich are not the opposite of the poor, but the corrupters of the poor. Mr. Ward turns in young Harry Graves and thus makes a lifelong misery for him as an ex-convict, while his son Dick seduces Gusta and introduces her to a life of tawdry misery. The rich prove to be very much like the poor, only they have more money, and this money insulates them from the world and prevents them from growing morally. It also keeps Dick Ward out of jail when he embezzles even more than Harry Graves, in a parallel that is none the less effective for being obvious and artificial.

As a tract, like *Resurrection*, the book indicted a whole society. Archie returns to town trained by his army duty in the Philippines only to shoot and dream of romantic adventures, and mere chance is all that is needed to make him a criminal; thus both romance and the army are ugly. Elizabeth, feeling as useless as the young Jane Addams, tries to join the Organized Charities, only to discover that its object is to ease the conscience of the rich and not the misery of the poor. Whitlock's withering contempt for such institutions is nicely summed up in the quotation from John O'Reilly, (p. 288):

> The organized charity, scrimped and iced,
> In the name of a cautious, statistical Christ—

And Elizabeth soon learns from Marriott the value of personal charity both for the giver and the receiver. The book is a tract against all the legal malfunctions that Altgeld so detested, the delays and technicalities and abuses that let the guilty go free and punished the innocent. It is also a tract against all the institutions Whitlock had come to dislike in his painful career as a lawyer: capital punishment, a corrupt capitalism, maltreatment of prisoners and the poor, and respectable morality. Most of all, it is a tract against all institutions and their inane prattlings about moral principles like law and order, duty and justice. An examination of this last hatred shows just how much of an imaginative achievement the book was.

The problem at the heart of the novel is best examined historically. Poverty, as a concept, seemed to many people in the nineteenth century as almost un-American. The poor, like the poor of "Acres of Diamonds," were poor because they were shiftless, thriftless, lazy, and immoral—and, besides, God intended it that way. Charity if given at all should be as unpleasant as possible, to encourage a quick return to productivity on the part of the poor. The approach was didactic, abstract, deductive, and appropriate if at all only to a rural environment where all could have their own farms. In opposition to this view, reformers and progressives like Jane Addams, Stanton Coit, Jacob Riis, B. O. Flower, and others publicized a newer approach for an industrial society. The poor, they held, should be investigated firsthand, without theories; when they had gathered the facts, they insisted that poverty was not always the fault of the individual but often the fault of society. The environment, and its economic forces, suddenly became more important than whether a man drank. Indeed, some rash souls even suggested that drink was a result of poverty, rather than a cause.[11]

BY THE TIME WHITLOCK WROTE *The Turn of the Balance*, these newer students of the subject had evolved certain doctrines; the merit of Whitlock's book is that, almost entirely from his own observation, he wrote the imaginative counterpart of these newer statements, putting them in an unforgettable form and achieving a far wider audience than the more austere sociological reports ever could. Thus, Edward A. Ross, who stressed the mutual interdependence and complexity of modern industrial society and the impersonal nature of modern sins like graft, adulteration of food, and stock fixing. Iniquity, he said, could flourish "even while men are getting better. Briber and boodler and grafter are often 'good men,' judged by the old tests, and would have passed for virtuous in the American community of seventy years ago." According to Ross, the new sinners were often "pure and kindhearted, loving in their families, faithful to their friends, and generous to the needy"; this paragon was the man who was "the respectable, exemplary, trusted personage who, strategically placed at the focus of a spiderweb of fiduciary relations, is able from his office-chair to pick a thousand pockets, poison a thousand sick, pollute a thousand minds, or imperil a thousand lives." Americans seemed incapable of realizing a corporate wrong, only a personal one, and so the men hidden by their corporations received little community disapproval. Such offenders Ross labeled "criminaloids" and the need to stop their activities a great public necessity.[12]

On another front, serious students were discovering that the saloon was not the den of thieves and drunkards that moral literature declared it to be. The whole issue, wrote Raymond Calkins, "is a social phenomenon to be studied wholly apart from ethical considerations"—which is just what his predecessors did not do. The saloon, he found, was the poor man's club, for along with much that was injurious it also provided "a measure of fellowship and recreation for which he would look elsewhere in vain." John Koren, using reports from Hull House, found that quite often drinking was not even the chief attraction for saloon-goers—that the lavatory, the food, and in many cases the recreational facilities like cards, pool tables, pianos, and so on were most important. "The saloon is here the workingman's club," he quoted Ernest Carroll Moore, "in which many of his leisure hours are spent, and in which he finds more of the things that approximate luxury than in his home, almost more than he finds in any other public place in the ward." The saloon is warm in winter, cool in summer, but most of all, "it is the society of his fellows that he must have." His home is ugly and his food bad, and he has no friends there; come to the saloon, he finds friendship, gossip, loans, and often food, fuel, clothes, and political jobs.[13]

At their highest level, the new doctrines were evolving slowly in the mind of Charles Horton Cooley, a scholar at the University of Michigan whom Whitlock probably never heard of. Cooley stressed the organic nature of society, with each component inseparable from the whole and necessary to the whole. Society and the individual were complementary, and anyone who tried to discuss one separate from the other was misguided. In *Human Nature and the Social Order* (1902), he stressed his idea of the "looking-glass self," that is, the way a man formed his character being patterned on what he sees in the environment around him. Suddenly, one's appearance to others, their appearance to him, and his conception of his appearance to them—not to mention feelings like pride and mortification—had more importance than vice and laziness and sin. In *Social Organization* (1909), his best-known book, he discussed such things as the relativity of moral values, his faith in democracy, and the importance of primary groups like the family, the neighborhood, and the work group in forming character. In *Social Process* (1918), he largely restated his earlier views and emphasized his faith in empirical data and his distrust of *a priori* reasoning in sociology.[14] His work had great importance in the history of sociology, but its value here is less grand: It tells us just exactly what Whitlock was doing in his character development, in particular the development of Archie Koerner from likable young man just back from the army to murderer in the electric chair.

The following are the elements that make Whitlock's insight remarkable for its time: the knowledge of the institutionalization of business and charity, with its effect on both businessman and poor man; the realization that men went to saloons for social rather than ethical reasons, with the more important corollary that the actions of these men in general were normal, explicable, and much like the actions of men with more money; and the sense, inductively derived, that men were not born much of anything at all, but became good or bad, and developed their personalities, from the environment. Thus, when Archie Koerner returns from the army, he is without a job and otherwise just a normal boy with a taste for adventure. The army taught him to shoot, but little else. The Koerner house is no sanctuary, for Reinhold is there with his stump of a leg, always complaining. The only place of welcome is the warm neighborhood saloon, where he meets men of his age and interests. There he becomes friendly with men who have minor prison records and is arrested on suspicion for a crime he knows nothing about. Once he is in jail, the police and his father simply assume his guilt, whether he is convicted or not. Only Marriott and Gusta assume anything else. Out of jail, Archie can find solace and respect only with his old gang. Society rejects him quite openly as a sinner to be shunned, and (p. 131) "it dawned on Archie that here was a little quarter of the world where he was wanted, where he was made to feel at home . . ." In particular, he becomes friendly with his former cellmate Mason and Curly Jackson, and they initiate their new friend into the world of crime. He meets important criminals, becomes knowledgeable in the argot, familiar with the status requirements of underworld hierarchy, and learns that the hatred of certain police pursues him regardless of his acts. His first crime, cracking a post-office safe with Curly, gives him some status of his own and a symbol of his belonging:

a nickname, "Dutch." Mason is framed for one of Archie's crimes, but then Archie is caught again and goes to jail once more. He is there brutalized, tortured, and victimized by the deputy warden and his lackeys, and the likable boy is soon quite capable of killing. On his release, a particularly obnoxious policeman, Kouka, decides he is guilty of a brutal murder and hounds him. Archie can take it no longer, shoots Kouka—the army taught him well—and for that he is electrocuted. Not sinful, but neutral, he has developed along the lines laid out by his environment and formed his character on the characters of those in his primary groups—especially the saloon—and the jail. American fiction, and certainly American realism, had never done this before, even with middle-class people. Whitlock did it in the underworld, and did it with minor characters as well: Gusta, by accident lovely and miserable, cannot fight off Dick Ward, and so she goes under; Dick Ward, the clubman and debauchee whose money and associations only make him more worthless with every passing day; Stephen Ward, a rich broker who has a conscience, but whose wife and business both paralyze his ability to do good; Elizabeth Ward, who barely survives her environment because she loves Marriott, one who provides a looking glass she cannot ignore; and Mrs. Ward, the obnoxious society woman incapable of unselfish thought, shuddering at what others might say. All of these people develop in a way Cooley would have understood and applauded, but Whitlock discovered his technique from his firsthand suffering, not from a book.

The institutionalization Whitlock detested is even more obvious in the book and is a vital aspect of his thought and its development. Many progressives had a streak of anarchism and individualism in their natures, and they felt most keenly not some vague social deprivation but a particular, individual one. "My friend Sam," not "the poor," was on their consciences; a specific case, not a general one. Industrialization had split workers from employers, givers of charity from the getters, the just from the unjust, and to Whitlock the symbol of this growing estrangement was the institution and its fatuous slogans. Society regarded the Law as a monolith of righteousness; to Whitlock, it was but the sum of the whims of very human men named McWhorter, Bostwick, Sharlow, and Glassford, whims which sent men to jail for twenty years instead of two because the judge had fought with his wife, say, or as in Reinhold Koerner's case reversed a personal-injury claim because of the judge's past service to a railroad and his desire for a vacation. Prison was another monolith, the house of sinners; but Whitlock saw only individuals, and in Chapter Eight he portrays in good realistic fashion the neatly individualized group of men Mrs. Ward can see only as an ugly group. The men turn out to have conversational peculiarities, marital problems, and legitimate grievances that make them people, just like Mrs. Ward. Even the men on Death Row are people to Whitlock, and he describes them as such (pp. 578 *ff.*). Most obvious perhaps is Whitlock's distaste for institutionalization in habits of thought and character. Marriott is always being offended by the conventional platitudes about law, order, charity, duty, justice, and so on. For the men who mouth such nonsense have not thought about what they are saying, they have only accepted what others tell them. Eades, the prosecutor, is the supreme example of the upright young defender of social conventions, and is their ablest propagator. He is, of course, put firmly in his place: Elizabeth chooses Marriott instead, for (p. 602) ". . . one can't marry an institution, you know . . ."

The book was a remarkable achievement in imaginative insight, but Whitlock awaited its reception with "a good deal of secret dread and trembling, I confess, for I am sure to be dreadfully criticized . . ." He was right. The storm broke quickly and generated great force. The book became a sensation almost overnight, was widely discussed, and was passionately praised by progressives and damned by policemen and prison wardens everywhere. Wardens denied the paddling, water cure, hanging by wrists, and other tortures Archie experienced; policemen objected to the evil Kouka and his fellow officers, who were somewhat too evil for full believability. The criminals of course were too good, and people objected to their being made more appealing than the judges and policemen. When Steffens privately made some of these criticisms, Whitlock replied: "I get so sick of cant and hypocrisy among business men and newspaper editors and preachers and the better element generally that I long for something that is real; hence the sight of a real thief is often a consolation." Explanation, perhaps, but hardly a justification on aesthetic grounds. He

also admitted another overemphasis: he had been unfair to Christians, because "the Christians have been so very unchristian to me
that I react in their spirit."[15]

Progressives everywhere were overjoyed, and with remarkable
unanimity they agreed about the nature of his achievement and in
so doing showed just how permeated they all were with Tolstoy.
Darrow wrote that it was "a remarkable book. In power, in
insight, in art and above all in its broad and tender sympathies it
stands with Tolstoy's Resurrection. But while it is all that can be
found in Resurrection, it is still a great deal more. Whitlock knows
the lawyer's side of his story as Tolstoy could not. And the lawyer
is infinitely wiser than the preacher can be." Jane Addams,
Howells, Frederic Howe's wife Marie Jenney, Upton Sinclair, Jack
London, and Charles Edward Russell all agreed. Whitlock of
course knew as much about Tolstoy as his readers. One of his first
acts was to send a copy of his book to Yasnaya Polyana.[16]

As realism in the aesthetic sense, the book was admittedly
unbalanced; but to certain readers its realism was unmistakable,
and they wrote Whitlock with great praise. The best of these
letters, in fact the most remarkable letter in all of Whitlock's
papers, came from inmate Grant Evans, Western Penitentiary,
Allegheny City, Pennsylvania:

> Candidly, my object in penning you this missive is my grateful
> appreciation of the merit of your popular book, "The Turn of the
> Balance," which I have just read. The book has created here quite
> a sensation among the inmates; all desire to read it . . . The
> consensus of opinion of veterans in crime, the accidental criminal
> as well as those whose crimes are purely legal, who can see them-
> selves mirrored in its pages, all concur in the opinion that it is
> true to life. And at this juncture I wish to say that several other
> prisoners knowing of my intention to write you, have asked me to
> put stress on this particular phase of the book, namely, its graphic
> and realistic descriptions and the sidelights it throws on criminal
> jurisprudence . . . Thus I say that the Turn of the Balance
> ostensibly under a veneer of fiction is a real classic satire on our
> modern system of Pharasaism, a conscientious arraignment of our
> farcical judicial system and the "Holier than thou" hypocrisy of
> conventional society of today and in the last analysis it knocks the

props away from the theoretical balderdash profusely indulged by canting sentimentalists. The stir and comment this particular book has caused in the underworld and the powers that prey is proof positive that it has struck home thereby diagnosing those psychic symptoms in the social and body politic, that insidious malady in the occultism of erring and criminal human nature with a possible solution . . . My own experience of more than twenty years spent among powers that prey during which time I have studied criminology and penology from the vantage ground where the ammunition was the thickest; therefore, being one of them among them and always in intimate association with them, should qualify me to give an authoritative opinion. In a broad and ethical sense, I regard the book as a high class contribution to standard criminology and penology as the moral aspect of the question is cleverly conceived and I sincerely hope that judges especially, and all those who have to do with the administration of law and justice will also read it . . .[17]

The progressives and the prisoners were in agreement, and Howells gave the book his benediction as art.[18]

THE CHIEF LITERARY RESULT of his new success was the willingness of publishers to commission him for books. He continued writing short stories and occasional essays, but he simply did not have the time for a new novel. He had, however, long cherished an interest in Abraham Lincoln and had once gone to considerable trouble and expense to get a copy of Billy Herndon's life, unexpurgated. Soon he had a chance to prove his devotion. Early in 1908, Mark A. De Wolfe Howe, the editor of the Beacon Biographies for Small, Maynard & Co., wrote to ask him if he would write a brief life, about 20,000 words, for the series. The book required no original research but offered rather a graceful introduction to the man for the general reader. Whitlock, although an ill mayor at the time, accepted by return mail, much to Howe's delight. Whitlock went to work quickly, for his heart was fully committed, and he soon waded through eleven lives of Lincoln— though he had little respect for most of them. He took a great glee particularly in parts of Herndon's biography, for he shared many prejudices with Lincoln's devoted law partner. He was especially pleased to note that the Springfield preachers almost unanimously opposed Lincoln, as did the respectable people. As most of the respectable people proved to be related to Nell and the Brainerds, that part of the story proved a bit ticklish, since Nell's sense of humor wavered in the face of her husband's quips about the stuffiness of her ancestors. Despite his wife's pained silences, Whitlock loved the writing of this book, for he found in Lincoln another of his heroes, a man who had lived and had by his living proved that a beautiful life was possible and, thus, that Whitlock's own ideals were not totally unrealizable. Naturally his enthusiasm carried him away, and the first draft of his book ran to over 60,000 words. October was the month of truth, and he slaved in misery over his creation, slowly whittling it down to 30,000. Then he wrote Howe in distress, asking that he have to cut no more. Howe immediately told him to stop cutting and send along what he had, much to Whitlock's relief. On November 11 he finished, and by December he was deep into the galleys.[19]

In its own small way, Whitlock's *Abraham Lincoln* was also a document of the progressive era. Whitlock disliked the plaster-saint Lincoln erected with such great care by J. G. Holland, John Hay, John Nicolay, and their imitators. Like Herndon, he loved Lincoln as a man of democracy, of distinctly earthy origins and unpretentious demeanor, a Western hero unafraid of tests of strength either in wrestling or debate. With the exception of an occasional minor story contributed by doddering old Springfield inhabitants, most of Whitlock's material came from Herndon, some of it shorn of extreme expression and all of it without Herndon's bawdy undertone. Herndon had created a folk hero, a noble Daniel Boone; Whitlock took this folk hero and made him a symbol of the best that is in all men. Whitlock also shared some of Herndon's radical social views, as well as his dislike of Stephen Douglas; naturally he also shared Herndon's sour views on Springfield Respectability. He did not, however, express himself in the choleric way in which Herndon had, for example, dissected Mary Todd Lincoln. Whitlock passed over Mrs. Lincoln's shortcomings quickly, as he did also the question of Lincoln's religious views. He did not ignore these questions, but he did not stress them. His one real error was his acceptance of Herndon's version of the

Anne Rutledge love affair and the resulting melancholia, a story gravely suspect to most later historians. But these minor historiographical points now matter little; what does matter is that the progressive Whitlock identified with democratic Republican Herndon; the result clearly demonstrated that his progressivism had a free-soil and even abolitionist lineage of which he was proud.[20]

After his Lincoln was safely published and well received, Whitlock turned most of his literary energies to more political topics and his book publications were simply collections of previously published work. The editors at Bobbs-Merrill were anxious to keep his name before the public and agreed to publish a volume of his short stories. When the stories were gathered, they proved to be more than enough for two volumes, and so they were divided; one volume, *The Gold Brick*, was issued in 1910, while the second, *The Fall Guy*, was postponed until 1912. Many of the stories were jejune early work dating back to the 1890's, with awkward sentimentalization and often a maudlin moralizing which marred them. Like Howells, Whitlock on his bad days tended to write sermons disguised as fiction, and the reading of some stories is a far more painful experience than anything in his novels. The better ones, like the title story for *The Fall Guy*, "Reform in the First," and "The Preacher's Son" are saved either because they lack a moral completely, and merely tell a good story, or else have the moral so embedded in convincing characterization that it retains force and effectiveness. Whitlock's short work is rarely distinguished, however, and these collections are better left forgotten.

Of considerably more importance is Whitlock's slow and painful composition of his autobiography. For five years, John S. Phillips of *McClure's* and later the *American Magazine* had been asking for a series of reminiscences, both about his past career and about his life as mayor. Through Phillips and his magazines Whitlock first met Lincoln Steffens and then Albert Jay Nock, and these men also thought that the sketches would be worth writing. Finally, as Nock and Whitlock quickly became friends, Nock was assigned by Phillips to coax the story from the harried and often ill mayor. His duties were slowly driving Whitlock to distraction, and it soon became Nock's job to calm him down and start him writing. He wanted, he wrote, "something informal and rather personal,—subjective,—showing some of the steps in your progress toward your philosophy." Although depressed by the attacks of the good people and the clergy, and in the midst of an important battle over street-car fares, Whitlock agreed. No such project would be complete without at least one serious period of depression and nervous illness, but this time Whitlock outdid himself. In early January, 1911, he came down with his case of appendicitis and was all but immobile for a month.[21]

The next year was a tragi-comedy of nerves. Nock, a former Episcopalian minister only recently hired by the *American*, soon learned that the mayor was often a walking bruise from his official duties. The two friends soon knew each other well enough to write letters in the Yiddish dialect of Potash and Perlmutter, the creations of Montague Glass. Whitlock was Mawruss, Nock was Abe, Nell was Minnie, and Nock's close friend Ruth Robinson was Rosie; each was thus named after a leading character in *Potash and Perlmutter*. The first letters show Nock trying to josh Whitlock into writing, scoffing gently about deadlines and the mechanical difficulties of publishing the articles. Soon, however, he made the mistake of telling Whitlock about the lack of response to the articles, measured by letters to the magazines. Whitlock quite unjustifiedly exploded in one of his worst displays of temper. He completely misunderstood Nock, took offense, and thus showed to what extent this most gentlemanly of men had been pushed by the pressures of his office. Nock was appalled at the unwarranted response, tried desperately to patch up the firm of Abe and Mawruss, and finally succeeded. The whole affair makes painful reading in the Whitlock-Nock correspondence, but viewed from a different vantage point, it tells much about Whitlock's character. Nock told his Rosie all about Whitlock, and his letters to her show us the man more objectively. At first, Whitlock "is never effusive, never gives the least chance of being thought insincere," and "one does not know him long without discovering what a gentle, patient, affectionate, disciplined man he is . . ." That was in April 1912. By October, Nock is writing that Whitlock's summer "has been the hardest of his whole life . . ." Two months later: "Brand is morose. There is typhoid fever here and his maid is laid up with a suspected case. So he and his Minnie have worked themselves into a blue funk and been innoculated with this infernal serum treatment. All he needs is a stiff upper lip."[22]

Nock soon discovered that the blue funks came too regularly for the mayor to perform many of his official duties. Certainly they left no time for writing memoirs. By January 1913, the start of Whitlock's last year in office, it was plain that if the magazine wanted any more articles something drastic was needed. Nock was in many ways the least practical of men, tending at times toward nervous hypochondria himself, but compared to poor Mawruss he was a pillar of strength. "This afternoon I have spent helping him clean up his desk of an accumulation of letters reaching back over a month. He simply looks at them and groans,—the most helpless man you ever laid eyes on." Nock sat down and made the nationally famous mayor sort out his papers and weed out the few that demanded personal attention, then teamed up with the city stenographer and got the repies written quickly. Soon the office resembled an orderly workshop. "He's a fearful fellow; can't run an office to save his soul. His gratitude was pathetic. There was method in my taking hold, for as long as that job was hanging over him he was no good for anything else; while now he will turn in and work on our stuff in great shape." That's what he thought. The next day Whitlock was convinced he had a cold. "By the powers, I'd hate to be his Minnie, even if he is the sweetest soul on earth. The poor chap has so many notions and is so unearthly helpless." Whitlock stayed more or less helpless, and Nock finally had to reorganize the whole office. By the time he was through he had answered letters months overdue and even introduced some of the efficiency techniques of Frank Gilbreth, about whom he in turn was writing for the *American*. By 1913, he was successful, and *Forty Years of It* finally reached print. Without Nock, it never would have attained book length; appropriately, he was asked to contribute an introduction, and did so.[23]

The resulting book showed the stresses involved in its composition. The time sequences are hopelessly confused, men appear and reappear in no apparent order, and ideas wander about as though they were vaguely perplexed and not entirely sure why they are where they are. Much of it was apparently written in one draft, with only the most minor of revisions, in contrast to virtually everything else Whitlock ever wrote, and the resulting prose is not so much written as spoken. The style is that of a man sitting down over port and re-creating some past experiences and present ideas to several friends who are sympathetic and undemanding. The book includes history that never happened, conversation that probably occurred but for which the author is not sure he was there or not, and the whole series of ideas that he had worked out, often with greater clarity, in earlier articles. The book is thoroughly unbalanced; to cite only one example, Grandfather Brand has several chapters while Whitlock's wives and mother have not even a footnote. As autobiography in its strictest sense, it left much to be desired.

But it offers more. Its principles of organization are unconventional but effective, and they make the book one of the most important documents of the progressive era. Its first principle is the simple literary device of the standard *Bildungsroman*. Ever since Goethe's *Wilhelm Meister,* and even before, works of art have been created which center about the intellectual, spiritual, and artistic growth of a young artist; life, the young man usually knows, is an art, and the book traces the course of his growth to the point where he knows how to live. The hero is often unheroic, dreamy and reflective and somewhat off to the side of life, spectatorial rather than involved. He usually begins as something of a blank, a *tabula rasa,* living in the country away from all that is exciting, alluring, and important in life. Slowly, and with pain, he becomes initiated, often through a picaresque journey to people and places which will teach him something. His family frequently is vulgar and philistine—or they live in a vulgar and and philistine town— and the oppressed boy simply must go to the City to grow. Finally, he arrives there, changes and grows and often produces works of art, and then perhaps returns to his old home town—a convenient device for underlining just how much he has developed.[24]

Forty Years of It now appears more structured. Whitlock has none of the tumultuous love affairs that dot most books in the genre, and the conflict between generations is heavily muted, but the rest is there. Stultifying Urbana, with Grandfather alone a source of joy, oppresses even the ten-year-old boy who watches the prisoner being freed. Soon he begins to meet the men and places in his *Bildung:* Frank Hurd, the Whitechapel crowd, Altgeld, Jones, and so on. He watches the great riots of the Debs and Lemont rebellions, sees the Haymarket men pardoned, and writes his first stories. His ideas change and become unacceptable to

Urbana. Finally, he settles in Toledo and determines to bring that town to accept his ideas; and soon the city gets its own *Bildung*, through the speeches of the Independents. Like most books of the genre, this "novel" was written by a comparatively young man and the ending is unsatisfying, vague, and predictive, for the best is yet to come, and we must live on. The ending here is even poorer than usual because the course of development and the resulting philosophy of life get so shaken up together that the sense of development disappears, and only a discourse on ideas and visions remains. The city, symbolically, takes on the burden of the *Bildung* from the artist, but the handling of the transition is not entirely convincing.

A second principle of organization is the vision which permeates the book, first by suggestion through characters like Grandfather Brand and Frank Hurd, and finally explicitly stated. Analysis of this vision shows how far Whitlock and his friends had come since the days when "Acres of Diamonds" was public philosophy and Republicanism the religion of Urbana. Whitlock has developed the methods of this older thought, if not its content, to their final extent; but he has not changed them. He seems to sense the pragmatism that will be the predominant intellectual force of the next reformers when he remarks in passing that "this is a world of relativities, in which the absolute is the first impossibility." But he does not mean it, and the whole remainder of the book shows this. Scarcely two pages later he is taking refuge in the same intellectual garments that Conwell used, the sense of world harmony and integration that so permeates Henry George and Herbert Spencer and is so foreign to William James and John Dewey. "But there is a more fundamental law—that of the destructive power of force, which always defeats itself." The forces that govern men were still abstract, *a priori* formulations and not the products of a universe of chance. Jones saw, and Whitlock agreed, that "above all the laws men make with their political machines in their legislatures, there is a higher law, and that the Golden Rule is a rule of conduct deduced from that law." It is no accident that Whitlock's very words here reflect the speeches of the abolitionists. Nowhere do they look ahead to the New Deal. Whitlock is still thinking in Victorian terminology, and the attractiveness of his person and his vision should not blind students to the ancestry of his ideas and the fact that after him they did not develop further.[25]

Another aspect of his vision is a hatred for conventional reform. No conservative was ever as hard on some kinds of men—"indurated" is Whitlock's favorite word for them—who spend their lives telling others how to live and demanding that the police enforce their prejudices. Whitlock, as a man with a vision of personal liberty for everyone, frankly loathed them. These men came to him so often "that my whole view of life was quite in danger of distortion. It seemed that half the populace had set forth in a rage to reform mankind, and their first need was to get the mayor to use the police force to help them." Their favorite day was Monday, "and each new Monday morning seemed to have in reserve, for a nature that was trying to keep its faith in humanity, some fresh and theretofore unimagined instance of the depths of little meannesses to which human nature is capable of sinking." Naturally, Monday was miserable because of the Toledo Sunday, when people had time and encouragement for thinking about the sins of their neighbors. Then they "could gorge on the huge Sunday noon dinner of roast beef, and then lie about all afternoon like pythons in a torpor which produced an indigestion so acute and lasting that for three days it passed very well for pious fervor and zeal for reform." To a man who was trying to liberate souls and make the life of a man a thing of beauty, pythons were unattractive.[26]

WITH HIS AUTOBIOGRAPHY safe in Albert Nock's hands, Whitlock turned once again to fiction and once again produced a work of unpublishable length and mediocre literary merit. "Karla" never did get published, despite the affection which the author expressed for it, and his national reputation as the muckraking author of *The Turn of the Balance*. In the story Whitlock combined both implicitly and explicitly most of the themes which had concerned his imagination, and it is for this reason and the resulting light it shines on progressive psychology—not for its literary merit—that the novelette is worth discussing. The chief characters are old Max Wohler and his attractive daugher Karla, a young and sensitive artist, Joe Garland, and two representatives of past and future; Dr.

Wayne, who stands for the best in the past, and the anarchist Peskov, who stands for the worst in the future. The Wohler family has *Das Kapital* for a family Bible, a deep commitment to philosophical and literary classics, and faith in socialism. Max, in short, is the best of the socialists; the rest of his group seem to be sectarians of the petty, religious variety Whitlock never had much use for. During a strike, Max goes and tries to calm the crowd; he is killed for his trouble. Peskov meanwhile returns to the house and all but rapes Karla, but she fights him off. He then goes and agitates, but returns with the authorities behind him; Karla hides him until they go away, and he flees.

The story, at times reminiscent of Conrad's political novels, is a study of how character evolves under the pressure of events. Karla is not really a central character. She scarcely ever speaks or does anything, and she deserves the title of the story chiefly because it is her choice to hide Peskov, who has assaulted her, because she thinks that by so doing she is acting as Max would have wished. Thus Max, as an example, has had a great and ennobling effect on her; but the theories that have surrounded her from birth have had almost no effect, the actual acts of people mean little to her—after all, she hated what Peskov did, both as a terrorist and rapist. She herself has done nothing to further the socialist cause and really seems quite bored with it. She is far more interested in Joe, who almost leaves her for aiding Peskov. She acts as she does because she knows what her beloved father would have done, and for that reason only. The effect of character on a person can be ennobling. Presumably, Whitlock looked at his grandfather, Frank Hurd, Golden Rule Jones, and the rest in like manner.

Psychologically, the story is illuminating, for it tells us what Whitlock saw as the central motive for a great life and for progressive action, why he concentrated so much on education and the setting of a good example, and why much progressivism was destined in the 1930's and later to turn to conservative individualism rather than New Deal collectivism. Examples, after all, can be set only by individuals, and acts which ennoble a person can be done only by individual decision. The crowd, in the story, is a mob of people who kill the great and noble Max. It is nothing to emulate, and indeed frightens all who see it. Only Max, the liver of the good and exemplary life, and Karla, who formed her character on his, remain.[27]

Whitlock sent the manuscript to Bobbs-Merrill, and, in the absence of H. H. Howland, a minor editor accepted it and began editorial work. Howland soon returned, found the story too brief and of too low a literary quality, and gently advised Whitlock that he should withdraw it. The story meant much to Whitlock, and he said so, but he agreed to defer publication and put it away for good. As it turned out, he did not publish any more fiction for a decade, and "Karla" provided a rather depressing end to this, the first phase of Whitlock's career as a writer of fiction.

❲ CHAPTER 7

The Life of Art (II):
Home Rule (1907·1910)

N O MATTER HOW MUCH HE TRIED to transform life in his art, Whitlock still found himself deep in the midst of a most unromantic reality. He could toy with ideas as did other intellectuals and novelists, but unlike them he also held public office and had to test his convictions on the proving ground of democratic politics; he succeeded, at least partially, because of the way he could fuse life and literature and because he was so persuasive that his audience soon shared the same predilections for romanticizing reality. Sadly, but inevitably, however, he gave up literature to concentrate on politics. Although his short stories continued to appear for years after his first election, he did little more actual writing except for his autobiography; instead, he used his artistic skills to compel people to vote for him.

He succeeded remarkably well. His first term, with its labor troubles, its charges of vice and corruption, and its fights over trolley fares, might well have made his dream of a free city impossible simply because he might not be re-elected. He need not have worried. His character and his real achievements proved more than adequate as a counterbalance, and, despite the dirt exposed in such loving detail on the pages of opposition newspapers, he could again campaign with reasonable confidence.

The 1907 Independent platform called for typical Toledo progressive goals. It requested nonpartisanship on the local level, with
nomination by popular petition and not by announced candidacy.
It asked for reasonable, modest salaries for officials, a judiciary
with no involvement in politics, the regulation of public-service
corporation prices, and those progressive hobby horses: the initiative, referendum, and recall. It demanded that the city be given the
legal right to own natural monopolies. It asked for the elimination
of graft from public printing. Most important for the future, it
called for an end to extensions of franchises for the Rail-Light
unless they guaranteed a three-cent fare, universal transfers, good
service, and reasonable compensation for the use of city bridges.[1]

The *Bee* made a point of publicizing its view of the Rail-
Light's business position and stake in the election. In two years, it
said, $10,000,000 in bonds would fall due, and the year after that
most of the franchises would expire. The company was capitalized
for $30,000,000, and fully two thirds if not more of that was
water. The company was in desperate shape, therefore, because
without a renewal of the franchises the stock was worthless and
the bonds worth hardly thirty cents on the dollar. In short, the
company was at the mercy of the Independents, since past experience had demonstrated that the company could not win. Joined
with them were the "Gas Merger Crowds," whose stock had been
bought by Big-Con (as they called the public-utility trust) and
their usual establishment allies.[2] The *Bee*, as usual, was somewhat
premature in its assessment, but not wrong. The trolley company
was in deep trouble, both politically and financially, and was exceedingly unpopular for reasons that were not always its fault. But
the 1907 campaign, like so many before it, was fought on vice and
tolerance more than monopoly; that issue would assume far more
importance later.

Whitlock, with his usual indifference to his own political success, went on a long vacation that summer and was not involved
in most of the petty squabbling that a few of his supporters indulged in. Excessive purity, as well as personal abrasiveness, was
a persistent factor in Independent ranks, and during the 1907
election the chief point at issue among Whitlock's followers was
whether or not one could be an Independent without signing the
platform. The faction that wrote the platform called for signa-

tures, while a large dissident group attacked this blatant bossism. The dissidents, apparently including some disappointed office seekers, included Percy Jones, Lyman Wachenheimer, William Cowell, Lewis W. Morgan, D. J. O'Rourke, John B. Merrill, and L. F. Towers. Naturally, the *Blade* and the *Times* egged them on as much as they dared. One chief grievance was the platform plank on salaries. The stated maximum for a city official was given as $4,000 per year, and the framers of the platform—E. B. Southard, Amos McDonnell, and M. W. Madge—apparently chose this sum to slap at Wachenheimer and City Solicitor Northrup, who were both earning more than that at the time. The argument would be minor and unimportant since everyone agreed that Whitlock should be renominated, but this sort of in-fighting unfortunately lasted; it bore fruit at its most sour in 1913, when Whitlock retired. Most of the newspapers in 1907 agreed that the men in the dissident group were those most devoted to Whitlock, but as he was away he never mentioned the quarrel, so his actual position—if he had one—is unknown.[3]

Despite this sort of pettiness, the campaign demonstrated that Whitlock had finally discovered the true basis for his campaigns. He spoke regularly as often as four or five times a day, and "it was the universal comment during the campaign that the meetings had almost a religious order." To the Reverend Mr. Charles Ferguson, he described these meetings again as "religious meetings in the best sense, and your own religion of democracy is being more and more exemplified in the spirit of the people of this town. I am doing little more than representing that spirit." He had, however, more work of education to do. "It has not yet expressed itself in those material forms, beautiful and artistic, which I hope to see it express itself in ere long."[4]

Whatever he was doing, whether encouraging prostitution and un-American labor unions, as his enemies declared, or the kingdom of God, as he thought, it worked. Whitlock was re-elected easily in a large Independent landslide that gave the party ten council seats to six for the usually victorious Republicans. The final returns gave Whitlock 15,787, Bartley (Rep.) 9,277, Stevenson (Dem.) 1,060, and Devine (Soc.) 672. Bartley carried only the fourth ward and ran close only in the seventh; clearly, Whitlock had appeal among all classes, not just the laborers and the foreign-born. Peter Witt, the acid-tongued populist of Cleveland, cabled his interpretation: "Dear Brand, your election again demonstrated that while men in rags never destroyed a Government, men in boiled shirts never saved one . . ." Whitlock, using in turn his own imagination, was less funny and only slightly more accurate. He wrote to Daniel Kiefer: "Our victory here was not a victory for me so much as it was a victory for all the people, and my only ambition is to make it mean just that. The issue was sharply drawn between the people themselves and privilege, and the people won gloriously."[5]

Shortly after the election, he began to cement his relationships with the Democratic machine of Cleveland mayor Tom Johnson and his associates, a group that came to include Peter Witt, Frederic C. Howe, Newton D. Baker, and Edward Bemis. Whitlock's Independent principles in no way prevented his alliances with such progressive forces, and in practice the two more radical northern cities worked effectively together against the more rural and conservative central and southern coalitions that traditionally dominated Ohio. The men worked together during campaigns, nominated each other in Democratic conventions, and were one faction in the eyes of their opponents. Thus, Tom Johnson and Governor Pattison were among the first politicians Whitlock saw after his first election, and four Clevelanders were among the first men invited to speak in the regular meetings in Golden Rule Hall.[6]

Aside from the friendships and ideologies which bound the leaders of the two cities, specific problems soon developed which Whitlock knew little about and which Johnson and his staff had confronted earlier. Whitlock always welcomed advice from these trusted friends, even sought it frequently. Late in 1906 he asked Johnson for his advice on an issue that cropped up again and again, the construction of the Cherry Street Bridge. The City Council had located the bridge at Cherry and Main streets, and Whitlock had approved, although with some doubt and hesitation, since some people wished to have the bridge built in another location. In his message of approval, he had said that he would like to have a referendum on the measure if that were possible, but that he knew of no legal means of conducting one. Some of the people who were upset over the issue had then pointed out to Whitlock that matters of policy in Cleveland were often decided by popular vote, and why did not Toledo have a chance to be as democratic as its sister city? Johnson's reply to Whitlock has not survived, but the latter's request only underlined the dependence he felt on precedents set in Cleveland.[7]

Unfortunately, the Cherry Street Bridge was not the worst of the problems of 1907. Nell was pregnant again, and the couple dearly wanted a child. Near the end of June she went to the hospital, but the baby died shortly after birth. Both husband and wife were all but prostrated. She was brave, Whitlock wrote Octavia, but their grief was deep and did not much improve with the passing days. "There was a moment on that day, just a week ago, when the world reeled, and I thought that if all was well with Nell I would ask no more." She was well, at least physically, and he was grateful, "but it is bitter to have had hands on such a pretty little girl, and then to lose her. There was something so ironical about it, something so mocking; Nell said that we have lived a little story which Hardy might have written—only have written." It is hardly any wonder that, when Nell was well enough to travel, the couple went north for a vacation and left the two factions of Independents to squabble about whether or not to support the platform. Whitlock had more important things on his mind and probably did not think about the town for several weeks.[8]

City problems traditionally are no respecters of mayors or their personal tragedies, however, and, as the two recovered, city tax problems once again took over the mayor's time. In a gesture to the smallest of entrepreneurs, he vetoed a tax on pedlars because he thought such taxes unfair to the poor. In his May tax message to the council, and in his budget, he made an announced effort to place the burden on those most able to bear it. The only man who paid his rightful tax, he said, was the man who owned his own home—if that home were small. But large mansions and business establishments, however, were not what he, unlike many socialists, disliked most. Whitlock was most scornful of the large areas of low-taxed land which people held as speculations and did not develop. The obvious results, he said, were the discouragement of improvements to the land and the reward of neglect. He also attacked untaxed franchises, but empty land received most of the scorn. Quite aside from the fact that these issues took up his time in 1907 and later, they are important also as indices of just how far Whitlock went in the ruling ideology of Ohio reform: the single-tax theories of Henry George.[9]

In his lifetime of campaigning for political reform, Henry George had concentrated on four policies, and these policies—rather than single-tax theories—gave his supporters in this most loyal of single-tax states their programs of action. He always stressed absolute free trade, the abolition of private-property values in land, the repeal of discriminatory taxes, and public ownership of public utilities. In addition to these four policies, he had certain bedrock beliefs which reappear in the thought of his followers. He believed that "the government should be restricted as nearly as possible to the preservation of order and the administration of justice." He looked toward a utopia that was both Christian and socialist in the welfare sense, "a Christian republic in the full grand meaning of the words." He disliked any concept of class struggle, for all people were equal in their interests and aims if once monopoly were destroyed, so "there is no conflict between capital and labor." He saw no flaws in capitalism as a system, and "believed that job opportunities were withheld and poverty induced by reason of wrong-headed policies and exploitative institutions . . ." Repeatedly, he stressed personal freedom. The panacea for poverty, he said, was not the single tax, but "freedom. What I see in the single tax is the means of securing that industrial freedom which will make possible other triumphs of freedom . . ."[10]

George and his Ohio followers shared many enemies. The socialists always disliked them, the wealthy in general detested and feared them, and the church except for a few mavericks opposed them. George's difficulties concerning Archbishop Corrigan and the excommunication of his loyal supporter, Father McGlynn, were accurate rehearsals of the troubles which Whitlock and the Cleveland reformers encountered later with the forces of religion in Ohio.

Finally, the intellectual approach which George used was the typical nineteenth-century device of deductive reasoning. It is perhaps misleading to speak too much of the "philosophy" of a political activist—especially in the case of the less cerebral men who campaigned in Ohio. Yet, acknowledging this caveat, the Georgist "philosophy" was to make dogmatic, abstract statements and then work from these. George did not look around him, pick up factual data, and then theorize. He proclaimed an ideal principle, "The equal right of all men to the use of the land is as clear as their right to breathe the air—it is a right proclaimed by the fact of their existence" (or some other such principle), and then applied this to what he saw, in the manner of his teacher and subsequent detractor, Herbert Spencer. Practice, especially with Brand Whitlock, often deviated from these principles, if only because Whitlock was too deeply concerned with people to consider them less important than principles. His practice, however, should not obscure the fact that he believed in the principles and often thought he was applying them, even when he was not.[11]

Georgist policies had the most immediate influence in the political arena. Despite his fame for the single tax, George had been devoted to free trade for an even longer period and had at first emphasized the latter far more. Whitlock considered his own conversion to free trade a major step in his education, but, by the time he and his friends were in office, free-trade policy was only a means of expressing a greater concern. The tariff was a special interest. So was the tax structure, since it protected big business and extracted money from poorer homeowners. So was the natural monopoly, like natural gas or a trolley or electricity. All Georgist campaigning thus tended to become a simple policy: a campaign against special interest. Every Georgist measure was an attempt to restore equal opportunity, to open the gates to every man to obtain the good life, and to eliminate the road blocks of special interest.

The Georgists did not campaign against wicked people, but rather against the situations which they felt made special privilege inevitable. Since the single-taxers regularly shared both ideas and precedents—at least in Cleveland and Toledo—their ideas were naturally alike, so the result of a look at all of them is a composite, intellectual portrait of one variety of progressive vision. "It is to *economic change,* and not to political change, that the people must look for the solution of this problem," Tom Johnson wrote. "Not *lawbreakers,* but *lawmakers* are responsible for bad economic conditions . . ." The existence of a natural monopoly meant, to most politicians, franchises to be granted. Any franchise, the Georgists maintained, was an invitation to corruption in the bribery of politicians by businessmen. "When a private business can live only by bribery, then the logical conclusion is that we can't have that kind of private business," Frederic Howe reasoned about the conditions that confronted Cleveland, Toledo, and much of the nation. "Everywhere, the cause of corruption is the same. It is privilege, not wealth; franchises, not business; the few, not the many, that have overthrown our cities within the past few years." The only solution was government ownership of all industries that could not be run competitively. The temptation, not the man tempted, was the villain. Lincoln Steffens, who was as friendly to the Cleveland reformers as he was to Whitlock, and the man who made Tom Johnson famous as "the best Mayor of the best-governed city in the United States," put the position succinctly to a questioning bishop. "Most people, you know, say it was Adam. But Adam, you remember, he said that it was Eve, the woman; she did it. And Eve said, no, no, it wasn't she; it was the serpent. And that's where you clergy have stuck ever since. You blame the serpent, Satan. Now I come and I am trying to show you that it was, it is, the apple."[12]

Municipal ownership would dispose of the apple. There is, Howe proclaimed, "a well-defined line of demarcation between the functions which should be performed by the city and those which should be left to private control. *That line is fixed by monopoly.* Whatever is of necessity a monopoly should be a public monopoly . . ." In Cleveland as well as Toledo the war was fought against the street-car combines. In other cities at various times, natural-gas, electric, and railroad monopolies all came under attack. At the same time, the attempts at a fairer assessment of property, particularly in Cleveland, aroused great opposition. Few writers have emphasized that the single tax in practice was usually a campaign for fair taxation. The assessors wished to discourage land speculation, so they raised rates on unimproved land. They wished to prevent discriminatory rates for trusts, so they insisted on one-hundred-per-cent evaluation and taxed corporate properties as heavily as they did private homes. Nowhere did they try to seize land and make it public property.[13]

The result was an almost mystic urban utopia that captivated the imagination. George was always a city man, from his birth in Philadelphia to his death in New York. His followers developed the city into a mystique that, in its most devout moments, had elements of a religious incantation. Baker called the program of his urban utopia "civitism," which he defined as a combination of "home rule and the Golden Rule for Cleveland." Whitlock wrote of Johnson that "he knew intuitively that the city in all ages has been the outpost of civilization, and that if the problem of democracy is to be solved at all it is to be solved first in the city." Frederic Howe devoted almost half his life to a vision of the city beautiful. In book after book he explored the possibilities in America and abroad for urban development, always with the hope that the city would be the intellectual and cultural center of society. "The possibility of a free, orderly, and beautiful city became to me an absorbing passion," Howe wrote. He had "an architectonic vision of what a city might be." He saw it as "a thing with a mind, with a conscious purpose, seeing far in advance of the present and taking precautions for the future." He "dreamed about them." In his most famous book on the subject, *The City, The Hope of Democracy*, a book which Whitlock read, reread, and quoted with great admiration, Howe became a psalmist. The city "is an organism capable of conscious and concerted action, responsive, ready and intelligent." It is "El Dorado, the promised land which fires the imagination," the one thing which "has given the world culture, enlightenment, and education along with industry and commercial opportunity."[14]

These beliefs attain greater importance in perspective, for they are the source of the almost fanatical localism which dominated these men. This faith in the city was a major factor in their opposition to almost all governmental action coming from outside the local community. During these years, the issue was stated in two words: home rule. Newton Baker's biographer has pointed out that Baker's "interest in local autonomy was so profound that he believed *self*-government more important than *good* government," since under it a people could at least educate themselves. With measures imposed from Washington, neither happiness nor education could come. Johnson said that "the most pressing of all civic problems is that of municipal home rule by the people themselves." All the evils of monopoly and special privilege resulted from outside interference. Whitlock agreed. "The first requisite" of municipal reform is "home rule; that is, the people of the city must have the right to decide how they themselves are to be governed, how they are to raise their taxes, how they are to control their public utilities, and all that sort of thing." As Howe neatly phrased the Georgist position: "If our analysis of conditions has been correct, the trouble with our cities is not too much democracy, but too little democracy; not too little state supervision, but too much state supervision."[15]

To achieve the realization of their vision, the progressives needed to go to Columbus and fight for the legal right to erect their utopia. During the years of Whitlock's first two terms, the chief legislative means to this goal was known as the Paine Bill, after Toledo Republican Louis H. Paine, who introduced it. The landslide that swept both Whitlock and Democratic Governor Pattison into office gave Johnson and his friends at the state house hope for their bill. In the Senate, Toledo Independent Sylvester Lamb held the deciding vote, so the progressives could demand large concessions for his support. They were successful, and Frederic Howe became chairman of the committee on committees and promptly packed the appropriate committees with his own men. In the House, however, the Republicans retained control, and despite Republican authorship of the bill its Toledo sponsorship was more than enough to stigmatize it. Despite the revolt of a few Republican Independents, the majority party held firm enough to the reins of power to mute all clamor for change. The session began hopefully as Pattison asked for such legislation in his inaugural, and the Association of Mayors had prepared a version of the bill which received all but complete approval from Attorney General Wade Ellis, who had written the code of 1902. The Paine Bill called for single men to replace committees in the direction of public works and public safety and gave the power of appointment of these men and the city solicitor to the mayor. It asked that the merit system be extended to cover all departments, that city tax commissions be reinstated and chosen by the mayor, and that the cities be allowed to enact public ownership of utilities if they wished. It also called for the elimination of red tape in the granting of franchises. Two other bills were also introduced with some of the same provisions, in the hope that at least one could get through. The attempt was doomed, as hostile House committees and railway lobbyists quickly went to work and emasculated the bills so badly that Johnson had his men withdraw support.[16]

After Whitlock's re-election, Johnson had his men try again.

This time the reformers used their experience from past defeats. Instead of an omnibus bill stamped with the brand of Cleveland and Toledo, they separated the parts of the bill and gave them to men who did not come from Cleveland and Toledo. Behind-the-scenes maneuvering obtained enough Independent Republican support to complement large Democratic majorities in favor of the reforms, and the measure finally passed. Whitlock was of course pleased, for the new law gave him the right to appoint the directors of public safety and public service and thus made them directly responsible to him, and through him to the people. In an article for the *Bee*, he announced to Toledo his approval and compared the new system to the federal government, with its responsible executive head and appointive cabinet; it was scarcely Frederic Howe's urban utopia, but it was a start.[17] The rest of the session depressed him, however, for progressive legislation on the initiative and referendum did not win approval, and the Anti-Saloon League lobby was more active and successful than it had any right to be.[18]

Meanwhile, the successful politician was submerged under a pile of requests for his name, his presence, and his voice. In early January, 1908, he traveled east, speaking and visiting his old friends.[19] The visit to Lincoln Steffens was particularly welcome. Aside from the pleasures of renewed friendship, the two men managed to obtain a commission from the Newspaper Enterprise Association to attend both the Republican and Democratic conventions and turn in eight hundred words per day on the proceedings. Whitlock predictably found far more to admire in William Jennings Bryan than in William Howard Taft, for all his doubts about Bryan's abilities. "We were well paid and had lots of fun besides," he wrote later. At the same time, he found that certain of his friends had been using his name to drum up support for the forthcoming gubernatorial campaign, and he promptly squelched the maneuver. Such a movement as an Independent campaign for governor, he wrote in a widely distributed formal letter, "cannot be artificially organized; it cannot be constructed and given to the people." Rather, such a movement must "come out of the people spontaneously, as it were, and whenever the people are ripe for such a splendid demonstration of democracy, the movement will come and the candidates will be found easily enough." Meanwhile, the Republican-Democratic partisanship was a cruel farce, and the people had to be educated about the need for spontaneous democracy. Whitlock's view had more than its share of naïveté, but that is the way, more or less, he had become mayor of Toledo, and he was apparently sincere in thinking governors were spawned in similar fashion. Certainly his views say more for his idealism than they do for his political intelligence.[20]

The national election campaign itself put him in something of a quandary. Late in September, Eugene Debs came to Toledo in his Red Special, whistle-stopping for votes. The two men, friendly by nature and sharing midwestern radical backgrounds, were cordial during their meeting, and Whitlock thought Debs "without any doubt the most intelligent and, possibly, the most practical man running for President this fall." He even contributed $5 to the campaign and received three cheers for his gesture. Debs "is a wonderful personality—full of enthusiasm and fire, and with the biggest heart that I know of." Unfortunately, the socialists as a group were too "authoritarian" for him, although their earnestness and devotion to principles appealed to him; realism dictated that the only real choice was between Taft and Bryan. Theodore Roosevelt's bombast quite disgusted him, but the "most sickening thing in the whole campaign has been the cynical, shameless admission on the part of the Tories that Taft is their man, and that his promises to carry out the Roosevelt policies—whatever that means—are but the usual pre-election hypocrisies of the campaigner." Thus, he eventually moved unenthusiastically toward Bryan, since no alternative seemed to offer itself. But the man who went for the Gold Democrats in 1896 was still far from any kind of populism.[21]

The state elections, while scarcely cause for jubilation, were destined to give progressives at least a feeble ray of hope. If Bryan was too radical and irresponsible, Judson Harmon looked too much like Grover Cleveland in his tendency toward high-minded immobility. Tom Johnson had no love for Harmon and said so, loudly and not in good temper. He preferred Whitlock, and when that prospect seemed increasingly unlikely, he gave his support to the moderately progressive Atlee Pomerene. The only other Democrat visible, John Welty, soon gave up, and the preconvention battle was long and hard. With his past career as a successful government and railroad lawyer, Harmon had the support of most of the conservative Democrats, but Johnson knew that he was firmly opposed to measures of direct legislation, such as the initiative and referendum, and this made the man a pariah in Johnson's eyes. In a typical case of political compromise, Harmon received the nomination and Johnson dictated much of his platform; so the Democrats had a conservative man running on a progressive platform. Johnson finally controlled himself enough to give his support, and the party went into the election reasonably well united. It was lucky. Despite a victorious William Howard Taft as a native-son winner of the Presidency, the Republicans were rocked in midcampaign by a scandal involving Senator Foraker and the Standard Oil Company; Harmon managed to squeak into office by a narrow margin, taking a few more scattered Democrats in with him than would otherwise have been expected. His administration proved capable but unspectacular and as a rule received little attention from the mayor of Toledo. But it was the first full Democratic term in many years, was heartening to the faithful, and was an omen of things to come. Reform now had an outside chance of statewide support.[22]

Whatever his political interests, however, Whitlock never ceased his traveling around the country, his speechmaking, and his visiting of his few close friends. In January he visited Buffalo and Chicago, then stopped off at East Aurora to see Elbert Hubbard. For a week he was sick in bed, meanwhile planning one of his longest and most rewarding trips east. In early February he went to Boston to see Steffens and some of his other friends, particularly Mark A. De Wolfe Howe, who had commissioned Whitlock's book on Lincoln. He and Nell took a Pullman through the Berkshires, enjoying the mountains and alive to the beauty of the snow on the hilltops. They arrived in Boston on a warm afternoon, greeted Steffens, and went with him to the Touraine, a hotel quite "luxuriously velvet-carpeted and soft and overheated and vulgar . . ." Then came a mad and whirling three days, begun by a dinner at the City Club, where three or four hundred men discussed, "in a lofty and wholly unintelligent and inefficient way, a new city charter." Whitlock spoke briefly, then went with Steffens to a Lincoln Day celebration at Faneuil Hall, where both men spoke. They and their wives then had a late supper with a small group of Proper

Bostonians, where Steffens persisted in asking questions that called for radical, anarchistic answers; it was, he explained later, all part of his scheme to educate Boston.

Three days later they arrived in New York. The next day Whitlock and Nell went to renew their friendship with Howells, in his new and sparsely decorated apartment on West 57th Street. A "mild and depressing" gentleman from Milwaukee, whose name Whitlock never did catch, was there to cast a pall over the meeting, and about all Whitlock recalled later was the nervous Mrs. Howells's fluttering in and out in a black dress about thirty years out of style. He did manage to take Howells aside for a chat, however, and they discussed and largely agreed on their political views, while Howells, with more kindness than perception, told his young disciple that he and Robert Herrick were "the two most hopeful figures in American literature." Later, Whitlock attended a wedding and the theatre, and then he and Nell set out for Washington.[23]

As soon as he could, he made an appointment to see the President. When he arrived at the White House, he took his place among the personages who were also waiting. Soon Roosevelt came in in his energetic way, glared about him, and came up to ask Whitlock to remain. He quickly, and in a loud voice, disposed of the senators and other visitors, purposefully making it impossible for them to have quiet, undercover confidential talk with him.

When the others were gone, Roosevelt pointed a finger at Whitlock, screwed up his face and stared at him myopically: "I'll tell you where we differ. You think no one should be killed; I think the world would be a good deal better off if some undesirable people were out of it!" Whitlock enjoyed the chat, or rather the presidential monologue—whatever the President's views on capital punishment—and he found Roosevelt fully aware of events in Toledo and sympathetic toward reform there.

At one point, Roosevelt startled his caller by asking, point blank: "What do you think is the greatest thing I have done?"

It was a tough question, especially since Whitlock did not always agree with either Roosevelt or some of his followers.

"Well, sir," he finally answered, "I think that the greatest thing you have done has been to create a new sense of decency in the public life in this country."

Whitlock was perfectly sincere, and Roosevelt patently enjoyed the answer. "That is what I think, and that is what I wanted to do." They then sat down to a long chat that included such old topics as John Hay's hatred of senators and Mark Hanna's less-than-perfectly-devout opinion of his protégé McKinley.[24]

Whitlock's trip ended on the last day of his thirty-ninth year, and the approaching birthday left him feeling old and useless; he returned to Toledo and quickly regained his good humor. Octavia had sent him Jane Carlyle's letters and a long letter of her own for a present, and the city-hall reporters gave him forty "gorgeous red carnations." Most touching of all, in one primary school in town, all the little children made birthday greetings for their favorite mayor, each greeting card with a four-leaf clover. The greetings, all bound together, also had childish best wishes laboriously copied on them. The whole affair left the sentimental mayor on the verge of tears.[25]

Unfortunately for Whitlock's temper and digestion, 1909 was one of those years that began well and then deteriorated. Shortly after the arrival of the four-leaf clovers, Whitlock discovered that the Anti-Saloon League was after him in earnest. Fed up with his unwillingness to pursue drinkers into their dirty holes, the prohibitionists announced their intention of getting a state law pushed through which would allow the removal of mayors who would not enforce state ordinances. Their frank and announced intention was to dispose of Whitlock. As if that were not enough, Nell's mother arrived with the summer heat, adding to his burdens those of a son-in-law, lest Whitlock had had any doubts. She claimed to be ill of rheumatism and soon planted herself in the room usually reserved for Octavia's visits. She brought with her "a trained nurse, and flowers, and medicine, and all the paraphernalia of invalidism." Whitlock had little sympathy. "Her attack, I think, is due to the long emotional debauch in which Springfield recently indulged under the name of the Billy Sunday Revival, the exhaustion of which revived in her rheumatic diathesis, and in others what physical ills I know not . . ." To compensate for these problems, Whitlock began solacing himself with Carlyle and allowed himself a good spate of hatred for poor Froude, whose attempt at an honest biography of the man made Whitlock sputter with contempt. All in all, he was dyspeptic about the immediate future. "I need a rest; my roving over the country and incessant shouting all the winter brought its inevitable result this spring, and for nearly two months I have been miserable . . ." The summer sun cheered him up slightly, but the thought of "the gloomy and hateful prospect of another campaign" was more than he wished to bear. He hated being mayor and wished only for the leisure to write. But his sense of duty simply would not let him stop.[26]

And the mayor's office would not leave him alone. He apparently contracted with Bobbs-Merrill in 1909 for a book on "the free city"—to sum up his vision in much the same way that Fred Howe did in his books—but the crusaders against just about everything never let him alone, and the book was never written. He managed a brief visit to the Michigan resort of Wequetonsing, and enjoyed a meeting with his new friend Robert Hunter, but such fleeting pleasures could not compensate for the daily drudgery of his office during one of Toledo's hottest summers. "The very devil seems to have taken general and personal command of things about here, and I have been tried beyond endurance. At the Mayor's office—the place is a veritable mother of dead dogs!—there has been one continuous stream of unreasonable complaints, all the nastiness of politics, and positive, brutal insult! I never knew such a time in the years I have been there, and how I long to get out!"[27]

The end of the summer saw the first signs of the problem that dominated Whitlock's last years in office. After simmering on a back burner since the early Jones administrations, the issue of Rail-Light franchises was slowly coming to a boil as the expiration dates for the earlier franchises slowly arrived. From April through July, the *Bee* ran a long series on the company and the amount of water it contained. By late September, the mayor began to take charge of the campaign, basing his moves, as usual, on the precedents set in Cleveland. His first move was to write to Peter Witt to ask him to find out how much the tax valuation of the Lucas County railroad was—to use as ammunition during the coming campaign, if they said what he thought they would say. Witt answered that he gave Whitlock's letter to Cleveland's expert on everything, Edward Bemis, and this letter marks the entrance of Bemis into the Toledo battles. Meanwhile, Witt advised that the best way to impress the electorate would be to get the railroad values for Indiana, then to have a map made of Ohio and Indiana showing the same railroad in both states and writing the figure of the values placed per mile on the road by both states. The results would be impressive: "The Indiana values will be considerably higher when in fact it [sic] ought to be less, for the great values that attach to railroads are, as you know, the terminal facilities in large cities. Ohio, of course, has more of such places. The Lake Shore terminal in Toledo is worth more than all the terminals of that line in Indiana." Witt also volunteered advice, useful later, on the tactics of explaining tax rates; his experience in tax problems in Cleveland proved invaluable for the considerably less sophisticated mayor of Toledo.[28]

Nothing, however, was important enough to interrupt Toledo's biennial sport, for 1909 was once again an election year. The friction within Independent ranks, which caused no little pain in 1907, became a bit more severe. The key man was a new Independent, Cornell Schreiber. His supporters, including Oscar Sabin, Otto N. Clemmons, Phil Birkenhauer, Amos McDonnall and Stanley Kryzaniak, helped him receive the nomination for city solicitor, over the vehement protests of many of Whitlock's closest friends, led by the mayor's secretary, Bernard Dailey. Aside from a few irresponsible charges about forming machines and deserting Independent dogma, neither side shed more light than heat in the debate, and in fact the friction seems to have been chiefly personal. But both sides fell in behind Whitlock, and both were attacked for nominating a man so obviously under Boss Negley Cochran's thumb, a man so dreamy and indecisive, a man so soft on vice, and so on, through the usual round of charge and countercharge. There were occasional surprises, as when Percy Jones came out in support of Republican candidate David T. Davies and when a phony independent ticket took the ballot name away from the real Independents; the latter had to take refuge under a new name, the Toledo Independent Ticket. Perhaps most intriguing was a local case of life imitating art. In "The Gold Brick," Whitlock had written of a cartoonist who had sold out to the opposition and had begun to attack, in his drawings, a mayor (a cross between Johnson and Jones) whom he really loved. In 1909, Sid Smith, who two years earlier had drawn for Cochran in the *News-Bee*, had been hired away by Hearst interests and was soon drawing anti-Whitlock cartoons for the Toledo *Times*. Oddly enough, the cartoons degenerated in both cases: in the story, because the artist's heart was not in it; in real life, because the *Times* had no Negley Cochran to give its cartoonist the ideas he could not think up for himself.

The campaign itself was rough, and Whitlock lost a good deal of both patience and charity under the repeated provocations. David Davies he called "a typical ward-heeling, saloon-campaigning, gang politician who walks 'gallus' and talks tough, and for thirteen and a half years has been holding some office or other." The real reason for the intensity of the campaign was the increasing desperation of the Rail-Light, most of whose franchises would expire during 1910. Rail-Light money bought the *Times* and turned it into an anti-Whitlock scandal sheet, and the mayor scarcely needed such a provocation to imagine countless plots against himself and the people on the part of the greedy capitalists —notions all the more enticing for being partly true. In a year in which reform suffered its worst setbacks in years—including the defeat of Tom Johnson—Whitlock managed once again to win a sweeping victory. The Toledo council had three Republicans to thirteen Independents; Davies managed to carry only the seventh ward and was close only in the fourth, fifth, and thirteenth wards (the last his home ward). The final results were: Whitlock, 15,582; Davies, 10,580; Patterson (Soc.), 741; Eger (Dem.), 495; and Scheble (I.V.), 128.[29] As Steffens wrote him in doleful congratulations: "You won. You alone were victorious this year. All the rest of us were beaten . . . I have felt the defeat of Mayor Tom deeper than I care to say . . ."[30]

Whitlock as usual felt both overwhelmed and sarcastic. Within two weeks of the election his desk was piled high with requests for offices, which in turn was nothing compared to the "pest of parsons and pugilists who are trying to moralize or demoralize the town . . . I was roundly berated by the opposition newspapers during the campaign for my golf—for the fact not for the quality, in which latter all of their animadversion might have been well-deserved." For all his wit, however, the defeat of Tom Johnson hurt deeply, and severely strained the deep democratic faith that Whitlock tried hard to share with Johnson. "I knew just how you felt and could feel for you," he wrote Johnson's chief deputy, Newton Baker. "I have felt rather sneaking myself to think that I was elected and old Tom was beaten." They read the news of the defeat "with tears in our eyes." He knew, he continued, "that it is all for the best and that the people are right in the long run; I understand the philosophy and believe it fully—as long as everything is going all right, which is the way, I presume, with most people's philosophy, but thank God, I am like the good old-fashioned machine politicians in this, that I like to see my friends win." Whatever his attitude to events in other cities, however, he was soon deep in a number of city problems. During the first months of his new term, he found himself active in the revision of local tax schedules, in the reorganization of the city administration along the lines of the Paine Bill, and in the ever-present controversy over the Cherry Street Bridge. In addition to all this, a lady politely but firmly requested him to recommend her verses to "Dean Howell." The mayor politely but firmly refused.[31]

Under such circumstances, the public-speaking duties of the public man took him out of Toledo and its local affairs with gratifying regularity. He protested valiantly that "I don't like this lecturing business anyhow," and was graphic about what it did to him: ". . . you sit there during the long dinner with your digestive processes absolutely at a standstill because your insides are already full of apprehension over your own speech"—but still he spoke, as though helpless to change. Obviously, whatever his qualms, he enjoyed escaping his responsibilities whenever he could. Not only did he speak, he traveled about the country as though in flight, actually looking for engagements. Early in January, 1910, he and Nell made a quick trip to Washington and New York, and "saw everybody, from our poor, fat, subservient butter-ball of a President, up to Mr. Howells." The visit with Howells proved particularly pleasant, as daughter Mildred, son John, and little baby grandson Billie made a family portrait delightful to the man who never had children of his own. Howells made a point of telling Whitlock that he was writing one of his *North American Review* blessings for his disciple, and he asked for copies of Whitlock's books and short stories. His own copies were then at Kittery.[32]

No matter how far Whitlock traveled, however, Toledo's problems remained. The chief villain in 1910 was once again the Anti-Saloon League, with its Black Bill for the removal of all mayors unwilling to enforce state laws. Whitlock was deeply concerned, and with good reason. Early in March he made a rather desperate, last-minute attempt to get national opposition to the bill from his friends. He asked Clarence Darrow, for example, to write a letter against the bill for the Scripps-McRae League and concluded: "If they try this on me, as I have no doubt they will, I am wondering whether I will fight or whether I will have nerve enough to put my theory of non-resistance to the supreme test." As the legislature worked on, apparently inexorably, he became gloomier and gloomier. As he wrote Steffens: "I have thought over the matter until my mind works in a circle and I can't find a tangent anywhere." He could see only three alternatives, should the bill pass: ". . . first, I might resign, which would be cowardice; secondly, I might attempt to enforce all the laws, which would be tyranny; thirdly, I might go on in the way I have done, which might mean removal and humiliation." He might look at the prospect of the end of his mayoral career as an attractive one under most circumstances, but not this one. "Upon the whole I am quite unhappy and miserable though I wouldn't admit that much to anyone else." Fortunately, Whitlock achieved salvation by the narrowest of margins. The bill passed the House, and was defeated in the Senate by a vote of seventeen to seventeen; a motion to reconsider it was then lost by the same vote.[33]

In contrast, the Cherry Street Bridge controversy, while full of irritation and exasperation, at least had moments of slapstick and did not threaten the mayor's job. Briefly, the issue was quite simple: the present bridge was plainly too low for the ice that had to flow under it each spring when the thaw came and the water often rose to flood height. Everyone admitted four years earlier that the bridge was unsafe and needed replacement. Since then, the whole business had been tied up in the courts, and many people seemed terribly bothered when Whitlock did not accept the lowest bid submitted—because he thought the company was not reliable. Aside from the gray hairs the haggling gave the mayor, the whole business illustrates the pettiness that motivates democratic taxpayers when they have the time, money, and befogged mental processes to make life miserable for city officials. The sole redeeming virtue of the affair was the cast of characters. One Harvey P. Platt led the fight, a crank so pure that even his lawyer deserted him partway through the case. Whitlock referred to him as "the antediluvian who is spending his declining years fighting this new bridge. From the fact he has already dragged out this contest to an extent equal to the Civil War we have known all along that he would not quit fighting until he is dead." Platt's motives remained obscure in the haze of legalities. He apparently wanted the new bridge built somewhere else and on a different plan. Logic, however, is foreign to many aged crusaders, and even this is hypothesis. The other star for the opposition was the "Hungarian pettifogger, Geza Farkas," who was apparently imported by the Platt group for unspecified mischief. Farkas was an alien who had left Hungary chiefly because he was wanted for embezzlement; "he was not extradited because the lawyer over there seems to have heard something about the Golden Rule and said he didn't care to prosecute him." Farkas, once in Toledo, was a leader of the campaign of suit bringing, but "before they could qualify him as a tax payer" a couple that was leading the battle "had to convey a lot to him, which, judging from Farkas's past record, they will never get back." Obviously progressivism was not the least of Toledo's attractions to him, although Farkas soon passed mercifully enough into oblivion, his cause lost with the mayor's temper.[34]

At the same time, the Rail-Light controversy became hotter. Late in March, company president Albion Lang offered to open the monopoly's books, in the desperate hope that he could thus win new franchises. Whitlock accepted without making any promises. He promptly contacted Newton Baker and begged for advice; Baker replied at some length, urging that he make all moves carefully and emphasizing the need for the city to retain as much control over the negotiations and the whole system as was possible. Always ready to rely on earlier Cleveland experience, Whitlock then hired the thoroughly experienced accounting company of Nau, Tanner and Rusk to go over the company books, and they promptly did so. Judging from the conciliatory tone of his letters, Albion Lang gave them every assistance and seemed ready at all times to comply with reasonable requests from the mayor's office.[35]

But whatever his intentions locally, Whitlock always found his attention drawn toward the state elections that were approaching.

Steffens and the other journalists who knew a good story had established his national eminence long ago; they wrote glowingly of Toledo and Whitlock whether the mayor actually accompished anything or not. Within the state everyone at least knew his name, for, after Tom Johnson, Whitlock was the most obvious target for any complaints about growing vice, immorality, and radicalism. That was part of the trouble; the other part was the Toledo insistence on Independent rather than Democratic principles. That policies in Toledo and Cleveland, the Democratic bastion, were all but identical and that the leaders were all close friends did not lessen the suspicion aroused by Whitlock's name when the time came for electing the faithful to important offices. That everyone also knew he was a Democrat nationally did not seem to make much difference. Local politics was the bread and butter that fed the petty chieftains, and Whitlock was notoriously uncharitable when it came to that sort of food. He soon had his reward.

Whatever support Whitlock had within the Democratic Party came strictly from the Toledo and Cleveland counties, and with the defeat of Tom Johnson, Newton Baker and Peter Witt now manned the cheering stations. On May 28, Baker wrote to Whitlock that "a few enlightened people in this state are hoping that some sort of political upheaval will take place which will result in your being sent to the Senate of the United States." Baker frankly admitted that he was one of the conspirators: ". . . while I don't know how much that effort would further your opportunity to study Russian literature or in any other way contribute to your personal happiness, I do know that it will be good for the Senate and enormously good for me." Whitlock did nothing to discourage him. He would accept the position, he wrote a week later, "if it came in such a manner to leave me free to represent the people." He would prefer a Senate seat to the mayoralty because "the position would be more congenial to my taste" than an executive position, "although I have hoped that at the end of this term as Mayor, I could get out and devote myself to my literary work, which is my first and only love." He was, in other words, courting a draft with minimum modesty but unwilling to bestir himself much. Besides, whatever his occasional naïveté, he sometimes had a firm grasp on practical politics: he was "too radical" for Ohio Democrats and had "about as much chance of being elected senator as [he did] of being chosen Premier of Great Britain . . ." The convention simply would not endorse him: ". . . if it were to endorse a radical, it would more readily turn to Pomerene than to me," for "he has always preserved that superstition known as party regularity."[36]

In the days before popular election of senators, the fall state campaign was only for the governorship and the legislature; the latter would then choose the senators. Governor Harmon, as an honest and capable middle-of-the-roader, received renomination as a matter of course at the Dayton Democratic Convention in June. He did not inspire the radicals one way or the other. He simply bored them, and they saw no sense in fighting him. Newton Baker could have had the nomination for attorney general but he declined. The Democratic platform proved to be a compromise one. It stressed: efficiency and economy; ratification of the income-tax amendment, initiative, and referendum; regulation of all public utilities; and direct election of United States senators. Harmon was at most lukewarm about these latter planks. Baker had fought hard for his favorite ideas, but took his defeat in good grace, and he and Harmon united behind the ticket, which included Atlee Pomerene for lieutenant governor. Whitlock was thoroughly uninspired by the whole affair. "It is known, of course, that I support Harmon," he wrote Baker, "though the enthusiasm of my support is not riotous or even exuberant . . ." Peter Witt was characteristically less subtle. Harmon is "a four flusher," he wrote Whitlock, without specifying details.[37]

In the campaign the Republicans were badly split, and Harmon slaughtered the Republican-machine candidate, Warren G. Harding, by over 100,000 votes, pulling most of his ticket along with him, a remarkable achievement in Republican Ohio. The Democrats even managed to obtain a legislative edge of eighty-eight to sixty-three, and so to them fell the choice of a successor to Senator Charles Dick. Immediately politicians started creeping out of the wormholes of the party mansion, eager for the only high office open to men without the degrading and often discouraging necessity of a popular campaign. John R. McLean all but openly tried to buy friends, so strong were the habits of the past; Congressman Carl Anderson claimed wide labor support; scattered votes were favorable toward former governor James E. Campbell,

Colonel James Kilbourne, John J. Lentz, and M. A. Daugherty. Baker of course was for Whitlock. But the two leading candidates were Edward W. Hanley and Atlee Pomerene. Hanley was the son of an Irish laborer who had worked his way up in the business world before entering politics. He was all but boss of Dayton County and had Congressman James M. Cox as campaign chairman. He had close ties to certain utility interests, however, and was more conservative even than Harmon. Pomerene, on the other hand, although so colorless as to be almost invisible, had long been a friend of Tom Johnson and had enjoyed his support in earlier campaigns. Although progressive only in a stolid, unspectacular way, he looked positively promising next to the competition. Baker assessed the situation: due to the strength of the Hanley candidacy, he wrote Whitlock, the Cuyahoga delegation would have to come out strong at first for Pomerene, even though preferring Whitlock, for fear that Hanley might win. The only chance Baker saw would be for Whitlock to emerge as a dark horse in the event of a Pomerene-Hanley deadlock.[38]

Whitlock apparently never raised his hopes too high. "The democracy of this state may be depended upon to send either a lawyer who would be in the category of those known to the police if he were not of that profession, or some distinguished example of dignified neutrality in a long frock coat and with an orotund delivery," he wrote nastily to Albert Nock. "So bid the East be of good cheer, the long list of bright crooks and dull nonentities which Ohio has furnished the nation, will not be broken now." Presumably Hanley was the crook and Pomerene the nonentity, although the remark does seem a bit extreme, with some little sign of the frustrated aspiration that lay behind it. After a bitter series of debates, Pomerene squeaked to victory and Hanley took his defeat with great ill grace. James Cox promptly endorsed the victor, who actually had views more like his own than did his own candidate. Newton Baker and the *Bee* were both pleased. Tom Johnson's endorsement was no longer the kiss of death, and reform democracy finally seemed to be winning a few statewide elections. Whitlock apparently kept his skeptical snorts to himself and his close friends.[39]

Now he had no excuse for ignoring local problems.

CHAPTER 8

The Life of Art (III):

Street Cars (1910-1913)

THE POSTELECTION LULL did in fact give Whitlock time to assess himself and his terms in office, and he liked much of what he saw. Indignant about persistent reports that municipal ownership was a failure in Toledo, he wrote Louis Post to make sure that single-tax editor was correctly informed. He pointed with pride to the new waterworks, which more than paid for itself and was working to the satisfaction of the entire city; to the new garbage plant; and even to the cemetery, which actually turned back $6,000 a year to the city. But most of the city beautiful was still under construction, some of it scarcely past the dream stage. The Cherry Street Bridge case was still in court, but late in November the City Council voted to issue bonds to provide for a new city hall, which, plus a proposed new Memorial Building, would hopefully go up "in the vicinity of our Court House and these three will make the beginning of a civic center." Naturally, the literary man found traces of irony in the situation. The odd part of the matter he wrote to his consulting architect, Arnold Brunner, was that the Business Men's Club and the Chamber of Commerce were now behind these plans; Whitlock had proposed the plans in his first weeks as mayor and had received no encouragement what-

ever. "All this amuses me the more because the Business Men's
Club and the Chamber of Commerce have always assumed that I
didn't know how to do anything but write books and dream
dreams," and they were sure that he did not "do either of these very
well although they do not read nor dream even when they sleep;
there are, however, some good fellows among them and I am
anxious to get them interested in helping me carry forward these
plans and I don't care anything about the credit."[1]

But the real issue that was taking up his time, costing him
sleep, and ruining his digestion was the inevitable street-car feud.
By December he was so involved that he finally did actually manage to cancel his schedule of speaking engagements—probably the
chief beneficial result for his personal life. Time was slowly running
out for the company, and the long battle begun in the early years
of the Jones administration at last had an end in sight. The company was in trouble and everyone knew it. The panic of 1907 and
the added shock of Whitlock's re-election had sent the price of its
stock down from 19⅜ shortly before election day to 9 by the end
of the year. Even that was not all. The bonds, $4,866,000 worth,
fell from 93½ to 84 by the first week in December, and at the
January meeting president H. A. Everett called the previous year's
activity "unsatisfactory" and said that the company would omit
dividends. Money was tight in Toledo at the time, and this action
may have meant no more than that no local banks were able to
offer credit, so politics may not have been entirely to blame. At
any rate, Everett predicted a profitable 1908. He was wrong. The
company defaulted interest payments on the bonds in July, and
the price sagged to 79. Whatever the cause, Rail-Light was perilously close to bankruptcy.

To the bondholders, it all seemed like a temporary embarrassment, and few considered the possibility of watered stock. The
local businessmen knew that their own credit was tight, and they
assumed that the company was basically sound in finances and
engineering. They then banded together, and made arrangements
for the 5-per-cent bonds maturing in 1909 to become 6-per-cent
bonds due in 1912. They also arranged among themselves to deposit extant securities with a committee, to make sure that no one
began foreclosure proceedings. They then hired the firm of Ford,
Bacon & Co. of New York to come and analyze the property.

They in turn recommended a $3,000,000 improvement and modernization to get the company on its feet again. Unfortunately, the company could never raise a cent without an extension of the franchises, for no one dared invest in a concern that would soon lose its right to operate except at the whim of a reform mayor. To the company, accustomed as it was to the business habits of the nineteenth century, the whole matter was unendurable. Albion Lang, its chief spokesman, again and again decried the involvement of a public service in politics. Franchises, he said, should be perpetual and above politics; when they were not, confusion reigned and proper business was impossible. "No developing community of size and importance should tolerate a state of affairs which makes impossible the upbuilding of the public utilities with capital borrowed at reasonable rates. It is desirable in the highest degree that the financing of public utilities corporations shall be conducted on a basis that will maintain the integrity of their capital investment and secure a reasonable return thereon." From a business standpoint, Lang was perfectly right. No matter how high-minded the company might be, it simply could not give good service without adequate capital—and that required franchises.

Where Rail-Light really lost its battle was in the area now known as public relations. In many cities corrupt politics was more than enough to drive an honest and high-minded businessman to despair, but Toledo was not corrupt in its politics and everyone knew it. Yet the best vote-getting issue, campaign after campaign, was the water in Rail-Light stock. The Independents won again and again on this one issue, with the support of Negley Cochran and the *Bee* and its successor, the *News-Bee*. The company made little effort to improve its image but, instead, retreated into a little hole and snarled threats about what the politicians and the people were doing to honest capitalism. Lang and his friends knew they had done nothing wrong, morally or criminally. They were not stock waterers, and they tended to take personally charges that the stock they held was watered. Naturally the men who were guilty and who had gained all the profits were long since dead or moved away, and Lang was left with his water. Both sides were right: the stock was watered, and yet the company did not have enough money to give good service. The city would not renew the franchise because the stock was watered, among other things. Yet without the renewal, men who bought stock and bonds in good faith were penalized, and the city received poorer and poorer transportation. It was a vicious circle, and blame is a concept irrelevant to it.[2]

The *News-Bee* was deadly in its analysis of Rail-Light finances and its assessment of the amount of water. It took the company's annual report for 1908 and extracted the official item of $755,424.66 for interest charges (in 1912 the figure was $755,425). Figured at 5 per cent, the presumed investment necessitating such charges was $15,108,533. The *News-Bee* then pointed out that by any reasonable, that is, non-company, assessment, the proper value of company properties was at most $6,000,000, or $300,000 for interest. The rest was water, and thus the people were being overcharged $455,424.66 per year or $1,250 per day for what was the unearned increment of social value in company franchises obtained through population increase. Thus, as Cochran pointed out as loudly as possible, renewal of franchise meant maintainance of these bloated bonds and a continuance of the $1,250-per-day payment from the robbed citizens. He never let up, and the following headlines tell their own story: THE BIG CON'S BIG CON GAME, A CHAPTER IN FRENZIED FINANCE, THE SPIRIT OF '76 AND '09, THE COW THAT GIVES GOOD MILK, and THE SAME OLD LEOPARD AND THE SAME OLD SPOTS. Cochran's figures if anything were conservative. Whitlock and his Cleveland advisers generally used $25,000,000–$30,000,000 as the total figure of investment in Rail-Light and $4,000,000 or $5,000,000 as the actual value, thus leaving $20,000,000 or more water. By any reckoning, the company was more than half water, and the people thought that figure low.[3]

Thus, when Mr. John H. Flynn, an investor in Rail-Light, made a public complaint to the mayor, he received a blunt and public reply. The company, Whitlock said, had $15,000,000 in stock and $14,500,000 in bonds, and yet their property was worth only about $5,000,000. "The company has 109 miles of track in the city, and, therefore, is capitalized for about $207,000 a mile." Since railroads generally cost only about $50,000 per mile, "you will agree, I think, that the enterprise under notice represents rather a striking instance of over-capitalization." Thus, its stock does not sell for anything "because it is not worth anything, and I know of no reason in law or in ethics why the people of the City of Toledo should be expected to pay an exorbitant rate for a public service in order to enrich those who have speculated in this stock." While he acknowledged that many innocent people might now own stock, having bought in good faith, he saw no reason why Toledo should bail them out of their difficulties. It had no more liability than the owner of stolen property has if he finds his property in the hands of a guiltless third party. They are his and he should have them back. Whitlock and the people would settle the matter fairly when they had the necessary power. Until then he could and would do nothing.[4] While in this whole affair one can understand the position of Whitlock and the town, one should also recognize that the majority of stockholders did act in good faith and were losing their investments. Whitlock's prejudices to the contrary notwithstanding, this was no case of black and white, right and wrong, as he invariably viewed it. Sympathy, caustic or otherwise, would not refill a bank account.

In this spirit Whitlock put Cleveland accountant Carl Nau and his firm to work examining company books and properties. He demanded an inventory of all property and received it. After checking it, he planned to use it in taking up the subject of proper valuation. On November 10, several of the more important franchises ran out, and he promptly notified the company that they were trespassers on the city streets, but that the city would suffer their continued operation if they operated in such a way as to contribute to the public welfare. City experts were working as fast as they could to establish a *modus vivendi* of rent in lieu of franchise, as a way of forcing low fares one way or another. Under such provocation, Lang kept his temper at least publicly far better than most of his fellow businessmen might have. He wrote the mayor a polite letter asking that Whitlock draw up a model law that would satisfy the city and then pass it along to the Rail-Light for modifications. The company also sent out feelers for a plan, long discussed in Ohio, that would channel "excess" trolley profits into the city treasury rather than reduce fares. Whitlock as usual asked for advice about this and received it. Louis Post opposed it as an unjust tax on the riders. Baker agreed, saying that it also encouraged wealthy taxpayers to look for dodges, that it was probably illegal, and haphazard at best. The dying Tom Johnson opposed it too, calling it one more aspect of the old fight against in-direct taxation. The single tax appears in these arguments masked and hidden but noticeable to those familiar with the doctrine.[5]

The temporary result was a stalemate. Whitlock and his staff wanted municipal ownership, but the laws of the state of Ohio would not permit this. If they did, said City Solicitor Cornell Schreiber, the city "would compel the street railway to accept a franchise we think fair." Whitlock, as was his habit, summed the fight up in his own words: "The truth is that the public utility com-panies are stronger than the city, and it will not be until the people become more powerful than privilege that they will have laws passed by the legislature giving the city the authority it needs." That this mighty gorgon of privilege was all but bankrupt, had omitted both stock and bond payments several times, and was scarcely able to keep cars on the streets made no impression on him. His mind and his metaphors had long ago solidified, and the facts of the situation no longer bothered him. Lang was wholly justified as a businessman in saying that the deteriorating service was due to company inability to raise capital, and that service would become poorer without a franchise. There the matter rested when, in January 1911, both Whitlock and his mother entered the hospital for operations. His appendicitis kept him inactive until the end of February.[6]

The chief issue, aside from municipal ownership and the frankly conflicting ethical values involved, was the proper evalua-tion of Rail-Light property. In June 1910, Lang proposed an evaluation that would include the so-called "Chicago Plan," where 50 per cent of the value of an unexpired franchise, replaced by a general franchise, would be credited to the company. To Whit-lock, this was like dividing virtue into halves and selling off one piece of it, and he would not listen. For one thing, he replied, the city could not delegate its authority to a board of engineers, as Lang proposed. For another, nothing intangible had value to the company. That, as any single-taxer could tell you, was unearned increment and the property of the people. To Whitlock proper property was tangible, and, as he had the power, his say, *ipso facto*, became operational law. Carl Nau made his preliminary report in October, and Whitlock announced publicly and accu-rately: "With the report of Nau, Tanner and Rusk and the inven-tory we have made more progress than any city that has considered the question, and Toledo will enter the negotiations better equipped than any other city in which a franchise has been considered." Whatever their faults in assessing the problem, the city could not be faulted for inadequate facts. It knew at least as much about the company as the company did.

Immediately after his illness, Whitlock conferred with Baker and with the progressive, trouble-shooting economist Edward Bemis, who was making a career of advising sympathetic city administrations on intricate social problems. Then he sat down with Lang and his attorney, Rathbun Fuller, and began long weeks of tough negotiations. Early in April the Rail-Light flatly refused even to discuss the three-cent fare, the heart of Whitlock's plan. The other major issues, the amount of city control and the length of the franchises, then took up most of the time, and the conferees sensibly put off discussion of the tougher issues of evaluation and rates until the other issues were settled. The men then reached agreement on matters like parallel franchises, service improvements, the legal rights of successor companies, routing, the extension of existing lines, and so on. Lang even made one major concession: He acknowledged absolute control of direct city service to the city, enabling it to fix the frequency of runs. Whitlock hailed this concession warmly, for not only was it a gesture in the right direction, it also took the whole gnarled question of routing out of the conference and left it to a city czar for later settlement. That, however, was the only bright spot in these early negotiations, for the issue of evaluation kept popping up. After weeks of squabbling, Whitlock and Lang agreed on evaluation by engineers, one picked by each side and a third man neutral. The third man was a sore point. Lang insisted on a qualified engineer; the city suggested Federal District Court Judge John M. Killits. Neither side seemed ready to budge.[7]

All was never entirely sober in midwestern cities, however, and, despite all the turmoil, comedy was always entering town. In 1911 much of it was called Billy Sunday. He arrived in Toledo in April for a big revival and promptly started a little war. In a public prayer he was quoted by the Whitlock-hating *Times* as saying: "Oh Lord bless the mayor of Toledo although he is not a Christian." That was good for all kinds of pious needling about Toledo vice, the mayor's religion, and so on. The chief trouble was that the whole business was a fabrication. Sunday, when he heard about it, promptly denied the prayer, said that he had prayed, "Lord, save our mayor, if he is not a Christian," and then added to the reporter: "I have met him and he is a good fellow." Oddly enough, Sunday and Whitlock apparently had a friendly meeting, and when Whitlock explained the Toledo vice problems to him, Sunday frankly if privately admitted that he himself did not know how to solve the problems and would probably do no better if he had the mayor's job. Even that was not the least of the mayor's weighty concerns. In the midst of the controversy he received a letter from Mr. James E. Gabrin of Boston, in which this unknown gentleman declared that he had a "fancy to western girls" and asked the mayor to find him one, blonde or brunette and full of fun, so he could marry her.[8]

Despite his status as Christian and marriage broker, Whitlock's negotiations dragged on interminably. By the early days of July, one of the most severe heat waves in history settled on the city, and on July 2 the thermometer read 99.5°. The town experienced an ice shortage, general misery, and several deaths. In the middle of the soggy weather, Lang turned down Judge Killits. Although Killits was an admirable man, Lang said, he was simply not well versed in the technical issues necessary for proper evaluation. Two weeks later, Lang summed up his own version of the course of events. The company and the city had met fourteen times, he said, and thrashed out certain tentative agreements, "among the most important being reserving to the City the authority to control service, the power to purchase the property when authorized to do so, the details to be agreed upon later, and you assented to eliminate or change many matters to which we objected." The chief issue remaining was settling just who was competent or knowledgeable enough to arbitrate sensitive issues. "I contend that a competent person to appraise the street railway property in Toledo must be, first, an electrical engineer; for our business, unlike Cleveland, Detroit and most other cities, is to furnish electric current for operating street railways as well as lighting streets and dwellings, and for power purposes in the City as well as outside, and it is developed in varying quantities by the same machinery from four different power stations and from a storage battery used jointly and intermittently." The power, transmitted overhead and underground both, required both poles and conduits. "Some of our property is also used for heating houses, and for the manufacture of gas for illuminating and fuel purposes, all of which must be taken into account in such an appraisal." Thus the man had to be trained in both mechanical and civil engineering and have had some field experience. Assuming that both sides were honestly trying to solve a tough problem—and there was no reason for not assuming good faith on both sides— the real conflict was plain: Lang, an experienced capitalist who believed in the profit motive and a just return on capital, thought in terms of depreciation, overexpansion, current expenses, and a legitimate return on an honest investment; Whitlock, Bemis and Baker thought in terms of the single tax, unearned increments, the exploitation of the workers and the citizens, and the powers that preyed. To Lang, politicians made honest business impossible; to Whitlock, businessmen never took the people into account and always tried for excess profits. Both sides were partially right, and both sides exaggerated. Neither side was really communicating efficiently to the other. But, in view of the common business practices of the time and the shaky condition of his company, Lang was more than reasonable. Baker, however, reacted characteristically to Lang's refusal of Killits: "I think you can now adhere boldly to the position that the railway company does not desire fair arbitration," Baker wrote Whitlock immediately. All the men as qualified as Lang wished were tools of the companies. Where else could such men be found, except as specialists working for utilities? Both sides had a point.[9]

There, for the rest of the year, the controversy rested, and Whitlock and the newspapers occupied themselves with other things until after the election. Small matters took up time, such as a brief flurry of interest in charges of an abuse of city funds by one of the city officials. The issue, apparently based partly on misunderstanding and partly on a desire to create a diversion by those who wanted the utilities problem forgotten, soon died out as a four-day newspaper scandal, and Whitlock was apparently right in shrugging it off as partisan politics. Of more personal importance was a scheme Whitlock was slowly hatching for a trip to Europe. "I have a plan and I want you to help me in it," he wrote Albert Nock, "the purpose of which is to enable me to retire gracefully

from the scene of political action at the end of my present term."
He wished to go abroad "and write some articles about certain
European cities," not travel letters nor anything conventional,
"but to point out some of the things that foreign cities are doing
that ought to be done in American cities, things we think are
radical over here but have long been done over there." Not the
least of his desires was his intention to show "something of the
progress of civilization by means of the city, for civilization has
been, for good and ill, just what the cities have been." Would
Nock try to interest a magazine in the project, using Whitlock's
vast experience in city politics as an appropriate business reference? "I want to announce it in such a way that it will appear to
be an excellent business proposition for you know that the American public will yield anything for the sake of a business proposition." Finally, scandal, business or heat wave notwithstanding,
Whitlock's doctors ordered him on a vacation, so late in August
he went off to the cool resort of Wequetonsing with its lovely golf
course. There, Whitlock was just starting to unwind when word
came from Toledo that seven men, three of them intimate friends,
had drowned when their launch was run down by a freighter. That
finished the vacation. He had only just seen them buried when his
father went to the hospital for an operation. Whitlock himself was
sick and in bed during much of September and October.[10]

Elections, however, waited for nobody's funeral or vacation,
and the 1911 elections were particularly important: Not only was
Whitlock's office at stake, but also the seats to the Ohio Constitutional Convention. The Constitution of 1851 provided for regular
opportunities to revise itself every twenty years. 1911 was the
third such opportunity, and progressives desperately hoped to take
advantage of it. The agitation for municipal home rule, initiative,
referendum and recall, protection for workingmen, woman suffrage, tax reform, etc., moved various of the politically conscious
men in the state. One of the leaders of the progressives, Herbert S.
Bigelow, had been working for such changes for some time, and—
with the backing of the single-tax Joseph Fels Fund of America—
he, Daniel Kiefer, and others associated with progressivism began
to organize support for their reforms. In June 1911, Bigelow
formed the Progressive Constitutional League and asked Whitlock
to accept its presidency. The group specialized in two issues: di-

rect legislation and municipal home rule. Alarmed conservatives, led by Allen Ripley Foote, attempted to organize opposition—with little apparent success. Other eminent progressives, including Washington Gladden, organized other groups. When nominations were complete, the *News-Bee* counted 286 declared progressives, 120 conservatives, and 13 unknown, but emphasized that the progressivism of many was suspect and that no one should relax.[11]

Meanwhile Whitlock himself easily won renomination for Mayor, while the Republicans named Carl H. Keller, the Democrats C. B. Ashley, and the Socialists W. F. Ries as their candidates. The campaign followed the now-familiar round of wild charges about vice, a dreamy, do-nothing mayor, bossism, and the futility of Whitlock's stand on the Rail-Light problem. *News-Bee* propaganda seemed to have taken its toll, however; even the formerly hostile *Blade* was approaching the Independent position; by 1913 it would even have kind words for Whitlock and parts of his program. As Whitlock described this, his final electoral victory, he had held the Independent forces "and even made some gains among the respectables, but three or four thousand of the workers went into the Socialist Party," and thus Ries received 5,000 votes. Whitlock had predicted as much, to the disbelief of his associates, but he was not depressed. "It is all right, of course, and I am rather glad of it in a way, for to my mind it insures the permanence of a radical movement of some sort in Toledo, for when the inevitable dissolution of the Independent Movement comes there will be a Socialist group, probably by that time become opportunist, to carry on the work. I shall run for mayor no more . . ." The final returns gave Whitlock 11,590 votes, for a plurality of 3,059 over Keller. Ries, the Socialist, received more than 5,000 votes, almost double the number received by the lowly Democrat Ashley. Not the least incredible part of the election, to those who see politics in terms of economic struggles or status revolutions, was that the Toledo version of the archetypal Boss, Walter F. Brown, easily led the group of constitutional convention delegates in popularity. As the *Blade* noted, "If it had not happened it would have been declared impossible." Another oddity: The Democrats came in a contemptible fourth in both total votes and in council seats; along with Ries's substantial vote, the Socialists elected two councilmen to the Democrats' one.[12]

In early January, 1912, the convention met, and immediately set its tone by electing Whitlock's single-taxer friend Herbert Bigelow president, after a brief fight. Many notable politicians, including Whitlock and some from out of state, spoke, but the heart of the convention was in the issues. One by one, the delegates framed amendments to the Ohio constitution for separate submission to the voters: liquor licensing, initiative and referendum, capital punishment, home rule, tax reforms, and labor laws all received approval along with a number of lesser issues. A total of forty-two amendments survived opposition and were placed on the ballot. To Bigelow, at least, the political phase of the social gospel was at its height: "Oh, my friends," he pleaded for support for the initiative and referendum, "we are striking down tyranny. We are forging the greatest tools democracy ever had. We are building grander institutions for freedom and for humanity than the world has ever known. We are engaged not only in an important civic work. Our task is a profoundly religious one." The results were gratifying to the progressives; and Whitlock, Bigelow, Baker, and Democratic gubernatorial nominee James M. Cox all stumped the state in support of the work of the convention.

Nine of the amendments were of major importance, and these absorbed most of the popular interest. The liquor-licensing law aroused the drys, and woman suffrage the men. The initiative and referendum and the welfare laws irritated some conservative business interests. The judiciary reforms, the call for primary elections, good roads, and municipal home rule each had its little group of proponents and opponents. The resulting vote, despite all the clamor, was light, but if nothing else it showed the results of the long education in progressivism. In Lucas County, a dozen years of Sam Jones and Brand Whitlock had so educated the citizens that every amendment passed—not so in the state. Eight amendments failed, including two Whitlock had campaigned for for years: woman suffrage and the abolition of capital punishment; the other issues were of little national significance, one signifying that racial prejudice was not yet dead and others that good roads uncluttered by billboards were still dreams of the future. On the whole, however, it was a victory for the progressives. The city beautiful was one step closer to reality.[13]

Whitlock's own success in the November 1911 elections all

but ended the Rail-Light battle. With two more years of an Independent mayor assured, Frank R. Coates, newly elected replacement for Albion Lang, and his company realized that they had very little left with which to fight. Stockholders certainly were in on the secret, for the stock sagged to 2½ by December 12. Three days after the election, W. W. Miller, lawyer for the bondholders and creditors, announced that a plan for reorganization was being studied. Whitlock immediately began to take a hard line and to talk about the measures that he was prepared to take. On December 8, Miller announced his plan: The company would reduce the common stock more than six times, to $2,000,000; it would exchange $6,000,000 of the bonds and $1,500,000 of floating debt for new bonds and preferred stock; it would redeem the rest of the bonds at the rate of $350 for each $1000 held. The plan would thus reduce what was $34,000,000 outstanding to $21,000,000. On December 11 the company submitted to Whitlock more detailed proposals. These included: five-cent tickets, 6 for 25¢, with universal transfers; a twenty-five-year franchise; the fixing of the valuation of railway property at $8,000,000, or else the establishment of a committee to adjust this sum, with Killits—previously rejected—as the key third man (Edward Bemis was Whitlock's choice for city representative); the results established by the Killits committee would be mutually binding; the city could always have the right to inspect company books; the net earnings of the company after 8 per cent would be placed in escrow, and, when the sum thus saved reached $250,000, a lower rate of 7 tickets for 25¢ would go into effect automatically, with universal transfers; if earnings still exceeded 8 per cent, then 5¢ per ticket and 5 tickets for 15¢ would be the rate; if at any time the earnings fell below 8 per cent and the fund sank to $50,000, then the next higher fare level would go into effect; the city could reasonably regulate service; it could buy on six months' notice all railroad properties at assessed valuation; and the mayor or his representative might be a member of the board of directors of the company. There were also a few other minor points. Baker, when informed of the proposals, scorned them. He said that the sum of valuation, as well as what was evaluated, was absurd, that fares should be lower for single tickets and not only for five- or six-ticket purchases, and that the company argument would prevent a referendum on valuation be-

fore the granting of a twenty-five-year franchise. Given their whip
hand, the mayor and his friends were obviously in no mood for
compromise.[14]

The *News-Bee* also rejected the offer as a "goldbrick," because it did not include such facilities as power houses, conduits,
and other of the Light aspects of Rail-Light. Whitlock agreed:
"The rate of fare should be based on the valuation of all the
property and not merely on the valuation of the street structures
and rolling stock," and he thought $8,000,000 an absurd valua-
tion for just the street structures and cars. He told Rathbun Fuller:
"You have not made a single substantial concession to the city."
At that, Cornell Schreiber declared war and battered the already
groggy Rail-Light. He asked the council to pass a straight three-cent
ordinance, and they did. He then prepared to bring suit against the
company for not paying $250-a-day rent on the streets where
franchises had expired. Finally, he declared that the city would
defend in court any citizen ejected from any car for not paying
more than 3¢. "The company has not been fair with the city at
any time," he proclaimed, "and its actions recently prove that it
does not intend to be fair. THE CITY MUST FIGHT . . . There will be
no let-up in this battle." That did it. Rail-Light counsel Barton
Smith immediately wired W. W. Miller, and Miller went to obtain
a receivership application; it was filed in Cleveland on January 4.
Miller then went to Toledo and offered to accept a three-cent fare
during the four rush hours (5:30 to 7:30 a.m., 4:30 to 6:30
p.m.), and charge 5¢—6 for 25¢—at all other times. This concession would last ninety days, to discover if adequate returns
were in fact possible at the low rate. In return, Miller asked Whitlock not to sign the three-cent fare ordinance and to suspend the
rental charge. Whitlock agreed. The *News-Bee* headlined, CITY
WINS THREE-CENT FARE, and went on to proclaim the great victory. Whitlock inevitably translated the event into his own language: "But greater than all is that moral victory which comes
from the recognition by the company of the principle for which
this city has so very long contested." Even the *Blade* rejoiced.
Privately, Whitlock was more subdued but none the less relieved.
"The arrangement we entered into, however, was but a temporary
one pending the solution of the whole franchise problem," he
wrote. "The city has not granted, and, under this arrangement, does

not grant any franchise or any rights to the company, but merely forbears, without formal action, to take the drastic course that might have been expected" in order to follow Schreiber's emergency laws. "I consider the temporary arrangement a very good one, though it does not at all provide for all things that should be provided for, and must be provided for when we come to consider an ordinance granting a permanent franchise . . ."[15]

The fight was all but over. After much squabbling between stockholders and bondholders about who would hold the bag full of water, the company found itself absorbed by the efficient public utilities operators, Henry L. Doherty & Company. Doherty engineers instituted modern business practices, while refinancing the stocks and bonds; the new company became the Toledo Traction, Light and Power Company, and everyone breathed a sigh of relief. The water was gone, service seemed to be improving, and even public relations received some belated attention. Few at the time noticed that the death of Rail-Light also deprived the Independents of their most important issue.[16]

With the transit issue all but settled, Whitlock could devote himself to less fatiguing matters. He kept working on his idea of a paid trip to Europe. He worked, with more or less success, on his autobiography and the galleys of *The Fall Guy*. He began his speechmaking again. One problem, remaining from the street-car business, was the status of the salary of Edward Bemis, the expert who had worked so hard to help Cleveland and Toledo progressivism. Whitlock's utter inefficiency and his dilatory answering of correspondence left Bemis wringing his hands in a doleful series of letters, asking what he was to do next, and when he would be paid. Whitlock, predictably, apologized profusely from the bottom of his heart and did nothing, while Bemis fretted away. Of equal importance was the reappearance of Curly Williams and his prompt incarceration in a Cleveland jail for burglary. "I don't know whether he was guilty or not," Whitlock wrote sadly to Mayor Baker. "I don't suppose anybody does, possibly he doesn't know himself . . ." Would Baker please consider a pardon? Whatever the time of year, Whitlock was still the father of all the waifs and strays of the city.[17]

Meanwhile, national politics soon distracted everyone from local affairs. William Howard Taft's bungling of several sensitive

issues and his fatuous defense of his mistakes caused first Robert
M. La Follette and then Theodore Roosevelt to campaign for
control either of a new, progressive Republican Party or a third
party based on progressive principles. Ohio, with its awareness of
new ideas and its oversupply of stand-pat Republicans like its own
native-son President, was a natural place for agitation, and the
Roosevelt boom began early. The best-known progressives, however, remained aloof, and the movement for Roosevelt fell into the
hands of those, such as Walter Brown, who had highly dubious
credentials. Not the least of the reasons for the progressives' lack
of interest was the sudden rise of Governor Woodrow Wilson of
New Jersey, who held out the promise of a rejuvenated and liberal
Democratic Party. One of Wilson's closest friends was Newton D.
Baker, and Baker lost no time in getting to work on his friends to
line up support. Within Ohio, Judson Harmon also had presidential aspirations, and the first move of the Ohio Wilson men was to
spike Harmon; they did so effectively. That done, they discovered
a new state leader of stature in James M. Cox. Whitlock celebrated the early maneuvering characteristically, as a letter from
Louis Post makes clear: "I am sorry indeed to learn of your
illness, and with something so annoying as whooping cough. I
found this bad enough when I had it in my very early youth, but to
have it as a grown man and a real Mayor, seems to climax all
whooping cough jokes that I ever heard of."[18]

Whitlock recovered more quickly than usual and was able to
sit on the platform when the tireless William Jennings Bryan came
through on a campaign tour. Bryan had Whitlock's public respect
and approval—if not his private—and Whitlock also secretly endorsed Bryan's attack on Harmon, perhaps also his attack on
Theodore Roosevelt. With Roosevelt, in fact, Whitlock was playing the reluctant debutante, and the wily Teddy used all his charm
to get Whitlock compromised and compliant. One warm and
pleasant evening in June, Roosevelt spoke before 15,000 people in
the old Toledo Terminal Building. Whitlock attended with Chief
of Police Perry Knapp to make sure that there was no disorder. As
soon as Roosevelt heard that the Independent and progressive
mayor was up and about, he sent a policeman to summon him.
Whitlock knew immediately what was in Roosevelt's mind and
refused politely, saying they would meet later for dinner at Mar-

shall Sheppey's. The officer left, then returned. Roosevelt insisted, and when Roosevelt insisted few could refuse. Whitlock walked down the middle of the hall to be greeted like a long-lost brother, and to the roars of the crowd he had his hand wrung and his back slapped. He left as soon as possible.

Then, at the Republican Convention in Chicago, Roosevelt tried again. The men had many mutual friends, and some of them immediately informed Roosevelt that Whitlock was there. The summons came, and Whitlock went. He entered Roosevelt's hotel room, and there, against the wall near the window, was a small table holding eight books. Four of them were by Brand Whitlock. Bert Taylor, the man who had brought Whitlock, pointed them out and said how well known Whitlock was.

"Yes, Bert, but four out of eight are too many. I might possibly have swallowed one, but four—no, not that. My vanity has reached no such self-flattering proportion."

The Colonel came in, "full of beans, very energetic, snapping his teeth, shaking hands vigorously and talking volubly about all sorts of things." He talked about the campaign for a while and of his faith in reform, and then gestured toward Whitlock's books.

"It is such books as those that have taught me this, and given me this belief and faith."

Whitlock was embarrassed half to death, for it was all so blatant. "Insincerity is a terrible thing, and I was sorry he had resorted to this palpable and cheap device to flatter and win me. For there was something about him that one couldn't help liking. He was so full of life and so human; there was such a magnetism in his personality."

The suit failed, and Wilson won the bride. Single-taxers all but unanimously rallied behind the man who held so many of Henry George's ideas: the value of individual enterprise, minimum government, competition, free trade, and the dislike of large and powerful economic organizations. Not least influential in deciding Whitlock for Wilson were the constant letters from his closest friends, for although Ben Lindsey and Jane Addams went for Roosevelt, Newton Baker, Frederic C. Howe, Albert Jay Nock, and Louis Brandeis were all strong for Wilson and all made sure that Whitlock knew it. Consequently the Bull Moose nomination for governor, several times pressed on Whitlock, held no allure, and he refused it. He came out publicly for Wilson early in October.[19]

Election or not, Whitlock was going to go to Europe. The Scripps-McRae syndicate of newspapers, which included the *News-Bee*, agreed to pay him $3,000 for a series of articles on the cities he visited and what experience they had to offer American cities. Not content merely with that, Whitlock was also in contact with the *Century* in New York in hopes that he could rework his experiences once again for magazine distribution, free of the rather irksome length requirements of the newspapers. He finally sailed on October 9 on the *Lusitania* and greatly enjoyed the voyage. Despite heavy seas and a broken turbine, the ship made good progress, and Whitlock was not sick the whole time. One of the reasons for his pleasure was the presence on board of several British Members of Parliament. Whitlock became particulaily friendly with Liberal member Francis Neilson, in an acquaintanceship that, through Whitlock's friendship also with Albert Jay Nock, led to the founding of the single-tax journal, the *Freeman*, in 1920.[20]

The record of Whitlock's itinerary indicates that he chatted and ate his way across the Continent, giving precious little time to study of the city. In Dublin, "the wits of that witty city gave me a dinner"; in Glasgow, "the Lord Provost entertained the Lord Mayor of Dublin and me at dinner," while the "venerable Dean of Guild conversed with me half through the meal under the impression that I was the Mayor of Toledo in Spain, asking me about Spanish customs on which I was unable to enlighten him!" In London, a group of M.P.'s, led by T. P. O'Connor, gave him another dinner, charming and flattering their visitor thoroughly. Unfortunately, of the thirty odd M.P.'s present, not one came from the right. "The Tories naturally would not have anything to do with me," and he could only conclude that "if they really knew about me they could only put up their monocles and stare with that expression that resembles so much a large Herkimer cheese." Despite his affection for Neilson and his Liberal friends, his total impression of Britain was negative: "Nor was I impressed much by British manners, which are not nearly so kindly as ours, if they are in a way so much more formal. . . ." When they said thank you, they didn't mean thank you, "they mean that you should be thankful that a Britisher spoke to you. The caste, the snobbishness of it, and the cold formalism of a dead state religion are overpowering. And the women! How ugly they are! What hands and feet and noses, and what clothes!"[21]

The resulting articles were quite short and scarcely memorable, for Whitlock merely approved what anyone familiar with his work would predict he would approve, with appropriate local color. He praised the single-taxers whenever they had been influential, as in Glasgow; he applauded municipal ownership of public utilities and the cheap fares that went with it; and he commented on municipal slaughterhouses, water purification, and refuse collection and disposal. In Glasgow he talked of firemen and slums, in Liverpool of the trolleys, in Dublin of the lack of freedom, in London of the lack of shame, and in Paris of its inspirational qualities. Nothing in the British Isles or France excited him nearly so much as the city life in Brussels and Germany, however, and the articles picked up slightly when Whitlock talked of Brussels' abolition of capital punishment, its system of cooperatives, and its idea that the city was "the citadel of our liberties." He was all but infatuated with Germany, where the cities were "clean, orderly, and there is everywhere the mark of efficiency and of an enlightened economy" and where the people had an excellent "civic spirit." Hamburg, a true free city, especially appealed to him. His final conclusions indicated that progressives found in Europe pretty much what they wanted to find in America in the years before they went abroad. "But there is much that we may learn from those efficiently governed towns, and principally, in a broad sense, first, that all communal functions should be discharged and all public utilities be conducted by the public and in the public interest," he wrote. "Secondly, that politics, in the professional and partisan sense, should be excluded from municipal government, considering the dogmatism with which he and the other selected solely for their ability to do the particular work required." Americans, Whitlock concluded, must become "practical, empirical," and not be "befuddled with theories"—an amusing statement, considering the dogmatism with which he and the other Ohio progressives pursued their tax theories when in office. Certainly there is no evidence that Whitlock found any new ideas in Europe.[22]

Early in December, Whitlock returned, greeted by a tumultuous reception in Toledo. Woodrow Wilson was triumphantly preparing to enter the White House, and James M. Cox the Governor's Mansion. On the national level, progressivism was at its height, and on the state level the tide had not yet begun to recede. On the local level, however, time was running out. Everyone in Toledo knew Whitlock would not run again, although some may have hoped for a draft. Without him even the few remaining possibilities for progressivism diminished weekly, as an increasing number of deaths decimated the leadership of the Independents. Even the street-car issue was "in status quo," quietly solving itself. The January preliminary report of Carl Nau's firm, now Nau, Rusk & Swearingen, showed that the lower rates during rush hours swelled the company passenger total by over 3,000,000 riders in the nine-month period, indicating that lower rates would still enable a profit through an increased patronage. Receipts were only $28,000 less than in the measurement period. The April report for the whole year 1912 concluded that, on the basis of an evaluation of $5,000,000, the company earned more than $224,000 in excess of a 6-per-cent return on investment and that on such a basis fares could go still lower. Privately, however, Nau told Whitlock that this figure probably could not survive an exhaustive evaluation. As of April 26, and based on admittedly arbitrary figures, he thought that a three-cent fare was impossible, but that a three-cent rush-hour fare and 7 tickets for 25¢ for the rest of the day would probably return a fair profit. That was only slightly different from the three-cent rush-hour, 6-for-25¢ rest-of-the-day fare then in force, and as Whitlock was "quite comfortable" with that situation, no further action seemed really necessary. Increasingly, therefore, Whitlock did less and less as mayor. Oddly enough, he began to find the job even more unpleasant than in earlier years.[23]

Naturally the prohibitionists were back, and the Methodist-Presbyterian hunt for vice was reaching a climax. Clergymen and their more upright parishioners were panting in anticipation of the end of the Independent movement and the return of a devout churchman to City Hall. In his revulsion, Whitlock wrote a congratulatory note to sometime correspondent H. L. Mencken, whose piece in the Smart Set on "The American and His Morals" had come as a breath of fresh air. "Just now we are being edified in this community by a display of puritanism on the part of a coterie of the righteous who call themselves the South End League, and spend Sunday evenings with motor car searchlights and flashlight photography," or, so they said, "hunting out spooners in the parks, an instance of psychic lasciviousness which is a little bit worse than anything I have noted in my experience." No one could have any idea "how this whole thing is getting on my nerves"; Mencken's article was a great relief. "When I get out of here next January, I am going to hunt up some country, if there is one, where puritanism is unknown, and live there for six months in the hope that I may get the odors of it out of my garments." Given the deaths of his friends, the quiet of the chief issue of his four terms, and the sheer dirt dug up by the churches, Whitlock's refusal to run was quite justified. His mission seemed all but over, he wanted desperately to begin writing again, and he was terribly tired. Put another way: His soul hurt. One friend at dinner, on hearing of his reasons for retiring, said: "But I thought you didn't mind criticism! I always supposed that after a while one became callous."

His good friend, Bishop Williams of Detroit, was at the table, and Whitlock always remembered his reply.

"Yes, callous," he remarked, "or—raw."

Precisely.[24]

A calmer life beckoned. The election of Woodrow Wilson meant that Newton Baker was suddenly an *éminence grise* whose advice was respected by the President-Elect. Baker, in turn, wanted nothing so much as to put his dear and bleeding friend in some safe little country where he could represent the United States, meet interesting people, and have plenty of time to write. When he first broached the subject, Whitlock was plainly interested, yet daintily Jeffersonian: "I don't want to get into this attitude of an office seeker, as you understand, for observation has taught me that that is a disastrous thing for a man's dignity and peace of mind," so perhaps the best thing "to do is to leave the notion of a place in the diplomatic service in your hands." The next day he wrote in a similar vein to Governor Cox, saying that "it has been an old dream of mine to be in the diplomatic service," and that he would very much like a post. He would naturally appreciate all efforts on his behalf, was glad Cox was friendly to the notion, and would tell Baker so if Cox did not mind. Meanwhile, he would sit by and hope for the best. Privately, the prospect cheered him up, and he could even demonstrate traces of his old sense of humor. Wilson, he wrote to a close friend, will no doubt be "too much of a covenanter for some of them down there, and it will be well if he is, though it occurred to me that in refusing membership in the golf club he was taking a step that you and I could not consciously approve, and that in abolishing wines from the White House table he was perhaps voluntarily depriving himself of little liberties" he might later have wished to indulge. "But, though the wine is banished from the table, as a good Presbyterian he would have, of course, a bottle in his closet, and this may not be altogether as serious a matter as it seems to be at first glance."[25]

Humor, however, was a rare indulgence that summer. With Whitlock's retirement, the Toledo Independents split into two violently quarreling factions, and the resulting campaign was a filthy amalgam of bigotry and vendetta. Nothing happened properly. The *Blade*, which in previous elections had often demonstrated irresponsibility and willingness to distort any fact in an effort to defeat progressive candidates, suddenly began acting like an intelligent and objective chronicler of events, and for this election is the most reliable newspaper. The *News-Bee*, which had given Whitlock vigorous support and had in general treated everyone but the street-car officials with perfect fairness, turned sour and irresponsible, as Negley Cochran went all but berserk in his hysterical cries about Cornell Schreiber. Cochran had always had a short temper, but he was a curious combination of populist and philistine businessman, and he proved unable to regard Toledo and the Independent Party as anything less than his personal fiefdom. The clergy provided the usual chorus of discontent about vice, but for once they were not the most depressing aspect of the campaign: That was supplied by the return to power of the American Protective Association—the anti-Catholic pressure group—as successful backers of Carl Keller, Republican mayoral candidate.

The *Blade* early signified its changed tone. "Toledo remembers and will always remember gratefully, the splendid service the independent party rendered the city when it was an independent party. It was born of a vital civic need and it did vital great good." But times had changed, and with the end of the street-car issue the party seemed more and more like a patronage-oriented national party. The editor frankly admitted that the *Blade* had been wrong in the past about the Independents, and the admission was a healthy sign of a new realism on the paper. Even Whitlock admitted privately that much of his work was completed, and that any responsible successor could simply keep the wheels moving to give Toledo good government. The Independents had always been a bit anarchic, never taking well to discipline, and Whitlock felt that if they deserved survival they should work out their salvation themselves. The result was a barnyard battle. The *Blade* wanted to initiate a broad, nonpartisan city government, based on a street-car proposal much like Whitlock's. The *News-Bee* wanted to continue the Independent movement, with, naturally enough, the *News-Bee* as the leader of the group. The *Blade* was apparently quite sincere in its scheme, and Cochran's total rejection of it doomed Toledo to a return to the corruption characteristic of the years before Jones.

Following custom, the regular Independents met and named Cornell Schreiber as the candidate to succeed Whitlock. All seemed well until Cochran found what he apparently had been looking for. He discovered that some Independents were trying to woo Democratic and Progressive support; such horrors were not to be borne, for they were the undemocratic connivings of machine men careless of principle and covetous of jobs. Cochran burst forth in loud and multicapitalized editorials decrying bossism, in an attempt to make Schreiber, whom he had never liked, into some sort of Tammany boss. He called a rump convention of pure Independents and named Whitlock as his candidate for mayor, a patent subterfuge that fooled no one. When Whitlock declined emphatically, Cochran persuaded Judge Charles E. Chittenden to replace him. He then all but ignored Republican candidate Keller and laced Schreiber, the "demon of darkness," with charges of personal corruption and ambition, none of which seemed to have any basis. After that, Cochran and the Keller supporters each sat on their own dunghill screeching at each other and at Schreiber and throwing whatever was available. The vice issue returned, as the prohibitionists united behind Keller. Religion returned, as the Guardians of Liberty, an A.P.A. successor, supported Keller and began a red-herring campaign for Bible reading in the public schools—a position opposed by Catholics. Even sex education came into the campaign, as a Catholic spokesman in turn decried those who would introduce it, saying that there were certain things which should never be mentioned to the pure in heart. Clearly no side had a monopoly of intelligence, but believers in Jones and Whitlock had little choice but to vote for Schreiber.[26]

At times, Whitlock could not take the whole mess seriously. "I have been so extremely busy playing golf this summer that I have not had time to answer your letter," he wrote to most of his correspondents that summer, for he was out of the campaign for the first time in over a decade. "Everybody in town is running for Mayor except you and me," he chortled. But this mood did not last, especially to close political friends. Both tickets had good men and good platform planks, he wrote Peter Witt, but "the movement has been thus broken by personal ambitions so that it will probably be of little force hereafter, at least for a long while. The situation makes me sick at heart, and I have come pretty nearly to despair of democracy." He was perfectly justified. Keller, the Guardians of Liberty, and the prohibitionists swept to victory with an absolute majority. Schreiber ran third, behind Chittenden. Every ward returned a Republican councilman. The Independents were permanently destroyed. Without Whitlock and the love people had for him and without the Rail-Light issue, the Independents retained no force, and the voting patterns returned to the days when the Republican factions could afford to fight over who would be elected. The new ethic that had motivated Whitlock and Jones, Johnson, Baker, and the rest could not survive when these men left. The people loved them but did not understand them. Political progressivism, it seemed, was based more on the politics of popularity than on a true desire for reform or innovation. People were disturbed about issues, to be sure, but only in a vague, unfocused way. What they wanted was someone capable of capturing their imagination by first seizing upon the issues and second by being himself an admirable person. They were in no sense ready to adopt complex intellectual positions unless those positions were phrased in their own language by people they respected. Whitlock had been able to carry all of Lucas County for all forty-two constitutional amendments, but without him there even Toledo, the core of his strength, could not vote correctly on issues he had educated them about for a dozen years. Politics in the progressive era was just like politics at any other time, confusing and unpredictable and always dependent on popular leaders. When the leaders espoused reform, reform was possible. When epigones espoused reform, it was not. The notion that American politics had tides of reform and reaction and that the age of Roosevelt and Wilson was a tide of reform seems utterly irrelevant. The notion that a status upheaval turned the white Anglo-Saxon middle class into reform as an expression of status resentment is flatly contradicted by Toledo experience. Finally, the notion that economic class divisions sparked reform seems laughable in a movement marked by labor support for a wealthy man like Jones, as are election statistics that show Whitlock receiving large majorities in almost every district while barely losing the one or two he did not carry. Personal popularity and a popular issue brought reform to Toledo; little else did.[27]

As if the election of Keller were not enough, Whitlock still had no news of his diplomatic appointment, except for embarrassing and premature reports in the newspapers. He knew that Baker was working on it, and he knew that Cox was favorable. But he also knew that some of the less cerebral Southern senators were opposed in principle to intellectuals in high office, particularly since the appointment of Walter Hines Page to England and the subsequent discovery that he had written books judged inimical to his native South. No Southern lawmaker wanted such a horror to reoccur, and Whitlock was fortunate that no senator had access to the friendly letters in his file from Negroes like Paul Lawrence Dunbar and W. E. B. DuBois. Ohio Democrats, in their turn, wanted offices for themselves and resented the consideration of an Independent who had all but wiped out their party in Toledo. For a long time nothing happened. Then Whitlock went to New York and called on Howells, and Howells asked about his appointment. Whitlock told him of the inertia of all concerned, and Howells was interested. Whitlock then visited his new publisher, Rutger Jewett of Appleton, and told him. Jewett immediately thought that the obvious thing to do was to get Howells to reopen the issue with a note commending Whitlock to President Wilson. Howells eventually did so. Wilson—whether from this note or from one of Baker's it is now impossible to tell—then wrote to Governor Cox. Cox gave his enthusiastic approval, and that settled it. Cox then called Whitlock on the telephone, on October 15, to say that Wilson would have Bryan send the appointment in shortly. His ambition finally achieved, Whitlock could afford to relax. Soon he was receiving cordial notes from the present Minister to Brussels, Theodore Marburg.[28]

A few loose ends remained. Led by Cornell Schreiber, the lame-duck City Council passed a bill requiring a flat three-cent fare on November 24, 1913, which Whitlock promptly signed. Such an abrupt action required the suspension of the rules and no prior notice to company or citizens, and, in view of Carl Nau's private opinion of the previous April, Whitlock's reasons for signing such a measure remain obscure. Presumably the Independents wanted to embarrass the new Republican regime, which had campaigned for the three-cent fare like all other parties; in retrospect, the whole affair seems unjustifiable. The law was never really enforced, and the whole matter wound up in a long court fight. No sooner was this clandestine little drama over than the Senate confirmed the nomination. Nell then entered the hospital for a minor operation. Whitlock discovered that, through Hamlin Garland, he had been elected to the National Institute of Arts and Letters. And finally, two days before Christmas, his father, Elias D. Whitlock, died. The few bonds keeping his heart in Toledo seemed to be snapping right on schedule.[29]

As of old, money haunted Whitlock, who had never had enough for much more than his few needs. Wealthy friends, hearing of his worries, offered to help out. The wealthy widow of a Minnesota hotel owner proposed to be a traveling companion on the boat and help with the expenses. Another man proposed that Whitlock take along his son as a private secretary and receive payment for the privilege from the father. Marshall Sheppey, a lifelong friend, did more than propose. He shipped his impover-ished friend off to a good New York tailor and had him fitted out to compete with the elite of Europe. The year ended in a rush. Whitlock found himself reading page proofs for his autobiography on New Year's Day, and then suddenly he was in Washington. He conferred with Wilson and Bryan at the White House, and then, on January 20, 1914, he sailed on the *Kronprinzessin Cecilie* to London, Paris, and Brussels. At last, he would have some peace and quiet in which to write.[30]

BOOK TWO

Ministre Protecteur

BELGIUM AND
FRANCE, (1914-1934)

CHAPTER 9

Best Girl of Europe (1914)

"LIVING IN BRUSSELS in the years before 1914 was to me curiously like living with one's best girl in the days of chivalry and romance," Albert Jay Nock wrote in his memoirs. Other cities had their attractions, he said, but when the train rolled into North Station and you took her in your arms you would not give her up for a harem of them. "Her ways and manners, are all just as you have been impatiently expecting to find them, and her face wears a jolly Flemish smile as you whisper in her ear the phrase of pure contentment: *Oost west, t'huis best.*"[1] Whitlock was soon equally entranced; as a democrat of most aristocratic taste and temperament, he was quite in love with the pomp and circumstance of life at a court.

The trip over was lengthy, with many stops. Chief among these was a trip to Paris, where Whitlock met his predecessor in Brussels, Theodore Marburg, and former governor Myron Herrick of Ohio, now American Ambassador to France. Herrick and Marburg, like most American diplomats in high posts, were quite wealthy, and the atmosphere at Paris was too opulent for Whitlock to be entirely comfortable. How, with his meager resources, could he ever survive in Brussels on the ridiculous American allowances? Finally, he pushed on for Brussels, where he was greeted by the whole legation staff. There he settled temporarily at the Hôtel Belle-Vue et de Flandre, and the enervating search for a suitable and inexpensive home began.

His first duty was to call on the Minister for Foreign Affairs and ask for an audience with the King. After a week, he received a letter informing him that His Majesty would be graciously pleased to grant the audience the following morning, and that the Palace would send suitable equipage. But what would he wear? Should he put on what Hugh Gibson, his secretary, referred to as "the simple garbage of an American citizen" or emulate Herrick and wear evening clothes? Walter Hines Page in London wore black knee breeches, silk stockings, and buckled shoes. Earlier Americans in Brussels had worn such oddities as specially designed outfits with gold braid, or satin knee breeches, cocked hats, and swords. Marburg recommended the breeches, sword, silk stockings, and buckled shoes, for he said they were required by court etiquette. Whitlock thought this ludicrous, and asked Gibson to make discreet inquiries. Gibson reported that Marburg's grandeur had simply amused the Court. Whitlock then discussed the matter with the British Minister Sir Francis Villiers, a charming old gentleman who represented both his country and realistic good taste.

"How are your calves?" asked Sir Francis. If they were up to the mark, Whitlock could safely wear breeches.

"Very thin and aristocratic," replied the Toledo democrat.

Then Villiers would by all means recommend trousers. The Grand Marshall, when consulted, agreed; Whitlock wore simple formal clothes, as all his predecessors had until the pompous Charles Page Bryan had complicated matters some years before.

Finally, Saturday morning, February 14, 1914, at eleven thirty, the thin aristocratic calves, accompanied by white gloves and an opera hat, waited in the lobby of the hotel. Soon the King's adjutant, Colonel Maes, in a uniform heavy with decorations, came, clicked his heels, bowed low, said "Son Excellence" and other terms full of respect. Followed by two other members of the legation staff, Whitlock left to confront two state coaches trimmed in gold, red, and black; high-strung, cream-colored horses; and coachmen in wigs and dove-colored liveries. Tall footmen let down the carriage steps, and Whitlock climbed in opposite Colo-

nel Maes in the leading carriage. Off they raced, all the way to the
Place Royale—which was around the corner. Grenadier guards
presented arms, buglers sounded, and through the gates they went.
Inside the palace were high white halls, statuary, glittering chandeliers, and a long, red carpet lined by tall footmen also in red—all
of whom had good, stout calves—with the lions of Belgium on
their collars. Then a turn, a climb up wide flights of stairs, and
Son Excellence met bowing military men and their clicking heels.
Then, slowly pacing, to the Count de Mérode, who welcomed him
and said he would inform the King. He disappeared through
closed white doors and soon returned. They passed through the
doors, and there, on the far side of a great *salle*, was the King. He
was tall and handsome, in a uniform with no decorations. He
looked kind and had a gentle, winning smile.

A bow at the start, another halfway, and then a third just
before the King. Behind him stood Davignon, Minister for Foreign
Affairs. He wore a resplendent uniform, with a noble sword almost as big as he was, and, Whitlock noted, a look of unutterable
boredom. The King spoke softly in English, and the men exchanged banalities about how their countries loved each other.
Whitlock presented his letter from President Wilson, then the two
men who accompanied him, whom the King already knew perfectly well. Next, like an old movie in reverse, the three men went
backward, bowing their three times and disappearing through the
doors. As Lady Villiers said an hour later when Whitlock had his
lunch at the British Legation, he was now "full blaown."

Full blown or not, he needed a house and had no money.
Marburg and Lars Anderson, his immediate predecessors, had
lived in the Palais d'Asche, an immense mansion that once had
been the home of Crown Prince Albert. The old place was most
impressive and had a magnificent staircase, but, as Albert himself
had remarked, "One can't live on a staircase." Anderson and
Marburg had lived on the staircase, as it were, for 85,000 francs a
year, unfurnished—and in Belgium that meant really unfurnished,
without chandeliers, fireplaces, or bathtubs. No one in Brussels,
Whitlock was assured, rented homes furnished, and he was about
to despair when an army colonel found himself suddenly transferred and had a home to rent, fully furnished, in the diplomatic
area. The place proved charming, four stories in the Quartier Léo-

pold at 74, rue de Trèves; rent was only 12,000 francs, or $2,400 a year. The American government was usually willing to pay $1,600 for use of a bottom floor as a chancellery, and so, by the middle of March, Whitlock was in some semblance of order.[2]

Just in time, for the season was underway. The diplomatic calendar was busy and crowded in the early spring of 1914, as the legations fêted one another, in between the royal signposts: one salon bleu at the Palace and another in the Summer Palace at Laeken. The new Chinese Republic sent representatives to Brussels, the King and Queen of Denmark visited, and toward the end the Lord Mayor of London, complete with his ancient coach and beefeaters, came to town. Never had the mayor of a provincial American city been amidst so much social splendor. The famous soirées at the home of old Prince Charles de Ligne; the musical gatherings at the Wittoucks', where Debussy played one afternoon, his fingernails striking the counter of the piano as he played; the Opéra at the Théâtre Royal de la Monnaie, which gave a complete *Ring of the Nibelung* and where a bugler would summon diners in the restaurant with the *Siegfried* motif for the resumption of the long performance. All these gave the culture-starved novelist a taste of life such as he had dreamed of but never expected to find. He, who was infatuated so often and so easily when faced with a man he thought great, fell in love once more with an entire country, an idea of aristocracy admist democracy, of culture loved by all the people.

The union of these elements appeared in the continual pageantry, perhaps, but most of all in the royal couple. King Albert and his Bavarian wife led a life almost Bohemian by most royal standards. They did not scorn intellectuals, and they patronized the arts to an extent unheard of during the reign of Léopold II. The party at Laeken Palace was typical. The summer palace had a little theatre of perhaps two hundred seats, seldom used since the days of Napoléon. The Queen had had it restored and personally arranged the entertainment for the party. Heldy sang, and Ysaÿe played and then conducted the second act of *Orphée,* with a theatre company from La Monnaie. The night was warm, with thick, purple shadows, and the setting "such an Elysian scene as no stage director could have contrived." The audience included the royal family, the King and Queen of Denmark, an English duke and duchess, and numerous lesser dignitaries. The scene captivated Whitlock's imagination, and one of Euridice's melodies always recalled "that warm and pregnant night," with its "shadowy dancers in their gauze" and "the shades whence Euridice was not to be wooed back to a world like this. Whenever that strain comes suddenly to memory, as strains of music will, it comes as a synthesis of all that is beautiful and sweet and evanescent, the *motif* that expressed the personality of the lovely and gracious woman who chose it as an offering to her guests."[3]

Laeken marked the beginning of summer, and as work at the legation was light the Whitlocks took a summer villa early in June. Bois Fleuri was only twenty minutes away by car, yet was so secluded that one could imagine oneself away from all the cares of the world. The villa was in modern French style, of red brick with white-stone trimmings and new enough to have all the desirable modern comforts. In a flowering wood, it even boasted a rose garden that seemed always to be in bloom. Victor, the gardener, lived in a little lodge close by with a fierce, caged Groenendael police dog for his companion. The Whitlocks could never quite make friends with the animal, but Victor knew his power, and entered the cage like a lion tamer to allow the dog to lick his face. Little paths went through the woods, and a peacefully nibbling rabbit dwelt close by. One day a scream of fear, and the sight of a dog slinking away, indicated that the rabbit was but the first of his compatriots to suffer that year. As yet largely undisturbed, the Whitlocks would often have dinner on the terrace in the twilight. One night they even heard a nightingale. Whitlock became so excited making sure that that was what he heard that he questioned Omer, his house servant, in three languages just to make sure: nightingale, *rossignol*, or *nachtegale?* That's what it was.[4]

The early summer drowsed along. Whitlock worked on the early chapters of a novel—his writing was one major reason he had become a diplomat in the first place—and in the afternoons he often went to Ravenstein for a round of golf. Americans, many of them old friends, visited on their holidays: George Ross and the Marshall Sheppeys of Toledo, and Mrs. Sarah M. Boyd of Milwaukee. Francis Neilson dropped his duties as Member of Parliament and came over to golf. In England, woman suffrage and the Ulster Rebellion excited everyone; in France the Caillaux murder case had Paris buzzing. News came through to Belgium and the American minister only in leisurely fashion, and he scarcely interrupted his novel and his golf to worry about the rest of Europe. Even when Omer interrupted him to announce, "Excellence, the Crown Prince of Austria has been assassinated at Sarajevo!" the occasion was important chiefly as a disturbance: Perhaps the Minister should go to the Austrian Legation and sign a book of condolences? In a land of nightingales, one could scarcely be bothered about the murder of heirs to thrones. The legation, in fact, could quite easily run itself. By midsummer, its clerk, Mr. Alexander P. Cruger, did most of the paper work; a Belgian legal adviser, Maître Gaston de Leval, had a good reputation as a lawyer and years of experience as adviser to American ministers; and Miss Caroline Larner, a state department employee on vacation, proved so worthy that Whitlock had her reassigned to the legation staff.[5]

The chief legation assistant was a young career diplomat, Hugh Gibson. Gibson was a jovial man of great energy, with a penchant for writing satire and light verse and a habit of making puns. He had been born in Los Angeles and educated at Pomona and the École Libre des Sciences Politiques in Paris. He entered the foreign service in 1908 and served as secretary in Honduras, Havana, London, and Washington. Like Whitlock, he was sent to Brussels chiefly to rest, before being assigned to a place where something happened. Gibson was, at least in peacetime, the least pompous of diplomats and was something of a Mad Hatter among the staid starched shirts. Joseph C. Grew remembered him as "that wild Indian" who pulled practical jokes at the Department of State: Once he pushed as many important buttons as possible and then ran and hid while the V.I.P.'s gathered and wondered why they were summoned. He also liked to claim credit for the notoriety of his name: the Gibson martini, he often said, was named after him, its inventor.[6]

But even Gibson was not the chief character of the diplomatic corps in Brussels. That distinction, by common consent, was reserved for the Spanish minister, the Marquis de Villalobar. He, as Count Carton de Wiart put it many years later, was "the most extraordinary personage in the diplomatic corps." Villalobar, to the amazement of everyone who knew the circumstances, was a congenital defective born into a highly placed Spanish aristocratic family. Accounts differ about just how defective he was. Herbert Hoover, for example, deprives him of ears, although several surviving pictures indicate either that Hoover was wrong or else that plastic surgery was more advanced then than seems likely. Most accounts do agree that he was born with a misshapen head and no hair, but that a cleverly designed wig made this difficult to notice; that he had only one hand he could show, the other resembling a goat's hoof—he kept both in gloves at all times; and that he had no legs. Apparently his feet—such as they were—came where his knees should have been, and only with the greatest difficulty did he get around on two artificial legs. Given these afflictions, it is little wonder that Villalobar had the most feared temper in the Spanish diplomatic corps, possibly in the whole corps, that he had an excessive vanity and sense of his rightful place, and that he would never let anyone see him in physical distress or notice his difficulties. Anyone who did, if on his staff, was recalled to Madrid the next day; anyone else experienced a frigidity of manner he was able to recall with a shudder for years. A Spanish tutor had educated Villalobar well, and sheer ability and will power had won him promotion. Of the entire corps, only he had the respect and admiration of both Germans and Belgians when war broke out.

But Villalobar carried himself well, and the careless might easily mistake him for normal, at least until he had to climb stairs. His pictures, in fact, make him look more like a Greek god than a cripple. Once, when he first appeared at the Madrid court—a young diplomatic official already booked for Washington and a minor post—a lady turned around quickly when she heard his name mentioned. As a girl, she had visited in his part of Spain, and she had always wondered what had become of the Villalobar monster she had heard so much about. It seemed that all through the countryside tales were whispered that talked of the Villalobar residence as some Glamis Castle, shadowed for years by some curse. Such a fascinating story, my dear Marquis, she said. Quite gave one the creeps. One heard it everywhere. Had the creature survived, or been killed off? Just what had happened?

"Madame," said the young Villalobar, a malicious smile twisting his face, "I am that monster." And he bowed low, shuffled away, leaving the lady wishing she had never been born.[7]

Whitlock never mentioned Villalobar's problems in all the thousands of pages his diary and books contain. The Marquis was then alive and would unquestionably have taken grave offense. Instead, when he tried to re-create the atmosphere of Brussels, Whitlock turned to the small events that attained symbolic importance from the later course of events. One evening late in March, Whitlock attended a formal dinner at the German Legation of Herr von Below-Saleski, also a new arrival in Brussels. A wriggling dachshund entertained the guests by accepting flattery from anyone who cared, in any language. As the guests chattered, Whitlock and von Below found themselves off in a corner full of objets d'art. The German offered Whitlock, as an ashtray, a silver bowl. As he put his ash in, Whitlock noticed a perfectly round hole on the rim, with jagged edges pushed inward. Obviously a bullet hole. He asked about it.

"Yes, a bullet hole," von Below answered. "In China, it stood on my desk, and one day during the riots a bullet came through the window and went right through it."

Other guests came to see. The bowl and its history proved an excellent subject of conversation, and the German had to repeat his tale several times. "I have never had a post," he said, "where there has not been trouble; in Turkey it was the Revolution, in China it was the Boxers. I am a bird of ill omen." Then he laughed, smiling up to his pointed black mustaches, and raised his cigarette delicately to his lips. "But now, I have the most tranquil post in Europe; nothing can happen in Brussels." Everyone agreed.[8]

Or, there was the time when everyone went out to Stockel for an airplane demonstration. Whitlock ate with Gibson and then they viewed the scene from the legation, which was ideally located for the display. The airplane was still a thing of wonder, and great flyers like Olieslager, a Belgian, and Pégoud, a Frenchman, could attract vast throngs for their displays of spirals, loops, and dangerous dives. One of the attractions was a woman in tights who went up with her husband and then came down in a parachute. The whole affair reminded Whitlock of a circus stunt, and he avoided watching it if he could. That particular day, when the children screamed in joy about the Vlieg machine, he and his companions at tea turned away. One woman shuddered. The plane disappeared, and they thought no more about it until a servant arrived:

"Excellence, the woman has been killed!" Whitlock did not believe it and dismissed the thought. But the next day the newspapers told of how the husband had knelt over the body of his wife, lying broken on the Stockel plain, and how he sobbed again and again, "Oh, my poor little doll! My poor little doll!" Whitlock noted later: "And because one life had come to so sudden an end there, on that tragic evening, the newspapers printed long columns giving all the details, and we were somehow depressed all day because death had struck so near."[9]

STILL, OMENS ARE THE STUFF OF DREAMS, and Brussels was at peace. Whitlock had four novels he wanted to write and was hard at work on what became, so much later, *J. Hardin & Son*. He could not be expected to pay much attention to the Balkans, which were in crisis regularly and had been for years. But one day he interrupted his work for lunch with Villalobar. The Spaniard arrived with a copy of the Austrian ultimatum to Serbia. When asked his opinion, Villalobar shrugged his stout shoulders. They speculated about the war and spoke of Belgium's good fortune at being neutral. "At any rate," Villalobar said as they were going out to lunch, "we have a comfortable *loge* from which to watch the performance." That was reassuring, and they were soon talking about the Caillaux case, French politics, life in Washington, and a visit the Spaniard had once made to Whitlock's Toledo. Villalobar then drove off to visit nearby. The next day was Sunday, and Whitlock and Nell drove to Antwerp to meet the *Lapland*, which was bringing over Mrs. Brainerd and Whitlock's mother for a visit. The Austrian ultimatum expired about the time the two old ladies entered the harbor. The next day they docked and talked of their trip while the idea of war was discussed with little fear that it might come. On Tuesday the papers printed the Austrian declaration of war, and the panic in Paris, Berlin, and London began, as men who saw the dangers tried to stop all the dominoes so carefully placed from falling together. Then Aunt Sarah Boyd—who was in Germany—returned, most indignant. No one would change her money, and everywhere troops jostled her. The legation was skeptical; everyone knew there had been no mobilization. Still indignant, she began to plan a trip to Dinant. Peace efforts failed, and faces in Brussels tensed; yet life still went on much as before. At Bois Fleuri, one thing seemed all-important: if war came, would Omer, the gentle, loyal Belgian servant, far too old to be a soldier and in the eleventh class of reserves, would Omer be called to the colors?[10]

At six o'clock in the morning at Bois Fleuri, Whitlock awoke to loud, insistent knocks on his door; it was August 1. He found Omer in the rough blue tunic, linen pantaloons, and *bonnet de police*—in uniform! Omer stood at attention and saluted.

"C'est la guerre, Excellence."

Suddenly the war was real, for one's friends were affected. Omer was in a hurry. He had to get to town, report, and leave for Liège. Whitlock fumbled through his clothes and gave him all his money in exchange for the news. The Germans had entered Luxembourg and were throwing down bridges. Whitlock offered to have Omer excused, as a legation employee. Omer replied: "I shall do my duty." They shook hands, Omer wearing his tender smile. Then he left. Sleep was impossible, so Whitlock dressed, ate his breakfast, and ordered the servants to prepare for the move back to Brussels. After only two months the summer idyll was over. He and Nell spent the day packing. Once he saw her looking out one of the large windows at ancient Tuvueren, its little red roofs warm in the sun. She was crying. "My poor little Tuvueren," she said.

They drove back with their mothers, the car flying a small silk flag to protect it from the authorities, who were already requisitioning all motor vehicles for the war. Troops and bustle were evident everywhere. Soon they had to worry about whether their money was worth anything, for the hoarding and inflation had begun. The newspapers were screaming about the "shameless barbarism" of the Germans and reporting the declaration of war on Germany. France and England, as well as Belgium, were mobilizing, and declarations of war seemed to be mere formalities. Jean Jaurès, the French socialist leader, had been assassinated; rumors had Caillaux dead too. Murder seemed commonplace, at least in the newspapers. The Whitlocks were very tired.

The next day the deluge descended. Hordes of Americans wandered into Brussels, all of them angry, distraught, frightened, and penniless, without a friend in town but the American minister. From all over the continent they came, in panic, demanding to know how to reach home. They told their tales of hardship to anyone who would listen; no one would take their money, no one would take their bags, and no one would get them ship passage. The German minister delivered the German ultimatum to the Belgian Foreign Minister; the King put the country on a war footing, issued new bank notes, and convoked an extraordinary session of the legislature. All telephone communication with France and Germany ceased. Even the socialists, some still panting from exhortations to pacifism and internationalism, turned patriot overnight and supported the King. The Americans did not know and did not care. "Even today," Richard Harding Davis wrote a few months later, "above the roar of the shells, the crash of falling walls, forts, forests, cathedrals, above the scream of shrapnel, the sobs of women and orphans, the cries of the wounded and dying, all over Europe, you still can hear the shrieks of the Americans calling for their lost suitcases."[11]

That night, Whitlock sent what became the first of almost daily messages to the Department of State. He was as confused as everyone else. "Situation here marked by great uncertainty and apprehension," he wrote. "Difficult secure any information on which to base definite estimate of probable developments. Great financial timidity among classes which has caused runs on all the banks . . ." Almost as he wrote, the Belgian government was drafting a refusal to the German ultimatum. No, they would not permit their soil to be violated by anyone; they were neutral, and Germany was one of the guarantors of that neutrality. Any such action was illegal and immoral. The Germans did not even wait. They crossed the Belgian borders near Visé.

Early on the morning of August 3, a telephone message came—Would Whitlock receive M. Klobukowski, the French minister? He would; they sent his subordinate, M. Fontarce, instead. He was haggard and pale, with dark circles under his eyes. Neither he nor anyone else at the French Legation had been to bed. They were as besieged by Frenchmen as the American Legation was by Americans. His whole manner answered all questions, and to Whitlock's mute interrogation he nodded sadly in confirmation. "Oui," he said, "c'est la guerre." He presented his chief's compliments and excuses. Would Whitlock take over the interests of the French in Brussels? Whitlock would be pleased to. He went upstairs and told Nell. She had her own problems. Her chief worry was Aunt Sarah, who was sadly shaken, and had decided to go home. The noise of clamoring Americans was everywhere and Cruger was turning out passports at top speed, but Aunt Sarah had to go. They bundled her, her maid Alice, and her luggage into a car and sent them off. Poor Alice was so flustered her black gown came all unbuttoned in the back, and she went off with her underclothes peeping out. In the afternoon, Klobukowski came over to confirm arrangements for the protection of his legation. But, as always, Americans seemed to think they were suffering most. One lady of foghorn voice and masculine assertiveness planted herself before the representative of that great country of which she was a patriotic member and all of whose important men she knew intimately. "If anything happens, you'll have to take care of me!" she bawled.

"I'm sure," Whitlock replied, bowing, "that Madame is abundantly able to take care of herself."[12]

By the fourth no one doubted that Germany would attack Belgium and France and was in fact doing so. Both France and England gave Belgium assurances that they would come to her assistance. More local communications were cut off. Belgian flags were flying everywhere. The civil guard had been mobilized to do garrison duty in the city. Everywhere crowds gathered to voice their enthusiastic support of their king and their country. At ten o'clock, Whitlock and Gibson went to the National Palace to see the King open the parliament. They met Sir Francis Villiers as they went in. The galleries were crowded, with even the wives of the ministers there. Below sat the senators and deputies, all quiet and in black, except for a few groups which were excitedly discussing invasions and ultimatums. A red-and-gold *fauteuil* awaited the King, and gold armchairs were set out for the Queen and Royal Family. After a few minutes, a voice shouted, "The Queen!" and the deputies sprang to their feet and fluttered white handkerchiefs, waved and shouted: "Long live the Queen! Long live the Queen!" She entered, lovely, gracious, and dressed in white, acknowledging the audience with curtsies. An old countess and the two young princes followed her. All sat down, the little Count of Flanders wriggling in his chair like any small boy in any country. Then the noises rose again, and the hoarse cries went up: "The King!"

Everyone stood, including the Queen, handkerchiefs waved again, and again the "Vive"s went up.

The King came in, booted and spurred, dressed in the fatigues of a lieutenant general, his saber clanking at his side. He went to the rostrum, made a smart military bow, clicked his heels, took off his white gloves, and without to-do began to read firmly from his notes. Everyone sat quietly. The King was shortsighted, wore a pince-nez, and had to hold his notes close. The Belgians no longer had a single party, he said, for all were united. As he spoke, supporting cries broke out and were quickly silenced. Addressing the gentlemen, he asked, ". . . are you irrevocably determined to maintain intact the sacred patrimony of our forefathers?" and all jumped to their feet and cried, "Oui! Oui! OUI!" The little Duke of Brabant sat, looking intently at his father. The King went on. "I have faith in our destiny. A nation which defends itself, which vindicates its integrity in the eyes of the world, that nation cannot perish. God will be with us in our great cause." Mad, passionate applause broke out, and handkerchiefs waved and mopped away tears. The King, Queen, and the Princes retired. Prime Minister de Broqueville, handsome, tall, slender in his black frock coat stood up. Quickly he told of the German ultimatum, of his reply, of the need for a vote for supplies. Then he struck the hard wood before him and ended: "The watchword is, To Arms!"

The drama was over. The voting remained, but the diplomats began to leave. Prince Koudacheff, the Russian minister, asked if Whitlock would protect Russian interests if evacuation or occupation occurred. Whitlock said he would be honored. Then the Nuncio, the only ambassador in Brussels and thus dean of the corps, called an impromptu meeting. In his soft, Italianate French he spoke of the possibility of the government retreating to Antwerp. If so, the diplomats must follow. Then, with Villiers and Villalobar, Whitlock left. Outside all was sunshine, as the men scurried about their business. At the legation, Washington had sent word that he might take over French interests, so long as that did not prevent taking over other interests should he be asked. Then came word from von Below: Would Whitlock be willing to take over German interests as well? He really had no choice. Within hours, frightened Germans were mingling with frightened Americans at the legation.[13]

By the fifth, the legation had more visitors than a hotel, as bewildered Americans demanded that Whitlock stop all this war nonsense and spare them the inconvenience that it was causing them. "I suppose I am to come right over here with my family in case of trouble," one man said, as dozens acted on the assumption. He was perhaps laughable, but what of the poor school teachers caught in Europe who had saved their pennies for years and who now could find no one to take even the few that remained? Or the honeymooning couple, with all their money invested in a long tourist ticket? His bride watching him proudly, the husband unfolded the long chain of coupons for hotels, railroads, steamships, and so on—all totally useless now. An old friend from Chicago came in, desperate for funds because no one would take his express check; Whitlock dug into his own pocket. The widow of Thomas Bailey Aldrich arrived with son and daughter-in-law. She had for some reason just traveled from Paris. Could she have a safe-conduct for the car? Whitlock was less than comforting, and said it would probably have been taken when they returned to the hotel. It was. But they were decent people and, while troublesome, were worth the trouble. A sister of J. J. Astor sailed in, heralding the approach of another breed. She disdained the weeping women about her, for she was an American and needed a passport. She poured out to Whitlock her indignation at the Germans, who were murdering and raping their way through Belgium, destroying women and children.

"That is buncombe," said the Minister.

"Why buncombe?" she demanded.

"You know they are not savages," he said.

She was beyond comfort, let alone reason. As Whitlock wrote later: "That particular specimen of super-elegant snobbism and cultivated neurasthenia is not to be comforted; was indeed shocked that any one, especially any American, should dare to contradict any statement she might make." What's more, she went on to say that her jewels were in Paris, and that the Minister was responsible for getting them.

The other Americans grew so numerous that Whitlock in desperation located a few responsible fellow citizens to help him work out a means of aiding them in an organized fashion. Daniel Heineman was an American engineer living in Brussels, and Millard K.

Shaler and William Hulse were American citizens resident in Brussels. Whitlock brought them together, added a few others including some from the legation, and the organization was launched. The men proved more than capable, which was just as well, for Whitlock himself was constitutionally unfit for such operations. He could barely keep the legation functioning and perform his official duties. The committee was soon finding shelter and food for all those in need. Meanwhile, word came back of the Belgian slaughter of German troops at Liège; for a while, false hopes seized the capital. Locally, crowds were destroying German shops. Outside of Chez Fritz, a big café, was the sign of the times: "Fritz is a good Luxembourger, but the house is Belgian."[14]

Yet even the war had its comic aspects. At eight thirty, a.m., August 6, Carton de Wiart, the Minister of Justice, arrived on a matter of supreme importance. Haggard and sleepless, he was nevertheless well groomed in his elegant high hat and frock coat. The Belgian government, he said, had reliable information that there was a wireless telegraph instrument on top of the German Legation. The gardes civiques had heard it during the night. The government wished to be correct, but there were no precedents. He proposed a formal inquiry with the Justices of the Court, with all things done in the most regular of manners.

"But," said Whitlock, "there is a much more practical method."

"What is it?"

"To go take a look. You'll come with me, won't you? Let's be off."

Carton was surprised but pleased. He went away to get a wireless expert and returned with a young man in rubber shoes. With Gibson and de Leval the three went over to the legation, routed out one of its few remaining occupants, and had him lead the way. He brought them to a trap door and supplied a rickety ladder. De Wiart eyed the ladder, thought of his frock coat, his high hat and his sense of dignity, and declined the honor. So Whitlock, Gibson, and the expert fearlessly ascended to the roof. The expert went about, clipping wires and no doubt raising havoc with the innocent telephone lines in the area. He could find nothing really suspicious. Then suddenly Whitlock saw the trap door almost at his feet begin to move. Slowly a head peered out, a

dark and handsome head with carefully combed hair and a mono-
cle in one astonished left eye. Then a high, tight collar, butterfly
cravat, smart coat, thin hands, manicured nails, a cigarette—the
villain turned out to be Felix Cavalcanti de Lacerda, Secretary of
the Brazilian Legation. He was speechless.

Whitlock spoke. "If I'm violating Brazilian territory, it's quite
by mistake and unintentional, and I apologize."

Cavalcanti laughed, appropriately enough, and said that his
chief had seen the men on the roof and had sent him up to investi-
gate. The Brazilian and German legations were next to each other.

Then, as they were talking, came a sudden rasping sound,
"Zssztt, Ssszzt, Zst-Zt-Zt-Ssst," exactly like a wireless sending out
dots and dashes. The expert pointed like a hunting dog and everyone fixed on the offending place. There was the culprit: a rusty
weather vane squeaking in the wind. The gardes civiques proved
to be disappointed.

The rest of the day involved shipping the Germans home, most
of the trouble being Gibson's responsibility. Carton de Wiart, who
pleased Whitlock by having a picture of Tolstoy in his office,
proved his humanity by harboring no hatred against the poor
civilians trapped in his country and was most cooperative in finding them trains. Gibson worked tirelessly for the poor refugees.
They in turn were pathetically grateful. Except for a few minor,
unfortunate incidents, they did in fact leave safely, a credit to
Belgian tolerance. The French minister, meanwhile, had a disagreement with Whitlock about the means of administering
French funds, and they amicably agreed to have French interests
handled by Villalobar. Shu-Tze, of the Chinese Legation, proved
less easy to deal with. When the little man came to talk of the
dangers of bombardment, Whitlock reminded him of his diplomatic immunities.

China knew more than America about war. But the cannons
had no eyes! he said.[15]

THE BELGIANS NO LONGER LAUGHED. The forts along
the Meuse held out heroically, and Belgians as they greeted each
other said with exhilaration, "The forts still hold out!" But the mo-
mentary victories could not last. Somehow the Belgians thought

they could win, so misinformed was the world in 1914. They were like the big officer of the garde civique who watched the legation. He asked Whitlock the news in his deep bass, and when Whitlock told him of the huge German losses his face lit up: "It is glorious! It is a day that will go down in history." It would, at that. In the midst of Liège's heroism, however, those in power were less optimistic, and retreat to Antwerp seemed more and more likely. Whitlock cabled Bryan for advice, but the reply was noncommital: "Move legation if desirable." Whitlock answered that he felt he could "render more real service" by remaining in Brussels but that he would like advice if the government moved; he preferred to say even if the corps diplomatique accompanied the government. Bryan cabled promptly: "Use your judgment on matter referred to."[16]

Then began what was but the first of a long series of diplomatic confrontations with both Germans and Belgians, for Whitlock soon found that America was to be the chief neutral. Henry Van Dyke, Minister to The Hague, had been asked by his German colleague to forward a message from his government to the Belgian government. The message spoke of the brave Belgian defense at Liège, of the German regret at having to violate Belgium to get at France, and suggested that now that Belgian honor had been satisfied the country should cease fighting and allow the Germans to pass through unmolested. Whitlock was appalled by the message and had no desire to relay it. He even doubted its authenticity, for he received it without code or other mark of genuineness. He cabled the Department of State for instructions and Van Dyke for confirmation. Meanwhile, he tested Belgian sentiment and found it negative. The message did prove genuine and eventually reached the Belgians officially through the Dutch, but Whitlock's actions relieved him of a nasty responsibility. As he had informed Bryan, the message was in fact "indignantly rejected."[17]

Behind the scenes, Whitlock worried about his wife and their mothers. Fortunately the ladies proved psychically a good deal more adaptable than their panic-stricken countrymen. Certainly Whitlock's mother, who had survived the rigors of life riding the Methodist circuit, was fully capable of weathering a war. Mrs. Brainerd had led a less demanding life, but one of her social attainments had been a knowledge of gin rummy, so she and her daughter taught the Methodist parson's wife the intricacies of the game. Occasionally also, Miss Larner or Villiers's daughter Marjorie would take the Minister for a drive or borrow a book and make conversation. Even that was not always so relaxing, however, for Brussels was anxiously waiting for further news from the front, and normal life was impossible. And the weather was utterly inappropriate for the carnage! The days were sunny and cloudless, for once without the incessant rain usual in summer. Whitlock's typical entry in his journal: "And lovely Brussels never so lovely, never to me so dear. A long day of tension, recognizable by all."[18]

One evening Whitlock was just sinking gratefully into his chaise longue when he received a telegram. The Belgian Foreign Office informed the American minister that the government was going to Antwerp immediately. Trains had been provided for the diplomatic corps. He jumped up and went to phone Villalobar. The Spaniard came over and they discussed the matter. He was indignant and said Villiers was too. They agreed to stay in Brussels and act in concert. Mme Carton de Wiart appeared and said she would not go either; she was too involved in relief work. Despite the interruptions, Whitlock had to inform Washington and see if Bryan had made up his mind about anything yet. He cabled that he planned to stay in Brussels despite the evacuation, since he was also in charge of German and English interests and did not feel he could abandon them. He would arrange for communication through the Consul General at Antwerp. Bryan replied, "Department approves your course of action," and left it at that temporarily. Then Wilson intervened, only to make life difficult. "President thinks it very important that American Legation should be removed immediately to Antwerp in order that our representative may be in immediate touch with the Belgian Government," Bryan wrote two days later. On August 24, Whitlock replied that he would make every effort to do as the President wished, "but it is absolutely impossible to move the legation under the existing circumstances . . ." Many nonbelligerents were also staying, he continued, and he was responsible for numbers of trapped English and German civilians.

There was also another matter. Whitlock on his trips around Brussels had noticed the pathetic attempts of the Belgians to dig an odd trench here and erect a flimsy, barbed-wire entanglement there. All troops in Brussels were those who were too old or young to be at the front, and no one seemed at all aware that the Germans could flatten them in minutes. Whitlock and Villalobar took it on themselves to see the King and Burgomaster Adolphe Max, to plead with them to allow the city to surrender without even token opposition. The result of a single shot could mean the destruction of Brussels, and no one wanted that. Fortunately, cool heads prevailed, and Max announced that the city would not defend itself. As Whitlock informed Bryan: "This service of course could not have been rendered had we been in Antwerp and under the circumstances the Department will not, I trust, consider me indelicate in saying that if I were to leave Brussels in this hour and take refuge in Antwerp, my action might be construed in an unfavorable light, and would, I am sure, be regretted by those whom I have been trying to help." It would also "leave wholly without diplomatic representation or protection a large number of our own and other foreign citizens." Left on his own, Bryan reverted to form and gave Whitlock his head: "Department must be guided by your judgment as to whether it is advisable to move legation from Brussels to Antwerp."[19]

Sir Francis Villiers represented a country at war, however, and he had to go. On August 19 he came formally to turn over his legation. Very calm, very British, the white-haired gentleman was displeased about his eviction. "A frightful bore!" he snorted, summing up the whole matter. Most of his archives were already in Whitlock's possession, and a few others would arrive. His British pride winced at the usual diplomatic formula of "under the protection of"—Britain could protect herself, after all—and so, in the exchange of letters confirming the arrangement, the words "in charge of" were substituted. Villiers said, "I shall lunch quietly at half past eleven, and motor over to Antwerp this afternoon." There was little more for the good friends to say. "I trust that it is only au revoir." Sir Francis then concluded: "But, I want you to know that I shall never forget you, and what you are doing for me now." They shook hands warmly. Friends are never neutral.

The next day the Germans arrived. Villalobar came over, excited as a boy, and he and Whitlock went several places, including the Italian Legation, to get a good view of the event. After odd delays and much confusion about the route the troops would take, they found a good vantage point near Ste. Gudule. Slowly the gray uniforms approached, black-and-white pennants fluttering from lances, past the silent crowds. The hussars chanted "Heil Dir im Siegeskranz" to the tune Anglo-Saxons associated with "God Save the King" and "America." The only other sounds were those of the horses' hoofs. "The scene had the allure of medievalism, something terrible too, that almost savage chant, and those gray hosts pouring down out of the middle ages into modern civilization." Villalobar turned, looked at him, and smiled. "We'll remember this scene," he said. They changed vantage points, only to discover the core of the army elsewhere, acres of soldiers, guns, horses, cannon; everywhere the men sang, a huge *Männerchor* in gray, followed by commissaries and a loud band. Never had the abandonment of Brussels seemed wiser than in the face of these well-trained masses.

At seven, Whitlock and Villalobar met to go to the Hôtel de Ville to make arrangements with the authorities. Everywhere German soldiers were scraping and bowing most formally; few seemed able to speak French, although some knew a little English. Poor, weary Adolphe Max, the Burgomaster, was there, the man who had to meet the invaders and somehow make the best of it. He had done his duty, he said, and would never forget the events of the day. No one would. Then he told of the attempts to salvage the remnants of the Belgian army around Antwerp. He had just finished when the German commander, General Thaddeus von Jarotsky, came in. He was a little bald man, with a gray, bristling mustache, fresh from his bath. He was still in riding boots and spurs, hearty and well satisfied with himself. After much crisp bowing, clicking of spurs, and rubbing of hands, the General proved most agreeable. Villalobar asked for the right to communicate with their respective governments, if possible in cipher. The General agreed quickly, in a curiously accented French, and accepted whatever they asked. It appeared, in fact, that he was hungry and wanted his dinner without difficulties; Whitlock and Villalobar thus got what they wanted, as did the General, who quickly retired to his table.

Meanwhile, the best girl of civilized Europe had lost her freshness. "Poor, poor little Belgium, and poor lovely Brussels! It is awful to witness the humiliation of a proud city."[20]

But Brussels never saw the worst, for it had managed to surrender peacefully. Other cities and towns were not so fortunate, and slowly the horrible stories filtered through. First the news of Visé, of Dinant, of Aerschot, and of Tamines arrived, each more miserable than the one before. Murders, burnings, looting, and rape, the stories varied only in detail. But, to the world, the worst example of German militarism was the destruction of Louvain. The Belgians had been retreating, and the Germans had occupied the town, taken hostages, and declared that any act of hostility— the possession of any weapon or any other act which might impede German progress—would result in the destruction of the town and its citizens, guilty as well as innocent. They usually made similar announcements in every town they occupied. At first only the usual petty thefts and harassments occurred, obviously unplanned acts of individual soldiers. Then, on Tuesday, August 25, an order commanded all townspeople to be indoors by eight, with doors unlocked and lights in the window. Soldiers disembarked all afternoon. Guns sounded in the distance, the sounds of a Belgian advance and a German retreat not far away. At dusk, two German groups mistook each other for the enemy in the confusion of the retreat. They opened fire, and the cry, "Man hat geschossen!" suddenly resounded everywhere. For some time, shots rang out at random throughout the town; some Belgians were as befuddled as the Germans and were glad at the thought that French or British troops might be near. They were not. Soldiers became enraged at what they regarded as franc-tireur tactics (the shooting by civilian snipers of soldiers), and the horror began. Houses were sprayed with bullets, people driven from their homes at gunpoint and massacred, fires set to drive out those who remained; everywhere the looting and killing went on. Nothing was spared. At the fabled old University, the pride of Cardinal Mercier and of Catholics everywhere, were more than 230,000 books, 750 medieval manuscripts, and one of the finest collections of incunabula in the world. It was systematically destroyed, as was the ancient church of St. Peter. Covered with ashes from the burning homes whose wine cellars they had just plundered, for days drunken German soldiers tormented the civilians of Louvain. Some of the Belgians were simply abused out of town; others were shot as they stood.

The next day, Whitlock and Villalobar went to see General the Baron Arthur von Lüttwitz about another matter. As they were about to leave, the General said: "A dreadful thing has occurred at Louvain. The general in command there was talking with the Burgomaster when the son of the Burgomaster shot the general, and the population began firing on the German troops." Whitlock did not at first understand what von Lüttwitz was talking about, so little had his earlier experience prepared him for such events. "And now, of course," the General continued, "we have to destroy the city. The orders are given and not one stone will be left on another." He lifted his hands in a gesture of regret. Soon the refugees began to stream in, numb at what they had seen. All Brussels shuddered. Slowly, Whitlock learned of the terribly specific examples. A young mother heard knocks on her door; her father and brother answered it and were shot. She took her eight-weeks-old baby, climbed the garden wall, found refuge with a friend for a night and a day. Then, as more houses began to go up in flames, she took her child and dodged bullets through most of her trek to Brussels. A widow told of how she and her niece, the latter about to give birth, had been taken from their house half dressed, driven from place to place, forced to kneel while Germans shoved guns into their breasts and kicked them. They were held prisoner for a while and returned to find their home ashes.

The most vivid memory Whitlock had was that of a priest, Mons. de Becker, Rector of the American College. Whitlock and Villalobar had secured the release of most of the surviving priests attached to the college, and on Friday de Becker came to thank the American minister. He had seen his fellow priests murdered and had come to Brussels in a filthy cart. He sat at Whitlock's table, his delicate face dignified and sad, his silver hair highlighted by his black soutane and scarlet sash. He spoke logically and calmly, slowly describing what he had seen. The home of his father had been burned, as had the home of his brother; his friends and colleagues had been murdered before his eyes and their bodies thrown into a cistern; long lines of townspeople had been marshaled together and systematically shot; the finest buildings of church and university were destroyed. And the library, all those precious volumes and manuscripts, burned. He tried to pronounce the word *bibliothèque:* ". . . la biblio," and he stopped and bit his lip; "La bib . . ." He tried to go on but could not, and he bowed his head to the table and finally wept.[21]

The Germans made no apologies. The use of terror was an accepted and established policy; posters telling of the penalties for all crimes had been printed months before the outbreak of the war. The Germans had a timetable, and it required great speed and quick success; any opposition impeded this schedule and had to be dealt with severely. But the Germans also had odd mental quirks which sound suspiciously like the products of a guilty conscience. With a passion for the letter of the law, they insisted that shooting by civilians was illegal and that it was organized from above. Soldiers were men in uniform, and they fought out in the open. All others were francs-tireurs, and the presence of one in a town condemned the town—thus presumably in the next town the inhabitants would stop this resistance on the part of the unchivalrous few. The idea that everything was organized conveniently enabled the Germans to blame all massacres on the Belgian government, since its orders had resulted in the treacherous acts and thus in the deserved reprisals. Perhaps more important were two other explanations. The German mind was trained to hate disorder and preferred organization to liberty. Where the State was supreme and all things run in Zentralen, individual acts had to be the result of orders from somewhere; men simply did not act on their own. Perhaps even more significant: All the destruction occurred at times of German defeats and looked like acts of revenge and frustration. Belgians doubtless fired some shots, and a reliable German source indicates that what the modern world knows as sniper tactics were at times threatening German advances. But the world could be forgiven for regarding German *Kultur* with a certain suspicion when examining its confrontation with the population and library of Louvain.[22]

For the most part, Whitlock felt helpless, and he could do little most of the time except rescue people supposedly under his protection, such as the American College priests. But the diplomatic community had all it could do just keeping track of its lines of communication with its own governments and deciding whether duty lay in evacuation or in making do and remaining. Bottaro-Costa was returning to Italy and Gravenskop-Castenskjöld was going back to Denmark; but Whitlock and Villalobar, the Chinese minister, and a few Central and South Americans were resolved to stay. Perhaps the most ticklish operation fell to Hugh Gibson, the nerveless and exuberant Secretary of the American Legation. Gibson seemed to revel in the thought of the danger around him and was quite willing to volunteer for the dangerous job of taking dispatches across the lines to Antwerp, to transmit them to Washington, and to pick up whatever Washington had sent. On another occasion he brought the pacifist Belgian count Woeste through the lines in a futile attempt to arrange a truce. On a third occasion he safely piloted the two elderly mothers back through the same route, leaving them secure in the hands of Richard Harding Davis and a trip home on the *Baltic*. Unfortunately, these trips of Gibson's increasingly disturbed the German authorities, who were convinced that he was smuggling suspicious materials of some vague sort or other, and this had unfortunate consequences for him later. Now, however, they just seemed like the brave acts of a young man doing his duty—which they were.[23]

Brussels natives heeded another kind of heroism. Whitlock, Gibson, and Villalobar, whatever their activities, were figures largely peripheral to what was happening in the city proper, and they suffered largely at second hand. The chief figure in the city, and the one who needed the most heroism, was the Burgomaster, M. Adolphe Max. He was a man of great composure and sang-froid, imperturbable, neat, discreet, small, and unspectacular. He was often incisive, and was capable of a glacial irony which he did not hesitate to use on the uncomprehending Germans. He had been born only a few months after Whitlock, on New Year's Eve 1869, the son of a prominent physician, and had grown up to become a liberal journalist and lawyer; he had become Burgomaster as one of the last wishes of the dying King Léopold. With the coming of the Germans, Max achieved the status of legend in Brussels. He opposed the invader politely but firmly at every opportunity, he allowed no offense by soldiers, however trivial, to escape official protest, and he all but single-handedly limited German demands for money from the Brussels banks. At first, he was helped by the German commander, General von Jarotsky, who from all accounts was a cordial, courteous man. Von Jarotsky even had the decency to say, when he left, that he regretted that circumstances had made him Max's enemy. He would have been honored to have been his friend. Unfortunately, von Jarotsky did not stay long, and his replacement, the huge, harsh, iron-jawed General von Lüttwitz, was no improvement from any civilized viewpoint. Within weeks, the new military governor was demanding changes in the agreement concerning German exactions of money from Brussels. Max, who had infuriated him several times by not seeming adequately impressed by von Lüttwitz's importance, refused. The German insisted, and when Max still refused he had him arrested and deported to Germany. Whitlock and Villalobar both attempted to intercede, but without success. The German appeared, seemed flushed with wine, laughed and as much as said it was none of their business. After much consultation among themselves, the bruxellois officials chose Max's deputy, M. Lemmonier, to act as his successor. Whitlock and M. Lemmonier had many meetings in subsequent months, as they became good friends. Whitlock, however, could do little but watch as the Acting Burgomaster was tormented and harassed by the Germans.[24]

But to Brussels and its few remaining diplomats the German military officials soon became more evil presences than actual people. They were soon an "ils," a "they" that referred not to any one person but to "messieurs les militaires," the military men who knew nothing about humanity and cared only for success in the war. Time after time, their requirements would overrule the saner and more civilized acts which the newer German civilian authorities preferred. These civilians were the men whom Whitlock, Villalobar, and the Belgians saw. The first civilian ruler was something of a legend before his arrival. The Field Marshal Baron von der Goltz Pasha was old and squat, with a heavy, mottled, scarred face that reminded the viewer of his lengthy career in the Near East, particularly in Turkey. He proved reasonably correct and too old and cynical to be troublesome. In a few months, he was replaced by Moritz von Bissing, but that is a story in itself. More important was the chief civilian assistant who arrived at the same time as the Marshal; he remained for the duration of the occupation, and Whitlock saw him almost daily. His name was Oscar Freiherr von der Lancken-Wakenitz.

Many people considered von der Lancken the finest flower of the German diplomatic corps. He was remarkably handsome, just over medium height, with neatly trimmed black hair, closely cropped mustache, and a well-groomed appearance. He was the envy of his colleagues in the Wilhelmstrasse, and the beau ideal of their marriageable female relatives. His fresh complexion belied the fact that he was about fifty years old, and, while he was always wary and on his guard, his face colored easily with emotions. He had spent ten years in Paris, had learned both French and the society manner perfectly, and was fluent in several other languages. At other times, he had served at Rome and Madrid and had somewhere picked up a respectable training in such rarefied subjects as philosophy, which he did not hesitate to use when Belgians disputed Germany's right to be in Belgium. Rumor said that the Foreign Office regarded him as capable of rising to the top and that Brussels was to be the difficult testing ground for his talents. If he succeeded in Germany's attempts to create a viable civilian regime that was a true part of the Empire, his future would be assured. Brussels, if it had to have any German, was fortunate to get von der Lancken, for whatever his faults of character he acted as a valuable buffer between the people and the diplomats on the one hand and the military on the other. And no group needed a buffer quite so much as "messieurs les militaires."[25]

But to average bruxellois, the character of their conquerors was less important than where the next meal was coming from. For the first time in memory, Whitlock could see on the streets women begging for food, and little children sometimes came to the legation to beg for a stray crust. Max, before his arrest, asked Whitlock and Villalobar to become patrons of a relief committee led by M. Ernest Solvay, who had made a sizable fortune with the "Solvay process" for making soda. This modest little man with his gray beard and blue eyes had long been interested in philanthropic work, and the popular school in the parc Léopold was already named after him. Whitlock could offer, more or less, the services of the committee—Heineman, Shaler, and Hulse—that he had helped form to handle distraught Americans and other tourists at the outbreak of the war. Heineman proved particularly useful: He had large financial interests in several countries, including Germany; he was fluent in German; best of all, he had that thing so impressive to German minds, a title, a Ph.D. from a German university—was, in fact, a German Herr Doktor. He was also wealthy and generous and willing to work long hours for nothing. Within months, whole groups of Americans, led by these men and others outside Belgium, would also be working just as long and for just as little pay. The result of these men getting together was the first step in the formation of probably the most massive attack on starvation the world had ever seen.[26]

Elsewhere in Brussels, two kinds of war went on, as it were, hand in hand. On the one side were the children and the jokers, who tortured the Germans whenever they could with their sense of humor, *la zwanze bruxellois*, in what became known as the "guerre d'épingle." They would deface German posters and torment German soldiers by mocking their movements. Thus, when the Germans were checked at the Marne, and the war slogged permanently into the mud, the children invented a new game: "Nach Paris." The little captain of a small band would line up his men, brandish his wooden sword, and shout "Achtung! Nach Paris!" Then the band would break out into the goose step and march—backward. The other side of the war were the psychically wounded: those in Brussels with relatives at the front or shot by the Germans or those who were otherwise brutalized in spirit. As Whitlock wrote, after speaking with a woman who was poring over a casualty list: "We were only beginning to learn what the war would do to us; just beginning to apprehend that the world could never again be what it had been—that all those who survived would be themselves mutilés, with wounds that would never heal." Even the Germans sometimes felt it, as Whitlock found once when he was speaking to a distinguished, cultured, educated officer who looked exhausted and miserable. "This thing," the German said to Whitlock, "this thing of standing old peasants up against the wall—well, it's no business for a gentleman!"[27]

Meanwhile the sensitive, dyspeptic American minister could only do his duty until he fell, and he worked tirelessly at a task for which he was constitutionally unfitted and physically inadequate. The peaceful post for a writer of novels had turned out to be an irony which as an artist he could scarcely bear thinking about. But, although he did not know it for years, his work was known outside of Belgium, and soon in many places he was as much a hero as he was for the people of Belgium—however unheroic he might have looked as he stood, tall and thin and a little anemic, his stomach growling and his head aching. As Walter Hines Page wrote to Colonel Edward M. House, the former mayor was of "the saving class of people to whom life becomes a bore unless they can help somebody. There's just such a fellow in Brussels—you may have heard of him, for his name is Whitlock. Stories of his showing himself a man come out of that closed-up city every week. To a really big man, it doesn't matter whether his post is a little post, or a big post, but if I were President, I'd give Whitlock a big post."[28] That time too would come. Meanwhile, people were starving and men did not have time to seem great.

⟨CHAPTER 10

Food (1914-1915)

BELGIAN RESISTANCE WAS BRAVE but largely futile. At best it bought time for France and England, but the price was high. Belgian troops suffered heavy casualties, while German troops destroyed large areas of land, more cities, and many civilians. Even before the fall of Antwerp in early October, Belgian officials were in the United States asking for aid of any available variety; a Comité Central and then a Comité National were formed within the country to give relief to the unemployed; finally, groups of men from Belgium and elsewhere met in England to attempt a major relief action. The British, while sympathetic toward the plight of the Belgians, had no wish to be supplying the Germans with grain, and they were at first unfriendly to any plans for the exportation of food. After much diplomatic maneuvering and the drafting of men, mostly Americans, into the service of the new organization, The Commission for Relief in Belgium—C.R.B.— quickly took shape. Its chief diplomatic protector outside Belgium was the American ambassador to London, Walter Hines Page; the organizing genius of the group was an unknown engineer who had made a fortune in mining, Herbert Clark Hoover. Inside Belgium, Whitlock would manage most of the Commission's diplomatic liaison with the German authorities, with the considerable help of Villalobar; Hugh Gibson would act as chief messenger and traveler between the occupied and unoccupied zones; and a group of Rhodes scholars, volunteering at the request of Hoover and Page, would manage much of the distribution.

The problem was immediate and serious. On October 16, Whitlock wired Bryan that Belgium, as a country that ordinarily produced only one sixth of its normal food consumption, was within two weeks of famine. "Winter is coming on and there are thousands who are without home and without hope"; relief was essential. The Germans had taken large stores of supplies to feed their own soldiers, and, with Belgium all but totally embargoed, new imports were impossible. In the Province of Hainaut, for example, the Germans had on August 23 taken 120 tons of wheat, 40 tons of bread, and large quantities of necessities such as sugar and coffee. Their levies continued until a deputation of the people begged Governor von der Goltz to stop. He did so. Then in early October, Dr. von Sandt, the civil governor of Brussels, informed the people that the Germans had food enough only for their own people, and that Belgians must take care of themselves; he suggested Holland. The Dutch declined for they had only enough to feed themselves. Soup kitchens appeared in Brussels, and many people soon were eating bread only one or two days a week. Industry was paralyzed, and large numbers could not pay for food even if it were obtainable. Conditions throughout the country were equally bad.[1]

On September 5, the men within Belgium organized, the Americans under the leadership of Heineman, Shaler, and Hulse and the Belgians under Solvay and Émile Francqui. Through his numerous German friends, Heineman was able to get the German commander, von der Goltz, to answer a request of Whitlock's in a way encouraging to the relief committee. On September 17, von der Goltz wrote Whitlock that his government would not levy further on Belgian stores and would not impound goods imported by the committee, but he warned that contraband found in any shipments would cause the confiscation of the whole, and he retained the right of Germany to supervise the allocation and distribution of the food. At this response, the committee sent Shaler— who was an old friend of Hoover's—to London with a credit of

$100,000 to buy two or three thousand tons of food, but the Belgian ambassador in London could not arrange for a permit to get the food through the British blockade. Shaler sought out Hoover for advice. Hoover suggested that the British might allow the food to be sent directly to Whitlock, if he would guarantee that only civilians would get it. Hoover then introduced Shaler to Walter Hines Page, and Page promptly obtained state department authorization for the moves. Then, with the aid of Spanish Ambassador to London Señor Merry del Val y Zulueta, Page managed to get Shaler his permit. Hoover then enjoyed several peaceful hours when he was sure his work was done. But his delusions about his freedom soon disappeared: Page telephoned and asked him to take over the whole operation permanently. After a night of prayer and consultation with his wife, the Quaker Hoover took the step and accepted. For the rest of his life he remained in public service.[2]

Hoover, characteristically, lost no time. Hugh Gibson had just arrived from Brussels, and the two men, soon close friends, set to work. Hoover contacted all his engineering friends, and soon Millard Hunsiker, Edgar Rickard, John F. Lucey, John Beaver White, Ben S. Allen, and of course Shaler, were hard at work. Page accepted the post of honorary chairman, and other diplomats gave their names when asked, with Americans, Spaniards, and Dutch most prominent. White suggested that in view of the large amounts of money involved, the Commission should engage public accountants, for the day when "some swine will rise up and say we either made a profit out of this business or that we stole the money"—as in fact some "swine" eventually did. When the announcement of these activities received newspaper publicity, an American student at Oxford, Perrin Galpin, came in to volunteer and suggested that his friends who were Rhodes scholars would willingly offer themselves. They did, and promptly went into Belgium with Heineman, Hulse, and Shaler. Hoover remained to face formidable tasks of organization. He had to build up food supplies so they could be shipped; he had to get the Germans and the British to agree not to molest the ships or their contents; he had to get blockade permits and the right to charter ships in wartime; he had to organize a worldwide charity to supply the money and goods the Belgians needed; he had to get money from countries already at war and in desperate need of money already, in order to subsidize the shipments; and he had to properly organize the Belgians for efficient distribution of the food.[3]

Not the least of Hoover's problems—and one he and Whitlock and their fellow workers faced again and again—was the working of the militarist mind, whether German, British, or French. Nothing else outlined the real issues of the war to an American liberal like Whitlock quite so much as the reaction that Englishmen like Lord Kitchener and Winston Churchill and Germans like von Tirpitz and von Lüttwitz shared toward the humanitarian attempt to feed the starving Belgians. The German militarists said that they would gladly feed the Belgians, if only the illegal British blockade were lifted. Otherwise, they could not be expected to deprive German civilians in order to feed Belgian civilians. They frankly believed that the thought of millions of starving neutrals or civilians would force the British to allow food to be imported. Thus, they maintained that allowing the C.R.B. to bring in food weakened the pressure on the British. They also feared that spies would infiltrate the movement. Finally, they hated the Belgians for keeping German armies from crushing France in the first weeks of the war. General von Lüttwitz, as military governor, was frank: If the allies did not do their duty and feed the Belgians, he said, "they are responsible for anything that may happen. If there are bread riots, the natural thing would be for us to drive the whole civil population into some restricted area"—such as Luxembourg—"build a barbed wire fence around them, and leave them to starve in accordance with the policy of their allies."

The British militarists were equally obtuse to any demands of simple humanity. The Germans had a moral obligation to feed the people of the countries they occupied, they said, and would have to do so if the C.R.B. did not operate. All the Relief accomplished was to take the pressure off the Germans. They claimed that Relief ships drained power from the necessities of war, that the Germans would face insurrections if starvation came to occupied areas, and that this would help the British war effort. In practice, while the Germans did at times infringe upon their agreements with the Relief, the few documented incidents seem to have been unintentional and the result of poor communication rather than deliberate misrepresentation. The British actually made more trouble, for they trusted the Germans not at all, and at times—with honorable exceptions—seemed quite willing to see poor, bleeding Belgium starve even while they were waging war supposedly to protect her neutrality from the vicious Hun. To cite one of countless examples, on December 3, 1914, Whitlock received a telegram saying that the British had been informed that German soldiers were eating Relief food while they stayed quartered in Belgian houses. It was just one of those "everlasting difficulties that pessimism, doubt and stupidity place in the way of our great work of revictualing," and there was no truth in it. "The German authorities are respecting our work and keeping all their engagements, and the organization of the Commission with its almost scientific method of distribution is such that it is practically impossible for our food to go to any but the suffering portion of the population." Never was the liberal hatred of the military and its mentality so justified. As American liberals at home soon discovered when the British brutally subdued Ireland, the war had little indeed to do with justice, morality, or scraps of paper.

The C.R.B. survived only because a few men of humanity in each country valued human lives more than the shibboleths of "military necessity." In his unsubtle way, Hoover all but browbeat influential men into support for his scheme. In England, Sir Edward Grey was friendly, and so were important officials like Lord Robert Cecil and Lord Eustace Percy; in France, President Poincaré and Aristide Briand, the Foreign Minister, balanced the militarists; and in Germany, Foreign Minister Gottlieb von Jagow and Interior Minister Theodor Lewald somewhat dampened the spirit of war horses like old von Tirpitz. Others managed to be persuaded, such as Lloyd George, who was most unfriendly at first, but who later changed under a Hoover barrage. Then there was the interesting case of Asquith. Asquith was not the most forceful of men and apparently soon found himself dominated by the military-minded. Hoover acted characteristically and typically: he sent a long letter to Will Irwin in New York, outlining the militarist position in the least friendly of lights, and then added: "Hold this until I send a cablegram releasing it, then blow the gaff, and let the work of revictualing go up in a loud report that shall resound over the world to England's detriment." Then he went to Asquith, argued his case, and added, "You have America's sym-

pathy only because America feels pity for the suffering Belgians."
Then he showed him the letter he had sent to Irwin, and said, "I
will send a telegram at once, and tomorrow morning the last
vestige of pity for England in America will disappear. Do you
want me to do it?"

Asquith was, after all, Prime Minister, and was not used to
being talked to that way; so he informed Hoover. Unfortunately
for his dignity, he was over a barrel and he knew it. "You told me
you were no diplomat, but I think you are an excellent one, only
your methods are not diplomatic."

Hoover had his permission.[4]

But belligerence could take Hoover only so far. Nothing was
more typical of the red tape, frustration, and misunderstanding
that Hoover had to overcome than the problem of German requisitions and British acceptance of German conditions. The original
letter from von der Goltz to Heineman and Whitlock, while promising much, specifically retained for Germany the right to oversee
food distribution. To the British and to Hoover also this was quite
unacceptable: A siphoning off of food would be all too easy and
would thus kill the whole project. Hoover asked Whitlock and
Villalobar to get von Bissing, who had replaced von der Goltz, to
modify the order, but von Bissing disliked Americans and Belgians and refused outright. Hoover then tried some of his undiplomatic diplomacy and went over von Bissing's head to Berlin. He
informed American Ambassador to Berlin James W. Gerard of
the requisitioning and the British attitude toward it; Gerard
promptly secured the authorization from the proper people. On
December 26, German Under Secretary for Foreign Affairs Arthur Zimmermann informed Gerard that "the Imperial Governor-
General in Belgium will issue without delay an order prohibiting
all the troops under his command from requisitioning food or
forage of any kind whatsoever which would require to be replaced
by importations by the American Committee for Belgian Relief"
and authorized Whitlock and Villalobar to do anything reasonable
to see that Germany kept her promise. Whitlock joyfully received
the news and passed it on to Hoover. Sir Edward Grey, in the
meantime, had written Hoover a stiff note on the wickedness of
Germans generally and the conditions which the C.R.B. had to
meet, but Gerard's work for the moment quieted him down. Von

Bissing gave a grudging acquiescence, and the coast seemed clear. Then von Bissing backed out. On March 12, 1915, he re-affirmed the guarantee against requisitioning imported food, but said that he could not agree that "every product obtained from our soil" was already being imported and thus not subject to requisi-tion; "in particular, it is not within my knowledge that oats, straw, hay, potatoes, fresh vegetables, and sugar are imported in such quantities that my prohibition should be extended to these articles also." If, he continued, the English insisted in stopping all requisi-tioning, "I regret that I am not in a position to give such a declara-tion . . ." Thus, all previous agreements were in effect invalid. Back to Gerard. Hoover was quite explicit: If "the Emperor him-self would interest himself in seeing that our humanitarian efforts are carried out," then the C.R.B. could proceed and the Belgians could be fed. While he did so, Lord Eustace Percy complained about the breach and said that any requisitioning "will lead us immediately to reconsider our whole attitude." More pressure on Gerard, who was not making much progress. A barrage of tele-grams sped between Berlin, Brussels, Washington, and London. Gerard finally got through to the next best thing to the Emperor, Foreign Minister von Jagow, and could tell Hoover that the For-eign Office had ordered von Bissing to agree. Hoover, however, should go to Brussels himself and do everything personally. He went at once. Von Bissing stalled, set up exceptions to the agree-ment, and generally complicated matters. The British did not like it and told Hoover so when he returned. But, using Whitlock as intermediary for the Americans and the intelligent von der Lancken as intermediary for the Germans, the parties finally reached agreement. Von Bissing soon broke it, but the Belgians could eat for a while longer. Similar difficulties plagued Hoover's shipping agreements, and despite all precautions several C.R.B. ships were sunk, with loss of men and cargo.[5]

Inside Brussels, things were hardly less confused and frustrat-ing. To Whitlock's great joy, food consigned to him was soon arriving at Rotterdam and, after innumerable complications, reaching Belgian stomachs. But his duties, while officially placing him in command, actually had little to do with distribution. The Rhodes scholars and engineer friends of Hoover did that. Unfor-tunately, Whitlock noted, the life of a diplomat was the life of a diplomat, and "the minor task of keeping peace in the family seemed, by some unkind fatality, to fall to the lot of the person who happened to be American Minister at Brussels, and seemed to offer a convenient human substance to absorb all the numerous shocks." Some tasks were relatively painless, if time-consuming. On November 29, 1914, Shaler and Hoover showed up with two distinguished representatives from the Rockefeller Foundation, Ernest Percy Bicknell and Wickliffe Rose. Hoover was his usual brusque, businesslike self, getting things done with a minimum of fuss, but he was full of the petty warfare that was going on in American charitable circles about which group or religious denomination would get credit for and control of Relief efforts. Bicknell and Rose grilled Whitlock for two hours about conditions, and all later chatted with Mme Carton de Wiart, who dropped in. During the next few days, Whitlock and Gibson chauffeured their visitors from soup kitchen to bread store, showing the men the extent of the suffering. Hoover was particularly impressed, and he and Émile Francqui, an old acquaintance from his China mining days, made preliminary banking arrangements for financing the Relief. Certainly the Rockefeller men were impressed. On Christmas Eve, Rose took Whitlock aside and said that he had been, as Whitlock wrote in his journal, "everywhere in Belgium, had seen everything, had taken no man's word for anything, had been in the homes of the poorest, and he spoke with tears in his eyes of their sufferings, their patience, their forbearance and charity." Whitlock was "moved and surprised." Of somewhat less importance were the visitors who came to Whitlock in all seriousness and proposed that he organize a committee to spray the battlefields with disinfectants. Certainly, the reform impulse did not completely die with the declaration of war.[6]

But visitors normally were real problems rather than minor irritations. Whitlock's own published account of his war years all but omitted the personal quarreling, bickering, and plain nastiness of individual members of the Relief and the diplomatic corps associated with it, but his frequent feeling of despair was in no small part due to such ignoble behavior. At the start, he was friendly enough with Gibson and Hoover, but that did not last. Even from the beginning, he had troubles with lesser figures. The American minister to the Hague, Henry Van Dyke, for example, was a prissy littérateur with an unbounded sense of his own importance, and no one found him enjoyable to work with. Whitlock scorned him, called him "Reverend" in private, and after one of Van Dyke's more absurd posturings, wrote: "Van Dyke has assumed entire charge of the question of revictualing and will issue his orders to all ministries, ministers, presidents, kings, emperors, field-marshalls, generals and civilians. Most wonderful to behold." At the same time, Jarvis E. Bell, briefly a member of the Relief in the early months, took a violent dislike to Dannie Heineman and often came ranting to Whitlock with his opinions. After one particularly nasty session, Whitlock could only record that "Bell is dreadful: talks all the time, and his sentences never have verbs, no end, no aim, no result," and yet "Hoover sent him here to take charge. I think he is an ignorant man, and a poseur." Then, as for himself, he could only sigh: "What a life for a peaceful man to have to lead!" Heineman, who was undeniably capable, somehow seemed to bring out the worst in several people. Shortly after Bell's tirade, the most terrible temper in Brussels walked into the legation. Villalobar was furious and subjected Whitlock to half an hour of table beating, something Whitlock would have tolerated from no one else. Heineman, it soon appeared, had sent out letters on stationery that did not have Villalobar's name in the correct position; "I am the one who started all this," he raged with something less than complete accuracy. "What a scene this mad, touchy Spaniard made. A great troublemaker over trifles," Whitlock wrote later. Villalobar demanded an interview with Hoover, Francqui, and Lambert to settle the matter. When Whitlock told Francqui all about it, the Belgian simply remarked, "He has Heineman on the brain, as the Brussels people say."

Hoover caused enormous friction. He could speak nothing but English. He was tactless and without sympathy for men with problems unconcerned with his own. He constantly deprecated any attempt to thank him for his work, yet displayed great pique if he were ever treated with less than the greatest deference. Whitlock did respect him greatly, but complained time after time that Hoover was trying to be with and impossible to conciliate if he were irritated. Whitlock had a far smaller sense of his own importance, had great tact, and had learned to speak French fluently, so he inevitably found himself caught in the middle, soothing

Hoover, or Francqui, or Villalobar, or von der Lancken, or some other ruffled official. With Hoover, perhaps the most serious problem was the difference in personality. When the Belgians did not display the proper gratitude to Hoover and his men, Hoover displayed his frame of mind. "Our real difficulty lies in the lack of esteem and consideration which the C.R.B. possesses as an *institution* in itself," he wrote Whitlock. "It has always been my belief, that a great work cannot be done by individuals but only by institutions and the association with a successful institution is sufficient gratification for any individual." Praise not Hoover, but be unspeakably glad for the organization that was all but synonymous with his name! He wished no praise for himself, of course, but "the prestige of the institution has somehow got to be built up and constantly safeguarded." Naturally, "I am not inspired by any desire to receive for myself or my associates gratitude for what has been done, but I do believe that a true understanding of the role of this commission and its dominating vital importance, will facilitate the task to which we are all devoted."[7] That was not the sort of humility Whitlock was accustomed to.

Even without Hoover around the Relief posed many problems. Sometimes they solved themselves, more or less. The easiest problem looked hardest to the outsider: How to organize a country for relief? That Belgian civil government Whitlock so admired when he toured Europe before the war was composed of 2,633 communes, or municipalities. The C.R.B. took over this organization as it stood. Each of these municipalities was accustomed to governing itself. Each had a common council, and within the council was a mayor and several échevins, or, roughly, commissioners, who headed the various departments. The communes were grouped into 233 cantons, the cantons into 41 arrondissements, and the arrondissements into 9 provinces—these latter usually coextensive with the old principalities. Here and there the Germans had arrested a mayor or shot a council head, but for the most part the system, previously so efficient, remained intact. The Relief, led by Francqui, used the existing apparatus. This stout, nervous man, genial yet dignified, a natural leader with much banking experience, and shrewd and tough enough to match Hoover, worked closely with Whitlock and became a good friend. Under him, the food was distributed with all the efficiency that proved possible.[8]

Far more serious problems accompanied the issue of the *Passierscheine*. These passes presumably enabled C.R.B. men to come and go as their duties demanded. Unfortunately, the signature of von der Goltz or von Bissing did not seem to matter much to the sentries, and men frequently found themselves stopped, delayed, or imprisoned while performing their duties. Confronted by the evidence, the civilian authorities could only shrug, for in Brussels as everywhere in the German Empire, military necessity overruled the promises and honor of the civilian rulers. "Messieurs les militaires" commanded, and it was done. Whatever their intentions, von Bissing and von der Lancken were frequently unable to overrule the military, and the sometimes deplorable treatment of Relief officials was often not their fault, hard though this may have been to believe for those men who came from countries where civilian control of the military was a guaranteed freedom. Two incidents, however, achieved enough attention to get the two civilians doing what little they could by way of issuing orders. One morning, when proper passes were promised at least to men of the standing of Whitlock and Villalobar, the latter stormed in and told Whitlock that their passes only permitted them to go into certain parts of Belgium, with gasoline subject to requisition at all times. Both complained, and new *Passierscheine* arrived. These permitted travel only for the inspection of Relief activity, i.e., food distribution. Whitlock refused this also; the Marquis had a thoroughly grouchy disposition by this time and was in no mood for nonsense.

"Monsieur," he informed the man who presented the insulting document to him, "I am no flour merchant; I will not accept it."

The chastened representative, unable to cope with such utter contempt, went away, and soon yet another set of passes arrived. Villalobar inspected the replacement. "No flour," he said. He accepted it, but he never let the Germans forget it. "Oh, as for me," he said to von der Lancken the next morning, "a poor little baker like me should never disturb a personage as eminent as you." He continued, rubbing it in as only he could, "you pay me too great an honor. During the French Revolution the republicans called Louis XVI, Marie Antoinette and the dauphin, the baker, the baker's wife, and the doughboy." And forever after, the poor baker selling flour reappeared in withering contempt whenever he wished to rub something into the German hide.[9]

The second incident underlined the contrast between the well-intentioned German civilian authorities and the brutal military. When the complaints about the *Passierscheine* came to a head, the Governor General assigned one of his officers, a Dr. Poigntner, to accompany the C.R.B. man. Both were equipped with the most fashionable passes. At the frontier, soldiers halted the car and began searching it. The German, in civilian clothes, protested and showed his pass. The guard told him to shut up. He protested again, and said explicitly who he was. He got his face smashed in for his trouble. He was then arrested and taken to the Kommandantur. He explained again, and was silenced. He was taken under guard to Antwerp and further mistreated. According to one report he had a broken nose, two black eyes, and unnamed other injuries. When he finally staggered back to Brussels, with a more intelligent understanding of C.R.B. problems, his superiors promptly threatened to have offending guards court-martialed. C.R.B. men thereafter carried "C.G.'s," *Passiercheine* with the personal signature of the Governor General, documents "much sought after for the sedative effect they exercised on sentinels."[10]

Such incidents were bad enough, but at least they were reasonably open and above board. Much more was not. Whitlock always had the uncanny sensation that someone was at his elbow, watching. At night, furtive shadows came and went, and figures stood half concealed in doorways. Men would meet and then glance about to make sure of privacy before talking, and no one dared gossip on the trams. Suddenly at the legation would appear someone with a tale of desperation. How to get letters to England? Or: I am a French soldier, can't you help me get back? Or a newspaper man or woman would arrive, often with impressive credentials, asking for a frank statement about real conditions in Belgium or an assessment of von Bissing as a ruler. Often Whitlock could say, with all his Whitechapel sarcasm, "Wait until you can speak French without a German accent, and then come back," but the whole series of episodes got on his nerves. "Their poor ruses were so transparent! How much of the German taxpayer's money has been expended in the purchase of scoundrels! And all wasted!" Everywhere people suddenly found themselves denounced, often for no reason but a private animus, arrested, and then tried, deported, or shot. The guilty and the innocent suffered

with the impartiality of war. The vast and vaunted German efficiency Whitlock viewed as a joke. It knew only one word: "ver-
boten." Instead of simple guideposts, a series of prohibitions. The
best example was the park in the center of Brussels. The Germans
had taken it from the people for the use of officers, and one day
Whitlock went to one of the entrances: "I counted twenty-six sign-
boards, of many colors with their various verbotens. Before the
war the only signs I recall were those reminding the public that
certain places were reserved for the children to play in. But then
the Belgians had learned liberty in their communal system, and
had their own pride in their own park." In short, "the very air is
poisoned with militarism," and "one has a constant sense of personal discomfort, one is everywhere ill at ease, one cannot voice
one's own thoughts. There is a menace everywhere, and in this
poisoned atmosphere one suffocates."[11]

At times, he rallied, often through the indestructible children.
One he could never forget was the moppet of four, of mixed
Belgian and American ancestry, a small girl he was trying to get
out of the war zone. Finally, her *Passierschein* came through, and
she made her last visit to the legation. She had, she whispered, a
secret; in fact, a goodbye present. She obtained the Minister's ear
and whispered in it quite softly that in her muff she had hidden
two chocolate bonbons, one for her, and one for the Minister. A
few days later, Christmas descended cold and sharp, and the C.R.B.
did what it could for less fortunate children. Suddenly the word
spread through Brussels: A ship was coming, from American children to Belgian children; Christmas would not be so joyless as had
been feared. Belgian tunes were forbidden, so all gathered around a
tree supplied by Lewis Richards and sang "The Star Spangled
Banner." There was even real cake and *gâteau de beurre*, obtained
from heaven knew where. The children were wild with delight,
and all day messages of gratitude poured into the old legation.

Even the mail from home had its moments. Normally, this
consisted of large quantities of requests that the Minister find
someone's friend or relative. Increasingly, it held often lucrative
requests that he write up his experiences and send them out for the
world to see. But every once in a while a citizen with an imperfect
understanding of world affairs would inquire about problems
which concerned them. Early in 1915, for example, Whitlock

wrote two letters that indicate how he sometimes spent his mornings. "Dear Madam," he wrote to Anna Jarvis, "Your letter written on the 6th October reached me only today. It is exceedingly difficult for me to advise you what to do in order to establish Mother's Day in Belgium at this time . . ." And two months later, he wrote to Mr. Joseph N. Wells of Toledo: "Dear Sir. I should indeed be happy to place you in correspondence with some young Belgian man who is a collector of stamps, but inasmuch as all postal service in Belgium is suspended, it would be impossible for you to exchange letters with anyone."[12]

The Brussels children's Christmas of 1914 was the start of an episode that only a literary man like Whitlock could appreciate fully. Reliable newspapers were banned in Brussels, and yet somehow the news of the Minister's sympathies and the sympathies of most of his countrymen were known in every corner of the city and soon throughout the country too. Brussels political figures were all but totally muzzled; Burgomaster Adolphe Max was in exile in Germany, where his intransigence could not strengthen his fellow citizens. All Belgians lived in constant fear of the Germans and could do little openly. But the American Legation was a privileged sanctuary. Whitlock was accredited to a government that was not there, to be sure, but the Germans respected his diplomatic immunities and those of the people under his protection, with only minor harassment. He represented the largest neutral power in the world, and he was the most conspicuous leader of the Relief. The Germans did not wish to offend him in either capacity. But with remarkable rapidity and no apparent planning, America and her minister slowly became powerful beyond all measurement to the imagination. Americans were the largest contributors to the charitable part of C.R.B. finances. Herbert Hoover was an American. The Rhodes scholars were Americans. The Spanish and the Dutch, of great importance to the operation, were all but invisible to the Belgians, and their representatives in Brussels made no pretense of being popular figures. But Whitlock was different, and his country had children who sent boatloads of gifts to the children of Belgium. The result was perhaps predictable, but no less overwhelming when it happened. When the Germans banned the Belgian flag, out came the Stars and Stripes; when they banned pictures of King Albert and his Queen, out came pictures of Woodrow Wilson and Whitlock; most apparent, and most touching, when they banned the celebration of Belgian holidays, the Belgians promptly began to celebrate every American holiday they could find. Brand Whitlock suddenly found himself the father of all the country.

Christmas began these customs, but New Year's Day 1915 confirmed them. Whitlock had asked for no manifestations, for fear that the Germans would be offended and that the people would suffer. Nevertheless, by tacit consent, there were all varieties of manifestations. One was particularly memorable. In the morning, at the legation door, stood uniformed Belgian policemen, in blue with smart képis, great blue capes, white gloves and swords. Baron Lambert, without Whitlock's knowledge, had put a blank book, handsomely bound in morocco, on the table; it was marked discreetly, 1 Janvier 1915. Whitlock asked his servant Gustave about it when he went out for his walk and received merely a knowing smile in return; the police saluted silently. All day the people came, alone, in pairs, in little groups. Those from the Quartier Léopold came in formal dress, with frock coats and high hats. Others arrived in Sunday best, with American flags for boutonnières; some had pictures of Wilson or Whitlock instead. They walked in, signed their names, left cards, lifted their hats to the Minister if he was there, and went away without a word. Those who had no time to wait in line to sign left their cards, and the latch in the door clicked steadily all day long. Brussels was as classless in its affections as Toledo had been: The cards included the engraved names of princes, noblemen, and the oldest families; some were simply tradesmen's business cards; some were pieces of cardboard, for many of the poor of course had no cards. Some had simply "P.F." marked on them for "pour féliciter," or perhaps "Félicitations et Remerciements" or a more involved message. Some were marked, in the rough hand of a Flemish workman, "Dank." All day they came, not only with cards and signatures but with bouquets of flowers so full of orchids and roses that by dark the legation smelled like a bower. All the Americans in town came to visit too, as did Villalobar and most of the diplomatic corps. For a whole nation, America and her minister were coming to symbolize freedom, peace, and the humane life.[13]

Once begun, the customs became permanent. On February 14,

Whitlock noticed that the American flag was everywhere. One Belgian told him that the people were celebrating the first anniversary of the day Whitlock presented his credentials to the King. Perhaps, for some, that was true. But it turned out that for the majority, it was a celebration of the great American national holiday, St. Valentine's Day, and all day the cards and the flowers—and even some personal gifts—came in. Then apparently the news went around that February 14 had no major significance for Americans, and the response was automatic. On February 20 a Belgian police sergeant came to the legation. What arrangements did the Minister want made for the great festival on Monday? "Ça sera quelque chose de colossal!" he said. Whitlock was in despair at the thought of the German reaction. Gibson went after Francqui and Lemonnier, to get them to stop it. An alderman called to request the Minister to accept a valuable Van Dyck sketch. Whitlock, so involved was he in matters like Wilson's submarine notes to the Germans, the status of men attached to the legation, passes, and such, had forgotten the vital fact: February 22 was the great American holiday, the birthday of President Washington! It turned out to be a lovely day, and the first thing Whitlock saw when he got up was the Belgian sergeant, in gloves, sword, and so on, directing the crowds in front of the legation. Looking on were more crowds, including many known German spies. Again the cards poured in and the flowers accumulated, sent by children and hospitals and schools as well as the public. Deeply touching, and enough to worry a chronic worrier to distraction. Would von Bissing object? If he did, he kept quiet about it.[14]

Such displays moved the Minister greatly, but they did not entirely improve the humor of a man who kept receiving news which disturbed him. From America, he received word of Theodore Roosevelt's irresponsibly belligerent attacks on President Wilson's neutrality policy, and all his old distrust of Roosevelt returned. Roosevelt was "an incorrigible and inveterate romanticist. He has worn many uniforms, carried many swords, and ridden about on horses, no doubt pretending at the time, or playing like a child, that he was at the head of a vast army, continually dramatizing himself, imagining himself to be like the heroes in the boys' story-books." Roosevelt had no idea what the European war was all about, and his Spanish-American exploits only deceived him further. Like most people, he did not know what war was; such people "imagine it can be carried on in some clean pretty fashion, as it is carried on in books and pictures. They cannot realize the horrors, the degradations, the unspeakable and ferocious cruelty of it all." Even more depressing to Whitlock was news of a more personal nature: His brother Frank, who had been studying medicine in Philadelphia, had died suddenly. The news reached him only two days before the St. Valentine's Day display. Just as depressing in its way, and longer lasting, was the whole atmosphere of occupied Belgium. Sometimes Whitlock could forget about it for a while, but often he could not, and visitors reminded him of it. Albert Jay Nock visited for several days in February, but could scarcely stay ten days. The atmosphere choked him, he told his old friend. It was choking everyone, and the end was not in sight.[15]

America, capable at times of depressing Whitlock though always retaining its symbolic virtues for the Belgians, shared the spotlight—in Whitlock—with three other symbols of the Belgium that was and would be. Characteristically, the minister who had idolized his grandfather, Frank Hurd, Altgeld, Jones, and Woodrow Wilson soon came to idolize, in much the same way as the Belgians, these three symbols. The first was most obvious, yet most distant from Brussels. The quiet, tolerant Catholic King of the Belgians, Albert, had rallied his people bravely at the start of the war, and he and his queen were maintaining an exile government behind the French and English lines. Albert was made to be respected. A quiet boy, lonely and retiring, he had shown nevertheless a strong sense of mischief when a student, and his sense of dignity, though strong, never quite overwhelmed his sense of humor. Incognito, he had in peacetime inspected his country's economic conditions and had shocked court circles by driving trains and donning miners' suits for descents into coal pits. He was widely traveled and had visited America and much of Europe as a part of his education. He had also come at a most opportune time: The Belgians had a very domestic notion of what was proper in royalty, and the misfortunes of King Léopold's private life had contributed greatly to his unpopularity. Albert made his entire country happy by marrying the Duchess of Bavaria, Princess Elizabeth, in a love match that had nothing to do with reasons of state. When he ascended the throne, he was the best of democratic monarchs; like the American minister, he was democratic in politics, aristocratic in taste, and libertarian by temperament. He cultivated the arts, preferred work among the poor to court ritual, and never stopped repeating that a prince "is merely a man who has more duties to fulfill" than other men. The people of occupied Brussels all but worshipped him.[16]

Albert, however, was in exile. Désiré Félicien François Joseph Cardinal Mercier definitely was not. The son of an impoverished tanner who died early, the young man had early shown both brilliance and piety, and with the support of local priests he had managed to get a good, rigorous, classical Catholic education. A true ascetic repelled by anything suggesting the sensuous, he came as close to being a living saint as anyone in Belgium; his intellect equaled his piety, and while still in his twenties he became adept at the intricacies of moral philosophy. In his early thirties he became Professor of Thomistic Philosophy at the University of Louvain and was soon a popular and respected teacher as well as a brilliant expounder of the unfamiliar doctrine of Aquinas. He was also psychologically understanding and humane. As one of his students remembered, he had a way with him. Once the student had been lax in preparing a thesis handed in to the imposing Mercier. A few days later, the summons to a coffee-time conference came. Once there, the student listened intently to the fascinating conversation, all but forgetting his fears. Only at the end did Mercier say goodbye and hand back the thesis. On the cover he had written, "II Thess. III-10." The student rushed back to his cubicle and found the passage: "For even when we were with you, this we commanded you, that if any would not work, neither should he eat."

Such a man became Archbishop in 1906 and Cardinal in 1907, by then thoroughly learned in neurology, chemistry, mathematics, and biology, as well as in his specialties. Then came the war and the utter destruction of his beloved Louvain, its cathedral, and irreplaceable library. Many students were killed. Except for a trip to Rome, Mercier stayed with his flock and slowly drove von Bissing almost to distraction and very close to indiscretion. In one of the more incredible minor chapters of Belgian wartime history, he even engaged the cultivated von der Lancken in a debate over the philosophical justifications for certain German acts; as men died and were deported, these two intellectual leaders of their peoples in Belgium debated, among other things, the categorical imperative. But what converted all Belgians to the Cardinal, if not his religion, was his Christmas 1914 message to the Belgian people: "Patriotism and Endurance." Read in every church under his jurisdiction, it made von Bissing furious, caused numerous arrests of minor clergy, and, but for von der Lancken's intervention, might well have resulted in the Cardinal's deportation to Germany. Whitlock, like Belgium, was thrilled and captivated. Belgium, Mercier said, had kept faith with her friends by defending her independence: Germany broke her word even as Belgium kept hers. At such a time, duty required him to tell those who relied on him of their duties to this occupying power. "This power is not a legitimate authority, and consequently at the bottom of your heart you owe it neither respect, attachment, nor obedience. The sole legitimate authority in Belgium is that which belongs to our King, to his Government, and to the representatives of the nation." No one else could properly claim allegiance.

In his view, the acts of the occupying power were without legal force, but such as were conducive to the public interest should be obeyed "as long as they neither conflict with the liberty of our conscience, nor with our patriotic duty . . ." Belgians should devote themselves to the common interest and by their patriotism show that they had not forgotten their religion or their country. "The religion of Christ made patriotism a law. There can be no perfect Christian who is not a perfect patriot." The whole tone of frank distaste for the invaders, of quiet assurance that they would have but a short stay, and the exhortation to suffer only those laws which they themselves found proper naturally caused an eruption, but von Bissing knew—except on rare occasions when he completely lost his temper—that any harm done to Mercier would cause a worldwide condemnation. It would also alienate Catholic Germans, whose devotion to Prussian militarism was notoriously weak. But Mercier would never quit, and all through the occupation at the proper times he delivered messages to his flock, calming them and encouraging patience—a function von Bissing could never comprehend, for he saw only the implied contempt.[17]

Seven weeks later, the Cardinal came to the legation to thank

both Whitlock and America for their efforts on behalf of his people. Tall, strong and spare, he came in wearing a long black
soutane with red piping and sash; he walked in long, quick strides,
kicking vigorously out at the skirt with each step, as though it held
him back. He had won Whitlock already, and the meeting was
most cordial. To the American, here was a man of strength and
tolerance, democratic in his asceticism and utter lack of preten-
tion, yet a Prince of the Church: roughly the same combination of
democracy and aristocracy that Albert had and that Whitlock so
admired. Indeed, but for the Cardinal red, "he would have recalled some tall, gaunt, simple, affectionate Irish priest, whose life
was passed in obscure toil among the poor, in humble homes, amid
lowly lives whose every care and preoccupation he knew and sympathized with." Mercier was the sort of man who would be "going
about at night alone in all weathers, unsparing of himself, visiting
the sick and the imprisoned, forgetting to eat, accustomed to long,
weary vigils, and of an independence that needed none of the
reliances or approvals of this earth." To Whitlock, his greatness
was obvious. "In his mere presence one felt all little things shrivel
up, and wondered why small annoyances should fret and irritate;
and when he had gone the impalpable influences of his lofty spirit
hung for hours about one in the air." His personality, "alone and
of itself, proved the superiority of moral over physical force."[18]

But even the Cardinal did not infuriate von Bissing so much as
the presence, week after week, of the little clandestine newssheet,
La Libre Belgique. All Whitlock knew was that, at "regularly
irregular" intervals, the paper appeared in the mailboxes of the
legations of the United States, Spain, and the Netherlands—and at
the Kommandantur. Only years after the war did most of the story
become common knowledge, in this, one of the most incredible
cloak-and-dagger exploits of any war. The occupation forces had
forbidden any papers not censored by the Kommandantur, and
instead published their own doctored propaganda papers. The appearance of one of these so angered certain bruxellois that they
began the new paper. They were a motley group, destined for
years of decimation, heroism, and fear. Victor Jourdain, an old,
heavy man in his seventies, had a long career behind him as a
Catholic pacifist agitator; Eugène Van Doren, the brother-in-law
of Jourdain's son, was a middle-aged and thoroughly myopic fa-

ther of five; the Abbé de Moor, a black-haired man who was strong as a horse, was a good friend with wide underground acquaintance—he was in close contact with the exiled Belgian government, with the British Intelligence Service, and with Edith Cavell's organization for getting stranded French, Belgian, and British soldiers across the frontier; Père Paquet was a Jesuit who in peacetime was a charity organizer; Julie Van Doren, Eugène's spinster daughter, was also his loyal secretary; Arthur Allard, a quiet, middle-aged craftsman, was the regular printer; Philippe Baucq was a young and utterly fearless architect, also in the Cavell group and destined to die with Miss Cavell; and Gabrielle Petit, a heroine to her entire country, was the niece of a de Moor neighbor, who had just turned twenty-one and still looked seventeen. She organized a spy network for British Intelligence and belonged to the Cavell group, along with her newspaper activities. She went before a firing squad utterly unrepentant, with a loud and withering scorn for the Germans. A motley group, to be sure, but none the less effective for that.

The early leaders first forged their plans in the clandestine printing and distributing of "Patriotism and Endurance." That operation successful, they began *La Libre Belgique* with a characteristic flair. The Abbé de Moor had a young and pretty sister of wit and discretion; she lived close to Van Doren. De Moor went to see her and bought a large, pale-pink envelope on the way—an envelope lined with unmistakably feminine, pastel-tinted paper. He explained his plan to his sister and cautioned her not to wait for an answer. Half an hour later a smartly dressed girl in a heavy veil came up shyly to the stalwart sentry at von Bissing's offices in the old Ministry of Agriculture.

"Is the Freiherr von Bissing in?" she asked in a soft German. "It's a very personal matter . . ." And she took the perfumed envelope from her purse.

A young orderly nearby grinned in instant comprehension. "Yes, Fräulein. His Excellency is in. What can I do for you?"

"You would be very kind to hand him this," she said sweetly, and added, "It is very important. It is for him personally."

The man was agreeable, and the girl said she would return the next day for her answer. A few minutes later, von Bissing got his first copy of *La Libre Belgique*.

Von Bissing at first did not take the threat very seriously, but he soon changed his mind; the sheet, despite numerous arrests, searches, interrogations, and executions somehow managed to stay alive throughout the war. The Belgians were physically beaten, but they never gave up. Whitlock regularly received his copies.[19]

Meanwhile affairs became more and more tense between the Germans and the Americans, both outside the country and in Brussels. The sinking of American ships, most notably the *Lusitania*, caused great dismay both in Washington and Brussels. Because dispatches apparently took two weeks to come from Washington to him, Whitlock learned of the events only after considerable delay; when he did, he could only mourn his own lost friends, such as Elbert Hubbard, who went to the bottom, and live in constant apprehension that war would be declared. He and the others attached to the legation lived with their bags packed, expecting orders to leave at any moment; Whitlock anticipated them by shipping his most valuable manuscripts and papers to Van Dyke at The Hague for safekeeping. The Belgians were equally apprehensive, for they knew where their food came from and who kept them alive. Every day they passed by the legation to make sure the flag was still flying. If it were not, they knew war was at hand.[20]

But, depressing as the submarine war became, it was less important to Whitlock and his peace of mind than the war of nerves waged by von Bissing and the petty German bureaucrats against the C.R.B. Indeed, Whitlock more than half suspected that some minor officials accused C.R.B. men of imaginary crimes only to demonstrate their zeal to von Bissing and thus win promotion. But the real cause of friction was von Bissing's all but uncontrollable desire to place every possible activity under close German scrutiny and require that everything be done the German way. On April 14, 1915, Whitlock received word at the legation that a German representative of von Bissing had arrived at a meeting of the Belgian Red Cross and notified the people that they were removed from their posts and that von Bissing proposed to take over the Red Cross and run it through a delegate he would name, who would also have the backing of the army. The Red Cross representatives promptly came to the most obvious assistant. Fortunately,

Villalobar drove up almost immediately afterward and had the whole story repeated to him. He and Whitlock discussed the situation, which of course was officially none of their business, and agreed that a polite letter of protest from the Red Cross to von Bissing was about all that could be done, aside from an official protest to the International Red Cross in Geneva. As Villalobar remarked, it was but one more example of German stupidity, and there was little to be done.

But the Red Cross was not what was really bothering von Bissing. The next day, Whitlock and Villalobar went to see von der Lancken, and the latter explained that von Bissing was thoroughly annoyed by the activities of the Comité National, which had slowly achieved a kind of independent status as dispenser of C.R.B. food. Von Bissing could not tolerate this threat to his self-esteem and wished to take the operation over, although von der Lancken stressed that the Germans had great admiration for the organization of the C.R.B. The two diplomats tried to point out to von der Lancken that the Belgians were, after all, convinced of ultimate German defeat and merely trying to set up organizations that would allow their country to eat and themselves to gain a reputation for having helped their country in the war. Von der Lancken was far more intelligent than his boss and understood the situation. The whole matter was put off for the moment until von Bissing's demands could be put onto paper. As they were leaving, Villalobar reminded the German that the Belgians were indomitable. Von der Lancken started, then said: "Yes, we know that after our experience with Cardinal Mercier." Apparently heroes could be appreciated on both sides.

Several days later, Whitlock and Villalobar returned. Von der Lancken, dressed in a very light, blue-gray fatigue jacket with the ribbon of the Iron Cross, dark trousers strapped under his shoes, and spurs, began by matching his dress with a long, formal oration which reviewed the whole food operation. He also presented them with copies. Despite possible blunders on the part of a few men, the record of the Comité National was on the whole admirable, as the Germans admitted. In fact the organization had apparently been so efficient as to excite German envy, for they prided themselves on planning and organization. Furthermore, their inveterately suspicious natures saw spies everywhere, and they could not believe that the C.R.B. did not have its share. So far as Whitlock could tell, nothing could be more untrue, but as he sighed privately, an idea once lodged in the German mind was all but impossible to remove. The real motive soon came out: the Germans wanted to take over the C.R.B., just as they had the Red Cross, but could not quite persuade the diplomats of their right to do so, especially in the face of their own guarantees that they would not. Finally, in classic style, a few phrases were put onto paper for mutual enlightenment, the talk turned to the Belgian climate, and the crisis was put off for another day. Several meetings—including Belgian representatives—did not entirely clear the air, although the Red Cross was obviously lost. Whitlock predictably felt the whole matter internally. As he wrote dolefully: "Half sick this morning, partook of two resisting dishes at Cornet's last night, when one would have sufficed. They resisted all night."[21]

The accumulation of frustrations—the *Lusitania*, the C.R.B., the petty diplomatic round, Germans in general—all these finally drove Whitlock to sit down one night and sum up, in a notably acid portrait, occupied Brussels and its ruler. To Whitlock, von Bissing was an old man over seventy who looked like an aged drill sergeant. A man about five foot eight or ten, thin and stiff, with the hands of a workingman, he had a hard, round head, straight in back, with brown skin stretched over its bones and shaved smooth—all but the black moustache which gave a sinister look. The jaw was set firmly, and small, cruel, watery eyes glared out under hair plastered down by water or grease on the cannonball head. The old man spoke no English and little French and had no ideas beyond those of the Prussian militarist. He was untouched by either liberalism or modern ideas and found his satisfactions in a vain display of numerous ugly decorations. He could not even take a walk without his clanking saber. His men were so afraid of him that they did not dare to talk about important matters with him, so that, often, diplomatic appeals that reached the Kommandantur did not reach his desk. Von der Lancken, once when von Bissing was away, indiscreetly admitted that things would go easier until his return. Von Bissing was also violent in temper, and at times von der Lancken had to go to some desperate lengths to repair the damage his boss had created in minutes of anger. Von Bissing also had enormous pride, and he could never forgive Hoover for going over his head to Berlin for the C.R.B. Oddly enough, he could never quite understand the full nature of C.R.B. activities and apparently for many months firmly believed that it was little more than a soup-kitchen arrangement. Heineman, the only American he seemed able to talk to at all cordially, purposely did nothing to disabuse him of the idea.

He also demonstrated his usual incomprehension both of Belgium and of human psychology, not to mention common sense, by some of his acts. He apparently had ambitions for ruling Belgium as a normal German province, and, as normal German provinces had industrial activity, he ordered that Belgians resume their occupations. Of course, Germany had dismantled most of the factories and taken them to Germany, and the import-export restrictions firmly prevented the commerce vital to industry, but he could see no connection. He had ambitions for prestige in intellectual circles and made much propaganda by ordering that museums remain open and concerts be held, but Belgians avoided the institutions they had so prized before the war and refused to enter any place with German guards visible. Even agriculture, which the Belgians had organized far better than the Germans ever could, seemed open to his interference, and here he caused Whitlock and Hoover and their men many hours of frustration by his stupid meddling.

His city soon matched his personality. Five or six thousand spies hurried about, denouncing whom they pleased, and the courts convicted often enough on accusation, without proof. No householder was safe from the agents or their judges, or from the many soldiers who felt themselves insulted by a glance. When even the legal penalty was not sufficient, von Bissing might well add to it, in the most humiliating way he could. Even children were not safe, but were subject to arrest for imitating goose steps or otherwise mocking the troops. The occupation government, as anyone not from Germany knew, was a bureaucratic nightmare. The Germans were always losing important papers, filed away safely and promptly lost, and then demanding new copies and blaming the sender for negligence. And every day, the hated *affiches* announced new indignities, new rules, and new deaths for "trahison de guerre." Even the sarcastic minister had to fall silent, after a while, in the face of so much he hated. Only rarely would he burst out: "He is another Duke of Alva for this land, without either the courage or the intelligence of a Duke of Alva."[22]

Food problems unfortunately had a habit not of being solved but of simply walking around the block, disappearing only to reappear from another direction. Personalities were always a concern. Whitlock respected Hoover from the beginning, despite the obvious disparity in most of their interests. "I admire this man Hoover, who has a genius for organization and for getting things done, and beneath all, with his great intelligence, he has a wonderful human heart." Whitlock had written this soon after their first meeting. He repeated his approval the next June: ". . . the more I see of this excellent man the more I like him." But others did not get on nearly so well with Hoover, and even Whitlock's feelings soon changed. Particularly unfortunate was the antipathy that Villalobar and Hoover, those strong and eccentric personalities, soon took to each other. Whitlock found that before confronting the cases of the C.R.B. or the requisitionings, or whatever other problems were at hand, he had first to try to get these two of his most important colleagues on speaking terms. When the English, in June, demanded new assurances on the part of the Germans that crops would remain in Belgian hands and that the C.R.B. would function undisturbed, the first problems of diplomacy were at home in Brussels. In conference with Villalobar and Hoover and several Belgian and American members, Whitlock and the men decided on another stopgap plan. The Comité National would write to Whitlock and Villalobar saying that the C.R.B. must know what purchases to make for the period after the middle of August, when the new harvest was in.

A few days later Hoover came storming in again, furious at the treatment of his boys by the Germans. He was also, predictably enough, furious with Villalobar, who, he was convinced, was poisoning German minds against him and the C.R.B. He made one of his frequent threats to resign and stop the whole business, which he could do in a minute since the British trusted no one else. But of course he would not do so, simply because he cared too much for the Belgians. The next day Villalobar showed up and assured Whitlock that whatever Hoover might think about him, he admired Hoover and thought the Relief had to continue. Whitlock then went with him to see von der Lancken. The Ger-

man was cordial and received their notes in good humor; Whitlock
did most of the talking. The whole problem boiled down to one
question: what would the Germans do with the new crop? After
some verbal fencing, Whitlock started talking about specifics.

"What proportion of the food stock required by the Belgians
for a year will the new crop provide?"

"Roughly speaking about a fifth," von der Lancken replied.
"In normal times Belgium had to import four fifths of her food-
stuffs."

"Very well," Whitlock went on. "I will make you a proposition. The new crop is one fifth of the new supply for the coming
year. You can do one of two things. You can leave that one fifth
to the Belgians and the Commission for Relief in Belgium will
furnish the other four-fifths, and you will get in addition and very
cheaply—for the crop does not amount really to so very much—
the credit for having been just and generous. Or you can take that
one fifth and then import yourselves from Germany four fifths to
make up the deficit."

Von der Lancken thought for a moment and gave the obvious
answer. But then he added, "If we give you the one fifth, what
assurance have we that when the Belgians have eaten that up, the
English won't come in?"

Whitlock replied: "You are perfectly right to say that, and I am
prepared to say that the English will give satisfactory assurances."

Villalobar agreed, and the two decided they would set about
getting the necessary assurances as soon as possible. As they were
leaving, Whitlock said to Villalobar, "Don't get into another fight
until I see you again!"

The Spaniard replied, "Oh, I'll never get into fights any more;
I am a good boy."

That remained to be seen.[23]

Good humor at best lasted an hour or two. The next day they
returned to von der Lancken. Von Bissing, he said, had agreed in
principle that the new crop should go to the Belgians. Then he
uttered his sinister "but" and went on to say that von Bissing
wanted to put his pet idea into force, that is, reorganize the efficient Belgian system of distribution along the lines of the centrali-
zation customary in Germany. They talked and argued, but, as
von der Lancken said, von Bissing never changed his mind at all

easily, and they simply abandoned the problem for the day. The next morning, with Hoover and the Belgian leaders—Solvay, Francqui, Lambert, and Janssen—Whitlock and Villalobar drew up a plan for their demands. Then back to von der Lancken. For hours the men argued with each other, while Whitlock apparently spent most of his time looking out the window in despair. Finally Francqui, as practical as Hoover and with a better sense of humor, looked up and asked in a naïve way, "Baron, may I ask you a question?"

"Why certainly," said von der Lancken.

"His excellency the Governor-General wishes to buy the crop, does he not?"

"Yes, indeed."

"And with what?"

All of German efficiency had never thought of money, let alone such petty matters as price fluctuations, freight charges, storage costs, and so on. Von der Lancken thought for a while and said they would sell it to the Communes.

"But the Communes have no money."

Finally, Francqui broke his own impasse by saying that he would somehow find the money if it were necessary, and they finally got some semblance of an agreement down on paper. In brief, the Relief promised to continue imports until the 1916 harvest and thus keep the civil population fed; the Germans would in return allow the Belgians to keep what they grew, at least of wheat and rye. The decision on distribution was put off; von Bissing would decide and communicate his wishes later.

As Whitlock was leaving, Oscar Crosby, one of the American representatives, sauntered over and said: "Francqui talks too much. It is terrible; he gets off the question and makes it very difficult."

As he left, Francqui in turn came up and whispered: "That Crosby, there, is a stupid fellow; he almost ruined our business!"

Whitlock apparently just sighed and said nothing.[24]

The next day the English began making trouble. Hoover was advised by Page in London that the government was preparing drastic action against the C.R.B. activities if German assurances about the 1915 harvest did not come quickly. Hoover immediately wired back that any precipitous action might well imperil negotiations that had been going fairly well. The news made Whitlock half sick. The next few days marked some improvement in German-C.R.B. relations, but even that proved brief. The day after Whitlock had spent considerable time cheering a downcast Hoover (June 24, 1915), von der Lancken suffered a loss of his usual urbanity and acted like nothing so much as Villalobar in a tantrum. He appeared suddenly, dressed in full regalia, complete with jingling spurs, and prepared for a most undiplomatic protest. Apparently, several days earlier, when things had been going badly, de Leval had drawn up a stinging note to the Germans. Whitlock had refused to sign it, and things had become better. But someone sent the unsigned letter off by mistake, and, although attempts were made to get it back, the Germans chose to make an issue of the matter. Possibly von der Lancken was in a bad mood due to von Bissing, who was not the easiest superior in the world; perhaps it was just his hatred of de Leval, a Belgian under American protection who never hid his hatred of Germans, and who never failed to anger von der Lancken. Whitlock calmed the man, and that problem turned the corner.[25]

Then another problem arrived. Von Bissing summoned the Belgians to a conference and then conferred by standing in full-dress uniform and orating at them at length from a written statement. He apparently had shifted his objections to the meetings of the subcommittees of the Comité National, which had been conducted without German presence. He proposed that each meeting have a German officer present to oversee crop distribution at this decentralized level. Whitlock and Villalobar delayed, while both they and the Belgians fumed. Whitlock, as usual, maintained his diplomatic exterior and raged in his journal: "I am sick to death of the whole miserable business, and of the effort to deal with the Prussians. They are mentally immature; they do evil for the pleasure of doing it—evil for evil's sake; and they seem in a fair way, too, to dominate the world with their rascality."

July 4 provided its usual opportunity for the Belgians to leave their cards and flowers and wear little American flags. Burgomaster Lemmonier called and made a short and moving speech. Whitlock responded, and then the Belgian presented Nell with a lovely brooch with the American flag in platinum and enamel, the stripes of diamonds and rubies. The heart of Brussels certainly had not grown colder. In the afternoon, forty of the C.R.B. men arrived at

Ravenstein golf course for a party, along with Villalobar and Van Vollenhoven, the Dutch representative on the C.R.B. So many came, in fact, that extra tables were needed. Afterward the men put on mock orations and heard a few words from the diplomats. No one could manage the wretched music for the American national anthem, so they compromised by singing America's only real indigenous music—Negro songs.

But that was at best only an interval. Problems returned immediately, and exasperatingly. Discussions of German desires were proceeding smoothly enough when Whitlock and the others discovered that, while the French translation of von Bissing's latest note had all the important verbs in the conditional, thus implying that the demands were not necessarily final, the original had contained none of this softness. As von der Lancken had done the translation himself, and as he was perfectly fluent in both tongues, the dishonesty seemed patent and intentional, and Whitlock grew sour on the cultivated German. Then von der Lancken did it again. On July 9, Whitlock was having his portrait done by the Belgian portrait painter C. J. Watelet, when de Leval burst in saying come at once, the Germans had reneged; 30,000 Belgians had resigned, the C.R.B. was over, finally finished, the end was at hand. Whitlock rushed back to the legation again to find Villalobar, Francqui, and Lambert. They were calmer. Apparently the original orders placing Germans on the committees had gone out, despite a von der Lancken promise of delay. It was a plain breach of faith. Whitlock was furious, at least as much about the moral principles involved and the personal honor impugned as about the food itself—his liberal ideas and postures were withering, but were far from dead. He and Villalobar decided to protest, but separately. Villalobar went first and apparently had a long talk with the German. Whatever he said did the trick, if, as seems likely, there was a trick. When Whitlock arrived, in a mood far from conciliatory, von der Lancken greeted him effusively; it was all a mistake, "messieurs les militaires" were impetuous, didn't he know? His cher collègue shouldn't worry another minute, all had been fixed. Villalobar's ability obviously had its advantages. Meanwhile Whitlock brooded on von der Lancken's "twisted, tortuous ways, his insincerity, his disingenuousness . . ."[26]

The effect of this almost daily buffeting, this atmosphere that was the opposite of the liberal world of his own creation, was naturally to make Whitlock withdraw when he could. He would at times meet his painter, or haunt his favorite bookstores, or retire to Ravenstein to play golf. But most often he would commune with his diary; that at least would not betray him. Much of Belgium and the United States regarded him as a hero; he regarded himself as a tired novelist impotently fending off an unfriendly world. Edward Eyre Hunt, a C.R.B. representative who visited Whitlock at the legation, left a touching portrait of this unwilling symbol of freedom and his country. The legation seal was dingy, Hunt reported, and the flag drooped weakly; the streets were empty and it rained; the offices were gloomy. (It all sounds suspiciously like bad romantic poetry, but may be accurate.) Inside, Hunt found Whitlock, tired and worn, sitting before a gas grate where he apparently worked for hours, rarely going out. His face, of academic severity, was accentuated by his thinness, and his eyes had the tense look of "a man constantly straining to see something too close to him." He seemed like a cloistral American gentleman who had been sacrificed to the crude practicalities of the real world. Obviously happier in a library than in an office, he should have been in a university, not a legation. The dry, mechanical precision of his speech rarely changed in pitch or tempo.

"How do they make maple sugar back home?" Whitlock had asked.

Hunt described the process as well as he could, adding that after too much sugar a bit of sour pickle could renew the appetite for more. "But why do you ask me that?"

"I had just reached a 'sugaring off' episode in my novel when the war began, and I have often wondered since how we used to make maple sugar in Ohio."[27]

Clearly, the depression was worse than anything Whitlock had suffered in Toledo, and no Nock was at hand to clear up the desk; no Steffens arrived for a cheery chat; and no visits to Howells could renew confidence and spirit. A once progressive, optimistic American was slowly dying; the body might live on, but the spirit would be noticeably different. Maple sugar offered little solace in the Brussels of July 1915. Whitlock was becoming a mutilé.

((CHAPTER 11

"Dead Hearts and

Poisoned Minds"

(1 9 1 5 ʹ 1 9 1 6)

OWARD THE END OF JULY, as the unwelcomed first anniversary of the start of the war drew near, Whitlock made several indications to von der Lancken that he would enjoy a visit to the front—or at least that he would like to make one. He had made this request several times before, with no effect, but apparently the Germans now regarded themselves as fully dug in and in little danger of a defeat, so von der Lancken set about to arrange the trip. Finally, on the afternoon of July 20, von der Lancken, Whitlock and Villalobar, accompanied by Count Harrach, an urbane and civilized sculptor and linguist, set out from von der Lancken's office in his big gray automobile, flying the insignia of the German government. In such company, Whitlock and Villalobar were unrecognizable and received none of the warm welcoming waves to which they were accustomed when they traveled under their own flags.

A heavy rain had been falling, but they sped anyway, down the usual road to Hal, with the muffler off. They reached Tournai at about five o'clock and went to the cathedral, which the artist in Harrach was eager to see; the church was worthy of the stop, an eleventh-century medieval creation whose five towers dominated the town.

"You know," said Villalobar, as he and Whitlock strolled down the nave, "when you enter a church for the first time, if you make a wish, it will come true."

Whitlock made a wish.

They then went to a little pâtisserie for tea. The patronne was full of curiosity about her visitors but not precisely servile. Villalobar and Whitlock were apparently American, and the others were German officers. She was bright and talkative, and Villalobar soon nicknamed her Madame Talleyrand. Then von der Lancken said, "We have come to see your beautiful cathedral."

The woman replied quickly, "Yes, and since you have destroyed the beautiful cathedral of Rheims I hope you will spare ours!"

Von der Lancken was abnormally sensitive about charges of German animality, and he promptly turned red. The rest of them only laughed at him, and the talk continued without incident. They then continued toward Lille. The road passed through Avernus, and, as the car proceeded into the zone where most of the fighting had taken place, the desolation deepened. Belgium could still have an air of beauty, whatever the military conditions were, but occupied France was a mess. Few figures appeared, except for women and hobbling old men, and the obvious degradation permanently scarred Whitlock. Brussels wore down the spirit by its atmosphere, but it at least had not been destroyed and neither had the spirit of the bruxellois. In France, everyone had given up. By the time they entered the town, the sounds of war were all around them. These would continue until the visitors left the war zone at the end of their trip. Avernus itself was even worse. All normal life was gone, and what remained consisted chiefly of swaggering soldiers. "Everywhere the dirty grey uniforms, the brutish common soldiers, officers swanking about or dashing by at reckless speed in their big grey automobiles—and that sad, idle, gaping, dazed population! And everywhere dirt, the disgusting dirt of war, that seems to sift into every crevice, every crack and cover everything!"

They drove at once to the Kommandantur, where Harrach obtained the necessary identification papers and passes while the others observed the depressing scene. Harrach soon returned with the news that Crown Prince Rupprecht of Bavaria, commander of the district, had invited them to dinner that night. Villalobar confided to Whitlock that he dreaded the prospect, and Whitlock had to reply that he dreaded it even more; the Prince was reputedly quite anti-American. They went to the Hôtel Europe, where von der Lancken's and Villalobar's orderlies had gone ahead with the luggage. There they shaved and dressed; on Villalobar's advice, Whitlock had brought his formal clothes, senseless as they seemed on a trip to the front, and so was not caught completely off his guard by the invitation. Cannon boomed regularly as they drove to a suburb of Lille, picking up Harrach's brother-in-law as a guide on the way—he was an aide-de-camp of the Crown Prince. Then they continued on into an old upper-class district to a château. There, an old servant in long gray coat, with two rows of brass buttons, bald head, and habitual stoop led them to a salon. The place was furnished in wretched taste, and the vain and conceited little French physician who owned it even had a bust of himself still sitting there, complete with a pince-nez on its marble nose. German officers began filtering in, and there were formal introductions. Then a thin man, almost as tall as Whitlock, entered in a gray fatigue jacket and dark-blue trousers with wide stripes down his legs. They all bowed low to the German prince.

They talked, as diplomats in Europe usually talked, in French. Rupprecht spoke it with an accent more refined than was the norm with Prussians, and he seemed sincere and cordial in manner, with none of the coarse exaggeration that was all too common with some German officers and aristocrats. After a few minutes of the usual banalities, a wide glass door swung open, and they all went into the dining room for a relatively informal meal, chiefly of roast chicken and ice cream. Afterward, a solemn servant passed around cigars and cigarettes and kept a candle ready to light them. Instead of coffee, the Germans had beer, and the supply was refreshed steadily throughout the evening. Rupprecht spoke for a while with Villalobar, and Whitlock with the Count; then the groups rejoined each other. The Crown Prince, it turned out, had been often to America and hoped some day to return, for he had a deep interest in the country.

The next morning Whitlock awoke to the sound of a cannon; men outside were trying to shoot down a lone airplane flying overhead. He could not go back to sleep and stayed awake for a skimpy breakfast of poor tea and crackers. Soon, the party's official escort for the day, a German captain, arrived in the courtyard in a large gray car with a black, red, and white target on the lantern in front and the Crown Prince's coat of arms on the side. They roared off at great speed, and at each sentinel that tried to stop the car for inspection one of the Germans in the car shouted roughly, each time snapping the guard to attention and silence. Often the driver did not even wait for the removal of some of the wooden barricades, but swung onto sidewalks and lawns and roared past. Finally, on the road to Armentières, they again began passing the dreary scenes of military life. At last, they stopped at a château to pick up an aide-de-camp of the commanding general in the area; etiquette required his presence. The whole area was desolate; the regular sound of shrapnel never stopped. The car halted while the guide explained the trench system to the visitors.

Then they left the cars and began to walk through the neglected fields, overgrown with grass, weeds, and flowers. On every side, soldiers were made to keep busy digging trenches for a retreat no one expected. Barbed-wire entanglements were everywhere. They reached the huts where the captain in charge of the area lived, nearby his men. To get through the town to the trenches they had to proceed through the walls of the deserted houses; the Germans had knocked holes through so that their men could quickly escape the bullets and shrapnel that flew constantly about. Inside the houses, Whitlock saw all the sordid belongings of the people who had been deposed so brutally. They went through house after house, occasionally finding a solitary picture or a lace curtain in place as the sole reminders that peaceful farmers had been living there a year earlier. They even came across a wounded soldier eating a solitary breakfast in the rear of one house. As he jerked to attention, Whitlock saw flies competing for his piece of black bread and the can of grease he was slowly consuming. The man had his head so bandaged he resembled a turbaned African.

Finally they reached the trenches and went down into them. Each was about six feet deep and a yard wide, very cleanly cut into the fresh clay and floored with rough boards. The trench they were in went directly through an old graveyard, and in the center, high over head, a great Golgotha reared itself—a huge crucifix hung on a wooden cross, with the white body of Christ spotted again and again by bullet holes. The arms of the cross were splintered, and the Christ could barely hang on; he had a great, black hole in one side. At every turn they passed soldiers, who would flatten themselves against the walls to let the visitors past, then return to their drudgery. In one small area a puppy was chained; it shivered with affection when Whitlock petted it. Instead of pin-ups, at least in open view, the walls had occasional pictures of men like the Kaiser and von Hindenburg. Some of the trenches even had names, most often after Paris streets. The soldiers seemed dull, numb, and stared, if they stared at all, without curiosity. Everything was as neat as humanly possible under the circumstances, yet everyhere flies covered the walls of the trenches; occasionally, little green toads hopped about. Possibly the trenches had been cleaned up in expectation of diplomatic visitors; perhaps it was only German efficiency manifest in a lull in the fighting. Finally, Whitlock reached the front trench and had a glimpse of the English encampment not far away. Despite the heat and the difficulties of walking even with normal legs, Villalobar made the whole trip without a murmur, displaying his usual tenacity. They returned the way they came. Whitlock was more subdued than usual. "Somebody says that every man has two countries, his own and France," he said to Villalobar.

"That is what the Germans think," Villalobar answered.

Whitlock was in no mood for humor, even black humor. "I wondered if I were sentimental, too easily moved," he wrote later. But, "over and above all the horrors of war we had seen, the waste and destruction and desolation, the immense folly of it all, the sense of the moral indignity that had been heaped upon these people weighed most heavily upon men, the dumb sorrows of that conquered people, conquered, broken, passed under the yoke . . ." He never forgot it.[1]

The trip to the front all but completed the first stage of the effect of war on Whitlock. Arriving as a sensitive libertarian and artist, he had seen little more horrible than the workings of the Methodist mind and the execution of convicted criminals. He knew both slums and mansions at first hand, but this exposure had not much affected his indignation at seeing injustice or his faith that men of good will could democratically establish a nation of free cities, all working for the betterment of mankind. He had not been too noticeably naïve, but rather buoyant and optimistic by nature. The war and the occupation were slowly changing both his character and his social views. On the first anniversary of the German invasion, he wrote down his own state of mind in his journal, and demonstrated that, while sadness and resignation were perhaps approaching, he was still capable of indignation and libertarian shock at military tactics. The Germans had swept down upon "this poor, dear little country, committing every crime, every abhorrence, every outrage," and the effect on the life of the Belgians "has been death." A year ago, they had had peace, contentment and liberty. "The Government of the free communes had made it, during the centuries, a liberty-loving, self-governing, democratic people." And then, for no reason, "that grey horde came with fire and sword, laying waste to the land, pillaging, looting, murdering, raping—it is even yet wholly inconceivable that in our day such a thing could be. History knows no such crime." Brussels, the best girl of its devoted visitor, was sadly changed. No workmen abounded, building anew; shops were empty, with no new hats or styles; soap, toothbrushes, medicines, and cigarettes were scarce; and living costs were four times what they had been the year before. Animals and food were dying off. "The streets are dead; no life in them—people dragging about, staring aimlessly, and every block a squad or a company of the grey—that dirty, hideous grey!—uniformed last reserves tramping stolidly, stupidly, brutally along, in their heavy hobnailed boots." One of the most beautiful cities in Europe had been laid waste, and the barbarians had even brought along the aesthetic symbols of their triumph: "They have built kiosks for the vendors of German newspapers, books and publications everywhere, hideous things of clashing colors; and they have stuck up everywhere their garish red, white and black sentry-boxes like monstrous barbershop signs." There were no free press, post, telephone, or any of the little signs of liberty anywhere; a Reign of Terror had supplanted any Bill of Rights. "It is a year I don't like to look back upon. I don't know how I have lived through it or how much longer this must be endured. And I am the most privileged man in Belgium, and my soul sickens every day and my heart grows hot with impotent rage at what these Germans do."[2]

Life in Brussels dragged on, more and more of the same. Von der Lancken was occasionally petulant, complaining as the political chief of the occupation forces about the conduct of this or that member of the C.R.B. and threatening that the Germans would be forced to take measures of a more or less drastic nature. Hoover would descend regularly, either furious with rage or in deep depression, depending on which German or English government official was making his life miserable with petty bureaucratic stupidities. C.R.B. men in their turn would arrive for a meal and a conference and tell of the suffering they had seen and the indignities they had suffered from German guards. A scheme for the revival of Belgian industry made some progress and took up a great deal of time, but it came to nought in the face of German desire to exploit it and English fear that they would succeed. Life in Brussels, in fact, was less a miniature picture of the war than a negative of it, for, when events were going on of military importance, little happened behind the lines. The great Allied offensive of September 1915 at Champagne, Artois, and Loos raised great hopes and took away soldiers on leave, but little else. "We know nothing, only that Brussels is drained of officers; they swagger in their floating capes along the boulevards no more, and their club, the old Hotel Astoria, is empty." Which was just as well, for Whitlock's frail constitution had gone on one of its periodic strikes; beginning in the middle of September, he was confined to his bed under doctor's orders, and he stayed there most of the time for the next few weeks. Unfortunately, this illness deprived him of all but a symbolic role in the most famous incident of the occupation.[3]

EDITH CAVELL had experienced her own version of the transition from Victorian religious faith to active charity in the world. She was born in rural England, the daughter of an impoverished Anglican curate who ministered to a wretched and suffering village even poorer than he. The serious child, one of four, was brought up in a manner both puritan and spartan; the rigor of life at the parsonage included family prayers at eight daily (with even the maid in attendance) and three separate services each Sunday. As an adult, she became as tolerant as her family was intolerant, but her upbringing did give her a certain inescapable legacy: She had a compulsive urge to be doing good, and she had not the trace of a sense of humor. She was small, scarcely 110 pounds, but when her will had fixed on a job it was quite indomitable, and she was accustomed to doing things in her own way and succeeding. For five years in the 1890's, she was governess to an aristocratic Brussels family; she then returned to England, obtained nursing training, and spent years in the London slums practicing her new profession. In 1907 she returned to Brussels as chief matron of a nurses' training school, an institution vitally needed in a country where a nurse ranked just below chambermaid on the social scale and where no person of any respectability would think of making it à career. She was still full of duty and empty of humor and was stiff, unbending, formal. Despite this, her example and tenacity began the profession of nursing in Belgium and established it as permanently as it was possible to do so, given the short period of time available before the outbreak of the war. On vacation when the war broke out, she was true to her sense of duty. She returned and, during the occupation, stayed and cared for the sick, whether they were Belgian, English, French, or German.

Soon after occupation, the Germans demanded the names of all men over eighteen who were in the hospital and required them all to report for deportation and a German prison when they were well. The nurses for the most part ignored the order. Soon afterward, led by Edith Cavell and outsiders like the Princess Marie de Croÿ and her brother, an organization sprang up, as if from nothing, to help soldiers to get through the lines and back to their homelands or armies. At first, the border guards were inefficient, and bribery and carelessness helped the conspirators. In time, the smugglers managed to make contact with other underground operations, including British and Belgian Intelligence and the *Libre Belgique* group. Indeed, the de Croÿs, Philippe Baucq, and Gabrielle Petit were in more than one group, and Edith Cavell was certainly acquainted with, if not directly involved in, much of this clandestine activity. But security tightened, and spies soon abounded. Two of them betrayed the organization: Georges Gaston Quien, a Frenchman freed from prison by the Germans to spy for them, and Armand Jeannes, a former employee of one of the leaders of the organization. The Prince de Croÿ, probably the most important of the group, barely escaped to Holland; his sister Princess Marie, Countess Jeanne de Belleville, associates Mlle

Louise Thuliez, and Mme Ada Bodart, architect Baucq, Edith Cavell, and many others were arrested. When the Germans caught her, Edith Cavell had by reliable accounts assisted over two hundred soldiers to escape.[4]

Whitlock, the protector of British interests in Brussels, seems scarcely to have noticed the arrests at first. He no doubt heard of them, in a general way, but most of those involved were Belgians or French and thus officially none of his business. The name of Edith Cavell could have meant little or nothing to him then, and there is no reason why he should have done much. With his Western liberal assumptions still largely intact, he no doubt felt distress at the arrest of a woman, especially a nurse, but also assumed that internment in Germany would be the only logical result. Civilized men did not kill women. The C.R.B. was having its usual troubles, and he was wholly absorbed in them. Not until Walter Hines Page cabled a query from London did he take notice of the case. He then, on August 31, 1915, wrote to von der Lancken asking the reasons for Miss Cavell's arrest and asking permission for M. Gaston de Leval, legal adviser to the American Legation, to confer with her and get someone to defend her. No reply came for ten days, so Whitlock wrote again, repeating his request and emphasizing the need for speed. On September 12, or in immediate reply to the second request, von der Lancken reported that Miss Cavell had been arrested on August 5 and that she was imprisoned at St. Gilles. She had confessed to hiding English and French soldiers and to helping them and others of military age to cross the border. Her defense had been entrusted to Attorney Mr. Braun, and de Leval would not be allowed to see her. Shortly thereafter, Whitlock was in bed, sick, and had to continue his efforts from there, usually through Hugh Gibson.

On September 21, Whitlock cabled what information he had to Page and promised to do all that he could. By October 9, he had to inform Page that the case was indeed serious, and that a good deal of its seriousness was due to Miss Cavell herself. Devout and humorless Victorian ladies did not tell lies, and Miss Cavell was as truthful as a model five-year-old. The Germans hardly had to try to trick her, as she readily admitted everything she had done, supplied accurate details, and with not even the threat of torture gave her accusers everything they needed to establish that she had committed the crime described in paragraph 90 of the German military code as "dem Feinde Mannschaften zuführen" (leading men of military age to the enemy). Paragraph 58 of the same code condemned to death anyone "who, with the intention of helping the hostile power, or of causing harm to the German or Allied troops, is guilty of the crimes of paragraph 90." On such charges, her release was out of the question. On October 11, Whitlock told Page of the request of the prosecution for the death penalty and of his hopes that the actual sentence would not be that severe. The trial, as far as he could determine from her Belgian attorney, had been fair.[5]

Then began the chain of events that sent a chill of horror throughout the civilized world. On the morning of October 11, Whitlock sent Gibson over to the Politische Abteilung for the facts, and Gibson was informed that no sentence had been pronounced and that in all probability none would be for a day or two. They promised to keep the American Legation informed. Repeated calls, usually answered by a Mr. Conrad, received the same answer. Then, sometime after eight o'clock in the evening, unidentified sources—probably the Belgian director of St. Gilles and/or several of Miss Cavell's nursing friends—sent word to de Leval and Gibson that shortly before the last call to Conrad, the court had definitely passed sentence and that Miss Cavell and several others had been condemned to death. The two men told Whitlock and then went to Villalobar, the only diplomat with force of character, position, and influence enough with the Germans to command their respect. Villalobar was dining with Baron Lambert, and, when things were explained to him, he agreed to come instantly. The three of them went to the Abteilung, armed also with notes Whitlock had written hurriedly pleading for Miss Cavell. Naturally, that late at night no one of importance was at the Abteilung, so they sent messengers after von der Lancken. Soon he arrived with Count Harrach and von Falkenhausen. Told the news, von der Lancken said the whole thing sounded highly unlikely and he was more interested in the source of such information—which Gibson would not give him—than in its truth. Certainly, he said, nothing would be done before morning. He was apparently quite sincere in this belief and cannot be held responsible for the acts of his superiors. Finally, at the urging of Gibson and Villalobar, he called the presiding judge of the Court Martial and discovered that the report was correct. Then Gibson presented his case, arguing that the woman had not committed espionage, that she was a woman, and that death even in the worst of circumstances was extraordinary. He also mentioned the ill effects on public opinion and the possibility of reprisals. Villalobar supported him vigorously. Under this pressure, von der Lancken went personally to the new military governor, a table-pounding militarist named von Sauberzweig. This commander had no sympathy for the pleas of softhearted diplomats, and he threw Whitlock's plea on the floor without reading it. In disgust, von der Lancken later reported—and there is no reason to doubt him—that he said to von Sauberzweig: ". . . then her blood be on your head and that of your children." He then returned to tell Gibson and Villalobar that he was powerless, that the decision had been made by "messieurs les militaires" and that, unlike Villalobar, a German officer of minor importance like himself could not communicate with his sovereign even in such a serious matter. He seemed quite nervous about the whole business and refused even to take Whitlock's note from Gibson. Whitlock, back at the legation fuming and sick, blamed him somewhat unfairly.[6]

Midnight came, and Gibson returned with the story of the events of the evening. Nell sat downstairs, administering hot milk to some of Miss Cavell's female friends, who were close to hysterics. Mr. H. Stirling T. Gahan, a clergyman, went to administer the comfort that he could and on the twelfth informed Whitlock of the calm bravery with which Miss Cavell met her death. The same day, Whitlock sadly informed Page of the execution and expressed his hatred in the pages of his journal: "And oh, to be out of sight forever of that hideous, grey German uniform, symbol of every cowardly brutality of which the dead hearts and poisoned minds of old, old men can conceive. Frightfulness!" A small footnote might have comforted him somewhat. The world condemnation of the act so got on the nerves of von Sauberzweig that he took to drinking far more than was good for him and to muttering that he only did his duty, yet was condemned as "a monster all over the world" and "a murderer; a second Duke of Alva," and the "most infamous of men."[7] Clearly the Germans had felt guilty about the matter from the beginning, for whatever the strictly legal accountability of Miss Cavell, no one free from doubts on the matter would have had her executed so hurriedly, so irregularly, and behind such a smoke screen of misleading information. The execution was one of the worst blunders of the military administration and did more to rouse world opinion than any event since the sinking of the *Lusitania*.

The rage of the world was all but equaled by the German counterreaction. Whitlock had sent copies of the diplomatic correspondence to Page in London, and Page being almost belligerently pro-British, the English immediately received copies and had Reuters publish them for the world to see. Von der Lancken immediately called Whitlock in, and the American went, against his doctor's orders. The Baron was pink from his morning ride, booted, his chest heavy with the Iron Cross and various ribbons. He had a large dossier under his arm, and he looked dark and glowering. "I am most unhappy to have to say to you," he began solemnly, and went on to talk of German tolerance for the diplomatic community in Brussels and the serious breach of etiquette involved in publishing secret and confidential communications. Yes, perhaps "messieurs les militaires" were putting pressure on the civilians, in their irritation at the unfavorable publicity. Certainly the Baron was disturbed at least as much by the fact that de Leval's reports, and even his presence, were involved in the publications; de Leval was a Belgian who hated Germans, made no secret of his hatred, and yet enjoyed the protection of the American Legation. He would have to go, von der Lancken insisted; with equal force, Whitlock refused to let von Sauberzweig touch him. At worst, Washington would be informed, de Leval would be formally labeled *persona non grata* and sent to Holland for the duration. As for the publication of the documents, Whitlock had not authorized it, and said he was in no way responsible. Later, Secretary of State Lansing concurred with Whitlock's actions, said that he also had not authorized publication, and agreed that de Leval should go to Holland. The Germans, meanwhile, published *affiches* of their own giving a misleading account of the whole business which presumably fooled few. As a diplomatic furor, the case soon died down, and the departure of de Leval removed one thorn from German-American relations. Yet another remained: Hugh Gibson had always been almost as frank and open as de

Leval in his dislike for the Germans, and his energetic efforts for Edith Cavell had not endeared him to them in the least. Von der Lancken would take language from Villalobar that he would not take from Gibson, and he soon had a confirmed distaste for the young American. Later, he even insisted that Gibson's activities had made it harder for him to try to intervene with Sauberzweig. This seems unlikely, and no detailed contemporary evidence supports it. Yet, undeniably, Gibson was *persona non grata* at the Politische Abteilung, and his later recall was at least partially the result of his work for Edith Cavell. In this context it is significant that, even aside from their work in Belgium, Gibson and de Leval were the writers of the two reports most critical of the Germans in the collection Page so stupidly published in London. On the basis of these reports alone, the Germans might have conceived enough animus to demand the recall of the men.[8]

The case had a further, strictly minor, result, but one dear to Whitlock. The reports of the case reaching Holland and America mentioned the Minister's health and told of his sickness. Lansing soon heard of it and cabled that the Department of State "highly appreciated" the way in which Whitlock had discharged his duties, and, "realizing the responsibility and the strain under which you have been working," told him that "if you so desire you may take advantage of the leave of absence to which you are entitled and visit the United States." Whitlock had not asked for the leave, but was overjoyed at the prospect of some rest and a breath of free air, so he accepted, and left as soon as his other duties would permit. Early in November, he departed for Holland.[9]

By November 8, he was at The Hague, visiting Van Dyke and others at the legation and motoring around the country. The next day he called on Sir Alan Johnstone, a "likeable Englishman" who said that the war would last two years longer and that life would never again be what it was. With that slim comfort, he drove to Rotterdam in a driving rain and boarded the *Ryndam* for a rough trip across the North Sea, a trip that enabled Whitlock to spot six floating mines and experience the thorough searches required by the British navy of all vessels near the war zones. Despite these, and despite a blackout rule on board, Whitlock was glad to get out of German territory and be where he could hear his own language spoken and at least a few of his own views supported. After several days along the British coast, the ship left Falmouth and was soon in a vicious gale that scattered the Whitlocks' possessions all over the cabin and gave him and Nell the privilege of hearing "champagne bottles exploding with a loud pop" without human assistance. Whitlock scarcely minded. In the next few days, as he relaxed and acquired his sea legs, representatives of William Randolph Hearst came and offered him $2,000 per article for the story of his Belgian experiences, to be printed in *Cosmopolitan:* ". . . impossible to accept, of course." Yet even at sea his duties would not let him alone. On November 15, Hoover sent a marconi telling of the activities of a second-generation German-American member of the C.R.B. who had apparently been working for German Intelligence and who had seriously compromised perfectly innocent members of the C.R.B. This man denounced five of the C.R.B. leaders for anti-German activities which turned out to be nothing worse than the utterance of anti-German gossip and a misunderstood joke. Von Bissing was furious and made a great row, and it was all Hoover could do to calm him down and get him to allow the feeding to continue. Hoover had the man recalled and sent home quickly and quietly; there, he set about denouncing Hoover and doing what he could to cause trouble. Whitlock, fortunately for his nerves, was out of the mess, and knew of it only at second hand.[10]

By November 24, he had arrived in New York quarantine, and the next day was able to spend "Thanksgiving Day in good old New York," with visitors such as Albert Jay Nock, Francis Neilson, Arthur Henry, Irvin Cobb, and others; he also made frequent tours of the city like any other tourist. On the twenty-sixth he had his inevitable cold and was seeing Dr. Holbrook Curtis about it, but for once was not taking it seriously. That night he had dinner with William Dean Howells, and he found his beloved old mentor "as young, as bright and as charming as ever." Others invited him to the Army-Navy game, but Dr. Curtis said a firm no, so Whitlock passed the day pleasantly with Colonel House, Melville Stone, Mark Sullivan, and Dudley Field Malone. On the twenty-eighth, he again had lunch with House, in a group that included Secretary of State Lansing and his wife. Whitlock liked Lansing immediately, found much depth in him, and thought him "charming, very able," and "forceful." Soon after, he took a train to Washington.[11]

On November 30 he began getting acquainted with official Washington, as he conferred with Third Assistant Secretary of State William Phillips and Belgian Ambassador to the United States Havenith. In the evening he dined with the Lansings, the Haveniths, French Ambassador Jusserand, Frank L. Polk, and Mrs. John W. Foster. These preliminaries over, he saw President Wilson the next morning at the White House. Whitlock frankly idolized Wilson and probably made no effort to hide his sentiments, and Wilson liked nothing better than total commitment from loyal subordinates. The meeting went well, and Wilson approved Whitlock's actions in Belgium. When told of Belgium's faith in the American President, Wilson seemed quite touched; both men were frank and cordial, and the talk ranged over everything from golf to philosophy. Wilson asked Whitlock to let him know when he was to sail back. When Whitlock mentioned a possible second visit to Washington a few years later, Wilson was quite pessimistic about his chances for re-election and said, "I'm afraid I shan't be here then." Afterward, Whitlock had a talk with Wilson's secretary Joe Tumulty and went for a walk with Ben Allen. He also found himself swamped by invitations and became increasingly aware of how much publicity he had obtained for his conduct. That evening, he dined at the French Embassy, again with the Haveniths and Jusserands.[12]

He then made a quick trip to Ohio, where he received the fruits of all the publicity his work had obtained. He saw the few who were left of his family—his mother and brother Will—and visited with friends like Newton Baker and Peter Witt. He was back in New York by December 21 and sailed a week later on the Rotterdam. On board were Colonel House, Marshall Langhorne, then legation secretary at The Hague, publisher George H. Doran, and Commander Karl Boy-Ed, naval attaché at the German Legation in Washington, whose recall had been requested by Wilson for apparently unneutral activity prejudicial to American interests. The presence of Boy-Ed presented something of a tactical problem, and Colonel House asked Whitlock how they should treat him. Whitlock, by now a seasoned diplomat and always a thorough gentleman, replied that nothing was ever lost by being polite; and by so acting the men found Boy-Ed good-natured, clever, and witty. Whitlock chatted with many of his fellow travelers, but particularly with House, Doran, and Langhorne. Yet, oddly enough, Boy-Ed received much of the space given the trip in Whitlock's diary. Whitlock found the man astonishingly sentimental and not a little Americanized, whatever charges Washington might have made against him. One day, as the two men were leaning over the rail, they began talking about American women. "I could never marry a German girl," Boy-Ed said. "They have no style; they don't know how to dress." He disliked the sort of women praised in his country, in the style of the "Kinder, Küche, Kirche" philosophy, who went about in aprons all day, carrying keys and smelling of the kitchen. Whitlock, faced with a German made human by personal contact and recognizable emotions, was touched. "I like this man, and feel sorry for him. Every one avoids him on the ship—I do not." In his own diary, Colonel House recorded even kinder sentiments about Whitlock: "I can better understand now why Whitlock has made such a success in Belgium under difficulties. He has the kindly human instinct," House wrote. "He is not given to hate or recrimination. He can see the other man's point of view and he is not absorbed with his own ego. He knows literature and the fine arts." Finally, House concluded: "He knows our political institutions and our people and their aspirations, and he is in every way a worthy representative of the United States during these troublous times. When peace comes I think the President should send him higher up."[13]

The ship soon reached Britain, where the paralyzingly slow searches for contraband began. Whitlock became annoyed by the whole affair and categorically refused to allow himself to be searched, claiming diplomatic immunity and demanding proper treatment. Despite constant attempts by British officers, he largely succeeded in fending them off. By January 9 he was in Rotterdam, and the next morning he was off for Brussels, arriving at the legation at eight a.m. After dinner and a talk with Gibson and Miss Larner, he went to bed, tired but not at all sure he was glad to be back. The next day, he and Gibson made the ritual calls on von der Lancken and Villalobar, who were glad to see Whitlock and pleasant to talk to again. Brussels, however, was just a little bit sadder. The war went on, no end was in sight, and the Germans had recently annulled one more of their promises: Now soldiers could be quartered in private homes. The city was cheered, however, by the return of the chief symbol of freedom and justice; word had been spread that he was gone for good, and the city had feared the worst. Whitlock scarcely had time to be surprised. Sir Edward Grey was threatening to stop the C.R.B. once again; a C.R.B. man in Liège had to be dismissed for consorting too enthusiastically with Germans there; and his favorite bookseller, whose shop had often been a refuge, had died of heart disease while Whitlock was away. Soon he was conferring regularly with Francqui of the Comité National and Walcott of the Rockefeller group and discussing new German demands for money with Lemmonier. He had a wearying amount of mail to read and, as protector of British interests, had further problems quite aside from the C.R.B.: Mr. Grant-Watson was being harassed by the Germans for no better reason than that his passport was English; and Sir Edward Grey, confused by a letter of Gibson's, and for no obviously compelling reason, picked that time to request all English women to leave occupied territory. The British governesses, teachers, and other women in the area promptly besieged the American Legation, all of them wondering what would become of them. The vacation was over.[14]

On January 23, Whitlock conferred at length with Francqui, and then the two of them went to see von der Lancken in an attempt to iron out the latest difficulties. The German proved sympathetic and promised to see von Bissing about the matter. He was, however, genuinely puzzled by Grey's fuss about the English women—who had not been maltreated—and he had complaints to make about Gibson. The next day, Whitlock and von der Lancken ate at Trois Fontaines with the Governor General and a few of his staff. The meal proved unexpectedly pleasant, and von Bissing impressed Whitlock as a "very solid old Prussian officer, firm and perhaps severe at times, but with the drive of duty, and very strong with his seventy-two years." They were both fluent in French, and told each other stories; the General laughed with delight at some of Whitlock's. He appeared unconcerned about the C.R.B. and said, "That will work itself out," much to Whitlock's relief. In fact, the American enjoyed himself, and he revised his assessment of the man so hated by the Belgians. "Were one to know him without the prejudice that attaches to everything the Germans do nowadays, I am sure one could like him. But then, one likes most people when one really knows them."[15]

But his immediate concern was a telegram from Lansing:

STRICTLY CONFIDENTIAL. MARYE HAVING RESIGNED THE PRESIDENT DESIRES TO APPOINT YOU AS AMBASSADOR TO RUSSIA AND WISHES TO KNOW THAT YOU WOULD ACCEPT BEFORE REQUESTING RECOGNITION OF THE RUSSIAN GOVERNMENT.

It was, of course, an immense compliment, the firmest possible official endorsement of his conduct by a President and Secretary who both had his respect, and that was pleasing. But the problems the offer raised were heartbreaking. The post was a full ambassadorial one, not a mere ministry, but the honor was diluted by the obvious financial requirements of an ambassador to an empire; Whitlock had only a slender income. Furthermore, to the Belgians he was the symbol of resistance, and his presence was a psychological necessity to them. Every day as he walked about, sad faces smiled their one smile of the day as he and Nell went by, and Whitlock had only recently been reminded of his importance by the ready rumors that he had deserted them while he was on leave. The evident joy his return brought meant much to him. He loved Brussels and did not want to desert her when she needed him. Sadly, he gave up the idea: "Have practically decided not to accept the Petrograd mission, for these reasons. 1. I couldn't afford it from the monetary point of view, 2. I must finish my work here and not desert my poor Belgians, and 3. I don't wish to live in Petrograd." This was just as well from another point of view; 1917 was less than a year away, and then even wartime Brussels would look calm in comparison to the Russian Revolution.[16]

Almost at the same moment, German dislike of Hugh Gibson reached the point of requiring his dismissal. Gibson had been on the suspected list for some time, ever since his frequent trips across the frontier in the confused opening weeks of the war. The Germans were convinced that he was reporting more than absolutely necessary to the Belgian government and carrying nonneutral matter under the protection of his diplomatic immunity. His frank support of the Belgians in the occupation did nothing to alleviate these suspicions, and von der Lancken soon made almost as many complaints to Whitlock about Gibson as he had about de Leval. Gibson's and de Leval's Edith Cavell maneuvers had irritated von der Lancken, and he was successful in getting de Leval out because of them; Gibson was next on the list. While Whitlock was away, things came to a head. Gibson was involved in an unpleasant incident with border guards, was charged with improper acts while performing his C.R.B. duties, and—possibly unknown to him—had been named as a witness in espionage proceedings then in progress against a Belgian and was due for interrogation. Whitlock had been away and now only discovered these charges in stages. On January 23, von der Lancken took Whitlock aside and said that he had reliable reports that Gibson was having goods shipped in in large and illegal quantities. Gibson denied it, and Whitlock dismissed the charge as a typical product of German suspiciousness. Then, on February 7, von der Lancken requested Whitlock's presence at once: Gibson must leave immediately, he said; both he and the Governor General insisted. By the tenth, Whitlock had as much of the story as it seemed possible to reconstruct. Gibson, he wrote, was a swashbuckler of the Theodore Roosevelt type, a young and romantic man excellent in time of peace, but too unstable in times of war. Apparently, on top of his bad reputation for German baiting and his involvement in the espionage trial, he had been out riding with a Belgian girl and had been showing off his diplomatic prowess to her by defying German sentries—or so Whitlock was told; Gibson never published a defense. Utterly unrepentant, he had even threatened to withdraw, which was both insulting to the Germans and exactly what they wanted anyway. Whitlock thought a little tact could have avoided many of Gibson's troubles. "He is so touchy on all points of honor, but honor cannot set a leg, or take away the grief of a wound, or feed the Belgians. One can't live according to the code duello, and I can't get him to be patient and await events and let old Nemesis take care of his enemies. He is truculent and impetuous, always wishes to rattle the sabre in the scabbard, and if I had gone to Petrograd he would have lasted here no more than two weeks."[17]

But, considering their eagerness to dispose of Gibson, the Germans proved oddly troublesome in actually letting him go. Perhaps they were fearful that he would publish his experiences and score propaganda points in the war for public opinion—which is

just what Gibson did. First, he had great trouble getting his passports, as von der Lancken became suddenly difficult and uncooperative. Then, on February 13, Gibson was told he could go, but
that he had to exit via train through Germany, spending a night in
Cologne and possibly losing some of his diplomatic privileges.
Whitlock was furious: "I have seldom been so enraged as I was at
this shabby and insulting treatment." He complained vigorously to
von der Lancken and the German agreed to try to make the
change; the excuse was that the Dutch border was closed, which
was transparent nonsense. "The whole nasty row made me sick—
and I feel tonight as I used to feel after a Monday in the Mayor's
office." For three days nothing happened, and then on the seventeenth Villalobar came and reported that von der Lancken had
been having trouble again with von Sauberzweig, who did not
want Gibson let out. Von der Lancken managed to arrange matters only by getting von Bissing's approval; Whitlock was skeptical, and said he would believe everything was all right only when
Gibson was actually across the border. There was one comfort,
however: Von der Lancken heartily subscribed to the world opinion of von Sauberzweig and referred to him, in Villalobar's presence, as "a dirty pig." The Spaniard also reported that Prince
Rupprecht had told the Kaiser of the visit the two of them had
made to the front, and the German ruler had been so delighted at
the thought of their being under fire that he wanted to award them
each the Iron Cross, first class. The Spanish ambassador had been
hard put to get him to postpone the honor until after the war.
"How droll to find myself a military hero all of a sudden!" Whitlock wrote that night.[18]

On the fifteenth, word arrived that the Germans were worried
about Gibson's becoming a chargé at Le Havre when he left occupied territory and wished Whitlock's assurances that this would
not happen. Whitlock agreed that it would only exacerbate ill
feeling, and he did what he could to advise Washington against
such a move. The next day, Heineman called and said that von der
Lancken had promised Gibson, Hulse, and himself exit permits
for the eighteenth. He turned out to be right, and at ten that
morning, Gibson left "amid the restrained sadness there is in all
parting and abandoned us to a dull day of dreary rain . . ." Gibson
went to London, joined the embassy there, and became a close

friend of Hoover, going on to a distinguished diplomatic career. Unfortunately, he could never get over the idea that Whitlock had somehow betrayed him, and more than once expressed privately his dissatisfaction with Whitlock. He never printed his views, but his close friendship with Hoover gave him that authoritative defender, and the highly colored, acidulous, and factually erroneous accounts in Hoover's *Memoirs* and *An American Epic* presumably tell Gibson's side of the story. The whole episode was highly regrettable and due more to divergent personalities rubbing each other the wrong way in a time of great stress than to a real deficiency in character or ability on anyone's part. The one small note of humor was unwittingly sounded by von der Lancken. On February 28, he solemnly informed Whitlock that Gibson had been involved in smuggling English soldiers disguised as American chauffeurs over the border when Whitlock was in the U.S. As far as Whitlock knew, the charge was ridiculous, and he laughed in his face; with that, the matter was more or less over.[19]

Unfortunately, even with Gibson gone, the atmosphere was still poisoned, and the story of the C.R.B. became both the grandeur of the achievement of feeding the Belgians and the misery of the petty personal vindictiveness, ambition, and back-biting of many of the men involved. With most of the basic machinery set up and conditions relatively stabilized, men of one country began trying to edge out of control men from another. Individuals began trying for diplomatic coups that would give them status after the war. Men without cars snapped at the privileges of men with cars. It may have looked very grand and heroic to watching Americans, but to the men involved the job was endless, unpleasant, thankless, and nerve-shattering.

The symbolic event for the worsening of relations was a trip proposed by Villalobar that would take him, Francqui, and Lambert to London ostensibly to improve liaison but actually to make a private diplomatic attempt at peace, and incidentally to try to undercut Whitlock and Americans generally in the C.R.B. Apparently these men, as well as von der Lancken, had hatched the idea that the Germans might withdraw voluntarily from Belgium as a gesture of good will and that Brussels could then serve as the place for the signing of a peace treaty. In that event, Villalobar and his colleagues hoped to go down in history as key makers of the Treaty of Brussels. It was no secret that Villalobar was inordinately ambitious and that he would have liked the King of Spain to play a major role at the conference table. Ultimately, he wanted to replace Merry del Val y Zulueta as Spanish Ambassador in London, and he hoped that his appearance in London and a subsequent trip to Madrid would allow him to achieve the coup of the war. Whitlock alternated between raucous laughter at the scheme and the thought that it was a beautiful dream. Certainly he did not want to go, and he did not much care if the others did. So, after much unpleasant haggling with the Germans about new guarantees demanded by the British, the men left.[20]

In London, Hoover had troubles of his own. The exiled Belgian government was paying no attention to his requests for Belgian-owned but British-registered ships. The French were willing to give none of their fleet to aid the feeding of northern France and were unwilling to permit use of captured German ships. Whitlock, as far as Hoover was concerned, was too sensitive and ill-adapted to the rougher requirements of diplomacy, and with Gibson out of Belgium Hoover had no one close to him in the occupied area. The Germans had apparently repudiated the December 1915 agreement not to requisition native food, and von Bissing was once more not cooperating. The British had reduced the permits for food imports so much that people were actually starving, including children. The C.R.B., run by foreign neutrals, chiefly the United States, was the object of suspicion to the Comité National, a Belgian group that was responsible for actual, in-the-field distribution. The English wished extension of the C.R.B. responsibility, and the Belgians wished it constricted. Finally, certain militarist and spy-minded Englishmen had decided that Hoover and his men were really German spies. Thus, when the group arrived in London, accompanied by Gibson, Hoover was thoroughly irritated with anyone and everyone who was so stupidly making charity difficult. Gibson may well not have known of Villalobar's peace ambitions; he told Hoover that the reason for the visit was a plan to allow the Comité National to take over the C.R.B. activities. Hoover and his advisers welcomed the plan and sent letters to the chief diplomats concerned resigning responsibility.

They did not like the idea. Page protested, Francqui was unenthusiastic, and, most important, Sir Edward Grey felt that

Hoover was the only man the British government could trust. He had begun the work, he had run it, and despite all the canards had satisfied the Cabinet about as well as anyone could have satisfied it. Likewise the Germans did not want the organization changed. They did not like the Belgians, did not trust them, and were quite opposed to giving them any status whatever. Only a neutral group, at least nominally under the private rather than official auspices, would satisfy them. Hoover, in short, could not dispose of his problems. He rescinded his resignation and the C.R.B. went on. Whitlock learned of these events early in March, but not until Hoover himself arrived on March 22 did he get most of the story of what had happened in London. Villalobar had gone into personal diplomacy with vigor, going over the head of Merry del Val—thus offending him greatly—to see Sir Edward Grey. Grey had refused flatly. The next day Villalobar had eaten with the Asquiths and said quite openly that the Comité National was a government within a government and was doing political work for the Allies in Belgium. Mrs. Asquith promptly told Hoover, and that least diplomatic of men told the proud and haughty Spaniard what he thought of such tactics, thus confirming the hatred Villalobar already had for him. Then Lambert again infuriated Hoover by saying to everyone in London who would listen that the C.R.B. was run by nice college boys who were living a high life in Belgium, roaring around in cars and living in châteaux. Hoover informed the Baron that a little more of that and the C.R.B. would lose the confidence and support of the British cabinet and that the result would be starvation, since no Belgian group could hope for Grey's support. The three of them, Hoover reported, really came to London to see if all Americans could not be eliminated from the operation. Under such circumstances, both men could be pardoned for nervous outbreaks of indignation, frustration, and a feeling that all the effort was being expended for a people who did not care and were not even grateful. Whitlock's journal is full of such outbreaks.[21]

On the twenty-sixth, the roving ambassadors returned, full of their own variety of good cheer. Villalobar had a lame arm and a severe cold. He admitted that he had had a little disagreement with Hoover but bore no ill will. Page, however, he had found quite pompous, and he did not like the American ambassador's delivery of an oration at him instead of an interview. Afterward,

Villalobar had visited Madrid and the Belgian King and Queen at La Panne; the latter, he reported in his inimitable English, were living "in anguish poverty." Francqui arrived later on, and for four hours gave his side of the story. He feared Whitlock might bear some ill will—as well he might have—but Whitlock assured him he did not. Francqui was, however, quite embittered himself against those "deux cochons," Gibson and Lewis Richards. "Gibson is no friend of yours," he said. "He has conspired to have you displaced." And Richards, he added, was "une brebis galeuse" (a black sheep who gossiped). To Whitlock all this was scarcely news, and he did what he could to soothe ruffled sensibilities. Fortunately, the gruff, generous, and witty Francqui thought most highly of Hoover, and Hoover returned the respect. "Good Lord," Francqui said to Whitlock, "if Hoover told me to take a walk three times a day in the Grande Place, I would take it." Francqui also was easily the most dependable of the Belgians, as well as the most important, and he, Hoover, and Whitlock could have held the group more or less together in all but the greatest of emergencies. Still, Villalobar and Lambert and the others did not help.[22]

In the midst of it all, Whitlock's personal affairs became all but ritualized. He and Nell took regular walks all over the city; if she did not come, he might well go to an out-of-the-way bookstore, or, increasingly, to the home of one of several Belgian painters he had befriended. One of them was even doing his portrait. He ate almost daily with members of the diplomatic community, the C.R.B., or visiting American groups; certain of these people, such as S. S. McClure, he would gladly have seen choke on dessert. He welcomed the first of his replacements for his dead Pekingese Mieke, another Pekingese he named Kin Kung—"this word is my best Chinese derived from Encyclopedia Britannica, and means Golden Duke"—and eventually a companion, Taï Taï; the dogs now came on the walks, too. As the guns began at Verdun, Brussels was full of the wildest war rumors, and Whitlock dutifully kept track of them, along with countless repetitions of "no news," meaning that nothing solid and uncensored had arrived either by pouch or courier. And of course, he was regularly cold, depressed, and sick. It rained or snowed often in Brussels. The journal soon filled with lengthy descriptions of the weather, its effect on his nervous system, and the difficulties of golfing at

Ravenstein under the circumstances. Finally, early in April, he came down with a severely swollen foot which the doctors diagnosed as "épanchement de synovie" and Whitlock called "water on the foot." On April 11 he still had enough of a sense of humor left to draw a caricature of himself with the foot in a huge bandage and at rest on a chair. The illness persisted for over a month and required several of the regular C.R.B. meetings to be held at the legation, since Whitlock was immobilized. Considering it all, one is only surprised that Whitlock did not become a good deal more waspish than he actually was.[23]

News, in fact, almost always meant a new problem in German-American relations or the course of the war. The various ships torpedoed with Americans aboard, most recently the *Sussex*; the time of famine in northern France, which made life in Brussels a picnic by comparison; the capture of Sir Robert Casement and the Easter Rebellion in Ireland; the Verdun offensive; the Battle of Jutland: All these events were news and usually bad news. Despite his dislike for the Germans and his affection for the Belgian people, furthermore, Whitlock was not yet an interventionist. He remained, like his liberal friends Francis Neilson and Albert Jay Nock, opposed to militarism everywhere, and he had no illusions about the glories of English democratic institutions, particularly with people like Churchill and Carson in the Cabinet; and when Asquith fell and Lloyd George came to power with Tory backing, he all but completely despaired. Politically he was so closely in tune with Wilson's mind that he scarcely had an independent position at all. Knowing the futility of war at first hand, he knew that America might well be better off neutral. But his chief concern, like Wilson's, was in the realm of morality and law, and like his abolitionist grandfather he was willing to let events take their course so long as he could follow his conscience and act properly. So, when enthusiastic C.R.B. people praised Theodore Roosevelt and derided Wilson, he cringed inwardly and only recovered when another one of Wilson's stately protests reached Brussels. At times, he had a better grasp of Wilson's and America's problems from long distance than did many at close range. As he wrote after a long discussion of an exchange of notes with the Germans: "Poor Wilson! The American people wish him to have a vigorous foreign policy, to make bold, brave stands, take strong measures,

etc., but they do not want war. And a break now means war."
With such rapport, it is little wonder that, for months, rumors of a
vice-presidential nomination in 1916 had been circulating; Whitlock several times asked friends, especially House, to scotch them,
with obvious success. Still, even Wilson did not know what would
happen next, and the early months of 1916 were tense everywhere. Whitlock was so ready for the summons home that he
started packing in anticipation; when he tried to box his books, he
discovered that he had accumulated an estimated 3,000 of them.
The break would have to be delayed awhile.[24]

Whatever the world was doing, Brussels officials went through
their almost weekly charade of complaints about the C.R.B. and
the German treatment of it. To the British, the Germans were
robbing the country of potatoes, fodder, fish, trees, dogs, and
whatever. To the Germans, the whole problem was a small matter
of a few soldiers, returning from the terrors of the Verdun campaign, who disregarded their orders and stole a few pigs, chickens,
and eggs. The men in Brussels were of course in the middle,
regardless of nationality. Von der Lancken, von Falkenhausen,
and von Moltke, and even von Bissing, whatever their military
rank, were civilians in their present offices. In a Germany dominated by war, "messieurs les militaires" overruled them constantly, and von Sauberzweig, von Sandt, and von Lumm (whom
Francqui always carefully called von Lump) made their lives miserable more than once. Von der Lancken would make a promise,
and, as far as can be known now, try with all honesty to keep it,
only to find himself ignored by a general and quite helpless. Even
von Bissing was not omnipotent, however much the bruxellois
hated him. When the English persisted in their complaints, the
charade would begin: Whitlock and Villalobar would go to von
der Lancken for a reiteration of promises not to requisition food,
von der Lancken would promise more or less and insist on taking
the issue to von Bissing. The old man would then promise just
enough to keep the British civil, but usually would add a few
clauses that could be open to misinterpretation. Then all would go
well, until some "militaire" decided that a theft was necessary for
the war effort. In would go the complaints, usually much exaggerated, to London. Then Hoover would arrive in despair to find out
what was going on, or a diplomat or C.R.B. man would rush to

London to deny the charge. Then the play would begin again. After the return of Villalobar, Lambert, and Francqui from London, meetings were held with von der Lancken, preliminary notes agreed upon, and the matter submitted to von Bissing. Whitlock did not often meet the Governor General, and took careful notes when he did. On this particular occasion, von Bissing received Whitlock, von der Lancken, and Villalobar on May 13 at the old Ministry of Arts and Sciences. He was quite cordial, then produced a manuscript in French, which he began to read. He was quite unsteady in the language and always wrote his words first when he had to use it. Over the drone of his mispronunciations, Whitlock could hear bellowing German officers outside shouting commands to a goose-stepping group and a band playing nearby. Much to everyone's relief, the address was abnormally innocuous, and Whitlock was positively shamed by it, so pessimistic was he about von Bissing's attitude toward the C.R.B. No, the Germans did not insist on taking Belgian food, nor on having officers present at meetings of the C.R.B. All they insisted upon were regular reports on what was going on, the precise formula to be agreed upon in a later talk between Whitlock and von der Lancken. Even von der Lancken was satisfied: Von Bissing's attitude supported his own, and that meant that in the bureaucratic jungle of centralized German officialdom, he had scored a victory over the military men. But perhaps the most significant aspect of the whole proceeding was Whitlock's attitude to von Bissing, now many degrees changed from his original loathing. As Newton Baker pointed out years later, here was Whitlock hating the sin, yet loving the sinner, once he came to know him and understand him: It was Walter Crosby, or Curly Jackson, or one of his fictional criminals all over again. As he wrote in his journal that night: "It seems but just to add that each time I see General von Bissing he makes a better impression. He is Prussian, but he lives according to his principles, is not unkind as to heart, and Belgium, occupied, might have a worse Governor."[25]

AT TIMES THE GERMANS seemed more agreeable than the Belgians. Only days after the meeting with von Bissing, Whitlock found himself involved in a feud between Hoover and the Belgian in charge of the Comité National clothing distribution, Emmanuel Janssen. Janssen apparently had little use for Americans, however charitable, and despite the $3,000,000 worth of clothes sent from America he refused to let any American delegates have a role in the distribution. "Ah well!" Whitlock mused. "The Belgians will hate us as badly as the Germans or the English the next thing! To be sure, gratitude is rare, and obligation hard to endure!" Part of the trouble was William B. Poland, director of the C.R.B. in Belgium, and an almost daily visitor at the legation. Like Hoover, Poland was a man who got things done, but with a minimum of tact and little ability to get along with touchy people. "I think most of the ill-feeling in the C.R.B. is due to his sensitiveness and his exactions and his tendency to listen to evil gossip." But Janssen was quite as bad and was enormously conceited in addition. He had no sense of what publicity about Belgium in America had done toward getting the country food and clothes and no recognition of the fact that Hoover's request for an American delegate was perfectly justified. Janssen, "little squirt that he is," would not hear of it, and was quite nasty. Hoover did his best to settle the affair, but then Janssen sent an ill-mannered letter to Poland, and everything flared up again. As usual, the event died down to a subdued unpleasantness, and the feeding went on.[26]

Even social events were constrained and unnatural. The diplomatic community, such as was left in Brussels, had all but abandoned the usual protocol, but the members nevertheless saw each other unofficially at irregular intervals and at times came together for special occasions, more or less pleasant. Whitlock went to two of these gatherings at the end of spring. On June 1, he and Villalobar left for Malines, for a goodbye luncheon in honor of the Papal Nuncio, dean of the diplomatic corps, who had been recalled. They drove into the pretty garden in the court of Cardinal Mercier's palace and entered the reception room where generations of Cardinals peered down from the walls—with a portrait of Mercier just finished. They were received by his secretary and half a dozen monseigneurs, in black soutanes and magenta sashes, and then almost immediately the most eminent symbol of Belgian resistance strode in, tall, vigorous, alive, and alert, with his red cap and a long, red, silken cape flowing from his shoulders. He was as spare and ascetic in appearance as he was in fact, yet with a humorous mouth. He made a "distinguished presence, quiet and very simple, natural, sincere, warm and generous of impulse, manly, good, and yet clerical, very democratic, cordial—putting everyone at ease, and exceedingly clever, too." Without ceremony they went into the large, barren hall for lunch; the Cardinal waved his hand carelessly at the broken ceiling and the scattered wreckage and said with a knowing smile that he must apologize, but that he was not responsible. They sat down with Whitlock on the Cardinal's left, and after grace the Cardinal and the American talked at some length. Mercier was full of appreciation for America and hoped to visit the country when the war was over. He was quite impressed with Hoover (as was everyone) and had formed a good opinion of the American delegates he had seen. Whitlock in turn complimented him for his activities and said that he was happy to see a church which had so often been attacked for helping the strong against the weak, the autocrat against the democrat, stand, in the person of the Cardinal, for freedom and justice. He regretted that the church in Italy did not seem to be in the same position. Mercier replied that on his recent trip to Italy he had urged the Pope to range the church on the side of humanity and progress, but had made no impression. He was sad about the whole matter. "A word would suffice," he said, "one word. But he has not seized the opportunity," and he sat silent, thinking. The meal ended with speeches by the Cardinal and the Nuncio.[27]

The second gathering was less enjoyable but more typical of life in an occupied country. One Sunday late in May, Villalobar arrived at the legation, unhappy. Von der Lancken, it appeared, had asked him to entertain in honor of Mme von Bissing, who had recently arrived at Trois Fontaines. As he talked to Whitlock, Villalobar threw up his hands, pouted, and said, "How German!" Von der Lancken had said such a courtesy would please von Bissing. Villalobar had tried to wriggle off the hook: He was unprepared to give a dinner, but perhaps a tea or luncheon would do? The Governor General did not like them, said von der Lancken. Villalobar had turned a bit green inside, but, ever the good diplomat, he had had to agree. Now, would Nell consent to help him, as well as the Minister? Of course, in such a situation one could do nothing, and Whitlock agreed. Nell was for the moment unconsulted. Then the two men sat and discussed for a long time the mysteries of German character. Two days after the dinner with Mercier, Villalobar did his unflinching best. All his men were in scarlet livery with powdered heads, and for the first time since the war Whitlock donned tails and a white waistcoat. Most of the guests were German, in gray field uniforms with ugly white crosses for decoration. Von Bissing, sporting a whole row of them, turned out to have a dowdy, thin little wife, oddly enough of partly English descent and able to speak English perfectly. Nell and she were half of the female contingent. Naturally Villalobar was angry at the thought of having been so imposed upon, and, just as naturally he looked pleased and affable and managed to carry the whole thing off as a gentleman. Such performances were no doubt a good part of the reason why he had more influence on the Germans than his fellow diplomats did.[28]

The 1916 season thus had little pleasure to look back upon, but to Whitlock's relief, he finally found someone in the C.R.B. group whom he could both respect and love. Indeed, almost everyone could respect and love Vernon Kellogg, the soft-spoken, diplomatic, gentle, kind, and considerate entomologist who was midway in a career that brought him world fame as scientist and humanitarian. A native of Kansas, and a Phi Beta Kappa of the state university, Kellogg had studied at Cornell and in Germany and been a professor at Kansas and at Hoover's alma mater, Stanford. He had already done some service for the C.R.B. but had had to return to his duties at Stanford; then he gave up his job—and a book—to rejoin the group as Director of the Commission. With his fluency in both French and German, and his years in Germany to help, he almost singlehandedly saved the feeding operation in northern France and did much to keep the spirits of Whitlock and everyone else up in Belgium. With his charm, tact, and sense of humor, he was able to tone down the words and actions of some of the more exuberant young C.R.B. members, and he somehow managed to do it all without offending a soul. Indeed, he is the only person of importance in the whole C.R.B. operation of whom no one has ever complained. In circumstances capable of bringing out the worst qualities even of saints, Kellogg maintained his equilibrium and kept the friendship of everyone he met. Even Whitlock never managed that, as he himself recognized.[29]

((CHAPTER 12

"What a Lovely World
It Would Be . . ."

(1 9 1 6 - 1 9 1 7)

N O MATTER HOW UNPLEASANT it might seem, however, life with the C.R.B. and the Comité National never
became as difficult as life under the Germans, and Whitlock joined
most of Brussels in fuming about the German mentality, its obtuse-
ness, its ignorance of Anglo-Saxon values, its deference to the military, and its countless other ways of acting that rubbed Brussels the
wrong way. It was bad enough to be occupied; but, as the war
dragged on and German military officials became less and less sure
of victory, life was more difficult for everyone. By the time America
entered the war in the spring of 1917, the exactions and persecu-
tions in the city had gone several inches beyond the tolerable.

At the beginning, most difficulties and tragedies were little
ones. At Nivelles, a poor keeper of pigeons had no food for his
carriers and had to kill them. He cut off their heads, and his
children put them on a window sill and wrote underneath: *Morts
pour la Patrie*. The Germans were not amused, and they sent the
man to the Kommandantur for fifteen days, fining him two hundred francs. There were the German officers who went to one
of the most famous stock farms in Brussels, put a half-dozen
stallions in with each other, watched the fight, and then hamstrung

328

them wantonly, amid loud laughter. There was the artist friend of Whitlock's who ran out of food and turned on the gas in despair. There was the pension visited by German officers and their mistresses; the paying Belgians promptly moved out, and the Germans refused to pay when one mistress decided she had been insulted—before this, the servants all had quit, and the proprietor and his wife had waited on the officers themselves. There were the estaminets which had to close by nine; German officers would get to drinking and forbid the shutdown at the ordered time; if the owner insisted, he was arrested for insulting the uniform; if he did not, he was arrested for operating after hours. There were the two French aviators helped by a professor; arrested in civilian clothes, they insisted they were not spies but prisoners of war, and they pointed out the professor when the Germans promised he would never be molested—he was promptly given ten years at hard labor. And then, there was poor Le Jeune, the barber. He kept dreaming the Germans were after him and asked the Minister to protect him. Whitlock comforted him briefly, then sent him away. A few days later he sat bolt upright in bed, his eyes staring, and pointed into the darkness.

"They're there! They're starting! They're starting!"

"What?" asked his wife.

"The guillotine! The guillotine! They can't kill me; I must find the minister; he will protect me!"

The poor woman called a policeman, a Belgian who assured Le Jeune that they would go together to find Whitlock and then took him away; he was soon in an asylum, and the doctors said it was hopeless. Small tragedies, but they mounted up.[1]

But the Germans went out looking for irritation, and nothing is so infuriating as the sublime assumption that only the way things are done at home is the proper way for doing them away from home. Late in 1914, Baron von Lüttwitz posted an *affiche* that said that "l'heure normale de l'Europe central," or time in Germany, would henceforth be "l'heure pour toute l'agglomération bruxelloise" and that the Belgians must under pain of penalty advance their timepieces "d'environ 56 minutes." Under this edict all the public clocks were advanced, and no one in Brussels paid the least attention. Asked the time, a person on the street would look at the local clock, subtract an hour, give the time, and be precisely understood. Naturally for the legations that meant trouble. Dealing with the Belgians required Belgian time, and dealing with the Germans required German time, and often Whitlock forgot which was fast and which slow and arrived somewhere two hours early or late, amid much apologies. *La zwanze bruxelloise* summed it up: "The Kaiser says, 'Advance on Paris,' but they don't advance. Then, 'Advance on Calais,' but they don't advance. Then 'Advance on Cracow,' but they don't advance there either; then he says, 'Advance the Brussels clocks one hour!'" When summer came, the Germans insisted on using "l'heure d'été," or Daylight Saving Time, thus getting two hours ahead of Brussels' normal time, for the Belgians had not yet adopted that practice. Whitlock began missing meetings and lunches by hours. The Belgians compromised part way: The French adopted "l'heure d'été," and with this Allied gesture, the bruxellois could come within an hour of German time, and they soon did so; people began speaking of "l'heure Havre." That still left an hour. Finally Villalobar solved the problem as well as it could be solved. The clock on the Hôtel de Ville was controlled by the Germans, yet the clock was one dear to Belgian hearts. The perfect diplomat thus had a solution. He simply spoke to all concerned of "l'heure de l'Hôtel de Ville." The Germans could say nothing, for that was their time; the Belgians were proud of the distinction, for it was their clock.²

Despite occasional grim humor, matters became steadily worse. For Whitlock, one of the signs of increasing German rigor was the ever-growing German hatred of the English. "We are going to continue this war," said a German official to him, "until one can travel around the earth without seeing Englishmen who act as if they owned it." Another time a general told him, his hands spasmodically becoming fists: "We shall destroy England if it takes twenty years." This hatred, born of commercial rivalry, of acute feelings of national inferiority, of plain jealousy, or of exasperation that a racially pure people should oppose Germany, or whatever, was always present in Brussels, and people who spoke English were inevitably sufferers from it. The prejudice certainly had its part in the decision to execute Edith Cavell, the only English person involved in that trial, and she knew it. Everyone knew it. But it did not mean anything until translated into human terms. One sweet-faced English woman had married a German years before the war, and the couple had prospered in England. But the man was an officer in the German reserves, and with the coming of war he received orders to go to Belgium. He went, with wife and children. Before long, he began neglecting his wife and then hating her; she was English, he said. Their two little boys were placed in a German school in Belgium, where they were tortured by German boys because of their English birth. Then the husband deserted his wife outright. She came to the protector of English interests in a desperate attempt to get herself and her two sons back to England to have them reared as Englishmen. Whitlock tried for the permission but could not get it. The Germans would not let her leave because she was English, and the English did not want her to enter England because she was German. Day after day she appeared at the legation, tears in her eyes, with two boys clinging to her skirts, always trying.[3]

Whitlock naturally sided with the Belgians, as he did with the underdogs and oppressed everywhere, although he was perfectly capable of making exceptions for Germans he knew to be decent, like von Bissing at times, von der Lancken perhaps more often, and von Moltke and von Falkenhausen frequently. But for the German nation as a whole he had little use as long as the war and the occupation went on. "What a lovely world it would be if there were no Germans in it," he wrote in the spring of 1915, and nothing altered the opinion. This presumption of guilt infuriated all Germans, many of whom after all no more wanted to be in Belgium than many French or English soldiers wanted to be in the trenches. They were drafted, or coerced by public opinion into volunteering, and knew nothing of the diplomatic and economic conniving that led to the war. Von der Lancken spoke for many of the better Germans when he, Whitlock, and Villalobar were together just prior to a German move from an office full of fine prints to the Ministry of Industry and Work. As he and Whitlock looked at the art, von der Lancken said, "Are you taking a general look around before the general déménagement?"

Whitlock said he was just admiring the prints. Von der Lancken then said bitterly, "If we were the barbarians they say we are, I should take them away with me."

As Whitlock noted later; "That talk of barbarians has hit him on the raw; he is forever bringing it up."[4]

Perhaps he was forever bringing it up because the subject was forever coming up, due to German actions. As the war went on, and went badly if at all, the German attitude toughened. The little tragedies became bigger tragedies, and more and more promises were "annulled," and von Bissing and his aides soon came under further fire from Berlin for being too lenient. The Germans had always made trouble about the feeding, making promises and then breaking them, haggling for weeks about details, not preventing minor infractions on the part of soldiers, and so on. These problems, as well as those caused by British counterparts, took up much of Whitlock's time. But German acts in requisitioning food were often unplanned, accidental, the whim of one man or the result of a failure in communication. Increasingly, the German treatment of Belgium became less chaotic, more organized, and thus productive of more resentment on the part of the Belgians and more disapproval and indignation on the part of neutrals like Whitlock.

The new German plans went on roughly at the same time, but the first to take serious form was the plan to split the Belgian people. The history of the little country was full of bitter battles between socialists, liberals, and Catholics, and between Flemish-speaking and French-speaking Belgians. French was the dominant language of the educated men of the country, but Flemish was the language of a large portion of the peasantry and bourgeoisie in the areas around Ghent and Antwerp, in the west, and natives who spoke the language had long wanted official recognition of their origins. They especially wanted a major university with classes conducted in Flemish. The Germans, presumably to split the nation, destroy its sense of solidarity, and perhaps ultimately annex all or part of the country into Germany, tried to take advantage of the split. Their first move was to order the University of Ghent to give its courses only in Flemish—a move often demanded in years of peace by the Flamingants, bills to that effect having been introduced in the Belgian parliament long before the invasion. Naturally the invasion had united the country, and Flemish leaders like Acting Mayor Louis Franck of Antwerp, the presidents of the two great Flemish bunds, and the University's professors all protested immediately against this German move. *De Vlaamsche Leeuw*, the nearest Flemish counterpart of *La Libre*

Belgique, and the two most celebrated of the University's professors, historians Paul Frédéricq and Henri Pirenne, joined in. For their actions the professors were promptly deported to internment camps in Germany.

The story, probably apocryphal, went around Belgium that the Governor General ordered the two men before him. When Frédéricq entered, von Bissing spoke to him in Flemish and said, "You see, Professor, I have learned Flemish since I have been here."

The reply was in French: "And I," said Professor Frédéricq, "since you came, I have forgotten it."

Like many apocryphal stories, that one sums up the spirit of resistance better than mere truth. The old adage of Brabant held true: "Walloon and Flemish are the given names; the name of the family is Belgium."[5]

The second German attempt to invade the remaining rights of Belgian citizens was the attempted army draft of the summer of 1916. Soldiers were dying by the thousands on the Western front, and manpower within Germany was running short. Then, on July 27, a withered little man from Verviers came to the legation to tell Whitlock that the Germans had ordered all young men of German birth or parentage, who had become Belgian citizens before the war, to report for examination and induction into the army of the German Empire. Several hundred such men lived in the Brussels area and thousands more in other cities and provinces. The man became quite excited, as he begged the Minister to stop these outrages against international law and common decency. "Mais vous êtes notre Ministre Protecteur!" he would repeat again and again when Whitlock told of his helplessness. Once again, Toledo's "father of all" was being called upon to protect those in trouble.

Apparently a good many men had been notified of their coming draft in the Verviers, Nivelles, and Luxembourg areas. To support their claims, the Germans cited a law of July 22, 1913, which provided that citizens who opted for citizenship in another country lost their German citizenship; but with a certain peculiar logic, they said that all those who changed nationalities before this law went into effect on January 1, 1914, were not covered by it and thus were subject to service to the Empire. This interpretation could be, and was, opposed by many precedents written by German judges in the years before the war, by the Hague Convention, and by other agreements which stipulated almost as axiomatic that occupying powers were required to respect the laws already in force when occupation took place. The new German view offered, as its sole amusing element, the vision of German officers going to the United States to inform the thousands of German-American citizens who had emigrated there of their responsibilities. The whole mess became real for Whitlock when a young man came to the legation one day begging for help. He sat there, his dark eyes fixed on the Ministre Protecteur, his hands clasping and unclasping nervously. He was a young lawyer, and before the war he had been one of the men of promise in his field.

"Now," he said, "this." He spread his hands in despair. "I was born in Belgium," he said. "I grew up in Belgium; I went to school and college in Belgium; my friends, my associations, my sympathies are all Belgian; I took the oath of allegiance to Belgium; I am a Belgian citizen; I *am* a Belgian." He paused to get his self-control back. "I served in the Garde Civique; I pursued my law studies here; I was admitted to the bar. For a while I occupied a public position in the Belgian judicial service. And now, to say that I must serve in the German army, and fight against Belgium!"

Whitlock was officially helpless, but he chatted as calmly as he could with von der Lancken about it, and the German, who did not approve of the policy anyway, agreed to see what he could do. He told Whitlock to have the Belgians make their own official protest, for the record, and then behind the scene apparently got the order either revoked or unenforced. A similar attempt late in 1917 provoked protests from the Pope and the King of Spain, and the result was that by the end of the war very few Belgian citizens had actually been drafted. Nevertheless the threat was always there and gave everyone one more reason for disliking Germans.[6]

Next, the Germans all but raided the Brussels banks that they had pledged themselves not to interfere with. On July 5, 1916, Albert Janssen of the Banque Nationale came to the legation for advice and possible assistance. Apparently, at the start of the war the bank had transferred all its funds to London. Several of the branch banks throughout the country had been entered by German soldiers and money taken at gunpoint. The Germans asked the

Banque to reopen, and, when the directors protested the robberies, von der Goltz gave them a written promise that they would not be molested if they reopened. They, therefore, did open and soon accumulated several million German marks in deposits. Now, von Lumm was insisting that these funds be transferred to German banks in Germany. In that case the Germans could then subscribe new loans for the war effort, and the Belgians would thus be aiding the enemy of their country. The directors refused to cooperate, and von Lumm was getting more and more insistent. What made the whole business rankle even more, was that von Lumm, as head of the Berlin Reichsbank, had visited Brussels before the war and been wined, dined, and honored by his fellow bankers.

The pressure became higher during August, as the Bank Abteilung finally hit upon a method of getting the Belgian money without actually taking it by brute force. It wrote to the Banque ordering that the pledges which all Brussels banks had to deposit with the Bank Abteilung to continue in business had to be paid in actual cash in German marks at Berlin. By some coincidence the amount of security required was precisely that held by the Banque. The Banque naturally protested again, and after three weeks the Germans threatened to sequestrate and liquidate the Société Général, another large but unrelated Brussels bank. The directors of the two banks met hurriedly, amid panic among the depositors, and decided that rather than ruin two banks the Banque Nationale would give in. Finally a dozen armed German soldiers arrived to complete the deal and took with them, 600,-000,000 marks ($120,000,000) from the Banque and 200,000,000 marks from the Société. All financial Brussels was indignant and could talk of little else for days. The Germans, sticklers for form, called the affair a loan and offered interest. The Belgians angrily refused. Whitlock had to dig into his Toledo and Chicago criminal argot to express his own feelings, and he placed the Germans somewhere below the social status of yegg men.[7]

But of all the German outrages, nothing compared to the forced-labor drives. The early months of the war naturally resulted in the closing down of much Belgian industry and the resulting unemployment of thousands of workers. These men were called chômeurs, and because they were unemployed they were often dependent on the C.R.B. for all the necessities of life. Whitlock, as the

C.R.B. representative in the Brussels diplomatic corps, even apart from his symbolic status, was always aware of the problems of the chômeurs. But this group created problems quite aside from their feeding. They formed a restless and discontented proletariat, which the Germans with varying degrees of justification hated and feared and always pointed to in horror. More important, for a nation at arms they appeared a marvelous way to replenish the supply of manpower; every Belgian in a German factory would free a German for the front. In the early days of the war, when victory was supposed to be imminent and men were plentiful, no one much worried about the chômeurs. But as the war bogged down in the trench warfare of 1915–16 and battles like Verdun decimated whole regiments, the harsh military group, led by Ludendorff and von Hindenburg slowly choked off the power of the more reasonable civilians like von Bethman-Hollweg. Military necessity increasingly became the rule and "messieurs les militaires" the rulers. In northern France, in the Operationsgebiet, suffering was always most severe, and there too the labor drives were most harsh; soon however, the policy spread to the Etappengebiet (area between the front and pacified sectors), and then to the Okkupationsgebiet, in which Brussels was located.

At first the problems were chiefly those of delimitation. The C.R.B. wished to remain out of the way, whatever its private feelings, and the British demanded that they do so. Thus, several letters were exchanged between C.R.B. members and the Germans that made it clear that the C.R.B. was not to be used to aid the Germans by supplying lists of those receiving food or to hinder them in the enforcement of decrees. The Germans and the C.R.B. agreed quickly, and in return the C.R.B. received a promise— never kept even if often renewed—that men holding C.R.B. cards indicating they were employed in the food distribution would not be taken. Obviously such men were employed and were not chômeurs. By the time Whitlock left, over 1,000 C.R.B. men had been taken despite every precaution. Increasingly, the Germans did what they pleased and ignored all threats that the feeding would stop. The British and Americans had to acquiesce or let the Belgians and northern French starve. The announced German position was that the men who were not working should be offered work in the public interest and that men refusing such work would not receive relief. The Germans were the ones who defined "public interest," and their definitions rarely agreed with those of the Belgians. When the C.R.B. tried to feed such men, they often encountered German intervention. Sir Edward Grey protested; the Masters of the Lessines Quarries protested; Hoover, Kellogg, and Whitlock protested. Nothing. Military necessity, with few exceptions, prevailed. Both von Bissing and von der Lancken opposed the measures; von Hindenburg overruled them.[8]

At first, word of the labor drives came through by rumor. By mid-October, the C.R.B. men were discussing the seizures and how they would affect their conduct. But as they had little hard evidence, and nothing at all from within Brussels, they could only wait for the results of von der Lancken's trip to Berlin to plea for a halt in the operation. By November it was clear that the rumors were true and conditions serious. John A. Gade, William Poland, Vernon Kellogg, L. C. Wellington, Hallam Tuck, and others began giving firsthand verbal and written reports on the chômeurs, and they were not pretty. On October 27 the chief diplomats and Belgian leaders met with von der Lancken and his aides to discuss the matter. Von der Lancken said that in Germany young children and old men were working in the fields, while in Belgium many men of good health and of working age were doing nothing—as Whitlock had already noted in his diary. The Governor General had twice offered work for the chômeurs, and now due to the shortage of men in Germany was prepared to force them to accept. Unemployment was always a menace, and if the war lasted much longer all habits of work would be lost. The men would work in fields and quarries and such places but not in factories directly involved in military work or in the army. While the Germans no longer insisted on lists from the Comité National, they did insist that no families of seized workmen by punished by having food taken away. Whitlock and Villalobar said they would not think of depriving Belgians of food for acts required by the Germans. The discussion then continued until Francqui, who never got along with von der Lancken, said, "We are slaves." Von der Lancken bridled and said he could not permit such talk, and the incident died down.

Then, when the meeting was ending and all were weary, Villalobar sighed, said the war was lasting too long, and turned to von der Lancken. "Germany and England ought to end it."

Von der Lancken all but lost his aplomb, and he said almost with a cry of pain: "This abominable war ought to stop! We are ready to stop it. Why aren't the others ready for peace also?" It was the time of Wilson's peace overtures, and in fact the Allies were refusing peace offers at the time, whereas the Germans were being cooperative. But, for a single moment, everyone in the room could agree.[9]

By early November, Brussels was in an uproar over the sei-zures. The legation of the Ministre Protecteur was jammed by supplicants. Hoover was calling for a ringing protest, and Whit-lock feared to make one, lest he endanger the whole feeding oper-ation. The net seemed to be closing in, as men were taken from Audeghem, Vorst, Uccle, everywhere around Brussels. People came to tell of men seized and lined up. A soiled gray soldier had them march past him, and he counted off: "Left . . . Right . . ." Those told "Left" went on to Germany without a word to their families and those told "Right" were presumably too weak or too important to go, and could return. The weather was bitterly cold, one of the coldest winters in Brussels history, and men huddled about for hours with no warm clothing. Women fell at the knees of German soldiers, begging for their men, and were kicked for their questions. Could not the Minister do something about it? He could do very little but write it down in despair. Tuck reported with yet more gruesome detail. He had stood on the bridge at Mons and watched long trains of cattle cars, many of them open to the sky, pass beneath him. In them were Belgian miners going into slavery, singing *La Brabançonne* and *La Marseillaise* as they went. People gathered in crowds on the bridge and threw into the cars turnips, potatoes, or anything they could find; the men grabbed the raw vegetables and ate them ravenously. The crowd joined in the cries, while a lone German bridge sentinel bounced about imploring them to be still. Other delegates had similar tales. Tuck was so moved that he later quit the C.R.B. to join the British army and fight what he had seen.[10]

Always the people came to their minister. One was the wife of a barber in the rue Belliard who had been put in St. Gilles for possessing a forbidden publication. He had served his month's sentence and was expected momentarily. The next day she returned; her husband had not arrived, and all she had was a note saying he had been sent to Germany. For what crime she did not know; there had been no charge and no trial. He had left her a note, that was all; it concluded, "Courage, and no tears!" But her thin face was full of tears as she came to implore Whitlock, her dumb, half-witted child clinging to her. "Please, Excellence," she pleaded again and again, "please do something for my husband!" But Whitlock could do nothing for him, as she doubtless knew. Yet even she had her tale of friendship, of good people aiding their neighbors. Fined as the accomplice of her husband in possessing the publication, she could not raise the fifty marks. The day before, when she was away, the police had arrived and begun tearing the place apart, seizing furniture to cover the fine. The landlord had pleaded, vainly. Another roomer was a chorus girl in a cheap concert hall; she scraped together her last pfennigs and barely managed to buy off the police. The furniture was saved, so that the woman still had a chair and bed to use in her misery. Whitlock made dutiful inquiries and was told only that a trip to Germany would do the man good. Later he found that German officers who had frequented the man's shop had heard him making remarks about the Germans. "He's a joker," they told Whitlock, thus explaining why many were called and who was chosen.[11]

Brussels itself had its turn on January 20, 1917. For days police had been distributing cards to the people threatening fines if the offer of employment were refused. For once, most of the men who were notified were actual chômeurs. No *affiches* were posted, nothing proclaimed, except privately, to each person. Thus no response came, for no general provocation was offered. The night before, a blizzard had made the severe cold even worse; even women had received cards, and they joined the men in the Gare du Midi. The arrangements were made with Germanic thoroughness: Streets were barred, and a squadron of uhlans stood ready to keep order should the need arise. The men with cards were admitted quickly, and only rarely did a man full of joy emerge, free because of a defect that had in times past doubtless cast a pall over his whole life. The C.R.B. had permission to distribute food and clothing to the men chosen, and members did so before the poor men were hustled off to the cattle cars. The seizures went on for days and then stopped, for no more apparent reason than they began. Brussels was in fact spared the worst of the labor drives and was lucky by comparison. As far as Whitlock could determine, about 1,500 men were called, about 750 appeared, and about 300 were actually deported, but there are no surviving official records. The men were not all that had left. With the first word of the drives in the Operationsgebiet, Whitlock's liberal, optimistic, almost naïve spirit died; it had been much battered by the war, and its death came slowly. He was no longer the successor to Golden Rule Jones. "We hear constantly details of brutalities everywhere. It is all too sad—but my emotions are exhausted. I am ashamed to say that I am unmoved, somehow, by horror." The moment was an emotional watershed; from that point on it was all downhill.[12]

The drives did not take all the Minister's time, of course, although they naturally overshadowed most of it. He still continued his dining out, particularly enjoying meals with Josse Allard and Brussels painter Franz Van Holder. As soon as his foot and the weather permitted, and sometimes when both did not, he went to Ravenstein both for the change of scene and the golf. Even his staff changed. Gibson's departure had left Whitlock with far too many petty routine duties, and, when Miss Larner also had to leave, he was even more overwhelmed than he had been when Albert Nock rescued him at the Toledo mayor's office. Fortunately, Albert Billings Ruddock, who had had some experience with the embassy in Berlin and who knew German thoroughly, arrived on July 13, 1916. Whitlock was most relieved. "He is a good-looking, modest, capable-looking young chap, with a charming and quite pretty wife. I am sure we shall like them." He did, and remarked regularly about Mrs. Ruddock's beauty, the sight of which was one of his few remaining pleasures during the labor drives. Later, young Christian Herter, only recently out of Harvard, also arrived, to assist in the few months remaining before the American declaration of war. But no matter who came, trouble followed. After Ruddock's arrival, the Whitlocks rented a charming retreat in the faubourg of Uccle, which at least gave the illusion of rural peace even though only a short drive from the legation. Kin Kung was sick, and the veterinarian had suggested that the country would be better for the dog as well as its owners. It

was not; Whitlock had trouble sleeping in the sudden silence, and
Kin Kung was thoroughly homesick. He spent the night whimper-
ing miserably on Nell's lap.[13]

Naturally the back-biting in the C.R.B. also continued. The
most injurious quarrel was that between Francqui and Hoover,
which despite occasional protestations of devotion seemed to have
remained unchanged since it began years earlier in China. On July
28, Hoover arrived at the legation to discuss a letter of Francqui's
in which the Belgian requested that Hoover stay out of Belgium
and that American influence be diminished in the organization.
Hoover had sent the letter, with his warm endorsement, on to the
British Foreign Office, only to have them refuse and recognize
only Americans. Hoover was then disposed to be magnanimous.
On August 6, he returned, bitter this time about Francqui's persistence in trying to oust the Americans. On September 13, Whitlock ate with Kellogg and Hoover, and Hoover again was complaining, this time with more instances of "Francqui's pettiness
and double-dealing—all too disgusting to mention." On September 20, he repeated the charges. On October 29, in conversation
with Warren Gregory and Kellogg, Whitlock had a chance to re-
dress the balance. "Hoover, by his lack of tact, his tone of severity, has caused much of this trouble. Our Americans do not recognize that the position of the recipient of charity is so delicate that
the donor should not add to the embarrassment by criticism and
by intimations that there is lack of appreciation." Hoover wanted
to run things with a bull whip: ". . . he is a strong man with a
good heart, but lacks diplomacy in his dealings with Francqui."
Whitlock was inclined to say: "A plague on both your houses!"[14]

Not the least of the irritants was quite unconnected with
C.R.B. activity. Francqui was a liberal, with real ambitions for
postwar politics, and nothing looked more like a good political
machine than the well-organized, heroic, etc., C.R.B. apparatus.
The Belgian government in exile was largely Catholic, and the two
organizations often had uneasy relations because of Francqui's
well-known ambitions. By early November, 1916, the two finally
came to terms, more or less: In return for recognition as leader of
the official government within Belgium, Francqui agreed to abdi-
cate his power when the King returned; meanwhile he all but
demanded treatment not as a food czar but as head of state; was,

as Whitlock noted in disgust, "quite blown with pride . . ." At times Francqui made Hoover appear quite gentle and diplomatic by comparison. He took to speaking of the "American invasion" of his country and warned that Belgium had one ruler already and did not wish two. You know, he said to the heroically silent Minister, "I have written a book of more than six hundred pages—a history of the feeding" with all the details and a long chapter on the role of the protecting ministers. "I shall send you a copy. I write very easily. It is nothing for me to write five or six days at a time. And so I have produced my book. Does Hoover wish to risk being shown in his true colors in a book which will remain the standard history, which will be read all over the world?" It was quite a decision, if one had to decide at all, but Whitlock more or less made it: "The more one sees of Francqui," he wrote sometime later, "while admiring his brilliant mind, the less one respects him; the more one sees of Hoover, the more one respects and likes him."[15]

Unfortunately Hoover and Francqui were the rule rather than the exception. With the departure of the Papal Nuncio, the corps diplomatique needed a new official leader, but the new Nuncio proved quite inadequate both personally and administratively. He promptly demanded that he be made a co-patron of the Comité National and the C.R.B., the equal of Whitlock and Villalobar. Naturally that posed further political problems, for Francqui and Solvay were anticlerical, and so were many of the freemasons who held subordinate offices in the groups. On August 23, Whitlock finally made the expected social call on the man and found his worst fears confirmed. He found "a clever little popish politician fresh from Buenos Ayres, here now to cultivate Belgian popularity . . ." He could have his patronship if he wished, but "if this oily prince gets in, then I'm going to insist that Blancas and the Persian Minister, too, be made patrons." But oddly enough, the leading Catholic in the C.R.B., Villalobar, hated the man even more than liberals like Whitlock and Francqui. He was forever arriving at the legation to attack the Nuncio, just as Hoover was arriving to attack Francqui. As the Nuncio and Francqui were hardly backward in counterattacking, Whitlock found himself, as usual, in the middle, liked and trusted by neither side and trying to be diplomatic and civil to both. "Oh, the damnability of the damned human race!" he snorted to his journal after one such occasion.[16]

Even that was not all. The Dutch interests in Brussels were handled by Mynheer van Vollenhoven, the Dutch minister to Belgium, since the chief Dutch representative had left Brussels at the start of the war. Von der Lancken gives a rather tepid portrait of van Vollenhoven, saying that he was competent enough but ambitious and sensitive toward possible slights to his personal dignity —all of which should have made him quite at home in occupied Brussels. Whitlock grew to loathe him. On November 21, 1916, he noted that the man, "in order to promote that good feeling and those pleasant relations that diplomacy is supposed to cultivate, threatens to stop my supply of gasoline coming in unless the C.R.B. will give him gasoline also." Naturally that decision belonged to the English government, and not to Whitlock, but van Vollenhoven threatened anyway. "With the soul of a Dutch trader," he thought that the American government could force the British to get him his gasoline. "He would even stop the export of gasoline to Gerard at Berlin, in an effort to blackmail the American Government into asking the British Government, and so on, and so on . . ." Naturally van Vollenhoven's ambitions for status in the C.R.B. ran into Villalobar's determination to get most of the credit for himself, so the two men were scarcely speaking to each other. Whitlock was utterly disgusted. "They are not trying, either of them, to alleviate the dire suffering of the land, but to obtain decorations, and what they call credit . . . I am sick with loathing of the V. and the V.V.—dealing with them is like dealing with card cheats."[17]

With the Germans seizing workers and the neutrals biting backs, Whitlock's nerves all but disabled him. Never strong, often sick, he was quite out of his element in such an atmosphere, and it is a wonder that he did his job at all; it is extraordinary that he did it as well as he did. He was totally pessimistic. "For we here seem so despressed—the horror of the situation is beyond words," he wrote in December; "everyone discouraged, everyone blue, the iron hand of oppression bearing down harder every day—no end in sight, no possibility either of victory or peace—and a hard and terrible winter coming on. The physical suffering is great—and every home in Belgium is darkened by the latest shadow, a real terror exists . . ." With his highly tuned nervous system, retaliation was inevitable. His swollen foot of spring 1916 probably had a nervous origin, and so did his depression; worst of all were the blinding headaches he had after particularly wretched days, and they in turn led to bad nights and thus further headaches. Toledo might have looked good, even on a Monday morning, compared to this. Even when in reasonably good health, however, he never lost his sense of just how mean people could be, and his summation of the suspicions surrounding him just before he left Brussels was all too accurate: "Thought for the day: The Germans here regard us as spies, the English as traitors, the Americans as smugglers, the Belgians as domestiques, and the Spanish as interlopers." All of which left gentleman novelists a bit blue.[18]

STILL the world never left him alone. Aside from the crying women and complaining diplomats and enslaving Germans, more normal incidents demanded his attention. Dr. Telemachus Bull, an old and canny English dentist who also was an effective spy for his native country, was finally caught, although fast thinking by his housekeeper and ingenious defenses at his several trials enabled him to avoid the death sentence. Naturally, Whitlock did what he could, and he may well not have known the full depth of Bull's involvement. Somewhat less important, but more irritating and potentially serious, was the case of a C.R.B. man and his friends who became publicly drunk one evening and got into a row with German officers. Only painful sessions with von der Lancken and von Bissing managed to get exit permits for the men concerned. "Messieurs les militaires" did not take kindly to insults to the uniform. But his real concern was far away from him. The United States was electing a President, and all predictions were for the election of Charles Evans Hughes, the Republican, over President Wilson. Whitlock was deeply pessimistic and several times pre-dicted Hughes's victory. Early results seemed to bear him out, for at first it seemed that Hughes had won. Late returns from the West, particularly California, however, turned back the tide, and Wilson managed a narrow margin. Whitlock was overjoyed. It made for some change of plans, though; he was so sure of a Hughes victory and his own subsequent dismissal that he had made tentative plans for a trip to Switzerland and Scotland, where he hoped to find time to finish *J. Hardin & Son*. Once more, the book took second place to his duty.[19]

The situation in Britain was of almost as much concern, and it ended badly. Prime Minister Asquith and Sir Edward Grey had run the country on relatively liberal principles since before the war, and, while pacifist M.P.'s like Francis Neilson or John Morley might resign from office in protest against the war, liberalism seemed at least to be holding its own. No longer. Lloyd George cut the throat of the Liberal government and then returned himself as head of what amounted to a Tory regime, with Arthur Balfour replacing Grey. Whitlock knew many of the men involved, from his visit to England, and he thought the move meant the death of English liberalism, at least for a while. "I can't get it out of my head, this colossal betrayal of Lloyd George. He not only stabbed Asquith in the back, but he had led into the shambles all those working-people who trusted him." Yet Dick McGee, years before in the House of Commons, had told him that "Lloyd George was not a genuine radical, that he had no principles, no convictions; a lot of ability and energy, perhaps some sentimental sympathy with the poor because he had been poor, and hatred of the rich because he envied them and was not one of them, but that was all." The prediction, at least, came true. The party of Gladstone never recovered from the split between Lloyd George and Asquith, and was eventually eclipsed by the Labour Party.[20]

Increasingly too, events outside Belgium determined actions inside. The peace efforts of Wilson and House had come to naught, and the Germans prepared to renew the struggle even more strongly. On February 1, Whitlock received a summons to the Politische Abteilung to see von der Lancken about an urgent secret matter. Soon, he was waiting for the German in the room where he had waited so often before. Villalobar arrived, followed by van Vollenhoven. "It's the submarine war," Villalobar said. Von Moltke had told him.

Soon von der Lancken arrived, in gray uniform and puttees, pale, with dark circles under his eyes—the sign of trouble. He apologized for his lateness and had his visitors sit down. Some aides joined them. He had one of them read an official communication about the submarine warfare. He emphasized, afterward, that he and his government did not wish the feeding to stop; was there anything that they could do to insure its continuance?

Francqui and Warren Gregory were sent for and soon arrived. Obviously some consultation with C.R.B. men abroad, as well as with the British, French, and Dutch governments and the Belgian government was necessary. They quickly decided who would go where and which telegrams had to be sent. Von der Lancken promised all cooperation and said he would expedite passports. Whitlock went back to work on a telegram to Wilson. While there, Merritt Swift, a new attaché, arrived from Washington; he replaced Herter, who had to return to Berlin the next Monday.[21]

Then began a kind of diplomatic tragi-comedy, as in a barrage of conflicting telegrams no one anywhere seemed to have much idea about what should be done. Washington followed no clear line, and what messages it did send were often mutually incompatible and often arrived late, garbled, or in the wrong order. For days at a time Whitlock had no idea of what his government wanted, and had a great deal of justice in suspecting that it did not really know what it wanted. Sometimes the messages seemed the work of Lansing; more often they sounded like Hoover and all too often reflected Hoover's personal dislikes and ignored local conditions. Naturally Washington had its own problems, as it came closer and closer to a declaration of war, but that explanation did not make life for its representatives any easier. So, events took place almost at random, men struggled for personal power and status, and Whitlock, the least ambitious politically of any of the men in Brussels, simply formed a vague plan, stuck to it mainly in default of any better suggestions, and saw it work out and be justified by the course of events.

On February 3, Wilson handed German Ambassador von Bernstorff his passports and thus broke diplomatic relations. No word came as to what Whitlock should do. Diplomatically he no longer had any status, if he had had much even before the break. He was only a distinguished resident of a country that might soon be an enemy. Yet as a distinguished resident he was also a protector of the C.R.B., and both he and the Germans wanted that organization to continue. It was an all but intolerable situation, both personally and otherwise: Whitlock felt responsible not only for Belgian stomachs but for the many American C.R.B. men spread throughout Belgium and northern France, who might well suffer at the hands of the Germans should war start and no one be there to protect them. Somewhat at a loss, he once more gave orders to pack up and then tried to get word from the Germans. Von der Lancken was in Berlin, and von Moltke was polite but could do or say nothing. Whitlock took the flag from his car, but that was about all he could do. The only instructions that arrived told the C.R.B. men to remain at their posts. One important-looking telegram in cipher arrived, and, as they stood around, Herter slowly decoded it; everyone was tense. It turned out to be a correction of another message—naturally that message had not arrived. The next day it did get there and instructed Whitlock to turn over his interests to Villalobar and go to Le Havre. But, then, an insertion obviously made by Hoover said for him to stay unless the Germans objected. As he summed up his predicament: "I am in a difficult position. I should like to remain, if by so doing the revictualing can continue. I am ready to make any sort of sacrifice for the Belgians, but in what quality am I to remain? As a distinguished hostage, or what?" Naturally, amid the packing boxes and the brutal winter, he came down with a bad cold.[22]

Then came a series of meetings with von der Lancken in an attempt to arrange the transfer of C.R.B. personnel. He and von Bissing wanted Whitlock to stay, but as a distinguished chairman of the C.R.B. with no diplomatic status; he would also keep a half-dozen or so Americans with him. Unfortunately Whitlock could not shed his status like a snakeskin, just because the season changed; no one, including his government, could recognize such a move. Whitlock thought the best plan was to turn matters over to Spanish and Dutch interests and have those countries import men to replace departing Americans. Some suggestions had been offered that Swiss delegates take over, and that was acceptable to the Germans. Villalobar and van Vollenhoven, however, could scarcely conceal their dislike for any plan that would dilute their prestige or responsibilities. Whitlock's own ambitions were all literary, so he spent his time on somewhat more basic issues: Just how would he be able to leave, and when? He insisted on leaving, himself, only after all C.R.B. men were out and safe, although von der Lancken objected strongly. "Messieurs les militaires" could not permit men to leave who had been in the areas where war was being fought; the men would have to be quarantined. Whitlock would then wait. But that would be difficult. He would wait anyway. Opposed by a stubbornness as strong as his own, von der Lancken finally gave way, and when the time came the party had special rail facilities and included wives, children, servants, luggage, all consular and other official figures, and all the members and staff of the Chinese Legation. But that was still days away.[23]

Then word came from Hoover ordering departure. The message, smuggled in, could not be mentioned to the Germans, for officially it did not exist. When it finally did arrive officially, it still ordered immediate American departure; to von der Lancken's shock it seemed to indicate that the American departure was due to German insistence on the abridgment of C.R.B. privileges. Thus the onus of starvation was on him. He backtracked instantly, promised a restoration of privileges; the C.R.B. could act as before. Gregory said that in that case he would wire Hoover and tell him of the change in circumstances; that might change the orders. Francqui, met afterward, was soon told of Hoover's blunt orders and their effect on von der Lancken. For once he laughed at his rival and approved. Hoover, he said, "is the best diplomat of all of us!" A dubious judgment, and given too soon. Von der Lancken really had no room for maneuver: Washington had broken relations, and all the good will in the world could not keep the break from appearing in all areas of diplomatic contact. Besides, good will was in short supply in February 1917.[24]

Meanwhile, Hoover was wearing out Whitlock's patience. Relations between the two men had been more or less civil throughout the war, and Whitlock's journal is full of appreciative statements about Hoover and his abilities. Hoover, however, apparently thought Whitlock something of a dilettante, inadequate to the tough problems involved in dealing with the Germans. Hoover had no appreciation of Whitlock's true abilities chiefly because he did not care for literary men, had no use for them, and disliked being around them. Whitlock was to him that incomprehensible phenomenon, the artist; that meant that he was often sick, usually depressed, and generally unhappy about devoting himself to life when literature beckoned. His heart was in the right place, but it was soft; so was his head. Furthermore, Gibson was close to Hoover and resentful about Whitlock's treatment of him; that could only have increased Hoover's dissatisfaction with Whitlock. February 1917 seems to mark a kind of final break. Hoover's dislike of Villalobar made him try out several plans for keeping the Spaniard out of C.R.B. power; none of them worked, and by March 6 Whitlock's plan seemed to be winning support. That evening, at Gregory's, he, Nell, Gregory, and Kellogg made tentative final arrangements. Kellogg had received a smuggled dispatch from Hoover which abandoned Hoover's early plans and endorsed Whitlock's ideas without managing to name Whitlock as their author. The Dutch and Spanish delegates would simply replace the Americans within Belgium and northern France, and things would go on as before. Gregory recommended that the Dutch replacements be brought in as soon as possible, to make the transition smoother, and slowly have the Americans withdrawn. Kellogg hesitated; like Hoover, he may have harbored some romantic views about Americans staying on to the bitter end, whatever the world might do. "Don't be quixotic," Gregory said. Kellogg remained unconvinced; the government might have good ideas. "The Government," Whitlock said, "has no ideas on the revictualing that Hoover doesn't give it." Kellogg did not agree. Whitlock went over the ridiculous chain of conflicting telegrams, confused instructions, and so on. What, after all, could Washington know about Brussels? Everything pointed to Hoover's dislike of certain people, i.e., Villalobar and Francqui, as the only possible explanation of the confusion. Both Gregory and Kellogg laughed, finally convinced. Nell repeated, "The voice is Jacob's voice, but the hands are the hands of Esau." That they were.[25]

Whitlock for one was fed up. Personal prejudice, he thought, should have no place in determining policy when dozens of C.R.B. men might find themselves left behind in an enemy country. He could still remember the way the British were treated in 1914 and did not want men he was responsible for subjected to similar treatment. He had, he wrote, again and again pointed out the dangers of Hoover's policy and urged appropriate action for the continuance of the relief that would permit the men to leave. "But Hoover, though three thousand miles away, thinks he knows more than Gregory, or Kellogg, or I, or any one who is here, and seems able to impose his brutal will on the Department. If any horror occurs, I shall have only the melancholy satisfaction of being on record—and have to take the blame anyhow!"[26]

Finally, on Sunday, March 25, a message arrived from Washington that was relevant, clear, and unambiguous. Villalobar brought it, since it had been sent through the Spanish minister at The Hague:

At the request of the President I transmit instructions to you to leave Belgium immediately accompanied by the personnel of the Legation, by the American consular officers and by the American members of the Commission For Relief in Belgium stop The Department begs you to telegraph the probable date of your departure from Belgium as well as the route and your plans stop Your official residence should be in Havre with the personnel of Legation . . .

Then began the sudden chaos of goodbyes—a luncheon with von Bissing from the Germans and at the same time luncheon from Lemmonier and the Belgians, with a mad dash between meals, so as not to offend anyone. Cardinal Mercier called, expressed his great sorrow that Whitlock was leaving, and stayed for a brief but pleasant visit; Whitlock admired him as much as ever.[27]

April 2 was the day. In Villalobar's car they drove to the Gare du Nord. Despite a total news blackout concerning the moment of departure, all Brussels seemed to know. The crowds were everywhere, pressing up to the Ministre Protecteur, repeating, "Au revoir—et bientôt," again and again. Otherwise they were abnormally silent, for the Germans would take reprisals at any show of disturbance; yet many were in tears. Women offered the hands of their children for the Minister to shake, and he took all that he could. Then Francqui, Solvay, and Émile Janssen appeared, and Whitlock all but broke down. He was so involved with their lives and futures that he was almost unable to leave them. Finally he said, "It's only a little au revoir," and told Francqui, "We shall tell our tall stories again." Von Moltke oversaw the boarding of the train; Villalobar helped Nell on board; she was weary and weighed down by flowers. All the diplomatic corps that remained was on hand. As the train was about to pull out, Whitlock spotted Josse Allard back at the gate, unable to get through the crowd. Unthinkingly, Whitlock waved; the crowd took it for a general goodbye and began to wave back and shout. Whitlock fled inside, petrified that he had set off a demonstration. Villalobar took one of Nell's flowers, and then he and von Moltke got off. The train started.[28]

Whitlock's firmness had paid off, and for the seventy-five con-
suls, wives, servants, and other dependents of the American and
Chinese legations there was at least the comfort of a special train,
shepherded by the ever-courteous von Falkenhausen. Left behind
were only a handful of C.R.B. men, quarantined for a month
because Gregory had foolishly sent them into the Etappen; they
had written assurances that they could leave when the month was
up and meanwhile were helping with the feeding. On the train,
Whitlock found that despite his warnings several people were
loaded with messages and souvenirs that might well offend German border guards. His chief responsibility during the ride was to
confiscate as much of the material as he could and destroy it. Most
of the precautions proved unnecessary, as the Germans made only
sporadic inspections at the border. Then, at last, the train crossed
the Swiss border. "I felt like Christian when his burden rolled off
his back. The journey had been accomplished without incident,
with perfect courtesy on the part of the Germans, in less than
twenty hours . . ."29

Switzerland, Whitlock soon discovered, had more to offer than
freedom and peace. He delayed his trip to Le Havre in order to
pay a visit to symbolize his remaining literary and philosophical
affections. Living at the Hôtel Byron at Villeneuve was the greatest living writer in the tradition of Tolstoy, and the man who had
become something of a liberal conscience for Europe. Whitlock
may well not have known of Romain Rolland's work before the war;
few people did, even in Paris, until 1913. But Rolland as a liberal
was soon a name detested throughout war-mad France, for he was
not overwhelmed by the superpatriotism of his country and its
utter intolerance for all things German. He refused to denounce all
Germans; even the hero of *Jean-Christophe* had been born a German, and a whole people had not changed in a decade. He was a
man who, in his own phrase, remained "above the battle" from his
retreat in Switzerland, where he had been at the outbreak of the
war. He denounced atrocities and intolerance on both sides and
tried to keep liberal principles in the air. Naturally he was impar-
tially damned by everyone, and even old friends deserted him.
Whitlock, who shared his values so closely, may well have heard
of Rolland's attempts to air his views, in spite of the censors. But
he certainly had read *Jean-Christophe*, and could not have missed

the values behind that work. In it, an anarchistic free spirit, a musician, offends all good society in his desperate search for his art and its recognition. He is highly emotional and romantic, boorish at times and yet always true to the idealism that motivates his art. Intensely moral in his idiosyncratic way, he condemns corrupt Parisian society and the deadening effect of small-town life with equal vehemence. He is, in short, much like Whitlock and his various projections into fiction (if on a grander scale), from Davis McGowan to Gordon Marriott.

Whitlock had read *Jean-Christophe* in August 1916. On August 8, he had written in his journals a few notes of commentary and then concluded, "And what a book J.C. is! Nothing like it ever done before!" By the end of the month: "Finished Jean-Christophe—in tears. What a superb piece of work!" Thus, the book was one of the few read during the war that made much impression on Whitlock; indeed, he occasionally had fits of temper about how poor most of his reading was. Naturally he felt drawn to Rolland and wanted to see him; perhaps he was at least partially unaware of the attacks made on the man and did not know that he was being constantly watched, his phones tapped, and his mail opened by the French. On April 9, Whitlock phoned and asked permission to call. Yes, Rolland would be delighted.

Instead of the fierce, impetuous madman who must have created Jean-Christophe Krafft, Whitlock found a slight, timid, sensitive, modest little man, positively frail. He was thin, and was dressed in dark clothes, a lounging coat, and a clerical waistcoat buttoned to the throat; he looked more like a protestant pastor than a man who had enraged half of France. Whitlock could, however, read some lines of suffering in the delicate features of the finely modeled head, with its long, thin nose and scanty yellow moustache; a thin, nervous smile flitted about, wary of one more visitor who would disapprove. The interview began badly, and even when Whitlock offered his congratulations and said how much the book had meant to him, Rolland did not open up. They talked of his book, its ten years of writing, and how the author had worked it all out before starting. Then the talk turned inevitably to the war; Rolland had been talking to soldiers, including Germans, and spoke of the growing disenchantment and hatred of it in the trenches. France, he said, had been too happy before the war, and never had men had such liberty. But he spoke also of the trend to authoritarianism, especially in Allied countries, and of the indignities of the censorship that helped make his life miserable. "I grew to like Romain Rolland, so simple, so sincere, so fond of living and so intelligent, so far above the herd—he used the word again and again."

Rolland inquired of Whitlock's books, but unfortunately none were available during the war, for Whitlock had none with him, and Rolland read no English. French translations had been made, at least of *The Turn of the Balance*, and Whitlock promised to send a copy when he could find one. They then talked again about the whole miserable stupidity of the war and solved nothing, just as the war had done. By train time, the men were in as close rapport as might be hoped in such a short time. Rolland asked if he might accompany Whitlock to the station; as they were leaving, the poor, battered genius "took my hand, peered into my eyes, and with emotion thanked me for coming to see him. I was quite embarrassed by his eagerness." They walked to the station in quiet conversation. Rolland had one last disillusionment. Whitlock happened to mention a dispatch in the day's papers about former Secretary of State Bryan, who had apparently offered his services as a private to the American army. Rolland paused, "threw up his hands," and despaired at this new defection. "I explained Bryan to him then." One wonders just how he accomplished that . . .

The meeting marked one decisive change in Whitlock's own growth. The labor drives had destroyed his capacity for indignation or at least finished off what the war had begun. A second casualty was his faith in democratic man, his belief in the capacity of the masses for any sort of spiritual growth. Little had been more important to Golden Rule Jones and his successor than uplifting the poor man and giving him a spirit that could sing along with the Golden Rule Band. Now nothing was more remote from Whitlock's mind. Rolland and his book were the perfect expression of the reason for the change. Jean-Christophe had all the liberal qualities, but his story is full to overflowing with the loathing which mass man has for genius and which genius has for mass man. Even Sinclair Lewis, in the 1920's, appears like a petulant child when his caricatures of small-town and small-city life are placed against the story of Jean-Christophe Krafft and his withering scorn for the conformist, the panderer, and the wealthy dilettante. The meaning, reiterated throughout a book roughly the length of *War and Peace*, was inescapable and overwhelming. Genius and the common mentality are in inevitable and bruising conflict, and liberal values could only have application to the soul of the artist. He who did not create did not exist. The democratic genius had of necessity to become an elitist or succumb to the tide of stupidity. The war, in short, killed ideals as well as men. Thus Whitlock mused on Rolland: "Lonely, I say, because a great genius is always misunderstood, all the more so in a crazy time like this, with which his nature is wholly out of tune. But I left with that sense of benediction one has when one has been with a great personality, in the presence of a great soul." The self-righteous people were baying like wolves for the blood of their enemies. The man of genius alone had liberal values. He was right and they were wrong. Thus, to remain liberal a man suddenly, and perhaps unknowingly, had to become a conservative.[30]

The rest of Switzerland proved somewhat less inspiring. War or no war, the deadly diplomatic routines of calls, card leavings, dinners, and conferences went on, and naturally a man with as much experience as Whitlock was in great demand. He and Nell found themselves continually visiting, eating, and telling their stories to people who lacked the imagination to get any idea of what life was like behind the lines. One day shortly after the meeting with Rolland was perhaps typical. They ate at the house of Dexter, the American consular agent. His father and mother were there, and in the good old American style of hospitality they kept pressing the Whitlocks to eat, and eat, and eat the rich dishes full of mayonnaise and sauce béarnaise. Whitlock's stomach being the delicate instrument it was, it gave out with scarcely a struggle, but even the resolute Nell was unequal to the task. As they went away, she told Whitlock that she could not even bear to look at the mountains. "They look like heaped up dessert!" she said.[31]

More or less fortunately, Whitlock could not stay in neutral territory, for he had to rejoin the diplomats accredited to the exiled Belgian government. He had a good deal of trouble finding adequate railroad accommodations, the French having no particular liking for American diplomats. His insistence finally paid off, though, and he was informed by Haskell, the consul at Geneva, that he was the first foreign diplomat to get a sleeping car put through to Geneva. So, on Sunday, April 15, they boarded the ancient and thoroughly uncomfortable but private car for what became a bumpy ride to France. They entered the country with no difficulty, and everyone was extremely polite. The first sight of a French flag filled Whitlock with joy, for, given the opportunity, he was an instinctive Francophile. The next day they arrived in Paris, a Paris "smiling under a bright sun, gay with flags, the American flag most conspicuous of all, entwining its folds with the tri-color —Paris, the charming, the capital of the human mind!" At the station they were met by American Ambassador William Graves Sharp, several lesser American and French officials, and hordes of the mosquitoes of the press.

Whitlock was exhausted, "never so tired, or so soiled with travel," and a long wait for his trunks did not help his frame of mind. Finally he arrived at his hotel and washed. Then the press descended for what they called a press conference but what seemed to Whitlock more like a cross-examination. They "stood and baited" him, in the usual manner of reporters, "who seem to feel themselves authorized to interpellate public men impudently, and grow angry when one will not commit indiscretions and make a fool of oneself to create an American holiday." The French were somewhat more polite. Finally, one of the disgusted Americans said pettishly, "Well, I guess the photographers are the only ones to get anything out of this," and stalked out. Then he was due at the Embassy for tea, by special invitation. The salon was cold, bald and barren, most uninviting compared to the opulent surroundings which Myron Herrick's fortune had once provided. Soon, however, the room filled with Americans, "types of the idle who live abroad, for the most part, barren, useless, aimless lives, their patriotism a thing of flags and bunting." Sharp was of course there, "on his tip-toes most of the time, very heavy, impressed, keeping up appearances, consciously reassuring himself, 'I am the American Ambassador.'" Also there was Frederic C. Penfield, officially the ambassador to Austria-Hungary, good-looking in a rather ostentatious way, with a bristling moustache and a long frock coat; he "went teetering about, placing the tips of his fingers together—highly ambassadorial, pompous and important." Whitlock was obviously unimpressed. Penfield was "very affable, a man of good heart, with much innocuous conceit," but they were "empty men, both." Fortunately he found one consolation, in his meeting with Edith Wharton, whom he found "charming, and still pretty, and nicely groomed, and highly intelligent." He much enjoyed talking to her, especially when he found her to be an admirer of Romain Rolland.[32]

The next day he was back at the Embassy. By an unlucky chance, Whitlock happened to mention Myron Herrick, and it all but ruined his afternoon. Sharp loathed his predecessor and immediately took off on a long and detailed denunciation, complete with a minute examination of his motives and of Herrick's mistreatment of him. Like all curly-haired men, he said, Herrick was a villain. Unfortunately the Premier of France, Alexandre Ribot, was waiting for them, but Sharp went pompously on, airing his years-old grievances: Herrick had said he was not wealthy enough for the post; Herrick had tried to have him recalled; Herrick had even accused him of not knowing French! Neither of them spoke a word of French, but that was not the point; meanwhile, Ribot waited patiently on, and Whitlock squirmed. Finally Whitlock broke in, and Sharp managed to get some idea of the delay he was causing. Nevertheless, he paused to have his picture taken first. Eventually they took a cab to the Quai d'Orsay. Ribot chose to speak French to Whitlock. Sharp promptly bellowed, "Musseer Ribot speaks English better than we do," and so Ribot spoke to him; to Whitlock he spoke French, mostly on trivial matters, his work in Belgium, the course of the war, and so on. He was, Whitlock wrote, a fine old man with good intellectual capabilities despite his age; his face was sweet and kindly, and he was cultured and experienced, a fit man for France.

Whitlock finally left and went to meet his acquaintance from his visit to London in 1914, T. P. O'Connor. O'Connor brought news of the Irish Revolution and the British bungling of the affair, particularly in the matter of the executions. He had made a particular attempt, himself, to save Roger Casement, had even appealed directly to Asquith; but Asquith did not dare to interfere, though he was deeply troubled over the whole affair. Casement, smuggled to Ireland by Germans to raise a rebellion and thus divert British war power, Asquith thought clearly insane; Casement had left a diary, full of the most awful things—Asquith, typically, thanked

God he had not read it. Lloyd George, O'Connor reported, was not corrupt although one often disapproved of his methods; he was afraid of the Tories, though, particularly of Carson, and so was paralyzed. O'Connor thought freedom would come eventually, but perhaps only after another failure. Meanwhile, he did not think the government as constituted could last, for the pressures of the Irish and the war were too strong, and hatreds too great.[33]

On April 19, Whitlock finally set off for Le Havre, where the Belgian government was located for the duration of the war. There he found himself plunged into all the diplomatic and political maneuvers which had gone into limbo in Brussels; there, too, the struggle appeared far less grand, and Franco-Belgian human nature somewhat less worth saving than he had imagined, having once been confronted by the Germans and the grandeur of a brave little nation under siege.[34]

⟪ CHAPTER 13

Apotheosis (1 9 1 7 ˗ 1 9 1 2)

T HE TRAIN ARRIVED at Le Havre at ten thirty, and "dear old Sir Francis Villiers" and the Carton de Wiarts greeted the Whitlocks at the station. That greeting was the highpoint of the week; Whitlock soon found himself jammed into two little rooms in a crowded hotel which reminded him of "a rather cheap summer resort out of season, save that the hotel is not cheap." Le Havre was little better, "a filthy hole" that "might as well be Lima, Ohio—the streets, too wide for any beauty, full of clouds of swirling dust. Ugh! It blows between one's very teeth!" Fortunately no one asked his opinion. Le Havre was the official home of the Belgian government for the duration, and men of the diplomatic corps had little choice. They could stay in Le Havre or in nearby Ste.-Adresse. Even so, they were a hard day's drive from the King and Queen, who insisted on remaining at La Panne, on the little corner of Belgium that remained unconquered.[1]

Whitlock found himself overwhelmed by diplomatic chores. He had fourteen bags of mail awaiting him and numerous demands from Washington: they wanted Ruddock for service elsewhere; they wanted reports on German atrocities; they gave information about other members of the C.R.B.; Hoover sent a gruff,

characteristic telegram that as usual protested countless indignities, including Villalobar. But the new post also had its compensa-
tions, as Whitlock once again could meet casually with old friends
and dine without fear of a note from von der Lancken coming
with dessert. Villiers was a frequent companion, as before, but
with increasing frequency Whitlock also began to get acquainted
with the various members of the Belgian government in exile.
Foremost among these were: the socialist Minister of Intendance,
Émile Vandervelde; Paul Hymans, the protestant Minister of Foreign Affairs; Prime Minister Baron de Broqueville; and Henri
Carton de Wiart, Minister of Justice. As it turned out, the most
exciting member of the group was not a minister at all but the
irrepressible wife of the Minister of Justice.

Mme Carton de Wiart was a brilliant woman, flashing with
insights, entertaining, critical, and impervious to criticism. "Not at
all pretty, strange eyes, and dressed in a yellow plaid gown with a
string of enormous yellow beads about her neck," she told Whitlock that her husband's government was full of old fogies and said
that most of them should be shot and would be if the Belgians had
any spirit left after the war. She liked Lloyd George no better,
thought Le Havre too deadly dull and the Belgian ministers too
deadly stupid for her to remain among them. Whitlock frankly
agreed. He thought the government a group of "pin-headed and
pig-headed idiots," with only a few exceptions like Hymans and de
Broqueville, and perhaps de Wiart, although "his wife is brighter
than he is." The experience of talking to such a frank woman,
especially one who agreed with him so closely, Whitlock found
"like a fresh breeze that blows off the sea to the cliffs." Unfortunately, as the days wore on, the woman began to wear too, and
Whitlock found himself spluttering helplessly to himself in the
privacy of his journal. Mme de Wiart, it seemed, had taken a
liking to Whitlock, and when the Germans had imprisoned her for
some months she had passed the time by translating *Forty Years
of It* into French. Now that she was free, she wished to publish the
work; would Whitlock care to check it for minor errors? Whitlock
was trapped. He found the manuscript a mess, "full of silly errors,
due to her ignorance of English and of American life and history."
For days he worked on it, trying to get the very free translation
into some resemblance to what he had written. For two weeks he

did little else. Finally, she accepted the changes carelessly, utterly
unrepentant; and diplomacy forbade comment. A month later, an
industrious printer had the first copies out. Almost none of Whitlock's changes had been made. He could do little but grind his
teeth under his smile.[2]

But all was not misery, for Whitlock soon had a more pleasant
duty—a visit to the King at La Panne. Early in May, the Whitlocks and the Ruddocks motored out by invitation. The gallant,
debonair de Broqueville, who unfortunately was also suffering from
sciatica, received them; despite his pain he received Whitlock with
hearty hospitality and the next day escorted the party to the King.
La Panne was little more than a village, with a few desolate summer hotels serving as hospitals. Three wretched villas served as
what de Broqueville laughingly referred to as "The Palace of the
King." The King, tall, strong, and handsome in his khaki, greeted
the Minister shyly but with deep appreciation for what Whitlock
had done and represented in Belgium. Albert, nearsighted and
introverted, was at least as awkward as his visitor, and social
duties were a trial to him. Finally, he stammered out his appreciation and presented to Whitlock and his country the Order of Léopold I, the highest honor the King could confer. Whitlock was in
turn shaken, for his country normally did not permit its democratic
representatives to take such gifts—never having considered the
diplomatic harm that refusals might create. Fortunately, the King
had said "for your nation" as well as for you, so Whitlock took
the gift gracefully, hoping that Wilson or Lansing would later permit him to keep it.

The formalities more or less over, both men relaxed slightly,
in the knowledge of their vast areas of both temperamental and
intellectual agreement. The King, Whitlock knew, had been told
stories about certain American activities; he tried to explain as
many as he could, but the King waved the whole matter aside, as
if the mere mention of such pettiness should not concern men of
their intelligence. "Of course," he said, "I understand perfectly."
The King then launched into a discussion of President Wilson, the
man of power and stature who was, the King thought, "the only
statesman because he is the only one of all who looks ahead, who
plans, who tries to build for the future." They went on to discuss
public opinion and its role in a democracy, and then Whitlock told

the King that he had as much popularity and hold on his people as Wilson had. Yes, the King replied, "I have noted that Kings are popular when they are away from home and the farther away from home they are the more popular they become."

The conversation then drifted to the deportations and the other German acts against Belgium, and Whitlock told the King what he could. But that, apparently, the King largely knew already. Finally, Albert broached his real subject. America had supported Belgium nobly by its aid already, he noted, but after the war the needs of his country would scarcely be less. The problems of rebuilding would be great and the problems of maintaining independence even greater. Whitlock had great tact, and he immediately let the King know that he understood perfectly. Belgium's deliverance from Germany would not mean deliverance to France or England. Belgium would remain independent, and all the moral force at America's command would help her and other small countries in their desire to remain or become free. Even at the peace table, Whitlock assured the King, Wilson would support Belgium.

With politics out of the way, the men could rejoin the party for lunch, and there Whitlock again met the Queen, with her wistful, charming smile, her sensitive mouth, and the look of timidity and shrinking that dominated her frail figure; he kissed her hand. Then he met Crown Prince Léopold; the boy proved even more bashful than his parents, and out of mercy Whitlock refrained from talking to him. The Queen spoke for all of them: "I wish to thank you for all you have done; you have been so good to us and to our country." Not the least of the sad effects of the war was that it created so many feelings of despair and gratitude and embarrassment that it made simple conversation between congenial people awkward, even impossible. The expression of deep emotions became formal and stylized, even when meant devoutly. Fortunately, both countries were represented by men of sensibility, and words were unnecessary. The King and the American minister grew far closer in the years ahead.[3]

The King was not typical of people in the war area, however, and Whitlock's meeting with him was only a brief respite from the unpleasantness of life near the trenches. Whitlock's chief worry was getting suitable quarters, since his hotel was small and prohibitively expensive. Through the British consul they tried to get a charming spot owned by a Mme Trouvée, but that black-eyed Norman "at once adopted the tone common to most women when they talk business, namely that they are doing you a great favor, meanwhile demanding four prices for that which they are wild to sell." There was much talk of the beauty of the place and of how her husband, alas dead these many years, had so loved it; but his love did not seem worth 600 francs a month, no term less than three months, the lady reserving rights of visitation and all the vegetables in the garden. Whitlock cut off negotiations in disgust. Next he inspected a place at St.-Jouin, in a charming area, where La Belle Ernestine, the mistress of both Dumas, of Flaubert, and especially of de Maupassant, ran a restaurant and aged peacefully among her memories and her letters from famous men. She was getting fleshy and her hair was white, but her eyes were still beautiful and she was always interested in writers, so Whitlock saw all of her letters and photographs. De Maupassant, she said, had written *Pierre et Jean* here; in the book she herself appeared scarcely disguised as La Belle Augustine. She would be happy to have the Whitlocks stay, and the charm and quiet of the place deeply appealed to the Minister after the filth of Le Havre, but discreet inquiries disclosed that certain modern conveniences were lacking so far out in the country; as Whitlock's pioneering instincts had all withered, he had to refuse. The search thus went on, and not until summer did Whitlock finally find "a pleasant old French house with a high wall over which the lavender blooms of the wisteria vines fall" inside Le Havre. The place had a small garden and a large kitchen, and luck finally produced a fat and competent chef to fill up the latter, much to Whitlock's relief—and presumably Nell's. Even the house, however, could not make up for the town and its inhabitants, and Whitlock found himself "disgusted with the utter filth in which the French live." "Every morning on my walk I meet foul slatterns, servants, carrying loaves of bread stuck under their armpits," he wrote, then dwelt in compulsive detail on the physical appearance and other properties of that bread.[4]

Once settled, he was quickly to his desk and the tasks of the diplomat. Always being asked to speak at various public events, he frequently did so. Despite a bad headache, he gave one speech on La Fayette at the Fourth of July celebrations at his grave at Picpus Cemetery in Paris, thus beginning the germ of the idea that moved him to write that man's biography years later. He also performed a labor of love, giving "Notes sur les services du Docteur Kellogg" on July 29, 1917, to honor the man who probably did the most inside the lines to feed the French and Belgians. Occasionally he enjoyed himself at meals, as on the day after his La Fayette speech, when he had lunch with Edith Wharton at her apartment, in the company of Nell, Walter Berry, and Joseph Reinach, the "Polybe" of *Le Figaro*. But for the most part he was writing. The government wanted its atrocity report, and Whitlock worked hard to write it; much of it he later printed as chapters in *Belgium*. Most people doubtless expected tales of Germans barbecuing babies and ravishing women, but Whitlock would have none of that. As he wrote Newton Baker: "The worst of the German atrocities is not connoted by Aerschot, Dinant and Louvain alone. It is the long, slow torture, the systematic attempt not only to corrupt but to assassinate a nation's soul." On top of that, he was also trying to adapt his Lincoln biography for French readers and hopefully eyeing his partially finished manuscript of the Ohio novel.[5]

Soon he was settled into a schedule that included a walk with his wife and dogs—often in the rain—then a session at painting, then lunch with diplomats, Belgian politicians, or visitors, and later an afternoon and evening writing. *Belgium* progressed slowly but steadily, as he tried to model his work on Turgenev's *Annals of a Sportsman* and, so, in true realist fashion create an impression indirectly through what appeared to be a mere statement of facts. In doing so, he also printed an overwhelming number of footnotes full of documentary evidence, which somewhat overburdened the book whatever they did to strengthen its case. Perhaps more important, Whitlock toned down or eliminated all the friction and back-biting that had so marked much of the relationships between himself, Gibson, Hoover, Francqui, and Villalobar. The result was only part of the truth; in wartime, perhaps no more could be expected. After much dickering with publishers and agents, Whitlock finally saw the book published and widely serialized, although he turned down more lucrative offers from the yellow press. Appleton, and Rutger Jewett who had published *Forty*

Years of It, published the American edition and thus made permanent Whitlock's shift from Bobbs-Merrill.[6]

Social life, meanwhile, proved only erratically satisfying. Mrs. Whitelaw Reid arrived, nose in the air and money in the purse, to oversee that part of the world: ". . . a great snob, Mrs. W.R., but not unpleasant." A week later, Medill McCormick motored in, "profoundly persuaded of his own importance in the human scheme," a "tremendous egoist." Yet, in compensation, de Leval appeared—after a gap of two years—and though Whitlock was glad to see him he was not overjoyed at his Belgian friend's reports that Gibson and Hoover had been working against Whitlock whenever possible. Gibson, it appeared to Whitlock afterward, was "even a worse cad and a more miserable snake than I had ever supposed." But then, only two days later, came the unalloyed pleasure of a visit from Bishop Williams of Michigan, "dearest of men" and an old friend from Toledo days. After him things improved, as "white-haired, distinguished, charming, intelligent" Paul Hymans and his wife came to tea with the John van Schaicks. Van Schaick, in fact, so loved the Minister that he all but canonized him in his postwar book, *The Little Corner Never Conquered.* At regular intervals, Edith Wharton and Walter Berry came. Both shared many of Whitlock's prejudices and were thus doubly entertaining; one party with them included Mrs. Bernard Berenson.[7]

But of all the visitors and friends, none was so welcome as Colonel House, for few were as charming and none as knowledgeable as that elusive and discreet Texan. House arrived late in November, 1917, ready to praise *Belgium* sight unseen. He repeated some of the dirt about Gibson, but was even more severe about Hoover, for he was convinced that Hoover wanted the Republican nomination for President in 1920; the C.R.B., he thought, was being made into a political machine. Whitlock pooh-poohed such talk, for, much as Hoover grated on him at times, he did not think him capable of any such action. Unfortunately, House could stay only a few days, so, despite some delightful drives and long chats, Whitlock was soon left to his own devices.[8]

The opinions of House and de Leval on Hoover and Gibson received further support from Mme Carton de Wiart, who told Whitlock several days after House left that Hoover had attempted to influence the British government to have them put pressure on

Belgium to ask for Whitlock's recall, on the grounds that Whitlock was not firm enough, or something of the sort. She, as the wife of a high Belgian official, had seen the letters herself. The Belgians adored their minister, or so she reported, and had turned Britain and Hoover down indignantly. Apparently the British even asked for Villalobar's opinion: a mistake, since whatever friction there was between the Spaniard and Whitlock was as nothing to the ill feeling Villalobar had for Hoover. He handled Hoover "without gloves," reported Mme de Wiart. For Whitlock it all mattered very little, and he was weary of the whole subject, but her report confirmed what he had all along been reluctant to believe. So many different and unconnected sources, combined with what he himself saw, all agreed that Hoover and Gibson had done their best to have him removed for his treatment of Gibson, his unwillingness to jump at Hoover's every command, in short his acting like an intelligent man who knew his own mind and would not be treated like a vassal. "It is hard to work with snakes and cads like Gibson, after all the kindness I showed, or tried to show him . . . and, while I was recommending him for promotion to the Department, he was conspiring against me, or trying to—it is hard to keep down bitterness."[9]

The result of this reminder of ill will, combined with the war, which was then going badly for the Allies, and the conditions in Le Havre, moved Whitlock to a disgust he rarely allowed himself to show. The French patently detested the Belgians and disliked the English and Americans. Indeed, they seemed unfriendly to everyone, and willing to show it. At a time when English and American soldiers were dying for France, this was more than the Minister could take, for he saw at first hand just how un-noble the French were. The contrast with his countrymen infuriated him. "And America almost maudlin over the French! And our boys, our splendid boys, with a high ideal in their hearts, coming over here to throw away their lives for a dirty, filthy, immoral, corrupt, decadent, syphilitic, alcoholic race!" The world "has never seen such a low, contemptible, rascally, dishonest, thieving, crooked race as these Norman French"—this last a specific reference to the gouging innkeepers and other tradesmen in the Le Havre area. It is no wonder that he suffered from chronic dyspepsia throughout these months.[10]

Even as the gloom of the darkest days of the war departed in the face of arriving American troops and the successes of the 1918 campaigns, Whitlock's routine more or less continued. Nell occupied her mornings at the British Y.M.C.A. hut, chiefly selling cigarettes to Commonwealth troops, and during the afternoons visited hospitals to cheer up wounded American troops. Whitlock at times felt less useful. On one typical occasion a group of visiting congressmen demanded an audience with the King, and Whitlock had little choice but to go along; so "a huddle of men, dressed like farmers ready for corn-husking in the fields—rubber boots, leggings, sweaters, old caps, clothes faded, unbrushed, wrinkled, distinctly old, flannel shirts, and so on, they were all unshaven, uncombed" arrived to see Albert. They walked right up, trampling etiquette left and right, and shook hands vigorously, passionately eager to hear atrocity stories and gossip with royalty. "What are you talking, French or Belgian?" one of the dignitaries asked Whitlock. Another said, frankly: "I reckon you're mighty homesick. Why don't you go home?" The King, neither stuffy nor humorless, seemed actually to enjoy the whiff of the prairie after the tedium of court protocol. "They're strong men, used to grappling with problems, with nature's forces," he said approvingly to Whitlock afterward. Whitlock could not dispute that.[11]

Other visitors were less trying. Ray Stannard Baker, Walter Lippmann, Charles Edward Russell, and Ben Lindsey and his wife all called—on their way to important conferences elsewhere, since little of much importance ever happened at Le Havre. The Prince de Croÿ came and filled Whitlock in on many of the details of what really happened in the Edith Cavell and *La Libre Belgique* affairs —which he was in an excellent position to do since he had been a leader in both and had escaped only hours before a police dragnet went after him. The oldest friend of all was Clarence Darrow, who called one day in September, 1918, slightly older, fatter, and more wrinkled, but otherwise little changed. Darrow had been a hero in *Forty Years of It* but had become slightly tarnished in Whitlock's increasingly censorious eyes. "There were whispers—his private life, his relations with women—in short one began to have an instinctive feeling that something was wrong, though one knew not what. I discovered that my idol had feet of clay." But despite it all, Darrow had been a good friend and fascinating companion, and he now largely agreed with his old disciple about war and disillusionment and pessimism and his enthusiasm for the English. They traded ideas on their recent reading, and Whitlock learned something of the climate of opinion in wartime America. "On the whole, the happiest two hours I have spent in a year, an oasis in the midst of the wide and arid desert of dullness in which I live. Darrow has all of his old charm, and with all his faults I love him still."[12]

Darrow could not take Whitlock's mind off the course of the war for long. In April, things had looked so black that he and most of Le Havre had packed their bags and prepared to flee the German advance. By October, victory was in sight, and Germany's allies were caving in on all sides. On November 7, Omer, the old servant who had gone off to war in 1914 and who had shortly before rejoined his master in Le Havre, "came quietly in, with his little smile," and said that the peace had been signed. Whitlock was full of doubts and immediately tried desperately for confirmation. Omer was slightly premature, but in a matter of days the Kaiser had fled to asylum in Holland, and a cease-fire was declared. On November 16, Whitlock even received news that Rupprecht of Bavaria and the Baron von der Lancken had taken refuge in Villalobar's legation. The war was indeed over.[13]

Instantly all was a confusion of preparation for the return. Whitlock and Villiers rounded up cars, baggage, and maids, and on November 20, 1918, the two-day trip began; oddly enough, Whitlock found that the driver of his car was soldier George Statler of Cleveland, who had, he said, been the man who had driven Whitlock to the hospital the day his father died. The whole country was *en fête* and devastated, the joy of the people almost hiding the wreckage around them. As they drove into Brussels, a few of the townspeople recognized their minister and raised their hats. At the legation were the servants, Gustave and Joseph in livery, Colette and her husband, and Josephine, all eager to see their minister. The place was warm and filled with flowers, with heaps of cards and notes of welcome everywhere. When the dogs arrived in another car, they sniffed about eagerly and then raced and barked joyfully down the halls and through the salons, so glad were they to be back.

The next day, the diplomatic corps reunited to hear the King and watch him enter the city. The people were out en masse, led by the indefatigable Max, in full uniform with chapeau-bras and white plume, giving orders, waving his white-gloved hands and playing to the hilt the role of theatrical leader of his city. To the shouts of the crowd, the King, Queen, and their family entered with the band playing Sousa's *Washington Post March*. Troops of Britain, France, and the United States joined the procession. The French were slowly regaining their sense of humor: Each poilu had a little Belgian flag in the muzzle of his gun. Whitlock reacted like any contrary intellectual. "Strange! This day toward which I have looked and longed for more than four years, this day I have so long imagined, dramatising its scenes, has left me somehow unmoved; not indifferent to be sure, not uninterested, but untouched. It is the invariable rule of this our ironic life, with its eternally contrary spirit; perhaps it is because I have had too many emotions, and am tired, tired, tired, to the bone, and to the marrow of the bone." Later, on the way to the reception, Whitlock was recognized, and a grateful city began its cheers: "Vive l'Amérique! Vive l'Amérique! Vive Brond Weetlock!" Inside, he even managed to meet some soldiers from Toledo, who had been in the parade.

The next day, a Te Deum in Ste.-Gudule; the church was hung with banners and famous tapestries and was filled with a huge crowd. The Cardinal was older, thinner, and surrounded by scores of Jesuits; he could not see well, and he fumbled with his steel-rimmed pince-nez as a priest tried to light the page with a candle. As Mercier prayed, the King looked surreptitiously at his watch. Then the organ broke into "La Brabançonne" and the King went out to an immense ovation; the Cardinal, who had escorted him out, then returned to a similar outburst; then the diplomats filed out, and the third heroic symbol of wartime had his ovation: ". . . it almost swept me off my feet." Whitlock had retained his status as national hero. He conferred with the King and the Cardinal briefly and then went to dinner at Villalobar's. Nell, as before, had to preside for the bachelor Spaniard, and she did so in the single gown that had arrived in Brussels from Le Havre.[14]

Almost immediately, Whitlock found himself in the midst of the postwar political maneuvering. Even as the ceremonies continued, the French jockeyed for power within Belgium and Luxembourg and showed no desire to treat inhabitants of either country as members of a true nation. Industry destroyed by the war would need rebuilding; would French, British, or American money help? There must be a peace treaty: Surely Brussels would be the perfect site? Would Belgium recover her prewar neutrality or would she act independently and take sides? Immediately upon his reentry into Brussels, King Albert made the first changes by swearing in a new government containing three socialists, three liberals, and six Catholics. Among those closest to Whitlock, Hymans was Minister of Foreign Affairs. Baron Janssen was Minister of War, and Vandervelde was Minister of Justice. The new government was to take charge of the liberal reforms promised by the King, chief among them being universal manhood suffrage. Much of the country was nervous about this new leap into the dark; calmer than most, the King feared little and was in this, as in most things, several steps ahead of his countrymen.[15]

One of the first acts of the new government was to thank its benefactors, and, when such ceremonies are involved, ministers get gray. As anyone could have predicted, Herbert Hoover was the cause of most of the trouble. At the time, Hoover was exhausted, deeply involved as he was in trying to stop famines in much of Europe, particularly in what had been Serbia and Austria-Hungary. He had more important things to do than get medals. But Brussels had invited him, and apparently he had accepted some time ago, before the current emergency; he asked for a week's delay. The Belgian officials all but burst into tears. The King was giving a dinner in his honor; the City of Brussels had arranged a special ceremony before the Hôtel de Ville; all the city schoolchildren had their special parts in the thanksgiving and honoring; a banquet in his honor was scheduled for Saturday night, with lunch at the Foreign Office on Monday. M. Grégoire of the Foreign Office was in consternation as he pleaded with Whitlock to deny that Hoover would not come. Everything was arranged; even the schoolchildren had been notified. It was another Hoover gaffe, and Whitlock was less understanding than he should have been, considering what Hoover was doing. Nevertheless, since Whitlock was left with the mess, his ire is understandable. The inevitable happened; the square hung with banners honoring Hoover, and the events slowly approaching, "the father of all" manfully whipped up a quick speech explaining as best he could the hero's absence, complete with a telegram of regret that someone forged just for the occasion—Hoover having neglected to send anything polite enough to be read safely. But Whitlock did not like the telegram idea, and the whole idea of honoring absent guests seemed so ridiculous that the event was finally called off, saving the Minister from further embarrassment. Nevertheless, he never quite forgave Hoover. Max, when informed, took the most diplomatic of stands: The delay, he said, would simply allow them to do a better job next time.[16]

Next, it was Whitlock's turn to see if he could not offend. To the Belgians he was almost a saint, the great American who had fed and protected them. To Congress, he was simply a diplomat who might get his head turned by aristocratic frills, and so, like all American diplomats, he was forbidden to accept or wear decorations. The Belgians wished to honor him properly; the King had awarded him the Order of Léopold; Hymans advised him to wear it when he appeared before the formal session of the Chambers. He explained to Hymans that he could not and tried to make the stupid prejudices of provincial legislators comprehensible to a European. Whitlock had sent the ribbon to Washington; well then, Hymans would get him another for the occasion. It was all so difficult. Here he had had no legation supplied to him and no decent salary. He could not accept decorations nor wear a uniform. He would be the only one there in evening dress; next to van Vollenhoven and Villalobar, he would look "like a grocer at the wedding of his fat daughter."

Despite his embarrassments, the result was "in some ways, the most remarkable day of my life." All day on December 17, 1918, he worked on his speech, until late in the afternoon when he drove to front of the Palace of the Nations. Soon after, Villalobar, van Vollenhoven, and the Cardinal arrived, and they all met the senators. The Cardinal then went in, and, after a delay, "The Protecting Ministers!" were announced bv the usher; they entered to loud applause. Spectators were everywhere. Great *fauteuils* had been set out for the ministers on the floor of the House, below the tribune; Villalobar sat in the center with Whitlock on his right, van Vollenhoven on his left. Before them, in a semicircle of *fauteuils*, were all the ministers. Speeches flattering to America; cheers whenever Wilson's name was mentioned; Whitlock had to stand, the symbol of his country. As souvenirs, the three had promises that their busts would be modeled and placed in the hall of the Chamber, with replicas given to each; more applause. Villalobar read his speech, full of references to his "August Sovereign" who was such a passionate friend of the workingman. Then Whitlock, the chief symbol, the Ministre Protecteur of the nation, the human link between a nation in need and a nation symbolizing the shared values of the civilized world. The cheers were personal too, from the same throats that had whispered "Dank" on George Washington's birthday and the same hands that had waved at the car with the American flag. He was America, as far as they were concerned. He mentioned the Cardinal, and the hall resounded; he reminded a nation of its own great King, and the cries came forth again. By this time Whitlock and most of the crowd were in tears. No one paid much attention to van Vollenhoven's mercifully brief address. Everyone crowded around Whitlock to congratulate him. In everything but name, he was a Belgian saint.[17]

Whitlock the Belgians knew, Wilson they did not. But if their hearts went out to the man who had stayed with them, their aspirations were at one with those of the American President, with his idealistic calls for an end to the policies which seemed to have led to the war. And Wilson was coming. If he went to Paris, surely he would come to Brussels. Well, perhaps. Whitlock found himself beleaguered on all sides by questions of when and where Wilson would travel. Whitlock did not think it at all proper for Wilson to come to Europe at all, however much he admired and agreed with the man. Worse, the Department of State did not bother to keep him informed one way or the other, so he feared that he would be the last to know what Wilson would be doing. Yet if he said that to anyone, it would be too embarrassing and reflect on both the department and its representative. But the Belgians were all but irresistible. As Whitlock's fat French chef said to him one day, "It is no longer the ten commandments of the Lord that rule but the fourteen commandments of President Wilson." Brussels could hardly wait.[18]

Unfortunately it had to. On February 10, 1919, Wilson wrote that he would be unable to come to Brussels, and he wished Whitlock to present his regrets to the King. That was slighly offensive. Worse was the apparent slight given Belgium at Versailles, where the delegates of minor nations were often ignored; the slight was exacerbated when Geneva, not Brussels, was chosen as site for the League of Nations. Soon, newspapers were attacking Wilson and America openly, and all the good will Whitlock had stored up for years seemed to be evaporating. Once, Whitlock wrote sadly: "America was like a star to Belgium, the President a very god, and our flag a symbol of light. Now, as a result of Hoover's boorishness, the failure of the President to visit Belgium, his seeming contempt of Belgium, his action in having Geneva chosen instead of Brussels, and so on, we are the most unpopular nation in Belgium. And now if the Conference does nothing for this little land—it is finished, that's all." The criticism became so bad that the Queen felt she had to make amends. As she told Whitlock, "We know that President Wilson is our friend, that he is a good friend of Belgium. We know that. Maybe the people don't know it; the newspapers are so poor. These are anxious times!" The question apparently hung fire for weeks, as no one knew if Wilson really would come. Not until June 1919 was it announced, more or less definitely, that he was finally arriving. Almost simultaneously, Whitlock discovered that his neglect had not been intentional: Lansing offered him promotion to the Embassy at Rome. The flattered Minister promptly accepted.[19]

On June 18, Whitlock, the King, and the Queen drove to Adinkerke to meet Wilson's train. Troops were drawn up along the platforms of the little station, a band played, and amongst the flowers and red carpets the Burgomaster appeared impressive in his sash. An army of photographers and spectators was all that spoiled the scene. The train pulled in, and the President stepped out and smiled at Whitlock. Reverentially, a valet handed the President a freshly ironed high hat, and he put it on and stepped off as the band played "The Star-Spangled Banner" over and over. The Presidential party, which included Bernard Baruch and Margaret Wilson, made its way to the cars. Whitlock whispered that Wilson would find his hat most uncomfortable; Wilson thanked him with obvious relief: "I was not quite sure what would be expected," he said, and he put on a traveling hat someone found for him. The cars went through several of the devasted areas, stopping for the dignitaries to have lunch at a specifically erected tent. There, amid black flies that chewed the visitors severely, they consumed cold chicken with red wine. Wilson was quite gay, making several good jokes about Dr. Jowett of Oxford; the King and Queen were polite, having only the slightest of ideas just who this doctor was. Wilson was also quite critical of certain people he had met recently. Poincaré he called a "stinker," and Medill McCormick a "crook." The rest of the trip was less successful, at least for Whitlock. His car broke down twice, and he and his passengers fell far behind, much to his exasperation.

The next day, lunch at the legation, complete with bands playing outside and flowers and uniforms everywhere. Max, the Cardinal, Villalobar, the Hymans and other dignitaries assembled, to greet first the Wilson party and then the King and Queen. It was all very pleasant, light and entertaining, and the Queen was grateful that the Whitlocks had remembered her hay fever and omitted the customary roses. In the afternoon, the big reception at the Chamber of Deputies, with everyone again present, even Hoover. The usual speeches, with Wilson as usual taking top marks in Whitlock's book and deflating all the anti-American feeling with the simple gesture of announcing that the legation would be raised to an embassy. Then a trip to Malines and the Cardinal, the King racing the whole way and leaving more cautious drivers in his dust. The old Burgomaster of the town performed his cermonial duties, and Wilson signed the "Golden Book" and then entered the bombed-out university. There, in the tragic ruins of centuries of learning, a red carpet was spread in the old and now roofless library, and on it Wilson was made *Doctor honoris causa*. The President was deeply impressed. "Was ever a degree conferred in such circumstances?" he asked Whitlock. Then, back to Brussels and more festivities, including a reception for the diplomatic corps and dinner at the Palace. Whitlock managed to lose his car and so had to run the whole way home to get ready; Nell fortunately squeezed in with Villalobar. Thus, the brilliant finale found one very lame and tired Minister smiling as gamely as he could, thankful that nothing else had gone wrong.[20]

But with the President's departure, Whitlock was faced with a dilemma. If Brussels were to have an embassy, why should Whitlock go to Italy? De Margerie was preparing to become France's first ambassador in Brussels, and Villalobar was lobbying steadily for the privilege of becoming Spain's. Sir Francis Villiers was doing likewise. If nothing else, the war had centered enough attention on Belgium to get her numerous diplomatic promotions. Now America was joining in, and she, of all countries, was already represented by the most beloved foreigner in Brussels. "And you stay too," Villalobar had told him, "as ambassador. No need to go to Italy now." Whitlock needed little persuading. News from Italy was bad, and rumor had it that the American ambassador there needed armed troops to protect his house. Whitlock had little stomach for the conditions that soon produced Mussolini. In July he was moaning, "I am not very enthusiastic about going to Rome —dread it, in fact. If this legation is raised to an embassy, I'd rather remain here." His agony slowly increased, and finally he began to hedge his bets as much as he could. He sent a dispatch to Wilson about the new embassy, calling the President's attention to the ill feeling that might result if he were not made the first ambassador. Not the least of all the ill feeling would be in his own dyspeptic stomach, but he did not say that. Even his pride was a bit wounded, as he noticed the grand cordons decorating the new ambassadors who were once his fellow ministers—and who now took social precedence over the American at all functions. Clearly that would never do.[21]

Whatever the final decision, it would have to wait. Whitlock was granted leave on July 12 to come home, and Wilson said he would discuss the matter with him then. A few days later, the King suddenly added to Whitlock's pleasure: "I want to go to America," he said, "as soon as possible." Animated and smiling, and quite enthusiastic over the thought of going to the country he knew had helped Belgium so much, the King was also patently eager for an end to his official routine and a sample of American informality. Anyone who enjoyed midwestern congressmen was certainly ripe for a visit; the King said Whitlock should limit his official duties to three days and then see the country with him. It was the carte blanche for a highly enjoyable vacation for both men. Whitlock was quite delighted, and he arranged matters easily. Almost five years to the day from the invasion of Belgium, the two groups departed.[22]

Whitlock and Nell, Marie, Nell's maid, and the dogs left first, on the *Nieuw Amsterdam*, early in August. The boat, full of drunken, craps-playing soldiers returning home irritated them immensely, but they completed the voyage without serious incident and arrived in New York on August 29. They met briefly with their two mothers and Mrs. John M. Palmer, Nell's aunt and the widow of Whitlock's old law teacher. They could stay only to say hello, however, for Whitlock wanted to get to Washington as soon as he could and settle his status. In Washington, Wilson displayed the full confidence he had always had in Whitlock, said he understood completely, and repaid Whitlock's loyalty by assuring him he would return to Brussels as its first ambassador. Whitlock then tried to talk to Breckenridge Long, Third Assistant Secretary, about the arrangements for the royal tour, but Long quickly made it plain that he did not need advice from anyone. Whitlock then rejoined his entourage in New York, and they left immediately for a hotel in Briarcliff Manor, in Westchester County, New York, where he planned to wait until Congress approved his appointment. As he golfed and relaxed, Wilson went west on his ill-fated speaking tour in defense of his League of Nations; soon after the bill raising the legation to an embassy passed, Wilson returned to the White House a broken man, unable to exercise most Presidential duties. Nevertheless, he managed to sign the measure and send it to the Senate for confirmation. Senator Warren Harding obtained waiver of the usual procedure for his old acquaintance, and with unanimous consent of his colleagues it went through without even going to committee. Subsequent events went somewhat less smoothly. On October 2, just minutes before the arrival of the royal boat, Whitlock took his ambassadorial oath before Long in the group headquarters at the Waldorf. Afterward, lawyer Whitlock began to have grave doubts about whether or not Long had the authority to administer such an oath. Long affably agreed that he probably did not, but that no other procedure would get Whitlock into his position before King Albert's arrival. Finally, in a fit of nervous conscience, the new ambassador wandered down to a store in the Waldorf basement, found a notary, and swore himself in properly.[23]

The reception was something less than a diplomatic triumph, at least by European standards. Long was a nervous, socially insecure and unsophisticated man who still had not recovered from marriage to a wealthy woman. He was conceited, despite his deficiencies, and he and Vice-President Marshall provided a remarkably untutored welcoming committee. No one paid any attention to precedence, and only Nell knew the proper moment to curtsy. The other Americans found themselves quite ill at ease, and their attitude soon communicated itself to the royal party. The King and Queen remained as close to Whitlock as they could, as if for safety, while poor, timid Prince Léopold was as devoted to the new ambassador as a faithful dog. After the disembarkation, the party returned to the Waldorf, and at the official reception Long again distinguished himself. He had been officious with Nell at the dock, and now she took her revenge. As Long stood there, representing his President, legs wide apart, hands in his pockets, his morning-clothes tails plainly visible between his legs, she simply stared at him. He began to squirm and look about worriedly. She kept staring. Finally, he noticed that every Belgian in the room was standing at attention, and he stiffened up slightly. Finally, he even took his hands out of his pockets.

The next day, October 3, was the official welcome so the royal party had to go through the charade of boarding a local politician's yacht—loaded to the waterline with petty dignitaries—and once more disembark. Before they managed to, they almost sank; the greedy souls on board made such a rush to the sandwich plate on one side that the boat nearly went over. The official welcomer, Rodman Wanamaker, did not improve matters by slapping the King on the back occasionally and seizing his arm to introduce some of "the boys" to the visitor. Whitlock concluded the sail by getting a cinder badly stuck in his eye. Finally the party escaped; Mayor Hylan read an utterly tasteless speech, but spoke so badly that none of the Belgians could understand a word. Then he demonstrated his patriotism and intelligence by wrapping his guests in the American flag. The King went through it all with stoic nobility. Nothing seemed to bother him but the news of Wilson's illness and his inability to pay an official visit to the White House. "I feel like one who enters a man's house and doesn't pay his respects to his host," he told Whitlock.

The Department of State had arranged a tour that would have killed anyone but a Presidential candidate. The King did not like to complain about it, but the Queen was obviously too weak for any such ordeal, so Albert asked Whitlock if, perhaps, the orgy of visits and receptions might be somehow curtailed. Whitlock did not want to go through such nonsense any more than his guests, and he quickly had the worst of the plans canceled. Originally, the train of the party was to stop at every minor city from Buffalo to California; every stop but one at Toledo was soon canceled. The only hitch was Chicago, which the King wanted to see. State refused; they would not have him "insulted by that damn fool of a mayor," as Long put it about Big Bill Thompson, so even Chicago was omitted.

In the meantime, Whitlock got the name of an oculist, and, when consulted, that gentleman decided he had found a cyst. He then began puncturing here and there and finally went after the offending object with a pair of scissors. Whitlock finally came to his senses and made the man stop, but he was now in far worse pain; his eye was severely inflamed. The next day he consulted a German oculist, who made some unkind remarks about his predecessor, diagnosed conjunctivitis, and forbade Whitlock—to his immense relief—any more attendance at outdoor events. In succeeding days, while Albert dutifully went through schools and cemeteries, even made an airplane flight, Whitlock stayed safely at the Waldorf, recovering. The women and dogs remained at Briarcliff.

When the tour eventually began, the train with the royal party aboard stopped briefly in Boston and Toledo, but Whitlock's efforts had kept ceremonies to a minimum. The most memorable incident occurred at Gary, Indiana, where the train was on a siding. Whitlock heard a knock at his door, and, when he opened it, there suddenly was Curly Williams, his old client, criminal friend, and the inspiration for several of Whitlock's underworld "fictional" heroes (as Curly Jackson). Whitlock was all but panic-stricken. "I should have been glad to see him anywhere else; but here! It all flashed through my mind,—the time that I defended him for murder,—and acquitted him—and, in fact, his whole mad, wild career, as thief and safe-blower."

Curly said, "Don't worry; it is all right," and he threw back his coat, showing a detective badge. "I have been waiting for this moment for six years. I wanted to tell you that I had reformed; that I have been living a straight life from that time and that my reformation was entirely due to your influence. I have wanted to tell you; but you were away in Europe and I had no chance."

Whitlock asked him in, and Curly told how, when he last left prison, he had resolved to go straight and so had obtained a job as a detective with the New York Central Railroad. "I have told them all about my past," he said. "It is all clear, open and above-board—nothing hidden. They know all about me and I have made good. I am now Chief of their detectives and the greatest honor that ever came to me in my life was in having been chosen to guard the King from New York to Boston and to Chicago. I saw you at all those places; I saw you at Boston, at Buffalo, at Toledo; but I didn't want to show myself to you until I had done this job; and now that the King is here at Gary and safe, my work is over." Whitlock was deeply touched, as Curly stood there smiling his gold tooth at him. They chatted briefly about old times. Curly was living in Cleveland with a wife and daughter. Then he finally excused himself, saying as he left: "I don't arrest many men. I try not to, for I don't like to put them in prison. I seem to have a faculty for spotting pickpockets. When we reach any place, I can tell a 'gun' as far as I can see him. I jump into the crowd and I go up to him and say, 'Here, you are a pickpocket—get out of this,' and he goes. I have been successful." Then he left, with a smile and a wave of his hand. The incident made Whitlock both happy and relieved.

The rest of the trip was notably for the opportunities it gave the King to play Walter Mitty. He drove the engine on numerous occasions, as fast as he drove his car. He received the freedom of the City of Reno, and solemnly promised Whitlock he would return if he ever needed a divorce, since citizenship matters were all settled. They spent several days in California, while the King went up for another plane flight and Léopold tried out a motorcycle. They returned to Washington via Yosemite and the Grand Canyon. Whitlock was appalled by the "militant provincialism" of the capital and by the directionless air of life there without a functioning President. He met Earl Grey and Vice-President Marshall and enjoyed a talk with Alice Roosevelt Longworth, but only after extended negotiatons with Cary Grayson, Wilson's physician, did he manage to get the King an audience with the President. The ship sailed almost immediately afterward, with a most happy King: "This last month has been the happiest of my whole life," he told Whitlock. "I do not say that because you are the American Ambassador; I say it because it is the truth."

The idyll ended in mid-November when Max, a red carpet, and a small crowd welcomed the Whitlocks back to a cold, drab, and dull Brussels. Almost immediately, Whitlock found himself in the midst of the bitter political feuds that were racking the country. Belgium was prosperous and industry reviving quickly, but the political changes wrought by the war were taking their toll. The Catholic conservative party, the majority party before the war, was steadily losing ground to the socialists, who seemed to be making sharp advances all over Europe. The Liberal party, the obvious place for the sympathies of a man like Whitlock who disliked both the obscurantist right and the doctrinaire left, remained important, but only in a minority sense. One of its most influential leaders, Whitlock's old friend M. Paul Hymans, became quite close to Whitlock during their period, and Whitlock's journals are full of long and often doleful conversations between the two men about the forces that seemed to be destroying the world they loved. Some issues were peculiar to Belgium: The continuing schism between Flemish- and French-speaking elements, underground during the war, and the German attempts to exploit it, reappeared; at least as serious, the French campaign to control the country won numerous supporters, much to Whitlock's disgust, and only the bungling of French Ambassador de Margerie and of the French government prevented a possibly nasty showdown. Other issues were universal, as the socialists and many liberals campaigned for a broadening of the suffrage and an expansion of welfare measures, often bitterly opposed by the Catholics and the men around the King. Albert himself was far more liberal than his court—that perhaps is one reason he so enjoyed Whitlock's company.[24]

If politics in Belgium was disturbing, politics in America was disgusting, and events in his native land increasingly contributed to Whitlock's perennially sour stomach. His affection and admiration for Woodrow Wilson slowly disappeared as Wilson turned more and more intransigent and became critically ill. Whitlock, through House and other friends and correspondents, regularly speculated on events from second hand: He and Nell decided that feuding between the Wilson and Lansing women had caused the dismissal of the Secretary of State, for example. But Wilson's failure in getting the treaty ratified appalled Whitlock. One did not have to admire senators Borah and Lodge to see that Wilson's stubbornness had been the key to the defeat of the treaty. His subsequent behavior seemed inexcusable even to Whitlock, who had admired Wilson earlier to the point of reverence. "One stands aghast, wondering what blunder he will make next. He was a year and a half ago the most popular man in the world, hailed everywhere as a veritable Messiah; now he is cordially detested everywhere, and all because of his astounding tactlessness. He has been mostly right in everything, but has ruined himself and his own cause, and almost his country, by his stubbornness and by tactless blunders that a common ward-heeler would know better than to commit." He was just as disgusted at the men who had opposed Wilson, but that was small consolation. Never again would he have a politician for a hero.[25]

The events of the 1920 Presidential campaign only added to his disgust. Hoover, backed by his C.R.B. claque and no expertise, made himself foolish in trying, or certainly appearing to try, for the Republican nomination; and Whitlock took a certain grim satisfaction in seeing his failure. He took even more satisfaction in seeing Hiram Johnson defeated, "for that bigotted, ignorant, provincial and intellectually dishonest demagogue would have wrecked the government and disgraced the nation." The eventual winner, an old acquaintance from Ohio politics, was Warren G. Harding, "A man of common sense. He is in no sense brilliant, but we have had enough of brilliant genius in the White House, after Roosevelt and Wilson." Indeed, the proper man for the White House should be solid and mediocre, he thought, provided he has "good sense, sound and careful judgment, and good manners. All these Harding has." He was no more radical than most Ohio Presidential candidates, but he was at least "more honest than McKinley, not so much of a hypocrite and poser, but human and attractive personally." Colonel House had predicted his nomination on the cruise four years ago, and Marshall Sheppey had done the same on Whitlock's trip home.[26] At least the blunders would probably stop; Harding would simply do nothing, whereas Wilson was doing things wrong.

The Democrats did a little better, or a least did not step so far toward mediocrity as did the Republicans. Whitlock was glad that Governor Cox of Ohio received the nomination, "for I am fond of

Jim Cox; he is my friend, and has been three times Governor of my state, and a good Governor." He found the two candidates "about equal in merit, Cox being perhaps the abler, certainly the more liberal of the two, while Harding is more showy, and looks the part a little better. I think he will defeat Jim. If I were home I should vote for Jim Cox, however, and think that he would make the better President." The campaign, however, with its demagoguery about Ireland and its obfuscation of international issues, quite disgusted Whitlock, and in his increasing pessimism he all but despaired for his country. Americans "are simply in a spiteful mood with the President and think that they are hurting *him*, though Cox doesn't represent him or his ideas any more than Harding does. The people indeed, do not know what ideas Harding or Cox represents; neither do Harding or Cox. Great is democracy!"[27]

The treatment accorded to him by Washington scarcely helped this mood any. Sentimentalists ably marshaled by the funeral lobby were making loud cries for the return of Americans killed in the war, and the thought of exhuming all those bodies and shipping them back—all under his direction—was just a little more than Whitlock cared to dwell on. But even that did not threaten self-respect quite like the simple problems of trying to find an embassy and a place to live. The Whitlocks had been moving repeatedly, as owners demanded that the United States either buy the place or allow them to find buyers elsewhere. Often the American Embassy had the distinction of sporting a large *For Sale* sign on the front lawn. Congress in its usual provincialism, was not about to subsidize "cookie-pushers," and it showed far more enthusiasm for laws that would forbid ministers and ambassadors to serve wine than it did for paying for a suitable residence. Whenever he thought about it, Whitlock was almost beside himself. "The provincialism in America, compounded with arrant demagogy, and Anti-Saloon puerility, is simply nauseating and there is no hope; the country will never change, never grow up. There is a kind of perverted snobbishness in America that is hopeless; as Englishmen are proud of being seen in the company of a Duke, so Americans are proud of being seen in the company of a ragamuffin, because they think that that proves to the world that they are not snobbish."[28]

America might never change, but there was no denying that Whitlock had. The scars of the war were too great, and the optimistic democrat of "Golden Rule" Toledo had become if not the darkest of pessimists, at least a gently disillusioned and determinedly apolitical gentleman, with conservative opinions to match. Even before the end of the war, he was writing in despair at the decline of parliamentary government, the boobs that represented the people in every country, and the nations' utter incapacity to govern themselves properly. At times, he even gave the appearance of returning to a Darwinian racism, of the variety that so dominated men like Theodore Roosevelt and, indeed, probably the majority of public figures in prewar England and America. Certainly he detested the idea of unlimited immigration into the United States with all the vigor of a benighted Tory. Even his old ideas no longer had much attraction for him. As he wrote after reading in the London *Nation:* "Strange! How all has changed in this world! Or is it I? So much of their radicalism seems to silly to me now—much of it, not all. Am I growing old? Ah well, radicalism, like flirting, in a youth is attractive; in an old man it is disgusting." If it was, he soon disposed of it. His aversion to socialism, which had been strong enough even in Toledo days, tended to overshadow his former affection for common workers, as more and more Belgians seemed to have become militant, humorless, and demonstrating socialists. With Brussels racked by strikes, he snorted: "The attitude of labour everywhere throughout the world has been contemptible. The workers took advantage of the world's agony to demand increased wages, they worked in safety, far away from the noise of battle or the range of guns, and are called heroes by the blatherskite politicians for having 'won the war.' " The new frame of mind even showed up in his sympathies toward boxing. When Jack Dempsey disposed of Georges Carpentier, Whitlock was quite happy about it—and "disgusted with those mawkish Americans who were licking the boots of the French by shouting for Carpentier. There is a soft strain in America just now, as a result of prohibition, coeducation, woman suffrage, and sentimentalism, uplift, and that sort of rot." Shades of Theodore Roosevelt! As he wrote Steffens: "As you say, we have all been changed with this war. No human being, and certainly no intelligent human being, could go through it without having been changed in many particulars, and lucky are those who have not been changed by it for the worse."[29]

ONE PLEASANT INTERVAL THAT SUMMER was a visit from Colonel House, one of many which he made over the next decade. He and Whitlock had much in common, both temperamentally and politically, and Whitlock always looked forward to their meetings and enjoyed them. On August 16 they had dinner and a long talk. Whitlock told House that he would love to have the ambassadorship to England, but that he was afraid he did not have the money needed for the job. House promised to see what he could do if Cox were elected. They then went on to discuss Wilson and his achievements, and House asked him what estimate he thought history would make of Wilson. To his surprise, Whitlock answered that he thought Wilson would appear as a great orator but not a great statesman. Whitlock felt Wilson had failed as a statesman because he had not been able to put his ideas over. Lincoln, by contrast, had confronted problems of similar difficulty and solved them, so his place was secure. Wilson was a failure. House disagreed, but typically he kept his higher estimate of Wilson to himself. Whitlock then went on to say that Wilson's greatest mistake was his second marriage. Both he and Nell regarded Mrs. Galt as a jealous and ambitious woman, who, as Mrs. Wilson, was soon bent on breaking up every friendship the President had and leaving herself supreme. They did not deny her ability, but thought her quite untrained in the art of government and prone to accept advice only from those equally ignorant.[30]

But with Harding's victory, it did not seem to matter much what happened to Whitlock. His days were numbered for purely political reasons. He certainly wanted to stay on, and Washington knew it. The Belgian government wanted him to remain, and both the King and the Cardinal took the remarkable action of writing to Washington to make the nation's desires clear. The result was a foggy and vague feeling of discontent, since Harding acted as murkily as he spoke and no one knew from one day to the next what, if anything, he had on his mind. What looked like the key to the business was Marshall Sheppey, who was very close to both Whitlock and Harding. Sheppey had worked hard for Harding, so hard in fact that he had imported his New York tailor to Ohio to get the dowdy President-Elect looking something like a statesman. Harding even wore a Sheppey-ordered morning coat at his inaugural. And all Sheppey wanted, as he made clear to Harding, was that "my friend Brand" should stay on in Brussels. Period. Harding as usual vacillated, did not say yes or no, but kept talking about the requirements of politics. That meant that Hoover and George Harvey wanted the office for one of their men, Henry P. Fletcher, and they had the backing of Whitlock's old Toledo foe, Walter Brown; the apparent plea was to appoint Fletcher to Brussels until Paris fell vacant, then give Paris to Fletcher and Brussels to Hugh Gibson, who as a friend of Hoover naturally had an inside track. Whitlock's enemies were riding high, and were it not for Sheppey, he would probably have been dropped early in the Harding administration. As it was, he could stand the strain only so long, and when his demise seemed near he submitted his resignation. It was accepted promptly, effective December 31, 1921.[31]

It was a sad way to end a remarkable term of duty, but his world was leaving before him. Sir Francis Villiers had been retired as too old and ineffectual to serve England properly. Villalobar, in a ceremony that excited every malicious gossip in the city, found his loneliness all but unbearable, received papal dispensation, and married his cousin, the Marquise de Guimarey; Mercier married them at Malines. No longer did Nell need to serve as hostess for the larger affairs at the Spanish Embassy. But two relationships continued, as warm as ever. Whitlock saw the Cardinal regularly, had many long chats with the old gentleman, and at times, despite his anticlerical politics, felt the pull of Rome a good deal more strongly than he might have admitted. But Mercier was old, and he was at Malines rather than Brussels; King Albert was nearby, and with him and the Queen Whitlock had one of those rare friendships that history occasionally discovers, as the energetic soldier King, who loved fast cars and mountain climbing, who was a devout Catholic and yet a liberal in politics, became as close to his American ambassador as he was to anyone outside his own family. The symbolic heroes of wartime resistance had cemented their friendship on the American tour, and for Whitlock's last months in Brussels the Royal Family and he enjoyed each other's company frequently. Thus, on one typical occasion, Whitlock drove out to Laeken in the summer of 1920 to see the Queen. He was received by the Countess Élisabeth d'Oultremont, who led him into the familiar red Empire drawing room, where tea was set up. The Queen had left word that he was not to wait, so the Countess immediately poured him a cup. Soon the Queen arrived, dressed entirely in white. They had their tea together, and then Whitlock took Her Majesty to his favorite sporting ground. The six-hole golf course in the great park had been especially designed, but no one had as yet managed to cut any holes, let alone install cups or flags. The Queen had given orders about the matter, but no one had responded. "I don't know why," she said, with her odd and amusing helplessness. Together they berated servants comfortably and in general, and Whitlock chalked up the debility to the war. He himself admitted—all too honestly—that he had a dreadful time ever getting anything done, and called himself "too lazy for words." The Queen was quite grateful (perhaps at finding a congenial man who preferred talk to mountain climbing)and answered quickly, "So am I; I am just like that." They fumbled around the course, Whitlock fixing her tees and hunting her lost balls, both of them getting enough sun and exercise to make it worthwhile. They played the course twice, and Whitlock loved it. "She is a perfect dear, so simple, so feminine, and so pretty."

For dinner they went back to the Palace. He found Nell and the King downstairs, the King vaguely distressed at having to wear evening dress even with friends. They talked for a while, and the King ably defended his Alpine habits: "It changes one's thought. It is better than talking politics, and going to ceremonies, and listening to discourse, and looking at fat cattle." With that sort of an argument, one could hardly argue. The Queen finally came in and found herself the butt of jokes for having been late; she appealed for Whitlock's aid against her doting but energetic husband. They then sat down to a simple dinner without ceremony. After dinner, the Queen whispered loudly in the King's ear. "The photographs, oh yes!" he exclaimed and then went to a table and took two large, flat boxes and gave them to the Whitlocks. One was his photograph, framed in silver and with a crown above it and the inscription: "To the great and faithful friend of Belgium and excellent companion of our visit to the United States, Albert." The other, a similar picture of Her Majesty, was inscribed, "To

my dear Mr. and Mrs. Brand Whitlock, in true friendship. Elizabeth." The group then went out, Albert and Whitlock lit their
cigars, and they discussed democracy, Cox, the future of Europe,
France's unreasonable demands on Germany, Foch as a general,
the French character, and Belgian politics. The next day the
Queen gave Nell a message: "Tell Mr. Brand Whitlock that when
I make my reverence this afternoon, it shall be for him, and that
all through the ceremony I shall be thinking of our golf game."[32]

Washington of course could not have cared less. As Whitlock
made the sad journey to the Ministry of Foreign Affairs to make
sure that the Belgians would find his successor *persona grata*, the
official there said: "I am very moved! It is sad news. You know
that we have done all we could to keep you. You are so much
associated with our life, our history, that it is a sad event to lose
you." Whitlock could not have agreed more, but all he could say
was, "It doesn't matter," and get away as quickly as possible. At
the Embassy, all of Nell's employees were in tears with some
frequency, and the confusions of packing were everywhere. Villalobar was quite indignant at what he regarded as the shabby treatment of his colleague, but that also mattered little. Whitlock and
his wife were both physically and nervously exhausted and needed
a vacation even if they preferred to remain. America, the land of
Harding, prohibition, and philistinism, he could not stand the
thought of; England attracted him, but they had rules about dogs
too stringent to get Kinnie and Taï Taï in without a great deal of
trouble; most of France repelled him, for the memories of the
French interventions in Belgium were too recent. But finally, almost out of frustration, they engaged rooms at the Victoria Hotel,
Biarritz.

Then, just as Whitlock was getting severely depressed, he heard
of his last great honor. On Christmas Eve 1921, King Albert
broke all precedent by making a personal call on the departing
ambassador, the first time in living memory that royalty had paid
such homage. The red carpet out, the King arrived in uniform, but
wearing only his American decorations. Whitlock and his wife
conducted him into the stripped house, made habitable only by a
quick infusion of flowers. The King sat on the sofa, Whitlock and
Nell on chairs, while an aide sat stiffly in a corner. Albert could
not say often enough how much he regretted Whitlock's departure,

and he thanked him over and over again for what he did during the war; he begged Whitlock to consider him as a friend and to come back often—although Whitlock scarcely needed persuasion. But the King could not understand why America persisted in shifting ambassadors from posts where they were well liked and which they knew and understood. "Your husband," he told Nell, "knows Belgium better than most Belgians." He spoke also of his trip to America and the "harmonious ensemble" of the New York skyscrapers and the confetti showered on him on "Broad Street." They discussed politics, too, and the Congo, and possible trips to Africa. Then the King rose, and Whitlock said he would always be glad to be of service, with as much loyalty and devotion as a Belgian subject. With his quiet smile, the King said, "I should call on you as a friend." He gave his hand to Nell, and kissed hers, and was soon gone. The King of the Belgians had spent forty-five minutes on a Christmas Eve with a friend from another country.

The country did not forget either. During his lifetime the Brussels boulevard that was a continuation of the boulevard St. Michel was named after him. One day, a six-year-old child said innocently to his mother: "Why must we always walk along the Boulevard St. Michel? Why can't we go down the Boulevard St. Whitlock?"[34]

⟪ CHAPTER 14

The Best Has Been

(1 9 2 2 ' 1 9 3 4)

DESPITE THE CLAMOR and misery of war, Whitlock had kept up his literary interests as best he could. He had to give up his novel at the start of the war, but he read omnivorously whenever he could and fretted at the thought of the books he wanted to write. During his Le Havre exile, he tried to forget the miseries of that town by reading George Moore, Samuel Pepys, Charles Greville, Henry James, Lytton Strachey, and Frank Harris's book on Oscar Wilde; he also found himself both repelled and fascinated by the successive volumes coming from the cork-lined room of Marcel Proust. Perhaps his greatest find, with the possible exception of Proust, was "an amazing book, *Moby Dick, or the White Whale*, by Herman Melville, an American who wrote and published it at New York in 1851." He found it "one of the finest sea stories ever written," with "all the mystery, all the fascination, the very secret of the sea. Curious, too, it is, with long philosophizings, and almost scientific treatises on whales and whale-fishing, but a breathless tale of adventure at the same time."[1] Thus, just before its rediscovery by D. H. Lawrence and Raymond M. Weaver, Whitlock found for himself the rewards and exasperations of the book that has since become the sacred cow of American criticism.

But, even during the dark days of the war, Whitlock did more than read. He achieved an award that meant a great deal to him, membership in the American Academy of Arts and Letters, presumably as a novelist rather than a diplomat. Less happily, he also got involved in making French translations of his own works, a nerve-racking and thankless job that he should have avoided. At the same time he was completing *Belgium*, he worked at his French version of *Abraham Lincoln*, completing it on January 26, 1918. That experience apparently was not enough, and when he put the finishing touches on *Belgium* the next August he was still willing to let it be translated also. That step was his downfall. The tale of woe stretched over three years and endless spasms of dyspepsia. Whitlock thought that the French publisher, Payot, acted like a worthless crook: He hired an incompetent translator and then proved quite willing to print the ludicrous result of the man's work. Whitlock was horrified and had to pay for the translation out of his own pocket so he could throw it away; then he had to do the job himself. On top of that indignity, Payot insulted him regularly and demanded bribes for himself as well as the translator if the book were to be published at all. For a mild and polite man like Whitlock the whole affair was intolerable, and it was only made more so by his diplomatic status and his fears that should he ever assert his rights, his country might suffer. Of less trouble was Whitlock's own translation of some of the speeches given by Woodrow Wilson, which Wilson's postwar popularity produced a market for. That went without hitch.[2]

But most important to him was his own writing. For a while, that too went poorly. He contemplated writing a third volume of *Belgium* using his exile diaries, but the state of public opinion after the war did not seem appropriate for such a book, and he never wrote it. Perhaps more significant was his failure to write his long-promised study of Walt Whitman. Even before Whitlock went to Brussels, Hewitt Howland of Bobbs-Merrill had signed him to do the book in a series the company was publishing. Apparently Whitlock wrote only a few, unrevised chapters. Part of his problem was natural indolence combined with perilous health, but a man who had turned out 1,200 pages of best-selling memoirs was in a rather awkward position to plead such weak excuses. Far more serious was his slackening interest in Whitman and many of the ideas he represented. He wrote Howland: "I could have written a most enthusiastic book about him a decade or more ago, but since then I have grown older, and, if I have not grown wiser, I have learned a great many things, one of which is that all of old Walt's output was not poetry." He was afraid, he said, that Whitman lovers would draw and quarter him if he should make such a statement, yet he could not write the book without it. Perhaps. But more to the point was his somewhat defensive elitism; his new, war-weary conservatism now appeared in his literary ideals. Whitman, he told Howland, "made the writing of poetry seem too easy" with his affection for free verse and spontaneous emotion. Of course Whitman did not find it easy, but people did not realize that. Even more to the point, Whitlock had "serious doubts as to whether there is, or ever will be, any such thing as democratic art." He was afraid that "the rising tide of democracy" would sweep art away "along with a great many things that are, after all, in their nature, unfortunately, and perhaps unjustly, the possession of an elite." Great poets were often democratic in their assumptions and aspirations, as they should be, "but most of them have been read and admired and praised by the aristocrats more than by the democrats." The people could not usually appreciate great work, and with Whitman the problem was even greater, for he was too often a preacher and a demagogue, "and it is precisely when he was most consciously the democrat that he was least the poet." His work was vitiated in this inferior verse by propaganda, and "when propaganda comes in at the door art flies out of the window." That, coming from the admirer of Tolstoy and the author of *The Turn of the Balance!* Whitlock quite obviously had grown so pessimistic and so conservative that he no longer felt akin to Whitman. Even though he still proclaimed his allegiance, as in this letter, his journals no longer record days spent reading Whitman or his older literary enthusiasms. The war had exhausted his idealism.[3]

A sad and apologetic letter to Howland could more or less dispose of Whitman. His novel was more tenacious. Whitlock had finished roughly 30 per cent of his study of rural Ohio by the start of the war and had managed to work at it occasionally during his exile and the days after his return to Brussels. But as the book went on, he was more and more assailed by lack of self-confidence. As he wrote in March 1921: "I have been trying to write on my novel, and am sick with discouragement. The story slips through my fingers, and devilish doubts assail and torture me every minute that I write . . . It is horrible, horrible." After he left Brussels for Biarritz, his mood improved only slightly, as his burnt-out nerves mended only to leave him in states of "procrastination, weariness, laziness, postponements, debility, etc., etc.," as he wrote Jewett. Yet time and the change of place did help, and the end of diplomatic responsibilities was an unmixed blessing. By April 1922 he was even capable of joking about his book as having "some fairish portraiture of pompous, pusillanimous politi-cians and pustulous puritanical prohibitionists" in it, and he prom-ised his publisher he would keep him informed of the "progress of their purgatorial perfidiousness and pithecoid peregrinations." Within months, he completed the first draft and then began his painstaking revisions. Not until June 1923 had he finally revised the book, sent it to Jewett, received his comments, and corrected the galleys. Ten years after Whitlock began it, the book was pub-lished that fall.[4]

Despite frustration and delay, the result was Whitlock's best novel, a realistic distillation of his entire rural-Ohio experience. Macochee, his fictional name for the villages his father served in, is in this novel as close to Urbana as possible, complete even with the expatriate artist Josiah West, a barely concealed portrait of J. Q. A. Ward, who so loved his home town that he spent his life in Europe. Here, in complete detail, Whitlock portrayed the stupefy-ing dullness of the Methodist Sabbath, the nastiness of the back-biting respectability, the joyless life of a devout believer's son, and the stifled passions that make life miserable for those without the courage to rebel and leave. Its only real flaws are the occasional uses, mostly in the early pages, of inappropriate, flowery termi-nology of the variety that sometimes marred *The Thirteenth Dis-trict*; within a space of four pages (4–8), Whitlock used expres-sions like "prodigious expectoration," "sardonic ejaculations," "ma-ternal solicitude," "visage," "stricken fellow traveller," "glance of dubiety," "penetrate familiarly," and "medicament." These quib-bles aside, *J. Hardin & Son* is a novel fit to rank with *The Damna-tion of Theron Ware*, *The Bostonians*, and *The Rise of Silas Lapham* as one of the better works of American realism.

The structure of the book involves four closely interrelated designs. The book opens with Paul Hardin, its chief character, standing on the Hog Back, an area near Macochee that is the highest point in Ohio and thus the principal watershed for the surrounding area. Paul is musing on the fate of two raindrops that fall in precisely the wrong place and are forced forever to remain apart as they flow away from each other. The device could easily become maudlin, but it does not, and Whitlock does not pursue it but rather uses it only to underline the more important indications of his theme that will follow. The next paragraph makes Paul, rather than the ridge, the center of attention, and once again the theme of opposites occurs. Paul dominates the scene, but appears "to be the victim, rather than the lord, of the dreary scene" (p. 3). The reference appears trivial but indicates a second theme or problem in the book, the evaluation of Paul and his experience. In many ways Paul will become a "lord," rich, married to an attractive girl, and a commanding citizen in the town. Yet he will be miserably unhappy and the victim of whims that seem just as meaningless as the fine line that divides the raindrops from each other.

Next, the personal element appears. Paul has obtained a brief holiday because of the illness of his teacher, and thus a taste of freedom. Yet his father, ever the believer in duty, immediately takes advantage of the hours off to have his son do a job for him. Paul is naturally resentful and remains that way as the book goes on, giving life to the freedom vs. duty motif that dominates much of the later action, both between people and between value systems. Finally (p. 7), the appearance of a stagecoach full of actors and actresses, on which Paul hitches a ride, introduces the wild and outlawed imagination that both captivates Paul and later causes him great misery. It contrasts immediately with the "sheltered, prosperous Macocheean residences, standing there, remote from the desperate emergencies of life, comfortable, serene and respectable." Finally, in a scene that brings these themes together, J. Hardin refuses to let his son go to such a show as these actors intend to put on, for he is moral and dutiful and to him the imagination and joy are immoral and inappropriate for a life dedicated to God.

These opening themes, all of them appearing by page 14, could easily indicate another stereotyped battle between right and wrong, between good, sensitive people and bad, stupid people—a battle of the sort that severely hurt *The Turn of the Balance.* Whitlock has uses for his opening watershed imagery and its thematic applications, but having established it he sensibly lets it sit on the back of the reader's mind while he attends to his second structural plan, and for the rest of Book I he devotes himself to the standard form of the novel of initiation, as Paul Hardin slowly grows up to the point where he will be capable of trying to deal with these announced themes. J. Hardin is a true rural mentality, who will allow no drinking or smoking near him or his house, who rises early, believes devoutly, and operates on God's time rather than on anything so new-fangled as Daylight Saving Time. J. Hardin's world, more or less, is Macochee's, but soon two enduring forces challenge it sharply: One of the actresses in the stage gives birth to a girl everyone assumes to be illegitimate and then dies as the town biddies enjoy being scandalized; and two of the townsmen appear as more or less regular drinkers—Wade Powell, the easygoing lawyer from several of Whitlock's earlier stories, and Malcolm Dyer, his friend. Through them Paul comes to know of scandal in the world: Scandal is the word you apply to those who live in ways other than yourself.

For the moment however, scandal does not concern Paul. He is too worried about whether or not to break the Sabbath by going to the swimming hole with handsome young Billie Dyer, an object of his admiration. Billie (a free-living pagan, much like his father) mocks the values of J. Hardin. Paul, of course, would never dream of disobeying his father, much as he wants to, so Billie and some others go off without him. That evening, Paul learns that Billie caught his foot in some roots deep in the pond and drowned. It is his first meeting with the injustice of fate, with the motiveless evil that reappears in the book to haunt Paul whenever he seems on the brink of enjoying himself. He can find no solace in his father's religion, and the revival that follows Billie's death offers him no comfort. Reverend Sparrow's snortings and the bad breath of Mr. Popple seem to have no connection with either peace or God, and thus the values of respectable Macochee have no relevance for Paul's crisis. He has seen inexplicable evil, and nothing helps. His initiation has begun in earnest.

Then he meets the inevitable crisis of any young boy. First, he becomes infatuated with a girl older than himself who leads him on for lack of something better to do. The result, through no real fault of his own, is that he is expelled from school due to a misunderstanding and a hypocritical principal. His father immediately orders him to get to work, and, as he does so, his introduction to life continues more quickly than ever. He learns about the saloons and tastes beer and tobacco for the first time, much to his father's distress. These events are trivial. His next important discovery coincides neatly with Whitlock's own prejudices and discoveries: He learns that "respectable" people torment those they disapprove of, "because they are moral." The vehicle of this insight is the child of the dead actress Evelyn Walling. The town boys may know little about sex, but they know from their parents that Ellen is a "bastard," whatever that means, so they chase after her calling her by that name, making her miserable in every way. In the name of respectability and conformity they chase her into the pond, where she is rescued only by the intervention of Malcolm Dyer and Paul. Paul is hereditarily among the respectable; yet it is Dyer, hardly a respectable man, who performs the rescue. Clearly, issues like good and evil are beginning to become complicated. They become even more so when Dyer dies of pneumonia contracted in the rescue and becomes a hero whom Paul tries to imitate. At this point, with the world becoming hopelessly complex, Paul finishes his initiation into young adulthood by getting involved with a servant girl. Book I then closes, and Whitlock moves to a larger perspective.

That is, he portrays the real world of rural America in totality. In so doing, he introduces matter that would have distressed poor old Howells even more than the free-and-easy attitude toward sexual morality in Robert Herrick's *Together*—before *J. Hardin & Son*, the last major novel by one of Howells's disciples. Not only does Paul fornicate with Mat, the hired girl, and later on commit adultery with a married woman after he too has long since been married; but, also, Mat proves a bit too free with her favors even among the drinking set. When Mat openly takes up with Smoke, a mulatto hotel employee, she brings the themes of miscegenation and lynching into the realistic American novel in a serious way. Certainly Howells's own gingerly hint of such problems in *An Imperative Duty* offered scant precedent. And the

Southern Gothic school of William Faulkner and his imitators was not yet functioning.

Sex is but a small part of Paul's world. Far more important both in the context of the novel and as a measure of the changes in its author, is the sense of drift that permeates all the actions Paul makes. In *The Turn of the Balance,* Archie derives his satisfaction and values from his psychological need for a group with which he can identify and achieve a sense of belonging. Paul has gone a step beyond this. In the portrait of Archie Koerner the underlying assumption is that you can change a man if you can change the group, or the social influences, which determine his nature. But Paul is not so much a member of a recognizable group as a drifter among various pulls of the competing currents in his life. He suffers from a disease his creator apparently shared, a sense of almost total inability to control his fate, a sense of helpless floating, of torpor and ineffectuality. The man who saw nation after nation drift into war as though no one could do anything to stop the carnage created a leading character unable to control his life or his acts. With rare examples of indecisive rebellion, Paul obeys his father when he is young; his father seems stronger than he. Then he meets girls, and finds himself obeying them in turn; the girl who cries at the appropriate time gets him to marry her. A stronger personality leads him to invest money in the oil and gas boom, and through no effort or talent on his part he first goes broke, then strikes it rich. "Those odd little accidents of propinquity" (p. 338) bring Paul and Evelyn together. As Paul thinks, almost at the end of the book: "What insignificant circumstances turned the current of a human life this way or that! How at the mercy of banal accident was every man! A trivial happening, a mere idle word, a thousand and one things of which one was not aware at the time, might be determining factors in a career. At every moment of existence one was completely at the mercy of these perfectly appalling chances" (p. 418). Paul, in short, is one of the first appearances in modern American literature of the victim of circumstances. Only Stephen Crane and Theodore Dreiser of earlier American novelists recognized the theme, and both of them tended to see the world more or less as a mechanistic device —a world of chemical forces for Dreiser, a chill world begun and then forgotten by God for Crane. God, however much He might dominate the world of J. Hardin, is not present in Paul's world; nor are chemical or mechanical forces. There is just the drift of the current and the whim of the watershed. No wonder Whitlock was depressed and Paul confused. Both were psychically helpless.

On another level, the book is also a remarkably successful delineation of what happened in the United States between the Civil War and World War I. J. Hardin represents the older America of firm religion and pride in craftsmanship. His carriage shop is as much his church as the Methodist one. His men, who all take pride in their respected products, are fully satisfied. In J. Hardin's generation, one important change is already past, as religion has become more and more only an ethical concern. Thus, the churchgoers talk less and less about God, except in formal ways, and more and more about reforming their neighbor. The old religion is as old-fashioned as the prejudices of Hardin's generation eventually become; soon, his own prejudices, like his symbolically appropriate carriage shop, will appear equally outdated. For Hardin, the key expression of religion is prohibition; for one of his friends, it is silver coinage at 16 to 1. Either way, it means churches full of itinerant reformers, often men who have failed as clergymen. Time both favors and opposes these moralists. True, they will soon win the town, and eventually the country, to prohibition, but they are doomed, for they do not appeal to Paul's generation. Paul hates both sides and finds his father's prohibitionism and Charlie Parton's bribing for the liquor companies equally disgusting. He is in no way attracted to barflies, even when the men are those like Powell and Dyer, both of whom he normally likes. Paul represents yet a new generation, one that will have few religious or ethical concerns. He is simply distressed and uneasy, rootless and adrift. The nation will soon be speaking of those like him as part of the Roaring Twenties and then as the "irresponsibles" who harmed "the American way." However accurate his descriptions, Whitlock had created the type just in time for his country to produce real-life counterparts. Life persisted in imitating art. Business again reflected the change: J. Hardin, like all of older America, found himself squeezed out by a trust with modern methods. Paul represented yet a further improvement—he was the man who lived off his investments and allowed the work of others to produce his income. Like many young men and women in the twenties, Paul

Hardin found himself wealthy and emancipated enough to be free of everything but a guilty conscience.

One final note. The great realists, with certain exceptions in occasional works of James or Tolstoy, were quite free in allowing a point of view for the author and in not permitting their characters to go through life unguided. George Eliot usually left little doubt about her own opinions, and Howells was often scarcely less visible; no one reading *War and Peace* is ever in much doubt about whether Kutusov or Napoleon shares Tolstoy's view of history. Likewise, while Whitlock often lets his characters function more or less autonomously, he still reappears regularly to establish his own voice. It is a voice remarkably changed since the days when he was mayor. Certain elements remain: He still detests prohibitionists and other moral reformers for their faith in their own divine right to meddle in the lives of others. He still cannot resist mocking romantic novelists, and the figure of Mrs. Malcolm Dyer, the vague and neurasthenic morphine addict who consumes at a gulp a novel full of sensations is a fine minor achievement. But the key change reflects Whitlock's own intellectual development and his emotional exhaustion. Whereas, earlier, he had kept his scorn chiefly for the respectable middle class of protestant fundamentalists and crooked businessmen, here he indicts almost all humanity. In particular, the lower classes come off far worse in this novel than in earlier works. When J. Hardin loses his first election but then regains public respect in an assault on him by the wets, Whitlock says that "had the people been able to vote again on the morrow of the election, they doubtless would have shown the divine infallibility of their judgment by reversing their verdict of the day before" (p. 330)—a jibe that would have horrified Tom Johnson or Golden Rule Jones. Where once the middle class had the scorn of people like drinker Wade Powell, now Powell is snorting, "In a democracy, unscrupulous mediocrity can go far" (p. 353). And in case someone did not get the point, the rowdies who lynch Smoke or who pillory Paul and Evelyn when they are caught together in the milliner's shop look far worse than anyone likely to turn up in the saloons frequented by Curly Jackson or Archie Koerner. In the more conservative, pessimistic, and chaotic world of the ex-ambassador, the middle class has more or less absorbed the mob, and people in general are the objects of

scorn. Because of this, they must suffer, and no one in *J. Hardin &*
Son is ever happy for very long. Certainly Paul rarely is. The
strongest character, and in many ways the most sympathetically
portrayed, Evelyn Walling, is left at the end all but destitute, as
Paul leaves her just when she thinks happiness is near. As a
summation of America's transition into the twentieth century, this
book certainly found little to rejoice about either in the life of the
present or in the life of the future.

With such an achievement, and after so much difficulty and
pain of composition, Whitlock expected great things of his book.
After all he was getting old, he had one somewhat notorious and
best-selling novel behind him, and he was world-famous for his
later war work. The result all but broke his heart. The America
that was responding to the satires of Sinclair Lewis and Zona Gale
found little in his quiet and realistic delineations of the same
scenes and was simply blind to the artistic maturity and skill that
makes *J. Hardin & Son* seem in retrospect a more memorable
achievement than, say, *Main Street*. In an age that respected nothing so much as youth, he was old; in an age that was experimental
to the point of mania, he was practicing an old form; in an age
that was bent on enjoying itself, such a somber statement seemed
irrelevant. Even the sex and miscegenation themes were scarcely
titillating. Whitlock was incapable of even thinking of such treatment; he was disconsolate. "I have been for weeks and months so
depressed and disheartened by the failure of *J. Hardin & Son* to
make any impression, or to receive any recognition, that I have
seriously asked myself if there were really any use in going on at
all," he wrote his publisher. He would go on, of course, for he
really had little alternative: Writing was his profession, whether
he succeeded in it or not.[5]

When he was not at his desk, Whitlock found himself a more
or less settled member of the exiled American group in Europe.
He was known everywhere and was at times the recipient of further thanks—like membership in the Belgian Academy, a great
honor he received in October 1922—but more often he went from
hotel to hotel, stayed a few months, suffering from eye strain or
dyspepsia or the influx of American accents, and then packed up
and left. Biarritz and Brussels both had climates that irritated him,
and Vichy was attractive only for occasional summer cures. In-

creasingly, he grew to love Cannes, with occasional side trips to places like Menton. Gradually he and Nell began the routine of winter in Cannes, perhaps a spring or fall visit to Paris or Brussels, and summer at Vichy; except for occasional trips to America, they kept to this schedule for the next dozen years. Only rarely was his peace broken by official matters, as the governments in Washington were most inhospitable to Wilsonian Democrats. The only real call came in December 1923, when Eric Drummond of the League of Nations asked him to mediate in the Memel crisis. Whitlock refused with alacrity.[6]

The new Whitlock, still nervous and sensitive, but disillusioned, more aristocratic and less democratic, and becoming more and more an elitist like Romain Rolland, also had time in these many hotels to decide to make a decisive gesture toward an open acknowledgement of his new position. In his youth, religion had always been something hateful to him, a killer of joy and a bringer of reform. During the war, this hostility grew as he observed the obscurantism of certain Catholic groups and then declined whenever he met again the imposing figure of Cardinal Mercier, the living saint who captivated Whitlock. The obvious moral bankruptcy in many lives during the twenties worked on Whitlock in reverse. He loathed the new freedoms that seemed in practice to mean only bad manners and the new moralities that seemed to him but the old immoralities. He was not by nature a theologian, nor a moralist, although most intelligent Americans of his generation were something of both and frequently acted as if the terms were synonymous. Undeniably, he was interested in aesthetics, however, in the way he looked at the world and the way he lived —or tried to live. The result was a slow turning in the direction of Mercier, one that halted in the church of an old and dear friend from Toldeo days, the Rt. Reverend Charles D. Williams, Episcopal bishop of Michigan. Whitlock was soon displaying his new leanings all but unconsciously, as he began noting saints' days in his journal and the other important days of the church calendar. For months nothing else religious is there recorded, and in effect the lack of any sort of religious thought is at least as enlightening as Whitlock's conversion itself. He did not become an Episcopalian for religious reasons so much as for aesthetic distance, as a way of institutionalizing his distaste for life in the 1920's. At the same time, he decided to take a trip to the United States, to visit his family and his publisher, and to try to write a new novel. On October 18, 1922, he was "too sad for words at leaving Brussels and Belgium! And my own country, alas, has no attractions for me, nor for Nell either. I wish it were otherwise." A few days later, they sailed on the SS *Lapland* for New York, where Marshall Sheppey met them with his Rolls-Royce. They spent a night at the Ritz and went to the Beechwood Hotel in Summit, New Jersey, an inexpensive place near New York that Rutger Jewett had recommended. Whitlock was appalled by his native land. He hated the hurry, the cars, the ugliness, and the prohibitions. Even the pronunciation of the tongue infuriated him, and he could not snort enough about it. "It is all too utterly hideous, too inexpressibly, appallingly ugly and depressing." The villain was obvious. "The world has been made safe for democracy, but not for gentlemen, and we had better be content to take our little back seat, and sit down quietly, and look on contentedly, and watch the amusement the spectacle after all affords, at the mad rush and scramble of the vulgar and the cheeky, the bounders and the cads who are having their glorious day." Despite them, he settled down in Summit and worked on his novel. His mother arrived for a long visit and worried everyone by having an attack of arterial sclerosis. Then shortly after Christmas, he met Bishop Williams in New York, and for the first time publicly noted his interest in joining the Episcopal Church. Williams was delighted, and he suggested that Whitlock come to St. Luke's Church, Montclair, on New Year's Day 1923, where the Bishop would be visiting his good friend Luke White, the minister. Two days later, on a gloomy, wet day, Whitlock and his wife drove to the large Gothic church, met White, and after the service were received into the church at a private ceremony. He was back in Summit by eleven thirty. "This is a step we have contemplated for years, since youth, indeed, in some senses and ways, and I am solemnly glad it is taken. It was all perfect, and done by my dear old friend Bishop Williams." Six weeks later he received news that the Bishop was dead.[7]

On March 24, his novel finished and his affairs in order, he left America "without regret" on the *Nieuw Amsterdam* to begin anew the life of an exile. He went to Brussels and promptly got another boil on his nose; looking like a drunkard, he went to visit the King and Queen at Laeken and found the King nursing a wrist broken in a fall from his horse. Despite the pleasantries of commiseration, Whitlock found himself once again in the doldrums: ". . . the trouble is, I am not very sure about my work . . . That awful doubt assails me again, that deadly 'It will be no good' from which I have suffered now ever since the war. It quite paralyzes all effort at creation." He began writing on volume three of *Belgium*, a book he never did finish, and did some organizing for his next novel. Then the reviews of *J. Hardin & Son* began to arrive, and he had grounds for despair and for expressing his increasing disaffection for his time. Some objected to the sex, "as though there could be life, or arts, or much emotion without sex!" Some objected to his occasional use of long words. What upset him most, however, was the criticism he received for not having Paul get his divorce and marry Evelyn at the end of the book. "Aside from their totally missing the point of the story, and not seeing that Paul, with his nature and his environment could not have done this without bitterly regretting it, they all speak of divorce as though it were a perfectly normal, natural and satisfactory solution of a life problem, and as an artistic expedient."[8]

The publication of the book exhausted him, and along with his boils he also came down with lumbago. Despite this, he persevered just as he had in Belgium, and was soon making good progress. The new story was about *déracinés* and their empty lives; it involved the themes of the Indian-summer romance—after the manner of Howells—and the conflict between American and European mores as depicted in the behavior of a young girl—after the manner of Henry James. In a way, perhaps, such a novel was realistic, for it was the rendering of autobiography through the depiction of common detail and people. Yet, more important, such a book broke significantly with Whitlock's past work. However much such a life had been his, for his readers such creations could only be the stuff of romance and the detail as exotic as any trifle from a sentimentalist's Ruritania. Even more important, the emotional bias of such a work would probably not be democratic —for how could one speak favorably of democracy or of the common man with most of the action placed in Monte Carlo, Cannes, and similar places?[9]

The early pages of *Uprooted* quickly establish two important themes. Waldron, the leading character who closely resembles Whitlock, is chiefly a spectator, a man who will observe but who will probably not participate. He is old and experienced, a bit tired. His profession, like Whitlock's avocation, is painting, and his function in the book that of a painter, the man who observes character and renders it on canvas. He is also cut off from the life around him, for as an interpreter for the British army, he has seen the war from the beginning. The war experience proves decisive: He finds that he has nothing in common with the far younger men and women who played no role until 1917. The difference is partly that of age, but the war pervades everything: "He was conscious of a gulf that the war had opened between him and his youth; he felt somewhat mutilated in spirit, if not in body, like those poor chaps one saw in dirty blue uniforms along the avenues of Paris, or in faded khaki, selling matches in the streets of London" (p. 4). Psychically, Waldron is merely going through the motions, dabbling at life vicariously. As such he is the perfect mark for a fresh young American girl.

Betty Marsh is attractive, uninhibited, and bent on her freedom, patently representative of the 1920's. "I want to do everything!" she exclaims with her usual exuberance (p. 12). She flirts with any man she pleases, goes about most lightly chaperoned by a widow of highly uncertain antecedents, and in general acts like the average American girl or French cocotte. She falls in with a seedy prince and a parvenu American millionaire, and carouses with them even while cherishing affection for Waldron, as if to indicate that she cannot be all bad.

Given these themes—of the spectator sampling of life and of the generation gap caused by the war—the book then settles into an examination of what an intelligent spectator with scars can do when confronted by a Betty Marsh of the twenties. The response, perhaps implicit in Whitlock's deep admiration for King Albert and Cardinal Mercier, nevertheless comes as something of a shock to those who know him only as a progressive humanitarian. For *Uprooted* has a definite voice, as well as characters who more or less cooperate with that voice, and what they advocate is an aesthetic conservatism unfriendly to innovation and disdainful of modernism in manners, painting, or morals. This voice appears first in Waldron's astonishment at Betty, as he watches both fascinated and repelled by the new generation. It soon gains support from Waldron's (or Whitlock's) side remarks. His Paris studio is part of "a spacious world that was so sympathetic" (p. 39), littered as it was with paraphernalia of a past that was finally over. Here, Waldron can comfort himself. If he is not happy he is content, "which was even better, as being more likely to endure" (p. 40)—an idea utterly lost on the hedonists of Betty's age. Even so, he is full of "mal du pays" and "l'esprit d'emigré" (p. 45) and must constantly take refuge among two old and vitally important friends. For not only are Lady Agnes Drayton and Dorothy, Countess of Granvallon, important to Waldron because they are old friends, they are important also as providing the closest answer Whitlock can provide for life in the 1920's. Dorothy's world is "so much better than the new" (p. 64); in it Waldron can find settled principles, common standards of manners, and an unshakable and eminent history—none of which impresses Betty's generation. "Who was it," Waldron asks, "that said that he who is not of his own time has nothing but its misfortune?" (p. 69) and he clearly means that he will say it if no one else will. The result is a wryly self-conscious and amusing but none the less sincere nostalgia. "The world is sadly changed," Waldron once moans. Lady Agnes will not be improved upon: "The world, my dear Leslie, came to an end with the Boer War" (p. 71). But, after all, a sense of humor is just what the new generation also lacked. And so Waldron can frankly find his refuge: "I'm a kind of early Victorian," he says, a man who has "fallen on a degenerate age" (pp. 83, 85).

The plot is *Daisy Miller* updated and writ large, as Betty slowly entangles herself more or less innocently in the demimonde of Monte Carlo. Her slow deterioration, while it never reaches the disaster that the plot really requires, is nevertheless noticeable. Her chaperone is caught cheating at cards; her reputation suffers because of an innocent accident; and she is propositioned publicly by her seedy prince, whom she promptly slaps with good American lack of reticence in a public dining room. Everything seems to point to a Roman-fever retribution, but Betty survives, tarnished but married to a decent American dragged in by his hair at the last minute. She survives because she has what Daisy Miller lacked: the protection of Lady Agnes, whose sympathy Waldron obtains for her just in time. Lady Agnes has complete social impregnability and thus can protect whom she pleases, even the still highly reluctant and rebellious Betty. The moral is obvious, even flagrant: The new generation, to succeed, needs the guidance of the Victorian aristocracy, as though they were some sort of underprivileged Londoners needing Disraeli and his Tory democracy to lift them up. Meanwhile, the old generation can only lean back, secure in the knowledge that it is right even when it is impotent, and occasionally reach down into the melee and save some deserving soul.

The war had indeed left its scars, and none so deep as the one that made all men either old or young. An entire generation seemed to have disappeared, and the gulf was tremendous. As Lady Agnes says to Waldron, with that sense of humor that makes it easy to understand Whitlock's attraction to her breed: "You and I, my dear friend, belong to an old world, a dying world, perhaps; at any rate, a world in which it is decidedly too chill to have coffee on the terrace after dinner" (p. 308). Out on the terrace are Betty and her decent American; inside, like a spectator feeling a bit de trop, one can only sip and stare.

The effort of completing the book nearly killed Whitlock. In the middle of March, 1925, he had a bad case of flu and then compounded his miseries with pleurisy and intercostal neuralgia, becoming so sick he did not write again in his journal until August. The doctors ordered him to Le Zoûte to recover, and from there he found himself stewing about America's treatment of Belgian war debts—which he found disgusting—and the Scopes trial at Dayton, where his old friend Darrow and his old acquaintance Bryan were capturing the attention of the world with ideas fresh from the 1880's. He was too weak to do anything but watch, and recovery was slow. Nell found that the work of nursing him broke her down somewhat, and she was grateful for the chance of a cure at Vichy. They spent September there and then returned to Brussels after a stop in Paris. Soon, he was back at work on a new novel. He found the writing much easier this time, and by the next year he was in reasonably good health and almost jovial about his inert existence. He spent summer "in the most shameful and outrageous idleness." He wrote his new friend Albert Bigelow Paine, "I played golf all morning, and read Marcel Proust all afternoon;

never wrote a line nor did a bit of work. I finished my novel just before leaving Cannes, in the middle of June."[10]

I F *Uprooted* was Whitlock's *Daisy Miller*, then *Transplanted* was his *Portrait of a Lady*; and, as in James's case, the second work was much the more impressive. *Uprooted* is not a bad novel, but it suffers both from the weariness of its author and the rootlessness of its characters. Most realists functioned best in settled societies, where the nuances of social intercourse could be examined closely and where one character could react against another. *Uprooted* is too full of *déracinés*. It has no objective solidity or frame of reference outside the author's own voice. Characters do not so much develop as become static or deteriorate, and in so doing they do not compel interest the way they should. But once he caught his stride in writing about Europe Whitlock proved he could capture it adequately on paper, even with so outwardly banal a plot as the marriage of an American businessman's daughter into an old French noble family.

The odd thing about the novel is its split image of France.[11] Despite his conservative mood, Whitlock in no way romanticized the French or found in them or in their age some sort of cure-all for the ills of the time. Quite the contrary, for the Granvallon family is full of petty jealousies, conceits, stupidities, egos, and adulteries, and is ruled by a mama horrible enough for a Gothic romance. The family, in fact, is slowly dying from its own studied incompetence. Since it disdains business to such a degree that it is all but in hock, it must find wealthy wives to keep the estates going. Dorothy Manning, however, proves to be a little bit more than they bargained for, as she slowly realizes that French avarice and French willingness to view people as tools rather than as individuals surpass anything found in America—even as the French indict Americans for making the money the former so lust after. In such an atmosphere, Dorothy, like Isabel Archer, finds that her life is to be an initiation into the problem of evil, and her problem how to come to terms with it.

Dorothy manages, barely. Faced with her exclusion from the intimacies of the family—their sole interest is in her ability to supply male Catholic heirs and money—and by the adultery of her husband with his cousin, she finds solace in the other half of the image of France. The key symbol is Chaunois, the country estate of the family, which their incompetence has loaded with mortgages. At Chaunois, Dorothy manages to create for herself a France of the mind that gives her fragments to shore up against her ruin. On her first sight of the medieval pile, she "thrilled with a sense of feudal proprietorship, as she thought of herself as its châtelaine" (p. 4). The vision remains with her and provides her with imagery in any given situation, much like Mont-St.-Michel for Henry Adams or the Abbey of Thélème for Albert Jay Nock. Thus, at a dinner, Dorothy is all but overwhelmed by her position: "The whole scene had about it something so gallant, so graceful, as though it were of the XVIIIth century, authentic and of the epoch . . . She felt herself admired, approved, envied, surrounded by flattering consideration, and she felt uplifted, suddenly filled with joy of living" (p. 56). That was what had attracted her in the first place; she had married the Count "well, because she liked him, of course, but then, too, for all this about her, this château in the country, this life and all of its implications; she was the Countess Georges de Granvallon, no matter what" (p. 73).

Given Dorothy's self-knowledge, it is only a logical step to the core of the novel. The adultery symbolizes evil, known but not recognized by the entire family. To all onlookers, such activity is expected, and the wife must say nothing and keep the home and family warm for the erring male, whenever he wishes to return. Yet Dorothy is Anglo-Saxon, not Latin, and she cannot quite tolerate such an attitude, especially when she is the wife. She contemplates rebellion and is at times successful. She deprives her husband, even when he wants her. She even defies his great vegetable of a mother, an event which turns that lady purple and almost causes her wig to take flight. But her stroke of genius is both perfect for the daughter of an American businessman of the Rockefeller era and symbolically precise: She negotiates for the purchase of Chaunois in her own name and refuses to help keep the place in the family under any other conditions. She can accept France, but only on her own terms. Yet happiness, in morals or in life, recedes at its approach: "Contentment, friendship, a fair understanding, mutual respect and toleration, these are about the best that human nature can attain to" (p. 222). She would, in sort, remain content in the possession of a diminished thing. Pain in one form or another "was indeed the law of life" (p. 301). Having made her decision and acquired her refuge, she then fulfills her part of the bargain and produces, at Chaunois, the long-awaited male Catholic heir. The book is thus Whitlock's most mature statement of belief. Dorothy faces adultery, he faces the postwar world; she creates a world of the mind in which to find refuge and so does he, turning his back on all life but his art and visits to his friends. His values are hers, and just as she is all but overcome (pp. 245-6) at receiving the approval of royalty, Whitlock was all but overcome by his contacts with Albert and Mercier. He, who had once thought that all men could become as kings if only society could be run by "Golden Rule" mayors, now had little sympathy, or perhaps little but sympathy, for those who somehow had never succeeded. The world became hateful, full of people and events that jarred and did not solace. A man could only sit back, like the Leslie Waldron who appears in both novels, and paint portraits.

Such disillusionment soon colored all Whitlock's assessments of the contemporary world. He and Colonel House, for example, took particular delight in egging each other on to sarcasm about the current political scene. When news media pictured President Coolidge in a few patently fraudulent scenes of bucolic bliss, Whitlock took aim: "Coolidge, after taking his exercise on a mechanical horse, is, as the despatches inform us, now fishing for trout with worms. Fancy Washington mounting a mechanical horse, or Cleveland baiting his hook with a worm! What a noble cavalier and dashing sportsman! When he comes thundering at the head of his Black Horse cavalry, in full charge, riding hell for leather, who shall resist this magnetic and picturesque hero?" When House learned that Whitlock was gathering material for his biography of La Fayette, he found further instruction in contemporary mores. "I notice in the morning papers that a lady in Chicago sat in a tub of water for fifty hours, ten minutes and fifteen seconds thereby breaking the world's record," he informed Whitlock. "I am wondering whether in your life of La Fayette you could not find some real great exploit that would catch the imagination of the American people. Is it not possible that he sat with his bare feet on a cake of ice for twenty-four hours or, to save time, sat on a red hot stove for fifteen minutes? It would simplify your biography of him and you might make him one of the world's heros." House apparently did not look enough around him. "The lady in Chicago who sat for fifty hours, ten minutes and fifteen seconds in a tub deserves well of the nation of course," Whitlock replied, "and I yield to no man in my admiration for her, but I am committed to Mrs. Carmen Teggio, of New York, who climbed the 1,358 steps in the Woolworth Building in 13 minutes, thereby breaking the world's record." Besides, House should not be so provincial as to limit himself to America. "I think she will be nominated, unless, as a surprise at the eleventh hour, the woman who holds the record for staying longest *out* of a tub should turn up, and she would probably be disqualified on account of her nationality, which is, of course, French. I am speaking, mind you, of the Vice-Presidency; for President we must all rally round our old leader who sat so gallantly on the ball of the flagstaff of the building in New Jersey."[12]

House reserved his real weapons for the political scene, particularly for the man he knew had tried to undercut his friend. "It is too bad you are not seeing the pictures of Hoover, Mrs. Hoover and the little Hoovers with their pets, and that you are not reading of Hoover's love for humanity and devotion to the cause of suffering everywhere," he wrote Whitlock during the 1928 campaign. "It seems that he is entirely devoid of selfishness and what he has done has been without thought of Herbert Hoover. Another thing we did not realize that he dislikes to be praised or his good works brought to the attention of the public. This must be a grief to him for his friends day by day sing paeans to him throughout the land."[13]

Being away from politics, Whitlock more often than before found his distastes in books, and his diary records his assessment of American writers just as House's letters encapsulate American politicians. No one could match Jane Austen, except possibly Marcel Proust, who was a gentleman. He even found himself taking solace in the second-rate, if only it had some pretense to style or taste: ". . . after the vulgarity of Edna Ferber, the blackguardism of Sinclair Lewis, the filth and nastiness of Sherwood Anderson, the ponderous and elephantine seriousness of Theodore Dreiser, it [was] a relief" to read Zona Gale, despite her occasional faults. Yet even in such fits of temper, his critical apparatus could still function. A week later he wrote: "Tonight I finished

Sherwood Anderson's 'Dark Laughter.' It is vulgar, squalid, realism, but the man *can* write, no good denying that, and the book is strong, with a curious artistic note and inspiration in it. But it is a debased and debasing kind of art." Even with such talent before him, however, his aesthetic revulsion to the world of the 1920's could not be more explicit. "Oh, but I did have a dose, before returning to Jane Austen and Proust, of blackguards, bounders, tramps, hobos, hired girls sluttish and lustful, sweating black wenches, tough coons, buck niggers, greasy Jewesses—all that rotten stench of vulgarity that passes for art in America today! Whew! Steward, a basin!"[14]

Transplanted was Whitlock's last novel of value, for in the face of such vulgarity and with his weak constitution he did not have the stamina for real creation. He had planned a third novel, *Storm*, that would take the characters in *Transplanted* through the war and into the time of *Uprooted*, rounding out his European experiences in fictional form, but his flagging energies, and Rutger Jewett's warning that American readers were sick of the war decided him against the project, and he never began the novel. Instead, in his revulsion against the real life around him and the degrading art he read, he turned back on his own past, he began to repeat himself, and he finally went to his reading for material. The resulting novels sometimes have a certain charm and craftsmanship, but they are unimportant.

In *Big Matt*, Whitlock returned to the Illinois political scenes of his early adulthood and of *The Thirteenth District* to dabble in the moral problems and complexities of political life. Should the popular Governor John Wesley Blake trust his somewhat disreputable friend Big Matt Holt with the political office that Matt's devotion and his labors have earned him? Filling in the minor characters are the by-now usual collection of types that illustrated Whitlock's prejudices in his early fiction: the humorless Anti-Saloon League zealot, hot for reform; the earnest young idealistic lawyer, who always does his duty and wants to marry Blake's daughter too; the nasty newspaperman, always willing to shade the truth for a good or preferably scandalous story. There are, too, the usual snipes against public-utility companies and prisons, which no sort of 1920's conservatism ever removed from Whitlock's memory. Whitlock's emotional response to past events had changed little. Whatever he thought of the socialist agitations of the 1920's, he still sentimentalized the more colorful and devoted members of the political and social underworld, and the bribe-taking Big Matt is easily the most attractive figure in the book. But, as a discussion of the nature of evil, which seems to be at the core of the story, as it was in *Transplanted*, Big Matt is distinctly forgettable. Almost the only solution offered comes in one of the worst examples of dialogue in all Whitlock's later fiction, as Abraham Lincoln Johnson, an old, faithful, darky servant who has yassuhed himself through several hundred inferior novels, proposes the solution to Blake's problem. It appears that old Elijah Gates was the one successful governor in Johnson's bottomless memory. Gates was never troubled: "He wasn't skeert o' nothin', God or man or debil." He was so successful, Johnson says, " 'Peered to me it was 'cause he des na'chally tol' 'em all to go to hell, suh, and run it to suit hisself." With such deep insight into human nature, Gates had been re-elected three times and quit when he wanted to. "He wouldn't take no mo'. Said he was done tired o' bein' pestered" (pp. 154-5).

Having exhausted his memory, Whitlock turned to his reading, with uneven results. No one, of course, could write a realistic novel out of a library, and Whitlock did not try. *Narcissus*, his first romance, and the more charming and successful one, was a little rewriting of the legend of Antoon Van Dyck and his painting of the portrait of St. *Martin Dividing His Cloak*. The tale is a study, best read in a mildly psychological vein, of the qualities of a painter and of Whitlock in particular. In Rubens, the teacher, are the qualities of the successful man of affairs, willing to submit to the needs of time and place and to cater to those in power and those who supply wealth. He speaks for Whitlock's head, or conscience, and his little talk on art (pp. 82 *ff*.) is really a small sermon admonishing the wilder aesthetes of the 1920's on their mistakes. Van Dyck, in contrast, is both indolent and restless, gloomy, dissatisfied, and talented; he lacks all discipline and is only too eager to forget art for the charms of his mistress. He has many of Whitlock's own qualities, particularly the sensual indolence that all but enervates him for days and weeks on end. The story plays out the little plot, and it is impossible not to suspect that Whitlock was here toying with his own credo. Van Dyck, he writes, felt "a kind of nostalgia" come "over him, a longing for the unknown and undiscoverable country where one is happy and at peace" (p. 41). The essential inhabitant of this country was the aristocrat. Thus, exposed to all the rough democracy of the Flemish countryside, Van Dyck thinks only that "he would leave all this to other artists and look for the meaning of existence in patrician countenances" (p. 52). The result, for a painter who was also an artistocrat and more than a little vain, is that when he decides to paint the portrait of St. Martin, he disposes of all the humility and servility of the scene and decides to use himself instead. "Such Christian humility and democratic familiarity were not for him. This was to be the portrait of no poverty-stricken and squalid ascetic, cleaning the boots of a young common servant; this was to be a young, handsome, elegant, aristocratic saint" (p. 105). St. Martin thus has the face of Van Dyck and the clothes of an aristocrat in the picture, while the beggars look suitably despicable and criminal. The logical conclusion is that, whether consciously or unconsciously, Whitlock was painting at least a part of himself in Van Dyck's clothes, just as Van Dyck painted himself into his picture. If nothing else, such an interpretation would give an amusing footnote to Whitlock's fastidiousness about his own clothes and general appearance, as well as his rising distaste for the rabble.

The second romance began when Octavia sent him a copy of *Child of the Sea: and Life Among the Mormons* by Mrs. Elizabeth Whitney Williams, a book about Beaver Island, Michigan, and James Jesse Strang, the leader of a Mormon sect that took over the island in 1847. The result was *The Stranger on the Island,* the story of Pierre Lenoir, a French Canadian fugitive who lands on the island after apparently killing a man. There Pierre finds a mistress who happens to be the wife of an aged elder, an Indian friend, and a Mormon King Gorel who steals Pierre's mistress and is in turn shot by the enraged Pierre. The book is full of the usual attacks on a narrow, bigoted morality, and praise of the delights of living free of social restrictions. But despite the exotic scene, its people have changed little since Whitlock left Ohio, and the Mormons on the island seem like nothing so much as Methodists with three wives. Except for the sex that permeates much of the book, it would make a good children's adventure yarn, but nothing more. The book was a sad way for a competent realist to end his career in fiction.

Fortunately, the deteriorating quality apparent in some of Whitlock's later fiction is only a partial picture of his life at this time. He had once described himself to Jewett as a man who "lacks the inspiration to be a romanticist which he has ever sneakingly yearned to be," and a look at these novels tends to confirm such a judgment. But at the same time that romantic predilections were showing up in his fiction, they were also permeating his reading and guiding him to another field. Increasingly, in the postwar years he despaired of the novel and immersed himself in historical reading, particularly letters, diaries, and memoirs. Soon this rather aimless reading took on a distinct direction. Ever since that day when he had spoken at Picpus cemetery, Whitlock had toyed with the idea of writing a biography of La Fayette and over the years had acquired many of the books needed for such a project. Finally, he made up his mind, and, as booksellers, friends, and his publisher all received his commissions for finding rare volumes, he set to work. He began the actual writing on January 20, 1927, after years of reading. Soon he was thinking of nothing else. As he wrote in his journal, "I have never been so interested in writing anything in my life."[15]

The chief adventure involved in the writing was a visit to the place of La Fayette's birth, the château of Chavagnac in Auvergne. The event was enough to dislocate all but the strongest sensibilities. As he and Nell drove up to the old manor house, with its towers, an American school marm thrust her head out of an upper window and peered at them through her noseglasses. "Have you lost your way?" she demanded sharply. "No, not so far," Whitlock answered, getting out. She disappeared downstairs, and when she came out Whitlock put on the lofty airs of a diplomat, showed his card, and demanded to see the man in charge. A little Frenchman, who looked schoolmasterly, appeared and made proper arrangements for the Whitlocks to remain overnight and to see the buildings. Slowly, the terrible news filtered out to Whitlock. The château had been purchased by a group of rich Americans styling themselves "The La Fayette Memorial Society," and these well-meaning antiquarians promptly "restored" the place, apparently on the model of the Ritz Hotel. They installed a new donjon tower and a large wing full of dining rooms and kitchens. They cut down the terraces, made a rose garden, added a whole block of dormitory and school facilities. They put in Louis XVI furniture with oriental rugs and scattered bathrooms, porcelain and nickel-filled and complete with Turkish towels and little "guests towels" all over the house. As Whitlock wrote Albert Bigelow Paine: "The soul of the place is no longer La Fayette, but the bathroom; they show the bathrooms with immense pride, and then take you down into the cellar and show you the bath-tub that La Fayette used," a poor old portable tub with staves and bands. "They are triumphant over the bathrooms; you see we know how to do things in America better than anybody in the world, or in the whole range of human history, and since La Fayette, the poor boob, didn't know how to furnish and fit up a house and install the proper kind of bathrooms and modern conveniences, why, they've just got to go to it and show him how, regardless of cost."

So the Whitlocks sank into the soft and padded decor, wandered about the rose garden that La Fayette never saw, and looked at the greatly enlarged fish pond, amusing themselves at seeing how the new additions successfully blocked off the view of the dirty town which doubtless had no bathtubs but which La Fayette had been forced to see. They enjoyed dinner in the fully Americanized dining room and slept in the new bedroom that was naturally attached to a new bathroom. That is, they would have, had not an American boy been singing Negro songs and playing the mandolin for his girl outside their window. Whitlock finally had to get up and take a walk in the desperate hope that love would die out in time for him to sleep next to his modern bathroom.[16]

Back at his hotel, he worked feverishly and soon had a mountain of manuscript. The sources for a biography of La Fayette were enormous, and great quantities had been published. Any French nobleman who was literate and at all poor in his declining years had written a memoir, and from La Fayette's own age there were copious collections of letters to and from all the great figures. La Fayette himself had been a dutiful champion of the art of letter writing, and his long separations from his wife and friends had only increased the opportunities. Because, in part, of this overabundance the result was overwhelming: Whitlock's handwritten first draft ran to 550,000 words. He whittled the first typed version to 432,000 words, and two subsequent versions reduced it to 320,000 and 274,000 words. The final draft is scarcely half of the original and, as it is, fills two fat volumes, or about 900 pages.[17]

La Fayette is Whitlock's finest creative work, a notable example of romantic history worthy to stand on the shelves of Motley, Bancroft, Parkman, and Prescott. For his own biography it does not have the significance of The Turn of the Balance or J. Hardin & Son and did not really break new ground in La Fayette studies. Rather, like many of his predecessors, Whitlock took an enticing topic that was relatively well known and told its history in a way that had never been done before. Such achievements frequently were in the manner more than in the matter of which they wrote, and in such a context Whitlock's La Fayette is remarkably successful. As earlier romantics had done, Whitlock emphasized the physical surroundings of his scenes—because they were vital for the transmission of the proper picture of the experience—and the characters and their emotions—since close examination of these figures aided in the transmission of personal experience, which the romantics had greatly desired.[18] As Prescott exhorted himself, one must "keep in view the most important, stirring, affecting incidents . . . Above all, keep character,— & especially the pervading, dominant character of the hero in view. Omit no act or word of his that can illustrate it. Interest is created out of character. All other interest is not only inferior in kind, but in degree."[19] Naturally, to be completely appropriate, such a character had to be acting in some grand, cosmic event, so men involved with the rise of liberty or the conquest of a continent seem obvious choices.

The logical corollary of such a theme as portrait painting is the use of allied arts, and historians—who were often novelists or essayists before they were historians—have borrowed freely from painting and from the stage. They have paid meticulous attention to portraying the various qualities of a character and have even changed his expression to suit the need of the particular scene. These carefully made-up romantic heroes found themselves regularly on stage. Their chapters have often been vignettes, set in carefully delineated rooms, castles, or fields, complete with dramatic confrontations, soliloquies, and climaxes. Their books were even usually constructed along dramatic lines, with great events occurring, as it seemed, in "acts," often battles that could have been lifted straight out of Shakespeare's history plays. Frequently too, their characters had what Cotton Mather had called "Remarkables," as the heroes experienced "hair-breadth" escapes or great trials, thus enabling them to demonstrate their devotion, courage, and generosity and underscore by contrast the cowardice and cruelty of their enemies.

In descriptions of such actions, real-life heroes tend to become representative men for the nations and principles they embody. When they have vigor and energy, so do the countries and nations they represent. They are men of morality touched with emotion, abhorring the extremes of atheistic rationalism on the one hand and blind, zealous Catholicism on the other. Usually, the hero is also the incarnation of the people who believe in the national ideals, if these are democratic, and who, however lofty his moral elevation, is always in rapport with his people. He is natural and unaffected in character, a warm and passionate man with a delicately balanced sensibility, well equipped to appreciate the ideals that the historian shares and wishes to see become more popular. Often the hero is a military man, yet strangely at the same time he is usually a man of great domestic tenderness, as though he must share feminine sensitivities as well as the masculine proprieties— chief examples being Parkman's Wolfe and Bancroft's Jefferson. Also he must have a noble heart, combined with a certain "loftiness"—perhaps even a bit of hauteur, as in Motley's William or Bancroft's Washington. He must stand a bit apart from the rest of mankind, even as he represents mankind's best qualities. And, since he has been often deep in adversity, he must of necessity be able to stand alone, to have the will, endurance, and constancy to survive and remain great.

Whitlock and La Fayette fitted this pattern admirably. Whitlock did not have the benefits of New England birth and education, but he grew up in the parts of Ohio that were settled by New England Congregationalists and Methodists, and his heritage at least on his father's side was New England to the core. Even the Brands scarcely contradicted the pattern, for Joseph Carter Brand disliked slavery with all the fervor of a transcendentalist and moved to free territory to escape it. Furthermore, although Whit-

lock was largely self-educated, he shared with the earlier romantics two of their greatest interests: Emerson and Carlyle. In fact,
he read so much Carlyle in his early years that his letters were
often full of little else, and it was the author of *The French Revolution* and *Frederick the Great* who set many of the precedents
that American romantics followed. Also, Whitlock rebelled
against the sterile and inhibited religious forms in which he was
reared, and like the transcendentalists he preferred to formulate
his own religion in warm, emotional terms that took him to the
closest modern form of institutionalized religious emotion, the
Protestant Episcopal Church. He too was strongly individualistic
and liberal in his ideas, a man of letters by training and a painter
by avocation.

La Fayette was an all-but-perfect choice. He could easily represent the best of the French nation, devoted to his country yet
neither atheist nor ultramontane in his sympathies. He loved liberty, and he loved it in the most dramatic way possible, by always
being in uniform and ready to go wherever the opportunity seemed
ripe. He was an aristocrat who loved the people and enjoyed their
support most of his life. He was a warm and passionate man, both
heroic and gentle, and a devoted family man with a wife who
worshiped him and children who never deserted him. He also left
piles of documents, after having participated in some of the most
exciting events in world history. He had only two real flaws as a
romantic hero. First, his mental capacity was a bit low even for a
heroic general, a flaw which at times bored Whitlock and tried his
patience severely. Second, his career was dramatically unbalanced,
with the great climaxes occurring two acts too soon: in Act I, with
the American Revolution, and in Act II, with the French Revolution—both of which should ideally have been moved forward to
become Acts III and IV. Fortunately for Whitlock and his art, La
Fayette made his triumphal return journey to America at the
proper moment to provide an emotional catharsis at the end of his
long exile in the country (Whitlock's Act IV: Empire and Restoration). He also played a leading role in the revolution of 1830,
which provided an apparent ideological climax in the fall of the
Bourbons and the reign of Louis-Philippe. That Louis did not
measure up to La Fayette's standards caused French Republicans,
and La Fayette, considerable concern. This also provided an in-

appropriate ending, but neither history nor the French nation have been noted for qualities of cooperation, so the flaw in the drama is not Whitlock's fault. If it were any consolation, Motley had been plagued by similar problems and solved them no better.

The La Fayette that emerged was "an aristocrat to the finger tips," even though "he supported the popular cause," a man who was born a marquis of the Ancient Regime and who carried down the grand manner into the bourgeois age he somewhat unwillingly helped to usher in. As such, he belonged in the pantheon of Whitlock heroes not far from King Albert and Cardinal Mercier. In addition, La Fayette "was one of the founders of modern Liberalism and for a long time its leader in the world. Liberty was his religion and the passion of his life," yet he never prostrated himself before the people and never allowed private ambition to cheapen his actions. In good romantic fashion, Whitlock said he had attempted "a portrait of the man himself," and of his time; such a portrait "would reveal a consistency of principle and a continuity of purpose that endured unbroken down to the day when, with all his principles and his illusions unimpaired, he found rest at last in American soil brought over in the *Brandywine* to make a grave for him in Picpus" (I, vii-x).

In *La Fayette*, the scene opens in the rather Gothic atmosphere of the château at Chavagnac, during a severe winter; a wild wolf or similar animal is loose, and amidst the general terror of the house and village the little boy La Fayette is utterly unafraid. *He* will go out and slay the beast. He never quite manages, and another man finally does the job, but the scene has been set and personal qualities displayed. In the future, the Marquis will be without fear, he will always be ready to fight for what he believes in, and he will always be shocking the royal ladies around him. He will also have the sense of a painter; only a few pages later (I, 16) he will meet his young bride-to-be for the first time, he will bow, and in perfect imitation of a Watteau painting on the wall, he will kiss her hand and think her very nice. All his life will in effect imitate some kind of art in this way and will be a bit self-conscious as a result; but a life that imitates art might well provide the best subject for art. His does, and artistically his career in Whitlock's book advances as much by artistic devices as by activities. Chief among these artistic devices is the appropriate contrast, as Whitlock sketches La Fayette against succeeding backgrounds to outline his character and growth. Against the background of the dissipated court, he is grave and serious. Next to the practical Baron de Kalb, he is idealistic. Next to the austere and serious Washington he is young and ardent. Next to the despicable and cowardly Charles Lee, he is noble and brave. And next to Napoleon, he symbolizes an age: "With all his illusions, La Fayette was not often very far wrong in his moral estimates of men, and as they stood there an instant, measuring each other—those two ambitious and stubborn men, one with the aristocratic manner of the old regime, the other, with the democratic vulgarity of the new—he recognized the ruthless adventurer, brilliant and ill-bred" (II, 112). Thus, in a remarkable portrait appear two men, each character outlined by contrast to the other and each symbolizing an age and its qualities.

Among such portraits, Whitlock sometimes pokes fun at his leading characters and sometimes criticizes mores. Sometimes he shows himself capable of the supreme achievement of the realist even when he is writing romances: the creation of emotional reaction in the reader through the use of many small details. Thus, in describing the meeting of the young Frenchman with the austere and fatherly Washington—two men who loved each other deeply —Whitlock neatly contrasts French and Anglo-Saxon qualities, mildly satirizing both:

> When the news was brought to Valley Forge, the Marquis leapt into the saddle, galloped down the Berwyn road to headquarters, burst into the General's presence and with tears of joy threw his arms about the somewhat startled Anglo-Saxon and planted two kisses, one on each cheek of His Excellency. The Commander-in-Chief never flinched; he stood there stiffly and endured this ordeal with the grave composure that never failed him in difficult situations, and when he was released from the embrace, he shook the Marquis warmly by the hand, and congratulated him as the one who had done more than any other man, perhaps, to bring this great event to pass [I, 133].

Equally successful is the backhanded indictment of American civilian elements during the war, those greedy souls who cared only for the liberty of becoming rich. Thus, when the well-disciplined French troops spend time in Rhode Island, they are set off against both the rag-tag thievery of earlier American units and the avarice of the citizens:

> The fine discipline of the troops impressed the Americans, who had never seen anything like it; pigs and chickens ran unmolested through the camp; the French soldiers did not even pick the apples that hung over their tents. And as they paid on the nail in gold for everything the Rhode Islanders soon came to love the soldiers, and charged them exhorbitant prices [I, 209].

Finally, the sort of realism that Scott and Cooper both attempted, that of minute detail. Here again, Whitlock's own emotion is perfectly plain yet never stated, and the reader with imagination can scarcely keep from a strong response (the scene is a prison):

> They were all in rags, like beggars; Maubourg was reduced to a waistcoat and a pair of nankeen pantaloons made at Nivelles. Their miserable food was prepared in the guardroom and reeked with the odour of rank tobacco. They were not allowed knife or fork, but only a pewter spoon; the napkins they had brought with them were in rags. They drank their sour wine and dirty water from earthen pots, which, after each meal, were left in the corridor, exposed to dust and crawling with flies. The soldiers used these pots to wash in, but thoughtfully cleansed them once a fortnight with a wisp of straw [II, 40].

Equally apparent are both Whitlock's new dislike of the masses and his old devotion to liberal principles. When La Fayette is caught in a crowd during the French Revolution, the obvious reaction Whitlock expects is revulsion:

> The fiery July sun beat down on his head, the crowd bawled its *vivats* in his ears, and with hot breath puffed its felicitations in his face; men pawed him with dirty hands and slatternly women of the people insisted on hugging him and kissing his large cheeks; and, powerless, he made his slow way along in that fawning mob, smothered by the sweaty caresses of his fickle subjects, hustled

through that wide, dusty avenue as he was hustled through life, uncomfortable and reluctant, but complaisant and unresisting, by forces that he could never control [I, 331].

Here, a simple act not only evokes the reader's emotions, it symbolizes the course of the book, as La Fayette will be buffeted and pushed time and again by the uncontrollable masses, experience all sorts of unpleasantness, and still somehow emerge a smiling, liberal democrat. For La Fayette and his party are the vessels of virtue here, and in them Whitlock sees types for his own predicament in the 1920's. He describes the "Fayettistes": ". . . like liberal parties everywhere in times of stress and crisis, its very moderation made it weak; it had the wisest leaders and the fewest followers" (I, 347). For such as they, the symbolic home is Wittmold, the house of Madame de Tessé: "too republican for the right bank of the Rhine, and too Royalist for the left" (II, 89).

The result, *mutatis mutandis,* is a sublime figure as close to Whitlock in the 1920's as a military man could ever be to an unhealthy and retired gentleman diplomat. Caught between right and left, and lost somewhere in the rise of new generations, both men combined appearance and opinions that did not seem entirely congruous, so that the aging La Fayette often seems but the view in Whitlock's mirror:

Thus, with old age coming on, the peculiar charm that he had always exercised was unimpaired. The winning smile of his youth, the sense of humor, the enthusiasm of his generous illusions, even the old sarcasm and irony—all were there. There was something fascinating and at the same time perplexing in the curious contrast between his manner and his opinions. His manner was that of the Court under the old regime; he received peasants, working people and the poor who came to ask his favour or his assistance, with the same distinguished politeness that he showed to the great of the earth [II, 184].

Some may sneer, but only the parvenus find themselves chilled. "The people of the countryside quite adored him," and like a true aristocrat, he takes care of them when they are sick, and feeds them when they are hungry. He is in short the perfect type of the

aristocratic democrat. Nothing could be more appealing to Whitlock or the romantic man of letters.

Whitlock suffered his usual doubts about the book, but for the
first recorded time he also found himself involved with his hero
even at night. "Last night I dreamt of La F.," he wrote in his
journal early in 1928.

> I thought that he looked like Grandfather Brand: he was very old,
> & wore the uniform of a Brigadier General with a chaplain's
> shoulder straps. I asked him: "What of old de Kalb?" He replied:
> "He was a fine man."

The queries went on, but the dream La Fayette apparently confused one man with the chambermaid. Yet he was physically very
much there; as Whitlock continued: "He had blue eyes, an enormous nose—like that of the girl who sings soprano in the choir at
St. George's,—and was most charming."[20]

Whatever his dreams, for the first time in his life Whitlock
found himself getting all but unanimous praise from the reviewers,
and the book is still the best study of La Fayette of its length. As
both the popular and the scholarly press spoke with unanimity,
perhaps the most touching gesture came privately from Albert
Guérard, who had reviewed the book for the *Herald-Tribune*. He
wished to apologize, he wrote, because his editor had cut the most
adulatory parts of his review due to lack of space, and he wanted
Whitlock to know of his real opinion. "I liked most of all the
unconventional tone of sympathy and respect in which the whole
work is written. Unconventional: irony can become as stereotyped
as praise, and in the case of La Fayette, it has long been the
fashion never to mention him without a half-contemptuous smile
. . . In scope and scale, in seriousness of purpose and felicity of
treatment, your work deserved to be an American classic; and I
beg you to thank you for it as for a personal benefit."[21]

Whitlock scarcely had time to rest, no matter how good the
book was. In the middle of November, 1928, he received word
that his mother was dying in Urbana, aged 84. As quickly as
possible, he and Nell boarded the *Roma* at Villefranche and arrived in America on December 7. He went straight to Urbana and
found himself in what amounted to a family reunion, as Brands

and Brainerds and Whitlocks all converged on the little town. As soon as he entered Ohio, Whitlock found himself once more a hero, for the newspapers had put his mother's illness and his own return on the front pages, and even the reporters on the train went out of their way to be kind. Mrs. Elias D. Whitlock managed to hold on until he got there, and mother and son had several talks in the four days before she died peacefully. All of Urbana could not have been kinder, and Whitlock suffered acutely from nostalgia for his home town—one of the few recorded times in his life. He then went to Toledo and reunions with more friends. The mayor met him at the station, and everywhere reporters and photographers trailed him ("the art of these latter represents me, by the way, as an aged and decrepit valetudinarian"); he spoke to the town on the radio. He even managed a long talk with Curly, who was still obeying the law, so far as Whitlock could tell. Then he and Nell went back to New York to continue that pastime of old age—visiting. He saw House and Jewett and had a meeting with Al Smith, whom he found quite charming except for his appalling accent. He also enjoyed an extremely funny dinner where Will Rogers displayed his abilities.[22]

On February 2 they sailed once more for Europe, enjoying a conversation on one occasion with Gene Tunney, who happened to be on the train they took from the dock to Cannes. By the time they had settled once again, the visiting began in earnest. Ever since he started the writing of La Fayette, in fact, old figures out of the more exciting past had been coming to call. After a long break caused by their different positions on the war, he and Albert Jay Nock met accidentally, and the friendship sprang up again without a word about the break.[23] Rutger Jewett, Albert Bigelow Paine, and Émile Francqui also came around whenever they were in the area, and Jewett and Paine were also regular correspondents.[24] Some visits were not entirely successful. Francis Neilson, who had divorced his wife and married meat heiress Helen Swift, appeared with the new Mrs. Neilson in June 1928. Whether it was the divorce, or the war, or the money, Whitlock was unimpressed. "Frank Neilson was here too for a while, he and his wife, whom you will remember. For how could you forget her?" he wrote Marshall Sheppey. "Poor Frank! He was so much nicer before he got rich. Or so it seems: either he has changed or I have."[25]

On Clarence Darrow the verdict was mixed. A 1927 visit gave Whitlock a good deal of pleasure, but two years later, when Darrow and his wife called, the visit was less enthusiastic. Darrow was too nihilistic for Whitlock, finding value in nothing and willing to condemn anything. Mrs. Darrow was painfully provincial, and Whitlock found the several meetings trying, although he could do little to avoid them—Darrow was living nearby, writing his memoirs.[26] Only with Colonel House was Whitlock completely at ease, and unfortunately even that pleasure had its problems. Whitlock had kept up his correspondence with House, and had even proofread and offered extensive corrections and suggestions for the manuscript of House's papers, then being published by Charles Seymour. But poor House, the perfect gentleman, was married to an ardent reformer, and Whitlock found her a sore trial that all but ruined his visits with the Colonel. Even as Whitlock was writing *The Little Green Shutter*, his essay against prohibition, Mrs. House still proclaimed her faith in the Noble Experiment, while the Colonel held his tongue like a gentleman. As Whitlock sighed: "He is delightful, but Mrs. H.! I never knew such an egregious bore in all my life."[27]

When not receiving visitors, Whitlock busied himself, whenever his health permitted, in a variety of literary jobs. *The Encyclopaedia Britannica* wanted him to do articles on democracy and King Albert. Jonathan Cape wanted him to write an introduction to Ed Howe's *The Story of a Country Town*, a dyspeptic and perverse herald of American realism when first published fifty years earlier. Whitlock agreed, although he did not like the novel. He also agreed to do introductions for books by Hamlin Garland, by now an old busybody with an indefatigable interest in writers' clubs and memorabilia, whose work had once had a slight resemblance to Whitlock's; by André Maurois, whose *Les Silences du Colonel Bramble* found a publisher through Whitlock's intervention with Rutger Jewett; and by Tolstoy and Conrad, two of his older enthusiasms, who were achieving the status of classics and coming out in new editions with introductions by other men of letters.

Increasingly too, he began again on longer projects. Occasionally he tried to work on volume three of *Belgium* but made little headway, and not even the fragment of manuscript he mentions

424 · A HERO IN SPITE OF HIMSELF
seems to have survived. He did quite a bit of research and some
writing for a new novel, a historical work about the abolitionist
period in Ohio—which he had heard so much about from Grandfather Brand. Unfortunately, when he was 62,000 words into it he
had lunch with Edith Wharton, and her merciless questioning so
shook his confidence that he never was able to get started again.
That manuscript, too, has disappeared. Fiction somehow seemed
unimportant to him after his critical success with *La Fayette*, and
he could not resist the idea of writing more history. His friends
were free with advice. House suggested that he write on King
Albert or James Madison. Nock, something of a historian in his
own right, insisted rightly enough that Whitlock was temperamentally perfect for a biography of Jefferson and kept at him to do
that. And Jewett wanted a short biography of Andrew Jackson for
a series that he was publishing. Under this pressure, Whitlock
began work on a long biography of Jefferson and a short one of
Jackson. Only fragments of both were ever completed.[28]

Politics, as always, kept him attentive and angry. His long
experience with Herbert Hoover had not endeared him to the
President either personally or politically, and, with loyal Democrats like House and Jewett and an old liberal, Nock, to feed him
information derogatory to Washington, he was soon expressing
himself vigorously. After one of Hoover's gaffes, he wrote House:
"Hoover is not a statesman but a businessman, and I know of no
instance in which a businessman ever succeeded as a statesman, or
even as a politician. Government is an art, not a business, and
Hoover has an unhappy and fatal facility for irremediably compli-
cating any political knot he tries to untangle with his clumsy fingers . . ." In the face of the depression and American inability to
climb out, he was soon talking as if he were in the 1880's again.
"I was thinking just the other day how foolish we Democrats had
been to give up our old theory of Free Trade, or tariff for revenue
only, and at the same time to have renounced Wilsonian principles," he told House. He thought the doctrines most applicable to
current circumstances, "the solution of our difficulties." Still, he
knew what was happening to his mind: "But I am beginning to
realize that I belong to another and a vanished epoch, and so do
you, by the way. We used to have statesmen; now we have pro-
moters. We used to have a Cleveland, a Thurman, a Culberson,

and a Lamar—but they are all gone . . ." One wonders what
Altgeld would have said about the inclusion of Cleveland. But he
had one solace: "We had the honour to serve the last President of
the old school, when presidents were gentlemen and scholars and
far other than the dynasty that has since succeeded."[29]

As the 1932 election approached, he grew shriller. "Hoover is
the worst, the most disgustingly hypocritical and appallingly incompetent President we have ever had, not even excepting the
odoriferous Harding. He is intellectually dishonest, and hasn't a
shred of principle to his name, in fact, doesn't know what a principle is." Naturally he was eager to do anything to see Hoover
beaten, and, while he preferred Newton Baker as the Democratic
Presidential nominee, he was willing to make an announcement
for his old acquaintance, Franklin Roosevelt. He had mixed emotions, however: "It is a difficult task; to tell the truth I am not so
enthusiastic over Roosevelt, although I like and trust him, as I
am eager to see Hoover beaten." As he wrote Jewett, in his most
comprehensive statement on the campaign, Roosevelt "is a nice
fellow and a gentleman, and I always had a great personal liking
for him, but I doubt seriously whether he has got the requisite grit
and backbone for what is going to be a gruelling task"—a judgment shared at the time by many in the United States, most fa-
mously by Walter Lippmann. "My choice would be Newton
Baker, but someone wrote me the other day that he is not in very
good health . . . He certainly has the best mind of any of them,
and no lack of backbone. Lord! I wish we had a Grover Cleveland, but that breed seems to have run out."[30] It is only slightly
uncharitable to point out that of all the men in contention, Hoover
most resembled Grover Cleveland. Cleveland, however, had never
tried to get Whitlock fired.

The New Deal quickly dissipated any support it had in Cannes.
Roosevelt's currency manipulations were "populist," and the abandonment of the gold standard "incomprehensible." "I suppose
that we shall be ruined. His later actions, his grandiose schemes,
are those of a cross between a Bull Moose and a Communist,
which is what he seems to be. Thus one more illusion fades, one
more ironic disappointment inflicts itself on one." Soon he was an
isolated if devoted member of the host of old Wilsonians and
single-taxers—Baker, Nock, and Neilson, to name but three—

who damned the New Deal and defended their old liberal principles. On July 4, he saw "a dictator on the throne who is doing his
best to ruin the country" and thought that "we may have to have
another War of Independence in order to determine whether or
not our old form of government is to be preserved." By the time of
the commodity dollar, he sounded like Hoover or a du Pont: ". . .
the fellow is simply a fatuous damn fool; drunk with power and
swollen with conceit, a cabotin and a demagogue, full of disingenuousness and duplicity, who enjoys the sensation of springing
some new and sensational surprise on the people every day or
so . . ." He even began sounding a bit anti-intellectual: "And then
the crew he's got about him—those adolescent professors and a lot
of intellectual snobs and parlour socialists: God save the State."
Even his literary tastes reflected his new politics, as he found
himself most enthusiastic over the conservative Whig gentleman
Lord Melbourne, and even considered writing his biography.[31]

Some of this acidulousness was simple intellectual dislike;
some of it was his own financial loss in the depression, although,
thanks to Marshall Sheppey's sound management, Whitlock lost
much less than he might have. Part of it was just old age. As
Whitlock snorted about the opinions of his old mainstay, Robert
Browning: "All this talk one constantly hears about growing old
gracefully is stuff and nonsense; there is no such thing as growing
old gracefully or any grace in old age. It is just about as graceful
as a withered, dried up mullen stalk in the fall . . . The best isn't
yet to be at all; the best has been, and now it is gone and there is
no way to bring it back." Most of the shrill and frustrated tone,
however, was due to illness, for throughout these years Whitlock's
constitution was giving out. The diseases that had kept him in bed
ever since he was studying for his admission to the bar were
gaining on him. Late in the twenties, his eyes gave him a great
deal of trouble, and Nell did not help matters by putting iodine
instead of argyrol in them on one occasion. He often had boils on
his nose, and frequently they impaired his vision, not to mention
his temper. Late in 1931, he was seized with violent pains in his
side and a severe chill, and the next morning he had a high fever.
A doctor diagnosed indigestion and prescribed a thin diet. Whitlock seemed to waste away under it, and in desperation Nell—
herself suffering from neuralgia and bad teeth—called in a second

physician. He diagnosed pleurisy, and Whitlock immediately began stuffing himself to get better. But even the visits of the King and Queen of Belgium were not enough for complete recovery. He was scarcely out of bed when he came down with shingles, again near his eyes. At times, he could find a kind of desperate humor in some of those who suffered with him. While taking a cure at Challes-les-Eaux, he and his companions went "through a most revolting process, first gurgling hot sulphur water in a room in which a score of Frenchmen are engaged in the same delectable occupation," as he wrote Jewett. "It is an inspiring sight to see them sitting in rows with their faces towards the wall, sipping that mephitic water and then reclining in large chairs, rolling their eyes to Heaven and making the most repulsive sounds in their throats." Under such stimulus, anyone might have cured himself, but Whitlock had no such luck. He came down with writer's cramp and found he could not write by hand at all. By early 1934 he was feeling seedy and depressed, his troubles compounded by an enlarged prostate that required his immediate hospitalization. As he wrote to Nock: "I have had the preliminary operation; the final one is to be performed in a few days I believe."[32]

He was dead when Nock got the letter.

H E D I E D O V E R W H E L M E D by a sense of failure. His great novel that he wished so much to write remained unwritten. The great deeds in which, as mayor and diplomat, he deserved to play a leading role, remained undone. Whatever the world might think of his actual successes, he was haunted by his own knowledge of the little he had actually accomplished. Illness had constantly oppressed him, his temperament deprived him of normal ambition, and circumstance could not always make up the loss. In a time of great passions, he had been detached and objective, an anti-hero looking on at life, not a giant moving events to suit his will. But Whitlock's own sadness should not blind others to his lasting merit. It is a supreme irony that a hero-worshipper should have found himself a hero, and however much he resisted the role he was in fact a hero to a city and a nation, and he deserved to be. For Brand Whitlock was great in what he represented. Like his great friends King Albert and Cardinal Mercier, he symbolized the saving virtues of a humanitarian civilization in a time desperately in need of those virtues. Coincidence placed him in a large city at perhaps the only time in American history when his diffident benevolence could command national attention; it then placed him in the one country in the world, at the one time in history, when his character was more important than his lack of energy and ambition. He did not desire such fame and responsibility, but he deserved his rewards and was equal to his opportunities. History will record that he was a decent human being who in spite of himself managed to lead a life of real value. The little boy asking about the Boulevard St. Whitlock was right in a way: Saints frequently have faults, but surely all of them are intermediaries between the world's suffering people and their fate.

Acknowledgments
and Sources

Acknowledgments

I SHOULD FIRST LIKE TO ACKNOWLEDGE the influence
of Mr. Robert Thornton on this book. When that gentleman heard of
my engagement, he kindly sent me Whitlock's letters and journals and
suggested that I do something about them on my honeymoon; I am not
yet sure how surprised he will be when he finds out what a long honeymoon that was. I also owe debts to Allan Nevins, Snowden Henry,
Hallam Tuck, Christian Herter, and to numerous librarians for answering my questions and assisting me with suggestions or introductions to
people or source collections.

I owe even greater debts to those men and institutions who have
granted me permission to quote from manuscripts in their possession.
Mr. James L. Brainerd allowed me unrestricted access to Whitlock's
papers and has placed no restrictions on my use of them, and neither
he nor any other of Whitlock's relatives has seen the manuscript. Mr.
Samuel A. Nock allowed me to quote from the papers of his father,
Albert Jay Nock; they were subsequently deposited at Yale University. The Library of Congress gave permission to quote from Whitlock's papers there; the Harvard College Library allowed the quotations from the Walter Hines Page Papers; the Columbia University
Library permitted quotation from manuscripts in the Lincoln Steffens

431

and Allan Nevins Collections; and the Yale University Library allowed me to quote from the Edward M. House Papers.

I owe my greatest debts to those friends who have advised me and humored me during the writing of this book. Louis Hartz retained his enthusiasm over the long stretch between seminar paper and doctoral dissertation, and I am grateful for his suggestions on Whitlock's American career. John Wells Davidson performed something of the ultimate scholarly sacrifice by not only telling me of a collection I would otherwise have missed, and by criticizing my Belgium draft, but also by showing me his pioneering unpublished paper on the start of C.R.B. activities; his work precedes mine in this area by several years even if it may someday bear a later publication date. My debt to Frank Freidel is greatest of all; his constant encouragement over many years, as this book swelled to a size well beyond its present weight, has meant more to me than even he perhaps knows. Mothers are perhaps unduly sensitive, but I have reached the point where I half expect him to be there to spank the first copy.

Intellectual debts are harder to pin down, but I should simply like to note that the work of Edmund Morgan, Walter Houghton, and Perry Miller came to my attention at a crucial stage, and I doubt that my interpretations would be what they are without their work. None of them has read the manuscript nor is in any way connected with possible errors in it.

In place of the usual fatuous remarks about the Angel in the House, I should simply like to record that Patricia Crunden took time off from her own work to help with several weeks of the research in the Library of Congress and with much of the editing.

Primary Sources

THE CHIEF SOURCES for a study of Brand Whitlock's American career are, of course, in the libraries containing papers by and about him. The Library of Congress has the largest collection. The Brand Whitlock Papers there total over 40,000 pieces; the majority of these are for his American period. The greatest bulk is for the years of his mayoralty. There are large scrapbooks of newspaper and magazine articles, many incoming letters, and voluminous letterbooks which contain all his official correspondence in carbon copy. Included in the general file are significant numbers of letters from the following figures: William Dean Howells, Clarence Darrow, Lincoln Steffens, Frederick U. Adams, Frederic C. Howe, Ben Lindsey, Peter Witt, Mark Sullivan, Arthur Henry, Louis Post, Herbert S. Bigelow, Daniel

Kiefer, B. O. Flower, Newton Baker, and Albert Jay Nock. Most of these letters, however, seem to have but a peripheral value for the biographies of the men involved; they do say much about Ohio reform, but the reader can discover most of what is in them in the pages of this book.

The Library of Congress also contains the papers of Clarence Darrow, Louis Post, Newton Baker, Ray Stannard Baker, and Ben Lindsey. Of these, the Darrow papers had a few items on Tolstoy and on Darrow's views on literature; the Lindsey papers were closed; and the others yielded little but general background material.

Only two other libraries have significant material for Whitlock's years up to 1914. The Albert Jay Nock Papers have been placed at Yale, although I made my notes when they were held privately. The Columbia University Library, in the Lincoln Steffens and Allan Nevins Collections, has items of great value not duplicated in Washington. Other libraries yielded a good many pieces of material, but all of insignificant value. Many of these minor letters and manuscripts merely duplicate material in Washington. They include: the Rutherford B. Hayes Library, Freemont, Ohio, which has one intriguing letter of reminiscence from Negley Cochran to Carl Matson; the American Academy of Arts and Letters, New York, which has a complete selection of Whitlock's published works, plus a few manuscripts, memorabilia, and such material; the New York Public Library, chiefly the *Century* Collection and the letters from Whitlock to its editors; the Indiana University Library, which has the Bobbs-Merrill papers; and the University of Southern California Library, which has the Hamlin Garland Papers. Other libraries have an occasional letter or two.

For the years after 1914, the chief primary sources are printed, although not always with meticulous accuracy. Allan Nevins has edited Whitlock's letters and journal in two volumes; the letters are most important for the years before and after the war, the journal for the war years. The Herbert Hoover Papers have twice been culled; George I. Gay and H. H. Fisher edited two large and ugly volumes, *Public Relations of the Committee for Relief in Belgium* (Stanford, 1929), and Hoover himself published *An American Epic* in four volumes, of which *The Relief of Belgium and Northern France, 1914-1930* (Chicago, 1959) is important for this book. The most important remaining papers from Hoover's collection, those of Hugh Gibson, are closed until 1971. I did find some material worthy of quotation in the Edward M. House Papers at Yale and the Walter Hines Page Papers at Harvard, and have quoted the best material in my notes. The Whitlock papers in the Library of Congress are very thin for the war years, although the postwar journal is there. The text of the war journal is in the Nevins papers, Columbia. The National Archives in Washington have much material in the Brussels Legation and London Embassy files (file number 848; there is more precise documentation in my footnotes). Some of these official documents were published in *Papers Relating to the Foreign Relations of the United States, Supplements 1914-1917, The World War* (Washington, 1928) and in the same series, *The Lansing Papers, 1914-1920* (Washington, 1939). These collections do not include Hoover's letters, however, nor many of the other documents cited in my text; these are interleaved with the Legation or Embassy files and other documents in the Archives.

Secondary Sources

THE LITERATURE ON OHIO POLITICS is both good and difficult to find. Of the best work relevant for Whitlock, only one of the dissertations has finally been published in full. Hoyt L. Warner's *Progressivism in Ohio, 1897-1917* (Columbus, 1964) was a remarkably able pioneering work as a Harvard dissertation in 1950. Unfortunately the delay in its publication made it somewhat outdated, for the author apparently included little material after that date, although such material is in his bibliography. He accepts Whitlock's own account of the "petition in boots," for example, even though Harvey Ford disproved this version in 1953. Warner also tends to accept the progressives on their own terms and evaluations, and to me the result is a bit romanticized. The reader should compare Warner's attitude and mine and make his own decision. Whatever he decides, he will find Warner's book an invaluable guide to Ohio in this period that will remain standard for many years. It is outstanding in its handling of state politics and has detailed bibliographies and notes.

The remaining dissertations most relevant to Whitlock's career are: Harvey Ford: "The Life and Times of Golden Rule Jones" (University of Michigan, 1953); Eugene C. Murdock: "Life of Tom L. Johnson" (Columbia University, 1951); and Philip R. Shriver: "The Making of a Moderate Progressive: Atlee Pomerene" (Columbia University, 1954). Parts of the Murdock thesis have been published as articles in various Ohio or single-tax journals, but all deserve book publication because of their permanent value. Ford's thesis was especially good. Students of the Toledo of this period should also consult the various issues of the *Northwest Ohio Quarterly*, especially for the years after 1950. The many articles there by Randolph C. Downes were particularly useful.

For the background of American literary sentimentality and the rise of realism, see: Herbert Ross Brown: *The Sentimental Novel in America, 1789-1860* (Durham, 1940); Alexander Cowie: "The Vogue of the Domestic Novel, 1850-1870," *South Atlantic Quarterly*, XLI, No. 4 (October 1942), 416-24; Fred Lewis Pattee: *The Feminine Fifties* (New York, 1940); and Floyd Stovall: "The Decline of Romantic Idealism, 1855-1871" and Robert P. Falk: "The Rise of Realism, 1871-1891," both in Harry Hayden Clark, ed.: *Transitions in American Literary History* (Durham, 1953). For Boyesen, see his *Literary and Social Silhouettes* (New York, 1894), especially pp. 71-2.

On realism in general, see: George J. Becker, ed.: *Documents of Modern Literary Realism* (Princeton, 1963); George J. Becker: "Realism: an Essay in Definition," *Modern Language Quarterly*, X, June 1949, 184-97; René Welleck: "Realism in Literary Scholarship," in *Concepts of Criticism* (New Haven, 1963), pp. 222-55; and Harry Levin: "What Is Realism?" and Bernard Bowron: "Realism in America," both in *Comparative Literature*, III (Summer 1951), 193-9, 268-85.

On the cult of Turgenev—a good measure of a man's realistic sympathies before Tolstoy's popularity—see Avrahm Yarmolinsky: *Turgenev: The Man, His Art and His Age* (rev. edn.; New York, 1963) for Turgenev himself, and Royal A. Gettman: "Turgenev in England and America," *Illinois Studies in Language and Literature*, XXVII, No. 2 (1941).

On realism and naturalism in America relevant to Whitlock, the best study, but one I find myself constantly disagreeing with, is Everett Carter: *Howells and the Age of Realism* (New York, 1954). See also Clarence A. Glasrud: *Hjalmar Hjorth Boyesen* (Northfield, Minn., 1963); and Lars Ahnebrink: *The Beginnings of Naturalism in American Fiction, 1891-1903* (Cambridge, 1950). Two studies by Whitlock's friends at the time are useful but overrated: William Dean Howells: *Criticism and Fiction* (New York, 1891) and Hamlin Garland: *Crumbling Idols* (Chicago & Cambridge, 1894).

For Howells's view of Tolstoy, see especially: "Lyof N. Tolstoi," *North American Review*, December 1908; "Editor's Study," *Harper's Monthly*, April 1886, pp. 808-10, on *My Religion* and *Anna Karenina; My Literary Passions* (New York, 1895), especially pp. 250-2; and Louis J. Budd: "William Dean Howells' Debt to Tolstoi," *American Slavic and East European Review*, IX, No. 4 (December 1950).

On the years after 1914 in Belgium and France, the only secondary source of lasting value is John Wells Davidson: "Brand Whitlock and Belgium Relief," still unpublished.

Notes

BOOK ONE
"The Father of All"
AMERICA, 1869-1913

CHAPTER 1: A Boy and His Grandfather
(1869-1890)

1. Brand Whitlock: *Forty Years of It* (New York, 1914), pp. 1-10. Hereafter cited as *40 Years*.
2. *Ibid.*, p. 12.
3. Allan Nevins, ed.: *The Letters of Brand Whitlock* (New York, 1936), p. 572. Hereafter cited as *Letters*.
4. *Ibid.*, p. 346. Whitlock several times made an extended study of his family genealogy in letters and documents, in a fashion far more detailed than seems to need repeating here. The most comprehensive statement, which goes back to 1620, is in Box 98, Brand Whitlock Papers, Library of Congress (hereafter cited as BWP-LC).
5. *40 Years*, pp. 25-6.
6. *Letters*, p. xxiii; *40 Years*, pp. 362-4.
7. Brand Whitlock: "Elias D. Whitlock," sketch dated May 29, 1929, BWP-LC, also partially reprinted in *Letters*, pp. xxiv-xxv.
8. Mrs. E. D. Whitlock to Ella Brainerd Whitlock, August 19, 1910, BWP-LC.
9. *Letters*, p. xxvi; *40 Years*, p. 23. See also the portraits of mothers

in the short stories collected in *The Gold Brick* (Indianapolis, 1910) and *The Fall Guy* (Indianapolis, 1912) and in the novel *J. Hardin & Son* (New York, 1923).

10. On poverty, see especially Will Whitlock to Brand Whitlock (hereafter cited as BW), March 10, 1901, BWP-LC, where he speaks of his poverty "which passeth all understanding" and even more where he shows his acute sensitivity over having a blue-collar job among men who do not care to read. Will loved reading and was quite proud of his abilities.

11. *40 Years*, pp. 12-23, 26-9.

12. Francis Elias Whitlock to BW, October 29, 1900, BWP-LC.

13. Elias D. Whitlock to BW, May 20, 1900, BWP-LC.

14. Philip D. Jordan: *Ohio Comes of Age, 1873-1900* (Vol. 5 of Carl Wittke, ed.: *The History of the State of Ohio*) (Columbus, 1943), pp. 21, 33, 155-61, and Chap. 6.

15. Clarence A. Glasrud: *Hjalmar Hjorth Boyesen* (Northfield, Minn., 1963), quotes from p. 23; from manuscripts in the Boyesen Papers.

16. *Letters*, p. xxiv; *40 Years*, pp. 24-5; Thomas Lloyd Reed: "J. Q. A. Ward, Sculptor," Ph.D. thesis, Harvard, 1947. Ward's *Reminiscent Sketch of a Boyhood Friend* (Urbana, 1908), deals with pre-Whitlock Urbana.

17. *40 Years*, pp. 322-7.

18. BW: *The Little Green Shutter* (New York, 1931), pp. 11-17.

19. "The Preacher's Son" is in *The Fall Guy*.

20. All of these stories are in *The Fall Guy*. Whitlock's only severe case of nostalgia came during his last visit in 1928, when he sailed from Cannes to bury his mother. See his journals, BWP-LC, for December 1928.

21. *J. Hardin & Son*, pp. 16, 35, 46-7, 52, 53.

22. Ibid., pp. 73, 83.

23. Ibid., pp. 124, 134, 179.

24. Ibid., p. 326.

25. *40 Years*, p. 161.

26. Ibid., pp. 270-2.

27. *Letters*, p. 540.

28. John H. Doyle: *A Story of Early Toledo* (Bowling Green, Ohio, 1919); Jessup W. Scott: "A Presentation of Causes . . . on the Great Lakes" (2nd ed., 1876); Randolph C. Downes: "Background and Development of Toledo," *Northwest Ohio Quarterly* (hereafter cited as *NWOhioQu*), XXX, No. 4 (Autumn, 1958). See also Chester McA. Destler: "The

Toledo Natural Gas Pipe-Line Controversy," *Quarterly Bulletin of the Historical Society of Northwestern Ohio,* XV, No. 2 (April, 1943).

29. Throughout most of his career, Whitlock or some woman near him, usually his wife, kept scrapbooks of his career, with the help of a clipping service; these books contain great quantities of relevant material by and about him. Whenever possible, I will give the dates of the articles and the newspaper or magazine involved, but these are not always clear, especially in the early years. As the scrapbooks are arranged, BWP-LC, in roughly chronological order, they should be easy to check simply from the dates. These are from the 1889 book.

30. BW: "Frank Hunt Hurd," a speech in typescript, BWP-LC; *40 Years,* pp. 29-36; *Letters,* p. xxvii.

CHAPTER 2: *The Education of a Whitechapel Wit* (1890-1896)

1. Theodore Dreiser: *The Titan* (Cleveland and New York, n.d.), pp. 4-7 and *passim.* Cowperwood's early career is in *The Financier;* Dreiser based him on Chicago traction magnate Samuel Yerkes. In *Newspaper Days,* Dreiser tells how he went to Chicago in 1890 and got a job on the *Herald* handing out Christmas gifts to the poor, although he wanted to be a reporter. He had to leave after Christmas because they needed no more reporters. After working briefly as a money collector, he finally pestered his way onto the *Globe.* Whitlock wrote to H. L. Mencken in 1916 that "I used to know Dreiser years ago"—presumably in Chicago, but he may not have known that Dreiser once worked as a charity dispenser on Whitlock's own paper and that the paper which turned down Dreiser's application to be a reporter hired Whitlock (*Letters,* p. 207). The letters from Dreiser in the Whitlock papers are mostly impersonal professional notes and indicate nothing except that Whitlock read and admired *Sister Carrie.*

2. Tracy E. Strevey: "Horatio Winslow Seymour," in the *Dictionary of American Biography* (hereafter cited as *DAB*); *40 Years,* p. 47.

3. Horatio W. Seymour: *Government and Co., Limited* (Chicago, 1895), pp. 25, 19, 21, 53, 54, 55; presumably a reprint of *Herald* editorials or a reworking of the paper's ideas.

4. Ibid., pp. 146, 44, 9, 26-7, 62, 95, 115.

5. Ibid., pp. 138, 146. Seymour to BW, September 7, 1919, BWP-LC, alludes to Whitlock's saying that Seymour influenced his life.
6. Ernest Poole: *Giants Gone: Men Who Made Chicago* (New York, 1943), p. 166.
7. Ibid., pp. 158-66 and *passim*; Willis John Abbott: *Carter Henry Harrison: A Memoir* (New York, 1895); Claudius O. Johnson: *Carter Henry Harrison I: Political Leader* (Chicago, 1928), *passim*, esp. Chap. 12 and pp. 188-200.
8. *40 Years*, pp. 40-2. For a list of members frequently mentioned as belonging to the Whitechapel Club, see Robert M. Crunden: "Brand Whitlock's American Career," Ph.D. thesis, Harvard, 1967, Chap. 2, *n.* 12.
9. *40 Years*, pp. 42-5; Drury Underwood: "The Whitechapel Club," *Chicago Record-Herald*, December 10, 1911.
10. Fred C. Kelly: *George Ade: Warmhearted Satirist* (Indianapolis, 1947), pp. 100-1; *Letters*, pp. xxviii-xxix; George Ade: "When Good Fellows Got Together," *Hearst's International Magazine*, LXXXII, February 1927, pp. 98 ff.
11. George Ade: untitled article, *Detroit Tribune*, June 4, 1911.
12. *40 Years*, pp. 42-9; Elmer Ellis: *Mr. Dooley's America* (New York, 1941), pp. 31-2, 47-54, and *passim*.
13. Underwood: "The Whitechapel Club."
14. *40 Years*, pp. 49-56.
15. All these stories are collected in *The Gold Brick*.
16. *Letters*, p. xxix. The only surviving document in Susan Brainerd's hand is a fragment of a high school essay, BWP-LC; all it shows about its author is that she was the only person Whitlock ever knew with an entirely legible hand. They were married June 29, 1892, and she died October 31, 1892.
17. *40 Years*, pp. 56-61.
18. *Letters*, pp. 2-3.
19. Ibid., p. 8.
20. Ibid., p. 3; *40 Years*, p. 87.
21. *40 Years*, pp. 86-90.
22. Ibid., pp. 36-40.
23. Ibid., pp. 64-70.
24. Edward C. Kirkland: *Dream and Thought in the Business Community, 1860-1900* (Chicago, 1964), pp. 7-9, quotes from same pages.
25. Ibid., pp. 11-24. See also Sidney Fine: *Laissez-Faire and the General-Welfare State* (Ann Arbor, 1956), pp. 52-3 and *passim*; these pages have also been heavily influenced by

Walter Houghton's quite remarkable study, *The Victorian Frame of Mind* (New Haven, 1957).

26. Irvin G. Wyllie: *The Self-Made Man in America* (New Brunswick, N.J., 954), Chaps. 2-4. See also Fine: *Laissez-Faire and the General-Welfare State*, Chap. 4. For Russell Conwell, see his *Acres of Diamonds*, with *His Life and Achievements* by Robert Shakleton (New York, 1915), chiefly pp. 17-21.

27. Thomas C. Cochran and William Miller: *The Age of Enterprise* (rev. edn.; New York, 1961), *passim*.

28. Henry David: *The History of the Haymarket Affair* (2nd edn.; New York, 1958), pp. 3-15 The classic description of Chicago life after the Haymarket affair is in Jane Addams: *Twenty Years at Hull House* (New York, 1961 edn.).

29. David: *The History of the Haymarket Affair*; Harry Barnard: *Eagle Forgotten* (Indianapolis and New York, 1962 edn.), pp. 77-8 and *passim*.

30. David: *The History of the Haymarket Affair* is an exhaustive account of everything relevant to the bombing; Barnard: *Eagle Forgotten* has a briefer summary.

31. E. H. Cady: *The Realist at War* (Syracuse, 1958), reprints Howells's letter, with quotes here from p. 74.

32. Barnard: *Eagle Forgotten*, Chap. 1, quotes from p. 18.

33. Ibid., Chaps. 2-6.

34. Ibid., pp. 75-121, quote from p. 118.

35. John P. Altgeld: *Oratory* (Chicago, 1915 edn.), pp. 24-32.

36. John P. Altgeld: "The Administration of Justice in Chicago," an open letter of February 12, 1889, in Henry M. Christman, ed.: *The Mind and Spirit of John Peter Altgeld* (hereafter cited as Christman: *Altgeld*) (Urbana, 1960).

37. John P. Altgeld: "What Shall We Do With Our Criminals?" in Christman: *Altgeld*.

38. John P. Altgeld: *Live Questions: Including Our Penal Machinery and Its Victims* (Chicago, 1890), pp. 168, 171, 179, 190, 195.

39. Barnard: *Eagle Forgotten*, Chap. 17.

40. Ibid., Chap. 18; John P. Altgeld: "Inaugural Address as Governor of Illinois," January 10, 1893, in Christman: *Altgeld*.

41. *Letters*, pp. xxix-xxxii; scrapbook, 1894-1902, BWP-LC.

42. Whitlock's early letter file, BWP-LC, is filed chronologically; the file contains far more incoming than outgoing letters but gives some indications of what he had to put up with. A few early clippings in the scrapbooks outline his legal progress.

444 · *Notes*

43. "Davis McGowan, Attorney at Law" is in the literary file, BWP-LC. The pieces are filed alphabetically by title.
44. Barnard: *Eagle Forgotten*, pp. 179-80; *40 Years*, pp. 92-4.
45. Barnard: *Eagle Forgotten*, pp. 180-2.
46. Ibid., Chap. 20.
47. *40 Years*, pp. 70-5.
48. Barnard: *Eagle Forgotten*, Chap. 23; John P. Altgeld: "Reasons for Pardoning Fielden, Neebe and Schwab, the So-Called Anarchists," June 26, 1893, in Christman: *Altgeld.*
49. The best accounts of the pardon and reaction are David: *The History of the Haymarket Affair*, Chap. 22, and Barnard: *Eagle Forgotten*, Chap. 24, and all quotes and information come from these books; much of the material is duplicated.
50. Ray Ginger: *Eugene V. Debs: A Biography* (orig. *The Bending Cross*) (New York, 1962) is the best study of Debs; see esp. pp. 1-135. Almont Lindsey: *The Pullman Strike* (Chicago, 1964 edn.) is best on the strike itself; see esp. Chaps. 1-4. Whitlock alludes to his own work in BW to Altgeld, December 31, 1894, BWP-LC; see also the scrapbooks, 1894-1902, BWP-LC.
51. Ibid. The quote is from Ginger, p. 125.
52. *40 Years*, pp. 90-2.
53. Ibid., pp. 94-101.

CHAPTER 3: *Life with the Iron Madonna*
(1897-1900)

1. Letters, general-correspondence file, BWP-LC.
2. Elizabeth Breckenridge: "John McAuley Palmer," *DAB*; John M. Palmer: *Personal Recollections of John M. Palmer, the Story of an Earnest Life* (Cincinnati, 1901), *passim*.
3. *40 Years*, pp. 61-4.
4. Scrapbooks and general letter files, 1893-6, BWP-LC; *Letters*, pp. 4-5; Seymour to BW, November 19, 1897, BWP-LC.
5. *Letters*, pp. 5-7; Mrs. Brainerd's comments are in the miscellaneous file, BWP-LC.
6. *Letters*, pp. 7-10; the last few lines are taken from the unpublished parts of this same letter, BW to Octavia, May 30, 1897, BWP-LC.
7. *Letters*, pp. 10-15. The poem is copied from an inscription in a volume of George Meredith's poems; it is the second of four stanzas dated December 25, 1897, BWP-LC.

8. Scrapbook, 1894-1902, BWP-LC; *Letters,* pp. 15-18; general correspondence for 1898, BWP-LC.
9. *Letters,* pp. 17-20; Whitlock's law register is in Box 62, BWP-LC, dated July 1897 through 1899.
10. *40 Years,* pp. 102-8; scrapbook, 1894-1902, BWP-LC.
11. *40 Years,* pp. 108-12.
12. *Letters,* pp. 15-20. "The Pardon of Thomas Whalen," drastically cut, was finally printed and is collected in *The Gold Brick;* "Blue Jacket" and "A Daughter of the Dunkards" were never finished, and they survive only in first draft, in pencil, BWP-LC.
13. Phillips to BW, September 11, 1896, answered immediately by the letter printed in *Letters,* pp. 3-4, followed in turn by Phillips to BW, October 17, 1896. All BWP-LC.
14. R. U. Johnson to BW, December 11, 1896, BWP-LC; BW to Phillips, December 14, 1896, BWP-LC; *Letters,* p. 6.
15. BW to Octavia, May 30, 1897, BWP-LC, quoting from the final pages of a letter partially printed in *Letters,* pp. 7-10. *Letters,* pp. 11-15, has Whitlock's discussion of his reading and his opinions.
16. For Boyesen, see the unprinted parts of BW to Octavia, August 2, 1898; Jordan to BW, September 26, 1898; *Atlantic Monthly* to BW, October 6, 1898; Jordan to BW, November 1, 1898; Stone Company to BW, January 5, 1899. All BWP-LC.
17. *40 Years,* pp. 79-86.
18. Irving Stone: *Clarence Darrow for the Defense* (New York, 1941), pp. 30-1. Darrow's autobiography is no help here at all; I have supplemented Stone by research in the Clarence Darrow Papers in the Library of Congress (hereafter cited as CDP-LC).
19. Darrow's remarks are from the lecture "Tolstoi," printed in *The Rubric,* I, No. 2 (January, 1902), copy in CDP-LC. In another speech on Tolstoy, CDP-LC, he calls him "a Christian and an agnostic and an unbeliever" (p. 5).
20. See esp. Darrow's "Tolstoi's *Resurrection,*" n.d., CDP-LC. On the face of it, Jones and Darrow had few qualities in common, and yet we know that at least once Jones went to Columbus just to hear Darrow lecture; and when Jones heard rumors that Darrow might run for office, he sent his support "in order that wider opportunity may be given for the preaching of this glorious gospel of human liberty . . . ," Jones to Darrow, February 13, 1903, CDP-LC.

21. Ernest Simmons: *Leo Tolstoy*, 2 vols. (New York, 1960 edn.), II, 250, 280-1, 123-5, 435, 198, 219, 335; Addams: *Twenty Years at Hull House*, Chap. 12; *40 Years*, p. 140.

22. For Tolstoy's opinion of Henry George, see Simmons: *Leo Tolstoy*, II, pp. 77, 200-1, 320, 392. For his opinion of Thoreau, see Leo Tolstoy: *Resurrection*, trans. Vera Traill (New York, 1961), p. 296, quotes from pp. 427-308.

23. Tolstoy: *Resurrection*, pp. 47, 21, 216, 227-8.

24. *Letters*, p. 18; "The Lynching of Lincoln Brooks" is a forty-four-page typescript, BWP-LC; "The Old House Across the Street" is reprinted in *The Fall Guy*.

25. *Letters*, p. 21. The *Munsey's* and *Ainslee's* correspondence is in the 1899 file for general correspondence, BWP-LC.

26. *Letters*, pp. 20-6 (June 27, 1899); parts of both information and quotation are from unpublished parts of this letter, BWP-LC; for Darrow's essay, see Clarence Darrow: *A Persian Pearl and Other Essays* (East Aurora, N.Y., 1899); Dunne to BW, November 11, 1899, BWP-LC; M. Roi is listed as Phillippe Henri Marie Jean Roi in *Letters*, p. 30.

27. Perry, Appleton, and Duffy to BW, late 1899-1900, BWP-LC; *Letters*, p. 29; Howells to BW, November 19, 1900, BWP-LC, like most of the Howells-Whitlock letters, is printed in *The Journal of the Rutgers University Library*, 1946, pp. 1-19 (hereafter cited as *Rutgers*).

28. For the basis of these comments on realism, see the bibliographical note, *supra*.

29. H. H. Boyesen: "Why We Have No Great Novelists," *Forum*, II (1886-1887), 615-22, reprinted in his *Literary and Social Silhouettes* (New York, 1894).

30. James D. Hart: *The Popular Book* (Berkeley and Los Angeles, 1961 edn.), *passim*, esp. Chaps. 7-11.

31. *Letters*, pp. 31-3. These pages include also Howells to Darrow, November 4, 1900.

32. Arthur M. Schlesinger: *The Rise of the City*, 1878-98 (Vol. 10 of A. M. Schlesinger and D. R. Fox, eds.: *A History of American Life*) (New York, 1933), Chaps. 1-4, quote p. 79.

33. Allan Nevins: *The Emergence of Modern America* (Vol. 8 of A. M. Schlesinger and D. R. Fox, eds., *A History of American Life*) (New York, 1927), Chap. 12.

34. Schlesinger: *The Rise of the City*, Chap. 12, esp. pp. 390-1.

35. James Bryce: *The American Commonwealth*, 2 vols. (New York, 1888), I, 608; Andrew D. White: "The Government of

American Cities," *Forum*, X (December, 1890), 357-72; E. L. Godkin: "A Key to Municipal Reform," *North American Review*, CLI (1890), 422-31; for a quick survey of early reform, 1875-1900, see Clifford W. Patton: *The Battle for Municipal Reform, Mobilization and Attack* (Washington, 1940).
36. Nevins: *The Emergence of Modern America*, p. 343; Charles Howard Hopkins: *The Rise of the Social Gospel in American Protestantism* (New Haven, 1940), esp. p. 24.
37. Washington Gladden: *Recollections* (Boston, 1909), *passim*, quote from p. 63.
38. Ibid., quotes from pp. 345, 371, 429. Harris Elwood Starr: "Washington Gladden," *DAB*, only sums up this book and adds nothing new.
39. Hopkins: *The Rise of the Social Gospel in American Protestantism* has a chapter on Herron; Clara M. Smertenko: "George Davis Herron," *DAB*; Harvey S. Ford: "The Life and Times of Golden Rule Jones" (hereafter cited as Ford: "Golden Rule Jones") (Ann Arbor, University Microfilms, 1953), Chap. 4, quote from p. 49.
40. Everett Walters: *Joseph Benson Foraker, an Uncompromising Republican* (Columbus, 1948), *passim*.
41. Ford: "Golden Rule Jones," Chaps. 5-6, quote from p. 107; Samuel M. Jones: *The New Right* (New York, 1899), *passim*. On the A.P.A., see Humphrey J. Desmond: *The A.P.A. Movement* (Washington, 1912), pp. 25-6, 67-8, and Donald L. Kinzer: *An Episode in Anti-Catholism* (Seattle, 1964), pp. 68, 98-9, 178. The organization claimed 7,000 voters in Toledo and 163,000 members in Ohio at this time.

CHAPTER 4: *Golden Rule Jones and the "Great Suspender"* (1900-1905)

1. Ford: "Golden Rule Jones," Chaps. 1-4.
2. Ibid., Chaps. 1-4, 7.
3. Ibid., Chap. 10. On Samuel Porter Jones, see William G. McLoughlin: *Modern Revivalism* (New York, 1959). Walter Brown had been a campaign manager for Whitlock in high school, and his sister Amy one of Whitlock's first crushes. They had adjoining law offices in the Gardner Building and remained personal friends—if political opponents—for life. See Whitlock's journal, March 4, 1929, BWP-LC.

4. *40 Years*, pp. 112-27.
5. Ibid., pp. 117-21.
6. Ibid.; *Toledo Times* (hereafter cited as *Times*), October 30, 1901.
7. Ford: "Golden Rule Jones," Chap. 13; *Toledo Blade* (hereafter cited as *Blade*), March 16, 1900; scrapbook, 1894-1902, BWP-LC.
8. Scrapbook, 1894-1902, BWP-LC. *Letters*, p. 26.
9. Ford: "Golden Rule Jones," Chap. 14.
10. I have followed the account of *Knisely vs. Jones*, 66 Ohio 453 (1902), given in Ford: "Golden Rule Jones," Chap. 14. For a printed discussion of the case viewed from a state perspective, see Hoyt Landon Warner: *Progressivism in Ohio, 1897-1917* (hereafter cited as Warner: *Progressivism in Ohio*) (Columbus, 1964), *passim*, esp. Chap. 5. A printed copy of Whitlock's brief in the case is in the BWP-LC.
11. Ibid.
12. Scrapbook, 1901-5, BWP-LC; Darrow to BW, March 17, 1902, BWP-LC. Darrow's firm until then was Altgeld, Darrow and Thompson.
13. All papers had lengthy stories on the case from June 19, 1902, on. The early scare stories are from the *Daily News* and *Bee* of that day; the descriptions of Whitlock in court are from the *Bee* and *Blade* of December 11, 1902.
14. See esp. the *Daily News*, February 25, 1903, and the *Bee* for February 28 and March 1.
15. Scrapbook, 1903, BWP-LC.
16. Ford: "Golden Rule Jones," Chap. 15; *40 Years*, pp. 126-7.
17. Ford: "Golden Rule Jones," Chap. 16.
18. *40 Years*, p. 139; Newton Baker: Introduction to *Letters*, pp. vii-viii; *Blade*, July 15, 1904.
19. Scrapbook, 1904, BWP-LC; Ford: "Golden Rule Jones," Chap. 16; Johnson Thurston to Allan Nevins, May 31, 1935, BWP-LC; *40 Years*, p. 177.
20. Ford: "Golden Rule Jones," Chap. 16; scrapbook, 1904-5, BWP-LC.
21. *Letters*, pp. 34-6; Sears to BW, June 27 and September 30, 1901; Howells to BW, May 29, 1901; Bowen-Merrill to BW, July 15, 1901; BW to Octavia, October 22, 1901. All BWP-LC. Nevins somewhat prematurely calls Whitlock's publishers the Bobbs-Merrill Co.
22. The long correspondence with H. H. Howland and other Bowen-

Merrill editors, for this and other years, including many later letters to and from William C. Bobbs, is in the general correspondence file, BWP-LC. The quote is from a letter of March 31, 1902; Howells refused in Howells to BW, April 19, 1902, BWP-LC; a brief discussion of the use of Howells's quote without permission is in *Rutgers*, p. 5.

23. See Everett Carter: *Howells and the Age of Realism* (Philadelphia and New York, 1954) for many of these points.

24. All these and subsequent early-draft quotations are from the relevant boxes of drafts, BWP-LC.

25. BW: *The Thirteenth District* (Indianapolis, 1902). For Whitlock's political lessons, see esp. pp. 45, 74, 93, 116-17, 148, 156, 236-8.

26. Cleveland to BW, September 14, 1903, copy in BWP-LC; *Letters*, pp. 36-7; BW to Octavia, January 2, 1903, BWP-LC.

27. *Letters*, pp. 37-8; Twain to Howells, August 12, 1902, copy of this postcard in BWP-LC.

28. BW to Octavia, January 2, 1903, BWP-LC.

29. Howells to Whitlock, February 11, 1904, *Rutgers*, p. 10. *Her Infinite Variety* was published by what was then Bobbs-Merrill—successor to Bowen-Merrill—(Indianapolis, 1904) in January.

30. Sears to BW, July 22, 1903 and February 3, 1904, BWP-LC.

31. *Letters*, p. 39; Howells to BW, November 25, 1904, BWP-LC.

CHAPTER 5: *The Life of Art (I): Sin* (1905-1907)

1. Steffens to BW, March 29, 1905, BWP-LC; scrapbook, 1905, BWP-LC.

2. The quotation is from the *News-Bee*, November 4, 1905. According to the *Blade*, November 14, the election results were Whitlock, 15, 326; Finch (Rep.) 10,517; Watts (Dem.) 1,329; and Reed (Soc.) 859. A splinter independent, Willard, received 331 votes. The congratulations are in the 1905 general-correspondence file, BWP-LC; Powers' telegram is dated November 14, 1905.

3. The invitations are in the general correspondence file, BWP-LC; the quotes are from *Letters*, p. 44.

4. *Cleveland Plain-Dealer*, December 5, 1905, and Warner: *Progressivism in Ohio*, p. 174 ff., discuss the meeting. For the quote, see *Times*, December 7, 1905.

5. Scrapbook, 1906, BWP-LC; quotes from *News-Bee*, January 9

and 22, 1906. On Whitlock and blue laws see *Times*, February 28, 1906.

6. Scrapbook, 1906, BWP-LC; the vetoes are in the general-correspondence file, BWP-LC, as dated.

7. James H. Rodabaugh: "Samuel M. Jones—Evangel of Equality," *Historical Society of Northwestern Ohio*, XV, No. 1 (January, 1943), pp. 17-46.

8. Census Reports, Vol. I, "Twelfth Census of the United States taken in the year 1900. William R. Merriam, Director; Population, Part I" (Washington, 1901), esp. pp. 776-7, 800-3, 868-9, 876-7, 950, 956-7, 959. It is significant that of the almost 30,000 foreign-born, 11,481 had been in the country over twenty years; 5,059, fifteen to nineteen years; 4,207, ten to fourteen years; and 3,494, six to nine years. The great majority thus were not recent arrivals, but established citizens. See also Randolph C. Downes: "Jones and Whitlock and the Promotion of Urban Democracy," *NWOhioQu*, XXVIII, No. 1. (Winter, 1955-6).

9. Randolph C. Downes: "The Rapid Transit and Electric Power Problems in Toledo in the 1890's," *NWOhioQu*, XXVI, No. 2 (Spring, 1954). For Toledo and the Rockefeller natural-gas dispute, see Henry Demarest Lloyd: *Wealth Against Commonwealth* (New York, 1901 edn.), pp. 305-68; and C. M. Destler: "The Toledo Natural Gas Pipe-Line Controversy," reprinted as Chap. 6 in his *American Radicalism 1865-1901* (New London, 1946).

10. Randolph C. Downes: "Watered Securities and the Independent Revolution in Toledo Politics, 1901-1907," *NWOhioQu*, XVIII, No. 2 (Spring 1956).

11. Ibid., No. 3 (Summer 1956).

12. Donald G. Bahna: "The Pope-Toledo Strike of 1907," *NWOhioQu*, XXXV, No. 3 (Summer 1963); scrapbook, 1906-7, BWP-LC.

13. Ibid., No. 4 (Fall 1963); Kline to BW, March 13, 1907, BWP-LC.

14. Scrapbook, 1906, BWP-LC.

15. *News-Bee*, March 24, 1906; *Blade*, March 26, 1906; *News-Bee*, April 2, 1906; *Times*, April 4, 1906.

16. Scrapbook, April 1906, BWP-LC; *Toledo Press* (hereafter cited as *Press*), January 30, 1907; scrapbook, June 1907, BWP-LC.

17. *Blade*, June 10 and 11, 1907; *Press*, July 26, 1907; *Citizen*, September 12 and September 27, 1907; *Blade*, September 30,

1907; scrapbook, October-November 1907, BWP-LC; *Blade,*
November 6, 1907.

18. "On The Enforcement of Law in Cities" was published in many
editions and in varying number of pages. I have seen no two
copies alike and see no sense in giving page references for
what was generally about twenty-odd pages in pamphlet form.
I have used the text in the BWP-LC, marked Third Edition,
Golden Rule Publishing Company, Toledo, and dated May 2,
1910.

19. The many notices of the pamphlet are in the scrapbooks; the
requests for copies are in the general-correspondence file. Both
BWP-LC. For Mencken, see the *Baltimore Evening Sun,*
November 28, 1912.

20. *News-Bee,* July 31, 1907.

21. For "the father of all," see *40 Years,* p. 219; *News-Bee,* October
1, 1910, for naturalization ceremony.

22. The description of the home is in the *News-Bee,* October 1,
1907; the remainder, as well as the next three anecdotes, are
from Minnie J. Reynolds: "The Golden Rule Mayor," *The
Designer,* April 1911.

23. Ibid.

24. *Letters,* p. 49; BW: "Thou Shalt Not Kill," pamphlet reprinted
from *The Reader,* February 19, 1906; scrapbook, early 1906,
BWP-LC.

25. Warner: *Progressivism in Ohio,* pp. 34-5, 75-7; BW: "What Good
Does It Do?" pamphlet reprinted from *Everybody's,* May
1907.

26. BW: "The Party Fetich," *Saturday Evening Post,* October 13,
1906.

27. This article was reprinted from the *Cleveland Press* as "Tom L.
Johnson's Wealth" in *The Public,* November 27, 1908, and as
"Is Tom Johnson Broke?" in *Fellowship,* March 1909; these
reprints are the texts used here.

28. Reynolds: "The Golden Rule Mayor" has the office inscription.

CHAPTER 6: *The Art of Life: the Underworld*
(1905-1913)

1. BW: "Golden Rule Jones," *World's Work,* VIII, September 1904,
5308-11. Whitlock's version and its later repetitions, especially
in his autobiography, have proved so artistically convincing
that historians have taken them at face value, so the pro-

gressives have come down to us pretty much as they conceived of themselves. This makes for a wonderful story but dubious history. Wendell Johnson: *Toledo's Non-Partisan Movement* (Toledo, 1922), *40 Years*, and all but one subsequent treatment of Toledo reform retain this romanticized view. Only Ford: "Golden Rule Jones" bothered to go back and find out from the sources what really happened. His explanation of Whitlock's account is a bad memory, which seems an oversimplification; but my facts depend on his work.

2. BW to Steffens, April 18, May 13, June 26, and July 6, 1905, Lincoln Steffens Papers, Columbia University (hereafter cited as LSP-CU). I have tried to make transcriptions as accurately as possible, but Whitlock and Steffens both wrote execrable hands, and Whitlock's comment, June 26, encapsulates the problem: "I could read your letter—but you can't read this—really I ought to use the typewriter."

3. BW to Steffens, October 19, 1905, LSP-CU.

4. BW to Steffens, October 28, 1905, LSP-CU; Ella Winter and Granville Hicks, eds.: *The Letters of Lincoln Steffens* (New York, 1939), pp. 171-2; Steffens to BW, November 16, 1905, BWP-LC.

5. Crosby to BW, November 15, 1904, is the best example, but see also the same for December 5, 1904, and February 2, 1906, BWP-LC.

6. The Curly letters, or letters in which Curly plays a role, are many. Most of them are in Whitlock's letterbooks, BWP-LC. The material used here is from BW to W. Kerfoot Stewart, March 12, 1907, 1LB (abbrev. for Letterbook no. 1, and so referred to hereafter; the letterbooks are a part of BWP-LC), p. 417, and two from BW to Laurance Chambers, March 21, 1907, 1LB, p. 456, and June 11, 1907, 1LB, p. 662. For a brief retrospective memoir, the source of some facts, and the cigar anecdote, see Whitlock's journals for December 19, 1928, BWP-LC.

7. *Letters*, p. 39; BW to W. A. White, June 3, 1907, 1LB, p. 647; *Letters*, pp. 44-5, 54-6.

8. BW to Mark Sullivan, March 12, 1907, 1LB; *Letters*, pp. 57-61; BW to W. C. Bobbs, November 6, 1906; Bobbs to BW, November 16, 1906; *Letters*, pp. 63-4. All BWP-LC, including copies of readers' comments.

9. All these and subsequent quotes are from the various drafts, BWP-LC. For some of the points on Whitlock's romantic

techniques, I am indebted to Robert Kiely and his forth-coming book on the romance.

10. As far as I can determine from the surviving mss., Whitlock intended the following to be chapters and then deleted them:
    (1) Chapter on the Brills, and a visit of Elizabeth to them.
    (2) Part of a chapter, Elizabeth and Dick together.
    (3) Elizabeth and Eades, mostly in conversation for a chapter.
    (4) Marriott and Eades see Wards off for Europe for whole chapter.
    (5) Long chapter, Marriott at home, and his first visit to Archie. Long scene in police blotter room.
    (6) Chapter, Eades thinking.
    (7) Another chapter on Elizabeth and the Brills; her thoughts.
    (8) Some fragments of Elizabeth; Eades with criminals.
    (9) Short chapter, Eades vs. Marriott in court.
    (10) Eades and Marriott talking in restaurant; very didactic.
    (11) Eades in action for a chapter.
    (12) Eades and Lamborn, talking; much analysis of Eades.
    (13) Brief chapter, Elizabeth in slums again.
    (14) Long fragment of a chapter, Eades and the law and his attitudes.
    (15) Short chapter, Eades and Elizabeth in church.
    Thus, quite obviously, Eades and Elizabeth suffered most in the cutting and were no longer able to balance the characters of Gusta and Marriott.

11. See esp. Robert H. Bremner: *From the Depths, The Discovery of Poverty in the United States* (New York, 1956) and three primary works: Robert Hunter: *Poverty*; Jacob A. Riis: *How The Other Half Lives* and *The Making of An American.*

12. Edward A. Ross: *Sin and Society* (Boston, 1907), *passim*, quotes from pp. 14, 29-30.

13. Raymond Calkins: *Substitutes for the Saloon* (Boston, 1901), esp. pp. 4, 25; John Koren: *Economic Aspects of the Liquor Problem* (Boston, 1899), esp. pp. 215-17. Both books were produced for The Committee of Fifty, Seth Low, President; Francis G. Peabody, Secretary.

14. For Cooley, I have relied chiefly on Cooley: *Social Organization* (New York, 1909) and two brief assessments: Richard Dewey: "Charles Horton Cooley: Pioneer in Psychosociology," in Harry Elmer Barnes, ed.: *An Introduction to the History of Sociology*

(Chicago, 1948), pp. 833-52; and Emory S. Bogardus: *The Development of Social Thought* (New York, 1940, 1960), Chap. 32.

15. BW to Octavia, January 14, 1907, BWP-LC; scrapbooks, BWP-LC; BW to Steffens, September 17, 1907, LSP-CU.

16. Jane Addams wrote that few books "have moved me more. I think I will put it with Tolstoi's 'Resurrection' and Gorky's 'Mother' in its genuine and stirring qualities." Howells wrote that no book since *The Octopus* had been so great, "unless it is Resurrection, which yours more favors through the resemblance which is natural from the subject." Marie Jenney Howe wrote that "no other book since Tolstoi's Resurrection has made so deep an impression upon my mind." Never to be outdone, Upton Sinclair wrote that he read the book as his last act at Helicon Hall. "It is an extraordinary piece of work, and if it does not become one of the best-sellers I shall be greatly disappointed. It is simple and natural—as true as life itself, and yet irresistible in its grip upon the reader. I know of nothing with which to compare it except Tolstoi's Resurrection, and it is a greater book than Resurrection." Russell was more graphic and less allusive: "Well, here is the truth; smashed square into our faces . . ."

Darrow to Bobbs-Merrill, n.d.; Addams to BW, February 8, 1909; Howells to BW, March 17, 1907; M. Howe to BW, March 27, 1907; Sinclair to Bobbs-Merrill, March 22, 1907; London to Bobbs-Merrill, April 6, 1907; Russell to Bobbs-Merrill, March 26, 1907. Copies or originals of above all BWP-LC. On the gift to Tolstoy, see BW to John Barry, March 29, 1907, 1LB, p. 487.

17. Evans to BW, September 6, 1907, original in BWP-LC, partial copy typed by Whitlock in LSP-CU. Evans was fortunate the Ohio Penitentiary confiscated the book and refused to let prisoners read it.

18. For Howells's public assessments, see "Editor's Diary," *North American Review*, CLXXXIV, April 1907, 781-3, and a survey of all Whitlock's fiction in "A Political Novelist and More," *North American Review*, CXCII, July 1910, 93-100.

19. *Letters*, pp. 53, 89-90, 93-4, 100; Howe to BW, February 19 and 25, 1908, BWP-LC; the penciled mss. of "Abraham Lincoln," 636 pages, are in the literary file, BWP-LC.

20. For Herndon, see David Donald: *Lincoln's Herndon* (New York, 1949); for recent Lincoln scholarship, see Richard N. Current:

The Lincoln Nobody Knows (New York, 1958); the best edition
of Herndon's book is edited by Paul Angle (New York, 1942).

21. General-correspondence file for letters from *American Magazine*
staff members, BWP-LC; for the Nock quote, see Nock to
BW, August 16, 1910, BWP-LC.

22. The Nock-Whitlock exchange is in BWP-LC; Whitlock's outraged letter to Nock is printed in *Letters*, pp. 160-2. For an
example of the Abe-Mawruss letters, see Francis J. Nock, ed.:
Selected Letters of Albert Jay Nock (Caldwell, Idaho, 1962),
pp. 24-5; the best of these remain unpublished, BWP-LC. On
the original characters, see Montague Glass: *Potash &
Perlmutter* (New York, 1909). The last quotes are from Nock
to Ruth Robinson, April 7, 1912, October 18, 1912, and
January 16, 1913, Nock Papers, Yale University (hereafter
cited as AJNP-YU).

23. Nock to Ruth Robinson, January 17, 18, 19, and 20, 1913,
AJNP-YU. See also Robert M. Crunden: *The Mind and Art
of Albert Jay Nock* (Chicago, 1964), p. 12.

24. See, for example, Susanne Howe: *Wilhelm Meister and His
English Kinsmen* (New York, 1930). I am heavily indebted
here to some lectures delivered at Harvard by Jerome Buckley
on the *Bildungsroman*. They are as yet unpublished.

25. *40 Years*, pp. 313, 315, 148.

26. Ibid., pp. 230-3.

27. "Karla" is filed with the other literary manuscripts, BWP-LC.

CHAPTER 7: *The Life of Art (II): Home Rule*
(1907-1910)

1. *News-Bee*, August 15, 1907.

2. Ibid., August 21, 1907.

3. Scrapbook, 1907, BWP-LC.

4. BW to W. S. Stuart, November 27, 1907, 2LB, p. 242; BW to
T. C. Wing, November 25, 1907, 2LB, p. 193; BW to Rev.
Charles Ferguson, December 12, 1907, 2LB p. 276; Ferguson
wrote *The Religion of Democracy*, which Whitlock had read
and apparently liked.

5. For the election results, see *Blade* for November 6 and *News-Bee*
for November 9, 1907. The Witt-to-BW telegram is November
6, 1907; BW to Kiefer, November 25, 1907. Both BWP-LC.

6. *Letters*, pp. 48, 52, 56-7. The four men were Witt, Howe, Rev.
Mr. Harris R. Cooley, and "Mr. Crane of the workhouse."

7. Ibid., pp. 65-6; scrapbook, 1907, BWP-LC.
8. BW to Octavia, July 9, 1907, BWP-LC.
9. *Times*, May 21, 1907.
10. Charles A. Barker: *Henry George* (New York, 1955). The first three quotations are from pp. 175, 211, and 246; the fourth is a paraphrase by Barker of a George speech, p. 247; the fifth is from p. 519.
11. On George's vision, see Henry George: *Progress and Poverty* (New York, 1942 edn.), pp. 383 ff.; on his church controversies, see Barker: *Henry George*, Chap. 16; on his deductive, *a priori* reasoning, see *Progress and Poverty*, *passim*, esp. p. 283, and *Henry George*, pp. 274, 449.
12. Thomas L. Johnson: *My Story* (New York, 1911), p. xxxviii; Frederic C. Howe: *The Confessions of A Reformer* (New York, 1925), p. 107, and *The City, the Hope of Democracy* (New York, 1905), p. 86; Lincoln Steffens: *The Struggle for Self-Government* (New York, 1906), p. 183, and *Autobiography* (New York, 1931), p. 574.
13. Howe: *The City, the Hope of Democracy*, p. 129. The literature on Ohio reform is extensive, and these battles form a large part of it. The path-breaking study was the series of articles by Robert Bremner in the *American Journal of Economics and Sociology*, VIII-XI, October 1948 through January 1952. They are now made obsolete by the publication of Warner: *Progressivism in Ohio*. See the bibliographical note for the dissertations on Jones, Johnson, and Pomerene.
14. C. H. Cramer: *Newton D. Baker* (Cleveland, 1961), p. 49; 40 *Years*, p. 172; Howe: *The Confessions of a Reformer*, pp. 113-14, and *The City . . .* , pp. 23-5.
15. Cramer: *Newton D. Baker*, p. 49; Johnson: *My Story*, p. 148; *Letters*, p. 114; Howe: *The City, The Hope of Democracy*, p. 163.
16. Warner: *Progressivism in Ohio*, pp. 176-7.
17. Ibid., pp. 193-4; *News-Bee*, April 25, 1908.
18. *Letters*, pp. 90-1.
19. BW to Howe, January 3, 1908, 2LB, p. 333; BW to Steffens, February 21, 1908, LSP-CU.
20. BW to Fred P. Johnson, 2LB, p. 523; BW to Fred P. Johnson, 2LB, p. 533; BW to John Barry for the newspaper articles, for message turning down nomination, see BW to Nick Port, etc., June 3, 1908, 2LB, p. 536.

21. *Letters,* pp. 96-7; BW to John Barry, September 29, 1908, 2LB, p. 679.

22. Warner: *Progressivism in Ohio,* Chap. 9; Hugh L. Nichols: "Judson Harmon," *Ohio Archaeological and Historical Quarterly,* XLI (1932); Philip R. Shriver: "The Making of a Moderate Progressive: Atlee Pomerene," Ph.D. thesis, Columbia, 1954.

23. BW to Steffens, January 25, 1909, LSP-CU; *Letters,* pp. 105-12.

24. *Letters,* p. 112; BW to Steffens, March 2, 1909, LSP-CU; BW: "Reminiscences" (of Theodore Roosevelt), n.d., an unpublished eleven-page typescript, Allan Nevins Papers, Columbia University (hereafter cited as ANP-CU).

25. *Letters,* p. 113; BW to Mrs. Della Galey, Greenwood Annex School, March 9, 1909, 3LB, p. 290. The children's greetings have survived and are in the general-correspondence file, BWP-LC.

26. *Blade,* March 30, 1909; *Letters,* pp. 115-16, supplemented by the unpublished portions of BW to Octavia, June 19, 1909, BWP-LC.

27. The free-city letters are in the July 1909 file, BWP-LC; BW to Octavia, July 2, 1909, BWP-LC; *Letters,* p. 116.

28. BW to Witt, September 30, 1909; Witt to BW, October 2, 1909. Both BWP-LC. On Cleveland's precedents, see the relevant portions of Warner: *Progressivism in Ohio;* Eugene C. Murdock: "Life of Tom L. Johnson," Ph.D. thesis, Columbia, 1951; and Carl Wittke: "Peter Witt, Tribune of the People," *Ohio Archaeological and Historical Quarterly,* LVIII, October 1949, 361-77.

29. *Letters,* pp. 118-20; scrapbook, September-November 1909, BWP-LC; BW to Ben Lindsey, September 20, 1909, BWP-LC; *Blade,* November 3, 1909.

30. Ella Winter and Granville Hicks, eds.: *The Letters of Lincoln Steffens,* 2 vols. (New York, 1938), I, 231-2.

31. BW to Winton Ingersoll, November 20, 1909, 3LB, p. 587; BW to Newton Baker, January 4, 1910, 3LB, p. 659; scrapbook, December 1909 to February 1910, BWP-LC; BW to Miss Dora A. Shull, February 28, 1910, 5LB, p. 20.

32. BW to Arthur C. Coit, January 6, 1910, 3LB, p. 670; BW to John D. Barry, January 26, 1910, 4LB, p. 22; *Letters,* pp. 128-9.

33. BW to Clarence Darrow, March 1, 1910, 5LB, p. 23; BW to Steffens, March 26, 1910, 5LB, pp. 51-2—the unpublished

parts of the letter printed in *Letters*, pp. 134-6; Bernard
Dailey to Louis Post, April 15, 1910, 5LB, p. 100.
34. *Times*, March 3, 1910, has a review of the controversy. BW to
K. F. Gill, April 29, 1910, 5LB, p. 123, and BW to Negley
Cochran, March 9, 1910, 5LB, p. 26, discuss Farkas et al.
35. Scrapbook, April–July 1910, BWP-LC; *News-Bee*, May 3, 1910;
Baker to BW, April 26, 1910; Lang to BW, July 5, 1910. All
BWP-LC.
36. Baker to BW, May 28, 1910, BWP-LC; BW to H. N. Rickey,
June 6, 1910, 5LB, p. 221.
37. Warner: *Progressivism in Ohio*, Chap. 10. BW to Baker, October
6, 1910; Witt to BW, October 6, 1910. Both BWP-LC.
38. Warner: *Progressivism in Ohio* Chap. 10; P. R. Shriver: "The
Making of a Moderate Progressive: Atlee Pomerene," esp.
Chaps. 12-13; Baker to BW, November 17, 1910, BWP-LC.
39. BW to A. J. Nock, December 1, 1910, 5LB, p. 71; Warner:
Progressivism in Ohio, Chap. 10.

CHAPTER 8: *The Life of Art (III): Street Cars*
(1910-1913)

1. *Letters*, p. 141; BW to Steffens, December 10, 1910, 6LB, p. 30;
BW to Arnold Brunner, December 12, 1910, 5LB, p. 89.
2. For the end of public speaking see BW to Arthur C. Coit, December 29, 1910, 6LB, p. 127; for the Rail-Light controversy,
I am heavily indebted to Randolph C. Downes: "Squeezing
the Water Out of the Toledo Railways and Light Company,
1907-1913" (hereafter cited as Downes: "Squeezing the
Water"), NWOhioQu, XXX, No. 1 (Winter 1957–8).
3. Ibid.
4. *Letters*, pp. 147-8.
5. Ibid., pp. 141-2. The Lang, Baker, Post, and Johnson letters are
all dated late December, 1910, BWP-LC. *Blade*, December
17, 1910, has Whitlock's proposals.
6. Downes: "Squeezing the Water"; Bernard Dailey to Mrs. Myron
B. Vorce, January 17, 1911, 6LB, p. 156; BW to Louis Post,
March 1, 1911, 6LB, p. 226.
7. Downes: "Squeezing the Water"; the Nau Report is in the
BWP-LC, very detailed, dated January 26, 1911; scrapbook,
March–April 1911, BWP-LC; *Blade*, April 13, 1911.
8. *Times* and *Blade*, April 17, 1911; BW to W. B. Morris, December
6, 1911, 6LB, p. 54; *Blade*, April 20, 1911.

9. *Blade,* July 3, 1911. Lang to BW, July 3 and July 25, 1911; Baker to BW, July 5, 1911. Both BWP-LC.

10. Scrapbook, March 1911, BWP-LC; BW to A. J. Nock, May 18, 1911, 6LB, p. 319; BW to Nickolas Roberts, September 8, 1911, BWP-LC.

   One of the odd aspects of Whitlock's mayoral career is his ignorance of, and lack of interest in, the technical aspects of urban reform. He apparently knew of Fred Howe's books and the laws enacted in Cleveland, but other experiments at home and abroad did not much interest him, whatever the tone of the letter here cited may indicate. Those interested in what Whitlock was lacking can consult Barry Karl: *Executive Reorganization and Reform in the New Deal* or Leonard White: *The City Manager,* for an introduction to this growing literature.

11. *News-Bee,* June 5, 1911; Warner: *Progressivism in Ohio,* pp. 295-300.

12. BW to George J. King, December 20, 1911, 6LB, p. 412; *Blade,* November 8, 1911. Final figures for the election are from *Blade,* November 16, 1911.

13. Warner: *Progressivism in Ohio,* Chap. 12.

14. Downes: "Squeezing the Water"; Company to Mayor, December 11, 1911, BWP-LC; *Times,* December 12, 1911; Baker to BW, December 14, 1911, BWP-LC.

15. Downes: "Squeezing the Water"; *News-Bee* and *Blade,* December 28, 1911; *Blade,* January 2, 1912; BW to Martin F. Jordan, January 5, 1912, BWP-LC.

16. Downes: "Squeezing the Water."

17. The Bemis letters are all BWP-LC, scattered through early 1912; BW to Baker, February 6, 1912, 8LB, p. 265.

18. Warner: *Progressivism in Ohio,* Chap. 13; Post to BW, April 16, 1912, BWP-LC.

19. *News-Bee,* May 8 and August 6, 1912; "Reminiscences," ANP-CU; *Letters,* pp. 152-6; Nock to BW, August 29, 1912; Brandeis to BW, September 3, 1912; Baker to BW, September 23, 1912, on Wilson. All BWP-LC. BW to H. J. Whigham, August 20, 1912, 8LB, p. 66, and BW to E. F. Swank, September 30, 1912, 8LB, p. 138, on Bull Moose overtures.

20. *Letters,* p. 154, including the unpublished parts of BW to M. Sheppey, September 20, 1912, BWP-LC. BW to Robert Underwood Johnson, January 27, March 12, and April 11,

460 · *Notes*

1913, and BW to Robert S. Yard, September 23, 1913 and May 29, 1914; all *Century* Collection, New York Public Library. BW to "Bob" (Cowell), October 13, 1913, and BW to Sheppey, October 14, 1913, BWP-LC.

21. *Letters,* p. 157; BW to H. H. Howland, January 13, 1913, 8LB, p. 253; BW to M. Nicholson, January 14, 1913, 8LB, p. 256; BW to Octavia, November 6, 1912, BWP-LC.

22. The articles apparently ran in many papers; the *News-Bee* version went from November 25, 1912, to January 11, 1913—about forty in all.

23. *Blade,* December 6, 1912; *News-Bee,* February 3, 1913; *Blade,* January 21 and April 29, 1913; Nau to BW, April 26, 1913, BWP-LC; *Letters,* pp. 162-3. Those men who died included Lyman Wachenheimer, E. B. Southard, Franklin Macomber, Oren Dunham, W. J. McCullough, Reynold Voit, Fred Shane, Frank Saunders, Harry Batch, James Wisler, and W. H. Maher.

24. BW to Mencken, June 16, 1913, 9LB, p. 252; *Letters,* pp. 166-7; *40 Years,* p. 351.

25. BW to Baker, March 12, 1913, 8LB, p. 495; *Letters,* p. 163. See also Baker to BW, March 19 and BW to Baker, March 22, 1913, BWP-LC; BW to H. W. Ashley, March 15, 1913, 9LB, p. 8, for Wilson quote.

26. Randolph Downes: "The Toledo Political-Religious Municipal Election of 1913 and the Death of the Independent Party," *NWOhioQu,* XXX, No. 3 (Summer 1958); *Letters,* pp. 166-7; scrapbook, Summer–Fall 1913, BWP-LC; Dailey to BW, September 2, and Cochran to BW, September 3, 1913, BWP-LC.

27. Downes: "The Toledo Political-Religious Municipal Election of 1913 and the Death of the Indepent Party"; BW to H. W. Ashley July 28, 1913, 9LB, p. 311; *Letters,* p. 170.

28. Scrapbook, 1913, BWP-LC. Whitlock was long known as a friend of Toledo Negroes and had a brief personal acquaintance with Dunbar, a rather pathetic Negro alcoholic who wrote verses that appealed to Howells and Whitlock. DuBois knew him only by reputation as a friend of the NAACP. For a brief comment on Senate opposition to the nomination, see the scrapbooks, BWP-LC, and B. Dailey to A. J. Nock, August 13, 1913, 9LB, p. 342. On Jewett and Howells, see Mildred Howells, ed.: *Life in Letters of William Dean Howells,* 2 vols. (Garden City, 1928), II, 339-41. See also Wilson to Cox, September 17, 1914, , and BW to Baker, October 15, 1913, and various let-

ters from Theodore Marburg, one prematurely sent on October 1; all BWP-LC.
29. *News-Bee* and *Blade*, November 25 and 27, 1913; 10LB for December 1913.
30. Negley D. Cochran to Carl Matson, October 16, 1939, in the Rutherford B. Hayes Library, Freemont, Ohio; miscellaneous letters, January 1914, BWP-LC.

BOOK TWO

Ministre Protecteur
BELGIUM AND FRANCE, 1914-1934

CHAPTER 9: *Best Girl of Europe* (1914)

1. Albert Jay Nock: *Memoirs of a Superfluous Man* (New York, 1943), p. 153.
2. *Letters*, pp. 175-8.
3. BW: *Belgium, a Personal Narrative* (hereafter cited as *Belgium*), 2 vols. (New York, 1919), I, Chap. 3, quote from p. 15.
4. Ibid., Chap. 4; BW to Maj. David Jewett Baker, Jr., March 29, 1915, BWP-LC.
5. Ibid., Chap. 5, p. 53.
6. Perrin C. Galpin, ed.: *Hugh Gibson, 1883-1954* (New York, 1956); Joseph C. Grew: *Turbulent Era, A Diplomatic Record of Forty Years*, ed. Walter Johnson, 2 vols. (Boston, 1952), I, 77. See also Edward Eyre Hunt: *War Bread* (New York, 1916), p. 186.
7. There is no biography. I have pieced this account together from the following: Count Carton de Wiart: *Souvenirs Politiques* (Brussels, 1948), pp. 180-1; Herbert Hoover: *The Memoirs of Herbert Hoover*, I, *Years of Adventure, 1874-1920* (New York, 1951), p. 206; Oscar Freiherr von der Lancken-Wakenitz: *Meine dreissig Dienstjahre, 1888-1918* (Berlin, 1931), pp. 164-7; and most important, and the source of the anecdote, Alexander Woollcott in *The New Yorker*, May 27, 1933.
8. *Belgium*, I, 1-3.
9. Ibid., Chap. 6.
10. Ibid., Chap. 7; *Letters*, p. 179.

11. Allan Nevins, ed.: *The Journal of Brand Whitlock* (hereafter cited as *Journal*) (New York, 1936), pp. 1-4; Richard Harding Davis: *With the Allies* (New York, 1914), p. 157.

12. *Papers relating to the Foreign Relations of the United States, 1914 Supplement, The World War* (hereafter cited as *Foreign Relations, The World War, 1914S or 1915S*) (Washington, 1928), pp. 30-1; *Journal*, pp. 4-7.

13. *Journal*, pp. 7-13.

14. *Journal*, pp. 13-16. Here, as elsewhere, these same events are discussed in the relevant portions of Whitlock's *Belgium*, based on the *Journal*, and in Hugh Gibson: *A Journal from Our Legation in Belgium* (New York, 1917).

15. *Journal*, pp. 18-21.

16. *Journal*, pp. 22-3; *Foreign Relations, The World War, 1914S*, pp. 45-9.

17. *Journal*, pp. 23-5; *Belgium*, I, Chap. 16; *Foreign Relations, The World War, 1914S*, pp. 51-3.

18. *Journal*, pp. 25-7.

19. *Journal*, pp. 32-5; *Foreign Relations, The World War, 1914S*, pp. 65-76; *Belgium*, I, 114-18.

20. *Journal*, pp. 36-45.

21. *Belgium*, I, 151-218.

22. James M. Read: *Atrocity Propaganda, 1914-19* (New Haven, 1941); *Belgium*, I, 230-1; Walter Bloem: *The Advance from Mons*, trans. G. C. Wynne (London, 1930), pp. 28, 41-4. See also Barbara Tuchman: *The Guns of August* (New York, 1962), Chap. 17, for a popular treatment.

23. *Belgium*, I, 259, 144, 270-1, 300, 326; Gibson: *A Journal from Our Legation in Belgium, passim.*

24. Oscar E. Millard and Auguste Vierset: *Burgomaster Max* (London, 1936), pp. 1-117. Vierset has also written the French counterpart of Whitlock's journal: *Mes Souvenirs sur l'Occupation allemande en Belgique* (Paris, 1932). Both books correct *Belgium* at several important points.

25. *Belgium*, I, 241-3; for von der Lancken, see John A. Gade: *The Life of Cardinal Mercier* (New York, 1934), pp. 150-1.

26. *Belgium*, I, 239-40, 297-8. A long report marked "Mr. President" in Box 57, BWP-LC, gives a detailed description of many of Whitlock's activities early in the war. On conditions in Belgium, see the reports in Box 59, dated August 30, 1917; 1914; and 1914, 1915.

27. *Belgium*, I, 263, 274, 330.

28. Burton J. Hendrick: *The Life and Letters of Walter Hines Page,* 3 vols. (New York, 1922), I, 334.

CHAPTER 10: *Food* (1914-1915)

1. A great many letters and documents relating to the formation of the Comité National and the C.R.B. are in Box 61, BWP-LC, marked "1914: Belgium: Relief"; an equally important group that also supplies information on London activity for the group is in the British Embassy Files in the National Archives, Washington (#848/47, C8.15 77). Published sources include Herbert Hoover: *An American Epic* (4 vols.), I, "The Relief of Belgium and Northern France, 1914-1920" (hereafter cited as Hoover: *Epic*) (Chicago, 1959), Chaps. 2-3; and *Foreign Relations, The World War,* pp. 811-12 and *passim.* The key material in the National Archives is BW to Page, October 16, 1914, and the official translation of von der Goltz to BW, also October 16, 1914, on Belgian needs and German guarantees. National Archives material will hereafter be cited as NAW; the stack area for all materials cited is 6B-3.

2. Hoover: *Epic,* pp. 1-3; *Journal,* p. 53; George I Gay, with the collaboration of H. H. Fisher, ed.: *Public Relations of the Commission for Relief in Belgium,* 2 vols. (hereafter cited as Gay: *Public Relations*) (Stanford, 1929), I, 6. Many newspaper reprints and cablegrams and a fifteen-page summary of events by Page are in the London Embassy Files, NAW; the emphasis in these papers is on Shaler. His own report is filed with the Brussels Legation Files, NAW (also with an 848 file number).

3. Hoover: *Epic,* pp. 2-5, 15. Whitlock found most of the Oxford students too brashly American and immature. BW to Hoover, December 17, 1914, Brussels Legation Files, NAW; BW to Page, December 19, 1914, British Embassy Files, NAW.

4. Hoover: *Epic,* Chaps. 5 and 11; *Foreign Relations, The World War, 1914S,* pp. 821 *ff.; Journal,* pp. 73, 77-8, including the quote on "The German authorities . . ." On another occasion, E. Grey to Page, November 13, 1914, complains about German requisitions; then Hoover to Page, November 14, 1914, firmly denies that the Germans interfered; and finally Page relays this assurance to Washington, November 14, 1914. All British Embassy Files, NAW. The process was repeated again and again, and Whitlock was frequently involved.

5. Hoover: *Epic,* Chap. 11; Gay: *Public Relations,* Chap. 8; *Foreign*

Relations, The World War, 1915S, pp. 1023 ff.; Gay: Public Relations, Chap. 5; Hoover: Epic, Chap. 13. Zimmermann to Gerard, December 31, 1914 (trans.); BW to Page, January 1, 1915; and Hoover to Page, January 6, 1915. All British Embassy Files (848/95), NAW.

6. Belgium, I, 362, 390; see also pp. 401-12. Journal, pp. 69-73, 81.
7. Journal, pp. 64, 76, 78-9. Hoover to BW, original dated June 25 (sic), 1915, Brussels Legation Files, NAW, copy dated June 25, 1915, BWP-LC. BW discusses Bell and Heineman at length in BW to Page, December 19, 1914, British Embassy Files, NAW. See also John Wells Davidson's pioneering but unpublished article, "Brand Whitlock and Belgium Relief" for the first scholarly exposition of some of the Hoover-Whitlock difficulties, and for information on Bell.
8. Belgium, I, 344 ff.
9. Ibid., pp. 364 ff.
10. Ibid., pp. 541-2; Journal, p. 88; for what was told Grew by Hugh Gibson in February 1915, see Grew: Turbulent Era, A Diplomatic Record of Forty Years, I, 180-1.
11. Belgium, I, 437-40; Journal, pp. 84-5.
12. Belgium, I, 412-16; BW to Anna Jarvis, February 19, 1915, and BW to J. M. Wells, April 20, 1915, BWP-LC. The little girl is identified as Miss de Sinçay, a great-granddaughter of General John A. Logan, in Letters, p. 547. File 848/49, London Embassy Files, NAW, has a great deal of material on the gift from American to Belgian children.
13. Belgium, I, 417-19; Journal, p. 83; BW to E. D. Libbey, March 22, 1915, BWP-LC; BW to Hoover, January 13, 1915, Brussels Legation Files, NAW.
14. Belgium, I, 507 ff.; Journal, pp. 99 ff.
15. Journal, pp. 83-4, 95, 97. BW to his mother, January 7, 1915 (misdated 1914); J. J. Mooney to BW, February 13, 1915, on Frank's death. Both BWP-LC.
16. I have relied on Albert's standard biography, Émile Cammaerts: Albert of Belgium, Defender of Right (New York, 1935), quote from p. 54.
17. For the letters with von der Lancken and much primary source material, see D. J. Cardinal Mercier: Cardinal Mercier's Own Story (New York, 1920). The best biography is Gade: The Life of Cardinal Mercier; the anecdote with the student is on p. 43; the "Patriotism and Endurance" quotes are from pp. 144-5. Originals of Mercier's speech are in BWP-LC.

18. *Belgium*, I, 420-3; *Journal*, p. 100.
19. *Belgium*, I, 643-5; the whole incredible story, which has somehow escaped Hollywood, is well told in Oscar E. Millard: *Underground News* (New York, 1938); for von Bissing's love letter, see pp. 43-4. Some copies of the paper have survived in the BWP-LC.
20. *Belgium*, I, 618; II, 50; *Journal*, pp. 149-50.
21. *Journal*, pp. 123-31.
22. Ibid., pp. 143-7.
23. BW to Page, December 1, 1914, London Embassy Files (848/48), NAW, expresses Whitlock's early delight with Hoover, as do several journal entries; *Journal*, pp. 81, 170, 104, 159-64; for German opinion of Villalobar; see von der Lancken: *Meine dreissig Dienstjahre*.
24. Von Bissing to BW, June 26, 1915, BW to von der Lancken, June 29, 1915, and BW to Page, August 9, 1915; all London Embassy Files (848/95), NAW; *Journal*, pp. 164-9; Davidson: "Brand Whitlock and Belgium Relief" treats this episode in greater detail.
25. *Journal*, pp. 171-2; for de Leval, see von der Lancken, *Meine dreissig Dienstjahre*, pp. 163-4.
26. *Journal*, pp. 172-8.
27. Edward Eyre Hunt: *War Bread* (New York, 1916), pp. 186-91.

CHAPTER 11: *"Dead Hearts and Poisoned Minds"* (1915-1916)

1. *Journal*, pp. 181-98.
2. Ibid., pp. 204-6.
3. Ibid., pp. 206-16, quote from p. 215.
4. Helen Judson: *Edith Cavell* (New York, 1941); Princess Marie de Croÿ: *War Memories* (London, 1932), esp. pp. 96, 102-6, 191 ff. A. E. Clark-Kennedy: *Edith Cavell: Pioneer and Patriot* (London, 1965) adds some new information, especially to the Brussels years.
5. *Papers relating to the Foreign Relations of the United States: The Lansing Papers, 1914-1920* (hereafter cited as *Foreign Relations, Lansing*), 2 vols. (Washington, 1939), I, 48 ff.; Judson: *Edith Cavell*; for the lawyer's story, see Sadi Kirschen: *Devant Les Conseils de Guerre Allemands* (Bruxelles, 1919).
6. *Foreign Relations, Lansing*, esp. p. 53; *Journal*, pp. 216-19; von der Lancken: *Meine dreissig Dienstjahre, passim*, esp. pp. 238 ff.;

de Croÿ: *War Memories*, pp. 191 *ff.*; Hugh Gibson: *A Journal from Our Legation in Belgium*, pp. 345 *ff.*; Belgium, II, Chaps. 7-10; Read: *Atrocity Propaganda*, Chap. 9.

7. *Foreign Relations, Lansing*, p. 53; *Journal*, pp. 217-19; Hoover: *Epic*, p. 241, quotes Vernon Kellogg on Sauberzweig; photostats of some of Edith Cavell's last letters are in Box 59, BWP-LC.

8. *Belgium*, II, Chaps. 11-12; *Foreign Relations, Lansing*, p. 53; von der Lancken: *Meine dreissig Dienstjahre*, pp. 161-4. Copies of the correspondence released by Page were printed and presented to Parliament, and a copy of this document is in the Walter Hines Page Papers, Harvard University (hereafter cited as WHPP-HU). On de Leval's departure, see also Gibson to de Leval, November 9, 1915, and de Leval to Gibson, n.d., copies in BWP-LC.

9. *Belgium*, II, 160-1.

10. Whitlock diaries, Allan Nevins Papers, Columbia University Library (hereafter cited as Diaries-CU), November 8, 1915–November 17, 1915. Whenever cited, these materials should be considered as unpublished portions of the same journal as that published by Nevins; the published version will be cited whenever possible. Hoover: *Epic*, pp. 148-53.

11. Diaries-CU, November 24 to 28, 1915; *Journal*, p. 226.

12. *Journal*, pp. 226-7.

13. Diaries-CU, December 3, 1915–January 4, 1916; *Journal*, pp. 227-8; for Boy-Ed, see Arthur S. Link: *Wilson, Confusions and Crises, 1915-1916* (Princeton, 1964), pp. 57-9; House diary, January 5, 1916, House Papers, Yale University (hereafter cited as EMHP-YU).

14. *Journal*, pp. 228-9; Diaries-CU, January 9–January 21, 1916; *Belgium*, II, 196-8.

15. *Journal*, pp. 230-32; Diaries-CU, January 23, 1916.

16. *Letters*, pp. 188-9; Diaries-CU, February 2–February 5, 1916.

17. Von der Lancken: *Meine dreissig Dienstjahre*, pp. 161-4; Diaries-CU, January 23 and February 10, 1916; *Journal*, pp. 234-6. I have given the story of Gibson's dismissal as accurately as possible, but, since the matter will come up again and again, both in this book and in general histories and biographies of the occupation, I would like to add the text of a somewhat misleading letter of Whitlock's to Col. House; it is dated February 7, 1916, is from the EMHP-YU, and continues the letter printed in *Letters*, pp. 189-90:

. . . von der Lancken told me this morning that the continued presence of Gibson here in Belgium was not desired by the German authorities. The ostensible reason that he assigned was that, some time ago, when I was in America, Gibson had some difficulty with a German sentinel and that as a result the military authorities were offended. I wish to say before the slightest shade of unfavorable impression can be created in your mind or at Washington that there is nothing whatever in this incident that reflects in the least on Gibson, nor is it even suggested by the Germans. The incident in itself is so trivial that it isn't worth a second's consideration; he told me all about it immediately on my return. He was riding one day when a stupid sentinel stopped him as he was about to ride over a railroad crossing; the sentinel threatened to arrest him, and Gibson spoke to an officer near by, informed him of his diplomatic capacity, and the officer rebuked the sentinel and told Gibson to ride on. Gibson himself informed the authorities at German headquarters of the incident, and supposed that disposed of it. It is indeed infantile in them to bring it up. I am certain, however, that it is merely a pretext for an action they have been contemplating a long while, and that the animus grows out of an earlier incident that occurred at the time of the burning of Louvain. Gibson had gone out there with two young secretaries of Legation, the Swedish and the Mexican, on the third day of the tragedy, and having witnessed some shooting, the German authorities wished him and his companions to make a deposition that the civilians had fired on the German troops. He declined and I supported him in his declination, and was later approved by Washington; thereupon the other two secretaries refused likewise to testify. The result was a certain feeling of resentment against Gibson which seems never to have disappeared. From time to time Lancken has made observations to me that indicated that he had an inimical feeling toward Gibson, but I have always dismissed the matter as too trivial for consideration. My opinion now is that this latest expression is a result of the recall of von Papen and of Boy-Ed, for in a conversation one morning immediately after my return Lancken told me that the foreign office in Berlin and especially the military authorities were very much offended by that recall and had thought of retaliating, but that he had dissuaded them from doing so. Considering these facts in their relation to each other and the demand made this morning it is easy to deduce the existence of a childish spite and desire to get even because of the von Papen and Boy-Ed affair, a little example of diplomatic tit for tat—such is the ire in great minds! Well, I told Lancken that they could do as they pleased of course but that if they made an incident of this business it would only react unfavorably against them in America and add another to the already long list of blunders they have committed . . . He personally agreed with this, but had, as they always have, recourse to the statement that the military authorities demanded it . . . and, to my very great personal regret, Gibson will go away; he agrees fully with me on this point. In all the time we have worked together we have never had a disagreement but have worked together in the most cordial and intimate and sympathetic relations . . . I wish to arrange it all so he will be subject to no unpleasantness whatever, and indeed so that he will receive what is surely due him, namely, some distinguishing mark of his government's confidence and approval. This is the point of this long preamble; that is what I wish you to help me accomplish. He is entitled, not only by seniority, but by long, devoted and very arduous service, to a promotion to first secretary of embassy . . . it makes me sad and lonely to think of his going away. I have grown to be fond of him in the time we have served together; experiences like this reveal men and he is of excellent material I assure you, with more than the making of a diplomat, and if he only had a rich wife he might easily be an ambassador some day.

Having seen the far more critical account of these incidents that Whitlock was writing in his journal, this letter may seem disingenuous in the extreme. Whitlock and Gibson did not get along at all well; the incidents which really annoyed the Germans are unmentioned, and the publication of the Cavell documents and Gibson's handling of that matter omitted. The letter is important, however, in showing Whitlock's sense of decency and fairness; here he recommended a man whom he much disliked, because he respected Gibson's great courage and his obvious natural abilities. Even more important, it contrasts glaringly with Gibson's subsequent efforts to have Whitlock removed from his post, which everyone from Col. House to Mme de Wiart soon repeated to Whitlock. It also shows conclusively that Hoover simply did not know what he was talking about when he discussed Whitlock and Gibson. The remarks Hoover makes, pp. 205-7 and elsewhere in volume I of his *Memoirs* and in *An American Epic*, are prejudiced and often in direct contradiction to facts Hoover might easily have checked. These are not the only places where Hoover's *Memoirs* are inaccurate.

18. Diaries-CU, February 14–February 17, 1916.
19. Diaries-CU, February 15, 16, and 28, 1916; *Journal*, p. 239.
20. *Journal*, pp. 236-9.
21. Hoover: *Epic*, Chap. 22; *Journal*, pp. 240, 244; Hoover to Page, February 24, 1916; "Procès-verbal of Conference . . . Commit-

tee for Relief in Belgium," dated Brussels, July 20, 1915; and Hoover to Page, March 18, 1916 enclosing Grey's refusal. All British Embassy Files, NAW (848/109). The friction did not stop here, nor was it limited to any particular time. Thus Hoover to Page, October 18, 1916, complains of the "systematic attempt" of the Belgians to take over from the Americans; BW to Hoover, November 29, 1916, tries to calm Hoover and says that Francqui is now grateful, etc. Both Brussels Legation Files, NAW. Hoover to BW, December 29, 1916, sums up his version of the feud with Francqui, also Brussels Legations Files, NAW.

Just what Gibson, Lambert, and Francqui were up to in London is a story in itself, and fortunately Page wrote it down in what is surely one of the most confused, even befuddled, letters ever written by that gullible Anglophile and unhappy man. The first quote is from his diary of February 25, 1916:

Villalobar, Lambert, Francqui—with the Villalobar-Lambert-German conspiracy against the Com. for Relief in Belgium—came; I advised Hoover to resign. He cannot come to giving up the work unless absolutely compelled to go. He offered to retire (with all the Americans) and leave the work to be done by the Belgian Comité National. Merry del Val and the Spanish members of the Commission stand with the Americans. He and I presented the matter to Sir E[dward] G[rey], who verbally said "No." Thus the conspiracy is dead. But there is a fear lest the unsatisfactory conduct of the Germans may cause the English to throw the whole work up and off. See my attached letter (never sent) to the President about Whitlock. The manufacture of a legend and its subsequent growth—what a commentary on public opinion. This "Saving Belgium–Whitlock" legend was in the first place manufactured by the Press Bureau of the Commission, in the newspapers of the U.S., to make the people there give liberally. Then it went to their head and to poor Whitlock's and will (I fancy) become a part of "History."

It will indeed. The second quote is from the letter of Page's to Wilson, marked "(never sent)" in Page's handwriting, dated February 22, 1916. Like the journal, it is in the Walter Hines Page Papers (WHPP-HU).

I have a most pitiful tale to write you; and I take it upon myself to write you because it is of the utmost importance that you should know it— for large political reasons; and, so far as I know, nobody else knows the whole story who will tell you—so many parts of it are incredible.

Seven or eight months ago, or more, the mailed fist knocked Whitlock out. His sympathy and eagerness to serve and his many attractive qualities —qualities which inspire not admiration only but affection—are housed in a dwelling of acute nerves; and the structure of this dwelling is far weaker than most of us who like him thought it was. I have lately learned that some years ago he suffered a complete nervous breakdown from wh. it long seemed doubtful if he wd. recover and it did take him a very long time to "come back." I hear that Mrs. Whitlock now sees some of the same symptoms and is very uneasy, as we all are. It has been coming to me from three independent sources that he has for a long time been incapable of real work; and since his return from the U.S. he has become distinctly worse. I am told that if one sees him casually one wd. suspect nothing wrong. But he sits in the house and broods day after day and week after week, unwilling to see anyone, unwilling, except fitfully, to put forth any effort, unwilling even to have others do anything. In the first place, the mailed fist was too much for him. Then, in his depleted condition, his reception in the U.S. completed the task of demoralization. It seemed, at first, to him that he is sure to be nominated for Vice-President, he being the savior of Belgium. And that came so easily and so spontaneously that it bred the pitiful hallucination that if he declined the nomination for the Vice-Presidency, they'll have to nominate him for President! This is the measure of the poor fellow's breakdown and nervous condition. His present unhappy, morbid mood, I am told, is to do nothing, least of all to do anything to cause comment or that costs effort, and to sit and wait till the nomination calls him.

Consequently the Spanish Minister in Brussels and a group of personally ambitious Belgians who wish to turn the Relief of Belgium to the furthering of their own political plans have simply "worked over" Whitlock, who, sitting alone in his house, doesn't know what has happened. Some time ago the British Gov't wrote me a letter complaining of the conduct of the German Military in extracting food from Belgium contrary to their agreement with the Commission, and asking for further guarantees. I informally sent this to Whitlock to take up with the German Governor-General. He wrote me that the matter wd. be all right. But now it turns out that the Spanish Minister in Brussels comes to London, accompanied by his Belgian friends, with the German answer to the British complaint, in wh. a plan for the reorganization of the Commission is laid down which seems sure to cause the British Government to shut down on the whole enterprise. They will talk about it here for a week or more. But, while Whitlock thinks that the thing is all right, these fellows have ruined the whole undertaking. I fear that Hoover and his group will resign, that the British Gov't will forbid the importation of more food, since the Germans really

break their guarantee; I fear that the Commission's days are almost numbered. — In this negotiation I have been careful to do nothing myself but
to transmit, without comment, the communication of the British Foreign
Office.

(There follows a paragraph on the legend that the U.S. fed
Belgium alone and how Whitlock is too sick for any politics;
then another on how "a real man" is needed in Brussels.)

The next important thing is, What is the best thing to do with
Whitlock? To Petrograd? No, he is not equal to it. Gibson the Secretary
of Legation at Brussels, has suggested that Willard be sent to Petrograd
and Whitlock to Madrid. Madrid is now the most restful place in Europe.
Whitlock wd. there probably gradually recover and (when his political
disease disappear [sic] by time and events) he wd [sic] become himself
again.

The information that reaches me is that Whitlock is mistaken in sup-
posing that the Germans wished Gibson to be transferred from Brussels.
It is possible that in this matter also Whitlock has been misinformed and
misled by the activities of the same people who wish to reorganize the
Commission.

Of this I wish you to make sure: Gibson and the American members of
the Commission who go to Brussels and those who have been living there
are every one dutifully and beautifully loyal to Whitlock. They will do
anything for him and anything to save him. They talk to nobody about
him except to the one or two who, they hope, may do something for him;
and they are all fond of him. But they see an impending catastrophe, wh.
they hope will be avoided.

(Then follow: his fears for the Commission; and his beliefs
that the British are justified, the Germans unspeakable, Hoover
self-sacrificing, that the typical Belgian is "a good deal of a
yellow dog," etc.)

So, poor Whitlock. If he cd. get to some quiet sanitorium, such as
Madrid, from all I hear he'd get over his hallucinations, write novels &
play golf and bow to the King and get right in time.

Walter Hines Page was capable of believing just about anything, and his whole career was a subject of great pain both to
Wilson and Col. House, who had to listen to the endless

record that always cracked on the issue of American support of the saintly British. But here Page achieves sublimity. The utterly baseless charges of Whitlock's inertia have an obvious core of truth in Whitlock's shaken nerves, and in his regular illnesses, but except for the Edith Cavell affair they never kept him from performing his duties, and it was a rare day indeed that he did not explore some part of Brussels, as his journal amply indicates. Gibson had simply poisoned Hoover's mind, and the two of them had convinced Page. The Presidential nonsense is too funny for refutation. The loyalty of the C.R.B. men was strictly to Hoover, and they would have done anything to get Whitlock out of Belgium and get Gibson in as minister. Whitlock did not cater to Hoover's ego and did not share his politics, and these plus Gibson's erroneous notions about his dismissal led to the above canards. No one can blame Whitlock for becoming bitter about Gibson and Hoover when he found out pieces of what happened in London. Not the least of the ironies of the whole miserable situation was that Page at times was far sicker and less reliable than Whitlock ever was and that he spent at least as much time at his desk writing letters. But that is another story.

22. *Journal*, pp. 247-8; Diaries-CU, March 26, 1916.
23. Diaries-CU, quote from February 15, 1916, entry; *Letters*, p. 192.
24. Diaries-CU, April 29, May 6–9, 1916; *Journal*, pp. 256, 227; *Letters*, p. 188.
25. *Journal*, pp. 260-1; Diaries-CU, May 13, 1916; N. Baker in *Letters*, p. xvii.
26. *Journal*, pp. 262-3; Diaries-CU, May 22, 1916.
27. *Journal*, pp. 265-8.
28. Ibid., pp. 264-5, 269.
29. *Belgium*, II, 317-20; *Vernon Kellogg, 1867-1937* (Washington, 1939)—a collection of tributes and facts by friends.

CHAPTER 12: *"What a Lovely World It Would Be . . ."* (1916-1917)

1. *Belgium*, II, 54, 55, 58, 62, 171-2.
2. Ibid., I, 372-4; II, 267-9.
3. Ibid. I, 380; II, 334.
4. *Journal*, pp. 133, 105.
5. *Belgium*, II, Chap. 20.

6. *Belgium*, II, 337-42; *Journal*, p. 281.
7. *Journal*, pp. 278-9, 283-4, 291; *Belgium*, II, 401-9.
8. Gay: *Public Relations*, II, Chap. 10; Hoover: *Epic*, pp. 154-60, 253-60, 273-82; *Letters*, p. 203.
9. *Journal*, pp. 305, 308-10 (October 27 misdated October 26 in the printed version, p. 308); see p. 306 for Whitlock's own description of the lounging chômeurs. Gay: *Public Relations*, II, Chap. 10 for many reports.
10. *Journal*, pp. 317-18, 322-33; *Letters*, p. 203; *Belgium*, II, 438.
11. *Belgium*, II, 653-4; for the labor drives in detail, with documents, see pp. 478-675; for von Bissing's position, see pp. 450-60.
12. *Journal*, pp. 345-6; 317; *Belgium*, II, 688-98.
13. Diaries-CU, July 13 and 29–31, 1916; *Letters*, p. 195; *Belgium*, II, 351, 371-2.
14. *Journal*, pp. 282, 284, 292, 296, 311. For more on Hoover and Francqui, see J. W. Davidson: "Brand Whitlock and Belgium Relief," pp. 29 ff.
15. *Journal*, pp. 313-15, 321-2. The book was never published so far as I have been able to determine.
16. *Journal*, pp. 287-8, 307-8; Diaries-CU, August 23, 1916.
17. Von der Lancken: *Meine dreissig Dienstjahre*, p. 167; *Journal*, pp. 324-5, 333-4; Diaries-CU, December 11, 1916. Whitlock to Gibson, August 24, 1917, BWP-LC, quotes Villalobar on van Vollenhoven after Whitlock's departure and a promotion: "Celui qui a grandi, gonflé, rougi et devenu brilliant comme une boule de fromage de Hollande, est notre ami van Vollenhoven."
18. *Journal*, pp. 331, 312; Diaries-CU, January 18, 1917.
19. De Croÿ: *War Memories*, p. 101; *Journal*, pp. 256, 262, 264, 304-7, 301-2; Diaries-CU, November 8, 1916.
20. *Journal*, pp. 331, 333; Diaries-CU, December 8, 1916.
21. *Journal*, pp. 348-9.
22. Ibid., pp. 351-3.
23. *Journal*, pp. 355-6. Von der Lancken to Villalobar, February 10, 1917; BW to Villalobar, February 12, 1917; von der Lancken to BW, February 25, 1917; BW to von der Lancken, February 26, 1917. All copied, BWP-LC. Many letters in 848/86, London Embassy Files, NAW, esp. Lansing to Page, March 11, 1917, on Hoover's influence in Washington, and Hoover to (no addressee), March 11, 1917, expressing his belligerence on withdrawal.
24. *Journal*, pp. 356-62.

25. Ibid., pp. 366-7. Despite it all, Whitlock still recommended Hoover to Newton Baker as a man of cabinet quality, January 17, 1917, BWP-LC: "You will find him at first the type of the strong-willed, indomitable American businessman and executive, but his hardness is all on the surface. He is a gentleman of a rather wide culture and immense amount of certain kinds of information, distinguished in his own calling as engineer, of a most democratic nature and with great human sympathies; his work in the Commission of course is one of the modern wonders of the world, if there are any more wonders in this world." Considering the circumstances, that is surely one of the most civilized gestures of this most uncivilized period.
26. Ibid., p. 368.
27. Ibid., p. 371; *Belgium*, II, 802-3.
28. *Belgium*, II, 811-13; *Journal*, pp. 374-5.
29. *Journal*, pp. 376-7.
30. For Rolland, aside from the Modern Library *Jean-Christophe*, see William Thomas Starr: *Romain Rolland and a World at War* (Evanston, 1956) and Romain Rolland: *Journey Within*, trans. Elsie Pell (New York, 1947). For Whitlock, see Diaries-CU, August 8 and 30, 1916; for the screed about his other reading, see *Journal*, p. 369, and pp. 384-7 for his visit to Rolland.
31. *Journal*, p. 387.
32. Diaries-CU, April 11-19, 1917; *Journal*, pp. 388-90.
33. *Journal*, pp. 391-4.
34. Diaries-CU, April 19, 1917.

CHAPTER 13: *Apotheosis* (1917-1921)

1. Diaries-CU, April 20-5, 1917.
2. *Journal*, pp. 395-6; Diaries-CU, April 21, June 6-19, July 25, 1917.
3. These paragraphs are based on *Journal*, pp. 399-412, but I must add a note here. I have been unable to find the originals for these printed pages in what I consider to be the key manuscript text for the journal at Columbia University; the passage has either been reconstructed from manuscripts not at Columbia or from other papers not technically a part of the journal. Likewise the entry for May 20, 1917, pp. 415-17, does not correspond to the version at Columbia. The printed text also has frequent omissions of important passages and a large number of misdated passages elsewhere in the book. Mrs. Whitlock and others who

read the text after editing may well be in part responsible for certain of these problems.

4. *Journal*, pp. 414-17, 432; *Letters*, pp. 232-3; Diaries-CU, September 18, 1917.

5. *Journal*, pp. 420, 425, 429; Diaries-CU has the three-page Kellogg speech in Vol. 11; *Letters*, pp. 234-41; on the German occupation, see also document #563, Whitlock to the Secretary of State, in Diaries-CU, Vol. 12.

6. *Letters*, pp. 236-40 Diaries-CU, September 19, 1917. There is an enormous correspondence dealing with Department of State permission to publish each chapter and the financial arrangement with agent Curtis Brown, beginning with George Creel to Whitlock, August 24, 1917, and continuing over many months, BWP-LC.

7. *Journal*, pp. 440, 441, 449, 457-8; Diaries-CU, August 15, October 15 and 17, November 11, 1917.

8. *Journal*, pp. 458-60. House was just as friendly to Whitlock in private as he was in public. In January, he had talked seriously with Wilson about Whitlock's ability to succeed Walter Page as Ambassador to London and had informed Whitlock about it in confidence (House to BW, January 17, 1917, EMHP-YU). When they met later, he repeated his friendly feelings in his diary, November 23, 1917. For Gibson, see also the penciled note on BW to House, December 2, 1917, and House's diary entry for December 3, 1917, which also concerns Hoover's ambitions. All EMHP-YU.

9. *Journal*, p. 461; Diaries-CU, November 30, 1917. See also the House material cited in note 8 above.

10. *Journal*, p. 462; Diaries-CU, December 8, 1917.

11. *Letters*, p. 263; Diaries-CU, December 27, 1917; John van Schaick, Jr.: *The Little Corner Never Conquered* (New York, 1922), p. 51; *Journal*, pp. 455-6.

12. *Journal*, pp. 489-91, 493, 500-2; Diaries-CU, April 18 and September 9, 1918.

13. *Journal*, pp. 479, 520; Diaries-CU, November 7, 1918.

14. *Journal*, pp. 521-7; Diaries-CU, November 23, 1918.

15. *Letters*, pp. 271-2; *Journal*, pp. 531, 534. For Whitlock's assessment of the Belgian socialists, see BW to Secretary of State, October 18, 1918, copy in BWP-LC.

16. *Journal*, pp. 532-6. Hoover to Francqui (via Sharp), December 2, 1918; BW to Hoover (via Sharp). *Letters*, pp. 272-3.

17. *Journal*, pp. 537-40; *Letters*, pp. 274-5; BW to Lansing, December

12, 1918, BWP-LC.

18. *Journal*, p. 530; *Letters*, pp. 273, 267; Wilson to BW, January 10 and February 28, 1919, BWP-LC.

19. *Journal*, pp. 552, 559, 560, 562; Lansing to BW, June 3, 1919, answered by letter, in *Letters*, p. 279. BW to House, May 2, 1919, EMHP-YU, has more on Belgian opinion and Whitlock's wretchedness about Versailles.

20. *Journal*, pp. 563-70; Diaries-CU, June 18, 1919.

21. *Journal*, pp. 572-7.

22. Ibid., pp. 575-9.

23. The entire report of the royal tour is taken from the journal, marked "Journal of the Royal Tour in America" in the BWP-LC. Mrs. Whitlock hid this manuscript from Prof. Nevins and then closed it when she gave it to the library. It is only recently open. All characterizations offered here, e.g., the one of Colby that follows, may be assumed to be Whitlock's, and not mine.

24. *Journal*, pp. 579-96, 643; Diaries-CU, April 11 and 15, 1920; for background on Belgium relations with Luxembourg and France —with several detailed reports to the Secretary of State—see documents dated 1920, BWP-LC. On L'Affaire de Margerie, see BW to Villiers, January 28, 1921, and BW to Secretary of State, January 8 and 13, 1921, BWP-LC.

25. *Journal*, pp. 587-91, 625-8.

26. Ibid., pp. 610-12; Diaries-CU, June 13, 1920.

27. *Journal*, pp. 615-16, 639.

28. Ibid., p. 605.

29. *Journal*, pp. 436-7, 482, 596-7, 699; Diaries-CU, July 25, 1918; *Letters*, p. 278.

30. House diary, EMHP-YU, August 16, 1920.

31. *Journal*, pp. 642-3, 679-80, 717, 719; Sheppey to BW, November 30, 1920, BWP-LC.

32. *Journal*. pp. 621, 685, 688, 618-19; Diaries-CU, July 20-1, 1920.

33. *Journal*, pp. 717-23.

34. Charles D'Ydewalle: *Albert and the Belgians* (New York, 1935), pp. 154-5.

CHAPTER 14: *The Best Has Been* (1922-1934)

1. *Journal*, p. 652.

2. Ibid., p. 467; Diaries-CU, January 26 and April 17, 1918, and April 29, 1921; *Letters*, p. 280. The Payot letters are voluminous; the problem begins in Payot to BW, January 14, 1919,

and BW to Payot, January 20, 1919, and drags on for months, BWP-LC.

3. *Letters*, pp. 289-92.
4. *Journal*, p. 654; *Letters*, pp. 340-2, 347.
5. *Letters*, p. 351.
6. Whitlock journals, 1922-34, BWP-LC (hereafter cited as Journals, BWP-LC); Drummond to BW, December 18 and 19, 1923, BWP-LC.
7. Journals (1922-3), quotes from October 18 and 30, 1922, and January 1, 1923, BWP-LC; Jewett to Nell, September 14, 1922, BWP-LC; *Letters*, pp. 341-3.
8. Journals (1923), quotes from March 24, July 5, and December 19, 1923, BWP-LC.
9. For Whitlock's sickness, see *Letters*, pp. 347, 373.
10. For the previous months, see the "make-up" entry, Journals, dated August 14, 1925, BWP-LC, including a brief memoir of Bryan; Nell to Jewett, several undated letters (1925), BWP-LC, describe the illness, as does *Letters*, pp. 367-8, 375; BW to Paine, October 4, 1926, describes the next summer and has quote, BWP-LC.
11. Whitlock always spoke of *Transplanted* as his "Belgian novel," and he obviously wrote it with his Belgian experiences in mind. He was terribly afraid of offending the Belgians, however, and so simply changed a few details to make the book French. See, *inter alia*, Journals, January 30, 1925, BWP-LC.
12. BW to House, June 22, 1927; House to BW, September 26, 1927; BW to House, May 31, 1928. All EMHP-YU.
13. House to BW, October 1, 1928. All BWP-LC.
14. Journals, December 21 and 27, 1926, BWP-LC; *Letters*, p. 398.
15. *Letters*, pp. 343, 374, 400-2; Journals, January 27, 1927, BWP-LC.
16. Ibid., pp. 410-12; Journals, June 24, 1927, BWP-LC.
17. *Letters*, pp. 421-2, 429, 450.
18. I am particularly indebted for this discussion and the pages following to David Levin: *History as Romantic Art* (New York, 1963).
19. Ibid., p. 10, quoting Prescott's Notebooks, X, p. 61, in the Massachusetts Historical Society.
20. Journals, January 23, 1928, BWP-LC.
21. Guérard to BW, October 30, 1929, BWP-LC.
22. *Letters*, pp. 429-31; Journals, November 1928–January 1929, BWP-LC.
23. Journals, February 1929, BWP-LC. On Nock, see especially

Letters, p. 393, and Journals, BWP-LC, September 22, 1927, September 17, 1928, and the following from March 6, 1933: "But Nock is a rum 'un. After all these long years I don't understand him. He is extraordinarily clever, a scholar, an excellent writer, and has a fine sense of humor. But he is remote, mysterious and queer. I don't know where he lives in America; I don't know at what hotel he is stopping now here at Cannes. And he is against everything. Roosevelt made a excellent inaugural address, but Nock poo-poos it and him. He is a kind of vague internationalist, with no patriotism and apparently no attachments. In short he baffles me, and after a while I grow tired of his queer ways, though I like him too."

24. Students of Nock and Edith Wharton will be interested in two comments on their lives by Jewett:

"Nock lunched with me last week. He is one of the most engaging souls I know and I cannot think of anyone with whom I disagree more. It is utterly impossible for me to follow him in many of his theories, or to come to conclusions which are not at right angles to his own." (Jewett to BW, January 30, 1916, BWP-LC.)

"Walter Berry's death has been a devastating experience, of course, for her. She has lost the great friend of her lifetime. What a great individual—which Edith Wharton is, whether you love or hate her—could see in a stuffed shirt like Berry is more than I have ever been able to grasp. Perhaps it is the proof of her greatness. If the gossip be true, he was guilty of the unforgivable sin and unworthy of such a friendship. I understand that by his will he left his ashes to her, but this is all she had possessed for years . . ." (Jewett to BW, December 6, 1927, BWP-LC.)

25. For Neilson, see *Letters*, p. 427, supplemented by the unpublished parts, BWP-LC.

26. For Darrow, see Journals, September 14, 1927, and December 1929; the longest statement is on December 14, 1929. All BWP-LC.

27. For House, see Journals, May 9, 1927, and March 18-19, 1930, BWP-LC. The comments on Mrs. House reappear regularly; the passage quoted here is from March 19, 1930, Journals, BWP-LC.

28. On the novel, see *Letters*, pp. 476, 481, 510, 532, and BW to Sheppey, March 10, 1931, BWP-LC; on *Belgium* III, see *Letters*, p. 492, and BW to Sheppey, May 3, 1931, BWP-LC;

for House, see House to BW, April 18, 1930, EMHP-YU, House to BW, December 6, 1929, BWP-LC, and *Letters*, pp. 485, 502; for Nock, see Nock to BW, May 22, 1929, December 11 and 23, 1930, BWP-LC; for Jewett, see Jewett to BW, August 17, 1933, BWP-LC; on the Jackson biography, see *Letters*, p. 566; the Jefferson and Jackson mss. are in ANP-CU.

29. BW to House, July 26, 1931, and Febuary 23, 1932, EMHP-YU.
30. Journals, June 19 and October 11, 1932, BWP-LC; the official statement on Roosevelt is in Box 86, BWP-LC; *Letters*, pp. 515, 530, 535.
31. Journals, May 2, July 4, and October 30, 1933, BWP-LC; Newton Baker visited on February 11, 1934, and Whitlock has a detailed description of his own anti-New Deal ideas; Nock agreed regularly by mail; for Melbourne, see *Letters*, pp. 505, 539.
32. *Letters*, pp. 419, 425, 493 (the letter to Nock is misdated, p. 574; the BWP-LC copy is dated May 16, 1934); for Whitlock's sicknesses, see Journals, April 25 and 29, 1928, May 12, 1932, November 17, 1932, March 4, 1933, and early 1934, BWP-LC.

Index

ABOUT THE AUTHOR

Robert Crunden was born in Jersey City, New Jersey, in 1940 and educated at The Kent School, Yale College (B.A. 1962), and Harvard University, where he received his Ph.D. in 1967 in the History of American Civilization. Since 1967 he has been Assistant Professor of History and American Studies at the University of Texas in Austin, and since 1968 Graduate Adviser in American Civilization. He is the author of *The Mind and Art of Albert Jay Nock,* published in 1964. Mr. Crunden is married, and he and his wife and their young daughter live in Austin.

A NOTE ON THE TYPE

This book was set on the Linotype in ELECTRA, a type face designed by W. A. Dwiggins. The Electra face is a simple and readable type suitable for printing books by present-day processes. It is not based on any historical model, and hence does not echo any particular time or fashion.

Composed, printed, and bound by
The Haddon Craftsmen, Inc., Scranton, Pennsylvania
Typography and binding design by

GUY FLEMING

DATE DUE

2/3

DEC 12 1977